Geographies of Empire

How did the major European imperial powers and indigenous populations experience imperialism and colonisation in the period 1880–1960? In this richly illustrated comparative account, Robin Butlin provides a comprehensive overview of the experiences of individual European imperial powers – British, French, Dutch, Spanish, Portuguese, Belgian, German and Italian – and the reactions of indigenous peoples. He explores the complex processes and discourses of colonialism, conquest and resistance from the height of empire through to decolonisation and sets these within the dynamics of the globalisation of political and economic power systems. He sheds new light on variations in the timing, nature and locations of European colonisations, and on key themes such as exploration and geographical knowledge; maps and mapping; demographics; land seizure and environmental modification; transport and communications; and resistance and independence movements. In so doing, he makes a major contribution to our understanding of colonisation and the end of empire.

ROBIN A. BUTLIN is Emeritus Professor of Geography at the University of Leeds. His previous publications include *Geography and Imperialism, 1820–1940* (co-edited with M. Bell and M. Heffernan, 1995), *Historical Geography: Through the Gates of Space and Time* (1993) and, co-edited with R. A. Dodgshon, *An Historical Geography of England and Wales* (2nd edn 1990), and *An Historical Geography of Europe* (1998).

CAMBRIDGE STUDIES IN HISTORICAL GEOGRAPHY

Series editors:

Alan R. H. Baker, Richard Dennis, Deryck Holdsworth

Cambridge Studies in Historical Geography encourages exploration of the philosophies, methodologies and techniques of historical geography and publishes the results of new research within all branches of the subject. It endeavours to secure the marriage of traditional scholarship with innovative approaches to problems and to sources, aiming in this way to provide a focus for the discipline and to contribute towards its development. The series is an international forum for publication in historical geography which also promotes contact with workers in cognate disciplines.

A full list of titles in the series can be found at www.cambridge.org/ historical geography

Geographies of Empire

European Empires and Colonies *c.* 1880–1960

ROBIN A. BUTLIN

CAMBRIDGE
UNIVERSITY PRESS

CAMBRIDGE UNIVERSITY PRESS

Cambridge, New York, Melbourne, Madrid, Cape Town, Singapore, São Paulo, Delhi

Cambridge University Press
The Edinburgh Building, Cambridge CB2 8RU, UK

Published in the United States of America by Cambridge University Press, New York

www.cambridge.org
Information on this title: www.cambridge.org/9780521740555

First published 2009

Printed in the United Kingdom at the University Press, Cambridge

A catalogue record for this publication is available from the British Library

Library of Congress Cataloguing in Publication data
Butlin, R. A. (Robin Alan), 1938–
   Geographies of empire : European empires and colonies, c. 1880–1960 / Robin A. Butlin.
     p. cm. – (Cambridge studies in historical geography)
   Includes bibliographical references and index.
   ISBN 978-0-521-80042-6 (hardback)   1. Europe–Colonies–History–19th
   century.   2. Europe–Colonies–History–20th century.   3. Europe–History,
   Military.   4. Military history, Modern–19th century.   5. Military history, Modern–20th
   century.   I. Title.   II. Series.
   JV105.B88 2009
   325′.309409041–dc22   2009014704

ISBN 978-0-521-80042-6 hardback
ISBN 978-0-521-74055-5 paperback

For Norma, Catherine, Ian, Richard, Martin, Ciosa, Sami, Tilly, Polly, Alfie, May, Crea, Ted and Tom

Contents

Figures

Preface

This book is one of a number of outcomes of my teaching and research interests in historical geography which have lasted for more than forty years, and of a more recent interest, starting about fifteen years ago, in the geographies of imperialism and colonialism. An initial curiosity about the historical geographies of imperialism and colonialism was sparked by my discovery of a series of books on the historical geography of the British Empire published between 1887 and 1925, notably C. P. Lucas's edited series on the *Historical Geography of the British Colonies* and H. B. George's *An Historical Geography of the British Empire* (see Butlin 1995). This led to my subsequent research projects into the links between geographical societies and imperialism and colonialism, specifically through the libraries and archives of the Royal Geographical Society in London and of geographical and historical societies in Australia and South Africa. The seeds for this work were sown and germinated at Loughborough University, notably in collaboration with Morag Bell and Mike Heffernan, in the early and mid-1990s, and their continued support and encouragement throughout this project is greatly appreciated. Additionally, between 1999 and 2005, the opportunity arose in the School of Geography at the University of Leeds for me to share some of my ideas on the differing experiences of European states and their empires and colonies with undergraduates in a third-year special option course on the Geographies of European Imperialism. To the successive groups of students who took that course I owe a great debt of gratitude for the stimulus and interest that they provided. One of my happy memories of the course was of a seminar on geographies of war and rebellion, led by a confident undergraduate actor dressed in the uniform of a British army officer from the Boer (South African) War, whose entry to the room was accompanied by loud military music that must have amused or (more likely) distracted other lecturers and classes in adjacent rooms.

There has been a great deal of important and innovative work in the past decade on many new aspects of the historical and cultural geographies of imperialism and colonialism by groups of very able geographers, working in Europe, Asia, Canada, Africa and Australia, linked with new insights afforded by, for example, postcolonial, gender, and indigenous perspectives, which has added to seminal work, conspicuously on Australia, Africa and Canada, which started in the 1980s. Neither of these substantial bodies of work has been as fully recognised and evaluated as it might have been outside the discipline of geography (Butlin 2002), and one of the purposes of this book is to attempt to showcase some of their insights for a wider audience, and to adjust, albeit slightly, the historiographical basis of broader writing on imperialism and colonialism about the period since *c.* 1880. Much of the notable work reviewed here, however, properly and necessarily digests a wide range of significant and seminal research and writings in other disciplines, conspicuously history, economic and social history, demographic history, and environmental history, and in a range of theoretical formulations. The broader context is that of trying in part through this book to meet the rapidly growing interest in the geographies and histories of former European empires and colonies and their postcolonial consequences, reflected in various media projects in Britain and linked publications (e.g. Ferguson 2003).

The chronological period covered by the book starts with the high imperialism of the late nineteenth and early twentieth centuries and finishes with the independence movements of the 1950s and 1960s. Its topical coverage is selective, perhaps even eclectic, necessitated by the limits of size of an individual book and one's range of interests and competencies, and it focuses primarily on spatial links, manifestations, discourses and processes. The individual chapters address questions of analytical frameworks; chronologies; demographies; land allocation and appropriation; geographical societies and their imperial links; empire, cultures of exploration and geographical knowledge; maps and mapping; geographies of civilising mission; environmental interaction; the arteries of empire; towns and cities; economic geographies; and decolonisation. Within these chapters are to be found accounts of resistance to, and acceptance and modification of, change, and attempts to hear the voices of both colonised and coloniser. Detailed coverage of major global and regional warfare has not been possible; nor has a comprehensive account of the wide range of institutions engaged with imperialism, though analysis is undertaken of the roles and characters of geographical societies.

One of the consistent and justified criticisms about many writings on empire is that they are too Eurocentric. Though this imbalance is now being redressed by a plethora of important work from 'subaltern' and similar perspectives, this book is written by a British scholar who has spent most of his working life in Britain, with additional experience of scholarly institutions and productions in Europe and North America, and with limited time in South Africa and Australia, and the book naturally reflects these experiences. Nonetheless, I have tried to represent and review alternative visions and perspectives, including those of other European countries.

Every attempt has been made to include a reasonably balanced narrative and analysis of significant parts and different experiences of the empires and colonies of European states, but geographical coverage has had to be selective to a degree, given the vast scales and spaces involved. The areas of major white settlement – the colonies such as Canada, Australia and South Africa which became Dominions and ultimately parts of the Commonwealth – have not been given the coverage that their extensively researched histories require because of space constraints, but selective narratives are provided of some of their major experiences and problems. Ireland's position as a colony and region is reviewed in Chapter 2, but the complexity and difference of that country's historical geography has meant that it does not figure prominently in this text.

I owe a great debt of gratitude to Dr Alan Baker, a good friend for more than forty years, and editor of the Cambridge Studies in Historical Geography series, who some years ago suggested that my interests in historical geographies of empire might be turned into a book, and whose encouragement in this and other scholarly projects, and whose own epic contributions to historical geography, have been of incalculable value.

In addition to his unfailing encouragement over many years, Joe Powell of Monash University in Melbourne also kindly undertook to offer critical comment on a first draft of this text, and these comments and suggestions encouraged me to rework a number of significant sections. I am grateful also for the comments on the manuscript by an anonymous referee from North America, and on Chapter 3 by Adrian Bailey of the School of Geography, University of Leeds.

The thinking that informs this work reflects a long period of encouragement and stimulus from colleagues at the wide range of institutions in which I have studied, researched and taught during a professional lifetime of scholarship. They include colleagues from the Geography Departments at the University of Liverpool, the University of Keele, University College, Dublin, the University of Nebraska, Queen Mary College (now Queen Mary) in the University of London, Loughborough University, Wolfson College, Cambridge, and the University of Leeds. Sir Alan Wilson, as Vice-Chancellor and fellow geographer, and successive heads of the School of Geography at the University of Leeds, provided, from 1998 onwards, further opportunities for me to teach and research, and I have been fortunate to have had there the scholarly support of colleagues which has enabled me to bring a number of projects to fruition. I have been singularly fortunate also in the encouragement that I have received in this and other projects from Richard Lawton, John Edwards, Tom Jones Hughes, Bob Dodgshon, Hugh Prince, Anngret Simms, Serge Courville, Alan Lester, Charles Withers, David Livingstone, Martin Purvis, Derek Gregory, Hugh Clout, Brian Graham, Graeme Wynn, Chris Christopher, Jehoshua Ben-Arieh, Haim Goren, Ruth Kark, Willie Smyth, Pat O'Flanagan, Tony Phillips, Roger Kain, Catherine Delano-Smith, George Revill, Paul Laxton, Iain Black, John Sheail, Philip Howell, Hans Renes, Elyze Smeets, and many other scholars.

I am also happy to have been one of the founders and members of two significant research groups: the Historical Geography Research Group of the Royal Geographical Society (with the Institute of British Geographers), and the International Conference of Historical Geographers (formerly CUKANZUS). These have grown and matured most impressively, and provide stimulating centres for debate in important research fields, and their meetings have provided invaluable opportunities for comparing research with scholars from around the world. I have been much helped in my work by many colleagues in Canada, the United States, Britain, Ireland, Israel, Palestine, France, Germany, Sweden, Italy, the Netherlands, Belgium, South Africa, Australia and Japan, and I extend my thanks to them all. I have also benefited greatly from support through research funding from the Economic and Social Research Council, the Royal Geographical Society (with the Institute of British Geographers), the British Academy, and, through a Research Fellowship and an Emeritus Research Fellowship, from the Leverhulme Trust.

My researches in this country have been greatly facilitated by support from libraries and librarians in many different universities, and by the librarians and archivists at the Royal Geographical Society, the University of Cambridge, the British Library, the Geography Department at the University of Stellenbosch, the Royal Historical Society of Victoria, the Queensland Geographical Society, and the Fryer Library at the University of Queensland.

I extend my warmest thanks to the cartographers Alison Manson and David Appleyard in the Graphics Unit at the School of Geography at the

University of Leeds for having taken great care with the drawing of the maps and diagrams for this book.

I am grateful also to Richard Fisher, Michael Watson, Helen Waterhouse and Chris Hills at Cambridge University Press for their encouragement of the project, for their professional advice, guidance and expertise, and for their patience.

Copyright permission from a number of authors and publishers is acknowledged in individual captions to maps, diagrams and photographs. In the preparation of the maps, use has been made of software from Mountain High Maps®Copyright© 1993 Digital Wisdom, Inc.

Unwavering support has been given by my wife Norma and our children Catherine, Ian and Richard, who over the years have patiently tolerated my academic routines, and found different and imaginative ways of drawing my attention to other goals and priorities, and to them and to our son- and daughters-in–law and our grandchildren I extend my deepest thanks.

Robin Butlin
31 May 2008

1 | Geography, imperialism and colonialism: concepts and frameworks

Aims

We have been witnesses of one of the most remarkable episodes in the history of the world. During the past eight years we have seen the bulk of the one barbarous continent [Africa] parcelled out among the most civilised Powers of Europe. (Keltie 1893: 1)

While these obscure struggles, often a grotesque mixture of savagery and farce, were fought out within the cultural context of traditional Zambesi society, the world outside was rapidly changing. The explosive industrialization of Europe and the United States spread its influence until eventually the armed struggles on the Zambesi became absorbed and transformed by the global economic revolution of nineteenth-century imperialism. (Newitt 1995: 298)

This opening sentence of a book on *The Partition of Africa* by J. Scott Keltie (Assistant Secretary to the Royal Geographical Society) gives a perspective on some of the assumptions underpinning the ambitions, failures and successes of European powers in their overseas territories in the late nineteenth century, articulated in this example by a distinguished senior member of a major geographical society. The words 'barbarous' and 'civilised' suggest assumptions about cultural superiority that were part of the dissemination of European 'civilisation' overseas, and the words 'parcelled out' imply an almost innocent diplomatic game. Keltie's book is, in fact, a helpful and generally even-handed chronicle of the history and geography of the 'scramble' for Africa, but it was written within a limited conceptual and explanatory framework. The second quotation, from Malyn Newitt's *History of Mozambique*, is a creditable summary, especially in the phrase 'a grotesque mixture of savagery and farce', of many experiences of imperialism and colonialism, and the increasingly global contexts in which they were enacted. The ideologies, processes and experiences of imperial and colonial expansion (and ultimately retraction) were in fact extremely complex, changed through time, and varied within and between colonial powers, the areas to which they laid claim, and their populations.

The purpose of this book is to identify and explain some of the main processes, geographical contexts and outcomes of European imperialism and colonialism within the time-frame *c.* 1880–1960. It draws on the traditions and outputs of historical and human (and to some extent physical) geography, and on a wide variety of works of historical scholarship. Its thematic focus is on the historical geographies of significant components of imperial and colonial change. These include: conceptual frameworks; the nature, timing and places of European and indigenous experience; assessments of numbers, compositions and movements of populations; the evaluation and appropriation of rights of use of indigenous land; links with the production of geographical knowledge (by exploration, mapping and the activities of learned societies); cultural assumptions and 'civilising' missions; environmental influences and interactions; communication and transport networks; metropolitan and colonial towns and cities; geographies of production and resource exploitation; and decolonisation.

A major component of this book is an attempted comparison between the historical geographies of the imperial and colonial experiences of the major European powers. While much of its content is about the British empire, it seeks, probably for the first time in a work on historical geography, to highlight and contrast the imperial and colonial experiences of the other powers such as Germany, France, Spain, Portugal, the Netherlands, Belgium and Italy, and in some measure Russia, and to make some comparison with the late developers in the imperial field, notably Japan and the United States. It seeks also to hear the voices of the indigenous populations of the countries subject to imperial policy and colonial management, and also of those more generally marginalised by these processes.

The book is aimed at a broad target, including undergraduate and graduate students and academic teachers and researchers in geography, history, and related subjects, together with a wider-ranging audience interested in imperial and colonial processes in the nineteenth and twentieth centuries.

Historical geography

The intellectual tradition on which the book is based – historical geography – incorporates reconstructions of changes in geographical spaces and places in the past. Historical geography has a long history dating back to at least the seventeenth century in Europe, but its more modern form developed from the beginning of the twentieth century. Historical geography incorporates a wide range of the perspectives and analytical tools of geography in identifying and understanding aspects of past life and environments. These include the character and construction of places, spaces and landscapes, the dynamics of human and environmental change, the appropriation and management of resources, geopolitical issues and conflicts including the determination of boundaries, the dissemination of cultural and belief systems, the varied roles of maps and mapping (as records, and tools of power), the nature of human settlements, gender and postcolonial perspectives, economic and trading links, modernity, cultures of exploration and 'discovery', the creation and development of geographical knowledge, and the roles of institutions and individuals in shaping the experiences of particular peoples and places. Most of these are covered in the individual chapters of this book. In its various thematic and regional narratives, sources used include maps, population data, field and landscape evidence, records of urban and rural development, national archives and official accounts, accounts of travel and exploration and the records of institutions such as geographical societies, and evidence of environmental change, by both human and natural agencies. This is not, however, the place for a reappraisal of the development of the subject and its many insights, for there are many useful and relevant recent accounts of its evolved present character and linked ideas (Butlin 1993; Graham and Nash 2000; Blunt and McEwan 2002; Baker 2003, 2005, 2007; Lambert and Lester 2006).

Different countries have their particular traditions and emphases within the sub-discipline of historical geography, and the geographical analysis of imperial and colonial issues within Europe started earlier in Britain and France than it did in Germany and Italy, for example, a feature reflective of the chronologies and trajectories of imperialism and colonialism in these countries. There is now, of course, a wider global comparison of these and related experiences, notably decolonisation.

Historical and cultural geographers have played a major part over the past two decades in the advancement of research and publications on imperialism and colonialism, and have located their research in both imperial metropoles and heartlands and distant 'peripheries', increasingly framed in the context of postcolonial approaches, and therefore offering new and different perspectives on the contrasting and complementary roles of actors from different cultural bases. Alison Blunt has emphasised the significance for the geographer of 'the spatiality of colonial power and its forms of knowledge, the spatial politics of representation and the material effects of colonialism in different places at different times' (Blunt 2005: 177), and has categorised the main contributions as cultures of imperialism, geographical research and education, whose major themes include: 'geographies of encounter, conquest, colonisation and settlement'; 'geographies of colonial representation in both written and visual forms'; 'the production of space in colonial and postcolonial cities'; 'the gendered, sexualised and racialised spaces of colonialism, colonial discourse and postcoloniality'; and 'geographies of migration, diaspora and transnationality' (Blunt 2005: 178).

Much of this work by geographers investigates the processes of production of colonial and postcolonial spaces. It has ranged from studies of individuals, households and families, through to trans-global and trans-imperial experiences by different kinds of colonised and coloniser. For the most part these studies are linked to imaginative interpretations of a wide range of evidence and representations, and fruitful analyses of situated experiences are examined within broader theoretical perspectives.

In recent times historical geography has made use of artistic and literary representations of geographical and landscape change, together with historical photographs, the records of the experience of individuals and of ethnic groups who interacted with colonisation processes, gender perspectives, the deconstruction of the symbolic meanings of maps, and evaluations of environmental interaction. Its practitioners have focused strongly on the regional and global experiences of imperialism and colonialism and their political and geopolitical contexts. Much of this research has been linked to studies of the histories of geographical thought and also to a wide range of theory (Graham and Nash 2000; Blunt and McEwan 2002; Cosgrove 1999, 2008; Driver 2001; Driver and Martins 2005; Harley 1998; Livingstone 1992, 2003; Withers 2001; Heffernan 1998c; Ryan 1997; Brayshay and Cleary 2002; Lambert and Lester 2006; Stafford 1999; Legg 2007; Powell 2000, 2004, 2007).

Strong links have also been made by geographers to contemporary issues of imperialism and colonialism. Powerful polemic narratives and post-colonial analyses of past and present problems in Afghanistan, Palestine and Iraq in the late twentieth and twenty-first centuries have been articulated, for example, by Derek Gregory, who has used a wide range of theory to engage with the profound, contorting and continually tragic events and processes of Western imperialism, notably in the aftermath of September 11, 2001 (Gregory 2004). Gregory's

purpose has been to try to understand what it was that those events in New York City and Washington triggered and, specifically, how they came to be shaped by a cluster of imaginative geographies into more or less *public* cultures of assumption, disposition and action … how did those imaginative geographies solidify architectures of enmity that contrived to set people in some places against people in other places? (Gregory 2004: 27–8)

Gregory (2004: 8) cites Nicholas Thomas on the significant links between culture and imperialism:

colonialism is not best understood primarily as a political or economic relationship that is legitimized or justified through ideologies of racism or progress. Rather, colonialism has always, equally importantly and deeply, been a cultural process; its discoveries and trespasses are imagined and energized through signs, metaphors and narratives; even what would seem its purest moments of profit and violence have been mediated and enframed by structures of meaning. (Thomas 1994: 2)

What those structures of meaning entail, and what forms they take, are questions to which answers are still being sought.

Ideas, processes, events and interactions operating within the complex kaleidoscope of imperialism and colonialism have been evaluated with a view to understanding what David Lambert and Alan Lester have called 'putative root causes' (the large canvas on which this book is produced requires this) and 'multiple colonial projects' (Lambert and Lester 2006: 8–9). They assert that:

In partial critique of the 'traditional' imperial history, 'new' imperial history recognizes that there was never a single European colonial project, whether it be the pursuit of industrial or 'gentlemanly' capitalism, or governmental geo-strategising. Neither, accordingly, was there a single discourse, or set of representations and practices of colonialism. Rather, the agendas of colonial interests, their representations of colonised places and peoples, and their practices in relation to them, were not only differentiated, but also often constructed in opposition to one another. (Lambert and Lester 2006: 9)

They and their contributors illustrate this point by detailing a series of imperial 'careerings' across the British empire by individuals bound directly or indirectly to the institutions and administration of empire, highlighting the complexity, varied scale, constitutions and compositions of personal imperial spaces and networks.

This impressive array of geographical scholarship has provided an intriguing and challenging set of ideas and presentations and has considerably advanced our understanding of colonial and imperial processes, and one aim of this chapter, and the book as a whole, is to expose these ideas to a wider range of recognition and debate.

Definitions

The major concepts which require definition are 'imperial' and 'colonial', 'imperialism' and 'colonialism'. 'Imperial' and 'imperialism' carry the connotation of control of an empire from a metropolitan place (London, Berlin, Paris, Madrid, Lisbon, for example), the empire comprising the metropole plus territories usually removed geographically from the metropolitan state and having, with the exception of settler colonies with a predominantly European population, very little in common with their cultures and production systems. 'Colonial'/'colonialism' applies to the specific locale(s) of overseas imperial control, including the means used on the ground, including European settlement, to suppress or modify indigenous cultures and modes of living. The two are clearly interlinked, but they do have different meanings. Engseng Ho, for example, suggests that:

> colonialism is the occupation of territory by foreign settlers, soldiers, or administrators. Colonies are possessions of master societies, so master and subject populations answer to different laws ... Imperialism, in contrast, is the projection of political power across large spaces, to include other states whatever the means: colonies, mercenaries, gunboats, missiles, client elites, proxy states, multilateral institutions, multinational alliances. (Ho 2004: 225)

James Sidaway has similarly pointed to the significance of locations for the multiple meanings and condition of imperialism and colonialism, citing Loomba's claim that definitions of imperialism and colonialism in terms of 'historical mutations' are in fact bettered by definitions based on space (Sidaway 1998: 6). The partial, discriminatory and interactive operations of colonialism and imperialism have been recognised by Stephen Howe in his book *Imperialism. A Very Short Introduction* (2002):

> In general, colonial conquest was nearly always partial, the processes of social and cultural change it sponsored or unleashed still more so. The ideologies of colonial expansion and rule, too, were far more varied and ambiguous than is routinely suggested in much current writing. To recognize and explore this is not to 'rehabilitate' the colonial record, nor to excuse or downplay the violence, oppression, and exploitation that marked almost all its passages. (Howe 2002: 125)

He argues that the relatively recent emphasis on cultural aspects of imperialism and colonialism has led to an understatement of the significance of economic and political forces, and that more attention should be paid to the 'political and legal systems of empires' in their variety, their component viewpoints and purposes, and in relation to questions of how political systems existing in and over colonial territories differed from those elsewhere. A distinction is also made between the intentions and the outcomes of colonial policy and action.

The idea of ambivalence in European conquests of distant places, proposed by Frederick Cooper, is also helpful and supportive of Howe's ideas. He claims that Europe's imperial and colonial activities and ideologies, notably those that attempted to distinguish between metropole and colony, the cultural superiority of the colonisers to that of the colonised, and the outward projection of knowledge, science and understanding, varied and fluctuated, and 'made the space of empire into a terrain where concepts were not only imported but also engaged and contested' (Cooper 2005: 4). While the terms 'imperial' and 'colonial' are widely used in this book, it is readily acknowledged that these are broad umbrella terms that in one sense can be unhelpful because of their implication of homogeneous process and all-embracing character in relation to what are in fact highly uneven and complex processes. At one level these are the outcome of quite small-scale, individual negotiations between ideologies and practices on the ground. On the other hand, the scale adopted in the book requires the qualified use of 'imperial' and colonial', and may help to make comparison with other published works whose narrative mainly operates at larger scales.

Imperial landscapes

One particular field of interest to historical geographers is the representation of landscapes of imperial and colonial territories through the evidence of written accounts, field investigation, maps, paintings, drawings, engravings and photographs. Mark Brayshay and Mark Cleary (2002: 5–10) have outlined the extent of landscape modification in the British empire, notably in the late and immediately post-Victorian era, noting that 'A pervasive theme ... is the argument that landscapes are shaped as much by the ideologies and philosophies of the peoples who create them as by the practical work that brings them into physical existence' (Brayshay and Cleary, 2002: 5).

Significant processes involved survey and mapping, plans for and the foundation of settlements, the effects of events such as gold rushes, the role of propaganda, the geographical imaginations of states and settlers, and interactions with indigenous cultures. Gareth Shaw and Paul Hudson have analysed the contents, production and distribution of colonial trade directories, with particular reference to Wellington, New Zealand, as sources of knowledge about colonial urban landscapes and as symbols

Fig. 1.1 Statue of Sir Stamford Raffles (1781–1826) on the east side of the Singapore River. Photo © R. A. Butlin.

of the industry and culture of the metropole and of colonies, of technical modernity (postal systems, printing systems), and of propaganda through exhibitions and displays (Shaw and Hudson 2002: 51–66). Their broader context was that of 'serving the needs of local communities, whilst at the same time acting as commercial windows on the manufactured goods of the mother country… The colonial trade directories were creating and reinforcing the commercial ties of empire, part of a network of information ties that bound centre and periphery together and helped to shape their respective identities' (Shaw and Hudson 2002: 53). Directories for Wellington from the 1860s show how the commercial and industrial landscapes of that city reflected a strong British influence, with many local companies acting as agents for British companies and some for Australian enterprises.

The effects of imperialism and colonialism on landscapes were reflected in the many buildings and statues erected in the colonies of European states, often in metropolitan style, or in a style which mixed local and imperial styles, and notably in their towns and cities. A parallel process also operated, with buildings and statues in metropolitan European states showing clear evidence of colonial and imperial themes.

The naming of places and streets was a familiar product of colonial activity. Within the British empire, many towns were named after Queen Victoria, a monarch of whom statues were also frequently found in towns at home and overseas. David Cannadine (2001: 103) stated that: 'Statues of Victoria (especially), and also of Edward VII, George V and George VI, were prominently placed in city squares and in front of government houses. From Cairo to Canberra, Wellington to Johannesburg, Vancouver to Valetta, the image of the queen–empress appeared, often in canopied magnificence', together with major constructions such as the railway terminus in Bombay, and the naming of many urban streets and places after British monarchs, politicians and administrators.

There were similar urban reflections of metropolitan authority in other European empires and colonies. In Algiers there was a square named after, and a statue of, General Bugeaud, the governor-general, a rue des Colons, and a place du Gouvernement (Çelik 1997: 183–4). David Prochaska has suggested a typology of colonial place names for the French colonial city of Bône in Algeria:

There were streets named after battles or personages of the Napoleonic era, especially concerning Napoleon's invasion of Egypt: rue Kléber, rue Castiglione, rue Josephine … there was another group of streets named after the Orleanists of the July Monarchy: rue Louis-Philippe, rue d'Orléans … Later in the century Third Republic people and places would supply the bulk of the street names in the new city and suburbs, such as Anatole France, Jean Jaurès, and Léon Gambetta. (Prochaska 1990: 209–10)

There were streets named after Christian saints, those that were Jewish in origin, and some had geographical names.

Far and away the largest group of street names referred to the French colonization of Bône, and in particular to the conquest and early occupation. First, there were the names of warships – frigates, brigantines, barks – which transported the French troops: rue Béarnaise, rue Suffren … Most numerous, however, were the streets named after those who had taken part: rue Damrémont, the general who first occupied Bône in 1830, rue Huder.

Villages in the region were also named after colonial military officers (Prochaska 1990: 210–11).

In Windhoek in Namibia (formerly German South-West Africa), there were streets named Kaiserstraße, Bulowstraße, Stübelstraße, Leutweinstraße, and a statue of Major Curt von François, who had 'led the massacre of scores of Witbooi women and children in the early morning of April 12, 1893' (Steinmetz and Hell 2006: 177). These symbolic landscapes of oppression were changed in many colonial countries on independence, with statues being removed and street names changed. The street names of European colonies were not, however, total replacements or innovations: they frequently existed alongside indigenously named streets and buildings.

Descriptions of colonial landscapes frequently reflected changing perceptions of exotic places, such as the tropics, and these have recently been subject to postcolonial analyses and interpretations, recognising that the tropics, as Felix Driver and Luciana Martins (2005: 4) put it, 'have long been the site for European fantasies of self-realization, projects of cultural imperialism, or the politics of human or environmental salvage. In the postcolonial world, these fantasies have if anything become more pervasive, if distinctly less enchanting.' European visions, encounters with, and mappings of the tropics by Europeans changed through time and with transactions of knowledge, processes that have been 'actually transformative of the European sense of culture and of history – of the temperate self' (Driver and Martins 2005: 5). The envisioning of the tropics was not always as exotic, picturesque and romantic, but sometimes as fearful and threatening, both for would-be settlers and visitors, and also for the populations of the European metropoles. This was evidenced, inter alia, by the perception of danger from tropical diseases, such as leprosy, and the development of tropical medicine in the late nineteenth century as 'the prime means by which this increasingly pathologized relation between tropical and temperate zones was to be described and regulated' (Edmond 2005: 181).

Geographical models of colonial settlement: R. C. Harris

In his essay on the simplification of Europe overseas, the geographer Cole Harris pointed to the initial differences between the physical and cultural environments of three of the mid-latitude regions settled from Europe from the seventeenth century – Canada, South Africa, and New England (Harris 1977). He argued that the differences that emerged between the emigrants in these places had more to do with the availability of land than it did with their historical cultural differences. A process of 'simplification' of European society led to the emergence of 'a remarkably homogeneous society' focused on the independent nuclear family. The landscape effect in the seventeenth, eighteenth and early nineteenth centuries was that 'similar farms and farmhouses, the homes of largely subsistence farmers and their families, were scattered in different patterns across the landscapes of these colonies, the reflection but also substantially the cause of the simple societies that inhabited them' (Harris 1977: 481–2).

Frugality, Harris (2002: 4) suggested, was one of the 'more explicit guidelines and theories' of British colonial government: 'The Crown would provide defence against external aggression, but internally colonies were to become fiscally independent as quickly as possible.' One of their early functions, outlined by Harris in the context of the transfer in 1849 of Vancouver Island by the British crown to the Hudson's Bay Company, was as supplier of raw materials to the metropole under the free trade policy introduced in 1846. Earl Grey, Secretary of State for the Colonies, 'was impressed by the image of colonies for a great power. He also thought that Britain had acquired responsibilities to British settlers who had chosen to relocate themselves within the empire and deserved the benefits of British protection, and also to Natives who would not be able to fend off these settlers and deserved to be protected from them' (Harris 2002: 5).

In addition to this pragmatic and principled view, broader, theory-based views, derived in part from the ideas of political economists such as Adam Smith and David Ricardo, were held by the British government and the Colonial Office 'about the relevance of land, labour and capital in colonial settings and about their bearing on colonial land policy' (Harris 2002: 5), linked to the ideas of Edward Gibbon Wakefield on the management of colonial land allocation through the encouragement of emigration from the metropole of people who would provide cheaper labour and eventually become landowners.

In an essay on postcolonial perspectives on the colonial dispossession of indigenous land and land rights, Harris (2004) placed particular emphasis on the colonial site, and the need for colonialism to be appraised through positioning

studies of colonialism in the actuality and materiality of colonial experience. As that experience comes into focus, its principal causes are to be assessed, among which may well be something like the culture of imperialism. To proceed the other way round is to impose a form of intellectual imperialism on the study of colonialism, a tendency to which the postcolonial literature inclines. (Harris 2004: 167)

The procedure took the form of a description and analysis of the dispossessions and expropriations of land in British Columbia, allocations of small quantities to reserves of indigenous peoples and much more of it to settlers, stimulated by the transition from trading to settled agricultural communities, the incentives of profit from capital, the spreading of geographical knowledge to distant places of the opportunities presented by these 'new' lands, and a series of geopolitical events that led to the establishment of the colonies of Vancouver Island (1849) and British Columbia (1858) (Harris 2004: 169, 178–80).

Supported by military power more effective than that of indigenous peoples, and with the interests of the British state handed to local politicians, assumptions were made about a simple civilised/savage dichotomy which 'by the mid-19th century … were powerfully reinforced by an increasingly strident racism and the achievements of industrial production'. Means of dispossession of native land and its allocation to settlers became more sophisticated, involving the use of maps and adaptations of English common law including individual property rights, and new settlement patterns and landscapes emerged in the second half of the nineteenth century, through this 'pervasive disciplinary technology' (Harris 2004: 171, 178).

According to Harris, the means of appropriation of native land owed much to ideologies and practices both in Britain and elsewhere in the British empire, even in other parts of Europe, including some rather ineffective consideration of the humanitarian rights of indigenous peoples that had been in the minds of Colonial Office officials in the 1830s and partially applied in New Zealand in the Treaty of Waitangi of 1840 (Harris 2002: 4). In these important studies by Harris the narrative of critical events and processes leads to considerations of relevant theory rather than the other way round. Bracken's use of the ideas of Heidegger and Derrida to explain the engagement by Gilbert Malcolm Sprout and his hired men with indigenous Aht people on the west coast of Vancouver Island at 'Alberni Canal' in August 1860 in terms of a 'zone of textual contradiction' is rejected by Harris, who is 'not convinced that it is necessary to let Heidegger and Derrida loose in Alberni Canal to expose the contradictions and the cultural overlaps and borrowings inherent in colonialism' (Harris 2002: xvii).

D. W. Meinig and *The Shaping of America.*

Donald Meinig, also a greatly respected geographer, has over a long period of time investigated the historical geographies of the regions and the totality of the United States, and the broader question of the expansion of American influence beyond its shores, particularly from the mid-nineteenth century. In 1982, in a short but perceptive essay, he looked at the basic components of imperialism and its geographical connotations, defining the five key parts as 'the exercise of ultimate *political* authority by the invader over the invaded'; a requirement for 'direct contact between agents of the two peoples' and inequality of power and status; culture change as an inevitable outcome of contact; 'imperial expansion is basically predatory'; and the requirement that 'in order to continue their domination at minimum cost and trouble, imperial rulers seek the allegiance of conquered peoples' (Meinig 1982: 72–3).

The geographical consequences of these, for Meinig, were manifest in 'spatial systems', 'locational distributions', 'man–land relationships', 'social ecologies' and 'cultural landscapes' (Meinig 1982: 74). No particular examples of the nature of American or European powers in practice are given in his short essay, but they are in his monumental four-volume treatise *The Shaping of America. A Geographical Perspective on 500 Years of History* (Meinig 1986, 1993, 1998, 2004), described by Wynn (2005: 625) as 'a remarkable achievement, one of the great accomplishments of twentieth century American geography'.

In the last two volumes (vol. III, *Transcontinental America, 1850–1915* and notably in vol. IV, *Global America, 1915–2000*) Meinig reviews the increasing geopolitical experience of the United States in the wider world, including continued activity in the Caribbean, increasing power in the Pacific, and the role of the United States as combatant in the First and Second World Wars. His narrative account includes recognition of the United States as a world economic and military power by the early twentieth century, its continuing involvement with the Caribbean – the 'American Mediterranean' – and Hawaii, and 'America's sudden extension across the Pacific and across the China seas' – seen by Meinig as 'entirely new and unplanned'. He states that the 'annexation of the Philippines was highly controversial at home and provocative abroad within a realm of intense Great Power competitions' (Meinig 2004: IV, 305). He further describes the participation of the United States in the two world wars, and its involvement in the process of peace-making at the end of both wars. Pertinent to the historical geographies of European colonialism was America's position in relation to Germany's lost colonies in Africa and the Pacific. Woodrow Wilson favoured mandated and trustee status for these colonies of which control would pass to Britain, Australia, New Zealand and Japan.

Meinig suggests that by the end of the First World War the continental United States 'had no further territorial ambitions, it shunned Greater Power alliances, and it refused to join the League of Nations that its president had so extensively shaped', coupled to a 'hatred of Bolshevism', but nonetheless expanded her navy 'with a declared aim of having the most powerful fleet in the world' (Meinig 2004: 313–14). American expansion into the Pacific inevitably conflicted with Japanese ambition, expressed by the Japanese invasion of China and annexation of Formosa, and later its defeat of Russia. Japan held a stronger position in the Western Pacific, East China Sea, Yellow Sea and Sea of Japan than the United States, whose interests focused increasingly on the 'American Mediterranean', and the Panama Canal and Hawaii. Meinig's explanation of the American geopolitics of the Pacific and of her attitudes to Europe is a credible narrative, as is his analysis of the geopolitics of the Second World War and its aftermath, which focuses on Japanese, German, American and British strategies. The role of the Pacific Ocean as a medium for the imperial and territorial aggrandisement of the United States and Japan in the early to mid-twentieth century, and later in the century as an ecological space, reflected in different forms of cartographic and other images, has also been innovatively narrated in Denis Cosgrove's fine essay (published posthumously in 2008) in a chapter on 'Seeing the Pacific'. He wrote that for Americans:

Fixing the date line at 180° had served to naturalize the Pacific as the world-historical fracture zone between West and East, figured as metonyms for civilization and barbarism, progress and decadence respectively, This spatiality superseded – while also incorporating – an earlier one that had translated the South Seas' distance from Europe into a historical and ethnographic regression from civilization. In both cases, dividing the Pacific between the eastern and western edges of a cylindrical projection world map with a restricted latitudinal range at once marginalizes and diminishes the Pacific as a world region. Only in the middle years of the last century, during the decisive struggle for imperial dominance, did the Pacific become a unitary space cartographically and in the Western geographical vision. (Cosgrove 2008: 202)

The Atlantic Charter of 1941 is seen to have included an important set of principles for the geopolitics of the world after the war, and contained, from an American perspective, 'anticolonial implications', counter to Churchill's ideas on the retention of empire and those of the Dutch and French. Meinig (2004: 347) suggests that 'Europeans had every reason to suspect that US anticolonialism was designed to open the world to freer trade – and its own economic dominance', and that in spite of her status at the end of the war there were some doubts in the United States about sustaining her powerful global position. The rest of Meinig's account of the United States as a global superpower from the end of the war empha-sises the significance of the Cold War and its events and consequences, and the process of decolonisation of the European empires fades, perhaps too quickly, into the background of his narrative.

Meinig's substantial, impressive, and very well written and illustrated account of the shaping of America has been widely applauded across dis-ciplines as an outstanding and innovative work of geographical scholar-ship. Wynn (2005: 621) suggests that it 'should be understood, at least in part, as a proclamation of both the importance of historical geography and the robustness of an American polity and society that was widely regarded as "coming apart" in the late 1960s and early 1970s'. Critics regret what they see variously as an overambitious grand-scale synthe-sis, the understatement of environmental and landscape history and of social/cultural agency, and also of more radical ways of explaining dif-ferent kinds of change. The historical imperial theme threads (at varying thickness) through much of this work and helps to evaluate the geopoliti-cal role of the United States in the changing world order in times when empires developed and collapsed, though there is surprisingly little on that trauma of decolonisation, including the Vietnam War (Wynn 2005; Baker 2005).

J. M. Blaut's *The Colonizer's Model of the World*

The essence of James Blaut's argument in *The Colonizer's Model of the World* (1993) is that explanations of political and economic ascendancies in the world in the early modern and modern periods have been exces-sively Eurocentric, and fail to take account of economic development, including proto-capitalism and proto-industrialisation in other continents, such as Asia. The global influence of Europe was explained by the pro-Eurocentrists in terms of the environmental disadvantages of tropical and arid climates, prohibiting economic development and enlightened govern-ment, seen against the advantages of the temperate climates and product-ive agricultural systems of Europe, linked to economic, political, scientific, technological and cultural sophistication. This he describes as Eurocentric diffusionism – the notion of a process whereby a perceived inherently superior culture and system of economic management was employed in the expansion of Europe overseas, starting in 1492 and reaching a zenith with European colonialism in the nineteenth and early twentieth centuries.

Blaut argues that two of the principal reasons for Europe's accelerating development from the fifteenth century onwards were its geographical location, notably relative to the Americas, especially to their supplies of silver, and the access to additional overseas colonial resources, including raw materials and labour, provided by European imperialism from the sixteenth century onwards.

In a later book – *Eight Eurocentric Historians* (Blaut 2000) – Blaut restated his criticism of four basic Eurocentric explanations of the acceleration of European wealth and power: religion, race, environment and culture, each of which had periods of prominence (religion in the early nineteenth century, followed by a combination of race, environment and culture, and finally by environment and culture). He saw the model of 'Classic Eurocentric diffusionism' as the prevailing philosophy and practice of colonialism. He argued, as before, that:

All of this … is wrong: it is false history and bad geography. Europe's environment is not better than the environments of other places – not more fruitful, more comfortable, more suitable for communication and trade, and the rest. Europe's culture did not, historically, have superior traits that would lead to more rapid progress than that achieved by other societies: individual traits like inventiveness, innovativeness, ethical behaviour, etc; collective traits like the family, the market, the city. The rise of Europe cannot be explained in this Eurocentric way. (Blaut 2000: 1–3)

In its place, Blaut proposed a non-Eurocentric model of world history. The base dateline is the year 1500, at which point in time he argues that 'Europe was not more advanced or more progressive than other civilizations', and beyond which the basic explanation for the rise of Europe is colonialism. This was not the result of superior expeditionary knowledge or advantage – other powers had explored the Indian and Pacific Oceans in the sixteenth and seventeenth centuries, and had maritime and littoral trading routes – but the consequence of European proximity to the gold and silver of the Americas. 'Europeans acquired the wealth from colonialism because of their location on the globe, not because they were somehow uniquely advanced, or progressive, or "venturesome"' (Blaut 2000: 10, 12).

Critical response to Blaut's arguments has varied. Sanderson (1998: 25–39) has strongly contested the main thesis in Blaut's *Colonizer's Model of the World*. He contends that Blaut's explanation of the rise of Europe to global prominence from the late fifteenth century in terms of the narrowness of the Atlantic (as opposed to the Pacific), leading, together with the Protestant Reformation, to capitalist trading systems and advanced political organisation ahead of the rest of the globe, is wrong. Sanderson sees Blaut's broad argument as a useful counter-balance to excessively Eurocentric explanations of the history of world systems, but thinks that in some areas Blaut goes too far: 'His claim that Africa was economically on a par with Europe and Asia is not only wrong; it is absurd. And his claim that it was merely Europe's geographical accessibility to the Americas that led to its success rings hollow' (Sanderson 1998: 26). Sanderson concludes with the proposal that Europe was becoming an advanced economic power in the world by 1500, on account of colonial activity, notably by Spain and Portugal, the beginning of the development of nation-states, a rapid rise in scientific knowledge, the development of industry in 'proto-industrial' form, and the advanced nature of financial institutions in Europe in centres such as Amsterdam and London (Sanderson, 1998: 30–3).

The one country outside Europe that had a similarly advanced economy and organisation was Japan, which experienced rapid economic and social capitalistic development from the mid-sixteenth century, and Sanderson uses its experience as a comparator for assessing Europe's advancement during a similar period of time. He claims that there were five 'preconditions' that distinguished the smaller economically advancing countries of Europe (notably Britain and the Netherlands) and Japan: their relative smallness of size, with lower costs of transport and administration than their larger neighbours; their geography, especially their coastlines which provided opportunities for marine transport; their temperate climates; their demographic history, especially population growth and urbanisation; and their developing political structures (Sanderson 1998: 36–7).

Imperialism and colonialism: issues, influences and explanations

The period of 'high' imperialism from the later nineteenth to the mid-twentieth century evidenced a complexity of changing and iterative relations between major European (and later American and Japanese) powers and lands beyond their own territories, frequently in distant parts of the globe. The imperial processes also included trans-imperial networks of contact and debate, and also links and debates between imperial state powers and states outside the imperial system, some of them part of 'informal' empires. Bayly has outlined the major analyses of the period of high imperialism or the 'second British empire', including those that welcomed its development, those that 'emphasized the ancient rights and liberties of settler communities of British subjects overseas', and the more sceptical writings of radicals and free-trade liberals, together with, in Asia and North Africa in particular, 'distinct indigenous traditions which viewed the expansion of the British Empire with a jaundiced eye' (Bayly 1999: 55, 56). Further developments from the 1880s to the First World War included an awareness of growing imperial powers in Europe, notably Germany and Russia, and other more distant powers such as Japan and the United States; recognition of developing nationalisms both in the British Dominion states such as Australia and in other imperial territories; together with accelerating issues of racism (Bayly 1999: 57).

J. R. Seeley, Regius Professor of History at Cambridge from 1869 to 1895, called for greater recognition of the significance of the 'English empire', or 'Greater Britain' as he called it, in the teaching of English history:

if we stand aloof a little and follow with our eyes the progress of the English State, the great governed society of the English people, in recent centuries, we shall be much more struck by another change, which is not only far greater but even more conspicuous, though it has always been less discussed, partly because it proceeded more gradually, partly because it excited less opposition. I mean the simple obvious fact of the extension of the English name into other countries of the globe, the foundation of Greater Britain.

There is something very characteristic in the indifference which we show towards this mighty phenomenon of the diffusion of our race and the expansion of our state. We seem, as it were, to have conquered and peopled half the world in a fit of absence of mind … nor have we even now ceased to think of ourselves as simply a race inhabiting an island off the northern coast of the Continent of Europe … This fixed way of thinking has influenced our historians … They do not perceive that in that century [the eighteenth] the history of England is not in England but in America and Asia. (Seeley 1883: 9–10)

Seeley, in this oft-quoted aphorism about the empire having been acquired in a fit of absence of mind, was not merely describing, as is sometimes thought, a process of imperial expansion, but voicing a complaint at the neglect of English imperialism by English historians. That having been said, it must also be noted that he later gave a similar and more direct view of the development of Britain in India: 'Our acquisition of India was made blindly. Nothing great that has ever been done by Englishmen was done so unintentionally, so accidentally, as the conquest of India. There has indeed been little enough of calculation or contrivance in our colonisation' (Seeley 1883: 207). He does, however, point to the likelihood of Indian independence: 'A time may conceivably come when it may be practicable to leave India to herself', and, with great prescience, 'The sudden withdrawal even of an oppressive Government is a dangerous experiment' (Seeley 1883: 224–5). Bernard Porter has placed Seeley's ideas on empire in pedagogic context, indicating that his appeal for the teaching of empire history to have a much more prominent place in the syllabuses of schools, colleges and universities went largely unheeded until after the First World War (Porter 2004: 49–50).

From one perspective, the general aim of imperial and colonial activity was political, economic and cultural dominance over indigenous or more recently arrived peoples in the colonial territories, with fragile sets of administrative controls and personnel put in place to maintain links with the metropolis and to implement what often were pragmatic and uncertain policies. Flimsy policies and attempts to put them into practice in widely differing environmental and social conditions were informed by the local knowledge both of Europeans and of indigenous people, and were supported, from afar and in situ, by an amalgam of individuals and institutions. These included explorers, cartographers and surveyors, administrators, traders, missionaries, and military and naval personnel, together with departments of government, and scientific, geographical and colonial settlement societies, whose nature and influence is expanded in later chapters of this book.

For much of the period of high imperialism, debate on the acquisition of colonial territories was conditioned by a number of major issues. These included the costs of acquiring and running a widely scattered empire; the eagerness to find mineral, natural biotic and agricultural resources that could assist the developing industrial economies of European countries such as Britain, Germany, France, and Belgium; and the creation of overseas markets for European industrial goods. Drayton identifies key targets as:

the opening of territory to commerce and exploitation; the creation of a revenue base to offset the expense of government; the preservation of internal order and the security of frontiers; the imposition, via laws, of British modes of labour, property, exchange and justice; and, in varying degrees, the support of Christianity, education, and sanitation, and the political consultation of 'responsible' local people. (Drayton 2000: 222)

The changing geopolitics of Europe was highly significant. Anxieties within Europe accelerated tensions over territorial control and were reflected in territorial 'scrambles' overseas, notably in Africa, and also in the influential roles of powerful individuals such as Bismarck, Ferry, King Leopold II, and ultimately Mussolini. Multinational conferences were convened that sought to co-ordinate the overseas commitments of Europeans and others, such as the Brussels Africa Conference of 1867 and the Berlin West Africa Conference of 1884–5. Both of these had unanticipated outcomes and were, inter alia, attended by European explorers and representatives of European geographical societies.

European colonial activities were increasingly global, through the rapid increase in the speed of travel and of communications, the advent of the steamship and the telegraphic system, and the effects of these technical innovations on the acquisition and dissemination of important economic, political and strategic information. The defence of the overseas realms was a permanent headache and continuing cost for the Europeans, closely bound up with rapid changes in war technology and with changes in military, naval, and – later on – air strategy. There have been many attempts at theorising on the impact of technology on imperial change, mainly at large scales, though regional or smaller-scale impacts, for example of irrigation canals in India (see Chapter 9), are equally significant and require further exploration.

Free trade

The economic advantages of free trade were reviewed by classical economists such as Adam Smith and David Ricardo, but the major incentive for Britain came with the repeal of the Corn Laws in 1846, after pressure from the Anti-Corn Law League, with an ensuing period of sixty-eight years in which Britain imposed no tariffs (Sheppard 2005: 159). This period from 1846 to 1914 partially overlapped the era of British and European high imperialism. The free trade policy adopted by Britain was initiated by the Anti-Corn Law League under the leadership of Richard Cobden, a Manchester textile factory owner. In his lectures on the political economy basis for free trade he 'drew on Adam Smith's principle, that trade extends the market, deliberately neglecting Ricardo's recently published principle of comparative advantage' (Sheppard 2005: 159).

The extent of the Manchester school's ideas and activities on the adoption of the free trade policy by Britain at this time is debatable, but the fact is that the repeal of the Corn Laws 'marked the moment when the regional interests of Manchester jumped scale to become the national interest, as the doctrine of free trade gained social legitimacy. This moment came to symbolize England's commitment to the free trade doctrine – the position in space-time at which free trade shifted from a discourse about the world to a world-changing performance' (Sheppard 2005: 163).

In the period 1862 to 1877 many other European countries became engaged in a series of bilaterally lowered tariff trade treaties, including France, Belgium, the Netherlands, the Hanseatic League, Prussia, the other German states, Austria, Switzerland, Spain, Norway and Sweden, though this phase was short-lived, with France, followed by others, moving back to protective measures from 1875. By the end of the century, most of the British settler colonies overseas, including Canada, Australia and New Zealand, all had tariff-protected economies.

Empirically based support for free trade policies in the contemporary era cannot, according to Sheppard, be easily drawn from the attempts of European states, notably Britain, to embrace free trade in the later nineteenth and early twentieth centuries because Britain had, in many cases, arranged trade advantages for her colonies, and her trading elsewhere was based on a comparative advantage in manufacturing, with other European states resorting to non-tariff devices to facilitate national advantage (Sheppard 2005: 164–8).

Bernard Porter has also made the point that free trade was not seen by many British contemporaries as compatible with an imperialism that included the formal acquisition and control of colonies:

> That last step, however, was in strict free-market terms, a retrograde one. Free trade, which was the flag Britain sailed under, was not supposed to be compatible with imperialism of this sort … it also created a practical problem. Nineteenth-century free marketeers were not only (theoretically) against colonial government; they were broadly unsympathetic to government of any kind. It was seen as an unproductive distraction from the real, 'manly', and important business of life, which was facilitating the production and exchange of products, so creating wealth for others and also, naturally, for themselves. (Porter 2004: 295)

Hobson and Lenin

The book by John Hobson (1858–1940) *Imperialism: A Study*, was published in 1902, and offered, as Hobson had done previously (in his newspaper articles, for example), a major critique of imperialism at a time when British imperialism was undergoing a major crisis. This crisis was attributed to Britain's failure to compete in industrial product markets with the United States and Germany, and to a global transition from merchant to industrial capitalism, so that 'the idea of the Empire became increasingly important as a fillip to the British balance of payments, as a source of gold and a set of assets to sustain the convertibility of sterling' (Kearns 1993: 9–15, 12).

Hobson's book was written during the Anglo-Boer War of 1899–1902, and identified imperialism with the expansion of Europe overseas in the period 1870–1900, because of the need to find outlets for the surplus capital produced by industrial intensification and domestic underconsumption, concluding that: 'imperialism is the endeavour of the great controllers of industry to broaden the channel for the flow of their surplus wealth by seeking foreign markets and foreign investments to take off the goods and capital they cannot sell or use at home' (Hobson 1902: 85; cited by Wesseling 2004: 146). This led to Hobson's contested idea of a change from settler and trading colonialism to an international imperialism, in which European states fought with the inhabitants of overseas territories, and competed between themselves, for control of desired territories.

This 'insane' moment in the development of world capitalism stood contrary to the principles of the British Liberal Party (of which Hobson was a member) and necessitated greater international co-operation and free trade rather than aggressive competition as a solution (Kearns 1993: 20). Hobson's argument is weakened by its eugenicist underpinnings, but current re-evaluations of the broader body of his work suggest that he overstated the perceived links between London financiers and politicians; that he focused too much on the imperial processes, including the flow of capital from metropole to poorer nations, rather than the flow to the wealthier settler colonies of Australia, Canada, and New Zealand, and to South America; that he does not explain the imperial trajectories of countries such as Italy which had very little surplus capital; that his proposed solution to even global development through capital used to peaceful and co-operative ends was rather naive (Cain and Hopkins, 1993: 16); and does not explain the later rise of the United States as an imperial power.

Aspects of his theory, though, have found favour with later commentators. Kearns, for example, suggests that on account of a crisis in industrial and finance capital, 'It seems likely that the increase in the size of Britain's formal empire in the late nineteenth century was largely a defensive measure to keep as much as possible of world trade under the terms of free trade conducted in sterling. This was the nature of the City's strategy' (Kearns 1993: 11). It was also symptomatic of the attraction of British 'parasitic' finance to new territory overseas, being part of an aggressive/militant, protectionist imperialism which would oppose a more internationalist philosophy and strategy, witnessed in the events and outcome of the Anglo-Boer War (Kearns 1993: 19).

Cain has pointed out, however, that Hobson had revised his views at a later stage and before the First World War, and was strongly influenced by the writings of Norman Angell (1938) to adopt a more optimistic stance in favour of capitalism. This attributed to European and American overseas investment the capability, through imperialism, of raising the standards of poorer nations, seeing imperialism 'not as a conspiracy of vested evil interests intent on exploiting the East and subverting democracy in the West', but as a means of transition to a better economic future within 'a capitalist universe, a step on the way to economic convergence, international government, and world peace' (Cain 2007: 28). Morag Bell has also suggested that 'by the First World War [Hobson] was writing more positively about the value of the empire to British trade' (Bell 1998: 166, n.16).

In the 1930s Hobson was cautioning that the rise of fascism in Germany and Italy exemplified a form of capitalist–military nationalism that opposed democracy, socialism and communism (as in Russia), and wrote that it was crucial for him that democracy and socialism needed to gain advantage before the likely catastrophe that would be the outcome of neo-capitalist imperialism (Cain 2007: 38). Anthony Webster suggests that Hobson offered 'an interpretation of British Imperialism which focussed principally upon metropolitan and economic interests as the main drivers of expansion' (Webster 2006: 47), and that these systems were of discriminating benefit to sections of the British populace, notably missionaries, military officers operating in the empire, arms manufacturers, and colonial civil servants (Webster 2006: 45–6).

Hobson's work was commended by V. I. Lenin in his book *Imperialism: The Highest Stage of Capitalism*, written in Zurich in 1916, and published in Russian in 1917. In the preface Lenin points to the difficult conditions (shortage of French, English and Russian literature to consult and difficulties of censorship) in which he wrote, but he also acknowledges the value that he gained from his 'use of the principal English work, *Imperialism*, J. A. Hobson's book, with all the care that, in my opinion, that work deserves' (Lenin 1948: 9).

Lenin extended the work of Karl Marx on late capitalism, and analysed the monopoly capitalism characteristic of advanced industrial economies at the beginning of the twentieth century, controlled by a small number of people, whose capital could not all be invested profitably in domestic or European economies, and required overseas investment in advantageous cost, labour, and profit conditions. His definition of imperialism was:

Imperialism is capitalism in that stage of development in which the domination of monopolies and finance capital has taken shape; in which the export of capital has acquired pronounced importance; in which the division of the world by the international trusts has begun, and in which the partition of all the territory of the earth by the greatest capitalist countries has been completed. (Lenin 1948: 109)

The world was dominated by monopoly capitalism, and the British free trading system had produced a dichotomy, between richer nations which had become parasites, and the poorer nations from which they extracted profit (Turnbull 1999: 386).

In Chapter IV, 'The export of capital', Lenin wrote:

As long as capitalism remains what it is, surplus capital will never be utilized for the purpose of raising the standard of living of the masses in a given country, for this would mean a decline in profits for the capitalists; it will be used for the purpose of increasing those profits by exporting capital abroad to the backward countries. In these backward countries profits are usually high, for capital is scarce, the price of land is relatively low, raw materials are cheap. The possibility of exporting capital is created by the fact that numerous backward countries have been drawn into the international capitalist intercourse; main railways have either been built or are being built there; the elementary conditions for industrial development have been created, etc. The necessity for exporting capital arises from the fact that in a few countries capitalism has become 'over-ripe' and (owing to the backward state of agriculture and the impoverished state of the masses) capital cannot find 'profitable' investment. (Lenin 1948: 77)

Although there were similarities between Hobson's and Lenin's ideas on the causes, consequences and dynamics of imperialism, such as the significance of capitalist financiers and domestic under-consumption and poverty in investment overseas, there are also differences in matters of geographical emphasis and the predicted future dynamics of capitalism.

Lenin's thesis, intended to explain the forms of economic development of continental European countries at a particular time in history, has many useful ideas, but has weaknesses: there is no clear idea of what might follow this 'highest form of capitalism'; it was written at a time when monopoly capital and trade protection were important elements of the economies of two of the fastest growing economies – Germany and the United States – and it assumes, incorrectly, that the outcome of investment of capital overseas by European states would be successful, for in some cases it was not. Particular criticism of Lenin's thesis came from the right-wing Austrian economist Joseph Schumpeter.

Schumpeter, notably in an essay of 1919 entitled 'The Sociology of Imperialisms', advanced the idea that imperialism was an anachronistic survivor in the modern period from a bygone age, but recognised that capitalism was rapidly increasing and that modern capitalist organisations and entrepreneurs could, however, promote imperialism, notably under conditions of protectionist regimes, but he 'did not believe that monopoly capitalism was inevitable or that it presaged the end of the capitalist system because it depended for its survival on protectionism and that was not intrinsic to capitalism' (Cain 2007: 31).

Schumpeter also supported the notion of recurring innovative economic or enterprise cycles, as postulated by Kondratiev and Mensch, and the geographer Peter Hugill has adapted these concepts, together with those of Goldstein and Kuznets, and Berry, Modelsky and Thompson (the last two in relation to the role of war), to propose a series of five 'clear hegemons, one in each of the five pairs of Kondratiev or world leadership cycles experienced in the past five hundred years: Portugal, Holland, England, Britain, and the United States' (Hugill 1993: 12–13). Recent work on gentlemanly capitalism and imperialism (see below) has revived interest in Hobson's ideas, particularly the roles of aristocratically led finance capitalists and investors, notably those operating from the City of London, but has also contested Hobson's thesis about the manipulation of politicians by finance capitalists (Webster 2006: 65).

The geographer David Harvey has applied Marxist concepts of the rise, accumulation and spatio-temporal fixes of capitalism to the development of modern and contemporary imperialism, characterising the period 1870 to 1945 as one of 'the rise of bourgeois imperialisms' and the forcing of surplus European capital outside Europe 'to swamp the world in a massive speculation of investment and trade' from 1870 onwards (Harvey 2003: 42–3), necessitating the development of empires and colonies in which this capital could be invested. The broad context has been summarised by Robert Dodgshon: 'the increasing tendency of investment capital from the nineteenth century onwards to seek a "spatial fix" by exploiting opportunities overseas forms part of a more general strategy whereby core areas can export or displace their problems geographically' (Dodgshon 1998: 195).

Spatial fixing is, however, not a simple process, not least because of the different constraints on states or polities as decision-makers in the imperial game, and investors of capital in the form of individuals and companies. Harvey (2003: 29, 32) points to the necessity of seeing:

the territorial and the capitalist logics of power as distinct from each other. Yet it is also undeniable that the two logics intertwine in complex and sometimes contradictory ways. The literature on imperialism and empire too often assumes an easy accord between them: that political–economic processes are guided by the strategies of state and empire and that states and empires always operate out of capitalistic motivations. In practice the two logics frequently tug against each other, sometimes to the point of outright antagonism.

The asymmetries both of natural resources and of wealth and power affect and change the functioning of the market, and their preservation is a familiar part of imperialist and colonialist processes.

Intriguingly, Harvey asserts that the imperialisms that began to take shape at the end of the nineteenth century were bourgeois imperialisms (rather than the last stage of capitalism). The mid-nineteenth-century revolutions at a time of capitalist crisis (whose initial solutions were long-term infrastructural investments and geographical expansion, notably via Atlantic trade) gave way to a global search for 'spatio-temporal fixes', and thus increased the consolidation of bourgeois power through a require-ment that the bourgeoisie 'either dissolve older imperialist forms (such as that of the Austro-Hungarian or Ottoman empires) or convert them (as in Britain) to a distinctively capitalist logic' (Harvey 2003: 43).

Robinson and Gallagher: the imperial mind and informal empire

Africa and the Victorians: The Official Mind of Imperialism, by Ronald Robinson and John Gallagher, was published in 1961, and their chapter on the partition of Africa in the *New Cambridge Modern History*, extended their thesis about the processes of British imperialism in Africa to those of other European powers (Robinson and Gallagher 1962: 593–640). The authors contended that much of the character of British imperialism derived from an informal and lower-costing free trade operating in infor-mal empire, and through the 'official minds' of administrators at the local frontiers of imperialism, rather than through activity and policy-making in the metropole. 'In spatial terms, theirs [Robinson and Gallagher's] was a centripetal, or as they called it, "ex-centric", analysis, since expansion-ary initiative moved from the colonial "edge" of the empire to the British "centre"' (Lambert and Lester 2006: 4), and found favour at a time when the independence movements in former European colonies and the Cold War were accelerating, and when greater scholarly emphasis was being placed on indigenous and non-European accounts and perspectives of imperial processes.

This work offered valuable and new perspectives on what have been labelled 'peripheral' or 'excentric' perspectives (Porter 1994: 51), including the attitudes of colonial officials. Their book on Africa and the Victorians stressed, against theories of Britain's appropriation of parts of Africa for economic motives, the importance of local resistance and pressure, notably the resistance in Egypt that prompted British occupation in 1882 and the events leading to the Anglo-Boer War, in the determination of British policy in Africa motivated by strategic considerations such as the protection of routes to India. The expansion of the British empire in Africa was a reflection inter alia of the decline in its informal empire and the 'need to counter the expansive tendencies of other industrialising nations which established themselves as world powers for the first time after 1870' (Cain and Hopkins 1993: 9). The other European imperial powers operating in Africa were there mainly to counter proto-nationalist movements, for example in Tunis, the Sudan, East Africa and the Congo basin (Flint 1999: 458).

This 'peripheral' thesis was widely influential, reflecting an opposition to Marxist ideologies and the need for a newer liberal thesis of imperialism that stressed more strongly the role of imperialist agents and indigenous polities at the imperial frontiers (Cain and Hopkins 1993: 9). Criticism of it has also been extensive, including questions about its seeming underestimation of economic imperialism, notably in West Africa, and the chronology of European imperial involvement in Africa (Flint 1999: 457). Robinson and Gallagher's work has been strongly influential in revising earlier analyses of the reasons and chronologies of European imperialism in the modern period.

'Gentlemanly capitalism'

The concept of 'gentlemanly capitalism' was proposed and developed by Cain and Hopkins in a series of articles and books published from the early 1980s onwards, and allocates a major role in the dispersion of finance capital to empire and colonies to a combination of English landowners and City of London financiers. They wished to counter-balance and replace existing 'peripheral' explanations for high imperialism with the 'centrifugal' thesis that 'the central weakness in existing accounts of overseas expansion and imperialism is that they underplay or misjudge the relationship between the British economy and Britain's presence abroad. Putting the metropolitan economy back at the centre of the analysis, we suggest, makes it possible to establish a new framework for interpreting Britain's historic role as a world power', thereby promoting the significance of the rise of services in Britain since 1850, disputing, inter alia, Marxist emphases on the rise and decline of industrialisation in the imperial process, and 'down-grading to some extent the importance of formal acquisitions, including the scramble for Africa, while bringing into better focus a vigorous and expanding informal presence, notably in areas of white settlement' (Cain and Hopkins 1993: 5, 12).

Difficulties arise partly from the problem of translating this alleged driving force of imperial investment and policy to the experiences of European imperial powers other than Britain, whose socio-cultural mixes were very different from those operating from London, and whose surplus capital available for investment overseas was also different. The amount of surplus capital available for overseas investment from Germany was limited, largely being absorbed for domestic development purposes, while there was surplus capital available for colonial investment from France.

There is also the problem, highlighted by Lambert and Lester, of accommodating the wide range of geographical differences of imperial experience in such a thesis, so that:

With their metropolitan focus, and the consequent marginalisation of both British and indigenous peoples in the colonies themselves, Cain and Hopkins still did not address the longstanding geographical problem of how to write about such vastly different places, processes and people as those contained within the ever-changing nineteenth-century British empire at the same time – how to link the local and particular (metropolitan and colonial) with the general and universal (imperialism). (Lambert and Lester, 2006: 4–5)

There are also problems with the underestimation of settler capital investment within the colonies themselves (McAloon 2002: 204–23), and with the explanation of expansion through military action at the imperial peripheries, in such places as southern Africa, on the basis of predominantly metropolitan influences.

Modernity

The concept of modernity has relevance to questions and processes of imperialism, and is characterised by a wide-ranging set of ideas and realities concerned with changes through time, notably in the 'modern' historical period, in places, societies, economies, cities, industries, scientific and religious knowledge, belief systems, and institutions. In the modern era there was greater global interconnection, notably through commerce and the exchanges of ideas, together with processes of erosion and modification of traditional beliefs and practices. The timescale of this set of changes starts in the late eighteenth century, and high imperialism from the later nineteenth century is part of it. While global scales of interaction affected the dynamics of trade, geopolitics and humanitarian movements for example, it is important to note that modernity was also part of a process that operated at very much smaller scales, each of whose local geographies and timescales were different. As Ogborn (1998: 1) puts it:

> Modernity is most often a matter for grand theory and for portentous pronouncements heralding either its origin or demise. It can, however, also be a matter of close investigations of the spaces and places of the past – and of the banks, newspapers, actresses and umbrellas that fill them – that try to connect these geographies to deep and wide social formations.

Bayly, in his seminal book on the birth of the modern world and global linkages, 'relativizes the "revolution of modernity" by showing that many different agencies and ideologies around the world empowered it in different ways and at different times' (Bayly 2004: 12). Simo has also linked the processes of imperialism and colonialism with modernisation, a process which was changing both Europe and its overseas territories at the same time (Simo 2005: 97).

Charles Withers, in his study of Scotland since 1520, engaged the concept of modernity in his analysis of the historical geographies of geographical knowledge in that country, drawing on Miles Ogborn's influential study of the spaces of modernity associated with London's geographies between 1680 and 1780. Both of these historical geographers emphasise the point that geographical differences and historical outcomes matter in modernity and that modernity's complex 'hybrid' relations are continually remade, contested and reconfigured through interaction. Ogborn suggests that 'there is no single history and no unitary geography of capitalism ... Instead there is the possibility of writing many histories and geographies, large and small, all of which can lay claim to versions of modernity's "complex multilinear" time and space' (Withers 2001: 24–5; Ogborn 1998: 13).

Pluralist explanations

The motives for imperialism and colonialism varied through time. As Bayly and others have suggested, no single argument can be adduced to explain the new imperialism of European countries in the late nineteenth and early twentieth centuries – such as Marxist-Leninist economic arguments, views on the significance of political changes, including the acceleration of nationalism and its territorial accompaniments, ideas about the significance of crises at the 'peripheries', diplomatic or political actions, or postcolonial perspectives. 'All these arguments', writes Bayly, 'seem to have some force at different places and at different times in the history of the new imperialism. It is probably fruitless to seek for one overarching explanation.' He suggests, though, that a general precondition for this new wave was the close link between imperialism and 'the more strident European nationalism … Imperialism and nationalism were part of the same phenomenon. Nationalism and conflict in Europe made states more aware of their competitors abroad and more inclined to stake out claims and prefer their own citizens' (Bayly 2004: 229–30).

Pluralistic explanations and understandings of imperialism and colonialism are also supported by Stoler and Cooper: 'Europe's colonies were never empty spaces to be made over in Europe's image or fashioned in its interests; nor, indeed, were European states self-contained entities that at one point projected themselves overseas. Europe was made of its imperial projects, as much as colonial encounters were shaped by conflicts within Europe itself' (Stoler and Cooper 1997: 1). Similarly, David Lambert and Alan Lester argue that '"new" imperial history recognises that there was never a single European colonial project, whether it be the pursuit of industrial or "gentlemanly" capitalism, or governmental geo-strategising. Neither, accordingly, was there a single discourse, or set of representations and practices of colonialism' (Lambert and Lester 2006: 9).

Within the individual states and regions of Europe there was much debate and disagreement about the desirability and practice of imperialism, both formal and informal. John Darwin, in a strongly persuasive discourse on the dynamics of British Victorian imperialism, suggests that even imperial India, thought to be the best example of formal imperial policy of acquisition and control, had been affected by a complex of different and changing motives: 'The motives for territorial expansion in India were not dissimilar from those animating settler or proconsular imperialism elsewhere: the desire of private interests to enlarge the political influence indispensable to commercial profit; the search for defensible and economical frontiers; the need to control or coerce recalcitrant frontier politics; the pre-emption of rival European influences' (Darwin 1997: 625–6). Many of the economic conditions of pre-colonial India were supportive of further European involvement. These included commercial transformations already underway, facilitating development roles for foreign traders; the inheritance by the East India Company in Bengal of an existing land revenue system; the existence of a military labour market in north India; and the commercial and political opportunities provided by the hinterland of India (Darwin 1997: 626).

British mid-Victorian imperialism, says Darwin, was driven by a capacity for overseas expansion greater than that of other European countries, by an 'interventionist ideology' underpinned by the energies of 'free trade, utilitarianism, evangelical Christianity and anti-slavery', by combinations of economic forces such as cheap long-term credit, the export of cheaply produced manufactured goods, and an increase in the number of emigrants, by sea- and land-based military power, and by the intelligence on Asian affairs sent back from India. These provided motives for seemingly unlimited opportunity for expansion overseas, though there were in fact many constraints that shaped the locations and events of British imperialism. Darwin suggests the concept of a 'bridgehead' – the varied means, including the experiences and agencies of individuals and institutions, which determined 'the reciprocal impulses which travelled between the centre and its diverse peripheries', constituting a 'hinge or "interface" between the metropole and a local periphery' which 'might be a commercial, settler, missionary or proconsular presence or a combination of all four' (Darwin 1997: 627–8). This notion has also been incorporated by the geographers David Lambert and Alan Lester in their book on imperial careers in the British empire in the nineteenth century (Lambert and Lester 2006: 5–9), in which they combine this notion of pluralistic explanation of imperial experiences with the concept of humanitarian networks operating across empire, through which the varied and often conflicting imperial projects interacted.

On balance Darwin favours, as explanation of the dynamics of British Victorian imperialism, a combination and modification of the 'official mind' and 'gentlemanly capitalism' theories, especially Gallagher and Robinson's ideas about the imperialism of free trade. He suggests 'that the engine of British expansion throughout the nineteenth century was the chaotic pluralism of private and sub-imperial interests: religious, commercial, strategic, humanitarian, scientific, speculative and migrational. The role of government was sometimes to facilitate, sometimes to regulate, this multiple expansive momentum' (Darwin 1997: 641).

Nation, state and imperialism

There was a major difference between those European powers that by the period of high imperialism from the 1880s onwards had long experience of nation-statehood and the control of colonies overseas, and those, notably new, nation-states such as Germany and Italy that did not. There has been much discussion on the definition, nature and history of the state in modern Europe and elsewhere. Bayly, reviewing the changing ideas of historians on the subject, argues that the modern state should not be regarded solely as a coherent 'homogeneous and all-seeing entity'; that state influence fluctuated considerably through the modern period; and that in the nineteenth century in particular there were many different voices 'increasingly speaking the language of the state', evidenced by Cecil Rhodes and missionary and millenarian movements (Bayly 2004: 252–3).

There are many ideas about the development of nationalism, some incorporating an evolutionary process from pre-existing cultural and political cores, others affirming that nationalism is essentially a modern phenomenon, an artificial construct by political powers and ideologies, linked, as Gellner claimed in his modernisation theory of nationalism, to economic processes such as industrialisation and urbanisation, moving eastwards in the nineteenth century and southwards from the late nineteenth and early twentieth centuries (Bayly 2004: 202–3; Gellner 1983).

The notion of nationalism preceding the formation of a state has also been disputed, with the reverse process being favoured, and another theory, by Benedict Anderson, attributes modern nationalism, especially in Indonesia, to the creation of imagined communities through the international spread of ideas via the printed word. Bayly has suggested three types of development of nationalism: evolution from earlier patriotic sentiments, evidenced in 'northern Vietnam, Korea, Japan, and Ethiopia'; a more abrupt emergence of nationalism in the nineteenth century, notably after about 1860, 'particularly in the complex large polities of eastern Eurasia and North Africa'; and areas of late coherent nationalism in 'the central Ottoman lands and parts of Austria-Hungary, Russia, and even parts of southern Ireland' (Bayly 2004: 204, 218–19).

Changing national identity and ambition were fundamental parts of the high imperialism associated with European states in the later nineteenth and early twentieth centuries. Simultaneously the populations and territories which were the focus of European imperialism continued to evolve their political and administrative systems and to redefine their objectives, frequently in expressions of nationalist aspirations in opposition to the imperial yokes.

The processes were not simple and most certainly not just one- or two-way, but a kaleidoscopic mixture of ideals and events. The period from about 1870 witnessed the intensification of European influence on existing imperial territories and the rapid acquisition of new territories, a process in which Japan and the United States also engaged. Bayly has pointed to the 'long-standing relationship' between nationalism and imperialism, which has necessitated reflection on the nature of nationality, and has argued that 'one general point, which seems obvious but has sometimes slipped from sight, is that the new imperialism was closely related to the more strident European nationalism ... imperialism and nationalism were part of the same phenomenon. Nationalism and conflict in Europe made states more aware of their competitors abroad and more inclined to stake out claims and prefer their own citizens' (Bayly 2004: 228–30). The geographer Michael Heffernan also takes this view in his review and analysis of the 'meaning of Europe':

Although legitimised by the age-old rhetoric of civilisation, commerce and religion, the yearning for new colonial space after *c.* 1880 sprang from an anxious and defensive European nationalism. Precise objectives varied, of course, but *fin-de-siècle* imperialism was often determined by fear that 'unclaimed' colonial territory would fall into the hands of rival powers. Colonies were coveted not for economic reasons but as symbols of an otherwise vulnerable national pride, tangible zones which could be coloured in the appropriate fashion on school atlases, wall maps, tea towels and a thousand other items of imperial propaganda. (Heffernan 1998c: 55)

Heffernan (1998c: 54–5) also shows that this imperial thrust at the end of the nineteenth century was one of three major features of Europe's 'geopolitical panic', the other two being the destruction of the free trade ideology by more protective national economic ideologies, and 'a fundamental reordering of the system of alliances'.

The reasons for the acceleration of German and Italian imperial ambition are complex. It has been argued that one of the causes of German colonial expansion was the desire to relieve population pressure and potential class discord by sending Germans overseas. This social imperialism was part of a mechanism, according to Bayly, by which 'Bismarck used overseas expansion as a tool of internal state building', in spite of which he 'did not see empire as an economic necessity for Germany *per se*' (Bayly 2004: 232). Imperial ambitions pre-dated the formation of the German Reich in 1871, 'nourished by a mix of ideologies and experiences, national dreams, and social contradictions' (Sandner and Rössler 1994: 115). Germany lost her colonies as quickly as she acquired them, becoming at the end of the First World War a 'postcolonial state in a still-colonial world' (Klotz 2005: 136).

The contexts and meaning of German national identity in the era of the Weimar Republic shifted during and after the First World War. During the war negative colonial tropes and metaphors were used to describe atrocities and attitudes on both sides, with German propaganda focusing on the colonial troops fighting for France and Britain and the instillation of fear in the minds of soldiers and populace about atrocities by these foreign troops. The removal of German colonies and the denial of a place for Germany in the new League of Nations were 'a reminder of the new global order and Germany's diminutive status within it. In a world that had for centuries been divided between colonizers and colonized, it seemed to many that Germany, no longer held to be "civilized" enough to be a colonizer, was now being reckoned among the colonized' (Klotz 2005: 141). A fear of reverse colonisation was stirred up by German youth groups who fanaticised about the supposed dangers and effects of the French deployment of colonial troops in the Rhine valley in 1921. This was a reflection of the German racism that would be even further promoted under the Nazis, and of a 'ghost that had long haunted the practitioners of empire: Africa colonizing Europe' (Klotz 2005: 141, 142). Klotz suggests that Germany's postcolonial experience came from a desire for restitution of her pre-war global status related to her 'racial standing', and led to the racist policies of National Socialism (Klotz 2005: 143).

Italy became a nation-state in 1870, and continued to redefine and practise changing concepts of national identity, some of which had been voiced earlier in the nineteenth century, into the late nineteenth and early twentieth centuries, and was involved as a colonial power in North and North-East Africa between 1883 and 1943. The ideology of Italian nationalism, linked to imperialism, included reference to historical heroes who had been involved in mercantilist trading and overseas exploration from the late medieval period onwards. Lucio Gambi suggests that: 'The evocation and exaltation of these historical precedents stood at the heart of Italian imperialism, and thereby made it different from that of other European nations. Of dubious historical validity these myths were nevertheless a source of fascination' (Gambi 1994: 75). They fed into the idea of the Mediterranean Sea as an Italian area of influence (*mare nostrum*) and, in relation to fascist ambitions for Libya, as Italy's 'fourth shore' (*quarta sponda*). Political and military ambitions underpinned Italian imperial and colonial policy after the First World War.

When Western imperial states attempted to administer overseas territories, they often built on existing local structures and ideologies. Concepts and practices of state governance, generally incorporating a central organisation of taxation and security, differed within Europe and between overseas places caught up in the imperial project, with the latter more involved with questions of migration and settlement, and in the British Dominion states, with greater emphasis on local state governance, as in Australia. The application of metropolitan legal systems overseas, however, gradually reduced the influence of local practice and custom – for the resolution of grievances, of systems of marriage, inheritance, and of regulated punishment, including those in regions of Muslim, Hindu and Buddhist cultures (Bayly 2004: 257, 260–5). Greater state influence was evidenced through the control of people and money, including taxation and the deployment of armed forces, together with the level of control facilitated by better communications, and states responded to public expectation of improvements in conditions of living, aided in this and more authoritative functions by new organs of administration, including government ministries.

Legal systems

European imperial and colonial expansion included the dissemination of legal authority, sometimes adapted to pre-existing indigenous systems. Law was one of the means by which European control and influence was formally imposed, including the legitimation of colonial taxation through the regulation of land rights. Lauren Benton has outlined the process:

The strategies of rule included aggressive attempts to impose legal systems intact. More common, though, were conscious efforts to retain elements of existing institutions and limit legal change as a way of sustaining social order. Conquered and colonized groups sought, in turn, to respond to the imposition of law in ways that included accommodation, advocacy within the system, subtle delegitimation, and outright rebellion. (Benton 2002: 2–3)

There were tensions and conflicts within areas of colonial jurisdiction, and between the colonies of different European (and other) states, leading to the operation of changing and complex systems over given areas. In North Africa French imperial and colonial administration had to deal with varied legal systems, including Islamic, Berber customary and Judaic law, which continued in operation, but under the assumed supremacy of French law. There were many different legal systems in India, including Hindu customary law, Anglo-Hindu law and English customary law. In the Dutch East Indies Dutch law governed the settlers and other

Europeans, and the indigenous inhabitants were subject to their own laws (Wesseling 2004: 51).

Laws existed in colonies not merely to govern and regulate people in specific places, but also in practice to facilitate a complicated array of global exchanges, some of them commercial and political, others cultural, including civil and criminal law. These legal processes may be viewed as 'patterns of structuring multiple legal authorities', a view that 'urges us to reimagine global structure as the institutional matrix constructed out of practice and shaped by conflict', and also to take a more nuanced view of the legal pluralism experienced in colonial situations, including the frequent crossing, by individual actors and sometimes by institutions, of boundaries between legal systems, and contested adjustments to specific legal systems, a process that Benson terms 'jurisdictional politics' (Benton 2002: 3; 4; 6–8, 10).

The focus within legal systems changed in time, with the links between state and religious law being a main focus of Islamic and Hispanic law in the seventeenth and eighteenth centuries, changing to greater emphasis by colonial powers on the role and nature of citizenship in the nineteenth century (Benton 2002: 14–15). Cultural differences and contested changes in jurisdiction were closely linked. Studies of case histories from India, West Africa, South Africa and Latin America are shown by Benton (1999: 563–88) to be indicative of a change over the three hundred years of European colonisation 'from a relatively fluid legal pluralism in which semi-autonomous legal authorities operated alongside state law, to a hierarchical model of legal pluralism in which state law subsumed in one way or another all jurisdictions, including "traditional" forums given special status by the state', the later stage quite often successfully used and appealed to by indigenous plaintiffs 'everywhere quick to perceive opportunity in this legal landscape' (Benton 1999: 563, 586). Evidence of this is provided by legal cases concerned with land rights and ownership and by cases related to the attempted control of morals and sexual behaviour, notably in the regulation of prostitution (see Chapter 11).

These trends were common to French, Dutch and British colonies, and were often reflected in tensions between agencies, for example, between the East India Company and the British parliament over Indian cases, various Dutch, British and African groups over legal issues in South Africa, and local and metropolitan legal administrators in relation to French West Africa (Benton, 1999: 586). In addition, Benton argues that 'it was the replication of these patterns of conflict that helped give rise to a global legal order – the interstate system – in which expectations about the location of legal authority became uniform across otherwise quite diverse polities' (Benton 1999: 588), that is in respect of recognition of rights by colonial states to the claimed territorial sovereignty of other colonial states and the creation of a framework of international order that facilitated exchange, including trade (Benton 2002: 25).

World systems and globalisation

One of the main issues engaging contemporary thinking is the concept of globalisation – the idea that over a period of time, starting perhaps in the sixteenth century, but accelerating from the eighteenth, a significant proportion of the world is caught up and interconnected with many other parts, places, economies and societies, largely through the processes and effects of modern capitalism, such as the movement of capital goods and people, and the exploitation of resources.

The linkage between economic and political development and the growth of global interconnections provided by trade, territorial ambition, and cultural systems, including expansions of religious beliefs, together with technological improvements in transport and communications, is important in understanding the growth of empires and colonies. An early attempt to link European economies and polities in a global context was that of Immanuel Wallerstein. He has written extensively about the emergence of a modern 'world-system', focused on north-western Europe. This became a 'core' area, influencing, through cyclical waves of capital accumulation, the economies and character of regions in the changing 'semi-periphery' and 'periphery', from the 'long' sixteenth and the seventeenth centuries, initially under mercantilism (including the agency of privileged trading companies and protective measures on imports), and from the eighteenth century under fully developed capitalism (Wallerstein 1974, 1980, 1989). The time-frame of this thesis has been disputed, with Dodgshon, among others, claiming that although there were early modern connections between European economies and those of the rest of the world, these were only 'still feeble flows that linked core and periphery over the sixteenth century' and that a fully fledged system did not develop until the nineteenth century (Dodgshon 1987: 347). Dodgshon has also more recently drawn attention to claims for the existence of earlier world-systems before 1500, such as a late medieval system incorporating an area of the 'Ottoman to north India region', and to the complexity of so-called core regions, offering the possibility of overlap of successive world systems

(Dodgshon 1998: 54–6). Nonetheless he contends that Wallerstein is correct in viewing the post-1500 system as distinctive from earlier systems,
while maintaining that 'its emergence as a functionally integrated system,
one capable of allocating economic roles to different sectors of the system,
needs to be delayed until the mid to late nineteenth century' (Dodgshon
1998: 72–4).

That the whole of the world and its spaces are bound up with and
profoundly affected by overarching processes of allocation, especially
through the market forces of capitalism, and that positive and negative
consequences flow from this process, is an attractive idea. Globalisation
cannot, however, be treated as a single force or set of processes initiated
from Europe: it is in fact a highly complex mix of motives and processes.
Doreen Massey has stated that 'Globalisation is not a single, all-embracing
movement (nor should it be imagined as some outward spread from
the West and other centres of economic power across a passive surface
of "space"). It is a making of space(s), an active reconfiguration and
meeting-up through practices and relations of a multitude of trajectories,
and it is there that lies the politics' (Massey 2005: 83).

This idea has been picked up by Lambert and Lester, who prefer the
idea of 'an imperial spatiality consisting of networks' rather than that of
world systems. They favour the idea of connected experiences that frequently are short-lived and changing – as reflected in the life experiences
of individual actors in the imperial theatre, lives that themselves 'produce
and alter the spatiality of empire' (Lambert and Lester 2006: 13). This network concept of space leads to a new concept of places not as bounded
and fixed entities, 'but rather specific juxtapositions or constellations of
multiple trajectories. These trajectories may be those of people, objects,
texts and ideas', and thus include individual experiences, cultures, representations and belief systems. Trajectories may develop formal identity,
in the shape of missionary, commercial or state institutions, for example;
others may be more ephemeral. This is quite a helpful yet difficult concept
to grasp, and it awaits exemplification, but Lambert and Lester confidently
assert that it still 'allows us to continue insisting on the unique "character"
of different places within the empire, and thus also to emphasise the obvious differences between metropolitan and colonial places' (Lambert and
Lester 2006: 14).

Historians have also re-examined the concept of globalisation. Cain and
Hopkins have suggested that worldwide or globalised systems of connection go back a long way, and point to four stages in the evolution of modern globalisation: 'archaic globalised networks', including early empires

linked to major religious movements such as Christianity and Islam; and a second phase of 'proto-globalisation' between 1600 and 1800, part of the widening imperial ambitions of European, Ottoman, and Chinese powers linked to ambitious mercantilist objectives and increasingly sophisticated administrative and taxation systems. The third phase is associated with industrialisation and the emergence of nation-states, and mainly comprises the modern era of European formal and informal 'high' imperialism in the nineteenth and early twentieth centuries; and the fourth phase is that of the demise of European empires and beyond: the postcolonial era (Cain and Hopkins 2007: 177–81; Hopkins 2002a: 1–10).

This chronology links gentlemanly and finance capitalism with imperialism, and also with cultural characteristics and dynamics of colonising and colonised peoples. Hopkins has claimed that in the modern period of global imperialism 'Overseas expansion nationalized the new internationalism by exporting national constitutions and religions and by extending national economies to distant parts of the world … The new international order was created partly by persuasion and partly by command: free trade delivered one; empire the other', and that the principal imperial systems of control were assimilation and association, used both separately and sometimes together (Hopkins, 2002a: 6). Hopkins has also highlighted the necessity of finding alternative approaches to historical globalisation, for example through non-Western perspectives, and of incorporating processes such as migration which are not confined by state boundaries (Hopkins 2002b: 21). Greater attention, in Hopkins' view, should be given to the dynamics of the nation-state in the nineteenth and twentieth centuries, to the growing sense of national identity, to national influence on imperial standards and criteria of measurement and of communication, to the role of emigrant communities, and to the significance of the ways in which local cultures and knowledge modified the processes and targets of imperialism, noting 'the ways in which a global presence was jointly produced, notwithstanding Western dominance', with local indigenous influences initiating and reshaping imperial goals and identities (Hopkins 2002b: 33).

Ethnology, with geography, history and other disciplines, became a tool of empire, influencing the survey of local populations and the determination of and response to anti-imperial actions, but merging, as part of the processes of globalisation, with knowledge and information systems at state, large region and imperial levels, through mapping and survey and the collection of statistics (Ballantyne 2002: 126, 129). The idea of trans-national imperial networks links well with the network concepts used in studies of the life-paths of individuals (Lambert and Lester 2006), the spread of evangelical missions, and of cartographic connections, in the last case linking the topographic survey of Ireland in the 1830s with the Great Trigonometrical Survey of India. Ballantyne describes globalisation as 'as much a state of mind as it is a series of financial transactions or shifts in technology that can be rendered in charts and graphs. Historians and social scientists alike could gain from devoting greater attention to the cultural and intellectual aspects of globalisations, past and present' (Ballantyne 2002: 131, 133).

The concept of globalisation has its limitations. One is the unevenness of penetration by capital and by economic and political power. Although from the seventeenth century the great trading companies of Europe such as the British and Dutch East India Companies opened up trading links with Asia, there remained, in Asia and elsewhere, places where the relations of production and exchange were very different, and this remained true into the nineteenth and early twentieth centuries. Cooper has suggested that:

it is salutary to get away from whatever tendencies there may have been to analyze social, economic, political, and cultural processes as if they took place in national or continental containers; but to adopt a language that implies that there is no container at all, except the planetary one, risks defining problems in different ways. The world has long been – and still is – a space where economic and political relations are very uneven; it is filled with lumps, places where power coalesces and where it does not. (Cooper 2005: 91–2)

Cooper also suggests that globalisation is an unhelpful concept in the sense that there are critical historical processes operating at smaller but nonetheless significant scales, which need as much attention as 'global' and more 'local' processes. Thus: 'The question is whether the changing meaning over time of spatial linkages can be better understood in some other way than globalisation' (Cooper 2005: 96). As an alternative to an explanatory narrative of the colonisation of Africa in the late nineteenth century, Cooper proposes a 'metahistory of integration' of Africa, an Africa that was subject to new borders, partially disruptive of existing trade routes, and also subject to disruption of externally linked trade networks, such as those across the Indian Ocean and the Sahara Desert, and thus to more of a de-globalisation than a globalisation process (Cooper 2005: 105).

Cooper's preference is for a concept of networks of cultural affiliation and change, not entirely bound by territorial limits imposed by colonialism, so that 'The spatial imagination of intellectuals, missionaries, and political activists, from the early nineteenth to the mid twentieth century was thus varied. It was neither global nor local, but was built out of specific lines of connection and posited regional, continental and transcontinental affinities. These affinities could narrow, expand, and narrow again' (Cooper 2005: 109). The case made is for more consideration to be given to the dynamics and spatial scales of commodity and cultural circuits, including the circuits of capital, rather than including all processes under the heading of 'globalisation'.

Postcolonialism

Postcolonialism is a term now used to encompass the events and consequences of imperialism and decolonisation, and a new pluralistic way of thinking and writing about different facets of imperialism, including issues such as race, gender and non-Western representations: that is, about different trajectories of experience. It is, as Massey (2005: 63) puts it, 'a move away from that imagination of space as a continuous surface that the coloniser, as the only active agent, crosses to find the to-be-colonised simply "there". This would be a space not as smooth surface but as the sphere of coexistence of a multiplicity of trajectories.' Robert Young (2003: 4) concurs: postcolonial cultural analysis has been much concerned with the development of theories that offer different and contesting perspectives than those from the West, and he states that postcolonial theory reflects not a single theory or practice but a complex 'related set of perspectives, which are juxtaposed against one another, on occasion contradictorily' (Young 2003: 6–7).

One of the main instigators and contributors to postcolonial analysis of imperial trajectories was Edward Said, notably through his seminal work *Orientalism*, published in 1978, together with *Culture and Imperialism*, published in 1993 (Said 1978, 1993), drawing on a wide theoretical base, notably on aspects of Foucault's notion of discourse and Gramsci's concept of cultural hegemony. The essence of his thesis, which has been both widely influential and strongly contested, is that the cultures of the Orient, as they have evolved through time, have been misrepresented by Western writers and cultures as stereotypical opposites of, and in many respects inferior to, Western cultures and ideologies (and hence seen as an 'Other'). This involves:

the hegemony of European ideas about the Orient, themselves reiterating European superiority over Oriental backwardness, usually overriding the possibility that a more independent, or more skeptical, thinker might have had quite different views on the matter. In a quite constant way, Orientalism depends for its strategy on this flexible *positional* superiority, which puts the westerner in a whole series of possible relationships with the Orient without ever losing him the upper hand. (Said 1978: 7)

He identifies significant connections between knowledge, including geographical knowledge, obtained through texts produced by geography, history, politics, economics, linguistics, anthropology, ethnography and an array of other literatures, and the Orientalist position (Childs and Williams 1997: 99).

Orientalism was, in many respects, a denigratory representation of the rich and complex cultures of the Middle East, as 'a place of decadence, corruption and menace', with 'the Christian west as an opposite – benign, masculine, civilised, moral and virtuous' (Webster 2006: 97). Notwithstanding the existence in the nineteenth and early twentieth centuries of what has been called an 'arabophile strand' of writing about lifestyles of individuals and groups (Thomas 1994: 26), the Orientalist position strengthened after 1948, and influenced Said's critical responses.

Critical response to Edward Said's *Orientalism* and *Culture and Imperialism* and to the broader body of postcolonial theory has been extensive, reflecting the intellectual power, stimulus and utility of Said's ideas about knowledge and power in orientalist and colonialist debates. Critics have pointed to the difficulty of generalising about colonialism and imperialism from a single geographical region; the absence of the role of women from this discourse; the lack of conventional historical context, method and data; the oversimplification of the highly complex and varied Western perception of the East, including an understanding of Islam; lack of detail on individual actors in the orientalist dramas; neglect of native agency and indigenous resistance, and also of representations through art forms such as painting, design, music, architecture and theatre (MacKenzie 1995; Washbrook 1999; Kennedy 1996; Childs and Williams 1997; Webster 2006).

Others, including Ernest Gellner and Robert Irwin, argued strongly that Western domination of the Orient was nowhere near as long as Said had claimed, and that it was more recent and uneven. They also argued that Palestine and Egypt, the focus of Said's writing, were weak examples because they only came under strong European influence from the nineteenth and early twentieth centuries, that major examples such as British India and Russian Asia were given less attention than they merited, and that the writings of some prominent German scholars on the East had been overlooked (Gellner 1993; Irwin 2006).

Said's writing was extremely influential on postcolonialist thinking from the 1980s, including constant 'subaltern' questioning of the significance of material evidence and knowledge systems that were seen as Western constructions. Cultural historians, geographers, and others adopted and adapted Said's ideas, and applied them to studies of cultures of exploration, survey and mapping, representations at exhibitions and institutions, humanitarian networks, infrastructures, the biographies of individuals, of gender, race and sex, of population movements, and economic and political interactions (Blunt and McEwan 2002: 1–6).

Gender, sexuality and colonialism

Facets of gender and sexuality within colonial societies have been increasingly studied by historians and by geographers. Levine (2007) has outlined some principal themes. These include the depiction, especially in Britain, of empire as a man's world, and of separate public and private spheres of activity for men and women; the assumption of the heterosexual family as the norm; the perceived dangers to women in primitive societies; opposition to practices such as sati, regulation of marriage age, and female infanticide; various aspects of images of masculinity and effeminacy; homosexual and homosocial practices among and between colonial and colonised men; the attempted regulation of intermarriage and of sexuality and associated transmitted diseases; and the roles of Western and non-Western women in the colonies. Levine argues that:

Gender, defined as social roles differently imposed upon men and women, shaped the worlds of colonialism deeply and in myriad ways. The expectations and the values of the multitudes of peoples involved – whether by choice or by force – in the colonial enterprise frequently clashed in this critical but slippery arena … gender considerations were always a point of negotiation and a critical issue within the colonies. This was no side issue, but a key and central organizing principle by which colonial rule was shaped and maintained. (Levine 2007: 164)

While gender aspects of Orientalism were underplayed by Said, they have been extensively developed by others within the wider compass of imperialism and colonialism. Patrick Wolfe suggests that:

As in so many areas, feminist scholars of imperialism have been obliged to labor the most elementary of points before being able to move on to more demanding questions. Thus they have had to remind us (or, at least, too many of us) that women were there too and that women have colonized and been colonized in different ways to men. Much of this work has been recuperative, rereading the imperial archive to disclose its female dimension. White women in the colonies have emerged in all their variety, exploding the stereotypical opposition that James Buzard has characterized as 'the Spinster Abroad and the Memsahib, the eccentric traveller and the pampered Hill Station denizen'. (Wolfe 1997: 416–17)

Wolfe also makes the point that common gender alone does not, in the view of women scholars from the former colonies, entitle Western feminists to 'transcend the colonial divide from which they themselves have historically benefited' (Wolfe 1997: 417). The writing of gender into studies of imperialism goes, of course, wider than feminist perspectives and the necessary evaluation of the roles of women from different cultures in imperial processes. It takes into account the greatly complex issues that require the recognition, as Angela Woollacot puts it in her study of gender and the British empire, of

gender as a foundational dynamic that shaped all aspects of empire from the conduct of war, to the drafting of statutes and regulations, to social and medical codes governing sexuality, to stories that appeared variously in *The Times* and in juvenile fiction. Ideas of gender, always linked to 'race' and class, were forged in the colonies as well as in the metropole and circulated constantly throughout the empire. (Woollacot 2006: 3)

The geographer Richard Phillips has studied aspects of race, class, gender, spaces, Western and non-Western identities and geography as revealed in adventure stories of the nineteenth and twentieth centuries (Phillips 1997), and of masculinity and empire with reference to the regulation of colonial prostitution (Phillips 2002). In his analysis of adventure stories, he states that 'Adventure stories chart masculinities contextually, in relation to particular constructions of class, race, sexuality and other forms of identity and geography. The masculinities mapped in British Victorian adventure, then, reflect a range of Victorian identities and geographies. They also reflect the specific form taken by adventure in that context' (Phillips, 1997: 45–6). In his study of the regulation of colonial sexuality, drawing on Hyam's maxim that 'The expansion of Europe was not only a matter of Christianity and commerce, it was also a matter of copulation and concubinage' (Phillips 2002: 47; Hyam 1990: 2), he shows the complexity of regulation and the significance of international networks of purity activists. Maps figured in the activities of the purist organisations. Phillips reproduces a map ('Sketch taken on the spot by Mr. Alfred S. Dyer, Dec. 30th, 1887') from the London journal the *Sentinel* from March 1888, entitled 'The Government *Versus* the Gospel at Bareilly' (a city in Uttar

Pradesh in India). The component parts of the map are labelled, respectively: 'Tents of the East Kent Regiment'; 'Tents of the General Camp Followers such as Tailors Shop-Keepers etc'; 'Public Road'; 'Temperance Tent'; 'The Soldiers' Lavatory'; 'Tents of Licensed Harlots Attached To The East Kent Regiment'; 'Native Christian Village'; 'Native Christian Church'; 'Government Brick-Yard and Native Dwellings'; and 'Private (European) Dwellings'. The author Dyer complains that 'While the Temperance tent is in a comparatively obscure corner, the tents of the Government harlots confront the troops from morning to night, separated from their own tents only by a public thoroughfare, without any trees or buildings interfering' (Phillips 2002: 57, 55).

The 'civilising mission'

An integral part of most imperial and colonial theories and practices was the so-called *mission civilisatrice* (civilising mission), a process determined by views that the indigenous peoples of the colonial territories were mostly inferior in mental, moral and practical capacity to white Europeans. Such people were for the most part thought to need training in basic arts and skills and also exposure to Western belief systems, notably various forms of Christianity, disseminated by missions and through education policies, which rarely recognised ability for sophisticated thinking and action and potential for self-government. These ideas were part of an extensive range of concepts in which racism of various kinds were embedded, and which fed both broader national and other agency policies towards the indigenous peoples of imperial territories, and the shaping of the attitudes of individual colonisers and colonised to questions of economic and humanitarian rights. Exclusion of non-white Europeans from basic human rights and experiences was a shameful part of much imperial experience, fed by the false scientific theories of racism and Social Darwinism, even during a century when the abolition of slavery and the slave trade was making progress (Morgan and Hawkins 2004: 14). This subject is more extensively dealt with in Chapter 8.

This chapter has reviewed a wide range of concepts and explanations of imperialism and colonialism, and the next chapter employs some of these ideas to identify and explain the kaleidoscopic geographical patterns and sequences of Europe's overseas links, especially in the later nineteenth and early twentieth centuries.

2 | Chronologies, spaces and places

The geographical interest of this country [French Indo-China] consists in the immense rivers by which it is intersected, and to whose alluvial bounty it for the most part owes its origin, and to the mystery which still overhangs its interior recesses; there on the confines of China, Burma, Siam, and Annam, wild and little known tribes inhabit the pathless mountains, and unexplored rivers thunder down profound ravines. Its commercial interest lies in the competition which it has engendered between rival European nations for the easiest approaches to the remote but populous provinces of Western China, on whose borders it lies; and the immemorial but lengthy caravan routes conducting to which it is sought to supersede by the agency of steam locomotion by river or by land. Its political interest lies in the fact that within the last thirty years the ownership of this vast tract, obeying the universal law by which the hitherto hidden corners of the world are gradually yielding up their secrets to civilisation – has changed and is even now changing hands; the conquest of the French having placed them in possession of the whole of its eastern face from Cambodia to Tongking, and the acquisition of Upper Burma by the British having brought the latter into similar contact both with China herself and with the frontiers of the one surviving independent Asiatic kingdom, that now separates England from France in the Far East, viz., Siam. (Curzon 1893: 97–8)

This opening section of an article published in 1893 in the *Geographical Journal* by George Curzon, later Viceroy of India and president of the Royal Geographical Society, summarises some of the main elements in European imperial activity towards the end of the nineteenth century: acquisition of geographical knowledge, the development of trade, the 'civilising' mission, and European political dominance of remote but geopolitically significant regions. This chapter is mainly about geopolitical processes, incorporated within a detailed narrative and analytical account of the geographies and chronologies of the spread of Europe overseas in the late nineteenth and early to mid-twentieth centuries, principally in Central, South and South-East Asia, Africa, Australasia, the Pacific and the Caribbean. It attempts to unfold the complexities and spatial dynamics of interactions between European powers, between colonisers and colonised, and the developing powers of Russia, the United States and Japan.

Europe and imperialism

One of the major energies affecting intra- and extra-European geopolitics in the late nineteenth and early twentieth centuries was change in the relative strengths of political and economic power. Key components included the rise and unification of Germany as a military and economic power, the defeat of France in the Franco-Prussian War and the establishment of the French Third Republic, the abasement of Austria, the unification of Italy, the rising influence of Russia, and the development of the United States and Japan as world powers. At the core of European imperialism was the redefinition of national character and identity, bound up with inter-state rivalry, shifting political alliances and oppositions, an increasingly global scale of trade, and territorial consolidation and aggrandisement within and beyond Europe.

The European 'upheavals' of the 1860s and beyond characterised a period of instability and uncertainty, which 'was only worsened by the failure of any obviously dominant power or combination of powers to emerge. Countries such as Britain, Portugal and Belgium found

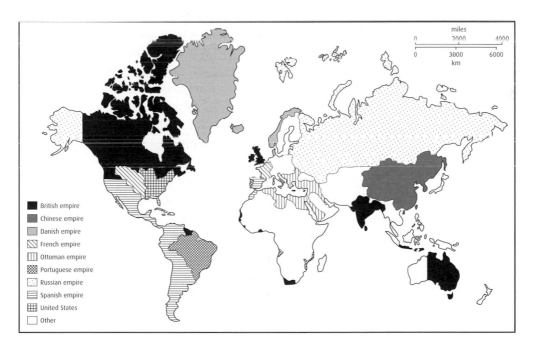

Fig. 2.1 The world in 1800. Source: Christopher (1999: 13).
By permission of and © John Wiley and Sons.

themselves jockeying for position' (Porter 1994: 70–1). A consequence was
the speeding up of the acquisition of territory and resources overseas as
alternative means of gaining advantage over rival European states. These
overseas engagements were not always the outcome of a carefully constructed geopolitical and imperial policy, but were in part opportunistic
responses to unfolding events, both in Europe and overseas, and related
to changing metropolitan ideas about the roles of empire and colonies.
Issues with which European states were engaged included the establishment of suitable balances of power politics, within Europe and overseas;
the development and sustenance of national prestige, nationalism, and
international status linked both positively and negatively to imperialism;
cultural and humanitarian obligations to improve, inform and educate
the supposedly weaker populations of overseas territories; and the maintenance of military and naval power to protect trade routes and settlements
(Porter 1994).

European perception of national space and global position had sharpened after the Renaissance, conspicuously from the seventeenth century,
when 'the shaping and representation of geographical space, including
landscape design, became a central component of the exercise of abso-
lutist state power', reflected in the compilation of new maps which were
'carefully constructed self-portraits of the new European nation-states
designed to legitimate their territorial authority' (Heffernan 1998c: 17).
In the late eighteenth century detailed territorial and topographic mapping of states such as France and Britain got underway, and new maps and
information were being compiled from voyages of discovery and land-
based explorations and military expeditions in the eighteenth and early
nineteenth centuries which informed the imperial and colonial strategies
of European states.

By the early eighteenth century the major political powers in Europe
were Britain, France, Austria, Prussia and Russia, three of which (Britain,
France and Russia) had non-European empires (Heffernan 1998c: 26–7).
The French revolution of 1789 and the period of Napoleon's domination
changed perceptions of time and space and the ideologies of state administration, and the idea of a united Europe was advanced by war, notably
by Napoleon's campaigns (Heffernan 1998c: 35, 39). In 1815, the year of
the Congress of Vienna (the name given to not one but a series of diplomatic meetings between September 1814 and June 1815, in which attempts
were made to compose a peaceful and stable Europe in the aftermath of a
long revolutionary period), the main powers in Europe remained Britain,
Prussia, the Austrian empire, France and Russia. The main force for

change was popular nationalism, the tensions of which underpinned the widespread revolutions of 1848, ' "the springtime of nations" which swept away the last vestiges of the European *ancien régime* in the name of liberalism, democracy and popular nationalism' (Heffernan 1998a: 154).

The nineteenth century witnessed an intensification of European rivalry both internally and overseas, the former evidenced by the Franco-Prussian War and the rise of Germany as a new, united empire, and the continued generation through nationalism of 'ever more divisiveness and rancour after 1870 not only within Europe but around the world, as the European powers sought competitive advantage by conquering more and more colonial territory. European nationalism and European imperialism thus reached their twin peaks in the same period' (Heffernan, 1998a: 154–5). The relative sizes of European and US colonies *c.* 1900 are shown in Table 2.1.

The largest of the empires was the British empire, which had increased in size by over 2 million square miles/5,178,000 km^2 since 1860. It covered nearly a quarter of the earth's surface, and was substantially larger than the French, German, Dutch and Portuguese empires.

The progressive industrialisation of different European countries was an important factor influencing the course of economic, demographic and imperial development. Population increase, emigration to colonies, and the search for further markets for industrial produce, were important issues. The population of Europe, excluding Russia, rose from 146 million (15.3 per cent of the world's total) in 1800 to 209 million (16.8 per cent) in 1850, 295 million in 1900 (18.1 per cent), and 395 million (15.6 per cent) in 1950 (Ogden 1998: 182–8). The annual growth rate for Europe was about 0.63 per cent from 1750 to 1850, and was most strongly experienced in Britain, though most other European countries underwent rapid population growth in the nineteenth century. France was different, owing to a decline in fertility from the later eighteenth century, and slower population growth in the nineteenth century as a consequence.

There is a long history of migration from Europe to lands overseas. There was significant emigration from Spain and Portugal to the Americas and (in the case of Portugal) to Africa and Asia, from the Netherlands to the West and East Indies, and from Britain to all parts of her developing empire from the sixteenth and seventeenth centuries. There were major migrations from Europe in the nineteenth and early twentieth centuries – about 60 million between 1840 and 1940 – of which about 45 million went to the New Worlds of North and South America, and also to parts of the growing European colonies overseas, conspicuously Australia and New Zealand (see Chapter 3).

Table 2.1 The relative sizes of European and US colonies c. 1900

	Number of colonies	Area						Population	
		Metropole			Colonies			Metropole	Colonies
		sq. miles	km²		sq. miles	km²			
UK	50	120,979	313,334		11,605,328	30,004,596		40,559,954	345,222,239
France	33	528,595	968,513		3,740,756	9,684,817		38,517,711	56,401,860
Germany	13	540,867	2,660,228		1,027,120	2,936,536		52,279,901	14,687,000
Netherlands	3	12,648	32,758		782,862	2,027,612		5,074,632	35,115,711
Portugal	9	36,038	93,337		801,100	2,074,839		5,049,729	9,148,707
Spain	3	197,670	511,962		243,887	631,638		17,565,632	136,000
Italy	2	110,646	286,571		188,500	488,212		31,856,675	850,000
Russia	3	8,660,395	22,421,762		255,550	661,618		128,932,173	15,684,000
USA	6	3,557,000	9,212,630		172,091	445,713		77,000,000	10,544,517

(*Source:* Hobson 1902/*Statesman's Yearbook*, 1900)

Fig. 2.2 European and other empires in 1914. Source: Fieldhouse (1982: 240).
By permission of and © Palgrave Macmillan.

European global influence had also been shown by the role of maritime states and port cities in the inhumane slave trade, which by 1820 had involved the shipping of 8 million slaves from Africa to British, Dutch, Portuguese and French colonial territories, mainly to the Caribbean and North America (Ogden 1998: 196).

The roots of industrialisation in Europe lay in a distant past, but the acceleration of proto-industry in the sixteenth, seventeenth and eighteenth centuries led to a further intensive period of industrial change, based on coal and steam power, from the eighteenth century, which included the production of new forms of transport, including the railway, and the mass production of a range of goods, including textiles, for which overseas markets were actively sought. The rates of industrial production increased dramatically, and significant inroads were made, for example by British textiles, into the Indian market, with the quantities of textiles being exported from Britain to India increasing from a million metres of cloth in 1814 to 13 million in 1820 and two billion in 1890, and with dire consequences for Indian textile producers in an unequal system of trading (Wesseling 2004: 25).

The development of such a global system of trade was facilitated by new technologies applied first to sailing ships and then to steamships made of iron and later of steel, and later by refrigeration. Sizes of cargoes and travelling times between European and colonial ports and the costs of transport were reduced substantially, though much of the feeding of export cargoes into overseas ports was dependent on local transport systems. Military power was increased by the availability of new weapons such as the Maxim gun. Changes in transport and communications are dealt with at greater length in Chapter 10.

The imperialist expression of national identities and ambitions was also linked to a series of trade depressions in the last thirty years of the nineteenth century. These in turn led European governments to move away from free trade systems to heavy economic protection by discriminatory tariffs and trade restrictions, about which there was much debate. Economic growth in Britain, and later in France and Germany, had produced policies of protection for domestic industry and production systems at the beginning of the nineteenth century. This changed to free trade with Britain's repeal of the Corn Laws (which forbade the import of foreign grain) in 1846, and the British–French Cobden–Chevalier Treaty of 1860. At the end of the century there was a reversion to protectionist policies for trade, put in place in Germany in 1879, in France in 1881, and in Italy in 1877, marking an end to the free trade period (Wesseling 2004: 28–9).

By the end of the nineteenth century Europe had two-thirds of the world's estimated imports and one half of all exports, imports being mainly foodstuffs, other agricultural products used in industry, and minerals, and exports being mainly industrial products and capital goods. The intensity of colonial mining enterprises and plantation agriculture also increased at the end of the century, further expanding and intensifying the levels of colonial exploitation.

A significant influence on the globalisation of European power was the greater stability of monetary systems, including the introduction of national currencies and national banks, and the gradual links to defined precious metal standards, partly for the purpose of facilitating international transfers of currency. The responsibility for the issue of national currency in England from 1844 was with the Bank of England, and England committed to the gold standard in 1821, with other countries continuing with the bi-metallic standards of gold and silver. Germany committed to the gold standard in the year of German unification – 1871 – and nearly all other advanced countries had followed suit by 1880, and Japan after 1900 (Wesseling, 2004: 28–9).

Britain's empires and colonies

By the beginning of the nineteenth century Britain's former empire had shrunk, mainly through the loss of its former North American colonies after the American Revolution of 1776. Growing imperial targets included India, in which the British East India Company had been active since the early seventeenth century; Australia, where British settlement had begun since the establishment of a penal colony on the south-east coast, at Sydney cove, in 1788; New Zealand; Canada; and colonies in the West Indies. Africa, in which the British presence remained small during the first part of the nineteenth century, became, however, a major imperial and colonial arena later in the century.

The general factors that have to be understood in any attempted explanation of British imperialism and colonialism in the later nineteenth and the twentieth centuries include variations in and heated debates about political and economic policy, the activities of pressure groups such as political parties, commercial groups such as traders and Chambers of Commerce, complex relationships and negotiations with other European states, and a wide range of humanitarian issues, notably the abolition of slavery. The mechanisms of extending colonial power included support for merchants and companies operating overseas, the giving of protectorate status, and in some cases indirect rule through the agency of leaders of indigenous peoples, annexation, acceptance of mandates, establishment of administrative agencies, support for settlement, military and naval action, diplomatic exchange and international conferences, and the production of information and propaganda.

In the nineteenth and early twentieth centuries the British empire 'was a diverse and scattered assortment of territories, some hugely valuable in commercial or strategic terms, others of little more than psychological value. No single policy connected them, no studied philosophy of governance reigned over them all' (Levine 2007: 85). British colonial policy was a mixture of deliberate policy and pragmatic reaction to events, opportunities and perceived threats. Levine has questioned the validity of Seeley's 'fit of absence of mind' thesis about the development of the British empire: 'Yet given the vast areas brought under British control during the course of the century and under leadership from a variety of political positions, the image of a reluctant or accidental imperialism is not awfully persuasive' (Levine 2007: 82). While pointing also to the role of extemporised responses by Britain in relation to some overseas territories, Levine contends that even these instances were considered within broader imperial and colonial strategies (Levine 2007: 83). These mixed motives produced a complex array of types of colony, including settler colonies, colonies acquired by military activity but governed by local rulers, treaty ports, and the parts of Britain's 'informal empire' (Levine 2007: 85).

In the second half of the nineteenth century Britain remained a some-what reluctant imperialist, resorting to formal annexation of overseas territories only when it was deemed absolutely necessary, and mainly in support of existing commercial (free trade) and strategic interests. Porter (1996: 74, 79) explains that in the period 1875–90 annexation was more frequently used because of greater threats to British interests, especially her trading interests, from other European states, which produced a means of supporting the export of industrial goods: 'to make sure of their export outlets by securing them politically'. Fear and pessimism about Britain's future informed British colonial policy, deriving from anxieties about economic and national wellbeing, but nonetheless imperial activity remained more pragmatic than programmatic (Porter 1996: 81–2).

Military actions played an increasingly larger role in British imperial experience. Major actions in the second half of the nineteenth century and the early twentieth century included the Second Burma War (1852–3), action against the Indian Uprising/Mutiny (1857–8), the Ambeyla Expedition (1863), the Third Maori War (1863–72), the Abyssinian Expedition, (1867–8), the Zulu War (1879), the Second Afghan War (1878–80), the First Boer War (1880–1), action in Egypt and the Sudan (1882–99), action on the Indian frontiers (1883–97), the Third Ashanti War (1895–96), and the South African (Boer) War (1899–1902). Most of these were against indigen-ous peoples and polities, and indigenous troops were an important part of the British army, notably the Indian army, which was widely deployed in colonial warfare.

The 'northern archipelago'

An important question about British imperial and colonial policies is the status of Ireland, and to a lesser extent of Scotland and Wales. Although from 1801 to its independence in 1922 Ireland was part of the Union, Irish experience in the nineteenth and early twentieth centuries bore many of the hallmarks of a colonial relationship with Britain, and continued an older (and equally disputed) colonial status dating back to Norman times, but accelerating rapidly from the late fifteenth century.

Debate about Ireland's colonial status in the late medieval/early modern period has been developed and illustrated in W. J. Smyth's monumental and seminal work *Map-Making, Landscapes and Memory: A Geography of Colonial and Early Modern Ireland c. 1530–1750* (Smyth 2006). Smyth shows how Ireland changed through interaction with English colonial aspirations, invasions and plantation settlements, while retaining aspects of Gaelic culture and language. 'Ireland's cultural geography was, therefore, plural. But its political geography was increasingly represented and simplified as a battle for hegemony between an expansive English national culture and a defensive but resistant Gaelic/Irish world, seeking its own legislative and cultural autonomy' (Smyth 2006: 7). The transformation of Ireland to a colonial territory largely controlled by England (seen as a centralised state) is shown, according to Smyth, by exercise of colonial ideology, authority and dominance by England, inequality of social relationships, segregation, pressure for cultural change, especially in language and religion, and various forms of economic imperialism and of landscape change, leading to a type of 'mixed settlement' (Smyth 2006: 9–14). Smyth works 'on the supposition that Ireland can be regarded as "colonial" in the sense defined for this era, and that the island must be located within the wider historical and geographical frame of Western colonial capitalism. Ireland was systematically colonized in an early modern context, which saw the expansion of the Spanish and Portuguese, as well as the English, empires' (Smyth 2006: 12–13). Comment on this exegesis has been positive (Kearns 2008; Andrews 2008; Clayton 2008; Smyth 2008).

Ireland in the nineteenth century had constitutionally become more strongly tied to England by the Act of Union, effective from 1801, and there has been extensive debate about the question of Ireland's colonial status from 1801 to independence in 1922. Howe (2000) has intensively reviewed the historiography of this question as seen by different individuals and political groups in and beyond Ireland. His own position is that medieval and especially early modern Ireland is best viewed in the context of the 'north European archipelago' (the 'British Isles') and the expansion of an early state (England) from a core area not only into Ireland but also Scotland and Wales. The determination of Ireland's colonial status in the early modern period

> begins from the British-Irish civil wars of 1640–91. A fully-fledged, fairly secure United Kingdom political authority over the entire archipelago was only finally achieved with the end of the Williamite war – or, some would say, only with the suppression of the Jacobite Highland clans after 1746. The most profound impact of these events, beyond the immediate political and demographic shifts, was perhaps cultural, with the Irish language starting its long retreat, the religious faith of the majority embattled and subordinated, and the customs and social institutions of 'Englishness' strongly identified with status, wealth and power. (Howe 2000: 31)

Howe states also that the patterns of cultural colonialism in Ireland in the late seventeenth and the eighteenth century 'were always complex and contested, rather than forming a mere manichean opposition of colonisers and colonised' (Howe 2000: 30). The extent to which the Union changed Ireland's colonial status is debatable. Howe contends that notwithstanding the constitutional change brought by Union, within which 'For the next 150 years Ireland was legislatively to be part of a unitary kingdom: on a constitutional level, at least the never clearly defined "colonial" status of Ireland had ended' (Howe 2000: 36). However, factors such as language, religion, systems of administration, including parliament, and the police force point, in Howe's view, to a 'curiously hybrid' state, redolent of a process of internal colonialism as advanced by Hechter, but countered by the argument 'that even if Ireland's juridical status, cultural complexion and so on were not colonial ones during the nineteenth century, nonetheless important aspects of British policy-making treated it as part of the external imperial system' (Howe 2000: 37; Hechter 1975).

The British perspective on Ireland and the British empire, particularly during debate on Home Rule, might seem to have been more closely linked to concern with the outcome for Britain and British nationality than for a broader empire and its future character, but Howe argues that British political discourses on Ireland in the nineteenth and 'early twentieth centuries neither fitted "some generalised colonial model" nor a model of political management of Britain' (Howe 2000: 65, 67–8). This perceived ambivalent position of Ireland has also been supported by Kearns, who states that:

Irish nationalism posed a direct challenge to the integrity of the two spatial units to which British loyalties were addressed: the united kingdom of Great Britain and Ireland, and the British Empire of Great Britain and its colonies. Ireland was in some respects a province and in others a colony. This ambivalence affected Irish nationalism in so far as it was based on the rejection of British domination. (Kearns 2003: 204)

In addition to the question of Ireland's colonial status, we must also recognise the material contribution of Ireland to the broader British empire (and perhaps others too) through trade, emigration and the settlement of large numbers of its population, through service in Britain's armies overseas (and sometimes in the armies of its opponents, as in the Boer War), and as missionaries, doctors, teachers and administrators (such as Roger Casement).

Scotland and Wales occupied different positions from Ireland within the British imperial context. They became constitutionally part of the United Kingdom at an earlier stage than Ireland. The crowns of Scotland

and England were united in 1603 and the parliaments by the Treaty of Union of 1707. Wales was united with England by the Act of Union of 1535. The Treaty of Union between England and Scotland seems to have undermined neither a distinct Scottish sense of national identity nor a strong commitment to the British empire. Forsyth (1995: 11) argues that:

Throughout the course of the nineteenth century, even at the height of imperial involvement there remained a quite distinct Scottish national identity, which coloured the views of Scotland's political classes to the imperial mission and the political system based on the treaty of union. Incorporating union it may have been, but the general view of Scotland's place in that union, not only that Scotland as a nation had not been subsumed by England, but more particularly as can be seen from the pronouncements of Scottish politicians and contemporaneous commentators that there were limits to infringement of England on Scotland.

Commitment to preservation and advancement of key aspects of Scottish culture such as law, education and religion coexisted with commitment to moral and material progress in the British empire through missionary and medical work, administration, promotion of trade and markets for the export of Scottish industrial products, the development of tea and cotton plantations and the conservation of woodland and forests. There was, as Finlay has shown, much popular support for Scotland's imperial roles in the period *c.* 1850–1918, providing 'an alternative focus for Scottish identity which helped to unify an increasingly divided nation', evidenced through popular newspapers, novels, children's comics, advertising for consumer products, and a variety of organisations, including youth movements and learned societies (Finlay 1995: 13, 17–19). Scotland's participation in the affairs and ideologies of the British empire and the refinement of a Scottish sense of nationality were interactive processes. Charles Withers has suggested that:

whilst acknowledging that Scotland played a part in the making of the British empire and, thus, of Britishness from the mid-nineteenth century, national identity was also being made in the geographical exploration of Scotland's own body politic for purposes of social amelioration. The culture of exploration in geography was played out in the dark 'heart of empire', Britain's teeming and ill-understood cities, just as much as it was in the unknown spaces of 'darkest Africa'. (Withers 2001: 171–2)

Cities in Scotland, notably Glasgow, evidenced strong links with empire in their built environments, cultural activities and businesses. MacKenzie has shown that there were many links between Glasgow – the 'second city of empire' – and the British empire in the later nineteenth century, claiming that 'few cities were as closely connected with imperial commerce as Glasgow', but on the downside was the fact that 'the disintegration of empire and the loss of markets which were sentimentally, if not fiscally, protected produced the collapse of the city's industrial base' (MacKenzie, 1999: 216).

The position of Wales within Britain and empire is not dissimilar from that of Ireland, in the sense of having experienced early 'colonial' conquest from the thirteenth century and of the preservation of a distinctive language and culture beyond the formalised link with England, in the case of Wales from the Act of Union of 1535, coupled with a strong but changing nationalism. Wales's experience of the broader British empire was similar to that of Scotland in material terms, with Welsh industries – coal and metals in particular – deriving much benefit from the major markets created by empire. Williams (1985: 180) states that 'It is against this massive growth of an industrial Wales of British and imperial character that every other Welsh phenomenon should be set.' As in Scotland the materiality of empire had its urban expressions, notably 'the noble and squalid city of Cardiff, with Swansea and Newport at its heels…the artery of empire and the jugular vein of capitalist Wales, within which every other Wales had to live' (Williams, 1985: 223). There were within the British empire Welsh administrators, missionaries, teachers, doctors and settlers, although little seems to be published on these subjects in the recently expanding literature on high imperialism. Formal institutional expressions of Welsh and Scottish nationalism in the interwar period of the twentieth century were the foundation of the Welsh Party, Plaid Cymru, in 1925 and the Scottish National Party in 1934: 'Ireland, Scotland and Wales were flexing their national muscles as the British Empire lost its force' (McCrone 1997: 593).

Britain in Africa

Prior to and during the 'scramble' for Africa in the later nineteenth century there existed many areas controlled by indigenous powers, some of which are shown in Fig. 2.3. Many of them had been removed by the beginning of the First World War, though some continued to exist under a form of European indirect rule.

West Africa

By the beginning of the nineteenth century Britain already had a long-established presence in South Africa, and smaller footholds in West

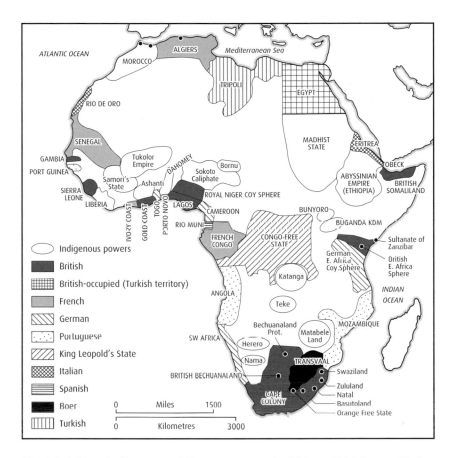

Fig. 2.3 African indigenous and European powers in Africa *c.* 1886. Source: Harlow and Carter 1999: 246. By permission and © Blackwell Publishers.

and East Africa, partly because of trading interests, partly because of the strong humanitarian motive of eliminating the slave trade. In West Africa, on the Windward Coast, Sierra Leone (named by the Portuguese as 'Serra Lyoa' – 'Lion Mountain' – during their explorations of the West African coast in the mid-fifteenth century) had been a major slave-trading area for 300 years, but was the site of a new freed slave colony from 1787, re-established in 1791 and funded from the Sierra Leone Company, with the former Granville Town renamed Freetown. The settlement was given by the Sierra Leone Company to the British government in 1807, the year in which Britain banned the slave trade, and it became a crown colony in 1808. An active campaign against the West African slave trade was led by the British navy, and many thousands of slaves, freed from captured vessels, were released into Sierra Leone. It became a British protectorate in 1896 (Hartwig 1991: 554–6).

The Gambia had developed from British and French forts of the seventeenth century. The territory along the Gambia River was disputed by the British and French during the eighteenth and nineteenth centuries, partly reflecting contrasting views of the slave trade. Britain had established a series of trading forts on the Gold Coast, and the settlements, including Bathurst the capital, were administered from 1821 to 1843 as a colony governed from Sierra Leone. In 1888 the area around Bathurst at the mouth of the Gambia River became a crown colony, with its northern boundaries with French Senegal established by a convention of 1889. Further extension of British influence was achieved for the upriver districts through indirect rule as a protectorate from 1894 (Michaud 1991a: 241–2).

The Gold Coast was the location of trading forts administered by the British in 1821–3, but concerns about the promotion of trade and the abolition of the slave trade made Britain take full control of the forts in 1843, and wars with the Asante people in 1863 and 1873–4 led to the formal establishment of the Gold Coast Colony in 1874. Concerns with French colonial expansion in the western Sudan and Dahomey in the early 1890s led to the British occupation of Asante in 1896 and the annexation of the Gold Coast in 1901 (Lynn 1991a: 104–5).

By 1830 British influence in the Niger Delta ('Oil Rivers') region was well established, and in a region where there was a major focus for trade in palm oil, and where trade with the interior was not permitted, African agents played key roles in the trading process. Another area of British commercial activity was the kingdom of Lagos to the west, where British concern was with the ending of the continuing slave trade. In 1861 Lagos became a British crown colony. There was no major concern from Britain to extend her control in this part of West Africa beyond appointing a consul in the Oil Rivers region. As Wesseling (1996: 187–8) states:

In the Oil Rivers the British presence remained confined for a time to a British consul. To make an impression the consul would now and then send a gunship upriver, which instilled some healthy respect in the local population, though not very much ... The British government was content to leave things at that. It was the period of 'informal empire' and of 'moral persuasion'. The Niger was important enough to be kept open for British trade, but not for shouldering the costs associated with a colonial administration.

Entrepreneurial and colonial development in Nigeria was promoted by Sir George Goldie (formerly Goldie Taubman), who in 1877, after a tempestuous early life, went to promote trade on the Niger by taking over a London palm oil trading company, which was retitled the West African

Company. Further mergers of British firms produced the United Africa Company in 1879, a company 'which was about to embark on a career not only of commercial but of political expansion. This company was to become Britain's imperial agent on the Niger' (Flint 1960: 32). There was keen competition between British and French traders for the upriver markets of the Niger operated by indigenous producers (in contrast to the delta where trading was between European companies and African merchants). Goldie further reorganised the company under the new name of the National African Company. Goldie's commercial and political ambitions for the Niger basin were manifest in his attendance at the Berlin West Africa Conference of 1884–5, at which the British Foreign Office strove for confirmation of British claims to the Niger and for the protection of British trade on the Congo River and its basin. Britain, initially reluctant to seek more control in the region, established a protectorate over the 'Niger Districts' in 1885, which included the coast of West Africa

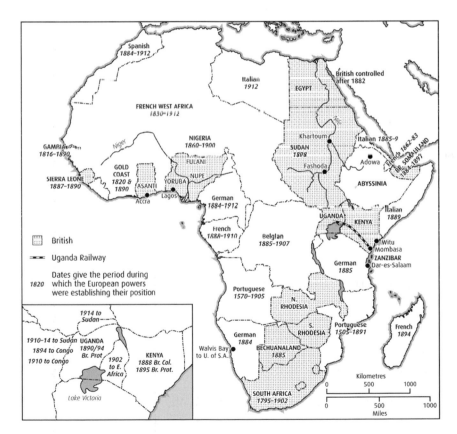

Fig. 2.4 The partition of Africa. Source: Lloyd (1984: 208).
By permission of and © Oxford University Press.

from Lagos to Cameroon, and the interior to the confluence of the Niger and the Benue rivers. To sustain British control of trade, Goldie's Royal Niger Company – the result of further company mergers – was established in 1886. A protectorate of Southern Nigeria was created in 1801, and of Northern Nigeria in 1900, and these were united in 1914 to form the protectorate of Nigeria (Wesseling 1996: 191–2).

East Africa

Zanzibar had been the main point of early British interest in East Africa on account of its active role in eliminating the slave trade, and also as an important focus of both trading routes from the African interior and sea routes from the Persian Gulf and the Indian Ocean. British explorers such as Speke, Livingstone, Cameron, Stanley, Grant and Baker in the mid-nineteenth century had used the mainland port of Bagamoyo as a starting point for their explorations inland, partly driven by their search for the source of the Nile, but Britain was reluctant to become involved in complex territorial geopolitics on the mainland. Portugal, which originally had trading links with East Africa, and France, whose major target after the resolution of British–French ambitions for the Nile valley was Madagascar, played no really active part in the division of East Africa after the 1862 treaty (which recognised the independence of the sultanates of Oman and Zanzibar). The main opponents for territorial control in the period of high imperialism were Britain and Germany. As elsewhere, the foundations were laid by exploration, by merchant companies and by energetic individuals, and the political interface of offices of government of these two European states intensified later in the century.

The contexts of development of European involvement in East Africa have been defined by Wesseling:

In the history of the partition of Africa the concept of East Africa therefore has a special meaning. In pre-colonial terms, it referred to an area that can be included in the sphere of influence of Zanzibar over East Africa; in colonial terms it was part of British and German Africa; in post-colonial terms, it comprises the modern states of Kenya, Uganda, Tanzania, Rwanda and Burundi. Even in this limited sense, it is still an area the size of western Europe. (Wesseling 1996: 133)

The basic geography of East Africa is a division between an isolated highland interior around the great lakes (Lakes Victoria, Rudolf, Albert, Edward and Tanganyika) and an accessible coastal region on the Indian Ocean which had long experienced the movement of people and goods through local and oceanic shipping and trading systems. Sailing routes along the coast and across the Indian Ocean was determined by the pattern of winds, mainly of the monsoons: the hot and dry north-east monsoon which occurs from late November to early February, and facilitates ships sailing from India, Saudi Arabia and south along the coast of East Africa; and the south-west monsoon, with winds more violent than the north-east monsoon, which blows from April to September, facilitating sailing in the opposite direction (Gilbert 2004: 133).

The British approach in East Africa was initially to give support to the sultan of Zanzibar, and promote British interests by means of a consul, but they were forced into further territorial evaluation by Germany. The Society for German Colonisation (Gesellschaft für Deutsche Kolonisation) had been founded in 1884, and the increased interest in East Africa was partly attributable to Karl Peters (1856–1918), a founder of the society, who had led a short-lived expedition in 1884 across the hinterlands of Bagamoyo and Dar es Salaam and claimed an area of 55,000 square miles for Germany (Wesseling 1996: 142, 145). A division of coastal mainland East Africa was agreed by Britain and Germany in 1886, the German territory (that became Tanganyika) lying to the south of the River Umba, and the British to the north, with the German protectorate of Witu to the north, in effect isolating the British territory (which would become Kenya), but this problem was removed by a further treaty of 1890, when Germany surrendered Witu and lessened the perceived threat to the Nile.

Zanzibar was subject to strong British influence, notably during the period from 1866 to 1887 when Sir John Kirk was British consul, and in 1873 the slave trade through Zanzibar was closed through British negotiation (by Sir Bartle Frere) with Sultan Seyyid Bargash of Zanzibar. In 1890 Britain proclaimed a formal protectorate over Zanzibar, and by the end of the nineteenth century Zanzibar was in effect a British colony and was 'left with only one crop, cloves, and only one buyer, Britain' (Shulman 1991: 677).

Elsewhere in East Africa, after a sequence of expeditions and missionary endeavours, the grant of an administration charter to the British East Africa Company in 1888, a treaty between Frederick Lugard and the *kabaka* of Buganda in 1890, and military intervention by Lugard in a civil war in 1892, Buganda became a British protectorate in 1894. To this the neighbouring kingdom of Bunyoro and adjacent territories were added in 1896, making up what was to become Uganda. The Uganda Agreement was made in 1900 by Sir Harry Johnston, by which the British government recognised the *kabaka* and council of chiefs of the Buganda people and granted them a substantial amount of autonomy, later extending this system of indirect rule to other kingdoms in this region (Michaud 1991b: 642).

As in West Africa, British interest was initially promoted not by government but by an individual and a trading company – the British East African Association, organised by Sir William Mackinnon, which in 1887 was granted a lease of the sultan of Zanzibar's coastal lands north of the River Umba, and in 1888 a charter was given to the East African Association under the title of the Imperial British East Africa Company. Further complications with Buganda, to the north-west of Lake Victoria, and 'a complex mixture of missionary and business interests with European diplomatic considerations, and Britain's decision to continue her occupation of Egypt, led to further activity in the area by Peters and to the Anglo-German agreement of July 1890' (Lynn 1991a: 107–9). In this, Heligoland was ceded to Germany in exchange for recognition of a British protectorate of Zanzibar, and a boundary change gave Britain control of Buganda.

Both Britain and Germany had achieved much of what they had wished, though the impact on indigenous peoples was traumatic, notably in German East Africa where Germany conducted eighty-four military campaigns in the period 1888–1902, in which at least 75,000 Africans were killed. Britain was also involved in military conflict, notably with retaliatory expeditions in western Kenya from 1894 to 1914 (Wesseling 1996: 168–9).

Egypt and the Sudan

Egypt, notably after the opening of the Suez Canal in 1869, was an important strategic point on the routes to India and the Far East, and had attracted the interest of France and Britain. After the short-lived French occupation from 1798 to 1801, Egypt became an autonomous country, but was still subject to financial intervention and control by British and European bankers and moneylenders, leading to much indebtedness. Britain had supported the Ottoman empire, of which Egypt was part, in order to sustain a blockage of French and Russian access to India. A nationalist uprising in 1882, however, led to British naval action and the occupation of Egypt. From 1883 Egypt was governed by the British agent and consul general, Sir Evelyn Baring (who became Lord Cromer). There were complications because of continuing French manipulation of the processing of Egypt's national debt, until a mutual agreement was made between Britain and France not to interfere with the other's interests in

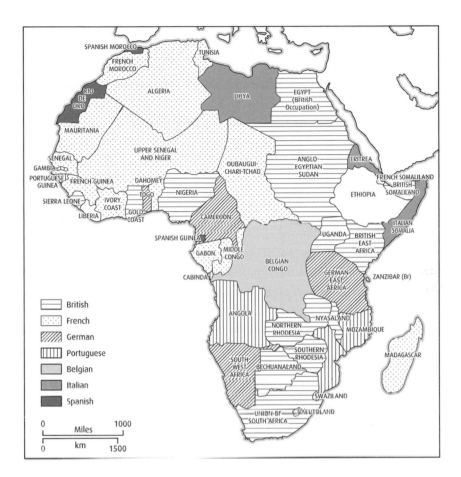

Fig. 2.5 Africa in 1914. Source: Christopher (1984: 29). By permission of the author.

Egypt and Morocco respectively. Nationalist movements began in Egypt in the late nineteenth century, and the First World War increased its strategic importance. Egypt was declared a formal protectorate of Britain in 1914 (Marsot 1991a: 193–5).

In the early nineteenth century the adjacent area of the Sudan comprised a collection of small independent states ruled by sultans. In 1821 the northern part was invaded by Egypt, which retained control until the early 1880s, when a rising by tribes in the west and centre of the country in an Islamic holy war led to the defeat of Anglo-Egyptian forces under the control of the British soldier General Charles Gordon, who died in the siege of Khartoum in January 1885. Thereafter, in 1895, the British General Kitchener commanded Anglo-Egyptian forces in a campaign up the Nile from Wadi Halfa to regain the Sudan, and in September 1898, in the battle of Omdurman opposite Khartoum, he routed the forces of the khalifa Abdallahi, killing 11,000 of the Khalif's men. A later attempt in 1898 by a French force led by Captain Marchand to re-establish a French base at the fort at Fashoda was also frustrated by Kitchener, ending French attempts to colonise the Sudan. The southern Sudan had been colonised by Christian missions, who built and ran churches and schools, the pupils of the latter, instructed in English, being given preference in employment in the Sudanese civil service over other Sudanese (Pollock 1991a: 16–19).

Central Africa

The British presence in Central Africa had been developed by missionary activity and trade during the nineteenth century, and by opposition to the slave trade. Missions were established with merchant financial support in 1875–6 at Livingstonia by the Free Church of Scotland, the Church of Scotland at Blantyre, and the London Missionary Society at Ujiji (Porter 1991a: 114). In the later nineteenth century Central Africa was caught up in the strategic ambitions of Portugal and of the Transvaal, and the aftermath of the Berlin Conference of 1884–5. Portugal sought to intensify control and profit from Angola and Mozambique, made a claim to Nyasaland, sought control of access to the Zambezi, and created the Mozambique Company to exploit the territory's resources.

British ambitions to use the resources of Zambesia and contain the Transvaal were supported by the formation of the British South Africa Company by the capitalist entrepreneurs Cecil Rhodes and George Cawson, and by diplomatic negotiation. In 1889 a royal charter was given to Rhodes' British South Africa Company. The company was a major agent in European exploitation of resources, including minerals, in this region during the last decade of the nineteenth century. In 1890 the company sent 200 settlers, protected by police, to settle in Mashonaland, where they founded Salisbury (modern Harare). Mining rights had previously been obtained for Matabeleland.

The western border of Mozambique was agreed with Portugal in 1891. Nyasaland (modern Malawi), named after Lake Nyasa, was part of a larger British protectorate from 1889 to 1891, then 'Trans-Zambesia', and later entitled the 'British Central Africa Protectorate'. In 1904 this protectorate was assigned to the British Foreign Office and in 1907 named Nyasaland. Trans-Zambesia (an area covering modern Malawi, Zimbabwe and Zambia) was divided into three parts in 1895. Rhodesia was so named and recognised in 1895, and Northern Rhodesia (modern Zambia) was formally designated in 1897; Southern Rhodesia was so called from 1898. As elsewhere in Africa, these acquisitions by Europeans met with African opposition, including the risings of the Ndebele and Shona peoples in 1896–7.

Britain and India

The jewel in the British imperial crown was India, in which there had been Portuguese coastal trading 'factories' since the sixteenth century, and Dutch, French and British factories from the seventeenth century. British influence accelerated with the defeat in 1757 of the forces of the Nawab of Bengal by Robert Clive at the Battle of Plessey, and from then until the early nineteenth century the British East India Company expanded its control by negotiation, subsidy and military force, with the other European powers declining in influence in India. From a Western perspective, by the end of the eighteenth century the British government had asserted control of the East India Company's foreign policy and administration, and in 1813 the company's monopoly of trade with India was ended. By 1833 the East India Company was no longer a major trading institution, remaining as a vehicle for the extension of British control. The company ceased to exist after the Uprising/Mutiny of 1857.

In the mid-nineteenth century the British had made English the official language for teaching, established a new penal code, abolished sati, changed inheritance laws for Indian princes who died without heirs, promoted free trade and competition, and extended the transport infrastructure (Kaminsky 1991: 302). From an Indian perspective, as Washbrook has suggested, the period from *c.* 1818 to 1860 presented a different face, that is some slight evidence of response, at least in and around Calcutta (the British administrative capital of India) to the Anglicising process, but otherwise signs of modernisation were few. The economy did not advance, partly because of depression from *c.* 1825 to 1850, and consequent de-urbanisation, and because traditional systems of caste and religious belief deepened, and fundamentalist views were revived and extended in Hinduism and Islam (Washbrook 1999a: 395–7).

These anti-modernisation tendencies may be partly explained in terms of a strong counter-action and resistance to increasing British control, but partly also in terms of new Islamic and Hindu religious movements that developed through exposure to Christianity, with aspects of caste, royalty and community changing in relation to the influence of Western ideas.

Washbrook suggests, therefore, that from these new perspectives the nature of British rule in India looks rather different:

The predominant effects which it had (both intended and unintended) were less to transport British civilization to the East than to construct there a society founded on the perpetuation of 'Oriental' difference, as Edward Said has put it. India became a subordinate agricultural colony under the dominance of metropolitan, industrial Britain; its basic cultural institutions were disempowered and 'fixed' in unchanging traditional forms; its 'civil society' was subjected to the suzerainty of a military despotic state. (Washbrook 1999: 398)

Military power extended British control over a wider area of India during the nineteenth century, involving the conquest of Sind (1843), the Punjab (finally annexed in 1849) and – not without major difficulties, including the disastrous First Afghan War – extension of authority to the North-West Frontier, partly for fear of advance by Russian armies. After the Uprising/Mutiny of 1857 the East India Company was abolished, and rule over India passed to the British crown, with Queen Victoria declared Empress of India in 1877.

In India the main areas of British rule comprised 'British India' and 'Princely India'. 'British India' comprised about two-thirds of the most populous parts of the country and included the three large historical 'presidencies' – Calcutta, Bombay and Madras – which in turn were sub-divided into provinces and districts. Attempts were put in hand for consolidation, for example of the North-West Provinces, and also for the partition of Bengal in the late nineteenth and early twentieth centuries (Christopher, 1999: 40–1). The 703 Princely States occupied one-third of India by 1914, but they varied in size and power. After 1857 they kept some independence but recognised British suzerainty, and as far as international relations were concerned they were totally subservient to the British government (Smith 1914: 246–7). After the founding of the Indian Congress in 1885 a series of constitutional acts over a period of about fifty years led slowly towards the greater participation of Indians in the operation of the Raj, culminating in the Government of India Act of 1935 (Stockwell 1991a: 168).

Ceylon, the large island south-east of India, was the home of an ancient civilisation, and the focus of trading interest by the Portuguese and then the Dutch, becoming British through the Treaty of Amiens (1802). Britain influenced the abolition of slavery, the advent of free trade, and the development of plantations, an administrative system and a modern infrastructure, financed partly from British sources but also by indigenous capitalists.

Britain in South-East Asia and the Pacific

The British East India Company acquired the island of Penang off the Malay peninsula in 1786. To this was added the mainland areas of Province Wellesley in 1811, Singapore in 1819, and Malacca in 1824, these being combined as the Straits Settlements in 1826, which in turn became a crown colony in 1867. Further additions were Labuan, off the coast of north-west Borneo, in 1906, Christmas Island (1900), and the Cocos-Keeling Islands in the Indian Ocean (1903) (Christopher 1999: 76). Singapore occupied an important position for trade and defence on the Strait of Malacca, and Sir Stamford Raffles secured Singapore Island for the East Indian Company, where the settlement of Singapore was founded in 1819.

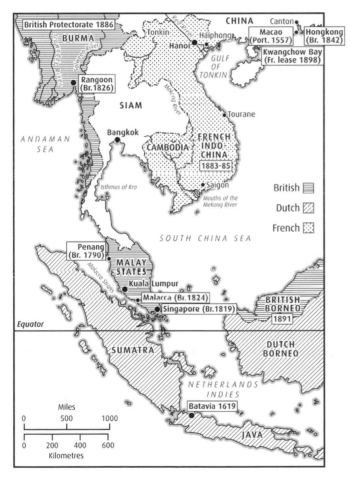

Fig. 2.6. European expansion into South-East Asia by 1914.
Source: Fieldhouse (1982: 219). By permission of and
© Palgrave Macmillan.

Singapore became a major trading base and administrative capital, greatly benefiting from the opening of the Suez Canal. The Federated Malay States were constituted in 1895 from the protected states of Perak, Selangor, Negri Sembilan and Pahang, with Kedah, Kelantan, Perlis and Trengganu (from Siam) in 1909. Johore became a protectorate in 1914 (Christopher 1999: 76).

Burma also had an ancient civilisation and strong Hindu and Buddhist cultures long before it was affected by European colonialism. Burma was part of the theatre of British involvement in South-East Asia, 'brought about by Anglo-French rivalry and fluctuating Dutch power, by the needs of India and opportunities in China, by the attractions of South-East Asian trade and the reactions of South-East Asian societies' (Stockwell, 1999: 376–7). British anxiety about India, together with concern at the position of British merchants in Rangoon, and the eviction by the Burmese of a British garrison on Shahpuri Island in the River Naaf, led to the first Anglo-Burmese War from 1824 to 1826. The outcome of this devastating and costly war in territorial terms was the ceding to Britain of Arakan, Assam, and Tenasserim in Lower Burma (Stockwell 1999: 376). A second war in 1852 'was a more clinical operation. What had started as an attempt to force concessions from the Burmese led to further annexations: first the ports of Rangoon, Martaban, and Bassein; then their hinterland, the old kingdom of Pegu; and finally, a swathe of teak forests lying north of Prome' (Stockwell, 1999: 379–80). In 1862 Lower Burma was annexed by Britain, and after the third Anglo-Burmese War of 1885 the whole of Burma, including Upper Burma, was annexed by Britain and treated as part of British India.

The very large island of Borneo had been a focus of Portuguese and Dutch interest from the early seventeenth century. The Dutch expanded their territory through military activity to what became Dutch Borneo. Britain expanded control into the two areas of Sarawak and Sabah. The demarcation of Dutch and British territories was agreed in a treaty of 1891.

British colonies and protectorates in the Pacific had built up during the nineteenth century, partly as a result of missionary activity and ambition, and partly through geopolitical and economic rivalry with other European countries including France, Germany and the Netherlands. The scientific voyages in the Pacific in the late eighteenth and early nineteenth centuries, and the expansion of missionary work in the late eighteenth and early nineteenth century, were followed 'by traders, whalers, deserters, escaped convicts and others on the make or on the run from settlements in Australia and New Zealand' (Stockwell 1991b: 142). Gradually political and administrative control was brought by the British to many Pacific islands – islands that had suffered from devastating introduced diseases and from the voracious demands for labour from other islands, including Fiji, and from Queensland and Peru.

Britain, concerned at the presence of lawless migrants to Fiji from Australia and New Zealand, tried 'every expedient short of annexation which might secure the same end', but none was effective (Porter 1996: 60). Britain placed a consul on Fiji in 1858, annexed it in 1874, and it became a British colony subject to the High Commission of the Western Pacific in 1876. The Gilbert Islands became a protectorate in 1892 and a colony, with the Ellice Islands, in 1916. The Solomon Islands became a protectorate in 1893, the Pitcairn group became a colony from 1887, Tonga was a protected state from 1900, and the New Hebrides was administered as an Anglo-French Condominium from 1906. British New Guinea was annexed in 1884, and the Cook Islands, a protectorate from 1888, were transferred to New Zealand in 1901 (Stockwell 1991b: 143).

In addition, conscious of the need to maintain naval control of the sea routes to India through the navy, Britain established bases at Aden in

Fig. 2.7 Kolari chiefs, Sadara Makara, New Guinea, 1885 (Scratchley expedition) Lindt Collection, A1005–0026. By permission of and © the Royal Historical Society of Victoria, Melbourne, Australia.

1839–40, the Seychelles and Mauritius (both ceded to Britain by France in the Treaty of Paris, 1814), and Ceylon (1802), and what were to become major trading posts were established in Singapore (1819) and Hong Kong (1842–3).

Britain and the settlement colonies

The four major areas of British settlement overseas, in addition to the United States, were Canada, Australia, New Zealand and South Africa.

Canada

European contact with eastern Canada had been made in the late fifteenth and early sixteenth centuries, and significant events included the landing of John Cabot on the east coast in 1497, the expeditions of the French explorer Jacques Cartier from 1534, the claiming of Newfoundland for Britain by Sir Humphrey Gilbert in 1583, de Champlain's founding of the city of Québec in 1608, and the foundation of the Hudson's Bay Company in 1670. The rival territorial interests of Britain and France, in British North America and New France, and the increasing progress to independence of what became the United States, determined much of the early

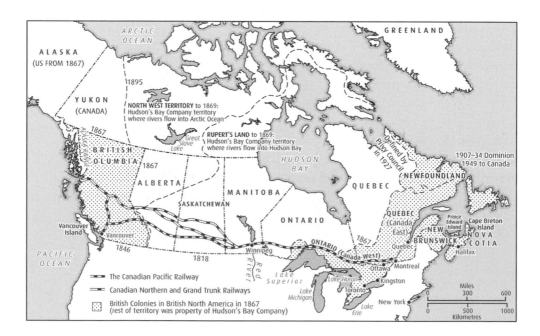

Fig. 2.8 Canada 1867–1949. Source: Lloyd (1984: 194).
By permission of and © Oxford University Press.

history of European settlement in the east. Major changes in territorial control included the division of the colony of Quebec into two parts – Upper Canada (in the west, now mainly the province of Ontario) and Lower Canada (in the east) – by the Constitution Act of 1791, and the two areas were united as Canada in 1841. The treaties of Utrecht (1713) and of Paris at the end of the Seven Years War (1756–63) enabled the large-scale transfer of territory from France to Britain. There were major changes in the relative sizes of French- and British-originated populations between 1791 and 1845, from a majority of inhabitants of French origin in 1791 to a majority of British origin by 1845.

The political geography in the eighteenth and nineteenth centuries of what became the Dominion of Canada was complex and dynamic, reflecting the political and imperial aspirations of the two main powers, Britain and the United States. Martin (1999: 522) has stated that by 1914 'Population had grown tenfold to just over 8 million, including the separate colony of Newfoundland. With that sole exception, all the Imperial territories had coalesced into the transcontinental Dominion of Canada, a self-governing entity within the Empire', while disputing the explanation that this process of change was simply one of British North America becoming Canada, imposing 'an unjustified coherence upon the British territories north of the United States' (Martin 1999: 523).

Ontario (Canada West), Quebec (Canada East), New Brunswick, and Nova Scotia were united as the Dominion of Canada in 1867 through the British North America Act (Constitution Act), to which were added the territories of the Hudson's Bay Company in 1869, Manitoba and the North-West Territories in 1870, British Columbia (which Vancouver Island had joined in 1866) in 1871, Prince Edward Island in 1873, the Yukon in 1898, and Saskatchewan and Alberta in 1905. These territorial consolidations reflected the necessity for a coherent federal administration and the outcomes of the rapid western expansion of Canadian settlement and infrastructure in the later nineteenth century. Newfoundland became a province of the Dominion of Canada in March 1949.

The Dominion of Canada faced many problems at the time of its creation. These included 'relations with the United States; the nature of its relationship with Great Britain; the strength of the provincial governments relative to the dominion government; and, above all, the presence of a large francophone majority in the heart of the country determined to preserve its language and culture. The most immediate problem was the empty west' (Sherill 1991: 111), a challenge met by the acquisition of the territory of the Hudson's Bay Company, major land grants to settlers, and the completion of the trans-continental Canadian Pacific Railway in 1885.

Australia

Australia is a continent with a very long history of human habitation, but European colonial interest dates from the eighteenth century, with James Cook's arrival in Botany Bay in 1770, and the establishment of the first British penal settlement in 1788. Several challenges faced policy-makers for Australian settlement, including the question of whether 'to treat the continent as a vast gaol and to what extent as a potentially useful colony' (Sturgis 1991a: 70), the latter in respect of the growing number of free settlers and the cost of transport to Australia. The transportation of prisoners to New South Wales was suspended in 1840. Progress of land take-up and settlement both along the coast and inland in pastoral areas led to the development of six colonies (New South Wales, Victoria, Tasmania, South Australia, Queensland and Western Australia) being given rights of responsible government between 1855 and 1890, and the Northern Territory, formerly part of the extensive original New South Wales and having been brought under the authority of South Australia from 1863 to 1911, and the Commonwealth government after 1911, being granted responsible government in 1978. The Australian Capital Territory (Canberra) was created in 1911.

In 1901 each of the original colonies became states in the process of federation and in the creation of the Commonwealth of Australia (Walmsley 1988: 57). As with other areas of white settlement in areas of European imperialism, the history of the advancement of land acquisition and use in Australia involved extensive and ruthless destruction of large fractions of the aboriginal population, with far-reaching consequences for that group and their rights of resource use, and for the complex question of national identity. This attitude to the aboriginal population of Australia was mainly shown by colonies and their settlers before about 1850 (and thus during British imperial administrations before federation), notably in Tasmania, in which a type of regulated ethnocide was practised across the island. Early in the twentieth century Australia was also caught up in the international eugenics movements which affected the treatment of aboriginal people by doctors, religious groups and social workers, and brought about the White Australia Policy, which was supported by trades unions on protectionist grounds and lasted until 1973. More overtly humanitarian attempts by missionaries and others to promote indigenous rights and welfare in the early nineteenth century – part of a series of connected efforts across the British empire – had limited success (Lester 2006: 229–41).

New Zealand

New Zealand, like Australia, had a long history of indigenous settlement and land use before European settlement from the late eighteenth and early nineteenth century by missionaries, traders, sealers and whalers. Polynesian peoples colonised New Zealand (Aotearoa) from the eleventh century, developing the Maori culture and a tribal/territorial system, and adapting their economy from a tropical to a more temperate environment. The colonial process intensified with the agency of the New Zealand Company, initiated by the colonial settlement theorist Edward Gibbon Wakefield from 1839 in the promotion of settlement and trade. Britain signed the highly controversial Treaty of Waitangi with Maori chiefs in 1840, which substantially appropriated Maori land, and in the same year annexed the South Island by right of discovery. Dalziel (1999: 578–9) has pointed to the significance of the treaty as 'the founding document of New Zealand as a bi-cultural society. Although it was repudiated by some British politicians, easily slipped from the consciousness of most settlers, and was ignored by the courts, it has always been regarded by Maori as a living document, a covenant of paramount importance in recognizing Maori rights and establishing a relationship with the Crown.' There were differences between the English and Maori versions of the treaty, and its interpretation and implementation by Britain were inconsistent and frequently contrary to the Maori interests, which were further eroded and marginalised by the rapid increase in the European population of New Zealand from 1840 to the end of the century, when 'The census of 1896 recorded 701,000 Europeans and just over 42,000 Maori. Thus colonialism marginalized Maori and ensured European dominance' (Dalziel 1999: 581–2).

British control over British nationals in New Zealand was for a period administered from New South Wales, and this authority was confirmed in 1823, but New Zealand became a separate crown colony in 1841 (Dalziel 1999: 576). Conflict between Maori and Europeans over land rights ensued on the North Island, notably in 1845–7 and from 1860 to 1872, in what were initially called the Maori Wars (later the Land or New Zealand Wars), with the British using *c.* 16,000 troops, a quarter of which were colonial (Sturgis 1991b: 74–5). After the wars the New Zealand economy accelerated through gold discoveries, and through sheep and dairy farming. The export of dairy produce and meat was facilitated by the advent of refrigeration in 1882. New Zealand was given Dominion status in 1907.

South Africa

The Dutch Cape Colony in South Africa became British territory in 1795 and in 1806, confirmed by an Anglo-Dutch Treaty of 1814, and in the nineteenth century the Cape was a crucial strategic British location for access to India and beyond. Significant migration from Britain to South Africa boosted the British settler numbers to over 10,000 in the 1820s. This exacerbated the tensions between Boer and British, leading to the Great Trek of 1835–7 and settlement by the Boer farmers in the east, which in turn brought Boer and Zulu people into conflict, with the battle of Blood River in December 1838 being a turning point. Thereafter the Boers occupied much of Zululand, and created their own republics of Natal Transvaal, and the Orange Free State (Wesseling 2004: 98–9). Britain annexed Natal in 1843 (which achieved self-government much later than the Cape, in 1892), the Orange Free State in 1847 and the Transvaal in 1877, but recognised the independence of the Orange Free State in conventions of 1852 and 1854. The conflict between Boer and Zulu transferred to a Zulu–British war, starting in January 1879, which resulted in great loss of Zulu and British life in battles at Ulendi and Rorke's Drift.

The colonies of South Africa were based on white settlement cores, and had achieved their status by fierce opposition to indigenous peoples and their land use rights. The Cape Colony had expanded eastwards through wars against the Xhosa and the annexation of their territory, and then by linking to Natal, with opposition from the Zulu. The final territorial conflict before South Africa was given Dominion status (in 1910) was between the Boers and the British – the Anglo-Boer War (1899–1902), following which the Orange Free State and the Transvaal were given self-government (in 1907), which ceased on the creation of the Union of South Africa.

Conflict between Britain and the people of territories under British imperial control intensified in the mid-nineteenth century in many contrasting parts of the British empire. As Lester has indicated: 'Both formal and "informal" components of Britain's empire were embroiled in contests associated with a more expansive imperial and capitalist phase. Each of these contests allowed for further undermining of humanitarian representations, the more emphatic adoption of settler discourses by powerful metropolitan groups, and the more forceful operation of colonial governance' (Lester 2001: 160–1). The outcome in each case was a stronger assertion of British control and the diminution of indigenous power and influence, but also the growth of seeds of nationalist aspiration in response.

France's empire and colonies

France had a long history of overseas colonisation, notably in North America and the Caribbean, with smaller outposts in India, Mauritius, Madagascar, the Seychelles and the coast of West Africa before the period of high imperialism in the later nineteenth and early twentieth centuries. Much of this was lost in the eighteenth and early nineteenth centuries. Andrew and Kanya-Forstner state that 'Left with only colonial trifles after Waterloo, France seemed to have lost all appetite for further imperial expansion. Over the next century, however, she was to build a second empire even larger than the first. Its construction began almost by accident' (Andrew and Kanya-Forstner 1981: 9).

The start of the new empire began with the invasion of Algiers in July 1830, followed by the establishment of other footholds in North Africa, the Comoros Islands in the Indian Ocean in 1843, and bases on the coast of the Red Sea. Further advances were made in Indo-China from the 1850s, and in Central and West Africa, Madagascar and the Pacific in the late nineteenth and early twentieth centuries. The final additions came in the form of the League of Nations mandates of Syria and Lebanon after the First World War.

French colonial policy in the nineteenth century was conditioned by both enthusiasm and strong opposition. The imperial enthusiasm of the Emperor Napoleon III ended with France's defeat in the Franco-Prussian War in 1870, but the republican Jules Ferry (1832–93) promoted the theory and practice of colonialism (Wesseling 2004: 132–3), with the acquisition of colonies in North Africa, Madagascar and French Indo-China. Ferry's imperial stance was manifest in support of French involvement in Tunisia (which caused the fall of his government in 1881), and, in his second ministry (1883–85) in the Congo (after Pierre de Brazza's expeditions), and in Indo-China. His most active period of pro-imperialism was in his second term as premier. His theory of imperialism focused on economic, humanitarian and political issues. He saw the empire as a provider of overseas markets for domestic industrial produce, and a target for humanitarian processes which were part of the *mission civilisatrice*. In a speech in 1884 in the Chamber of Deputies on the removal of the slave trade (abolished in France in 1848), he indicated that his priority were the political consequences for France in Europe if she did not take part in European expansion into Africa and Asia.

His opinions did not always convince his political contemporaries, or the French populace, evidenced by the effect of military losses in

South-East Asia in ending his second period as premier (Wesseling 2004: 132–3). It has been suggested that rather than promoting a logical and overt colonial policy, Ferry 'stumbled along reacting to events and initiatives undertaken by others. Thus people on the spot, often autonomous missionaries and businessmen, and especially adventurous military officers, set in motion imperial activities that Ferry later approved' (Haynes 1991: 216).

Andrew and Kanya-Forstner agree, suggesting that the colonial ambitions of Napoleon III and Ferry were less typical of French colonial processes than of the more 'fitful and sporadic' influences in the early phases by French army and naval officers operating in the proto-colonies, a kind of 'gigantic system of outdoor relief not, as in the British case, for the upper orders but for the armed services'. They argue that it was not until *c.* 1890 that initiative moved significantly though not exclusively to the metropole, motivated by 'the passions aroused by the scramble for Africa and the European rivalries which the scramble generated' (Andrew and Kanya-Forstner 1981: 10): that is, stronger nationalist sentiments. They also believe that the indifference of French governments to imperialism in the quarter-century before the First World War stemmed 'from the constitutional weaknesses of the pre-war Third Republic: transient governments with an average life-expectancy of nine months, [and] a poorly developed sense of cabinet responsibility' (Andrew and Kanya-Forstner 1981: 12).

The ideas of the economist Paul Léroy-Beaulieu (1843–1916) influenced politicians such as Léon Gambetta (1838–82) in his advocacy of the accumulation of colonies that might be exchanged for Alsace-Lorraine (lost in the Franco-Prussian War), and also as outlets for the export of the poor and undesirable elements of French society. Some of the impetus for French imperial initiatives came from the *parti colonial* – an entity made up of many different groups, including politicians and geographers from the universities and the Société de Géographie de Paris (SGP), and, from 1876, from the more business- and commerce-orientated Société de Géographie Commerciale de Paris which had split off from the SGP (see Chapter 6). A group of colonialists had been meeting informally in Paris between 1873 and 1896, but in the 1890s more formal committees – for Madagascar (started in 1895), Egypt (1895), French Asia (1901), French Morocco (1904) and French Oceania (1905) – were established that influenced French imperial policy, and also in due course considered and advised what French colonial policy, and geostrategy should be after the end of the First World War (Aldrich 1996: 163–4).

In France there was opposition to imperial policy, on the grounds of the overstretching of French resources, including people; more important domestic priorities such as the restoration of Alsace Lorraine; and, in the case of the geographer Élisée Reclus, a change of balance of imperial priorities to favour Africa instead of Indo- China, because Indo-China was much too distant for France to govern. Other dissenting voices included those of Anatole France the novelist, the Socialist Party leader Jean Jaurès, and the politician Georges Clemenceau (Aldrich 1996: 111–14). Socialists in particular objected to the economic exploitation of the resources and peoples of French colonies, and claimed that any profits from the colonies benefited only bourgeois capitalists and not the French nation as a whole.

By the eve of the First World War French policy was more focused on European continental geopolitics than on a wider empire, a priority being defence against further German invasion, notably in the aftermath of the loss of Alsace Lorraine in 1871 (Andrew and Kanya-Forstner 1981: 13–19). French colonial investment was small, and some imported food-stuffs, such as wine from Algeria, were resented, but industries such as sugar soap, metallurgical products and cotton products were exported from France to her imperial territories. The metropolitan administration of French overseas territories was complex, being divided between four different government ministries, a problem not resolved by the creation of an independent but low-calibre Ministry of Colonies in 1894, and the poor quality of French imperial administrators overseas.

In spite of all these constraints, however, the French empire did expand in the late nineteenth and early twentieth centuries, driven by European geopolitical issues and fears, and particularly by French public opinion, which showed the way in which 'the injured nationalism of French society made it vulnerable to a colonialism with which it was fundamentally out of sympathy', and 'sensitive to any slight to French prestige' (Andrew and Kanya-Forstner 1981: 29), notably after 1890, when French colonialism increased the territories of the French empire in Africa, South-East Asia and the Pacific.

France and North Africa

Algeria

In May 1830, partly because of the need to settle a debt to the *dey* of Algeria, incurred during the Napoleonic Wars, an insult by him to the French consul in 1827 and his destruction of the French trading posts at the Bastion de France in Algiers in the same year, and partly because of the need for a cause to boost the image of the unpopular king Charles X, France sent 653 ships and 34,000 soldiers to invade Algeria. They were strongly opposed by a large indigenous army, but soon gained control and took violent revenge on the inhabitants of Algiers, at the same time confiscating land and property. Initial French control in 1830 was restricted to the coastal cities of Oran and Bône, but by 1870 this had been extended to the whole of the coastal zone between Morocco and Tunisia, and inland to the Atlas Mountains (Aldrich 1996: 26–7).

This expansion met with strong opposition, notably by the tribal chief Emir Abd al-Qadir. The military campaigns of the French under General Bugeaud from the 1840s involved large numbers of soldiers: about 64,000 in 1840, increasing to over 100,000 in 1847, when Abd al-Qadir was sent into exile in France. The colonial energies of the French increased at the time of the July Monarchy, Napoleon III and the Second Empire, and the number of French settlers in Algeria increased from 27,000 in 1841 to 75,000 in 1845, and nearly 300,000 in 1860 (Marsot 1991b: 10). In 1871 France had almost total control of Algeria, which was divided into the three *départements* of Algiers, Oran and Constantine. French citizenship was granted to Algerian Jews in 1872, and in 1881 the three *départements* became constitutionally an integral part of France (Wesseling 1996: 13). The ruthless suppression of opposition by Algerian leaders and people led to Algeria becoming a major French settlement colony by the late nine-teenth century. European economic activity included the cultivation of vines, with the sedentary and nomadic Arab and Berber peoples largely confined to geographically, politically and socially marginal positions (Aldrich 1996: 28).

Tunisia

Tunisia, with a history of weak and corrupt administration, strong hill and desert nomadic peoples, a consistently weak economy, and a popula-tion resistant to attempted reform and higher taxation in the early 1860s, was in a poor economic state. It had been part of the French imperial scheme for control of the Maghrib, partly because of its strategic position on the Mediterranean relatively close to Sicily. There was growing interest in Tunisia by Italy, which had settlers there, and by Britain. Italian and British entrepreneurial agency in the sale of a major railway and a large estate, and an incursion by Tunisian tribesmen into Algeria in March 1881, led to a French invasion in April 1881 and protectorate status for

Tunisia in May of that year (Aldrich, 1996: 30). Tunisia became in effect another French colony, but after the First World War a nationalist movement for independence began with the help of the trade unions.

Morocco

Morocco became a French protectorate in 1912, and was the last piece of territory in Africa to come under French control. Morocco occupied a critical position at the western end of the Mediterranean south of the straits of Gibraltar, and had considerable mineral resources, including copper. In the nineteenth century both France and Spain had geostrategic and economic interests in Morocco, as did Germany and Britain. A Madrid Convention of 1880 had registered fourteen countries with 'most-favoured-nation' status for Morocco. With increasing competition between European powers for territory in Africa, the balance of power was partly shifted by the *entente cordiale* between Britain and France in 1904. Immediately prior to this there were French military incursions into Morocco from Algeria, some led by General Lyautey, a powerful military commander based in Algeria. As with Tunisia, France had supplied money to support the Moroccan sultanate, which by 1900 was so much in debt that the French took control of its financial affairs (Marsot 1991c: 411).

The Algeciras Act of 1906 was agreed by twelve European states, and recognised the special interest of France and Spain in Morocco. There was a major uprising in 1907, when France took advantage of the opportunity to suppress rebel activity, and did so again in 1911. In 1912 France formally gained Morocco as a protectorate, having agreed to appease Germany – which had economic and strategic interests in Morocco – by the allocation of 107,000 square miles of territory in the French Congo (Townsend 1941: 131). Lyautey was appointed as French Resident-General, though active opposition to the French continued until the mid-1930s (Aldrich 1996: 35).

French West Africa and Equatorial Africa

South of the Sahara France took control of vast areas of West and Equatorial Africa during the later nineteenth century. These did not form part of a logical French plan for acquisitions of specific areas of sub-Saharan Africa as part of her empire, for 'most land was acquired at the expense of armed forays, negotiations with African chieftains and great efforts to secure posts over which the French flag had tentatively been raised'

(Aldrich 1996: 36). This activity was spurred by the tensions between European powers that led to the 'scramble' for Africa, by the initiatives of individual soldiers, traders, and missionaries, and by the ideologies of a *mission civilisatrice*.

French West Africa comprised the vast territories largely appropriated by the French between about 1885 and 1905, including eight territories formerly named Niger Colony (Niger), Ivory Coast, Dahomey (Benin), Mauritania, French Sudan (Mali), Upper Volta (Burkina-Faso), Togoland and Senegal. At the beginning of the nineteenth century France had only coastal bases, at Gorée and Saint-Louis in Senegal and slave-trade bases on the coast of the Gulf of Guinea. From these, through military initiative and local diplomacy, France expanded control into the interior. From *c.* 1880 to 1900 French influence developed by treaty and military action. From 1900 to 1914, African attempts to retain sovereignty failed, and experiments were made with new administrative systems. The major objectives of the West Africans remained the recovery of their former autonomy, the expulsion of Europeans, opposition to the iniquities of the colonial system and attempts to find some degree of accommodation with that system (Gueye 1990: 68).

Initial French impetus was in the area of Casamance, south of the Gambia River, by military activity along the Casamance River, including the establishment of forts, and the defeat of the Islamic Wolof people in 1886. This was accompanied by increased trading by French companies, particularly of groundnuts and rubber in the 1880s and early 1890s. Local labourers were forced to endure harsh working conditions in the collection of rubber (Aldrich 1996: 38). The French advance was strongly opposed, but was enhanced by General Louis Faidherbe (1818–89), who was posted to Senegal in 1852, and became governor in 1854, and who had a broad vision of French imperial development in West Africa. This required the extension of French control from bases such as Senegal to 'the whole hin-terland of West Africa from Algeria to the Congo' (Fieldhouse 1982: 214).

In the 1880s and 1890s French control spread to the Sudan, with its fabled city of Timbuktu, to Upper Niger (Niger) and Lake Chad, southwards from Bamako to the Ivory Coast (Côte d'Ivoire), and both south from Senegal and inland from the coast of the southern Rivers region through conquest of the Muslim stronghold at Fouta Djalon to create French Guinea, northwards and eastwards to create Upper Volta, and inland to the territory of Dahomey. The vast territory of Mauritania, mostly made up of the Sahara Desert, came under French influence from *c.* 1900 to 1934 (Aldrich 1996: 48), and part of the former German territories of Togoland and Cameroon became mandated French colonies at the end of the First World War (Aldrich 1996: 38–9).

The main component countries of French Equatorial Africa (Afrique Équatoriale Française) were Gabon, Middle (Moyen) Congo (People's Republic of the Congo), Ubangi-Chari (Central African Republic), and Chad. French interest in this thinly populated large area of 2.5 million square kilometres (976,000 square miles) dates back to missionary activity in the seventeenth and eighteenth centuries. From the early nineteenth century, partly because of a will to eradicate the slave trade and partly to advance commercial prospects, France's interest increased, and treaties were negotiated with tribal chiefs in coastal regions, further treaties following the expeditions by the explorer de Brazza on the Congo and Ogooué rivers. Thereafter France completed the shaping of her central African empire through treaties with Portugal, the Congo Free State, and others stemming from the Berlin Conference of 1884–5, the effect of the Fashoda crisis of 1898, and the granting of a large area of the French Congo to Germany in 1911 (Cherkaoui 1991a: 229).

From about 1891 the region was named the French Congo, and in 1910 this was changed to French Equatorial Africa. The administration of this large area was not supported directly by funding from the French state, which was not in favour of direct investment, so development was implemented through the familiar process of concessions to forty-two private companies, who in the event invested little in the areas which they were allocated, and for which they paid small rents and received 15 per cent of the profits.

Cherkaoui (1991a: 229–30) states that 'The companies were completely unregulated and notorious for exploiting native Africans. The concessionary exploitation of natural resources by the use of forced labour, combined with heavy taxation of the natives and the frequent recruitment of porters, caused enormous resentment and a local depression. The decline of rubber prices precipitated a crisis of the concessionary system', rubber and ivory having been the main exports. Conditions improved after 1910, the year in which this huge French territory was consolidated into one unit.

French territories in East Africa

French Somaliland is a very small territory in North-East Africa, with a shoreline on the strait of Bab el-Mandeb and the Gulf of Aden, comprising what for the French in the mid-nineteenth century was an area producing perfumes and spices in demand in Europe. It was also a key strategic location as a coaling and naval station for French ships before and after the opening of the Suez Canal in 1869, and notably as a base connected with French colonial expansion in South-East Asia. French interest dated from 1855, and various purchases and treaties were combined in 1884–5 to create French Somaliland, in a context of increasing British involvement in Egypt (1882) and Somalia (1884). Aldrich (1996: 59–60) has highlighted the significance to the economy and the French purse of its modern port structures, the new railway from Djibouti to Addis Ababa in Ethiopia, completed in 1917, the trading of arms and ammunition, also mainly with Ethiopia, and salt mining.

The boundaries of French Somaliland with British Somalia, Ethiopia and Eritrea were established between 1888 and 1901. Most economic activity was at the coast, and the inland territory was occupied by the Issa and Afar peoples, who were subject to inter-tribal power struggles over most of the late nineteenth century and the first half of the twentieth, a process that weakened opposition to the French. In 1958 French Somaliland became a French Overseas Territory, and in 1967 the name changed to the French Territory of the Afars and Issas (Cherkaoui 1991b: 176).

French islands in the Indian Ocean

Madagascar

Although France, unlike Britain and Germany, and at an earlier date Portugal, had no direct imperial interest in East Africa, it was drawn into the interplay of geopolitical and commercial interests in the later nineteenth century. France had attempted to establish settlements in Madagascar on the island of St Marie and at Fort Dauphin from the mid-seventeenth century, but it was not until 1751 that France colonised St Marie and established trading posts along the east coast. The island was a base for European piracy in the eighteenth century, and was actively involved in the slave trade.

The indigenous peoples were highly resistant to European attempts to control and exploit them, but successive monarchs of the Hova (Merina) kingdom between 1782 and 1828 encouraged modernisation through new technology and new ideologies, and allowed European missions, teachers and technologists to migrate to the island, resulting in widespread high levels of education. The monarchy itself remained oligarchic, and implemented by military strength and the use of slavery (Wesseling 1996: 165–6). In 1883, however, France, which already had imperial control of Réunion and some of the islands off Madagascar, took exception to a law of 1881 in which Madagascar sought to ban French ownership of land (a facility afforded in an earlier treaty of 1868), and a naval squadron bombarded several coastal towns, resulting in the Tamatave Treaty of 1885. By 1894, attacks on French residents on Madagascar had reached a point of crisis, and France first vacated the island, then returned with a naval force which took Tamatave and other ports and landed a large military force. This force, although decimated by fever, took the capital, Tananarive, and a short-lived treaty declared Madagascar a French protectorate. There was further resistance, which resulted in the annexation of Madagascar by France in June 1896. Two prominent colonial soldiers, Joseph Gallieni and Hubert Lyautey, were appointed governor-general and deputy governor-general (Wesseling 1996: 166–7). French control of the relatively small population of Madagascar (*c.* three million in 1911, of which over 15,000 were Europeans who had mainly come via Réunion or Mauritius) was mainly through missionary work and schools, but France introduced hardly any economic innovation other than protective import tariffs – inducing price rises – and an unsuccessful land allocation scheme for would-be colonial immigrants (Wesseling 2004: 177).

Réunion

Réunion, originally named Bourbon, had been a French colony since 1643. Coffee and spice plantations, which were worked with African slave labour, had been established by settlers from 1662, and sugar cane was introduced in the late seventeenth century. After short-term control of Bourbon by Britain during the Napoleonic Wars, the French resumed control through a treaty of 1825, and it was named Réunion. In 1848 the French abolished slavery, and a substitute labour force for the plantations was provided through the importing of contract labour from East Africa, India and Indo-China (Olson, 1991a: 521).

Mauritius

Mauritius, east of Madagascar in the Indian Ocean, had been settled for a short time by Dutch colonists in the mid-seventeenth century, but this and other Dutch colonial settlement projects were unsuccessful, and they abandoned Mauritius in 1710. In 1715 control was claimed by the French East India Company, and in 1764 the island, with sugar plantations and a population largely made up of slaves, became a French crown colony. At the beginning of the nineteenth century the harassment of British ships in the Indian Ocean by French pirates and privateers led to the invasion of Mauritius by the British navy and an accompanying army in 1810, during the Napoleonic Wars, and Britain took control under the Treaty of Paris of 1814. The sugar plantations became very productive, but lost their slave labour force when Britain abolished slavery in 1833, these labourers being replaced by contract labour from India. At the end of the nineteenth century Britain extended the representation on the council of government of French–Mauritian landowners, and then of the (majority) Indian–Mauritian populations (Olson 1991b: 401).

French Indo-China

In the second half of the nineteenth century France, together with other European powers such as Britain and Germany, and the United States, increased their economic and strategic interest in South-East Asia and the Pacific. There had been French involvement in Indo-China through missionary activity in Annam in the early seventeenth century and the commercial activity of the French East India Company. By the early nineteenth century there was a small number of French commercial trading bases in India.

The experiences of the French, like the British, in Indo-China and South-East Asia more generally, involved more than military conquest and colonisation. The broader context included changes in the balances of European influence and rivalry in the region, industrialisation, major improvements in communications, a growing interest in India and China, and the modernisation of Japan (Tarling 1999: 2).

Tarling has also reminded us that Europeans were not the sole actors in this region. There was Islamic influence from Arabia, and the United States was also becoming a significant player. Most important were 'the peoples of Southeast Asia themselves, who interacted with the Europeans and with others in a variety of ways, fighting, resisting, accommodating, adapting, turning and being turned to account, with greater or less vision, wisdom or acumen, at the popular and élite levels' (Tarling 1999: 2). Also significant were the contrasts between the European geographical concepts of polities, places and the people who lived in them, and the greater importance attached by indigenous peoples to less territorial and more personal concepts of affiliation, including personal allegiances, courts, core and periphery links and overlapping hierarchies, so that European attempts at designation and delineation of territorial boundaries were nearly always resisted.

French expansion in Indo-China, according to Fieldhouse, was unlike that of Britain, which had existing bases, and 'is difficult to explain in terms of the expansion of an existing nucleus. Like French power in Algeria it was partly accidental, partly the result of metropolitan decisions' (Fieldhouse 1982: 74). French policy was affected by British imperial activity in South-East Asia. It has been argued that the opportunities for French expansion in the area were influenced by their exclusion from India by the British, by rivalry with Britain for influence in Vietnam, by civil war in Vietnam in the late eighteenth century, by the bringing of French warships to the area to protect trade to the newly opened China, and by the persecution of French and Spanish Catholic missionaries.

There was little metropolitan enthusiasm for French expansion in Asia, but an active presence was established by the missionaries, the navy and the army, traders, and local officials (Tarling, 1999: 37). A French–Spanish force took Tourane Danang in Cochin China in 1858, and, being unable to move inland to Hué, moved south and took Saigon in 1859, which remained under siege by an Annamite army until relieved in 1861 by Admiral Bonard. In 1862 Bonard agreed a treaty, ratified in France, by which Annam ceded the three provinces of East Cochin China to France, leaving the three western provinces isolated and as sources of opposition, and these were annexed by the French in 1867. French protectorate status for Cambodia was agreed in 1863.

In 1866 a scientific expedition – the Mekong Exploration Commission – was sent by the French to the middle and upper Mekong from Saigon, led by Doudart de Legrée (who died during the expedition, in March 1868) and Francis Garnier, and returned via China in 1868, showing that because of rapids the middle Mekong could not be used for transport and trade, but that better prospects were offered by the Red River (Fleuve Rouge) for links with China (Keay 2005a and b).

As a consequence of this expedition, the French looked to Tonkin and the Red River as a means of access to China, and after an initial attempt led by Garnier (who was killed in the action) to capture Hanoi and other cities of the Tonkin delta, and continued opposition from Annamites and Chinese pirate groups (Black Flags), they signed the Convention of Tiensin in May 1884. In this the Chinese agreed to withdraw troops from Tonkin, but the war continued, and it was not until June 1885 that the final definitive treaty was signed. By this time Annam (central Vietnam) and Tongking (northern Vietnam) had been designated French protectorates.

After the establishment of French authority to the east and south, the landlocked country of Laos became a target for the French, partly because of British and Siamese interest, and in 1886 a treaty was signed with Siam which registered French claims to Laos, and a consulate under Auguste Pavie was established in Luang Prabang. Luang Prabang was attacked in 1887 by Black Flag and Tai Khao forces. This was countered by French troops, and in 1893, with French warships blockading Bangkok, Siam conceded to France the territories east of the Mekong. Laos became a French protectorate, and it was added to the Government-General of French Indo-China in 1897. Laos was not greatly affected by French colonialism, retaining its king in Luang Prabang, while subject to administration in eight provinces, the whole protectorate being governed by a French resident. In contrast, Cochin China was a resource-rich region, including the major rice-growing areas of the Mekong delta and the southern ranges of the Annamese cordillera, where a plantation economy producing tea, coffee, rubber, oil palm and sugar cane was developed. The French had a major colonial impact on Cochin China through the development of Saigon as a major colonial city, and of plantations by French and Vietnamese landowners.

The story of French Indo-China in the twentieth century is complex, and revolves around both broader international and local issues. Each of the main territories experienced nationalist movements and bloody conflicts, in which the conflicts between international powers, notably France and the United States, and the indigenous nationalist movements finally ended the colonial presence.

French colonial territories in the Pacific

French imperial activity in the Pacific in the nineteenth and early twentieth centuries continued early European geographical and commercial interest from the late fifteenth century onwards, to which were added missionary activity and the scientific voyages of the eighteenth and early nineteenth centuries. Changing geostrategic and commercial challenges and opportunities in the nineteenth and early twentieth centuries included the opening of links with China and Japan, the rise of the United States as a major trading power, better access to Asia and the Pacific for European and Middle Eastern states through the Suez Canal, faster naval and merchant ships, more rapid means of communication, and concerns to protect existing and promote new colonial interests.

Rivalry between France and Britain was a significant factor. In the nineteenth century the main targets of the French were Tahiti and the

Marquesas Islands in French Polynesia in the south-west Pacific, together with the smaller islands of Wallis and Fortuna, and New Caledonia and the Loyalty Islands in the Melanesian cultural area of the South Pacific. Tahiti had acquired the image of an exotic idyll, notably after the voyages by Bougainville and La Pérouse in the eighteenth century, but as Aldrich has indicated, these images were deceptive, for 'the noble savages suffered from a variety of diseases, typhoons and other natural disasters often buffeted their islands, tribal warfare was endemic. And the Polynesians had a more structured and complicated society and culture than met the eye of many travellers: hierarchical divisions between nobles and commoners, taboos and traditions, a complex cosmology' (Aldrich 1990: 2).

Thirty British missionaries, including four ordained ministers, reached Tahiti in March 1797, but in 1835 French missionaries were refused permission to land and work there. In 1842 a French ship commanded by a naval officer, Admiral Du Petit-Thouars, arrived in Tahiti, and by threatening to bombard the island, obtained an apology for the expulsion of two Catholic missionaries and also gained favoured-nation trading rights. Du Petit-Thouars returned to the Marquesas Islands in May 1842 and annexed Fatu Hiva and the south-eastern Marquesas, then sailed to Papeete, which he reached in August 1842, and, demanding rights of settlement, trading and missionary work, obtained agreement for Tahiti to become a French protectorate, an action only confirmed from Paris in 1843 and translated to an annexation in 1890 (Aldrich 1990: 21–4).

The islands of Grande Terre and the Isle of Pines in New Caledonia were annexed for France by the French naval officer Febvrier-Despointes in 1853. These were followed by the Loyalty Islands, in an attempt by the French to thwart British interest, obtain a key base on Pacific shipping routes, and also provide a location for a French penal colony. The islands of Wallis, Fortuna and Alofi were also of interest to Britain and Germany, but Wallis and Fortuna were made protectorates of France in 1886 and 1887. The three islands were annexed in 1913. The New Hebrides island groups unusually became jointly administered by Britain and France from 1906, a curious 'condominium' that persisted until 1980 (Aldrich 1990: 26, 30–1).

The Dutch empire and colonies

In the 1590s Dutch ships travelled to the West Indies, the Mediterranean and the East Indies. In 1600 they reached Japan, and in 1602 the Dutch

East India Company (Verenigde Ost-Indisch Compagnie or VOC) was founded through the amalgamation of smaller trading companies which had been active in Asia. It was given great power in its enabling charter, including the use of troops, diplomatic power, and the right of territorial appropriation. It relied heavily on local military and commercial agents, and had a monopoly of trade in Asia, in return for promoting Dutch economic and strategic interests. Its nominal control lay with its board of seventeen directors in Amsterdam, and the company was financed by share issues.

The Dutch East India Company had a very strong and widespread influence in South-East Asia, including India, Burma, Malaysia, Indochina and Siam, and founded a factory at Hirado in Japan in 1609. In 1605 the VOC captured Amboina and expelled the Portuguese from the Moluccas – formerly known as the Spice Islands – where the cloves, cinnamon, nutmeg, and pepper were produced that were luxuries much in demand in Europe. The Dutch were also active in Java and founded a major administrative settlement at Batavia in 1619.

The Dutch, through these two main trading companies, actively sought, won, and periodically lost, in conflicts with other European powers, settlement colonies in South America, North America, the Caribbean and South Africa, but were less involved with colonial settlement in Asia, partly on account of its distance from Europe. Continued interest in the economic resources of South-East Asia maintained an active Dutch trading and military presence, and by the beginning of the eighteenth century the Dutch had a strong presence in western Sumatra and in Java, and a weaker hold in eastern Indonesia. Dutch control was extended more widely in the nineteenth century to include parts of Borneo and New Guinea, and a larger area of Sumatra. A decline in profits had caused the dissolution of the VOC in 1799, and the transfer of its assets to the Batavian Republic.

The Cape Colony in South Africa was lost to the English in 1794, and the invasion of the Dutch Republic by France in 1795 ushered in a period of French control of Dutch territory, including the Dutch East Indies, but from 1811 to 1816 Britain took control of the East Indies. It was not until the Convention of London (following the Congress of Vienna) that the Dutch had the Dutch East Indies restored to them, and the Anglo-Dutch Treaty of 1824 agreed on the division of East Asia by the Dutch and the English, in effect forming a Dutch Indonesia and an English Malaysia (Wesseling 2004: 105).

James and Schrauwers have summarised the Dutch colonial experience from the late nineteenth century:

The Netherlands began the nineteenth century as a small agrarian nation with a tenuous hold on a large inherited colonial empire. Over the subsequent one hundred years, it remained an eddy in the larger currents of European history; handicapped by its small size, internal divisions, limited military might and slow industrialisation. Yet by the end of the century, a resurgent nationalist sentiment had emerged; hoping to recapture the patina of their golden era, they collectively cast their eyes out once again to the 'Greater Netherlands' created through that earlier Dutch diaspora. Under the guise of a new 'Ethical colonial policy', the Netherlands began an imperialistic consolidation of their Asian territories with a degree of force which shocked even the most inured of their colonial allies. (James and Schrauwers 2003: 53)

The core of the modern Dutch empire in South-East Asia was Java, and consolidation involved the incorporation of other parts of the region 'into what became a Java-based colonial state' (Booth 2008: 26). After the Java War (1825 to 1830), the Dutch introduced the 'cultivation system' (*cultuurstelsel*), a means of forcing indigenous producers, partly in lieu of tax, to grow certain commodities that were of value on world markets, notably coffee, sugar and indigo. These commodities were mainly sent to Amsterdam for sale, and the profits accrued to the Dutch state. By 1864 the cultivation system had ended for all crops save sugar and coffee, which were also removed from the system in 1890 and 1917 respectively (Wesseling 2004: 109).

By the beginning of the twentieth century the Dutch were concerned with consolidation of their position in the Dutch East Indies, in contrast to other European powers such as Britain, France and Germany whose empires and colonies were expanding. Wesseling has outlined the debate in the Netherlands at this time about whether it really was or should be an imperial state with an imperial policy. This reflected the idea that it was not a great power and that it was not greatly involved with industrial monopoly capitalism, relying on treaties with other European countries to respect their mutual interests and authority in the region, rather than direct action (other than for the 'pacification' of territories already under its control). 'The explanation for Dutch colonial policy', says Wesseling (2004: 141–2), 'must be sought in the Netherlands' peculiar position in the world. It was a colonial giant but a political dwarf. It played first fiddle in Asia, but merely hummed a little tune in the concert of Europe. This put Dutch colonialism in a class by itself.'

Dutch policy in the East Indies was thus mainly for securing the Dutch hold on existing colonial territory, frequently by force of arms,

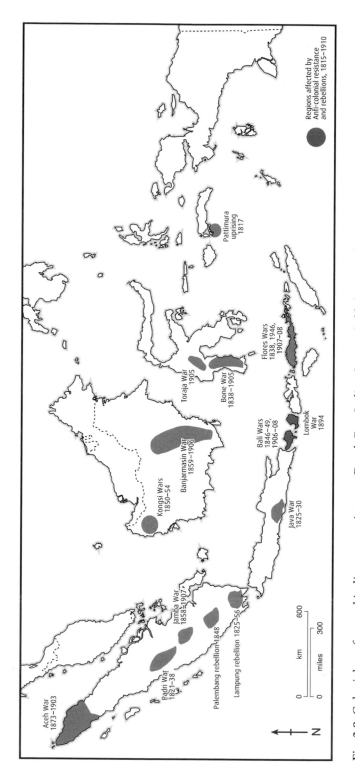

Fig. 2.9 Colonial warfare and indigenous resistance, Dutch East Indies. Source: Cribb (2000: 122). By permission of and © Taylor and Francis Books UK.

Regions affected by Anti-colonial resistance and rebellions, 1815–1910

Pattimura uprising 1817

Flores Wars 1838, 1946, 1907–08

Toraja War 1905

Bone War 1838–1905

Bali Wars 1846–49, 1906–08

Lombok War 1894

Banjarmasin War 1859–1906

Kongsi Wars 1850–54

Java War 1825–30

Jamba War 1858–1907

Padri War 1821–38

Palembang rebellion 1848

Lampung rebellion 1825–56

Aceh War 1873–1903

km
0   300   600
miles
0   300

N

and notably through the Aceh Wars on Sumatra from 1873 to 1903, and improving the security of areas that had remained independent. These actions aimed to establish Dutch sovereignty over the Islamic sultanate of Aceh and to eliminate piracy by the Acehnese. In the Sumatra Treaty of November 1871 Dutch sovereignty over Aceh was recognised by Britain, but the sultan of Aceh refused this recognition, and this, together with fears of possible Italian and American interest, set in train a long and complex series of military campaigns against the sultan of Aceh (Wesseling 2004: 211).

These bloody and lengthy campaigns, following the earlier actions by the Dutch in the 1820s and 1830s and continuing action in the mid- and late nineteenth century, involved large numbers of indigenous troops recruited by the Dutch from other islands in the archipelago, whose death rates were increased by tropical diseases. In these campaigns, the Dutch 'bombarded Kutaraja, cut off trade, sent 10,000 native troops recruited from other islands, burned villages, and drove the Islamic guerrillas into the mountains. The war finally sputtered out due to Acehnese exhaustion. The Netherlands treasury was nearly drained' (Marlay 1991a: 595).

Much of the action by the Dutch against indigenous peoples and their rulers was extremely violent and had a devastating effect: 'Those who resisted the imperial advance invariably found it a hopeless, if not suicidal enterprise. Several entire political entities, such as Bali, Aceh and Sulu, perished in paroxysms of frenzied violence. More than once poorly armed but dedicated and often religiously motivated warriors threw themselves against Gatling guns, heavy artillery, repeating rifles and the disciplined infantry forces of industrialized states' (Trocki 1994: 77). Resistance to Dutch authority was also widespread in areas of the archipelago peripheral to the Dutch administrative centre of Batavia on Java, such as Sulawesi, west Borneo, Bali, Flores and Ceram.

Other parts of the East Indies that were subject to Dutch consolidation of power at this time were the island of Lombok and its Balinese rulers, and then Bali itself in 1906; Djambi in south-east Sumatra; the Batak lands of north-west Sumatra; the Tana Boemboe states in south-east Borneo (first ceded to the Dutch in 1817, and then governed for them by their original rulers); Meliau and Benoet in western Borneo, annexed in 1909, and the states of Pinoh and then of Semitau in 1913 and 1916; Sumbawa and the sultanate of Boni in the Southern Celebes; and part of New Guinea (Wesseling 2004: 213–14).

The advances of European powers in the region ultimately required, after a period of expansion of influence, agreements on the delimitations of borders. The border line between Dutch West Borneo and British North Borneo was determined by treaty in 1891. Dutch interest in New Guinea accelerated in the nineteenth century, largely on account of fear of advances by Germany and Britain. The Dutch laid notional claim to the western half of the island in 1814. An attempt by the Australian colony of Queensland (concerned with other Australian colonies about German activity and about geostrategic power balances in the South Pacific) to annexe New Guinea in April 1883 was repudiated by the British government. In 1884 Germany claimed the north-east of New Guinea, and Britain the south-east, with a consequent need for the demarcation of boundaries between the territories claimed by these three European powers. A border was agreed between Britain and the Netherlands, after negotiations from 1893 to 1895, to be fixed as a line of longitude north from slightly to the east of 141° East, the point where the Bensbach River reached the south coast. The German part of the border was never formally agreed, at least until the German colony had been taken over by Australia at the end of the First World War (Cribb 2000: 121).

There were also boundary problems for the Timor Island region. Portugal had settlements on Timor and the island of Flores, and treaties with indigenous states on these islands and with local rulers on Solor and Adonari. Dutch interests dated back to the seventeenth century, mainly in the south-western part of Timor, but boundaries were not agreed with Portugal until 1859, when, after an exchange of territory to facilitate consolidation, Portugal retained East Timor together with Atauro and two enclaves in what was Dutch West Timor. By *c.* 1914 most of the Indonesian archipelago was in Dutch hands, and an age of capital-intensive economic development, conspicuously in agriculture and mining, began.

The West Indies/Greater and Lesser Antilles

From the late fifteenth century onwards there had been a European colonial presence, conspicuously of England, France, Spain, and the Netherlands, on some of the islands of the Caribbean Sea and later to the south in the lands that were to become the Guyanas in northern South America. Colonial impact was through the slave trade, the establishment of plantations for producing crops such as sugar and coffee, and in the case of France the establishment of penal colonies. Global humanitarian processes, politics and economic dynamics strongly influenced the European colonies in the Caribbean in the eighteenth and nineteenth centuries: notably, the abolition of slavery (by England in 1834, France in 1794 and again, after its reintroduction, in 1848, and by the Netherlands in 1863); the replacement of slaves by indentured labour from India, Africa and China; the market effects of sugar beet growing, particularly in France; and the advancement of the British Caribbean colonial economy from the beginning of the nineteenth century, in contrast to the more sluggish colonial Caribbean colonies of France and the Netherlands (Wesseling 2004: 79–80).

There were, however, depressions in the economies of the British West Indies, for example after the Napoleonic Wars. The late eighteenth and the nineteenth centuries were times of great turbulence in the European colonies in the West Indies, substantially conditioned by the fight by slaves, creoles and white humanitarians to end slavery, the opposition of the plantation owners to this process, and the search for an adequate formulation of new more equitable and democratic systems of landholding and political representation (Heuman 1999: 470–93; Hall 2002; Lambert 2005).

By the early nineteenth century the British West Indies comprised the older colonial islands of Barbados, Jamaica and the Leeward Islands, together with Dominica, St Vincent, Grenada and Tobago, which became part of the British empire in the mid-eighteenth century, and St Lucia, Trinidad and British Guiana, added in the early nineteenth century (Heuman 1999: 470). The French possessions in the West Indies (the French Antilles) had included Martinique, Guadaloupe, part of Saint-Christophe (St Kitts) up to 1713, Saint-Croix to 1733 (when it was sold to the Danish West India Company, and thereafter to the United States in 1917), Desirade, Marie Galante, Grenada and some smaller islands, together with the western part of Saint-Domingue (now Haiti and the Dominican Republic) and French Guyana in northern South America – a penal colony. The Netherlands also had colonies in the Caribbean, including Dutch Guyana (now Surinam) in the north-east of South America, together with the Netherlands Antilles (Curaçao, Aruba and Bonaire, just off the coast of South America), and the Leeward Islands of St Martin, St Eustatius, and Saba. The Spanish West Indies colonies included Cuba and Puerto Rico, Hispaniola having been declared independent in 1844, but with a complex history thereafter.

The Spanish colonies were lost at the end of the Spanish American war of 1898, with Cuba controlled by the United States from 1898 to 1902, then becoming independent. Puerto Rico was also transferred to the United States. In addition to geopolitical conflict between European powers in the region, there was also a long continuing indigenous and slave opposition to European rule and treatment of the labour force, evidenced in Puerto Rico and Cuba, as well as the slave revolt led by Toussaint l'Ouverture on French Saint-Domingue in 1798, the slave revolts of 1823 on Demarara, another on Jamaica in 1831, anti-census riots on Dominica in 1844, a labour strike in St Vincent in 1862, the Morant Bay rebellion on Jamaica by freed slaves in 1865, and riots in Barbados and Tobago in 1876.

German imperialism

Germany was, with Italy, the last of the European powers to acquire an overseas empire at the time of high imperialism, and lost it at the end of the First World War. The trajectory of German imperialism followed the pattern of countries like Britain, France and the Netherlands, in so far as the initial moves relied on merchant companies and individual explorers and entrepreneurs to evaluate resources and commercial trade possibilities in Africa and South-East Asia, and the formal role of an imperial agent was only adopted through protectorates and annexation quite late.

German colonial activity began after unification in 1871, notably during and after the Berlin West Africa Conference of 1884–5. Promoted by the explorer/imperialist Karl Peters and Otto von Bismarck, the diplomat, politician and first Chancellor of the new German empire from 1871 to 1890, Germany rapidly developed an imperial policy for the purpose of obtaining raw materials and markets, and establishing protective naval stations for promoting trade and commerce, and for strengthening Germany's strategic position in Europe against France and Russia. The ideological basis for German colonialism was outlined in publications by Friedrich Fabri in 1879 (*Bedarf Deutschland der Colonien?*) and William Hübbe-Schleiden in 1881 (*Deutsche Kolonisation*). Colonialism was strongly promoted by the Colonial Society – Kolonialverein – founded in 1882, and the Society for German Colonisation – Gesellschaft für Deutsche Kolonisation – founded in 1884. They merged in 1887 under the title of German Colonial Society (Deutsche Kolonialgesellschaft), and actively supported the new policies developed by Bismarck.

This colonial movement was also reflected in the work of German geographical societies, including those established for promoting commercial geography in the Hanseatic trading towns. Bismarck's motives included the diversion of France away from the issue of Alsace-Lorraine towards colonial possibilities in Africa and Asia; and, through a form of 'social imperialism', 'conserving the status quo at home, especially by pre-empting radical political change, and of protecting the nation-state externally, associating its security and overseas economic expansion, the acquisition of colonies, and naval power … Overseas expansion, involving colonial empire, sea power and access to new markets abroad, would generate greater domestic prosperity and make for social stability' (Porter 1994: 32–3). Such explanations are favoured in Hans-Ulrich Wehler's book *The German Empire 1871–1918*, first published in 1973. Opposing views place greater emphasis on the various pragmatic and opportunist aspects of Bismarck's colonialism, which reflected his refusal to see any purpose in a longer-term strategy for formal empire, and which precipitated his downfall in 1890.

After 1897 Germany's colonial policy, while clearly influenced by the colonial activities of other European states, notably France and Britain, still retained an ad hoc flavour (Wesseling 2004: 136). This is also reflected in the limited impact that German colonialism had on German settlement emigration, other than to North America, and on the German economy. Fieldhouse suggests that Germany was exceptional among the European colonial powers, in that its empire had a very short life, and that its experience is evidence of how 'a rich and efficient industrial power, though without any colonial experience, could master the complex problems of tropical colonization within a generation' (Fieldhouse 1982: 364). He also argues that Germany did not lose her colonies on account of particularly adverse treatment of indigenous peoples, and that colonies were not crucial to Germany's economic well-being.

Most of Germany's acquisition of colonial territory occurred in Bismarck's time as Chancellor. In the period from 1890 to 1906 there was less interest in colonies, though they were still acquired as part of a strategy, under Wilhelm II, of German *Weltpolitik*, and also characterised by brutal military action against the Herero people of South-West Africa in 1904–7 and the Maji-Maji rising in southern Tanganyika in 1905–6. Fieldhouse states that:

Germany lacked experienced colonial administrators and soldiers. Her agents tended to excess through fear. German resources in Africa were severely strained by these simultaneous risings, and reprisals were intended to prevent a recurrence. The Germans had no monopoly of 'frightfulness' in tackling such crises: the French in Algeria and the Western Sudan, the Belgians in the Congo and the British in the Egyptian Sudan used similar methods. (Fieldhouse 1966: 367)

Maybe so, but their methods, like others, are quite indefensible when seen from a humanitarian perspective.

Germany's colonial history began with the claiming of protectorate status for Lüderitzland in April 1884, in the core of what would shortly become German South-West Africa. In 1884 the Berlin West Africa conference was convened in Berlin, and in the same year Germany made German East Africa, Cameroon and Togoland protectorates, and annexed north-east New Guinea and what was named the Bismarck archipelago (including the Admiralty Islands). In 1886 Germany annexed the Marshall Islands, and in 1889 divided Samoa with Britain and the United States, and established naval bases in the Marianas, the Marshall Islands and Palau. In 1890 Germany agreed the Heligoland–Zanzibar Treaty with Britain. Kiaochow, on the south coast of the Shantung Peninsula in China, was attacked by German naval and military forces in November 1897, and part of the territory was leased to Germany in March 1898. Germany's short-lived overseas empire was therefore confined to Africa, South-East Asia and the Pacific.

Most of Germany's formal empire in Africa (Togo, Cameroon, South-West Africa and East Africa) was acquired within a space of a year (February 1884 to February 1885), during or immediately after the Berlin West Africa Conference. This lasted from 15 November 1884 to 26 February 1885, and was the outcome of discussions between Germany and France, against a background of contesting rights and claims between Britain, France, Germany, Belgium and Portugal, about the formal status of the International African Association promoted by King Leopold II of Belgium in 1876. The states represented at the Berlin Conference were Germany, France, the Habsburg empire, Belgium, Spain, Denmark, the United States, Italy, the Netherlands, Portugal, Russia and the Ottoman empire.

The issues raised included the question of free trade in the Congo basin, rights of navigation on the rivers Congo and Niger, and the procedures to be followed for determining new territory appropriated by European states along the African coast (Wesseling 1996: 114–15). Britain's strong position in relation to the Niger was quickly recognised, and the Congo became the focus of attention. The conclusion here was the approval of two areas of free trade, one being the Congo and its tributaries – an area from the west coast of Africa to the great lakes – and the other an eastern maritime zone, from the great lakes to the Indian Ocean.

Humanitarian issues were also discussed, but another critical matter was the discussion of procedures and formalities for new claims to territory inland from the coasts of Africa. This was resolved only in general terms, involving an agreement to notify other signatories to the final Act of the conference that they were taking over new territory, but as there was very little new territory left to appropriate, the resolution carried very little practical meaning (Wesseling 1996: 118).

Conflict in German South-West Africa in the early twentieth century

The Herero people of central German South-West Africa rose against the German military occupiers in January 1904, in protest against the appropriation of their land, the deaths of many cattle through epidemics, and hostile treatment by German settlers and administrators. In October 1904 the Nama people of the south of the country also began a revolt against the German colonial occupiers. Because of the threat that these uprisings posed to German authority and her international standing, the outcome was a campaign that was 'the largest and in every respect the costliest undertaken by Imperial Germany before World War I ... contemporary estimates numbered the Herero at between sixty and a hundred thousand people. Between six and eight thousand warriors targeted adult German male settlers, sparing German women and children, German missionaries, and non-German Europeans. The Herero killed about 125 men' (Hull 2005: 39). The outcome of these multi-phase campaigns was a high financial cost and great loss of life on both sides. An estimated 1,500 German volunteer troops died.

For the Africans, the war was catastrophic. It is estimated that 75 to 80 per cent of the Herero died, and 50 per cent of the Nama (whose population was around 20,000) in 1904. SWA was the first genocide of the twentieth century. Survivors were stripped of their rights, condemned to forced labour, and subjected to an openly racist regime until 1915, when the colony fell to Allied troops from South Africa during the First World War. (Hull 2005: 39–40)

Hull has suggested that the campaign by the German armies against the Herero and Nama was not a deliberately intended act of genocide, but the product of a particularly German type of military campaign, requiring swift and total victory and the neglect of prisoners of war and civilians. She contends also that an important symbolic feature of these military actions, common to many European countries but seen in extreme form in Germany, was that the army 'represented state authority', and 'Kaiser Wilhelm had elevated it to the chief bulwark of the monarchy. In the context of *Weltpolitik*, the revolt in SWA assumed national security dimensions that only reinforced the symbolic importance of military success

and the use of the military to punish offenders against state authority'
(Hull 2005: 44).

Restitution claims have been made by the Herero, notably in the centenary year 2004, leading to renewed categorisation of these awful events as
a genocidal forerunner of the Holocaust of the Second World War. Krüger
has questioned, however, whether the term genocide can be applied to
these massacres, and argues that it cannot in the strict sense of a deliberate national policy to eliminate African groups and cultures (Krüger
2005: 45–9).

Zimmerer, in contrast, claims that the racist ideology of Lothar von
Trotha, the German military commander, marked the campaign out
from other European military colonial activities, and that it was deliberate genocide. Thus, 'as a consequence of this ideology of a race war, the
German army shot men, women, and children, prisoners of war, and non-
combatants; it forced thousands to die of thirst in the Sandveld of the
Omaheke or in Southern Namibia during the anti-guerrilla war against the
Nama; and it killed hundreds through deliberate neglect in the concentration camps'. On this basis, he argues that this was genocide, that there is a
link forward and 'close proximity' to the later 'colonial' war of conquest in
Eastern Europe against Poland and the Soviet Union, and that there is not
just one 'road from Windhoek to Auschwitz' (Zimmerer 2005: 53–6).

Portugal's empire and colonies

The roots of Portuguese imperialism date to the early fifteenth century,
with a military expedition in 1415 to Ceuta on the north coast of Morocco
near the Straits of Gibraltar. Voyages of discovery, partly intended to find
routes to the spice wealth of the Far East and to investigate the economic
potential of Africa, were initiated in the fifteenth and sixteenth centuries.
The Cape of Good Hope was rounded in 1487 by Vasco da Gama, who then
sailed via the Mozambique Channel to East Africa and thence to Calicut
in south-west India, where valuable spices such as pepper, produced in
Kerala, and other spices traded from Indonesia, were to be found. The territorial and commercial ambitions of Prince Henry of Portugal promoted
voyages to the coasts of Africa and ultimately to the Far East, where, in
the early sixteenth century, the Portuguese founded trading settlements
in Malacca in 1511 and Macao in 1557.

Portuguese commerce and proselytising were thus extended to India,
South America, Brazil and Africa. The Treaty de Tordesillas of 1494 had

allocated lands in South America to the west of the treaty line to Spain and those to the east, including Brazil, to Portugal. During the sixteenth century, Portuguese interests had spread to Upper Guinea via the Cape Verde Islands off the west coast of Africa, and likewise in the Gulf of Guinea via the islands of Principe and São Tomé. There was gradual involvement in West Central Africa (Portuguese West Africa, ultimately Angola) via initial settlements in Luanda and Benguela. Angola was a major centre of Portuguese activity in Africa, and also supplied slaves for the Portuguese colony in Brazil (Olson 1991c: 502–3). On the east side of Africa Portuguese settlements were established along the coast of modern-day Mozambique with additional estates along the Zambezi valley, an area that eventually became Portuguese Africa. Elsewhere, posts were established at Goa and Gujerat in India, and Nagasaki in Japan.

The Portuguese empire started to decline from the seventeenth century. By the nineteenth century the main Portuguese imperial focus was on Portuguese East and West Africa. There was some 'success' in the export of materials and slaves, but the slave trade ended in 1888 because of anti–slavery movements elsewhere in Europe, including Britain. Brazil became independent in 1825, and activity elsewhere was constrained by the strategies and strength of European rivals, including Britain, France and the Netherlands. Gōa was lost in 1961 (seized by India) and the major remaining territories, Angola and Mozambique, became independent in 1975.

Fieldhouse has claimed that the Portuguese imperial experience

> abounded in paradoxes which made it difficult to compare with contemporaries. It was the oldest overseas empire; yet geographically the greater part of it was acquired only after 1884. For centuries it seemed likely to succumb to external attack or to Portuguese lethargy; yet it survived all others in the age of decolonization. Portugal was poor and militarily weak, never able to hold the larger colonies against their will; yet after the secession of Brazil in 1822 she lost nothing until India seized Goa and her other possessions in India in 1961. (Fieldhouse 1966: 349)

Fieldhouse suggests that Portugal's modern experience of imperialism dated from the 1880s, with the division of Africa between European imperial powers giving Portugal an opportunity for rebuilding the empire that she had largely lost.

The Portuguese presence in Angola and Mozambique was initially restricted to two coastal cities in Angola, Luanda and Benguela, to which were later added Moçâmedes and their respective hinterlands together with Lourenço Marques on the east coast, but with gradual expansion into the interior. The boundaries of Angola and Mozambique were fixed by a series of treaties with King Leopold of Belgium, and Britain and Germany, between 1886 and 1891. British activity in Bechuanaland from 1885, and the granting in 1899 of the charter to Rhodes' South Africa Company territory, eliminated the Portuguese idea of a trans-African territory.

The strategic importance of Delagoa Bay to the British enhanced the importance of the port of Lourenço Marques. Other European machinations to capture Portuguese coastal forts and ports, and the aims of the British to dominate Central Africa including the Shire and Mashonaland regions, led to a treaty by which Britain and others recognised the Portuguese African territories, notably Portuguese Guinea, Angola and Mozambique (Fieldhouse 1982: 350–1).

A cartographic representation of Portuguese ambition in Africa was the 'rose-coloured map' (*mapo côr de rosa*) drawn in 1886, in the aftermath of the Berlin Conference. This portrayed a Portuguese imperial territory, a 'Brazil in Africa', stretching from the west to the east coast of Central Africa. Ribeiro shows that:

> the Rose-Coloured Map was a Portuguese idea that conformed to the Europeanist impulses of the time. It failed because it disregarded the reality of the metropolis – a decadence and dependency in a peripheral Portugal … Drawn through a symbolic imperial perspective and with scant regard for its own political and economic implications, the Rose-Coloured Map was yet another vision of the empire as an imagination of the centre. (Ribeiro 2002: 150–1)

It was an illusionary metropolitan compensation for 'failed home-made dreams' of prosperity and development in Portugal at the end of the nineteenth century.

Wesseling has stated that the Anglo-Portuguese Treaty of 11 June 1891

> was a turning point in the history of Portuguese Africa. Great territorial dreams had been dashed for ever; Portugal was simply too poor and too weak to continue entertaining them. Even so, what Portugal did receive was sizable enough. After all, the treaty gave Angola and Mozambique rights to the greater part of the hinterland. In the end, Mozambique was almost one and a half times, and Angola almost two and a half times, the size of France. (Wesseling 1996: 299)

Portuguese imperial attitudes changed markedly in the twentieth century under the Estada Novo, which came into power after the military coup of 1926 initiated the Fascist regime of Salazar. Ribeiro has suggested that there were two prime aspects to the new philosophy, one of which produced an imaginary of a great Portuguese empire from Minho to Timor with an important metropolis at the centre. This was an image of Portugal reflected in school textbooks, where the misleading image presented was of Portugal as a major world power. While Portugal was seen as marginal by other European powers, the country reproduced the fiction that a Portuguese identity, consciously distanced from Europe, could be established and maintained through the medium of its history, especially the so-called golden age of exploration of Prince Henry the Navigator. This image, it believed, could also be reflected in and through its empire. The 'Salazar regime constructed itself as the legitimate heir to the civilizing mission of Portugal in the world'. A major Portuguese World Exhibition was opened at the beginning of the Second World War, in which 'The language used to define Portugal was grandiose. It did not correspond to reality but rather an image that was created of a mythical country put on display at the exhibition. There, the centre of the world and centre of the Portuguese world became one' (Ribeiro 2002: 159, 161).

Notwithstanding the long history of Portuguese exploration and settlement overseas, in Latin America, India, the Far East and Africa, by the end of the nineteenth century, in consequence of the formal treaty of independence of Brazil in 1825, and especially in the period from *c*. 1870 to 1885, there was much uncertainty of feeling about Portugal's continuing and prospective role as a colonial power. Historical geographies of all aspects of Portuguese imperialism and colonialism in the nineteenth and early twentieth centuries have to take note of this. Ribeiro (2002: 149) has stated, for example, that:

The theoretical complexity of the Portuguese presence in Africa cannot be reduced to a single explanation. The ghost of the break with Brazil haunted Portugal's relationship with its African colonies. It was a spectre that ran through the whole century, and came to be reflected both in the conception of the African empire, from a practical and symbolic point of view, and in the Portuguese presence in Europe.

The reasons for Portuguese imperialism have been debated. On the one hand there is a view which contends that there was no obvious economic motive, for the Portuguese made no profit from their colonies and did not succeed, except perhaps in a small way in Brazil, in establishing settlement colonies. An alternative perspective is that Portugal had economic interests to the fore in its colonial activities. Because of low agricultural productivity at home, colonies were developed to create protected markets and generate foreign currency, notably through the neo-mercantilism of the 1880s that developed from economic crisis in 1873, with the creation of a protective tariff in 1892, which promoted and increased trade with Africa (Wesseling 2004: 137–8). In the first three-quarters of the nineteenth century Portugal's colonies were regarded as sources of finance through trade and customs revenue, which could help fund development in the metropolis. In the last quarter of the century, however, the need to open up overseas markets for overproducing Portuguese industries, including the northern textile industry, changed colonial policy.

In the late nineteenth century, the Portuguese colonial economic policy was essentially one of finding outlets for the surplus goods of metropolitan industries, notably textiles, with little inclination or capital for investment other than to São Tomé and southern Mozambique, but 'after the republican revolution of 1910, the state took more positive measures throughout the empire to encourage a plantation sector based on migrant labour and to regulate the petty commodity production of African peasants' (Clarence- Smith 1979: 13).

The context of the world economic depression 'led to cut-throat competition for markets and increasing protectionism, including the famous "scramble for Africa"'. Portugal therefore vigorously pressed its claims to territory in the African continent and adopted extremely protectionist tariffs in 1892' (Clarence-Smith 1979: 13). Settlement and missionary work were two additional factors in this positive characterisation of Portuguese colonialism (Wesseling 2004: 137–8).

The Portuguese, like the French, had a policy of integration, with the empire controlled from Lisbon, but with various degrees of local autonomy given to colonial administrators for practical reasons, together with some incorporation of indigenous people into the lower end of the hierarchy. Initially, like other European powers, Portugal had given responsibility for capital investment, development and settlement to chartered companies such as the Mozambique, Niassa and Zambezia companies (Fieldhouse 1982: 351–2).

One of the features of Portuguese colonial practice that mirrored the operations of most other European powers, for example, was the exploitation of the indigenous labour force. A forced labour system existed in the Portuguese colonies, typified by very poor conditions, strict sanctions for non-compliance, low pay and a pace of reform significantly slower than in other European colonies. This was a feature, according to Fieldhouse (1982: 353–6), of the late survival of slave-trading and slavery in Portuguese colonies into the nineteenth century, which also slowed serious reform until 1926, though Portugal evaded the International Forced Labour Conventions of 1930 and 1946 and the Indigenous Worker Convention of 1936, which reflected both the lack of humanitarian activity and the archaic labour laws still in force at home. Portugal managed to obtain support for her currency by the profits in foreign exchange made from the export of tropical products and minerals from Angola and Mozambique, and the colonies also provided space for emigrant settlement.

The Spanish empire and colonies

Spain had a long history as a colonial power, dating back to the late sixteenth and early seventeenth centuries in the Greater Antilles, including Cuba, Puerto Rico and Hispaniola, expanding shortly afterwards into Central America, south-west North America and South America. Control of many of these colonies was lost during the early nineteenth century, partly because of Spain's isolation during the Napoleonic Wars and partly because of the rise of nationalist movements. At the end of these wars, and through the efforts of revolutionary movements from 1810 to 1830, Spain had by the end of the century lost all but her colonies in Puerto Rico, Cuba, and colonies in Africa and the Pacific. The Spanish-American War and the Cuban revolution combined, through the Treaty of Paris, to remove Cuba, Puerto Rico and Guam from Spain, with the Philippines being acquired by the United States in 1898, and the Marianas and Marshall Islands sold to Germany in 1899. There remained only the African colonies: Spanish Equatorial Guinea, Spanish Sahara, Spanish Equatorial Guinea and parts of Morocco – Spanish Morocco, plus Ceuta (a tiny outpost on the north coast of Morocco opposite Gibraltar), Melilla (a Spanish port on the Moroccan coast), and Ifni (a Spanish province of Morocco on the Atlantic coast). All of these colonies, with the exception of Ceuta and Melilla, were lost, mainly to Morocco, in the period from 1950 to 1976 (Olson 1991d: 581–2).

As with all other European colonial powers, there have been differing interpretations of Spain's motives for continuing to retain an empire in the late nineteenth and early twentieth centuries. According to Clarence-Smith,

Much of what has been written assumes that Spain had no economic motivation for colonial expansion and was simply clinging nostalgically to the tatters of former imperial glory. Madrid did at times withdraw into a kind of splendid isolation, but it is quite wrong to portray Spain as always clinging passively to the remnants of her former empire. At times, the Spaniards participated actively, even aggressively, in the general process of European expansion. (Clarence-Smith 1991: 71)

Clarence-Smith has outlined seven phases of Spanish colonial expansion in the nineteenth and twentieth centuries: the survival of empire

(1824 to *c*. 1850); imperial expansion (*c*. 1850–82); the scramble for colonies and neo-mercantilism (1882–98); the creation of an African empire (1898 to *c*. 1918); a period of fiscal deficits and foreign exchange extraction (*c*. 1918–36); the empire and the war economy (1936 to *c*. 1950); and the period of decolonisation and investment (*c*. 1950–76).

From 1824 to *c*. 1850 Spain focused on the retention of 'small but valuable possessions' (after her defeat by the forces of Simon Bolivar at Ayacucho in Peru in 1824, a key moment in the progress towards Peruvian and Spanish Latin American independence), such as Cuba, Puerto Rico and the Philippines. Considerable economic advantage accrued to Spain from the wealth of Cuba, notably in tobacco and sugar production, from Puerto Rico through sugar and coffee, and from the Philippines through sugar, tobacco and hemp. Earlier in the nineteenth century much of her colonial economy in the Antilles was supported by slave labour. Spain's significant participation in the slave trade, facilitated by the banning of the trade by Britain in 1807–8, bestowed economic benefits on such regions as Andalusia and Catalonia (Clarence-Smith 1991: 72–3). British opposition to the slave trade constrained Spanish ambitions to gain further territorial control in Africa beyond the small *presidios* at Ceuta and Melilla in North Africa.

From *c*. 1850 to 1882 greater domestic political and economic stability facilitated the development of a more energetic, expansive and planned Spanish colonial strategy, partly focused on attempts to win back influence over Spain's former South and Central American empire, further consolidate her territory in the Philippines, and secure territory in Morocco. The island of Fernando Po was occupied in 1858, as part of Spanish Equatorial Guinea, which had been ceded by Portugal to Spain in 1778. The benefits to Spain of the acquisition of these small areas were not great, but the wealth of richer colonies such as Cuba was used to fund colonial expansion, so that, for example, the budget deficit of the developing colony of Spanish Equatorial Guinea was paid by Cuba, the Philippines and Puerto Rico. Restrictive tariffs were introduced to facilitate the export of Spanish goods that were uncompetitively priced in European markets, though such restrictions were very difficult to introduce in the Philippines. There was major emigration from Spain to her colonies, notably Cuba, in this period, conspicuously from the Asturias, Galicia and the Canary Islands (Clarence-Smith 1991: 75).

From 1882 to 1898 'imperialist sentiment briefly caught alight in Spain in the form of the Africanista movement. The Africanistas were best known for their advocacy of expansion into North Africa. They also laid claim to huge areas of Western Africa' (Clarence-Smith 1991: 77), and had aspirations for a coaling station in East Africa, and rights of recognition in North Borneo and in the Pacific for control of the Micronesian archipelagos. But these ambitions were largely unrealised. Spain was the only European power during this period of heightened imperial ambition to emerge with a smaller empire than the one she had begun with. The major blow to Spain at this time was the loss of Cuba, Puerto Rico, the Philippines and Guam as a result of defeat in the Spanish-American War (initiated by the rebellion in Cuba and the perceived loss of American investment interests) of 1898. At the Paris peace conference in 1898, Spain agreed to Cuba becoming independent, for Guam and Puerto Rico to be annexed by the United States, and for the Philippines to be purchased by the United States. A consequent effect was the inability of Spain to sustain a presence in the Pacific, and she sold her possessions in the Marianas and Marshall Islands to Germany in 1899.

This was also a period of intensification of one-way protectionism (of the export of Spanish goods to colonies, but with high tariffs on exported colonial goods to Spain), which was one of the causes of the Spanish-American War. The attempts by Spain to create an African empire after 1898 'were frustrated by a combination of disillusionment at home and French diplomatic manoeuvres. This period constituted a low point in the awareness of and interest in the colonies, after the hectic years of Africanista propaganda, and there was little public support for further colonial expansion' (Clarence-Smith 1991: 79–82). From great ambitions for a more substantial presence in Morocco, Spain only obtained by treaty (in 1912) small areas in the north and south of that country, and the small enclaves of Villa Cisneros, Tarfaya, and La Guere on the Bay of Levrier in the western Sahara. In spite of the small size of these acquisitions, some economic benefit accrued to Spain from the iron mines in Rif, the fishing banks off the Saharan coast, and the cocoa plantations of Fernando Po. Spain's colonies in Africa were managed by systems very similar to those of her former empire, and these were thought to have been partly responsible for her defeat in 1898. A contrast was the prevalence of free trade for the colonies in North-West Africa, through international agreements to preserve free trade in Morocco. Elsewhere, notably in Spanish Equatorial Guinea, import duties were maintained, for example on cocoa exports to Spain.

The period from *c*. 1918 to 1936 was characterised by financial difficulties with the colonies, notably through fiscal deficits and problems with foreign exchange extraction. Spanish conflict with the tribes in the Rif Mountains of northern Morocco started in 1909, and accelerated until there was a major defeat for the Spanish army in the region in 1921, leading to the intensi-fication of the anti-Spanish rebellion, and a further escalation in military activity and costs, exacerbated by the world depression in the 1930s. A con-sequence for Spain was the decline in income from exports and emigrants' remittances, and the promotion of lower import duties on imported colo-nial products, though the adjustment processes to facilitate an increase in foreign exchange were complex (Clarence-Smith 1991: 81–2).

Major factors conditioning Spanish colonial policy and experience in the period 1936 to *c.* 1950 included the Civil War of 1936–9, the success of nationalist uprisings in the Canaries, North Africa, northern Morocco, southern Morocco and the western Sahara; the consideration by the Franco regime of the imperial advantages that might accrue through join-ing the Second World War on the side of the Axis powers; and the advan-tages of colonial possessions in the provision of foreign exchange and food to Spain during the Civil War. From 1950 to 1976,

Spain opened herself up to the capitalist world order, and her economy began to grow fast. Trade with Western nations blossomed, and abundant foreign exchange was provided through tourism and the remittances of workers in Western Europe…Imperial economic policy thus shifted towards a 'develop-mental' perspective, with a view to justifying Spain's colonial record before the United Nations and containing the growing demands for independence from the peoples of the colonies. (Clarence-Smith 1991: 83–4)

Decolonisation, initiated by Franco, was completed between 1956 and 1976, leaving only Ceuta and Melilla.

Belgium and the Congo

Belgium, like Germany, had no colonial ambitions at the start of the era of high imperialism, but the ambitions of one man – King Leopold II – led to the appropriation of the territory – as a private fiefdom – of what was the Congo Free State, to which at a later date were added Ruanda and Urundi which had formerly been German colonial territory.

Ewans divides Belgian colonial and postcolonial history into three periods:

The first, the Leopoldian era, was marked by unremitting exploitation and grave human rights abuses. In the second [from 1908], the Belgian era, human rights abuses continued, if on a less extreme scale, but the interests of the inhabitants were overwhelmingly neglected in favour of economic exploitation. In the third, the Mobutu era [from 1965], locally generated human rights abuses and exploitation were condoned by the former colonial power in its own economic interests. (Ewans 2003: 174)

As Fieldhouse states, 'Leopold II acquired the Congo not as a Belgian colony but as a private estate, and supported the assumption that the modern tropical colonization was motivated by economic greed by treating it as a mere business investment' (Fieldhouse 1982: 357). It was only after the Congo was taken over from Leopold by the Belgian state in 1908 – and renamed the Belgian Congo – that humanitarian issues were given greater priority. Leopold's motives were a combination of capitalist aspiration for wealth and a concern that Belgium should not be left out of the imperial geostrategies that were being adopted by other European powers, notably the Dutch. The indicators of the Belgian presence in the Congo Free State included promotion of the slave trade and the appropriation of land and resources, including human labour.

The exploitation of the considerable resources of the Congo through the granting of land in the south-east to private companies, and the holding of the rest of the Free State as state property with state (i.e. Leopold's) rights of exploitation, were the outcome of this intervention. Leopold's target of extracting profit from the Congo was achieved by investment in infrastructure for mining, and by extracting resources, notably natural rubber, palm oil and ivory, which could be obtained at low cost, specifically by forced labour working to product quotas. The profits were enhanced by the creation, contrary to the Berlin Treaty, of a monopoly for trade in two of the three sectors into which the Congo had been divided by Leopold – the *Domaine Privée* and the *Domaine de la Couronne* – in which only the state and its grantees could operate. Resources and profits from these two sectors were extracted either by Leopold's agents or by companies to which he had given concessions, notably the Katanga Company (Fieldhouse 1982: 358). The products gathered, particularly natural rubber, were obtained by the most heinous and inhumane methods, including severe penalties such as death and maiming for failure by local people to reach the quotas of production set by companies working on Leopold's behalf, notwithstanding the fact that the Congo Free State was based, at least in theory, on humanitarian principles.

The inhumane treatment of the forced labourers in the Congo received much attention in Europe and the United States. In Britain, the combination of a 1904 report by Roger Casement – a civil servant – and the protests and activities of the Congo Reform Association (set up by E. D. Morel) put pressure on Leopold to resolve the matter. Similar protests were made from Germany and the United States, including the pamphlet by Samuel Clemens (Mark Twain) *King Leopold's Soliloquy*, an imaginary monologue by Leopold, published in 1905. After an international commission assembled by Leopold reported in 1905, and confirmed the findings of Casement and others, the Belgian government insisted on taking over the governance of the Congo Free State, which it did in November 1908.

The atrocities in the Congo have been well documented, but for a long time the main critical voices came from outside Belgium, both in the late nineteenth and early twentieth centuries, and in the postcolonial era of the late twentieth and early twenty-first centuries. In his introduction to the second edition of his book *The King Incorporated. Leopold the Second and the Congo*, published in 1999, Neil Ascherson states that in the introduction to the first edition of the book, published in 1963, he had

remarked that the Belgians had avoided any real assessment of the Congolese past, and that Leopold II was still honoured as a national hero for his *mission civilisatrice*. It never occurred to me that this would remain the case more than thirty years later. But it is possible to visit the Africa museum at Tervuren without gathering a hint that the Congo was the site of one of the most atrocious and criminal regimes in history. (Ascherson 1999: 10)

The museum at Tervuren near Brussels was founded in 1910, and the neglect of the negative side of Belgian colonial experience was rectified by the creation of a major exhibition – 'La mémoire du Congo. Le temps colonial' – at the Musée Royale de l'Afrique Central at Tervuren from February to October 2005. The accompanying publication, with the same title, acknowledged the general silence (with a few dissenting voices such as those of a small number of missionaries) of the past in respect of the Congo atrocities under Leopold II (Vellut 2005a). Anthony Browne, writing in *The Times* about the exhibition under the heading 'Dark heart of Congo's former rulers returns to haunt them' (12 March 2005: 43), stated that:

For generations, Belgian children were taught to be proud of what their country gave the Congo – education, health-care, and civilisation. But 45 years after the Central African country regained its independence the Belgians are finally, and painfully, confronting a very different version of their colonial past: forced labour, mass murder and the routine severing of hands in what was probably the most bloody of all colonial regimes.

The enforcement of Congolese people in the collection of rubber was effected by keeping women and children hostage until sufficient rubber had been collected by the men of the community, any seeming shortfall being punished by the amputation of limbs or the killing of the men, women and children, sometimes directly, sometimes by starvation in the compounds in which they were confined.

Much of the 'discipline' was exercised by European officers and the Congolese in the Force Publique, 'a mercenary army which by 1905 contained 360 European officers of different nationalities and 16,000 Africans' (Fieldhouse 1966: 358). Poverty, starvation, mutilation, murder and disease are estimated to have reduced the population of the Congo by about half, from 20 million to about 10 million (a reduction greater than the total number of those killed in the First World War) during Leopold's twenty-three-year regime, but the figure has been disputed as too large, and estimates made that the losses were more of the order of 20–40 per cent (Vellut 2005b: 16).

The book by the American journalist Adam Hochschild, published in 1998 – *King Leopold's Ghost* (Hochschild 1998) – had helped to move the thoughts of Belgians towards different interpretations and narratives, and the book of the 2005 exhibition recognised this contribution, while at the same time pointing to some other individuals who had been trying to give voice to the awful experiences of Congo Africans (Vellut 2005b: 11–22; see also Marechal 2005: 43–50). One of the desperate ironies of these dreadful times was that the progenitor of these colonial crimes had also been the architect of the Berlin West Africa Conference, which had – at least nominally – claimed as one of its main concerns the humane treatment and advancement of the indigenous peoples of the Congo Free State.

Further evaluation needs to be made of Leopold's role in these matters: J.-L. Vellut (2005b) has suggested, for example, that this process of murder and maiming did not amount to genocide as experienced in Europe in the Second World War, as there was only a small number of Europeans in the Congo, including missionaries and engineers, at the time; that Leopold invested some of the profits from his Congo resources in research at the Liverpool School of Tropical Medicine that was to be of benefit to the Congolese; and that some of this money was also invested in the Belgian state.

After 1908, Belgian administration of the Belgian Congo, mainly through indirect rule, promoted more humanitarian processes of management, and the economic focus switched from ivory and rubber to mineral extraction. The transition took place from about 1915, when the profits made from ivory and rubber were exceeded by those from copper, diamonds, radium and uranium and from agricultural products such as palm oil, cotton and coffee, the latter produced on European plantations. By profiting from these products and not extracting money from the Congo to subsidise the metropolitan purse, Belgium, according to Fieldhouse (1966: 362–3), 'became a model colonial power after 1908. Her record appeared defective only after 1960, when it became clear that she had not prepared enough for Congolese independence', and was unprepared for the riots in Leopoldville in 1959. Belgium had also acquired the kingdoms of Ruanda and Burundi, which came under German influence and then indirect rule in the last decades of the nineteenth and the first decade of the twentieth century, but were won by Belgian-Congolese troops in 1916, becoming part of Belgian East Africa.

Italy as a colonial power

Italy, notwithstanding its historical role as the core of the Roman empire, was a late arrival on the modern imperial scene. Her late unification in 1870 delayed her participation in the global expansion of other European powers, but nonetheless there were overseas links through heavy emigration, for example, and colonial aspirations were enhanced by the appointment of Francesco Crispi as Prime Minister, whose policy, according to Wesseling (2004: 140), was that 'Italy had to have colonies, because the past demanded it and the future made it necessary'.

Italy's imperial ambitions were directed southwards to Africa and eastwards within Europe. The first steps were on the Red Sea coast, where in 1882 the Italian government established rights to the bay and port of Assab, which had been purchased in 1869 (the year of the opening of the Suez Canal) by the Rubattino shipping company, and an Italian colony established there. This was followed by Massawa, some 600 kilometres to the north on the Red Sea coast, captured in 1885, and in 1890 the territory of Eritrea was created, incorporating these two sites and part of their hinterland. The British and French had interests on the western coast of the Red Sea. The boundary between British and French Somaliland was confirmed in 1888, and the coast of Somaliland from Cape Guardafui at the Horn to Kismayo, some 1,000 km to the south, was granted in 1887 as an Italian protectorate by the sultan of Zanzibar, forming the base of what later would become Italian Somaliland, which took final shape through an Anglo-Italian agreement of 1925 (Wesseling 1996: 241). By 1900 Somalia had become divided between the British, French, Italians and Ethiopians, these European powers being largely confined to coastal territories.

In the late nineteenth century, Ethiopia, notably during the reign of the sovereign Menelik, supported by the Italians after their defeat at Dogali in 1887, was a space and economy strongly contested by European powers such as Britain, France, Italy, Switzerland, Austria and Russia. As Wesseling (1996: 243) puts it:

France let it be known that it felt a 'very sincere and disinterested friendship' and 'profound sympathy' for a proud nation that had for centuries so courageously defended its independence as well as the Christian faith … Queen Victoria had a gramophone record pressed for Menelik with a message of British goodwill. Russia stressed the religious bond between the Coptic and the Russian Orthodox churches and sent impressive gifts together with strange adventurers.

Italy's attempt to establish a protectorate over Ethiopia in a treaty of 1899 was followed by an intensification of attempts to extend her control, but these were ended by the heavy defeat of a large Italian military force by Menelik's army at the battle of Adawa in 1896. Subsequent manoeuvring between Britain, France and the Triple Alliance of Germany, Austria, and Italy, with the reconquest of the Sudan as a possibility for the British, was concluded in March 1896, when Britain invaded the Sudan, and in the tripartite treaty of 1906 Britain, France and Italy agreed to Ethiopian independence. After the First World War, Ethiopia became a member of the League of Nations (1923) and in 1930 Haile Selassie became emperor. Italian colonial interest was renewed under Mussolini, and in 1935 Italy attacked Addis Ababa, and in May 1936 annexed Ethiopia, which was combined with Eritrea and Italian Somaliland to create Italian East Africa (Pollock 1991b: 203–5).

A further addition to Italy's empire, on her 'fourth shore', was Tripolitania, the north-western part of Libya, which was taken from the Ottoman empire in 1911, being separated from the rest of Libya in 1919 as a colony, though reunited with Cyrenaica (the eastern part, whose capital was Benghazi) in 1934 to form a total Libyan colonial territory. In the 1920s and 1930s over 100,000 Italians were settled in Libya.

Russia, Japan and the United States

In the nineteenth and early twentieth centuries there were major new participants in imperial expansion in addition to those from western and southern Europe: Russia, Japan and the United States. Their histories of imperial ambition and achievement need to be outlined in order to understand the broader global position, especially where their interests abutted on to or conflicted with European imperial aims.

Russia was an emerging world power by the end of the nineteenth century, having slowly expanded from the fourteenth century from the Principality of Moscow, and in the nineteenth century adding territory to the south from the Ottoman empire and the Caucasian states. To these were added large areas of central and eastern Asia, notably the very large area of Turkestan, and acquisitions from China. Alaska had ceased to be Russian territory with its sale to the United States in 1867. Siberia became a Russian settlement colony.

The means used to annexe these additional territories were harsh and uncompromising. In the mid-nineteenth century, there had been much concern by Britain at Russia's advancement into Central Asia, notably the areas north of India, involving diplomatic and clandestine moves to avert any Russian interest in India itself – 'the Great Game'. This 'Great Game' of diplomacy and military geostrategy was played out in the period from 1837 onwards, with southward progress by the Russian armies with the annexation of Tashkent (1865), Samarkhand (1868), Bokhara (1868) and Khiva (1873), and the British, after their embarrassing defeat in their Afghan campaign in 1842, progressing northwards to take Sind (1843), Kashmir (1846), the Punjab (1849), and Baluchistan (1859). There were different responses from Britain to this perceived threat, one of which, labelled the 'Forward School', held the view that Britain needed to intervene, with a presence in Afghanistan, to thwart the Russian menace (O'Hara, Heffernan and Endfield 2005: 93).

By the beginning of the twentieth century this particular threat seemed to have lessened, but Russia's vulnerability to a different kind of counter-imperial action at the far eastern end of her imperial frontier was evidenced by defeat in the Russo-Japanese War of 1904–5. This was initiated by the Japanese attack on the Russian fleet at Port Arthur in northern China as a consequence of the Russian occupation of Manchuria and progress into North Korea, as part of an imperial ideology and search for areas of potential economic benefit. A peace treaty between the two, brokered by the United States, was signed at Portsmouth, New Hampshire in September 1905 (Christopher 1999: 51–3; Wesseling 2004: 142–6; Bassin 1999).

Japan, a country with limited areas for crop cultivation and an old feudal social structure, in which the prominent groups were territorial lords and aristocratic warriors – *samurai* – and isolated by a 'complex language with no close relatives and an intense consciousness of cultural uniqueness' (Kennedy 1989: 265), had little contact with the Western world before 1853. In that year the arrival of the American Commodore Perry with

US navy ships was followed in 1858 by access treaties with Western powers, which led internally to civil war, the outcome of which was the Meiji Restoration and a remarkable and rapid modernisation from 1868, including a new constitution, legal and banking systems, and the expansion of education and the development of a navy and an army under British and German tutelage. New infrastructure, including railways, was facilitated by industrial development (Kennedy 1989: 266).

As John Darwin states, 'The halting steps before 1868 to transform Japan along western lines had given way to a headlong rush towards European-style "modernity". In the race against time, the Japanese had become the champion sprinters' (Darwin 2007: 280), and they moved into the worlds of international trade, capitalist industrialisation and territorial imperialism, though industrial development was slowed by lack of capital, and agricultural reform by an inefficient structure. Kennedy claims that Japan's progress as both an economic and a territorial power was helped by her geographical location (away from other major imperial powers, yet close to China, Manchuria and Korea) and by her morale, so that:

the strong Japanese sense of cultural uniqueness, the traditions of emperor worship and the veneration of the state, the samurai ethos of military honour and valour, the emphasis upon discipline and fortitude, produced a political culture at once fiercely patriotic and unlikely to be deterred by sacrifices, and reinforced the Japanese impulse to expand into 'Greater East Asia', for strategical security as well as markets and raw materials. (Kennedy 1989: 267–8)

In spite of losses and costs, by the end of the Russo-Japanese War, Japan had become a significant power, partly with the financial and armaments aid of three other major powers – Britain, Germany and the United States. Japan had acquired the Kuril Islands from Russia by the Treaty of St Petersburg of 1875, together with Port Arthur, part of the Sakhalin peninsula and southern Manchuria, and had effective military occupation of Korea by the Portsmouth Treaty of 1905 (Korea was finally annexed to the Japanese empire in 1910).

The United States as an imperial power

According to Paul Kennedy, 'Of all the changes that were taking place in the global power balances during the later nineteenth and early twentieth centuries there can be no doubt that the most decisive one for the future was the growth of the United States' (Kennedy 1989: 312). With domestic political stability after the Civil War and the rapid development of vast raw material, agricultural and industrial resources, facilitated by territorial cohesion, absence of land-based threats, high capital invest-ment, fine infrastructure, including railways, and the advanced technolo-gies introduced by major companies, the United States was well ahead of any other country in the world. She was a major trader in the transat-lantic and global economy, and her military and naval assets were also substantial. Her industrial and trading positions were 'accompanied, per-haps inevitably, by a more assertive diplomacy and by an American-style rhetoric of *Weltpolitik*', linked to a sense of moral superiority, the Monroe Doctrine and its Manifest Destiny in relation to the lands of the Pacific Ocean (Kennedy 1989: 317).

The Monroe Doctrine stemmed from the confirmation by President James Monroe in his address to Congress on 2 December 1823 of the geopolitical policy of the United States in respect of non-intervention by the country in European affairs and colonies, and an assertion of non-tolerance of any attempts by European powers to expand their interests in states adjacent to the United States, including those of Latin America. This doctrine was enhanced by Theodore Roosevelt's 'Corollary' of 1905, which expressed concern at the pressure being used by European states to enforce the repayment of debts by Latin American countries, including the blockading of Venezuelan ports in 1902, and stated that the United States would vigorously oppose such perceived interference in the affairs of the Western Hemisphere. The late nineteenth and early twentieth cen-turies witnessed a strong and increased influence by the United Sates over its Latin American neighbours, notably those in the Caribbean, which became what was termed the 'American lake', a concept and practice that diminished in the 1930s, but elements of which continue to the present. Meinig (1998: 364) states that:

in the opening years of the twentieth century, the United States had transformed this Mediterranean into an American lake, its hegemony unchallenged. It did so in response to what it believed to be geopolitical necessities; it expanded upon these for economic advantages – and it generally considered its motivations to be in the best interests not only of Americans but of the peoples of this region. Yet in this realm of empire as in others there was always ample evidence of contradic-tions and resistances to such policies.

The imperial realities of the United States were evidenced by a num-ber of developments. These included the Spanish-American War of 1898 (initiated by a rebellion and the destruction of American businesses in Cuba from 1895), as a result of which the United States blockaded Cuban ports in May 1898, and besieged Santiago de Cuba. It also attacked and destroyed the Spanish fleet in the Philippines as a response to the

Philippine insurrection of February 1898, and fought in the consequent Philippine-American War of 1899–1902. The outcome of the Spanish-American War, after a Paris peace conference, was independence for Cuba, the annexation of Guam and Puerto Rico, which had been taken by the United States during the war, American possession of the whole of the Philippines (as opposed to just Luzon, presumably for commercial advantage), and control of Hawaii, which had been annexed in 1893. In effect the resolution by the United States Senate on 6 February 1899 was not only a ratification of the American–Spanish treaty of December 1898, brokered by France, but also an acceptance of the principle and practice of imperial acquisitions and an imperial role for the United States.

An imperial role for the United States was not, however, strongly supported at home. There was much fierce opposition in Congress and beyond, on grounds of the principle that the United States should not become an imperial power; the right of self-determination by the Filipino people; objection to the ruthless methods employed in suppression of the rebellion; and the possibility of Filipino immigration to the United States. The Spanish-American war is seen by Neil Smith as:

a watershed in the historical geography of U.S. expansionism. The national and state boundaries of the United States were effectively in place, even though several territories had yet to consummate statehood, and the geographical claims that resulted from the war were less about national consolidation than international colonization ... This marked the first and last serious foray by the United States into extraterritorial colonization. Thereafter, U.S. expansionism took an increasingly geo-economic rather than colonial form. The Spanish-American War therefore represents an anomaly, but it also marks the cusp of a radically different globalism. (Smith 2003: 30)

The United States came directly, as a result of the war, 'into the cross currents of international rivalries in the Far East, increased greatly the propensity for interference in the Caribbean, and forced the nation to deal with the many problems of colonial policy' (Andrade 1991: 578). Another outcome of the Spanish-American War was, on account of the long voyages by American fleets to and from the Pacific and Atlantic oceans, an increasing involvement in the affairs of what became the state of Panama, and the grant of the Panama Canal Zone 'in perpetuity' to the United States in the Hay–Bunau–Varilla Treaty of 1903.

The American position at the Versailles Peace Conference at the end of the First World War, ending in the treaty of 1919, was essentially one of limited interest in the future of European and American colonies, and then only concerned with the rights of colonised people and the fair arbitration of colonial claims. By the end of the Second World War the position was different, with President Roosevelt taking a strongly anti-colonialist line (Smith 2003: 370–1). The involvement of all the European imperial powers together with the United States and Japan in that war fundamentally changed the global geographies of imperialism and colonial settlement, and pointed the way towards a major wave of independence movements, more details of which are given in Chapter 13.

This chapter has mainly been concerned with the spatial manifestations of complex geopolitical processes that affected large numbers of people. The following chapter looks more closely at the populations of these imperial and colonial spaces.

3 | Numbers and movements of people

The British assumed that the census reflected the basic sociological facts of India. This it did, but through the enumerative modality, the project also objectified social, cultural, and linguistic differences among the peoples of India. The panoptical view that the British were constructing led to the reification of India as a polity in which conflict, from the point of view of the rulers, could only be controlled by the strong hand of the British. (Cohn 1996: 8)

Introduction

Millions of people were caught up, some deliberately but many of them unwittingly, in the dynamics of imperialism and colonial development. The interactions between imperial and colonial policies and of imperial and colonial peoples were, of course, extremely complex. They extended, as the above quotation from Bernard Cohn's book *Colonialism and its Forms of Knowledge* suggests, to such issues as the cultural and ideological underpinnings of enumeration and the classification of colonial populations, the promotion and restriction of migration, and concerns with disease and health. A full understanding of such phenomena and processes needs to go beyond 'essential' demographic 'facts' to more pluralistic interpretations of the production and circulation of different knowledge about populations (Bailey, 2005: 118–21).

The main themes of this chapter concern primarily the ideologies and methods of classification and counting of populations, migration trends and policies experienced and used by European powers, and the production and application of knowledge about diseases and famines in colonial contexts.

Enumeration and classification: colonial censuses, ideologies and practices

The counting and categorisation of populations and various aspects of national identities through censuses was an important characteristic of both metropolitan and colonial territories during the nineteenth and twentieth centuries, reflections of the process of modernisation and the production of the nation-state and its identity. A major aim was the production of knowledge, in this case about people, through the use of numbers and classifying frameworks of ethnic, cultural and regional characteristics, as means of power and discrimination (Anderson 1991: 184). The enumeration of indigenous and immigrant populations by European states in the period of high imperialism was linked with national identity, partly through willingness or reluctance to recognise ethnic groups, and the tendency when they were identified to use the data for apocalyptic predictions about dilution of national character, or worse.

Broad theoretical questions about the use of official population statistics and the measurement and regulating of populations have been raised by Foucault in *Discipline and Punish* (1977) and these ideas have been included, among others, in concepts of an extended population geography developed more recently by Legg (2005) and Philo (2005). Legg helpfully links a wide range of Foucault's concepts to his own research on India, and in a section on 'Scales of (Colonial) Biopolitics' looks at Indian experience, and that of other colonies, as 'places of particular types of biopolitics', and examples of 'power relations behind population management' (Legg 2005: 145). The biopolitical measurement and management of population included concepts of the supposed lesser ability of subject populations to review their own national demographic futures; censuses as means of control; the geographical imaginations and modes of use and outcomes of census data; the role of the state in population policy, that is the 'state technologies by which the state attempts to influence population patterns, whether of reproduction, health, productivity, or migration' (Legg 2005: 146); and comparisons of national demographic experiences. All of these will, in the future, provide bases for new insights into the 'biopolitics' of colonial populations.

The questions asked in the course of enumeration have been and remain highly contested and controversial, and have changed through time. Blum, in a study of the changing attempts at identity categorisation in France from the nineteenth century, points to the common history of debate among European states, dating from the mid-nineteenth century, about the use of ethnic categories in censuses. Contrasting the inclusive approach of the Austro-Hungarian empire with the excluding approach of the French, contested and developed in the 1870s, he argues that while the French recognised ethnic differences, 'they applied only to certain states and were not of great interest. From the French perspective, differences between regions did not need to be reflected or recorded statistically. What was important was to defend the unity of the French nation', with the two main categories of population being the citizen and the foreigner, reflecting places of birth and citizenship status (Blum 2002: 126–7).

The exceptions to this were, however, the French colonies, where ethnic distinctions were used in censuses, notably in Algeria, where Blum (2002: 129–30) has shown that although early population descriptions by the French military in the 1830s used a range of ethnic categories, such as Turks, Arabs, Mozabits, Kabyles and Algerian Jews, the increasing incorporation of Algeria into the French body politic led to more simple distinctions between Muslim and European populations. Also,

During the 1850s, the growing idea of an Algerian 'race', representing a fusion of the various European populations inhabiting the colony, began to threaten the French government, which was fearful of secessionist movements. Thus, a 1865 decree provided all Europeans who had lived in Algeria for at least three years the possibility of becoming French, while the 1889 law on nationality extended *jus solis* to any European child born in Algeria. By contrast, a person indigenous to Algeria could become French only with enormous difficulty. (Blum 2002: 129)

By the end of the nineteenth century the Algerian census contained only three cultural categories: 'French; French as a result of the Crémieux decree [of 1870 which gave French nationality to Jews living in the country]; and indigenous' (Blum 2002: 130). Ethnic categories have also been used in censuses for other French overseas territories, reflecting local population structures and mixes and also local political sensitivities.

Censuses were part of a broader imperial and colonial remit, for example by Britain in India, which Cohn has called 'the enumerative modality', a process of management by numbers, starting in the seventeenth century, and evidenced by the compilation of extensive 'lists of products, prices, customs and duties, weights and measures, and the values of various coins. A number was, for the British, a particular form of certainty to be held on to in a strange world' (Cohn 1996: 8). Formal censuses were taken from the mid-nineteenth century, especially in the aftermath of the Indian Uprising (Mutiny) of 1857–8, and for all the regions of British India in the period 1868–72. They were taken in 1881, and were followed thereafter by decennial censuses (Guha, 2003: 148).

Through the employment of indigenous census enumerators (Cohn suggests that there were over 500,000 of these by 1881) (Cohn 1996: 8) censuses also aided the development of new forms of national and regional identity, and therefore the formation of aims for independence and the overthrow of colonial rule. Anderson (1991) asserts that the three basic institutions on which colonialism was founded were the census, the map, and the museum, and of these Guha has suggested that the census, 'unlike the map and the museum ... was an institution that every adult male would encounter during his lifetime' (Guha 2003: 148). Guha has also emphasised that censuses were not simply a product of nineteenth-century British rule in India. There were, for example, enumerations from the seventeenth and eighteenth centuries during the Mughal empire, and population estimates were made under British colonial agency in the first half of the nineteenth century, including the census of the Bombay Presidency organised by W. H. Sykes, the 'Statistical Reporter to the Government of Bombay' in 1826 (Guha 2003: 151–60).

While the role of colonial governance in the collection of data and knowledge for more effective supervision and control is unquestionable, nonetheless anomalies exist that suggest that such a role varied between colonies: 'But if an Indian history of censuses and classifications is supposed to reveal colonial modernity in the nineteenth century, then what is one supposed to make of the fact that the first census in Kenya that counted indigenous people was conducted only in 1948, and that before then officials showed no interest in taking one?' (Cooper 2005: 143).

Of particular relevance to colonies was the production of differences: distinctions made in censuses between settlers, permanent or temporary, and 'others' – mainly indigenous inhabitants for whom some kind of control was thought to be necessary. As Kertzer and Arel (2002: 6) have stated, 'Knowledge was power, and the knowledge of the population produced by the census gave those in power insight into social conditions, allowing them to know the population and devise appropriate plans for dealing with them.' One of the important distinctions between metropolitan and colonial censuses, however, was the cultural categorisation of colonial subjects in, for example, colonial censuses of France, Britain and Belgium at times when such categorisation was absent from metropolitan censuses, often in racially descriptive or naming terms that were not familiar to the very people classified (Kertzer and Arel 2002: 10). Censuses that had been initiated and constructed primarily to evaluate numbers and characteristics of the home metropolitan populations were introduced to colonial territories.

One of the major elements of this attempt by colonial state authorities was to make populations knowable, to link them to the state and thereby make them governable, was the Herculean effort to divide the people into mutually exclusive and exhaustive identity categories…The European colonial powers (France, Britain, Belgium), who rejected cultural categorizations in their metropolitan censuses as incompatible with their imagined 'nation-states,' had no such qualms when faced with the daunting task of counting their colonial subjects. (Kertzer and Arel 2002: 9–10)

The varied concepts of race and related debates influenced the construction and development of enumeration and descriptive demographic schemes. Profound ideological and analytical problems are posed by the concept of race itself, and by its use in enumerative schemes. Race has unquestionably been a significant element of census-taking in the nineteenth and twentieth centuries, and includes the assumption, as Melissa Nobles has indicated, that to 'count by race presumes, of course, that there is something to be counted' (Nobles 2002: 46), a presumption clearly made by census-takers in the past and to a degree at present, even though now 'most agree that racial categories have no biological basis'. Racial categories used in past censuses have been used as bases for racial discrimination and racial theories and also for resistance to such a process, and in her analysis and comparison of race in American and Brazilian censuses, Nobles builds on the concept that 'treats race as a discourse, meaning that race is a set of shifting claims that describe and explain what race is and what it means' (Nobles 2002: 47, 48).

In addition to the differing concepts of race, there were practical difficulties with the inclusion of categories of race – however determined – into enumerative practice. In a study of race and Commonwealth censuses A. J. Christopher (2005: 104) states that 'colonial administrations, and indeed the Colonial Office, generally expected that a question on race should be included in population censuses. Thus practical race classifications had to simplify and limit observed differences to those which were regarded as politically and legally significant by administrators usually concerned more with reducing the costs of an enumeration than undertaking an anthropological enquiry.' Race classifications were used in censuses conducted for British colonies. Initially they were found in the Blue Books of statistics for individual colonies produced from 1821, but by 1871 most individual British colonies were conducting their own censuses and classifications. Common themes in the classification of racial types included attempts to identify former slave populations, the use of physical appearance, including skin colour, together with nationality, religion and language (Christopher 2005: 106). Classification of indigenous populations led to very complex and difficult taxonomies, and difficulties including the delimitation of caste types in India, and changes in the bases of such calculations made for incompatibility with subsequent censuses. Christopher has also documented the futile attempts initiated by the British governments to produce a census of the British empire between 1840 and 1940 (Christopher 2008).

In his statistical summary of censuses of colonial populations, Kuczynski portrayed the range and incompatibility of racial categories adopted by European imperial states. 'Most census reports of colonial and mandated areas contain some data on race. But few of the figures for the different territories are comparable. The reasons for the chaotic state of these statistics are manifold' (Kuczynski 1937: 10). He gave two main reasons. First was the process whereby 'more or less numerous members of the less favoured races succeed in being allocated to that race which is considered as the superior one', citing the examples of South Africa, Sierra Leone Granada, and British Malaya. Second, 'The incomparability due to differences in the meaning of the original data is enhanced very much by differences in the presentation of the data' (Kuczynski 1937: 10, 13). He pointed to the attempts by the French to standardise racial type representation in censuses across the French empire, but with some modification to allow for regional differences, but he concluded that this attempt 'to observe uniform fundamental distinctions by races for census purposes has thus failed completely' (Kuczynski 1937: 15).

The most potent and blatant example of the use of censuses for racial purposes is probably that of South Africa, though in a different way this may be matched by the omission of enumeration of aboriginal people in Australia, having been, as Fay Gale explained, 'excluded by the provisions of the Commonwealth Constitution (at federation in 1901) from the population to be counted by census. For this reason, they have not been included officially in any Commonwealth census, although Aborigines designated as "half-caste or less" have been included' (Gale 1969: 65). Some full-blooded aboriginal people were included in censuses on account of the difficulty of distinguishing them from people of part-aboriginal origin, and some attempts at fuller enumeration were made by individual colonies, but the figures nonetheless are inaccurate. They have been included from the 1971 census onwards.

South Africa has a long history, under colonial and Dominion status (from 1910), of attempts to define racial types in population descriptions and enumerations, with major consequences for the human and material rights of individuals and groups. A. J. Christopher has shown how initial distinctions made between 'Christian' and 'Heathen' evolved to 'Free' and 'Slave', then to 'European' and 'Coloured' categories:

Such bi-polar divisions became increasingly fragmented in the nineteenth century when, under the influence of anthropological taxonomy, ever more elaborate classifications were used in the censuses. Accordingly, in the last Cape Colonial census in 1904 seven major categories were employed, fragmented into over forty subdivisions. Although simplified at the Union, the census commissioners continued to employ a racial classification scheme, based on physical and social characteristics … Broadly some four groups were distinguished in the Union period, namely: White, or European, Native (later Bantu, Black or African), Coloured or Mixed, and Asian. (Christopher 1994: 17)

After 1948 the National Party government adopted even more complicated racial classifications for purposes of discrimination, spatial segregation, and differential allocation of resources – a vicious system of apartheid, which remained until 1991.

Similar problems attaching to the abuse of human rights through population enumeration and control systems were experienced in colonial and early federation Australia. Kraly and McQuilton (2005) have reviewed the use of population data by the colony/state of Victoria to administer settlement (including reserves), mobility, employment, marriage and cohabitation, health, crime, voting and education. Population counts or musters had been held in Sydney from 1788, Blue Book statistics were produced from 1822, and the first state-based central statistical office was created in Victoria in 1851. Aboriginal Australians were not counted or estimated in nineteenth-century censuses, and were excluded from the census counts after federation in 1901.

Kraly and McQuilton show, however, that there is useful alternative material in official reports, and they characterise relations with aboriginal people, as shown by an array of information sources, in graphic terms:

Although the early governors had been instructed to develop friendly relations with, and protect, the indigenous population, the story of Aboriginal affairs in Australia since the time of colonisation by the British is a confluence of frontier settlement and land claims, Christian zeal and Social Darwinism, liquor and rape, benevolence and malevolence, all told in chapters separated by political jurisdiction, political economy, and geography. (Kraly and McQuilton 2005: 229)

Legislation, notably the Aborigines Protection Act of 1886 for the 'protection' of aboriginal people in Victoria, had devastating effects. It was 'a classic example of Social Darwinism', which by attempting the separation of 'full-blood' from 'half-caste' Aborigines produced the devastating removal and splitting of families (Kraly and McQuilton 2005: 230).

Counting the populations of European colonial territories

There is surprisingly little recent work on the sizes and dynamics of European colonial populations through the high colonial period, and some of the major secondary sources are quite dated. Kuczynski (1937) calculated, inter alia, the populations of self-governing and non-self-governing areas of the world (according to the Economic Intelligence Service of the League of Nations statistics of 1934). He wrote that:

of a total world population of 2,080 millions, 270 millions, or 13 per cent. lives in colonial or mandated areas, and that 55 per cent. of these 270 millions live in Asia, 42 per cent. in Africa, and 3 per cent. in other continents ... It appears that of the total of 270 millions, one-quarter live under British administration, one-quarter under Dutch administration, one-quarter under French administration, and one-quarter under the administration of another power. (Kuczynski 1937: 1–2)

Using an ambivalent and inconsistent classification from French census material, Kuczynski estimated that in the French colonies in Africa in 1931 there was a population of 1,655,000 'Europeans and Assimilated' and 37,454,000 'natives'.

The equivalent figures given for French colonies in Asia were 80,000, and 24,411,000; for America (including Central and South America) 535,000 and 1,000, and for Oceania 40,000 and 117,000 (Kuczynski 1937: 13). A table estimating the white populations of colonial and mandated areas shows 'that the Whites, numbering about 4,500,000, constitute $1\frac{2}{3}$ per cent. of the total population of the colonial and mandated areas. But over 3,500,000 of these whites live in territories bordering the Mediterranean or Puerto Rico. In all other areas combined with a total population of 250,000 there are hardly 1,000,000 Whites' (Kuczynski 1937: 2).

Townsend (1941: 7–20) estimated the populations of European overseas territories in 1939. Britain's empire overseas contained 470 million people (as against a home-based population of 46.5 million) of whom 361 million were in India, 75 million in the 'dependent areas' and 34 million in the Dominions – Canada, Australia, New Zealand, and South Africa. France's overseas empire had about 65 million people, against 42 million in France. Belgian's imperial territory population was entirely in Africa, and numbered 13 million, against 8.3 million at home. By 1939 the Netherlands had a population of 8.5 million, as against 66 million in her overseas territories.

Portugal controlled an empire, in Africa and Asia, of 8.7 million people, from a domestic population of over 7 million. By 1939 Germany was hardly an imperial power, having lost all of its territory overseas at the end of the First World War, but in 1914 Germany had a colonial population of 13 million, mainly in Africa and the South Pacific, compared with a domestic population of 67.5 million. By 1939, its domestic population was 80 million. Spain had colonial territory in North Africa, Morocco and Guinea. Its home population was about 24 million and colonial population about 1 million. In 1939 Italy had a domestic population of 43.8 million and a colonial population of 10 million.

Many of the Europeans enumerated in overseas colonial territories did not stay permanently in those places. Many went on a temporary basis as administrators, military personnel, engineers, health and education specialists, missionaries, and those involved with particular agricultural, mining and infrastructural development (especially railways), and in due course returned to their countries of origin. Smaller numbers went to settle permanently in the colonies, with larger numbers going, under special settlement schemes, to the white colonies in particular. Wesseling (2004: 18) states that:

Typical examples of such settlement colonies were South Africa, Algeria, Kenya and Rhodesia and, on a more modest scale, German Southwest Africa and Angola. In France, colonial migration was directed overwhelmingly at Algeria. Of the 700,000 French people living in the colonies in 1914, 500,000 were living in Algeria. There were 25,000 French living in Morocco, making up slightly more than half the European population of this territory. In Tunisia there were more than 45,000 French, who made up almost one-third of the total European population, while Indochina had nearly 25,000 French inhabitants. The emigration of Germans and Italians to their colonies was negligible, however.

Natural population change within Europe's colonial territories

While small numbers of European migrants, many of them temporary, increased the populations of Europe's territories overseas, as did more significant numbers of Africans and Asians via the slave trade, and forced, indentured and free labour migration, probably the main factor governing population size was natural change. The overall demographic pattern was initially pre-industrial in character, and subject to massive depletion through a variety of human and environmental impacts such as drought and famine, together with other forms of environmental catastrophe and hazard, slave-trading and forced labour systems, and the vicissitudes of increasing exposure to world trading systems.

The dynamics of population characteristics obviously varied very widely within and between European colonial territories. The parts most remote from the metropolitan hearth experienced slow growth of European population, and varying degrees of indigenous population change. Imperial policy and practice reduced mortality rates in some colonial places through the introduction of various new types of tropical medicine, improved hygiene systems, including sewerage and clean water, and technological and infrastructural innovations such as modern irrigation, river control, railways systems and improved roads.

One basic set of population figures for Africa indicates:

> an overall increase in population from 120 million in 1880 to 129 million in 1900 and 142 million by 1920. However, apart from some parts of North and Southern Africa and possibly the Gold Coast, which witnessed an increase in the growth rate, most other parts of Africa, and especially the whole of middle Africa, witnessed a sharp decline in growth rate. Indeed, in spite of the increase in population numbers between 1880 and 1920, the rate of population growth declined to as low as about 0.25% by about 1900 and rose to an average of only 0.5% by 1920. (Caldwell 1990: 200)

The reasons for these trends include the suppression of revolts against colonial administrations, and the appropriation of large numbers of people as forced labour to work in regions of great difficulty, not least those severely affected by diseases (such as malaria and blackwater fever) unfamiliar in the labourers' home regions. They were forced to live and work in poor conditions, including the extremely hazardous working and living environments in and around the mines of southern Africa. Here the death rates per thousand for tropical Africans were recorded in 1905 at 130, as against 35 for Africans from the temperate south, and 20 for white people (Caldwell 1990: 201–2). There were also high mortality rates among African labourers on European-controlled plantations, especially in Central Africa, including the Congo Free State, the French Congo, and German Cameroon.

The population of what became the Belgian Congo had from the sixteenth century been steadily eroded by the slave trade, but from the mid-nineteenth century demographic decline rapidly accelerated with the depredations effected by the agents of King Leopold II of Belgium, notably through the use of enforced labour in the gathering of rubber and ivory.

The first census of 1924 numbered the population of the Belgian Congo at 10 million, including a very small percentage of Europeans, but the key issue is the unquestionable fact that this population represented a major reduction from the mid-1880s. Adam Hochschild (1998: 232–3), citing a Belgian government commission of 1919, has put the reduction of population in this period as 10 million – though this figure is disputed by Sanderson (2000: 332) – and he also cites evidence from 1907 and 1908 showing a major imbalance in local populations between women and children on the one hand, and much smaller numbers of adult men on the other. Roger Casement indicated in a report of 1904 a population reduction of about 3 million in this period, brought about by 'war', starvation, diseases and a lower birth rate. The population of about 10 million for 1924 had changed little by 1941 (10,354,000), with the number of Europeans in the population 27,800 (0.27 per cent). The European population had doubled between 1925 and 1929, but had fallen back by 1933 (Mason 1944: 246–7).

There was, according to Sanderson (2000), a major difference between accounts of the demography of the Congo. The 'official' state perspective was that population increased after 1925, perhaps as a consequence of pro-natalist policies put in place after the First World War, in contrast to an image in the Belgian demographic and colonial literature from 1885 to 1955 that the population was decreasing until the 1930s. The estimated population of the Belgian Congo in 1941 was 10,354,000, with 0.27 per cent Europeans, the majority from Belgium.

For the two decades following the First World War it is thought that the total population of Africa increased substantially, with figures of 142 million in 1920 and 165 million in 1935. The major influences were the intensification of mining and agriculture; an increase in the density of roads and railways; the impact of hospitals, initially run by missionaries; the more extensive use of drugs and medical treatments (developed in Europe in the late nineteenth century by pharmaceutical research and Schools of Tropical Medicine, and in Africa in the early twentieth century); and the development of rural clinics in such countries as Nigeria, Sierra Leone and Uganda.

The major reduction in mortality in Africa has been ascribed to:

attacking the period peaks in mortality caused by famine and epidemic disease. With gathering momentum from the early years of the century, the campaigns against epidemic disease apparently gained some success. The British attacked sleeping sickness by keeping the tsetse fly away from people, preventing game from using waterholes in inhabited areas, clearing bush, and, more spectacularly, moving populations, as they did from the foreshores of Lake Victoria. (Caldwell 1990: 203–4)

The decline in the death rate and the increase in population by 45 million between 1880 and 1935 led to large migrations of people from rural to urban and industrial areas and the spectacular growth of towns in sub-Saharan Africa, and further increases in population (to *c.* 200 million by the late 1940s and 400 million in the late 1970s) continued these urban and migratory trends (Caldwell 1990: 206).

Natural population change in India, and in the white settlement areas of the European empires, varied widely. India's population in the first census of 1871 was 203 million, 253,896,330 in 1881, and 287,314,671 in 1891. The figure for 1901 was 283,396,327, and for 1911 252,093,390. Before 1920 India's population was characterised by high death rates and high birth rates, giving rise to population increase, though much affected by endemic and epidemic disease outbreaks, natural disasters and famines. In the 1921 census the population total was 251,321,213. After 1920, the population of India increased rapidly, mainly through reduction in the death rates by preventative measures such as inoculation, so that by 1931 India's population had reached 278,977,238, and 318,660,580 in 1941.

In the major white settlement colonies – Dominions as they became – the fundamental demographic trends were different from those colonies with small resident European populations. Canada's population increased from 3,230,000 in 1861 to 4,833,000 in 1891, 5,371,315 in 1901, 7,206,643 in 1911 (Tinker 1995: 16), and about 7.5 million in 1914. In 1931 Canada had a population of 10,378,000 (Christopher 1988: 24). Immigration played a large part in population increase in the nineteenth and early twentieth centuries. From 1850 to 1896 there was a period of low immigration and high internal migration, followed in 1896–1913 by a major increase in immigration from 17,000 to 400,000. Thereafter immigration fell until 1945, and then picked up again (Beaujot 1998: 2–3).

The population of Australia increased dramatically from 405,356 in 1850 to 1,455,585 in 1860 (Tinker, 1995: 16). The white population was:

no more than a quarter of a million before the gold rushes of the 1850s, rising from 1.25 million in the early 1860s to 2.25 million in the early 1880s, and reaching 3.75 million by the turn of the century. In the critical years of the 1860s and 1870s when fertility first began to fall, this was essentially an immigrant population, less than half of all adults were native-born as late as 1891. (Caldwell and Ruzica 1978: 81)

In 1931 Australia had a population of 6,449,000 (Christopher, 1988: 24). The historical dynamics of population change in Australia have been reviewed by Powell (1988: 25), who showed that the birth rate in Australia had reduced by 40 per cent from about 43 per thousand by the beginning of the twentieth century, with a parallel decline in the population growth rate of 40 percent from 1860, leading to new immigration initiatives from 1907.

The main changes in population in New Zealand from the early nineteenth century were characterised by a diminution in the relative size of the Maori population and an expansion in the numbers of Europeans. Dalziel (1999: 581–2) estimates that in 1841 Europeans in New Zealand numbered about 2,000, compared with a Maori population of between 70,000 and 90,000. 'Musket warfare, increasing mortality rates, and declining fertility had taken a heavy toll. The treaty [of Waitangi] then became a licence for settlement on a scale undreamt of by the Maori. By 1858 the European population, at over 56,000, exceeded the Maori population, estimated at about 56,000.' In 1896 there were 701,000 Europeans and about 42,000 Maori. In 1931 New Zealand had a population of 1,443,000 (Christopher 1988: 24).

Population change in South-East Asia

Rates of population increase in South-East Asia were also generally characterised by pre-demographic transition processes. For South-East Asia in general, the pattern of demographic development was one of rapid population increase in the nineteenth and early twentieth centuries, at a rate greater than China and India. Booth (2008: 33) states that:

In all cases the annual average growth in population was well over one per cent, and in those regions which attracted substantial in-migration such as British Malaya it was over two per cent per annum. This rapid growth was due to a combination of high fertility, falling mortality compared with other parts of Asia and Africa, and especially in Burma and Malaya, high immigration.

Booth suggests that important components of demographic change in the region before 1950 included lower mortality in the nineteenth century than British India and Egypt, and a more ample supply of land and food, together with improved health regimes introduced by colonial governments before the 1920s, and the role of colonial government in reducing warfare and rebellion (Booth 2008: 34).

A study of Java in the nineteenth century has shown, however, that it experienced an unusually high rate of population increase, amounting to what has been called a population explosion, with an increase in estimated population from 3,647,000 in 1802 to 4.5 million in 1815, and 28.5 million in 1900 (Peper 1970: 71). These figures were derived from official estimates of the indigenous population in the nineteenth century, and Peper thought that they demonstrated an experience (if the basic figures were accurate) that might be unique in the population history of either Asia or Europe, but after a careful scrutiny of the population estimates and some of the causative factors in population change in Java, concluded that Java's population for *c.* 1800 was much higher than had been thought (8–10 million). The annual growth rate *c.* 1800–50 was between 0.5 and 1.0 per cent, and 'The view that there was an exceptionally rapid population growth in Java is to an important degree the product of an ethnocentric European approach to the history of Java' (Peper 1970: 84), particularly the overestimation of the impact of Western influence on demographic trends, through improvement in living and health conditions. Not all scholars agree with these figures. Elson (1999: 158–9) suggests a base population of 3–5 million at the end of the eighteenth century, growing rapidly to 40.9 million by 1930 at an average rate of 1.9 per cent per year, and similar rates of growth elsewhere. Thus:

in Malaya, a population of 250,000 in 1800 had risen to 3.8 million in 1931. In the Philippines, one of 2.5 million in 1830 had grown to 16.5 million by 1940. Burma's population more than doubled between 1891 and 1941. The component parts of French Indochina grew at rates around 2 per cent from the late nineteenth century on. Siam witnessed a similar rate of increase after the turn of the twentieth century. (Elson 1999: 158–9)

Much of the growth was due to migration, notably by Chinese to Borneo and the Malay states, Siam and the Philippines, Malays from the Indonesian archipelago to the western Malay peninsula, and Indians to Burma on a large scale. This notwithstanding, natural increase was also a factor through changes in birth and death rates. Tarling sees this phase of population increase in South-East Asia in the nineteenth and early twentieth centuries as a new development in the demographic history of the region, explained in general terms by a reduction in mortality, partly through a reduction in episodic warfare, and a small increase in fertility because of more peaceful conditions. Another factor affecting regional population change was increased internal migration, with efforts by the states to control migration and stabilise the rural workforce having only limited success, 'because despite an enduring stereotype of the territorially-rooted peasant household, mobility rather than permanency seems to have been a keynote of peasant life in this era as well as earlier ones' (Elson 1999: 160).

Migration within Burma, Siam, French Indo-China, the Philippines (notably Luzon), and east Java was strongly influenced by opportunities provided by new agricultural developments in the high colonial era, such as in the Irrawaddy delta in Burma and the Mekong delta regions of French Indo-China. Booth suggests that internal migration was important: 'there is abundant evidence that indigenous populations moved out of densely set-tled agricultural areas to colonise new lands everywhere in the region and that this movement was often facilitated by the introduction of individual land rights in the latter part of the nineteenth century which provided legal sanction to what had previously been rather ill-defined occupancy rights' (Booth 1980: 34). While much of this movement was spontaneous, there were also examples of the Dutch and French colonial governments creating programmes for land settlement in Sumatra and North Vietnam by peoples from densely populated areas in Java and South Vietnam (Booth 2008: 34).

French Indo-China

French Indo-China is not a homogeneous geographical or demographic region, but its incorporation into the French empire, starting in 1859, had profound demographic consequences. Comprising a series of plains and deltas separated east from west by the central Annamite Cordillera, French Indo-China incorporated the colony of Cochin China together with the protectorates of Annam, Tonkin, Cambodia and Laos. Prior to the coming of the French, the two basic geopolitical divisions were the area to the east of the Annamite Cordillera, including the Annamite king-dom of Tonkin, Annam, and Cochin China, and the area to the west of the Cordillera, mainly the Khmer empire, with its historical links with India, headed by Brahmins, and with a majority Buddhist population. These areas each experienced different population histories. Both areas had been populated by migrations from elsewhere in Asia,

but differences in efficiency of the agricultural techniques, the family and com-munity patterns, and the strength of the political units combined with differ-ences in climate, soil, and the hazards of disease to produce a cycle of growth and decline in the west but fairly continuous growth in the east. The Khmer empire at its height is supposed to have had a population of over four million, but by the beginning of the twentieth century the long periods of foreign and internal strife, accompanied by periodic epidemics and famines, had reduced the number of Cambodians to an estimated 1.2 million. The history of the Annamites, on the contrary, is one of continuing expansion. (Office of Population Research (OPR) 1945: 69)

The Annamites had migrated to the area of Tonkin and mixed with the Indonesian peoples of the river deltas, and were joined by immigrants from China, with a consequential further migration by the Annamites to southern Annam and Cochin China. Notwithstanding periodic demographic setbacks through famine, typhoons and drought, population increased over time, early nineteenth-century accounts of population size and distribution 'indicating the great density of population in the Tonkin and Annam deltas, the secondary concentration in Cochin China, and the relative emptiness of the rest of the country' (OPR 1945: 69–70).

Although the impact of the French in Indo-China was not as great as that of the British in Malaya or the Dutch in the Dutch East Indies, the effects of greater political stability and drainage and irrigation works in the Red River, Mekong and Tonkin deltas, together with medical advances and the gradual control of malaria and smallpox, led to an increase in population in the delta areas. The so-called censuses from 1876 to 1921 were little more than estimates of population, and those of 1926, 1931 and 1936 not much better. The evidence that they provide for the five countries of French Indo-China is of 'a general and fairly consistent population increase which appears plausible in the light of what is known concerning the economic and social conditions of the various areas', and the census estimate of 1936 'indicated a total population of 23.0 million, of which 72 per cent were Annamites, 13 per cent Cambodians, 6 per cent Thai, 1.4 per cent Chinese and other Asiatics, and 0.2 per cent Europeans and "assimilated"' (OPR 1945: 71).

The European and 'assimilated' group (Europeans plus Japanese and Filipinos) totalled 42,000, of whom 40 per cent had been in French Indo-China for about five years, about 26 per cent for fifteen years or more, and just over half of the total were soldiers, about a quarter were administrators, with smaller numbers in commerce, industry, mining and trade (OPR 1945: 72). The majority of this group of Europeans were French citizens who had been born in France, mainly in the Midi, Corsica and Brittany, with a significant number of others having been born in French India, other French colonies such as Réunion, and the Antilles (Studdart 1943: 251–2).

In comparison with other countries in South, South-East and East Asia at about the same date, the population of French Indo-China was smaller than that of China, India and the Dutch East Indies, but higher than that of Siam, Burma, Malaya and the Philippines, and with a mean density of population higher than Siam and Burma but lower than China and India, but much of Indo-China is mountainous and uncultivable (Studdart 1943: 211).

Migration and European empires

General features

International migration from home countries to territories of European overseas empires was a significant process in the development of the world

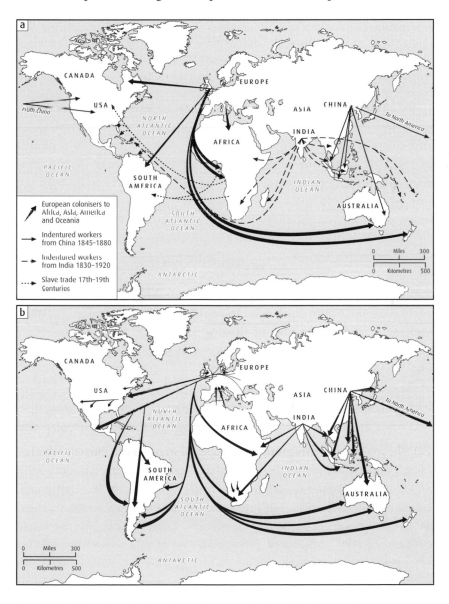

Fig. 3.1(a) Colonial migration from the seventeenth to the nineteenth century.
Fig. 3.1(b) Labour migration connected with industrialisation, 1850–1920.
Source: Castles and Miller (1993: 47, 54). By permission of and © Palgrave Macmillan.

economic system of the nineteenth and early twentieth centuries, and also in the process of modernisation of the nation-state or multinational state. The effects were profound:

> In earlier centuries, European emigration had radical and sometimes cata-strophic consequences for the indigenous populations of the lands that they settled; almost eliminating them in Australia and the United States, creating new *mestizo* populations of various shades in South America; introducing new variety by their own migration and by those of their African slaves and Asian indentured labourers throughout the world, from Trinidad to Fiji. (Coleman 2003: 719)

The basic processes influencing the character and dynamics of immi-grant and resident labour forces in the European imperial territories and colonies were linked to accelerating changes from pre-capitalist to capitalist economies and societies, a process 'whereby their econo-mies were internally disarticulated and integrated externally with the world-economy' (Knox and Agnew 1989: 240), involving a reorgani-sation of factors of production, including labour. While much of the migration literature dealing with the period from the mid-nineteenth century onwards focuses on transatlantic migration, McKeown (2004) and others (Lucassen 2007) have shown that this was just one of a series of major contemporary migration systems. Two of these were in north Asia and South-East Asia. In contrast to the transatlantic system, McKeown argues that most of the migrants in the Asian systems were free, and that the rhythms of migration were similar in the transatlantic and Asian systems.

These ideas have been debated. Prabhu Mohapatra (2007) has argued that the operation of Indian external migration was less free than McKeown suggests, because of its location within the British empire, and the use of indenture as

> a template for the 'contract' and debt-bonded migration of free labourers. This, at least, is suggested by overwhelming evidence from the bulk of so-called non-indentured migration from India to south-east Asia and Ceylon. For instance, the Kangani system in Malaya or the Maistry system in Burma or the Tundu system in Ceylon...functioned through systems of debt and advances, tying labourers to particular employers through the mediation of labour contractors. (Mohapatra 2007: 111)

Control was thus through terms and conditions of employment rather than initial coercion to emigration. Account has also to be taken of the fact that many Indian emigrants returned, and of the significance of non-European capital in South Asian migration.

Ulbe Bosma (2007) opposes the notion that free white labour migration was universal from the mid-nineteenth century, with transatlantic migrants frequently affected by state control or semi-indentured status: mechanisms of control that Bosma argues were 'increasingly navigated by a social Darwinist mindset' or a 'racist taxonomy' (2007: 117). All areas of colonial migration were thus influenced by a belief in a 'hierarchy of human races', in which 'black labour was enslaved, Asian labour indentured, whereas the apex was firmly held by the free white well-educated northern Europeans' (Bosma 2007: 117). Nonetheless there was considerable free/non-indentured migration from India and China in the period 1840–1940. The theory that most transatlantic migration was free and that migration from and within Asia and elsewhere was not has to be countered by such additional features as the recognition of state and commercial sponsorship of migration from Europe to North and South America, the inclusion of large numbers of (unfree) colonial soldiers as migrants, and the initiation by state agency of migration to Australia and Algeria (Bosma 2007: 122–3). Prabhu Mohapatra (2007: 115) concludes that 'McKeown's [2004] essay marks a major departure from the dominant Eurocentric perspectives on global migration flows, highlighting the quantitative and qualitative significance of non-European patterns of migration in shaping the evolution of global economic formations in the nineteenth and twentieth centuries'.

The main circuits of global migration from the mid-nineteenth to the mid-twentieth century include migrations of about 55–58 million from Europe to the Americas, to which can be added about 2.5 million from India, China, Japan and Africa; migrations of about 48–52 million from India and southern China to South-East Asia, the Indian Ocean Rim, and the South Pacific, to which can be added about 4 million from Africa, Europe, north-eastern Asia, and the Middle East; and migrations of about 46–51 million people to Manchuria, Siberia, Central Asia and Japan from north-east Asia and Russia (McKeown 2004: 156).

In this period there were about 19 million emigrants from India to South-East Asia, lands bordering the Indian Ocean and to the South Pacific. McKeown (2004: 157–8) states that:

most migration from India was to colonies throughout the British empire. Less than 10 per cent of this migration was indentured, although much of it was undertaken with assistance from colonial authorities, or under some form of debt obligation under *kangani* labour recruitment systems. Over 2 million Indians also migrated as merchants or other travellers not intending to work as labourers. Migration expanded with the increasing restriction of indenture contracts after 1908 and the abolishment of indenture in 1920. Nearly 4 million Indians travelled to Malaysia, over 8 million to Ceylon, over 15 million to Burma, and about 1 million to Africa, other parts of Southeast Asia, and Islands throughout the Indian and Pacific Oceans.

These were the main components of trans-oceanic migration, but there were also very large numbers of migrants involved in shorter-distance migration, within and beyond state frontiers, to places of employment in urban, industrial and agricultural areas. There was much movement of population within India under changing economic and political circumstances, for example to 'tea plantations in the south and northeast, to mines and textile-producing regions of Bengal, and to newly irrigated lands and urban areas throughout the subcontinent' (McKeown 2004: 161). In Africa there was a combination of internal migration (see below, pp. 152–3) of indigenous labour forces to plantations and mines in Central and southern Africa and to agricultural and urban areas in West and East Africa in the mid- and later nineteenth and twentieth centuries, and trans-oceanic migrations, mainly from Europe, the Middle East, China and India.

Much European migration was across the North Atlantic Ocean, including migration to Canada, a British colony. Some of this was encouraged by a range of colonial propaganda that compared Canada favourably, for example, with the United States and Australia. Serge Courville, in extensive studies of this phenomenon in relation to migration to Québec (2000, 2001, 2002), has shown that 'there was a colonial version of the American dream that was diffused throughout the British colonies, one whose themes were integral to the Quebec colonial discourse that was developed during the nineteenth century' (Courville 2001: 290). Against a background of large-scale overseas migration from European and other countries in the nineteenth century and migration of 15 million people from Britain and 5 million from Ireland, Courville points to the role of migration as a safety valve for overpopulation and as 'an important bulwark in the defence of the colonies and, along with the new free-trade policy of the 1840s, a way to build a "Greater Britain". By peopling the colonies and offering them the hope and the means of becoming true commercial partners, it was thought that the true integrity of the Empire would be assured' (Courville 2001: 290). Canada was promoted by reference to its relative proximity to Britain, its beauty and natural state, its beneficial climate, unlimited land and mineral resources, and its secure political state. Courville has focused on what he calls 'the dream transposed', that is the migration of significant numbers of French Canadians from Québec to the United States, which accelerated throughout the nineteenth century. The main tenets of Québec's counter-propaganda to retain French speakers, their religion and culture were 'the promotion of agriculture, a familial-centred society, and religion, more than through industry and commerce, which were considered to be foreign to French-Canadian identity' (Courville 2001: 298). Courville concludes that there were three types of colonial 'dream' influencing migration policy to and within Canada: the British, the American (to which the British dream was partly opposed) and the Québec dream, which 'was a fusion of these two dreams and demonstrates the connections the elite of Québec had with the outside world' (Courville 2001: 305).

A key component of the social and economic development of European overseas colonies was the nature, composition and dynamics of their labour forces. The economic well-being of a colony or any part of a European overseas empire depended on the establishment and maintenance of a labour force sufficiently large in size and possessed of appropriate skills to provide for the basic defensive, economic, educational and health needs of indigenous and European populations. In settler economies in temperate latitudes, much of the workforce was European. In tropical and equatorial regions, whether in settler or non-settler contexts, much of the labour force was made up of indigenous or immigrant peoples who were, by a variety of means and statutory or local controls, made to work under extremely difficult conditions. They made up essentially an unfree labour force, in that they themselves appear to have had little control over the terms and conditions of their employment, and they were therefore often treated as commodities in an exploitive chain of production.

It would appear at first sight that there is a close connection between European overseas expansion and the creation and enlargement of unfree labour forces, starting in the fifteenth century and continuing into the twentieth (even the twenty-first) century. The basic premise is that there was originally a generally free labour force whose use was increasingly appropriated by European capitalist and world market conditions and transformed to a condition of either total slavery or some degree of unfreedom. The living and working conditions of those made unfree were worsened through the imperialist modes of exploitation of people and resources, and were only ameliorated through such humanitarian processes as the slavery abolitionist movements of the eighteenth and nineteenth centuries.

This picture is inevitably far too broadly drawn, and incorporates elements that are difficult to prove. One difficulty is to establish the degrees of freedom of labour before the advent of European imperialism from the fifteenth century onwards, and, for the purpose of this book, before the heightened imperialism of the nineteenth and twentieth centuries. Emmer has suggested that 'Historically speaking, free labour was usually the exception and unfree labour the rule, especially when we consider non-European controlled labour systems' (Emmer 1997: 9). He suggests that the abolitionist perspective or ideology characteristic of much scholarship from Western Europe or North America is an obstacle to a fuller understanding of labour economics and conditions, and that 'in spite of all its personal, psychological and cultural drawbacks [slavery] was on the whole an *economically* advantageous institution for slaves and owners and that the ending of slavery in North America and the Caribbean usually depressed personal incomes rather than the reverse' (Emmer 1997: 14). This can obviously be strongly contested.

Numbers of migrants

It has been estimated that in the period from 1815 to 1930 about 52 million people emigrated from Europe to countries overseas (Baines 1994: 525). In the European overseas colonies there were about 100,000 European settlers in 1830; in 1880 there were about 700,000, of which 400,000 were in Algeria. By 1913 the European population in the overseas colonies was about 1.6 million, and in 1938 about 2.7 million. Etemad (1998: 458) has suggested that in the nineteenth century the European component was little more than 0.2 per cent of the population of the colonies, and under 0.5 per cent between 1913 and 1938. In contrast, in the period 1918–38 75 per cent of the population of the British Dominions was European and white. There were major contrasts between the tropical colonies, which had very few permanent European settlers, and the white settlement colonies in more temperate regions.

The percentages of population coming from Europe were: 0.1 per cent in Asia, and 0.4 per cent in sub-Saharan Africa. There were major concentrations of Europeans in the Maghrib in North Africa – about 7.5 per cent of the population in 1913 and 8.5 per cent (1.6 million) in 1938. The European component in Black Africa in 1913 was 0.2 per cent of the population and 0.4 per cent in 1938. The figures for Oceania were 2.1 per cent

Table 3.1 People from Europe in British Dominions (millions)

	1913	1938
Canada, including Newfoundland	7.726 (98.1%)	11.222 (98.2%)
South Africa	1.330 (21.4%)	2.085 (20.9%)
Australia	4.830 (98.6%)	6.9 (98.4%)
New Zealand	1.079 (95.1%)	1.528 (94.4%)

Source: Etemad 1998: 459.

in 1913 and 1.9 per cent in 1938. The figures for the British Dominions, as they had become, are shown in Table 3.1.

The distinctions were not, however, as simple as some of the figures might imply. Eighty per cent of the European residents in Algeria in 1938 had been born in that colony rather than having migrated there. Hence,

Algeria and South Africa appear to be mixed colonies where white settlers, numerically in the minority but nevertheless of a considerable number, deprived the indigenous populations of their land and subsoil rights. Algeria and South Africa would have become real settlement colonies if the European population had been more numerous than the native population, as had happened in North America and Oceania. (Etemad 1998: 460)

Christopher (1984: 123) estimated that there were about 25,000 Europeans in Africa at the beginning of the nineteenth century, but that by 1860 there were approximately 320,000, with the figure reaching 2.2 million by 1911, and peaking at about 6 million by 1960. The two major areas of European settlers in Africa were Algeria and South Africa. Algeria experienced high rates of immigration between 1841 and 1891. South Africa's population growth through immigration came later – after 1890 – peaking between 1900 and 1905. Portuguese Africa's inward migration peak occurred much later – from 1960 to 1973.

The balances of population in different parts of the European empires in the nineteenth and twentieth centuries were modified in the white minority colonies in the tropics by the initial employment of slave or coerced labour, and later by indentured labour and labourers working in so-called free market contexts. Indigenous people were widely employed as troops for the European armies stationed overseas: Etemad (1998: 462) suggests that in 1913 about 70 per cent of all colonial troops were soldiers who had been recruited locally.

The conditions under which forced labourers worked in agricultural, infrastructural and industrial projects in the European colonies were generally very poor, often resulting in high mortality rates: for example, in the gathering and initial processing of wild rubber in the Congo, and the construction of railways in Africa and India. Before the advent of rubber plantations in Malaya and the Dutch East Indies, rubber was gathered in its natural state in the Congo Free State for the concessionary Anglo-Belgian Rubber Company. Christopher (1984: 92–3) has described the consequential effects. 'Once the territory had been occupied the administration proceeded to extract goods and services from the Congolese. The villages close to transport routes were called upon to supply porters, canoe paddlers and food. Those further away were required to deliver rubber ... increases to production were achieved by varying taxes and prices and by forcing women and children to gather rubber.'

This process was intensified by the 1891 decree by the Congo Free State to appropriate to itself all 'vacant' land (land seemingly not occupied) and all its produce, so that villagers 'now found themselves obliged to spend days in the forest searching for a declining number of rubber vines, doing unpaid labour as porters, or working as woodcutters for the river steamers ... failure to deliver was marked by corporal punishment, collective fines in kind, imprisonment, or by punitive expeditions which burned villages and on occasions massacred the inhabitants' (Ascherson 1999: 102). Inhumane punishments also included whipping with the hippo-hide whip – the *chicotte* – and the amputation of hands and limbs of people living in villages that were deemed to have failed to meet their production quotas. The combination of punishment, severe working conditions, and the spread of disease, together with the labourers' lack of immunity to disease when forced to work on railway construction outside their own territories, lowered the population of the Congo by between 5 and 12 million.

Forms and causes of migration varied, but for our immediate purposes we will adopt a distinction between forced and voluntary migration. During the mercantilist phase of the development of the early capitalist world system from *c.* 1590 to the early nineteenth century, the major component was the trade of about 10 million slaves from West Africa to North America and the Caribbean, followed after abolition by major movements of indentured labourers from China, India and Japan to work on the European colonial plantations (Cohen 1995: 1–2). Parallel to these movements of unfree labourers, there was voluntary migration, some of it based on individual decisions and perceived opportunities, some of it on more organised forms of voluntary settlement overseas, conspicuously in what were known as colonies of settlement. Most of this occurred in temperate regions of the world, notably the British Dominions and North

America where the climatic conditions were thought to be conducive to the settlement of Europeans. Cohen (1995: 2) suggests that:

Britain was the only mercantile power to have made an unambiguous success of colonial settlement – if we understand success to be the establishment of a hegemonic presence. Other than in Quebec the French abroad were never concentrated in sufficient numbers. Even in Algeria and Indo-China, where there were substantial settlements, they were driven out by powerful anti-colonial movements … Essentially, this form of migration coincided with the period of European expansion and imperialism, and came to an end with the rise of the anti-colonial nationalist movements.

The majority of European migrants went to temperate regions such as North America, a minority to the tropical regions. Reasons for permanent and temporary emigration varied in different European regions, with, for example, a tendency for a higher proportion of emigrants from southern and eastern Europe to return than those from northern and western Europe (Baines 1994: 526). The main motives for emigration seem to have been the expectation of better economic conditions overseas and propaganda for emigration to particular regions. These two motives have been characterised as the 'relative income' and the 'information' hypotheses. Baines suggests that both of these rest on 'an underlying assumption that the emigrants were actors moving freely within a changing international economy', and that economic developments were linked to migration through the greater mobility of labour and capital, so that 'higher labour productivity in some countries led to a higher demand for labour. The gap in labour demand could be closed by migration – this assumption is implicit in the relative income hypothesis' (Baines 1994: 527, 540).

In practice, however, neither of these hypotheses takes us very far towards explaining the important question of the wide differences in and the detailed character of emigration from different parts of Europe. There are different scales at which international migration can be reviewed. Generally, figures for migration from one country and continent to another can start to indicate the broadest of trends and population transfers, but they do not necessarily help much with the understanding of either the complex mechanisms of migration or the processes of choice/compulsion.

As McKeown (2004: 179–80) has suggested, with reference to aggregate models and economic approaches to migration:

individuals making decisions (the 'free' migrants) are the basic unit of most economic and aggregate models, yet those studies have little understanding of the social conditions under which those decisions are made... A map of the world drawn from these geographically dispersed spaces and networks would look much different than the familiar mosaic of geographically discrete territories. They make up a world of complex and overlapping flows and nodes, none of which can be entirely captured within a single national or regional history.

Such complex mappings are largely beyond the scope and space limits of this book, however, where broader trends will be the main focus, albeit qualified by accounts of some regional and local migration experiences. Migration to provide labour is clearly an important component of global migrations in the nineteenth and twentieth centuries, and a partial fulfilment of the needs of colonial commercial economies.

Migration and the British empire

The greatest provider of migrants to the overseas territories of the British empire was Britain itself, and in other European countries too the metropolis was the greatest provider of colonial emigrants. Our understanding of the reasons for and patterns of emigration to overseas colonies is still far from complete. Harper (1999) has pointed out that ideas about emigration to the colonies fluctuated in the nineteenth century. The idea of migration as a safety valve for Malthusian concerns at a dangerously expanding population, and its implications for poverty, unemployment and social disturbance, which prevailed up to the 1830s, was then replaced by Wakefield's more positive concept of controlled emigration as a means of settling Britain's newer colonies, a philosophy that was operative for about thirty years. An influential figure at this time was Edward Gibbon Wakefield who, at a time of economic revival in Britain in the 1830s, advocated a deliberate policy of populating Britain's colonies through the use of money from the sale of land in the antipodean colonies to provide funding for systematic colonial emigration. His views were implemented by the National Colonisation Society, founded in 1830 (Harper 1999: 76). The Wakefield concept of paying for emigration by the sale of land in the colonies had in theory the advantage of reducing the cost to the British government, which had been reluctant to become directly involved in overseas migration schemes.

State involvement in emigration schemes was again in favour in the 1870s because of economic depression at home and a shortage of labour in the colonies. There was clearly no national agreement on emigration policy, and each proposal was contested. Wakefield's colonisation scheme was opposed on the grounds that able people were being selectively removed from the country, and there was a failure to address the needs of the poor. The government's main approach was 'to avoid positive intervention, while broadly sanctioning Imperial colonization and discouraging emigration to the United States. Legislation – either to impede or encourage an exodus – was infrequent and largely ineffective' at least until the twentieth century (Harper 1999: 76–7).

The specific details of migration to various parts of the British empire depended on economic stimulus, measures of financial support for travel and settlement, and in the most obvious cases (the transportation of convicts) on compulsion. Assisted migration did not always produce the quality of labour force that the recipient colonial administrators required. Those in the British colonies looking for labour to help them on their farms and other enterprises found voluntary migration, encouraged by family and other private contacts and with practical help, and sometimes by visits home and the use of agents, much more effective (Harper 1999: 83).

The discoveries of gold deposits in Australia and New Zealand in the 1850s and 1860s and of gold and diamonds in South Africa from the late 1860s were stimuli to specialist emigration, particularly by miners. Bounty and migrant assistance schemes had earlier encouraged the emigration to Australia of sections of the population who were not convicts, ensuring a better population mix. From the mid-nineteenth century onwards antipodean migration was facilitated by means of selection, nomination and land order schemes implemented by agents working in Britain.

In the case of Canada, migration schemes from Britain in the first half of the nineteenth century were 'organized primarily by individuals, commercial companies, and charitable societies' (Harper 1999: 79, 80). In the second half of the century the main agents for British migration overseas were 'national and provincial charities and self-help groups – over sixty of them in 1866 – which aimed to find colonial outlets for Britain's surplus female population, and destitute children, as well as the unemployed' (Harper 1999: 81). Action and agencies to increase the number of women migrating overseas increased after 1880, in the period of high imperialism, with women being seen as important contributors to the advance of empire. Emigration of working-class people to the empire, mainly to Canada, was greatly facilitated from 1890 to 1930 by the Salvation Army, which assisted about 200,000 such people to find new homes and work overseas (Harper 1999: 82).

Constantine (1999) has shown from shipping and census statistics that the pattern of overseas migration from Britain changed from the beginning of the twentieth century. One important characteristic was the reduction in emigration from Britain to the United States, dominant in the 1880s and 1890s, and the increase of emigration to parts of the British empire. The majority were destined for white settlement colonies, with Canada dominant *c.* 1905–38, but with Australia and New Zealand significant from 1914 onwards, to which must be added smaller numbers to South Africa. Other areas of empire with significant British populations in 1931 included Nigeria, Kenya, Northern Rhodesia, Tanganyika, Uganda and Nyasaland (Constantine 1999: 167–8). There were in Constantine's opinion two types of labour market for British migrants overseas. First, that in which indigenous labour was largely used to supply manual labour needs, and to which in consequence, as in India, mainly specialist and generally higher-ranking administrators and professionals were drawn. In contrast, a British labour force was attracted to settler colonies in the Dominions such as Australia, New Zealand and Canada, with South Africa being the main exception. Official recruiting systems were operated by the Dominions, with the British government playing a limited role before the First World War, but thereafter the recruiting of ex-soldiers and the Empire Settlement Act of 1922 led to increased imperial emigration from Britain, by the provision of assistance with voyages and settlement costs, mainly to Canada, Australia and New Zealand, with smaller numbers to South Africa and Southern Rhodesia. The Act of 1922 was renewed consistently in the 1930s and 1950s, with more realistic programmes of land settlement being introduced. People also moved from the Dominions to the metropole, with 92,745 Dominion-born people registered as living in Britain in the 1931 census (Constantine 1999: 170–4).

The second-largest source of overseas emigration to various parts of the British empire was British India, the most populous part of the empire in the nineteenth and twentieth centuries, followed by smaller but nonetheless significant numbers of migrants from Africa, China, and the Pacific islands. Northrup (1999: 89) suggests that: 'Before 1860 nearly all of these migrations were to supplement former slave populations in tropical sugar plantation colonies, but thereafter a growing share went into plantation labour in colonies that had never known slavery as well as into mining and railway construction.' All this was part of a process of development of new colonies and assisted migration to Australia, New Zealand and Africa. Many of the migrants to Asia, Africa and the Pacific were indentured labourers engaged under a range of contracts, mainly long-term, and the size of this indentured migrant labour force within the British empire remained at about 150,000 per decade from 1841 to 1914, the major recipient early in this period being Mauritius, then the Caribbean, and after 1890 African and South Pacific colonies.

Indentured labourers were also recruited from India for work in Natal and Fiji, and for plantations in Ceylon and Burma, and from India and China for plantations in the Malay Straits Settlements. Pacific islanders were 'recruited' as labourers for Queensland before the beginning of the White Australia Policy. Labour was also imported to Uganda from India and China for the building of the Uganda railway, and early in the twentieth century from China for gold mining in South Africa (Northrup 1999: 88–90). The factors influencing migration within the empire in the nineteenth and early twentieth centuries included the abolition of the slave trade in 1834, and the consequent release of slave labour from plantations in the West Indies and Mauritius and from slave ships from Africa; the Indian Uprising/ Mutiny of 1857; and instability in China in the first decade of the twentieth century.

Continuing humanitarian concerns for the conditions in which indentured workers operated were reflected in short-term constraints placed by the British government in the early 1840s on migration of indentured labourers from India to Mauritius and to the plantations in the West Indies. The annual number of Indian labourers allowed to migrate to Dutch Guiana, Fiji, East Africa, Ceylon, Burma, and the Straits Settlements increased substantially from about 300,000 in *c.* 1875 to over 425,000 by the end of the nineteenth century. In addition, there was large-scale labour migration within the empire, notably in India and Ceylon for the development of plantation estates (Northrup 1999: 90, 92).

Migration from India to other territories of the British empire was a complex phenomenon, as has been demonstrated in Gillion's study of migration from India to Fiji. Gillion shows that contract migration from India to Fiji under the indentured labour system began in 1879 and continued to 1916. 'The number of emigrants from India to Fiji under the Indian Emigration Acts was 60,965, the peak year being 1911 when 4,204 emigrants left for Fiji. 45,833 went from Calcutta and 15,132 from Madras. The number of arrivals in Fiji was 60,537' (Gillion 1956: 139). These numbers were increased by non-contract labourers and those who went to Fiji via New Caledonia or Australia and New Zealand. Migration resumed after the First World War.

These movements of labour were part of a globalising capitalist system which sought cheap labour for the development of various food and mineral commodities and their export to European states. These conditions were, as Northrup has indicated, accelerated by:

the strong push of social and economic misery. Most Indian migrants came from two areas feeling strong demographic and economic pressure – the Gangetic Plain of northern India and the environs of Madras in South India. Although ambition motivated some, desperation best explains the emigration of others. Population pressure, periodic famines, political upheavals, and changing economic conditions drove large numbers of Indians out of their ancestral villages and into the global labour market. (Northrup 1999: 93, 94)

One of the major debates in Queensland concerned the suitability of white labour for use in tropical agriculture, and the alternative use of black labourers (*kanakas* as they were called) recruited, often forcibly, from the Pacific Ocean island regions of Melanesia and Polynesia, for work in sugar plantations in Queensland (and Fiji), and exposing them to diseases to which they had no resistance and thus to very high mortality levels. This was an issue that had engaged attention over a wider geographical area, but the problem was highlighted in Queensland in the late nineteenth and early twentieth centuries. The debate at times was clearly discriminatory and racist in character, tapping into theories of acclimatisation. In 1939, in a book by A. Grenfell Price entitled *White Settlers in the Tropics*, Price included a section on Queensland, with details and contexts of the introduction of *kanakas* for the cultivation of sugar cane from the 1860s:

From the point of view of the Australian nation there were two fundamental arguments against the coloured labor system in Queensland: the undercutting of white labour and the appalling incidence of disease and death, which afflicted the Kanakas and through them the whites. From the outset the labouring classes of white Australians struggled against Kanaka labor, which they rightly saw was incompatible with the white standard of living and with free democratic ideals. Also, the rates of disease and death soon became deplorable…

The truth was that history, the history of the West Indies and the southern United States, was repeating itself. The island continent, which might have remained a protected human laboratory for the white races, had opened its doors to malaria, filariasis, hookworm, leprosy, and other forms of tropical disease, altogether the whites brought some 46,000 or 47,000 Kanakas to Australia. In addition, by 1887 60,000 persons, or one-fifteenth of the entire Australian population, were Chinese. The unique feature of Australian history is that the young Australian nation saw the dangers to the economic status and health of her citizens and carried out a long and difficult purification, despite the fight waged by north Queensland for the Kanakas and by the British government for the Chinese. (Price 1939: 60–1)

These sentiments are underpinned by the context of 'racial purity' subscribed to in Australia, attributed by Powell (1988: 26) to roots in 'Aboriginal ethnocide, the tragic history of the persecution suffered by Chinese goldminers, strenuous efforts of the growing union movement to destroy cheap labour competition, and the popular desire to deny entrance to people from countries with very low standards of living'. The debate over the expansion of Melanesian labour as against white labour for the development of sugar cane growing in Queensland was part of a wider issue which led ultimately to the adoption of a White Australia Policy through the agency of the Immigration Restriction Act of 1901.

The indentured labour migration within the British empire that had started in 1863 with migration from Pacific islands to Queensland continued until the first decade of the twentieth century when immigration was controlled by Australia, but larger movements involved migration from India:

a regulated system for recruiting indentured Indian labourers to work under white supervision on sugar, coffee, tea, cotton and rubber plantations in the West Indies, British Guiana, Mauritius, Fiji, Malaya and Natal had been developed since the 1830s. Less formally, many others migrated to Ceylon and Burma. Indentured labourers also worked in the coal mines and as domestic servants in Natal, and more were also brought into East Africa from 1896 (mainly from the Punjab) to construct and maintain the Uganda Railway (in aggregate nearly 40,000 by 1922). (Constantine 1999: 179)

The flow of emigrant contract labour from India to Fiji was substantially influenced by world sugar prices and the consequent demand for labour, mainly by large sugar companies such as the Colonial Sugar Refining Company, whose requests for specified numbers of labourers were sent via the Fiji government to the Fiji Government Emigration agent in India, and there were also agencies in Calcutta and Madras, and large numbers of sub-agents in and beyond those cities. Permission had to be granted by sub-magistrates. Formal processes to recruit labourers for work in Fiji and other overseas colonies were imposed because of the unpopularity of emigration from India. This in turn related to peasant inertia, communal and religious constraints, and the problem of breaking caste rules by emigrating, and fear of the unknown and of forcible conversion to Christianity (Gillion 1956: 140, 141–2).

Fluctuation in emigrant numbers was influenced by the state of crop harvests, with the fear of starvation, for example, generating much emigration from North India. Other economic and employment factors in different areas included the decline in emigration from Bengal and Bihar because of the attraction of railway construction and other infrastructural activities. In the south of India migration patterns from Madras were different. These included the easier recruitment of men, but not women, less reluctance to leave home for work farther afield, and a longer tradition of emigration to Ceylon, Burma and Malaya (Gillion 1956: 144, 149).

Non-economic factors promoting emigration to Fiji included a desire to escape the constraints of family and village community, or in the case of criminals to escape police attention, or because of family contacts in Fiji. Although the Fiji government specified the number of women to be recruited for emigration from India, in order to have a basis for family life among immigrants, the women made up about 44 per cent of emigrants from Calcutta and about 40 per cent from Madras, but it was rare for whole families to emigrate. There is strong evidence that there was resort to the abduction of women to give a better gender balance to migrant numbers, and this was also promoted by the higher fees paid to sub-agents for women emigrants. Gillion (1956: 149–50) notes, however, that 'While such practices were widespread, it is probable that the majority of female emigrants had already adopted independent lives. They were, for instance, widows or women who had been deserted or were escaping from bad husbands or tyrannical mothers-in-law. Emigration must have seemed to some of them an honourable alternative to a life of prostitution – a fresh start.'

Many of the people recruited for emigration to Fiji tended, not surprisingly, to be from agricultural castes, but there were also significant numbers from higher castes, the latter because of both better physical condition and also greater degrees of indebtedness in hard times. The age range of recruited emigrants was predominantly between 16 and 25. Although their general intention was to return to India, many of them stayed in Fiji where they enjoyed better living conditions.

There was also emigration from India to numerous other British colonies. Mauritius, a British colony ceded by France in 1814, experienced extensive migration from India from 1834, the year of emancipation, with the need for a labour force to replace the slaves used in the sugar plantations that had originally been established by the French East India Company in the early eighteenth century (Gillion 1956: 151).

Christopher (1992) has shown that immigration from India to Mauritius fluctuated, with peaks in 1843, 1859 and 1865, with a decline until 1910, when immigration was abolished. About 450,000 people migrated to Mauritius from India in the period 1834 to 1910. As elsewhere, the mixing of populations was a question of increasing interest to the controlling colonial power. The population data is provided by the Blue Books which from the 1830s use a three-fold classification, as elsewhere in other European colonies, of European, Free Black and Slave. This changed to a combined European and Free Black category and an Apprentices – freed slaves – category, to which was added a separate Indian category for the first census in 1846. An Indian–Mauritian category was introduced in 1891 to include those born on Mauritius. There were major problems through racial mixture, so that 'the distinction between European and Free Coloured was thought to be so blurred on the island that its reintroduction was not considered. As a result the category "general" was adopted to cover the physically diverse population ranging from European to African in origin, but which was largely French-speaking and Roman Catholic in faith' (Christopher 1992: 58).

The 1901 census 'marked a significant attempt to introduce a more systematic racial, or physical anthropological, classification at the insistence of the Secretary of State for the Colonies. The attempted disaggregation of the General category into: 1. European, whites, mixed and coloured; 2. African; 3. Chinese; was not a success' (Christopher 1992: 58). A more appropriate, self-identified ethnic group classification was not introduced until 1962. The total population of Mauritius increased from 96,945 in 1830 to 180,823 in 1851, 359,984 in 1881, 378,195 in 1901, 501,415 in 1952, and 826,199 in 1972.

The distinctiveness (relative to other European imperial migrations) of the indentured labour migrations, which were essential parts of the economic development of plantations and infrastructural developments in the tropical regions of the British empire, has been contested. Northrup suggests that in spite of kidnapping and other forms of illegal practice for labour recruitment, the process of recruiting indentured labourers was not, as some have asserted, akin to the 'recruitment' processes of the slave trade. He points out that most of the indentured labourers migrated from free choice, albeit to harsh conditions, and that 'theirs was less a new system of slavery than an old system of free labour revived to suit imperial needs in an industrial age'. Within the British imperial system, the rates of continued residence of these labourers and their rates of return to their home countries varied by time and place, and were influenced by, for example, white preference policies in the Transvaal and Australia that forced a high rate of return, as opposed to more liberal policies that enabled the settlement of labourers from Africa in the West Indies, and from India in Natal, British Guiana and Fiji (Northrup 1999: 95–6).

Cost factors influenced the distinction between indentured labour migration from less developed regions in the British empire to the growing plantation economies of tropical regions, in contrast to the bulk of migration in the British empire in the nineteenth century which was to countries in temperate latitudes where a relatively high standard of living could be sought, such as North America. The encouragement of white European settlement further afield required government subsidy of the cost of long-distance sea travel, and was facilitated by the preference of recipient countries for white immigrants.

The conditions in which migrants travelled to their destinations improved greatly with the introduction of larger steam-powered ships, and with better medical facilities and supervision on the ships, though passengers in the tropics, for example those travelling from India to the Caribbean, experienced higher death rates through disease up to about 1875. The system of indentured labour had provided essential support for the growing plantation economies of the British empire, but this phase of development ended by about 1920, on account of white preference policies, the sizes of European immigrant labour forces, and the decline of the sugar plantations, plus the banning, under nationalist pressure, of the indentured labour trade by the Indian government in 1916 (Northrup 1999: 97, 99).

The population of New Zealand at the time of the Treaty of Waitangi in 1841 has been estimated at *c.* 70–90,000 Maori and 2,000 Europeans, but as a consequence of the treaty and the perceived availability of land for settlement the European population had by 1858 overtaken that of the Maori, with *c.* 59,000 against *c.* 56,000. By 1896 the Maori population was 42,000, and the European 701,000 (Dalziel 1999: 581–2). This massive change in the sizes of the two groups of people drastically changed the balances of power and had a cultural impact. Another significant feature of New Zealand's demography in the late nineteenth and early twentieth centuries was the fact that although European men outnumbered women,

New Zealand was always promoted as a colony for women. European settlement coincided with the full flowering of the domestic ideology that emphasized woman's role within the home and community, and her moral influence … Propaganda was designed to attract women migrants and women were offered cheap and free passages and domestic work on arrival. Women saw themselves as partners in the colonial enterprise. (Dalziel 1999: 582)

Labour migration in South Africa

The binding of the mineral resources of colonial southern Africa into the world capitalist economy from the late nineteenth century had profound effects on labour migration and the living conditions of migrant labourers. Gold was discovered in central Transvaal in 1886, which, as Crush (1986: 27) has described, 'inaugurated an industrial revolution which was to transform the face of the sub-continent ... Thirty years after the first discoveries this "world the mine owners made" was the site of sixty working mines and the residence of a quarter of a million people. Of these some 200,000 were black migrant workers drawn from throughout the region.'

The system, which had a voracious appetite for the bodies and lives of African migrants, involved labourers moving from rural to industrial areas under the influence of market forces, while at the same time providing them with some measure of choice of work location (Crush 1986: 28). Crush's study of the migrant labour force moving from Swaziland westwards to the Witwatersrand identifies a beginning in 1898–9, promoted by famine, locust invasions and a rinderpest epidemic, followed by a period of both coercion and volition after the Anglo-Boer War, when migration increased rapidly, notably in 1907–8, because of 'the combined pressures of general economic depression, colonial coercion and chiefly inaction' (Crush 1986: 32).

The mines of the Witwatersrand tapped labour forces from a wide area, including Nyasaland, Northern Rhodesia, Tanganyika and Mozambique, together with many from the High Commission Territories. Their pay and conditions of work contrasted markedly with those of white British and South African technologists and managers (Constantine 1999: 180). Pollock and Agnew have estimated an African labour force of about 100,000 in the Rand gold mines before the Anglo-Boer War, a figure that was reached again after the repatriation by 1910 of 50,000 Chinese labourers brought in to make up African labour shortages after the war. Many of the African labourers were recruited by the Witwatersrand Native Labour Association and the Native Recruiting Corporation Limited (Pollock and Agnew 1963: 186).

Labour forces and labour migration in the French empire

France's first period of imperial involvement lasted from the sixteenth to the eighteenth century, during which most activity was focused on North America and the Caribbean. The second period of French imperial development, which focused on Africa and Indo-China, but also included the Caribbean and parts of the Pacific and India, began in 1830 with the conquest of Algiers, and accelerated during the period of European high imperialism from the 1870s onwards. At its zenith the French colonial empire included Algeria, Tunisia, Morocco, French West Africa, French Equatorial Africa, French Indo-China, Madagascar and the Comoros Islands in the Indian Ocean, French Guiana, five coastal enclaves in India, and, in the Pacific, the Society, Austral, Marquesa, Tuamotu and Gambier island groups (with Tahiti having the largest French population), together with a number of islands in the Caribbean. At the end of the First World War there were added the League of Nations mandates for Syria and Lebanon. By the start of the Second World War the French empire had a population of 69 million, and a total area of 12 million km² (Heffernan 1995a: 33–8).

As in other European countries, there were complex debates in France on reasons for and ideologies and models of colonisation and emigration. These included historic Roman models for settlement of retired soldiers in North Africa; the use of penal settlement to rid the metropole of unwanted paupers and dissidents; colonisation as part of a positive *mission civilisatrice*; and as a geopolitical device for advancing France's standing in Europe. France's low birth rates and fears about underpopulation, the limited extent of the worst forms of poverty, and levels of access to land, all reduced the push factors in overseas migration that operated more powerfully in other European countries, and frustrated French implementation of migration policies, but nonetheless resettlement schemes operated in French North Africa and New Caledonia.

Against pro-colonial settlement arguments there was a counterview that such a policy would have a harmful effect by depleting labour resources at home:

Those advocating colonial emigration often clashed with economic imperialists who sought a commercially profitable empire based on trade. From their perspective, colonies should be seen in purely economic terms. The use of scarce European labour to develop colonies was useless. This could easily be undertaken by indigenous people under European guidance. Civilian colonization was at best a diversion and at worst a costly drain on metropolitan and colonial resources. (Heffernan 1995a: 37)

Not all emigrants to French colonies were French. In the Maghrib colonies, there were migrants from southern European countries where there was overpopulation and poverty. Thus in 1886 there were 219,000 French citizens in Algeria and 211,000 people from other European countries, notably Spain (160,000), Italy (35,000 in 1886), and Malta (11,000 at the end of the 1890s) (Aldrich 1996: 144–5). There were, however, tensions between these immigrant groups. Aldrich (1996: 145) states that 'The French looked down on other migrants, Italians and Spaniards jostled each other for status, and Maltese remained at the bottom of the European hierarchy. Jews, who totalled 35,000 in 1830, were as poor as most of the Arabs and Europeans, but roundly despised by both groups.'

Compared with other European countries, notably Britain, France was less effective in the promotion of emigration from the metropole and settlement in imperial territories overseas. In the period of European high imperialism after *c.* 1870, the main settlement projects were in Algeria and New Caledonia. By a variety of processes, 170,000 Europeans had settled in Algeria by 1856, 630,000 by 1900, and 950,000 by 1936, compared with an indigenous population of about 4 million. In Tunisia there was an indigenous population of about 10 million, compared to a maximum French immigrant population of 10,000 in 1911 and 500,000 by the middle 1950s, most of the immigrant population being located in coastal towns (Heffernan 1995a: 35).

The development of French settlement in North Africa from the 1830s greatly modified existing population patterns and movements. A general feature of many colonial settlements in lowland, desert and mountain areas was their impact on nomadic and transhumant migration.

Although French policy in the period *c.* 1830 to 1880 was for intensification of settlement in Algeria, great difficulties were experienced by French settlers in working agricultural land themselves because of unfamiliarity with environmental and cultivation conditions, and they had to make use of indigenous labour (MacMaster 1995: 190). Before 1880 the removal of nomadic tribes from the plains, forcing them to work as sharecroppers on poorer land, had been part of French colonisation policy.

After 1880 there was a distinct move away from a farming economy, with mostly small settler farms, to one based on the development of large estates and more commercial production. 'Europeans in Algeria increased their lands from 765,000 hectares in 1870 to 1,912,000 in 1900 and 3,028,000 in 1954. Vine cultivation, which was the motor of the colonial economy (40 per cent of exports by value in 1913) increased from 40,000 hectares in 1880 to 400,000 in 1940 and was ten times more labour intensive than cereals' (MacMaster 1995: 190).

Parallel developments in Tunisia and Morocco occurred mainly in the early twentieth century. The two main types of labour migration associated with commercial farming in North Africa were seasonal migration – mainly by sedentary peasant Berbers from the interior mountain zones; and permanent labour migration by indigenous peoples from colonially dispossessed lands in the northern Maghrib to the periphery of the new large estates, 'where they constituted a reserve of cheap labour which was close enough to be hired on a daily basis' (MacMaster 1995: 193).

Labour migration in French North Africa was closely regulated, partly because of fear of indigenous insurrection, and of secessionist movements among Europeans. Regulation increased after 1880, when there was a labour shortage in the viticultural estates in Algeria. The establishment of the Native Code laws in 1881 mandated passes and the requirement of permission for migrants into and out of Algeria, and the laws also granted powers of summary seizure and fining to local magistrates. Travel permits were granted to seasonal labourers from the mountains, but denied to Algerians on the colonised plains so that they could be used as cheap labour for work on farms and roads.

In the early twentieth century, migration from the Maghrib to France increased to meet demands for labour in Marseilles, Paris and the coal-mining region of northern France. These numbers increased rapidly during and after the First World War, with large numbers of Algerians, Tunisians and Moroccans emigrating to be part either of the army or of the broader labour force. Complaints from French settlers about labour shortages in the Maghrib were not always justified in fact, and by the mid-1930s the rapid rate of increase of the indigenous population of Algeria had in any event solved the problem, at least from the settlers' perspective. The population increase in Algeria also increased rural and urban poverty and unemployment *c.* 1935–54, and in 1954 the outbreak of anti-colonial revolution began a phase of insensitive compulsory resettlement of about half of the Algerian rural population (MacMaster 1995: 193–4).

From 1864 New Caledonia in the Pacific was a major prison colony for France, with the 1901 census showing 10,500 convicts in the population, some convicted for minor crimes, others for political reasons. Participants in the insurrection at Kabyle in North Africa in 1870 were deported there, as were 4,000 participants in the Paris Commune who were sent to New Caledonia for penal resettlement after 1870–1. The island's population of French settlers had reached 54,000 by 1983 (Aldrich 1996: 146–7; Heffernan 1995a: 35). From the 1890s failure to attract voluntary settlers to New Caledonia led to the recruitment of contract labourers from Japan, Vietnam and Java.

In Indo-China there was a very much smaller immigrant French population, the total for the whole area being just under 5,000 at the end of the nineteenth century, the majority based in Saigon, Hanoi, Haiphong, and Phnom-Penh, though numbers were periodically increased by the arrival of French troops: for example, in 1888 there was a total of about

16,800 French soldiers in Tonkin, Annam, Cochin China and Cambodia (Heffernan 1995a: 35; Aldrich 1996: 148). The French population of French Indo-China at the end of the nineteenth century has been estimated as 0.18 per cent of the total population (Elson 1999: 179).

The French sub-Saharan African colonies had quite small European populations: in 1931 French Equatorial Africa had an overall population of 3.19 million, including 4,657 Europeans, and for French West Africa the equivalent figures were 16,078 and 14.57 million (Kuczynski 1937: 18).

Migration and the German colonies

Germany became an independent state in 1871, but before then there were, notwithstanding the diversity of political units, various 'ways in which global landscapes, real and imagined, affected the constructions of German national identity before unification' (Naranch 2005: 22–3). Emigration from Germany in the nineteenth and early twentieth centuries was partially rooted in concerns about the nature of the new nation-state; the consequences of homeland overpopulation; the dilution of German character through migration to areas of heterogeneous European migrant populations (as opposed to areas of focused German migration) and thus the possible dilution of German culture; and fantasies about ideal German settlement communities in exotic locations and their roles in developing colonial territories and their inhabitants. There were often, however, major differences between the expectations and images of the pre-colonial German period and the realities of its attempted colonial activity, what has been called 'the contrast between pre-colonial Germany's fantasy worlds and its modest, failure-prone experiments in overseas imperial conquest' (Naranch 2005: 24).

An important aspect of Germany's history of emigration relates to a much wider context than numbers and discrete sets of motives. Naranch draws attention to the work of Susanne Zantop and others on the fantasies of colonial conquest in Germany and the way in which that introduces a broader context for analysis:

By focussing on the historical processes and discursive patterns that helped shape Germans' perception of cultural difference and imperial power, practitioners of German colonial studies treat the period of formal colonial rule as an important episode in a larger story of social modernization, cultural change, and international conflict rather than a self-contained account of conservative social imperialism, middle-class aggressive nationalism, and short-lived colonial expansion that ended in failure during the First World War. (Naranch 2005: 22)

This wider context includes possible forward links between colonialism and National Socialism and its grievous impact.

Emigration from Germany in the nineteenth century was a concern not just for administrators but also for many individual families who struggled to explain why it was happening and what might be done to conserve a sense of national unity at home and maintain strong links with German communities overseas. From the mid-nineteenth century positive images of a German diaspora were presented by colonisation societies and by illustrated scientific magazines such as *Globus: Illustrierte Zeitschrift für Länder- und Völkerkunde*, published from 1862. *Globus* was similar in some respects to the publications and journals of contemporary European geographical societies, but with a stronger colonial advocacy. It was a middle-class publication that used the images and ideas of the 'German abroad' to promote familiarity and difference, the investigation of 'the familiar contours of the national Self, while exploring the strange but alluring landscape of the foreign Other' (Naranch 2005: 27).

In the period *c.* 1849–71 much attention was focused on the realities and possibilities of German migration to the Americas, to the Danube basin and to southern Russia, and on ideas of more formal links with the homeland. There was a significant semiotic change in terminology, with the first general term for emigrant (*Auswanderer*) being replaced by the more culturally and place specific term *Auslanddeutsche* (the German abroad), a term much used in literature aimed at the middle classes, encouraging thoughts of a more effective German presence overseas and stronger links between diaspora Germans and the metropole. These are what Naranch has identified as 'calls for the worldwide unification of the German cultural diaspora, the *Auslandsdeutschtum*' (Naranch 2005: 25–7, 35).

In a study of German colonial activity in Cameroon, David Simo has drawn attention to the contrasts and conflicts between German policy and practice for colonial development. In spite of the humanitarian principles enunciated at the Berlin Conference of 1884–5, the details of German impacts on Cameroon show that, at the beginning of the twentieth century,

the practice of colonial rule in Cameroon and the other German colonies had been contrary to the long-proclaimed goals of colonization and even to various decrees, regulations and laws that aimed to protect the natives from colonists' arbitrary practices… In the years just before the First World War, the chancellor and Kaiser Wilhelm II disregarded petitions from the Duala people concerning their forced removal from their land, in violation of signed treaties… As in Kafka's penal colony, colonial jurisdiction introduced procedures and penalties that were familiar to Europe but belonged to its past. (Simo 2005: 109–10)

A new German colonial policy was introduced through the newly founded Colonial Office in 1907 (replacing the Colonial Section of the Foreign Office), notably by its first director Bernhard Dernberg, a banker. He sought to improve the profitability of German colonies by the efficient use of natural resources and better treatment of indigenous peoples, and visited East Africa and South-West Africa, as well as the United States (to look at methods of growing cotton for possible use in Africa) (Henderson 1993: 100). In 1907 he had also appointed 'Professor Hans Meyer to take charge of a new geographical commission in the Colonial Office which was given the task of undertaking research into the geography of the overseas possessions. By 1914 the commission had sent out ten scientific expeditions to the colonies' (Henderson 1993: 103). Meyer privately funded a chair in colonial geography in Berlin in 1911. The period 1907 to 1914 was characterised by what Henderson (1993) has described as a 'policy of enlightened imperialism' attempted by Dernberg and his successors. In spite of the draconian measures taken to suppress indigenous uprisings, there were, it is claimed, signs of increasing concern at the health, welfare and treatment of indigenous people by German administrators (Henderson 1993: 114), though these claims have been strongly contested. An alternative view is that Dernberg's apparent concern for indigenous welfare, for example, was 'nothing more than an attempt to find a solution to the labour question which would serve the interests of monopoly capitalism more satisfactorily', and Dernberg was supportive of policies of expropriation of land and the imposition of ruinous taxes (Stoecker 1986g: 200).

The limited extent of German migration to its overseas colonial territories can be seen in estimates of colonial populations. Townsend's (1941: 177) estimates of African white population numbers against indigenous population numbers in 1913–14 are set out in Table 3.2.

The only German colony to experience significant immigration from Europe was German South-West Africa. 'The German colonial movement thought a golden future was in store for the colony and issued a lot of propaganda to that effect. This resulted in a modest amount of immigration on the part of German cattle breeders', but the optimism was broken by the Herero war – 'one of the most brutal wars in colonial history' (Wesseling 2004: 186).

Italian migration

Italy had more emigration in the period 1876–1976 than any other European country, the total being estimated at 26 million. The reasons

Table 3.2 The population of German colonial territories in Africa, 1913–14

Colony	Indigenous population	White population
German East Africa	7,645,770	5,336
South West Africa	80,556	14,830
Cameroon	3,326,132	1,871
Togoland	1,031,978	368

for this emigration were complex (Vecoli 1995: 114). Vecoli has identified three phases of Italian migration:

First, the classical period, 1876–1914, during which over half of the total emigration took place; second, the period of low emigration, 1915–1945; and third, the period of renewed migration, 1946–1976, which accounted for 25 per cent of the total. Of the 26 million emigrants between 1876 and 1976, some 52 per cent migrated to European countries (13.5 million), 44 per cent to the Americas (6 million to North America, 90 per cent of these to the USA, and 5 million to South America), 2 per cent to Africa and 1.5 per cent to Oceania, mainly Australia. (Vecoli 1995: 114)

One can see from these figures just how relatively small Italian migration was to her short-lived colonies in Africa, though the figures do not include temporary migration of military and administrative personnel, for example. The economic crisis of the 1880s influenced an emigration of over 1.3 million, partly conditioned by land poverty and by the advent of the devastating phylloxera virus in the vineyards.

Portuguese colonial migration

The size of the European population in Portuguese Africa in 1911 has been estimated at about 20,000, the majority living in Angola. The figure increased to 50,000 in *c*. 1935, but more dramatically to 126,000 by 1950 and 495,000 by 1970 as a result of an increase in immigration, including migrants redirected away from Brazil by the Portuguese government (Christopher 1984: 133).

Before 1850 the main component of Portuguese colonial migration was the slave trade from Africa to the Americas, with Mozambique, Angola and Guinea as major sources of slaves, and São Tomé, Principe and Cape Verde as transit points for these pitiable human cargoes (Ishemo 1995: 162). Coffee and cocoa plantations were introduced on a small scale at the beginning of the nineteenth century to São Tomé and Principe, two small islands in the Gulf of Guinea off the coast of Gabon, which had in effect been in Portugal's hands since the late fifteenth century, and where slaves had been imported to work sugar plantations early in the sixteenth century.

Notwithstanding the reduction in transatlantic slave trading from 1855 to 1875, increases in coffee and cocoa production were achieved with the use of slave labour. The importation and use of forced labour in all the Portuguese colonies was continued in the 1850s and 1860s under the guise of a new supposed status of *liberto*. This was a status bestowed in Mozambique, Cape Verde, São Tomé, Principe and Angola, in 1854, 1858, 1859, and 1869 (Ishemo 1995: 162). As Clarence-Smith (1979: 38) has stated, with reference to a decree relating to slaves in Angola in 1869, 'The distinction between a slave and a *liberto* was a hard one to make. Effectively, a *liberto* was no more than a slave who was guaranteed that he would be free by 1879', and because many understood that it meant instant liberation, it was 'followed by a wave of "insubordination" among the servile population of the south'.

In spite of the official abolition of slavery by Portugal in 1879, the slave trade continued, and slaves were illegally imported from Angola to work cocoa and coffee plantations in São Tomé, and sent from Mozambique to Réunion (a French colony) into the 1890s, in the guise of indentured labourers (Ishemo 1995: 162). From 1860 a policy of using indentured labour from various Portuguese colonies, notably the Cape Verde islands, was instrumental in sustaining and developing the plantation economy of São Tomé at times, for example in the early 1830s and mid-1860s, when there was major loss of population through famine. But slavery in one form or another was in effect the basis of much of the Portuguese colonial economy until about 1911, notably in Angola, São Tomé and Principe.

In the late nineteenth and early twentieth centuries the combination of a developing plantation economy, together with the construction of roads and railways, and heavy taxes levied on peasant farmers in the form of money and labour led to the extensive use of forced labour, notably in Mozambique and Angola. Because taxation was normally higher than wages, 'Taxation, therefore, was an instrument of forced labour. It created and reproduced conditions for labour migration and seasonal labour. When and how this labour was exploited depended on the level of capitalist development' (Ishemo 1995: 163).

Additional reasons for an increase in population migration in Africa were the developments in mining and in capitalist agriculture in Southern Africa, notably the labour requirements of the Transvaal gold mines and the mines and plantations of Southern Rhodesia, for which labour was provided from southern Mozambique, and by the beginning of the twentieth century from the whole of Mozambique. Restrictions on the areas from which labour could be recruited in Mozambique were agreed in 1913.

Linked to the export of labour was the use of Mozambican ports and railways by South Africa and Rhodesian capital. The Portuguese state benefited from fees paid for every worker recruited, and deferred wages paid in gold bullion by South Africa and sterling by Southern Rhodesia, but reimbursed in colonial *escudos* to returning workers after deducting tax. (Ishemo 1995: 163–4)

The advance of Portuguese capital investment in cocoa plantations in São Tomé and Principe between 1880 and 1910 was supported by the export of what were in effect slave labourers from Angola, but protest brought a substitution by labour from other Portuguese African territories. The forcible transportation of slave labour continued into the twentieth century, linked to the intensification of agricultural production on plantation *latifundia* on São Tomé and in Angola. Estimates suggest forced labour transfers to São Tomé of 80,000 from 1903 to 1970 (Ishemo 1995: 163–4).

Dutch colonial migration

The Dutch empire was mainly in South-East Asia, with Java as its main settlement base. Although there was severe famine in 1849–50 in central Java, the population of that island, according to Wesseling (2004: 108–9), 'grew quickly, rising from 4.5 million in 1815 to 12 million in 1850 and from nearly 20 million in 1880 to 29 million in 1900'. His figures are greatly different from those of Boomgaard (2002), who estimates the population of Java in 1850 as between 10 million and 13.8 million, and in 1900 as between 28.4 million and 29 million. His estimates for the population of the Indonesian archipelago are between 18.3 million and 25.8 million in 1850, and between 41.8 and 44.6 million in 1900, and for the Outer Islands or Provinces (Sumatra, Kalimantan, Sulawesi, the Maluku Islands and the lesser Sunda Islands) 8–12 million in 1850, and 13.4–15.6 million in 1900.

The European population in Indonesia showed a marked increase 'rising from 42,800 in 1860 to 44,200 in 1870 and again from 56,600 in 1880 to 90,800 in 1900. The number of Europeans in Indonesia more than doubled in the space of 30 years' (Wesseling, 2004: 218). By 1900 there were significant numbers of Dutch, European and Chinese in the larger cities, notably Batavia, which had 30,000 Chinese and 11,000 Europeans in a total population of 150,000 (Wesseling 2004: 218). There was a major gender imbalance within the European immigrant populations in the Dutch East Indies up to the mid-nineteenth century, when most of the Europeans immigrants were men, estimated as 43,000 in 1860, and a much smaller number of 1,000 women (Imhoff 2004: 338). This imbalance led to some inter-marriage with local women and to concubinage, but from the later nineteenth century there was an increase in the number of European women migrating to the East Indies, so that the European man/woman ratio was about 2:1. At the same time there was a tendency for more permanent settlement by Europeans, of whom there were about 91,000 in 1900, 170,000 in 1930, and 240,000 by 1942 (Imhoff 2004: 339). The overall trend reported by Imhoff (2004: 342) was that:

before World War I the migration to the Dutch East Indies consisted mainly of men who frequently came to the Dutch East Indies on a temporary assignment (either military or civil) and returned thereafter (the so-called *movers*), [but] *after* World War I the settlement in the Dutch East Indies became more and more of a 'permanent' character, with increasing family reunification and family formation migration, including also (young) married women (the so-called *stayers*).

Disease and health

An important aspect of interaction in European colonies between people and the challenging physical environments was the encounter by colonisers and colonised alike with tropical diseases, and also the attempts made to apply developing Western scientific and medical knowledge, sometimes linked with indigenous knowledge and practices, to the improvement of survival and living conditions. The history of medicine in European colonies and the metropoles is a rapidly developing topic with a vast literature, and only selected aspects will be considered here.

Recent evaluations of the links between science and empire have emphasised the changes in concept from core–periphery models, such as Basalla's three-stage model of Western imperial science (Basalla 1967: 616–22), to more complex and sophisticated models that accommodate the experiences of particular local interactions between colonisers and colonised. These include the difference between scientific independence as experienced in settler colonies such as Australia and those of tropical Africa; the concept of a 'moving metropolis'; the perception of science as a tool of cultural imperialism; the nuances of the spatial impacts of imperialism, including mapping; colonisation through knowledge and control of mind and body; interactions on disease, sexual health and gender identities; local adaptations of attempted transplantations of science; the effects of colonial expansion on botanical transfers; and the development of new ideas on medicine and environments (Harrison 2005).

MacLeod (2000: 5) has emphasised that:

spectacularly in India and Africa, the level of intellectual interaction between ruler and ruled, expert and populace, was vital, everyday and decisive. The ensuing relation was one of interdependence. Western science was, above all, a purveyor of solutions to the needs of imperial governments; at the same time, it could be, and was, assimilated and transformed by local and indigenous peoples into a body of knowledge for local empowerment.

A significant historiographical route in the history of colonialism, changing environments and interactions of disease and medicine, started with the concept of the 'Columbian exchange', which included the transfer of European pathogens to the peoples of the New Worlds of the Americas, Asia and the Pacific who lacked immunity and were devastated by them. To these processes was added the transfer of African diseases such as yellow fever and malaria to the Americas through the slave trade across the Atlantic Ocean from the sixteenth to the nineteenth century. This, according to Crosby, was one aspect of an even wider process of 'ecological imperialism', which included the transfer of plants and animals around the globe to (and to a lesser extent from) places of colonial settlement (Crosby 1972, 1986). John MacKenzie critically claims that in these and other works Crosby 'painted a picture of organisms of all sorts being marshalled, consciously and unconsciously... Mammals, birds, freshwater fish, insects, pathogens, trees, plants and weeds set about the creation of neo-Europes, exotic environments comprehensively overlaid with the extensive biota of the new conquerors', also noting that little attention had been paid to Africa, and that 'so little came back' (MacKenzie 1997: 219).

The indigenous populations of early imperial territories had frequently been decimated by introduced diseases and pests from the Old and New Worlds, including smallpox, which continued with devastating effect – for example, on the aboriginal population of Australia from 1789. The same happened with measles in Fiji in 1875 (Pawson 1990: 533). Territories such as Australia, New Zealand and the Pacific islands, were greatly affected by European diseases, to which indigenous inhabitants had no natural resistance, and these differed from parts of Africa and India, for example, where existing diseases were intensified through urbanisation, migration, population concentration through industrialisation, and environmental modification through irrigation schemes, the latter facilitating the spread of malaria. Fieldhouse has stated that 'India was ravaged by cholera (twenty-three million people may have died in epidemics between 1865 and 1949), by the plague (an estimated twelve million victims died in the great pandemic that started in 1896), and by malaria, influenza and tuberculosis', and there were significant increases in Africa from the mid-nineteenth century of sleeping sickness and malaria, and of rinderpest in animals (Fieldhouse 1996: 142). Parts of the European colonies were also affected by world pandemics. The great influenza pandemic of 1918–19, with a death toll of at least 20–30 million, spread from the United States to Europe, then Asia, North Africa and Australia, with a very much larger death toll than that associated with the normal regional morbidity rates from endemic influenza (Killingray 1994: 59–87).

Most of the instances of the devastating effects of Old World diseases on 'New World' populations were the accidental outcomes (rather than deliberate intentions) of the mixing of contrasting cultures. Diseases such as smallpox devastated the populations of what should be seen as sophisticated and politically efficient indigenous societies, and this process was a key factor of European expansion in the Americas, Australasia and Oceania, where the disease environments created by Europeans favoured the invader, as opposed to Africa where the environment was often (but not always) either equal or favoured the indigenous populations. The Polynesians in Hawaii – a sophisticated and well-organised society – initially resisted the first invasions by Europeans, but later were devastated by smallpox in the mid-nineteenth century when shipping and therefore access became quicker. Their restricted gene pool also made the Hawaiian population susceptible to leprosy (Hansen's disease). The Hawaiian islands had suffered from European diseases since 1778: 'when Captain Cook's ships loosed syphilis and gonorrhoea on the islands, the inhabitants had suffered one assault after another. New sicknesses broke out with awful regularity, to tear through the fragile brush of a population with little or no natural immunity. Never had Hawaiians encountered even "children's diseases" such as measles, mumps, and chicken pox, much less influenza or leprosy' (Tayman 2006: 24–5). Tayman estimates that within two decades ten thousand people on Oahu had died from venereal disease, and in 1805 an epidemic of typhoid fever struck 'killing more than five thousand and decimating the army of King Kamehameha I', followed in turn by influenza in 1826, which also had devastating effects in the year

1848 (Tayman 2006: 25). Smallpox reached Honolulu in February 1853, and in spite of the availability of vaccines the disease killed between ten and fifteen thousand people in just under a year.

Leprosy

One of the most enigmatic diseases to affect Hawaii and its neighbouring islands was leprosy (Hansen's disease). It had been known in the islands since the late eighteenth century, and could have been brought there from any number of sources. As Tayman (2006: 21) puts it:

By 1840 a thousand Hawaiians had sailed to sea on foreign ships, bound for ports in the Azores, Malaysia, the West Indies, and the southern coasts of India or Africa, all areas where leprosy was endemic. Any one of them might have returned home infected. Just as probably, the disease might have entered aboard a British whaling ship, or on one of the hundreds of American vessels that anchored off the islands' two principal ports in the years following the opening of the Japanese and Arctic whaling grounds.

Leprosy was historically a disease around which were constructed strategies of containment, mainly through stigmatisation, marginalisation and confinement of the sufferers in isolated places, as in the case of the Hawaiians who from 1866 were exiled to the settlement of Kalaupapa on the island of Molokai (Tayman 2006).

By the end of the nineteenth century strategies for containing leprosy were part of wider imperial processes for medical and social control (Worboys 2000), processes which were frequently contested between the propagators of Western and indigenous medicine, and which also changed as understanding of the causes of and remedies for many diseases changed with scientific discovery and broader cultural understanding. This was also a time when the acceleration of European imperialism and changes in medical science produced new representations of the tropics, of their links with temperate metropolitan regions, and of the roles of 'degenerative' diseases such as leprosy. This was a 'period in which knowledge of the tropical world received institutional expression in the formation of new disciplines, such as tropical medicine, which were closely allied with the requirements of colonial policy, including newly revived questions of colonisation' (Driver and Martins 2005: 17).

Edmond, in studies of the medical and cultural histories of leprosy, has shown that it was included in the late nineteenth century in the new constructs of tropical medicine, which 'as a category ignored diseases like measles and influenza that made terrible inroads into indigenous populations and concentrated instead on the diseases believed to be specific to tropical climates and to which Europeans were especially vulnerable' (Edmond 2005: 181; 2006). Uncertainty about the causes of leprosy and fears of a physical and moral degeneration through contagion, especially the fear of further spread to Europe, had led to various strategies of containment, including the creation of leper 'colonies', frequently on islands, in many overseas territories of European imperial powers such as India, Australia, New Zealand, South Africa (Robben Island), the Seychelles, French Guiana, the Belgian Congo, French Equatorial Africa and French Indo-China. Hawaii, an independent state until 1898, was severely affected by leprosy and other diseases, as shown above (Edmond 2006). Leprosy was not in fact solely a tropical disease, having long been evidenced in Europe, and 'was as much a European as a tropical disease and was feared to be returning to metropolitan centres' (Edmond 2005: 183).

The confirmation by Edward Hansen, working in Norway in the 1870s, of the *Mycobacterium leprae* as the cause of leprosy slowly changed its comprehension and treatment. In the 1860s an investigation by the Royal College of Physicians in London 'decided that the disease was hereditary, noncontagious and did not require segregation' (Worboys 2000: 213). Hansen's work, however, restored the concept of leprosy as contagious, but with weaker infectivity than previously thought. The Royal Commission on Leprosy in India of 1891 accepted it as a contagious disease, but 'decided against strict segregation because the infectivity of the disease was relatively weak. Already in India, leprosy had become a focus of medical missionary activity. Its Biblical associations gave it particular significance for Christians, while the perceived risks of caring for lepers offered opportunities to show dedication to the cause, if not martyrdom' (Worboys 2000: 213–14).

New concepts of the management of leprosy included parallels made with the treatment of tuberculosis – isolation and improvements in diet and living conditions. New technical discoveries included the use of a derivative of chaulmoogra oil, promoted by V. G. Heiser and L. Rogers who worked in the Philippines and India (Worboys 2000: 215). Worboys points also to 'the strength of research in the colonies, while the exchange of materials and ideas between the two men and other experts demonstrates the vitality of polycentric colonial research networks. These networks crossed political and geographical boundaries, and showed no evidence of any "tyranny of distance"', and were further evidenced by the foundation in 1923 of the British Empire Leprosy Relief Association (Worboys 2000: 215).

Public health and hygiene

An important factor in evaluating the role of Western colonial medicine, in the nineteenth and early twentieth centuries especially in the tropics, is its general neglect of indigenous medical practices. 'India', says Deepak Kumar, 'was the largest natural disease repository in the British Empire, yet its medical services (particularly the IMS [Indian Medical Service]) were not geared to meet this task. Its primary responsibility was to look after the troops and the European civil population ... Indian medical traditions were completely ignored and the study of indigenous drugs found no place in the medical curriculum of Indian universities' (Kumar 2006: 165–6). The IMS was also criticised for not having taken the opportunity to undertake research on disease in India.

Public health and hygiene policies were part of the imperial armoury for combating disease and poor health in densely populated urban areas. These were normally based on Western experience, practice and culture, with inevitable conflict when such practices were imposed on different cultures in relation, for example, to public hygiene, disease control, the burial of the dead, and attempts at regulating of prostitution. Yeoh (1992; 2003) has demonstrated the British colonial intention in Singapore at the end of the nineteenth century to reduce high mortality rates from tuberculosis, cholera, enteric fever, diarrhoea, smallpox, beriberi and malarial fevers by trying to change those Asiatic, especially Chinese, domestic practices which were deemed to be significant contributory factors, and by the introduction of new public water supplies, sewerage and urban reconstruction schemes. Chinese health and medical provisions, although used as a form of resistance to colonial urban control, were, however, recognised by the British and this gradually led to the advantageous use of these kinds of medicine and health provisions in the solution of urban health problems.

Not surprisingly, many of the early European efforts to control disease in colonies were targeted at Europeans, including military and naval personnel. Gradual progress was made, especially from the mid-nineteenth century, in the recognition and treatment of tropical diseases such as cholera, malaria and yellow fever, and in the remedial use of new botanical discoveries. Extensive studies, notably by Curtin (1989; 1998), have assessed the occurrence, effects and treatment of European troops who were serving in colonial locations. At the beginning of the nineteenth century the death rates of European troops from disease in colonial locations were high, but had declined on average by 90 per cent by 1913 (Curtin 1989: xvii). High death rates of over 100 per thousand had been experienced in the early to mid-nineteenth century, the highest being 483 in Sierra Leone, 170 in the Dutch East Indies, 164.66 in Senegal, 130 in Jamaica, 78.20 in Algeria, 71.41 in Bengal, 16.10 in Canada, and 8.55 in New Zealand. By the period 1909–13 the death rates were 5.56 for British West Africa, 24.40 for French Equatorial Africa, 41.12 for Cameroon, 21.99 for Morocco, 6.39 for the Dutch East Indies, 7.76 for Jamaica, 5.25 for Algeria and Tunisia, and 4.62 for India (Curtin 1989: 7–11). Although the figures reflect deaths both from disease and, directly and indirectly, from military action, the effects of tropical disease are clearly reflected in the first set of figures, and the dramatic improvement in the second. Major contributing factors were improvements in understanding tropical disease, the purification of drinking water (particularly important in relation to the prevention of cholera), better sewage systems, the application of quinine to the treatment of malaria, and the empirical reaction to yellow fever outbreaks by 'flight' – the movement of troops away from the source region.

Revolutionary changes in medicine and hygiene in the last third of the nineteenth century were followed by methods of mosquito eradication to counter yellow fever and malaria, and new prophylactic measures against malaria. Much progress was also made in the reduction of tuberculosis, pulmonary diseases, cholera, intestinal diseases, typhoid fever and venereal disease (Curtin 1989: 80–7).

Disease and war: the Anglo-Boer War 1899–1902

Specific military campaigns of the nineteenth and early twentieth centuries resulted in soldiers and civilians suffering death and injury from war, and also from related diseases, notably typhoid fever. Low-Beer, Smallman-Raynor and Cliff (2004) have shown, for example, that in the Anglo-Boer or South African War of 1899–1902 more than 60 per cent of all deaths from all groups were of refugee–civilians, notably children and women, and that measles was the major cause of death, with typhoid also a major killer. They suggest that 'The South African war and its disease history reflect the changing importance of military and refugee disease in the emergence of modern warfare: one characterized by the "typhoid campaigns", the other by measles in the camps' (Low-Beer *et al.* 2004: 223–4). The death rates of British soldiers from battle were 1.25 per cent, compared with 2.46 per cent from disease, and this may well have been the last war fought by European and empire troops in which there were more deaths from disease than from battle (characteristic of most previous conflicts) (Low-Beer *et al.* 2004: 227).

It is estimated that 450,000 British and empire troops took part, as against just over 87,000 Boers (including 2,000 foreign volunteers) (Low-Beer *et al.* 2004: 227; Pakenham 1992: 572), with a suggested total of '77, 000 military and civilian deaths (22,000 British and 7,000 Boer soldiers, and in addition over 28,000 Boer and over 20,000 blacks in the camps). The full mortality impacts of the war are shared between all groups in South Africa, British, Boer and Black' (Low-Beer *et al.* 2004: 230). The detailed analysis of mortality figures shows difference in the rates and chronologies of deaths in the Boer and black refugee camps, with mortality frequently the outcome of single-source epidemics in individual camps. One reason for measles being such a potent killer was the increasing number of people in the camps, which created a threshold for sustained incidence of measles in conjunction with deteriorating conditions, together with smaller-scale 'micro-geographical conditions affecting individual camps. These included the transmission between groups in the camp; overcrowding; malnutrition; the choice of camp site; ventilation; and levels of treatment and hygiene' (Low-Beer *et al.* 2004: 234, 239–40).

The costs of this war were great loss of life of large numbers of civilians as well as combatants, and the moral opprobrium heaped on Britain domestically and internationally for its failure, through lack of preparation, to take adequate measures to ensure the protection of life from disease, particularly measles, in the refugee camps, in spite of the general improvements that had taken place in the quality of nursing and general hygiene, and the understanding of germ theory and epidemics in the later nineteenth century.

Famine and hunger

The death of large numbers of people through famines is a recurrent theme in the narratives of human suffering in almost all parts of the globe throughout history, but is more familiarly associated with regions whose populations live and have lived at the margins of material existence. The histories of imperial territories bear sad and consistent testimony to this phenomenon, and to the debates on causes and means of relief. The accounts by European administrators illustrate not only the physical and cultural complexities of this phenomenon, but also their abject failure to understand the appropriate remedial measures.

Famines occurred in many of the overseas territories of European empires in the nineteenth and twentieth centuries. They were influenced by local or longer-term changes in weather and climate, and mortality rates were conditioned by the spread of famine-related disease such as cholera. Famine and its associated diseases disproportionately affected the poor and marginalised peasant cultivators and nomads, with survival often dependent on the inadequate famine relief strategies of the very classes responsible, through appropriation of land, labour and large quantities of agricultural produce, for their deprivation, indebtedness and vulnerability in times of dearth.

Attempts to explain the causes and effects of famines within the last 150 years or so have been varied and much debated. They include the initiating effects of climatic change, unusual seasonal variations in rainfall, bringing drought or flooding, and seismic events such as major volcanic eruptions. All of these require more research and evaluation. A fuller story can only be told when we add critical evaluations of demographic theories of crises of overpopulation and mortality, such as those of Malthus and Boserup, and when such phenomena as the related declines in birth rates and increases in migration are brought into the equation. In addition, we need further analyses of the nature and effects of epidemic diseases such as cholera and smallpox, theories of food entitlements and availability such as that of Amartya Sen (Arnold 1988: 29–46), and many aspects of the nature of peasant societies and the polities with which they become engaged.

Mike Davis (2002) has produced a powerful analysis of the sequences, causes and outcomes of major famines in the world, including those in Asia, Africa, China and the Middle East in the late Victorian period. He argues, from a 'political ecology' perspective, that these major famines were partly a consequence of major short- and long-term climatic fluctuations leading to drought (and sometimes flooding) and partly a consequence of the effects of global capitalism in driving up the prices of essential foodstuffs at times of scarcity, putting them out of reach of millions of starving people. At the same time the commercial processes operating on an international scale allowed both the stockpiling and export of food grains, often in and from the same areas where famine was rife and where they could have been used to palliative effect. Davis highlights the astonishing, dogmatic and indifferent attitudes of colonial administrators to the fate of the starving populations against a background of attempts to economise on the cost of imperial administration. He also draws attention to the significance of resistance to colonial authority, for it is 'imperative to consider the resistances, large and small, by which starving labourers and poor peasants attempted to foil the death sentences passed by grain speculators and colonial proconsuls' (Davis 2002: 11).

Famines strongly affected sedentary peasant cultivators in marginal areas, while nomadic pastoralists and some hunter-gatherers have been less vulnerable but not entirely free from famine. Nomadic pastoralists suffered from a gradual loss of access to grazing land by the increase in farming, in both Africa and Asia, and notably under colonial control, an example being the Tuareg nomads of West and North Africa who were marginalised by French colonial policy and action (Arnold 1988: 48–50). The vulnerability of one level of peasant societies to famine derives in part from their necessary dependence on market conditions for the availability of produce that they cannot provide themselves, with market prices for basic foodstuffs, land and rent conditioning their welfare through the agency of richer peasants and landowners, all of which is beyond their control: 'Peasant vulnerability to famine was not a self-induced nightmare, but a spectre present in the very structure of the agrarian order within which they were confined' (Arnold 1988: 58–9).

The cultural and social contexts in which Europeans saw famines in their colonies can be viewed as another example of their assumed superiority of knowledge, practice and energy, as against the supposedly inferior knowledge and status and passive apathy of 'Other' peoples. Hunger and famine were seen as a norm: 'Where once the Orient spoke of opulence now it only told of hunger. Famine became, in the West's perception, almost the normal state of all societies other than its own. The destitution that famine engendered, the exhaustion, the lethargy and the dependence that it bred, were seen as representative of Asian or African societies as a whole' (Arnold 1988: 131).

It would, however, be inaccurate to portray those who suffered from dearth and famine as passive recipients. As Hardiman (1996: 118) has argued, in his study of usury, dearth and famine in western India: 'the poor have time and again refused to accept that they were the hapless victims of fate. They saw very clearly that in times of dearth and famine the rich were the winners and they the losers, and quite logically – given the structure of their beliefs – sought to oppose what they assumed was divine support for the rich', through prayer and ritual, leading to tension and conflict.

Famines in India

India was an imperial territory that had suffered from famines over a very long period of time, but detailed studies of their demographic effects

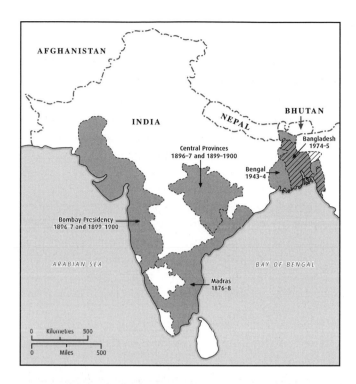

Fig. 3.2 Famine in India. Source: Dyson (1991a: 8). Permission given by the author and by the Population Investigation Committee.

were only possible after the beginning of censuses and related information in the last third of the nineteenth century. The total number of deaths in famines in India in the second half of the nineteenth century has been variously estimated at between 12.2 and 29.3 million (Arnold 1988: 20; Davis 2002: 7). Many famines occurred over quite small areas, but periodically very large-scale famines were experienced, such as those of 1876–8 – the 'Great Famine', which affected much of south, central and western India, the 1896–7 famine, the famines of 1899–1900 that affected the greater part of India, and the Bengal famine of 1943–4 (Dyson 1991a: 6–7).

The initial causes of the nineteenth-century famines were for the most part the variations in the timing and extent of the monsoon rains. As Arnold (1993: 388) puts it: 'So much hung upon the whim of the capricious monsoon, particularly in dry-cultivation areas, that almost as soon as it failed to arrive by the expected time landlords and wealthier peasant proprietors began to "cast off" their dependent labourers, and essential credit from moneylenders and traders quickly ceased.' Dyson concurs, attributing famine to drought consequent on the failure of the monsoon and its rains, notably of the south-west monsoon which normally occurs from June to October, a process characterised by scarcity of food and sharp rises in food prices (Dyson 1991a: 6). A major human factor, however, was the world depression in trade, which severely affected the parts of the Deccan where cotton was produced for export, having replaced more balanced local ecologies of grain production, with the paradox that India as a whole was producing larger than normal quantities of wheat and rice, but much of it for export (Davis 2002: 26). Another terrible irony, as Davis has stated, was that:

newly constructed railroads, lauded as institutional safeguards against famine, were instead used by merchants to ship grain inventories from outlying drought-stricken districts to central depots for hoarding (as well as protection from rioters). Likewise the telegraph ensured that price hikes were coordinated in a thousand towns at once, regardless of local supply trends. Moreover, British antipathy to price control invited anyone who had the money to join in the frenzy of grain speculation. (Davis 2002: 26)

Fig. 3.3 A corner of the Pettah Kitchen in Bangalore, Madras, South India. Over 3,000 people waiting for feeding during the famine of 1877.
By permission of and © the Royal Geographical Society, Picture Collection, S0002013.

Lord Lytton, the Viceroy of India, made no attempt to moderate grain prices or to provide famine relief, resting on British policy that in turn was based on the ideology of Thomas Malthus. Even Sir Richard Temple, lieutenant governor of Bengal, who in the drought years of 1873–4 had imported Burmese rice to Bengal and Bihar, changed to a non-interventionist stance when commissioned by Lytton to investigate the famine, becoming 'the implacable instrument of Lytton's frugality', and the policy was continued by later Viceroys such as Lord Elgin and Lord Curzon (Davis 2002: 36–7, 11).

A poor harvest in 1895, and the weakness of the monsoon in August and September had led to crop reduction and to famine in 1896–7, and this, together with the reduction in forest resources, also led to a weakening of many of the population who were then severely affected by cholera and other diseases, with a mortality rate of 21.18 per thousand. Hesitant application of the famine relief codes and practices by local British colonial administrators meant that official relief was less effective than it should have been, for during the nineteenth century British famine policy 'remained stubbornly subordinate to the development ethos' (Damodaran 1998: 877, 878, 884), adhering to the minimalist provisions of the Famine Commission of 1880. Notwithstanding the additional provision of finance by the Famine Fund, which paid for the construction of 10,000 miles of railways, the degree of relief of the effects of famine was very small (Davis: 2002: 142). Attempts to import the poorhouse or workhouse system from England to India as a means of famine relief were ineffective, partly because of lack of trust in the system by the tribal peoples of India, and partly because the relief provided was hopelessly inadequate.

There were attacks on grain storage depots in the Central Provinces and elsewhere which were put down by the army. Famine relief works were closed in August 1896 by the Commissioner of Chota Nagpur Division when the death rate from famine-linked diseases such as cholera, smallpox and dysentery was very high. The city of Bombay, which had grown rapidly in the 1880s and 1890s, suffered from the bubonic plague, starting in 1876, to which were added the effects of cholera. Attempts by the British to play down the effects of famine on the Indian population were gainsaid by reports from missionaries and the photographs of famine victims facilitated by the development of affordable cameras (Davis 2002: 147–9). The scale of death was almost unimaginable:

Famine mortality crested in March 1897. The next month Elgin himself conceded that 4.5 million poor people had perished. Behramji Malabari, the nationalist editor of the *Indian Spectator*, countered that the real number, plague victims included, was probably closer to 18 million. At the same time, the *Missionary Review of the World*, which ordinarily praised British philanthropy, denounced the double speak by which the government had downplayed the severity of the crisis and sabotaged missionary efforts to organize prompt international relief. (Davis 2002: 152)

Limited means of partially offsetting the lack of food by local populations included the search in the local ecosystem for 'famine foods' – edible materials that were normally used for medicinal purposes, some of which were taboo in normal conditions. In nineteenth-century India these included leaves, roots, grasses, seeds of the bamboo plant, wild rice, berries, fruits of trees and shrubs, small animals, rodents and reptiles (Arnold 1993: 390). Such strategies could, however, be eliminated via capitalist appropriation of resources and through colonial policy. Damodaran has shown, for example, that the forest economies of the tribal people of Chota Nagpur in south Bihar, with their rich sources of fruit from forest trees and shrubs, of which the fruit of the *mahua* tree was the most important, together with fish and game, and the growing of rice in valleys, provided some normal food sources and nutrition substitutes in times of food scarcity via a sophisticated knowledge of the jungle habitat. Groves of *sal* trees were reserved as consecrated space for forest gods and spirits (Damodaran 1998: 853–90). The peasants of the Tirunelveli district of South India also had a sophisticated system of using their ecological knowledge to advantage, of operating with sound political and market exchange systems, and taking advantage of colonially initiated improvements in road and railway systems to expand trade (Arnold 1988: 61–3).

The alienation of tribal land and the erosion of forest rights had begun in the eighteenth century with the superimposition of British colonial authority, the granting of land to traders, merchants, moneylenders and farmers, and the change of some villagers to agricultural labourer status. There was extensive destruction of forests in the nineteenth century and a consequent reduction in many of the food resources. Notwithstanding the fact that much of the destruction of forest was by private capitalist interests (for the production of railway sleepers, for example), attempts by government and state continued to remove relatively unharmful land-use rights, while paradoxically promoting 'a wholesale programme of forest reservation and exclusion' (Damodaran 1998: 864, 873–4).

Two of the major famines of the twentieth century were those in Bengal (1943–4) and Bangladesh (1974–5), with high mortality, particularly among young children. The Bengal famine, responsible for 3 million deaths, was the outcome of a number of coincident factors: proximity to the war with Japan in Burma, with high war expenditure, reduction in rice flows with the fall of Rangoon in 1942, partial failure of the rice harvest, and later in 1942 extensive damage to crops by a cyclone, heavy rain and fungal disease (Dyson 1991b: 279). A reduction in conceptions was an important demographic factor, as it was in the later Bangladesh famine. A major factor was the incompetence of the British colonial administration: 'Its bungling – including the imposition of restrictions on grain movements and incompetent interference in the rice market – did much to stimulate a market crisis' (Dyson 1991b: 279). Death rates were affected by a cholera epidemic in 1943, with a notable increase in malaria – the major cause of death – in 1943–4 (Dyson 1991b: 282). The Bangladesh famine of 1974–5 related to the economic consequences of the 1971 war of independence, inflation, dependency on food imports, and 'the severe monsoon flooding of July to September 1974, which destroyed much of both the minor *aus* rice crop (harvested in July–August) and the main *aman* harvest. There was widespread unemployment, hoarding of food, and rapidly escalating prices' (Dyson 1991b: 287).

Famines in Africa

In the period of high imperialism, famines occurred in the savannah lands of East Africa in the 1880s, notably the Ethiopian and Sudanese famine of 1888–92, the famine of 1896 in the northern Transvaal, the East African 'Great Famine of 1898–1900', and the Rumanara famine in Ruanda from 1916 to 1918 (Iliffe 1995: 209).

The Ethiopian famine of 1888–92 was one of a long sequence of famines dating back at least to the sixteenth century, but it has been described as 'perhaps the most serious and certainly the best documented famine in Ethiopian history', whose causes 'are to be found in a combination of natural calamities, a major epidemic of cattle plague or rinderpest, a harvest failure, and an outbreak of locusts and caterpillars' (Pankhurst 1966a: 98–9). The political context was one of warfare with the Egyptians in the 1870s, followed by conflict in the west with Dervishes/Sudanese, and in the north with Italians who were attempting to control and colonise the coastal lowlands, but who in doing so imported infected cattle. Rinderpest spread south in 1888–9 to all parts of the country and to neighbouring Somaliland. Very large numbers of cattle, goats and sheep died, including an estimated 90 per cent of the cattle in Ethiopia, thus removing most of the draught oxen (Pankhurst 1966a: 102–3).

The period 1888–9 was very hot and dry, with extensive crop failure. At the same time there were major swarms of locusts and caterpillars, plus very large numbers of rats, which destroyed what was left of the crops (Pankhurst 1966a: 119). Food prices rose, exacerbated by poor communication systems. Imported grain could not reach the mountainous interior, and palliative attempts by the emperor were limited in effect. Famine followed, accompanied by epidemic diseases: smallpox, typhus, cholera and dysentery. Weakened people were attacked and eaten by wild animals, including lions, leopards, wild dogs and hyenas, with vultures completing the grim process (Pankhurst 1966b: 272–3). Estimates place the overall loss of total population at 30 per cent, but the loss rate was much higher in individual regions. Some were totally depopulated, others lost at least 66 per cent of their inhabitants, and the effects were worst in areas of pastoralism, where alternative 'famine food' was not available. Raids by chiefs and by soldiers in search of grain or money were widespread, and migration was a major consequence of the famine (Pankhurst 1966b: 273–9).

Famine in Africa had a wide range of causes that varied with time and place. Climatic variation was a major cause, but warfare also contributed, as did insect infestation. There were locust invasions in 1931. The cattle epidemic rinderpest widely affected East and South Africa in the 1890s, killing up to 80 per cent of the cattle in some regions, and removing the most important food and exchange commodity of nomadic pastoralists (Arnold 1988: 23). In the nineteenth century major droughts occurred in East Africa in 1833, 1835–7, 1840–5, 1865, 1885, 1888–92 , and 1898–99, and in Central West Africa in 1835, 1837–41, 1857–60, 1867–9, 1879–84 and 1884–8, part of a cycle linking drought, famine and epidemic human and epizootic animal disease (Coquery-Vidrovitch 1988: 32).

The indirect effect of the First World War was a contributing factor in famines in French West Africa and French Equatorial Africa, partly through the requisitioning of basic foodstuffs for troops in those territories. Coquery-Vidrovitch (1990: 169) says that:

In Gabon, only a quarter of the compulsorily produced crops were left for local consumption. Even manioc (cassava) was exported from the Middle Congo and Oubangui-Chari. In AOF [French West Africa], as a consequence of the decision to export local staple crops, the authorities emptied the reserve granaries, which were already reduced by a succession of two years of semi-drought (1911–12) and one year of total aridity (1913). This drought had spread over the entire Sudan area, from Senegal to Wadai and Chad. From periodic shortages, the situation worsened to a devastating famine which claimed probably 250,000 to 300,000 victims.

Similarly, in French Equatorial Africa, devastating famine began in 1918, and the famine of 1922–5 severely affected the north, largely because of the compulsory sales of staples to support the building of the Congo–Océan railway, with outbreaks of smallpox and influenza decimating the population. Famine also affected Ruanda in 1928–9 after a drought (Coquery-Vidrovitch 1990: 169). In Angola the combination of drought, colonial wars and famines, recruitment for labour in railway construction, destruction of forests, and the appropriation of land for European plantations rendered the population vulnerable to smallpox and sleeping sickness, and there were major droughts, floods, and locust invasions *c.* 1900–10, and famines in 1911 and 1916. Coquery-Vidrovitch (1988: 36, 39) attributes the human agency for famines, epidemics and community disruption in Angola and French Equatorial Africa to European colonisation, and similar but less extensive demographic and welfare regression through colonisation in British and French West Africa.

In West Africa there were major famines in 1913–14 in the Sahel, and in French Equatorial Africa from 1918 to 1926. Most of these were caused by drought, and diseases such as smallpox spread rapidly among concentrations of the malnourished (Coquery-Vidrovitch 1988: 209). Devastating droughts occurred in 1901–3, 1913–14, 1930–3, and 1972–4. A common problem was the lack of an adequate local infrastructure, particularly roads, with which to concentrate food relief, or of the ability or willingness of administrations to identify and relieve hunger, as in the case of Niger in 1913 (Iliffe 1995: 238).

Famines in South–East Asia

Famines and subsistence crises occurred in Indonesia in the nineteenth and twentieth centuries, precipitated by drought and flood, and in some cases volcanic eruptions, such as that of Mount Tambora on Sumbawa Island in 1815, and the better-known eruption of Krakatoa in 1883. These crises were accompanied by high grain prices and epidemic and epizootic diseases. The volcanic eruption of Mount Tambora in 1815 'not only led to harvest failures and large-scale famines on the islands of Sumbawa, Lombok and Bali, but also to the so-called year without summer across the world' (Boomgaard 2002: 38).

Tree-ring data for Java from 1514 to 1929 provide information on wet and dry years, and there is also information on harvest failure, pests and disease in crops, and mortality figures from 1834 (Boomgaard 2002: 37). There were famines in three administrative areas (residencies) of Java in

1844–6 and 1849–50, the outcome of the reversal of monsoon seasons, and the advent of the Cultivation System – the Dutch policy of compelling peasant cultivation of coffee, indigo and sugar for European markets. In the Residency of Semarang on Java over 80,000 peasants died in the famine of 1849–50, and the Dutch East Indies were severely affected by the famine of 1896–7, a time of depression in world markets and disease in sugar and coffee plants (Davis 2002: 195–6).

The subsistence crises of this period were also characterised by cholera and smallpox epidemics. Subsistence crises occurred on Java in the periods 1873–5, 1880–3, 1900–2 and 1918–21. Boomgaard (2002: 42) suggests that after 1921 these crises eased in response to an improvement in Dutch colonial policy on famine relief, in contrast to their laissez-faire approach during the nineteenth century and their belief in removing obstructions to free market conditions as a solution, linked to imperfect understanding of the rice market and the reluctance of colonial administrators to admit to failure to deal effectively with famine.

Drought, famine and climatic anomalies: the El Niño Southern Oscillation (ENSO)

Research into the changes in climate that produced the droughts that triggered famines has produced important insights. Boomgard (2002: 42–3) has reviewed the effects on drought and famine in Java, including the droughts of 1876–8 and the droughts and harvest failures of 1918–19 as well as climatic anomalies experienced in Indonesia as a whole. He acknowledges the climatic agency of the El Niño Southern Oscillation (ENSO) on famines in Indonesia, but cautions that 'the analytical value of calling something an ENSO phenomenon remains limited, as not every drought is part of an El Niño effect, and not every El Niño produces a drought. It is perhaps more important to realise that the irregularities of the monsoons occur regularly, on average once every 3.4 years.' Others are more positive about possible links, as is shown below.

Grove pointed to the knowledge of what subsequently became known as the El Niño Southern Oscillation (ENSO) as early as 1816, when the botanical and medical services of the East India Company in India, St Helena and St Vincent analysed sophisticated statistical meteorological data in an attempt to understand the major drought of 1791 and to use tree-planting as a counter-measure to desiccation (Grove 1998). This understanding was linked to the global droughts between 1788 and 1833, and to their specific regional impacts, including the experiences of the settlement colony at Port Jackson in Australia (Grove 1998: 317).

Since the end of the nineteenth century, scientists have more fully understood the physical processes involved in changes in the normal configuration of wind and water in the Pacific Ocean. This involves easterly trade winds moving the warm water of the Pacific westwards, as a 'warm pool' in the region of Indonesia–Australasia, producing low pressure in the west, and the consequent upwelling of cold water, giving high pressure and colder than normal sea surface temperatures in the centre and east. This cold phase is known as La Niña. Against this, an anomaly exists when the situation is reversed, and trade winds collapse, the cold water upwelling along the equator ceases, and sea surface temperatures rise to become warmer than usual in the central and eastern Pacific, where pressure decreases and rising air leads to precipitation. This is termed El Niño – Spanish for 'Christ Child' – the local name given by Pacific fishermen in the nineteenth century to the anomalous upwelling of a warm water current around Christmas time, but later adopted to describe climatic behaviour over a wider area. Climatic anomalies affecting the timing and nature of the seasonal monsoon in India had been identified by Gilbert T. Walker, Director-General of the Observatories in India (the Indian Meteorological Department) from 1904.

Attempts to find climate links between the major Indian famines and monsoon anomalies commenced in 1877 during the famine of 1876–8, but Walker's work over thirty years prompted by the famine of 1899–1900 (both 1877 and 1899 were El Niño years), caused by the failure of the monsoon in 1899, established the significance of a Southern Oscillation. This was 'loosely speaking a tendency of the atmospheric pressure to "see-saw" between two "centres of action", one in the general vicinity of Indonesia, the other in the tropical-subtropical south-eastern Pacific Ocean', the waters off the coasts of Peru, Ecuador and Chile (Katz 2001: 97).

Later work, notably by Jacob Bjerknes, established further links between what had been labelled El Niño and the Southern Oscillation, and has further explained climatic anomalies such as droughts and floods in Pacific and Pacific-rim territories, and also those much further away, for example in South Africa, including changes in mid-latitude circulations. Subsequent research findings have been summarised by Davis (2002: 214–38). He graphically describes how, under El Niño conditions:

The central tropical Indian Ocean also catches a fever, which affects the strength and path of the monsoons. In big events, the normal geography and aridity and rainfall in the equatorial Pacific is reversed as thunderstorms flood the hyper-arid deserts of coastal Peru, while drought parches the usually humid jungles of Kalimantan and Papua. The monsoons fail to nourish agriculture in western India and southern Africa, while further afield drought holds northern China and northeastern Brazil in its grip. (Davis 2002: 216)

El Niño events are now thought to last for one to one and a half years, and to occur every two to seven years, but these link to other, longer climatic periodicities lasting for decades or even very much longer (Davis 2002: 234–5).

The Indian famines of 1876–8 and 1888–9 coincided, according to Nichols (1997), with El Niño events, as did the Ethiopian famine of 1888–9, with similar connections to major drought in Australia and Brazil in 1888. Davis asserts that out of the twenty-six droughts affecting India between 1871 and 1991 twenty-one can be linked to El Niño events, as can droughts in other regions such as South-East Asia, China and Africa, but the influence of El Niño could be more indirect, and its effects vary more widely in strength and character according to regional factors (Davis 2002: 246).

This chapter has examined many of the characteristics of population size and composition, of change and migration, and of aspects of diseases and famines to which many were subjected. The economic and social viability of many people depended, of course, on the resources available to them, the most important of which was land. The following chapter examines the patterns of land use, the tensions introduced by imperial and colonial policy and practice, and the consequent interactions with indigenous peoples.

4 | Patterns and shadows on the land

Despite considerable colonial reliance upon Aboriginal labour in a wide variety of crucial tasks, their traditional mode of existence represented an obstacle to the European mission to tame the bush, to compel the land to yield its financial potential. Foremost, Aborigines represented an obstacle to European development of Queensland merely by their occupation of land which the Europeans sought for themselves. Europeans considered the land to be unoccupied, they did not recognise Aboriginal right of occupancy, nor that they even *used* the land. (Palmer 2000: 117)

Introduction

In both settler and non-settler regions of empire, a key feature of European colonial territories overseas was the difference in attitude between colonial powers and indigenous populations on the question of rights of land occupation and use, as shown by the quotation above from Alison Palmer's study of Aborigine–European conflict in colonial Queensland and the German–Herero conflict in colonial South-West Africa. In this chapter we examine in detail the geographies of contested uses of land as a resource, and the resulting tensions and outcomes. The European attitude generally was that land not seen or thought to be in continuous occupation or cultivation was deemed to be empty land (in English legal terminology *terra nullius*) devoid of any legal or moral property rights, and therefore available for occupation under modified European systems of legal land tenure. In spite of a long tradition of communal use rights in many parts of Europe from the early middle ages onwards, the modernising influence of capitalist-inspired movements towards land appropriation and re-allocation into units of individual property ownership had a strong bearing on European attitudes to land rights and use overseas. This inevitably brought conflict with the communal and spiritual dimensions of indigenous attitudes to land.

Developing policies and practices

The actual experiences of coloniser and colonised varied temporally and spatially. The settlement policies and doctrines of European states evolved through time, as did the related question of the provision made for indigenous populations removed from their home bases, sometimes to prescribed places of residence – 'reservations' – or in other cases abandoned to the vicissitudes of market economies. The complexity of many aspects of European and indigenous population relations in the period of high imperialism has to be recognised. National policies for overseas economic enterprise, political relations and emigration policies, for example, all changed through time and from one place to another.

Much of the earlier history of European land settlement overseas involved policies adopted by the merchant companies to whom, in many cases, authority had been given for local affairs by governments anxious to avoid the political complexities, and particularly the cost, of overseas economic activities. There were, it has to be noted, some overseas colonial territories where there was little permanent European settlement other than for military and administrative purposes. India is an example, where relatively little appropriation of land and land-use rights by Europeans occurred over a long period of British influence, though systems of land tenure were manipulated for purposes of land tax revenue, and some land was sold or leased for coffee, tea and other forms of plantation.

The policy of British governments in the mid-nineteenth century laid foundations for developments later in the nineteenth and in the early twentieth century. Policies were developed for expansion of British trade overseas against a background philosophy of free trade and a confident global civilising, renovating and improving role for Britain. The House of Commons Select Committee on Aborigines reported in 1837 that Britain's role was to provide for other people in the world 'the opportunity of becoming partakers of that civilisation, that innocent commerce, that knowledge and that faith with which it has pleased a gracious Providence to bless our own country' (cited by Lynn, 1999b: 102).

These goals were intended to be achieved by free trade, which would promote the growth of British industry, expand British markets, improve the earning and raw material export capacities of overseas countries, and promote moral regeneration in less developed countries (Lynn, 1999b: 103). British free trade policy was intended to be disinterested, providing for access by all countries to international markets, and restrictive only in the sense of British private companies being supported when it was convenient for the government's political purposes. In practice, however, this disinterest has to be qualified, for Britain's globally dominant position in naval, military and economic power meant that she enjoyed better opportunities through free trade than almost any other power.

The basic underpinning of the promotion of Britain's global ambition was commercial gain, to which other civilising influences could readily be attached, such as missionary work and the abolition of the slave trade, notably in Central and East Africa. Thus: 'Trade, Christianity, education and constitutional principles were all vehicles whereby this was to be achieved, but trade, as even Livingstone admitted, was the primer' (Lynn 1999: 106, 107), supported, where necessary, by political diplomacy and naval activity. Much British promotion of commercial imperialism took place outside the existing colonial territories, in Latin America, the Middle East and China. Progressive inroads were also being made in a continent – Africa – in which Britain then had few footholds, but which was to become the focus of a great deal of imperial attention at the end of the nineteenth century. Preliminary footholds already existed in South Africa, but in the period *c.* 1840–1860 there was an expansion of trade with sub-Saharan tropical Africa. This was the intention: in practice, Britain was not dealing with a blank map, and existing powerful tribal, political and economic interests in both East and West Africa ensured only limited success in Britain's attempts to secure major trading benefits from these regions, at least until the very end of the nineteenth century.

Reinforcing these earlier attempts at commercial imperialism were the few basic overseas settlement policies developed by the British government, including that developed by Edward Gibbon Wakefield (see Chapter 3). His opinions were influential up to the 1860s, in spite of the government's reluctance to promote emigration. The money raised from land sales in the Antipodes was linked to two bounty schemes by the Colonial Office and the New South Wales government in 1832 and 1836 geared to the emigration of women, artisans and agricultural labourers, though the New South Wales government scheme was twice interrupted by financial difficulties before 1848. After 1850, as Harper has shown, one of the main influences on migration from Britain to the colonies, notably Canada, Australia and South Africa, was 'national and provincial charities and self-help groups – over sixty of them in 1886 – which aimed to find colonial outlets for Britain's surplus female population, and destitute children, as well as the unemployed' (Harper 1999: 81).

The interface between colonisers and colonised was of crucial significance, not only to Wakefield but to other colonial and humanitarian apologists including Herman Merivale, a Permanent Under-Secretary at the Colonial Office and formerly Drummond Professor of Political Economy at Oxford. In this latter capacity his lectures at Oxford in 1839, 1840 and 1841 had drawn attention to the problems and possibilities of interaction with indigenous peoples in settlement colonies, and the need to accommodate their use rights for land in the face of conflicting settler interest, a matter whose arbitration could best be left to metropolitan rather than local colonial legislative control, through the Colonial Office and the British governors of the settlement areas (Harris 2002: 6–7). Britain's civilising mission had also to ensure long-term land use and access rights for indigenous peoples, initially through a system of land reserves, but ultimately through the amalgamation of colonisers and colonised and the sustenance of indigenous populations (for he did not share the view that such groups were biologically predestined to decline and disappear), interrupting the cycles of appropriation of land by settlers. Merivale's views on the modernisation of indigenous peoples through a humanitarian colonialism were supported by liberal humanitarian thinking, which

> posited a universal humanity and before long (with proper instruction) a universal, civilised culture, a product of common sociocultural evolution – allowing next to no room for continuing cultural difference … The rights of property, an industrious labour force given to hard work and thrift, a free market, an ordered Christian society: this bourgeois vision set the agenda for the reform of the indolent British poor and for the liberation and civilisation of savage peoples overseas. (Harris 2002: 7, 9)

Such principles were not, however, widely applied in practice in British settlement colonies, evidenced by the conflicts of interest revealed in the versions of the Treaty of Waitangi in New Zealand in 1840, and in Australia. In effect, 'For all the theorizing about colonial land policy, the system as it emerged was essentially a set of ad hoc responses to particular pressures in particular colonies', the altruistic principles aired in mid-nineteenth-century British colonial thinking being overpowered by policies of local pragmatic and settler-biased schemes of land appropriation (Harris 2002: 14; see also Harris 2004: 165–82).

Weaver has shown the complexity of methods of land acquisition in British and American colonies in the later nineteenth century, and states that 'wherever desirable land remained with indigenous peoples and under British or American rule, governments supplemented or replaced with new tools the traditional legal technology for securing land' by war, treaties, boundary adjustments, trusteeship, and manipulation (Weaver

2003: 176). These included purchases by crown agents of vast amounts of land and the use of land courts and land confiscation in New Zealand; the acquisition of land added to the South African republics and the British colony of Natal by war, treaties, boundary adjustments and white trusteeship manipulation of tribal land; the purchase by the Canadian government of large areas of land from the Hudson's Bay Company; the suppression of indigenous interests by treaties; and the disposal of land by crown grants, sales and leases in Australia (Weaver 2003: 174–6).

New Zealand

The question of land appropriation in New Zealand by Britain and British settlers has some parallels with and some differences from Australia. During Captain James Cook's first voyage of exploration in the *Endeavour* to the South Pacific in 1768–71, a major feat was the mapping of the coastlines of New Zealand's two main islands. After making astronomical observations in Tahiti, Cook sailed south to New Zealand and around the two main islands, before sailing on to eastern Tasmania and the east coast of Australia, and bringing news of their resources to England. By the early nineteenth century the exploitation of some of those resources had begun, with ships from Australia, France and the United States putting in at anchorages on the North Island. During the period *c.* 1792–1840 there was substantial exploitation by Europeans and Americans of the seal and whale populations, and of many of the native tree species which were cut and used as spars for sailing ships and as timber for construction. Trade in such commodities as timber and flax, and in provisions such as potatoes and pork, increased over this time. Missionary settlement began on the North Island in 1814, and increased interest in the private acquisition of land was shown by Europeans and other colonists in the later 1830s. Inevitably this led to conflict with Maori notions of land use and use rights.

The Maori relationship with land was fundamentally different from that of the Europeans/*Pakeha*. Maori saw themselves not as owners of land but as custodians and users. Stokes (2002: 35–6), citing the Waitangi Tribunal's comments in the Muriwhenua Land Report of 1997, states that:

The fundamental purpose of Maori Law was to maintain appropriate relationships of people with their environment, their history and each other ... Maori saw themselves as users of the land rather than its owners ... they were born out of it, for the land was Papatuanuku, the mother earth who conceived the ancestors of the Maori people ... That land descends from ancestors is pivotal to understanding the Maori land-tenure system ... Maori customary tenure comprised a complex system of overlapping and interlocking usufructory rights; that is, rights of use and occupation, but with no right of alienation except in very special circumstances sanctioned by the community.

The advent of the *Pakeha* to New Zealand with trade and land settlement as their two main objectives was to produce major tensions over a wide range of use rights both of land and of sea. In 1840 the Treaty of Waitangi was signed, ushering in a period of contention over use rights that would last to the present day, and have a profound influence on the development of New Zealand's national identity. New Zealand was declared an independent country under Maori rule by means of the 1835 Declaration of Independence, which was signed by northern Maori chiefs. A private company (the New Zealand Company) sent representatives to New Zealand in 1839 to purchase land for a group of settlers who were to travel out from England in September of that year. In order to free up land rights and to have a formal treaty of agreement with the Maori, in a country that had been declared independent, processes were set in train for the drafting and signature of a treaty that would allow Britain to control and stabilise the country.

The Treaty of Waitangi was signed on Thursday 6 February 1840 at Waitangi on the Bay of Islands on the north-east coast of the North Island of New Zealand. In subsequent weeks it was taken to about fifty other locations in New Zealand and signed by Maori representatives, including five women. Its main functions were to transfer sovereignty over New Zealand to the British; to guarantee Maori right over lands and resources; and to give the Maori rights and privileges as British subjects (McKinnon 1997: 35–6). The Treaty was drafted in English, and translated by a missionary (Henry Williams) and his son in little over 24 hours, but there were problems over the translation of English words such as 'government' into Maori. The Maori chiefs signed the Maori version of the treaty, after some debate.

Shortly after the signing of the treaty, conflict arose from attempts at land purchase by European individuals and institutions, including the New Zealand Land Company, without obtaining the consent of the Maori who had use rights over it. White immigration and settlement was proceeding rapidly in New Zealand, and by 1860 *Pakeha* were equal in number to Maori. The survey and mapping of land led to conflict, for example at Wairau in 1834 when both Europeans and Maori died because of disagreement over land ownership.

Resistance to land sales and survey increased in the 1840s and 1850s, leading to an attempt to unite Maori opposition under a single king in the area of the Waikato confederation, which was a region whose settlement potential was recognised by *Pakeha*. This opposition to land sales and also to strategic road construction south from Auckland led to the use of British troops for road construction and the invasion of Waikato in 1863–4. The British campaign was successful and the Waikato region was substantially depopulated of Maori (Prickett and Stokes 1997: 38), leading to land confiscation and offers of land to military settlers.

In 1862 a Native Land Act was passed to determine land ownership and rights and to facilitate transfer of land to European settlers. In 1865 a Native Land Court was established, which provided in effect 'a new framework for extinguishing customary tenure' (Stokes 2002: 49). The court did not make provision for recognition of collective/communal land ownership and management. By the 1850s the crown – by far the largest and most potent agent in land alienation from the Maori in the nineteenth century – had acquired much of the land in the South Island, with some small amounts left as Maori reserves.

By 1910 there was little Maori land left on the North Island, and even that had been reduced by the start of the Second World War. In 1975, a Labour government in New Zealand instituted the Waitangi Tribunal to re-evaluate claims to breaches of the 1840 Treaty, but it was not initially intended to deal with historical claims. Historical and alienation claims were, however, admitted from 1985, and tribal groups (*iwi*) received back large areas of land and financial compensation for the loss of fishing rights. This positive development has more recently been countered by a racist ideology on the part of New Zealand's right-wing National Party (there were similar developments in Queensland in Australia) based on a recent court ruling on Maori rights of access to produce of the foreshore and seabed.

Australia

British interest in the settlement and colonisation of Australia dates in effect from the late eighteenth-century voyages of exploration by Captain James Cook, and later by Matthew Flinders and George Bass, in the Pacific. On his first voyage to the Pacific in 1768–71 in HMS *Endeavour*, Cook mapped the coastlines of the two main islands of New Zealand,

and the east coast of Australia (New Holland – so named because of Dutch discoveries in the seventeenth century). Although the main purpose of the voyage was astronomical (observation of the transit of the planet Venus in 1769), national pride, moderate economic aspiration, and rivalry with France and the United States led to encouragement by the Admiralty and the Royal Society for Cook to take possession of such land as might be possible. A caveat, in theory at least, was the request to obtain the consent of indigenous inhabitants before he did so.

In January 1770 Cook did lay claim to possession of Queen Charlotte Sound in New Zealand, and in the same year 'In August at Cape York Cook annexed the whole of the east coast of Australia from lat. 38°S. on the grounds, as explained later, that it was *terra nullius*, no person's land' (Williams 1998: 560). He gave the name New South Wales to the area of eastern Australia that he had charted, and the view that Botany Bay, where the *Endeavour* had landed in 1785, could be the site of effective British settlement was borne out by the decision to use the region as the site of a convict settlement. The first fleet with convicts arrived at Botany Bay in January 1788 (Williams, 1998: 566–7).

Grants of what was deemed to be crown land were made to officers of the colony from 1792, and to small numbers of free settlers, including released convicts, from 1795. Inevitably the appropriating approach of the British government to land rights and settlement, and to aboriginal customs – through what Williams (1998: 570) has called 'a dead end of comprehension' on the part of the Europeans – caused conflict with the aboriginal populations. The conflicts are indeed rooted in fundamental flaws in the British comprehension, in Australia, New Zealand, North America and elsewhere, of the belief systems, customs, environmental knowledge and land-use rights of indigenous peoples. An important factor was the 'white belief that either the natives themselves, or their culture, or both, were irrevocably doomed. Therefore the geography of dispossession in the case of the Australian Aborigines was really agonizingly simple, for the removal was usually swift and virtually complete' (Powell 1977: 96).

The Wakefield theories for systematic colonisation through sales of colonial land and careful supervision of type and location of settlements were implemented in South Australia in particular, and land became an influential medium for metropolitan–colony economic and social policy. Hence:

the argument envisaged linking Home and Colonial partners, economically, socially, and politically, by encouraging the specialized development of primary production in Australia based on the 'transplantation' of whole sectors of British society. Land, or at any rate the price of land, was the key. It was not to be given away: on the contrary, comparatively high minimum prices were required, though they might be 'regulated' in tune with supply and demand in the immigration market. And strong governmental control of 'agricultural areas' was expected. (Powell 1988b: 16)

The Wakefield policies for settlement included the maxims that land should be carefully surveyed before allocation and that settlement should preferably be undertaken by families: both of these were intended to counter the problems experienced elsewhere of speculative, squatter settlement and an overemphasis on populating new areas by convicts and bonded servants (Williams 1969: 4). In practice the surveying and layout of land-lots varied, though the American rectangular quarter-section grid seems to have been a model. Variations were also introduced by the individualistic views of such administrators as Governor Sir George Gipps in New South Wales in the period 1838–49, and also by pastoralist squatters in areas inland from the coast, notably in Victoria (Powell 1976: 27–8).

The actual practices of land allocation and layout were determined in effect by imperial legislation modified by local circumstances, including the attitudes of colonial governors and settlers, and the topography, soils and climate. On the whole, the basic principle of land alienation was by means of grants and orders from the crown, with quit-rents payable on secession. Early grants for freed convicts, sailor-settlers and free immigrants were made from 1789 onwards, and grants of town allotments were made in Sydney from 1811. A penal settlement was established at Port Arthur in Tasmania from 1830, mainly industrial in character and making use of the timber from surrounding woodland.

The notion of land sales to free settlers was introduced in 1825, in parallel with the earlier land-grant system, with maximum limits of purchase to 4,000 acres per individual and 5,000 acres per family. Free grants of land were abolished in 1831, with future disposal of crown land being by sale at auction, and this principle was developed in the Imperial Acts of 1842 and 1847, the former providing, under the Wakefield concept, funding of immigration from part of the proceeds of land sales.

The question of the basic rights of aboriginal populations seems to have been far from the minds of the organisers and architects of new settlements:

In South Australia where, as elsewhere in Australia, there were no treaties, the situation was quite different [from New Zealand]. The Colonial Office had insisted on Crown-appointed Protectors of Aborigines and on the obligation to extinguish Aboriginal title to lands in their possession, but once in Australia – half-way around the world from the Colonial Office – the South Australia Company concluded that the Aboriginals, a wandering people, did not possess any land. Therefore, it had not purchased land, had not granted reserves, and left the protector of Aborigines with nothing to do. (Harris 2002: 12)

Aboriginals on land under pastoral leases were often shot.

The complex pattern of land alienation and development in Australia reflected both colonial and private agency, including squatting. Before the mid-nineteenth century the main factors affecting settlement and land-use policy included ignorance of Australian environments, together with metropolitan imperial ideals of settlement and their translation into practice by local colonial officers in the Australian colonies. The main types of land settlement were government-initiated small settlements near the coast, and rapidly moving pastoral frontiers associated with large-scale commercial livestock farming. From the 1850s the gold rushes also introduced the principle of land allocation to yeoman-type farmers, so that

Fig. 4.1 Penal settlement, Port Arthur, Tasmania. This settlement was developed from a small timber station founded in 1830. Photo © R. A. Butlin.

politicians, notably in Victoria, 'waxed eloquent on the fabled yeoman, and between 1860 and about 1890 a bewildering succession of Land Acts was passed in the various colonies, ostensibly to produce desired cultural landscapes and social class' (Powell 1988b: 17).

From the 1870s a more liberal selection process accelerated the acquisition of what was deemed to be unoccupied land, but with stronger colonial governmental roles in the process in the period 1880–1900, with the application of improved communications, notably railways, and of applied agricultural science. Powell suggests that 'perhaps it is more accurate, however, to differentiate a growing trend towards *land management* from earlier aggressive sorties into *land development*' (Powell, 1988b: 17), leading to an intensification of agricultural settlement, increased use of short- and long-term leases, and of management of water resources and forests.

By 1901 public lands, including leased or licensed land, made up 94.2 per cent of the total, with private lands at 5.8 per cent. After federation in 1901 various land settlement schemes, including soldier settlement after the First World War and the British Empire Settlement Act of 1922, had limited success, but denser settlement schemes were nonetheless developed, in Western Australia and Queensland in particular. During the twentieth century up to about 1980 there was a conspicuous increase in private ownership, though leaseholds and crown lands occupied 83.7 per cent of the total (Powell 1998b: 19–20, 23).

South Africa

As in other colonial locations, the histories of settler colonialism in South Africa were complex, characterised by changing discourses on different topics (land, politics and geopolitics, and humanitarianism) between the major actors in the metropoles and at the frontier. One of the most important subjects of discourse and related actions was land:

The land, both as symbol and as reality, has had resonant implications in the history of South African society. Possession of land was, since 1652, a theme of contention between racially and ethnically defined participants, and remains so today. Whites not only sought to deprive blacks of the possession of their land, but also to transform the nature of land ownership itself. While Africans had practised a form of unequal communal tenure associated with landscapes of dispersed, self-sufficient homesteads (kraals), over much of the region whites substituted a landscape of individually owned, enclosed farmsteads and trading communities. But this was no smooth transition: the landscape was fiercely contested. (Lester 1998: 37)

The onset of European settlement in South Africa derived from the expedition sent by the Dutch East India Company in 1652, and the establishment of a small Dutch fort and colony at Cape Town on Table Bay on the Cape of Good Hope. The purpose of this initial settlement was for the provision of food and water and protection for Dutch ships travelling to the colonies in the East Indies. In 1657 the East India Company started a small agricultural settlement beyond the environs of Cape Town in the Liesbeeck River valley, the small allocations of land being farmed by former employees of the Dutch East India Company with the aid of slave labour from the East Indies (Christopher 1976: 30–41). Gradual expansion of arable farming and settlement took place eastwards in the last quarter of the seventeenth century, including the foundation of Stellenbosch and Drakenstein, and by the end of the century 1,500 square miles (3,885 km^2) of the South Western Cape had been settled. The use of slave labour expanded in the early eighteenth century between 1713 and 1721, after a smallpox epidemic among the indigenous Hottentot people.

The agricultural frontier was extended considerably in the eighteenth century with the expansion of livestock farming to the north and east of Cape Town, through various permissions for grazing, annual leasing, and some arable cultivation, consolidated in 1714 by the general leasing of grazing rights and specific rights of cultivation in the 'loan place' (Christopher 1976: 42, 47). This mechanism of land leasing did not give sufficient security of tenure; nor did it provide incentive to secure investment. Some improvements to tenure were made in 1732, but by the beginning of the nineteenth century population densities were still very low. Nonetheless there was a general change from European models of intensive farming, as practised by early Dutch, French and German settlers, to more extensive pastoral farming as the frontier moved eastwards and northwards during the eighteenth century. Allocations of land as stock farms of 2,500 hectares were being offered to European settlers by the end of the eighteenth century, in a process of land alienation from indigenous peoples that led to conflict.

The Cape Colony was occupied by the British from 1795 to 1803, and Britain again took control via a treaty of 1814. Population after 150 years of Dutch rule was still small – 76,865 (Europeans, 'Hottentots' and slaves) in a territory of 150,000 square miles (388,498 km^2), the greatest density being in and around Cape Town (Christopher 1976: 52).

Major developments, including the expansion of population and of cultivated and pastoral areas, took place between 1806 and 1860, with the figure of alienated land increasing from 11 million acres in 1806 to 100 million acres by 1860. The alienation of land from the indigenous inhabitants led to further conflict with Europeans: five wars were fought at the eastern border of the Cape Colony between 1811 and 1843. Immigration to South Africa was in part both cause and effect of the conflict, with policies of British settlement being developed to protect the eastern frontiers. In 1820, for example, a major settlement initiative involved the migration of 4,000 British settlers under the initiative of Lord Somerset, the governor of the Cape Colony, to the eastern frontier to act 'as a buffer between the dispersed Dutch settlement of the Colony and the Xhosa of Kaffraria' (Christopher 1976: 58, 64). An unusually representative cross-section of British society, they used Xhosian labour in the construction of their settlements. Later, colonists were allocated Xhosa lands cleared as a result of military response to so-called depredations by the Xhosa of settler livestock and property, notably in what was newly named as Queen Adelaide Province after the 'Sixth Frontier War' of 1834–5 (Lester 2000: 109–12). Thirty-six thousand people had immigrated to South Africa by 1860.

Appropriation of land continued throughout the nineteenth century as the frontiers of settlement and land use were extended, and Afrikaner settlers, who opposed British liberal attitudes (slavery had been abolished by Britain in 1834, and missionary activity was increasing) and land policies, moved inland across the Orange River to distance themselves from British control. They entered an area thought to be largely uninhabited by indigenous people, though there was already some European settlement there. From 1836 to 1864 the Afrikaner (Boer) farmers took part in the Great Trek (a major migration of Boer farmers and pastoralists east and noth-east from the Cape Colony frontier) as pioneer settlers or *voortrekkers*. They founded the Orange Free State in 1854 and the South African Republic (Transvaal) in 1848 and what is now Natal in 1838, as independent republics. The British, however, annexed Natal in 1843 and the Transvaal in 1877. After subsequent negotiations the three colonies became internally self-governing until the end of the century: Transvaal and the Orange Free State from 1884 and Natal from 1893.

Settlement and land development in these new territories mirrored earlier processes in the Cape Colony, though farm sizes were very much larger. After much confusion about conflicting and indeterminate land claims, very substantial areas of land were allocated to settlers. Christopher suggests that in Natal just fewer than 600 farms were granted by the British with an average of about 6,000 acres (14,829 ha) per farm, with larger allocations of 8,000 acres (19,772 ha) inland, and smaller farms in coastal areas where plantations were permitted (Christopher, 1976: 69–70).

In the period from 1806 to 1860, the overall impact of European control and colonisation on land ownership and use in the Cape Colony was massive. Christopher has estimated that about 40 per cent of the colony's land was European (47.8 million acres/11,814,137 ha, out of a total of 117.3 million acres/28,991,596 ha), and has pointed to two other significant changes in the period: the emancipation of slaves and a major wave of rebuilding and improvement (Christopher 1976: 76–8).

Fundamental to this extensive process of European expansion in South Africa was the appropriation of the land and rights of the African inhabitants. The first affected were the Khoisan peoples in the west: hunters and herders who had first contact with white settlers and who lost both land and livestock as European settlement was extended. They were decimated by European diseases, and became a population reduced 'to servitude, as servile tenant labourers on the newly established European-owned farms' (Christopher 2001: 9).

There was also conflict with the Xhosa, Bantu-speaking peoples who inhabited the better-quality lands to the east, who were 'less susceptible to European diseases and proved to be difficult to control militarily, and so to dispossess of their land and livestock. Consequently there ensued a long period of conflict from the 1770s to the 1870s, while colonial and local governments conquered the various indigenous chieftaincies and kingdoms of the subcontinent in a piecemeal fashion' (Christopher 2001: 10–11). There remained large numbers of indigenous populations in the colonial and republican lands of the east in the nineteenth century, resulting in the designation of areas of indigenous inhabitants as rural reserves, where they maintained their traditional chieftains and laws but under overall European control. Land was granted to African leaders under various conditions and means. Even though a kind of protectorate status was given to the indigenous peoples, the land had no indigenous rights of ownership or use attached, and thus it still technically remained government property, and could be removed from African use, the principle here being the familiar one of *terra nullius* (Christopher 2001: 17).

Between 1860 and 1914 there was a limited extension of the area of European settlement to the borders of the Kalahari Desert and to what was to become Rhodesia, and intensification of settlement and land use in areas already colonised. Christopher has showed that in the period

1860–1911 the area of European farms doubled, to a total of 227 million acres/561 million ha, and that there was a major expansion in livestock numbers and in exports, notably of wool (Christopher 1976: 116–17). This intensification of European control of land was in part stimulated by the discoveries of diamonds (in 1867 on the alluvial terraces of the Vaal River and in 1871 at Kimberley), and of gold in the Transvaal from 1872 and more spectacularly in the Witwatersrand fields in 1886, which caused a dramatic increase in population, wealth, internal demand for agricultural products, and financial support for the colonisation of Rhodesia (Pollock and Agnew 1963: 170–2; Christopher 1976: 122).

Colonisation of the arid interior of the Cape Colony was facilitated by the Crown Lands Act of 1860, which allowed land to be sold in blocks with a maximum size of 50,000 acres, thus accelerating the alienation of land. Varied rates of consolidation and filling-in of settlement – the main processes of settlement change in the rural areas of Natal, Transvaal and the Orange Free State – occurred in the period 1860–1914, with some advances towards the desert margins, partly under the influence of diamond mining at Kimberley, which led inter alia to sales of land by the Griquas (the earlier indigenous inhabitants) to Europeans in the early 1880s. In the late 1880s there was limited advance into the Kalahari Desert. In the area of the British Bechuanaland Protectorate north of the Molopo River, land was acquired and then allocated for European settlement in large farm areas by the British South Africa Company, totalling 3.8 million acres, though with only limited take-up by 1910 (Christopher 1976: 134–5).

The last stage of settlement on the distant frontiers of the Cape Colony came with the colonisation of Rhodesia. In 1888 Cecil Rhodes had acquired mining rights in Matabeleland, the homeland of the Ndebele people, and in 1889 his British South Africa Company obtained its charter and started a process of land appropriation with the acquisition of Mashonaland, in anticipation of new (but in fact, limited) mining possibilities, followed by the occupation of Matabeleland in 1893. Here allocation to European settlers consisted of 6,000 acre farms, and prospects for successful farming were greater than on the Eastern Highlands. Large blocks of land, one of 2 million acres, were, however, allocated to large investment companies by the British South Africa Company. The attempts to attract more settlers were intensified from 1907, emphasising prospects for cattle ranching and a welcome for a range of classes of settler, the outcome of which was that 'the number of Europeans engaged in agriculture increased from 14,007 to 23,606 in the period 1907–1911. In this manner approximately 10,000 acres had been alienated for each

member of the farming community' (Christopher 1976: 135–6). There
was very limited settlement north of the Zambezi, and the declaration
of South-West Africa as a German protectorate in 1885 effectively ended
the possibility of significant settlement from South Africa until 1915.
Christopher has stated that the closing of the European settlement frontier in southern Africa occurred by about 1910.

The effects of European land appropriation and settlement on African
populations and the subsequent in-filling of settlement varied from one
region to another. The best lands within the aegis of the Cape Colony
and its extensions had been appropriated by Europeans by about 1870.
Thereafter attempts to intensify use of land in Natal and the Cape of Good
Hope by means of irrigation and favourable land grants by both government and land colonisation companies were initially less successful than
later schemes dating from about 1902. In the Transvaal possibilities for
settlement intensification came with the dispossession of the African
Mapoch's people of 80,000 acres (32,375 ha) of good-quality and watered
land in 1883, resulting by 1904 in the settlement of 1,197 Europeans there
(Christopher 1976: 147–8).

In 1910 the Union of South Africa became a British Dominion, with the
four constituent colonies (the Cape, Natal, Transvaal and the Orange Free
State) giving up their rights of self-government. The Natives Land Act of
1913 confirmed the existing division of lands between African and White
populations, defined 8.9 million ha as native reserves, prohibited land
purchase by Africans outside these reserves other than in Cape Province,
confirming that the Act was 'officially conceived as a first stage in drawing
a permanent line between Africans and non-Africans' with some further
adjustments being made in the Native Trust and Land Act of 1936 that
accelerated the concept of segregation between African and white populations (Christopher 2001: 32–3).

Land management in French colonies

France was one of the oldest European imperial and colonial powers,
but her colonial interests accelerated afresh in the nineteenth century,
starting in North Africa and later spreading to Central and West Africa,
South-East Asia, and the Pacific. The dynamic of French imperial experience, is complex, and the basic chronologies of colonial spread have been
analysed earlier in Chapter 2. What is significant about French imperial
development and colonial settlement is that, probably more than any

other European power, France had a clear notion of the role and function of colonies and of its own *mission civilisatrice*. In essence this involved a centralisation of power and control in the metropole, and concerted attempts at standardisation of language and culture to a French model. French colonisation was often based on powerful military intervention.

It has been estimated that between 1830 and 1914 the French had appropriated almost half of Africa north of the Sahara, most of it comprising forest and waste land, whose management was in the hands of either settler communities or the state. About 10 per cent of this area was under arable cultivation, mainly by Europeans (Brett 1986: 271). Difficulties encountered in the attempted development of a settlement plan that would give security to the French colony and some economic return included a shortage of good-quality arable land; the complexities of land appropriation; and 'the presence of a disaffected indigenous population which was hostile to French rule and settlement, and which always greatly outnumbered the French colonists' (Christopher, 1984: 60).

Policy changed during the period of French control over Algeria, starting with the mistaken assumption that:

there would be abundant unalienated land, only to learn that the conquered territories were covered in layer on layer of indigenous custom and philosophy of landholding ... To acquire a public domain, the French resorted to a combination of tools, including conquest, expropriation, investigations of traditional title, and one-sided laws that freed up inalienable land held by tribes and Muslim religious orders. (Weaver 2003: 38)

Additional operative principles were that land should be granted, not sold, to settlers, that villages rather than individual farms would be the basis of colonisation, and small-scale rather than estate-scale enterprises would be the norm, coupled with use of a land-dispossessed Algerian labour force, reliance on state direction and a shortage of French and European settlers in the Algerian countryside (they preferred the towns) (Christopher 1984: 162). The consequent problem was: 'How do you make Algeria a French colony, and a colony administered as an integral part of the *metropole* at that? The initial French response was to offer prospective French settlers the inducement of free land. But relatively few accepted the offer, and of those who did, more would-be *colons*, or rural settlers, preferred to congregate in the cities than settle on the land' (Prochaska 1990a: 152).

The settlements established after the French conquest were initially quite small (400–1,000 ha), had defensive walls, and benefited from new drainage schemes and orchard plantations. Although the European rural population increased from 30,000 to 100,000 between 1840 and 1860, the figure declined to 90,000 in 1891, to which attempted redress was sought by an official colonisation programme from 1878 to 1904, and in

1881 the ambitious Project of Fifty Millions was launched to spend 50 million francs (£2 million) on 150 new villages. However, the pace of colonisation had slowed. Whereas some 264 villages had been established or enlarged in the 1870s only 107 were initiated in the 1880s while the number fell to a mere 46 in the following decade ... Thus by 1900 there were 700 colonisation villages housing some 189,000 Europeans on 2,000,000 ha of land, mainly situated on the plains of northern Algeria. (Christopher 1984: 165)

Thereafter agricultural colonisation was through purchase of Algerian land. Occupation and settlement lasted until Algeria became independent in July 1962, and was characterised by long and bitter conflict.

Sutton and Lawless, in their study of the regrouping of 2 million Algerians during the war of independence from 1954 to 1961, state that:

Regrouping as a policy was not new to Algeria or to the French army. It was used by French forces in Algeria during the nineteenth century to put down rebellions and to pave the way for settler colonisation. It enabled the colonial power to destroy resistance by weakening tribal structures and to appropriate the most fertile tribal land for European settlement. The strategy was practised again by the French army in Indo-China in their struggle against the nationalist forces of the Viet Minh immediately after the Second World War. (Sutton and Lawless 1978: 332)

Tunisia

France had a long-established trading link with Tunisia, but interest was intensified from 1862 onwards with the granting of a loan to Tunisia floated in Paris to support the lifestyle of the Bey. Italy's increasing ambition was also a geopolitical factor, and following the Congress of Berlin of 1878, with the support of Britain and Germany, France sent a large force to Tunisia in 1881 to subdue raids on the Algeria/Tunisia border, and declared an open protectorate in 1883. There had been European settlement in Tunisia before it became part of the French empire, and the colonial pattern of land exploitation was achieved through the speculative acquisition of large plantations worked by large Algerian labour forces – a familiar feature of colonial policy elsewhere. There was some reduction in the size of these colonial agricultural enterprises in the late nineteenth and early twentieth centuries through the sub-division of large estates for sale to speculators. A major commodity grown on the plantations was olives, for the production of olive oil (Christopher 1984: 166–7).

Morocco

The Spanish interest in Morocco was restricted by the Franco-Spanish Treaty of 1912 to a protectorate role over a northern coastal zone, 200 by 60 miles (320 by 96 km), together with the Ifni enclave and Cape Juby region in the south-west, on the Atlantic coast. It took France over twenty years to control and pacify Morocco, mainly under the influence of Marshall Lyautey, the first Resident-General who was in control from 1912 to 1916 and 1917 to 1926.

Lyautey was an important colonial theorist, who in a *Grand Rapport* of 1916 to the French Minister of War set out detailed plans for colonial development, including communications networks, industrial advancement, training of local labour and trade fairs to promote industry and agriculture (Salazar 1991. 372). Salazar has shown how

Lyautey, supported by Sultan Moulay Yussef (1912–27), simply aimed at making Morocco a model for developing countries: he drew his conception of social development from nineteenth-century social catholicism (Albert de Mun) that emphasized a belief in natural hierarchy, social solidarity and corporatism: 'Colonial action is social action' ... Lyautey's unique colonial doctrine was in fact deeply rooted in the French royalist tradition, which, from 1900 to 1930, shaped, along with Marxism, French intellectual elites. (Salazar 1991: 373)

Lyautey's practical basis for the colonisation of Morocco involved military subjugation, particularly of the more militant tribes of the Atlas and the south of the country, but also attempts at indigenous economic development. The potential for such development was, of course, dependent on the degree of 'pacification' of the regions or zones of Morocco, which Lyautey divided into three. First there was the completely pacified zone, where the work of European colonisation could proceed and where collaboration with local people was made possible. The second was a marginal zone between the first and the third (war zone), where the progress to peace was made by military action and intense political activity. The war zone, by definition, was an area of constant conflict and use of major military resources (Hoisington 1995: 55).

The pattern and process of French rural colonisation in Morocco was very different from that in Algeria and Tunisia, on account of its late establishment (1912) as a French protectorate, more marginal position in the French empire's administrative structure, and the basis on which land was acquired (by purchase from the Moroccans). Christopher (1984: 168) states that the 'French rural settlement of the country was remarkable for the speed with which it was accomplished in the years between the two world wars; it is also a rare example of colonial initiative in a period of neglected Empires.' A programme of colonisation was initiated by the Comité de Colonisation in 1916, with the sale of land to soldiers, recent immigrants and others, at a medium size of about 200–400 ha, larger estates being rejected, notably during Lyautey's time as Resident-General, but the average size of colonists' farms had lowered to 50 ha by 1953 through sales in smaller units after 1935. Most of the European settlement was scattered across the plains of northern and central Morocco (Christopher 1984: 168).

Land appropriation and allocation in French Indo-China

Details of land appropriation processes in French Indo-China have been studied, inter alia, by Mark Cleary, who identified land control as 'a key part of the French *mission civilisatrice* in colonial Indochina' (Cleary, 2003: 356). The improvement of agricultural output and attracting greater capital investment from the French metropole were the major objectives. In common with many other European powers, French land development policy started from the premise that land use under indigenous systems was wasteful, especially the various forms of shifting cultivation, and assumed that it could only be improved and rationalised by translation to private ownership. It was helpful to such a policy that the French metropolitan state under the Third Republic strongly supported the idea of the socio-economic benefits attaching to a predominantly peasant society: 'A metropolitan France dominated by the economic and cultural values of a numerous peasantry provided a model for the reshaping of the colonial periphery' (Cleary 2003: 356).

The French developed a series of 'land codes', which facilitated the appropriation, reallocation, and determination of land-use practices in colonial regions. In Indo-China the land codes were part of the civilising mission, primarily geared to an export economy and the promotion of both small family farms and plantations, together with infrastructural initiatives such as land drainage for better rice production on the lower Mekong (Cleary 2003: 357).

Cleary's study of the southern Vietnamese colony of Cochin China focuses on the improvement of land use for the commercial production of rice and rubber in the period *c.* 1900–40. The improvement ethic brought conflicts of interest both between smaller colonial settlers and the major commercial plantation groups such as Michelin, and in turn between the colonial state and the interests of the indigenous peoples, especially the Moi and Hmong *montagnard* hill peoples. A key feature of Cleary's study is the complexity of land legislation shown by documents in French colonial archives.

The French took control of Cochin China, at the southerly tip of Indo-China, between 1859 and 1883. With a low density of population, and as a target for immigration from Annam and Tonkin, in the north together with the significance of Saigon, its main urban centre for investment and port for export, it became a major focus for French colonial development. Cleary has distinguished three types of pre-colonial land tenure in the region: 'the heavily-settled lands of coastal and estuarine Tonkin and Annam, the "frontier" lands of Cochin China and the landholding systems of the *montagnard* groups in the interior' (Cleary 2003: 361). The pre-colonial landholding systems were primarily controlled by village communities, and comprised a mixture of communal and private ownership.

In the older-settled parts of Cochin China, Annam and Tonkin, there were three types of landholding: *tu dien* – communal land to which family use rights were attached; *cong dien* – lands for periodic redistribution to benefit the poor; and *tu dan diem* – lands which were used for income generation for ceremonial events. The systems characterising the land-use systems of the hill tribes were focused on use rights linked with and inherited through kinship and lineage groups. Hence: 'Rights to land were rarely documented and boundaries were neither surveyed nor registered. Instead, a knowledge of rights and boundaries was handed down through oral tradition and often imbued with particular spiritual and ancestral overtones … Land was held by stewardship rather than in outright ownership. It was neither a freely marketed nor a homogenous, tradable entity' (Cleary 2003: 362). The main agricultural system was the production of hill rice, based on shifting cultivation: a system which conflicted with the French notion of efficient and scientific use of land.

One aim of the French colonial administrators was to settle the area with farmers: initially the intention was that they should be French, but in practice, with the exception of those who took up land under a post-First World War policy for settlement of army veterans, the settlers were mainly Vietnamese. They were seen as the Indo-China equivalents of the French peasant farmers whose existence was a major part of contemporary French social and economic policy. Economic profitability was closely linked with agricultural production for export from the new rice fields of the Mekong and from the rubber plantations in the east. The radical land legislation required to effect this development commenced in 1885, with further refinements between 1886 and 1928.

The crux of this legislation was the recognition of the tensions between the two parts of French colonial development policy for this region, with 'fundamental contrasts between productive and speculative capital and between a small peasant and large-scale capitalist agriculture' (Cleary 2003: 363–4). The new land codes, while recognising indigenous use rights, facilitated the appropriation of lands deemed to have been vacated by the population, for example in Tonkin and Annam, that had departed during the time of French subjugation. Though indigenous rights were preserved in some of the *montagnard* lands, against the requests of large French companies for large land allocations, there was a stronger desire for the appropriation of land for rice-growing in the delta region. The determination of the size of land grants was a problem. Earlier large concessions were replaced by upper limits of concessionary land grants by the Land Office of 200 ha in 1909 then 500 ha in 1916, most of the grants additionally having conditions requiring the rapid development of cultivation. The size limits on land grants at once frustrated French settlers and colonial officials keen to speculate on the rubber-producing boom, and smaller farmers anxious not to be affected by the consequences of such land speculation.

The conflicting discourse of the major players in this drama typifies the contradictions of a policy aimed in the late nineteenth and earlier twentieth centuries at the development of rice production on small farms in the delta, and the creation of a French and Vietnamese landlord class, with dependent tenant-farmers an outcome of the failure of this policy (Cleary 2003: 364, 366).

In north-east Cochin China rubber plantations were developed on the *terres rouges* soils. Rubber trees were planted experimentally from 1905 around Saigon, but substantial development of rubber plantations started in earnest in the period *c.* 1921–5, and accelerated from 1928–33 (in the east of Cochin China). This new internationally tradable commodity brought added requirements for large-scale land allocations, and again brought tensions via anti-speculation sentiment and concern for indigenous land rights. Rubber required major capital investment for land clearing, tree purchase and planting, and for payment of labour, while there was also a delay of about seven years before planted trees produced significant amounts of rubber.

Land policy in the rubber-producing regions of Cochin China evolved from an initial tendency to accommodate large-scale capital investment by planters and plantation companies through large land grants, to a more regulated system, the latter partly an outcome of the amount of land left uncultivated on the larger estates. From 1928 levels of land grant of 300–1,000 ha, 1,000–4,000 ha, and over 4,000 ha could only be made with approval of Residential Officers, the Governor-General, and the Minister of the Colonies (Cleary 2003: 369). Notwithstanding this, the development of larger-scale rubber plantations undermined the government policy of encouragement to small farmers, and led to great complexities of land appropriation and sale in the *montagnard* regions which were more radically affected by rubber-growing than they had been by the increases in rice production in the delta.

There was some official protection of the lands used for shifting cultivation after 1924, and leases rather than sales of larger areas of land for rubber production were favoured. But by the 1930s it was proving more difficult to protect the use rights and shifting cultivation (*ray*) systems of the indigenous peoples such as the Moi and Hmong in the face of the growing demand for rubber plantations, and subsequently for timber, concession rights for which had also been incorporated into 1928 legislation. Cleary's important study of the changes in land-use rights in Cochin China through French colonial policy has interesting parallels:

Elsewhere in the French empire, most notably in North Africa, similar clashes over how landownership was conceived by different groups (as between, for example, the French administration in Algeria and its Islamic subjects) was an important outcome of the spread of colonial legislation. Certainly it can be argued that the land codes themselves provide a valuable base from which to examine colonial policy in southeast Asia. The Dutch in Sumatra and the British in Borneo and Malaya faced similar pressures in developing their land policies and in their dealings with both indigenous peoples and metropolitan capital. (Cleary 2003: 371–2)

The Dutch East Indies

The Dutch had been in South-East Asia from the sixteenth century, expanding in the seventeenth century after the establishment in 1602 by the States-General of the Netherlands of the United Netherlands Chartered East India Company or Dutch East India Company (VOC), a consolidation of a number of Dutch private trading joint stock companies already operating in the region. The VOC was given exclusive Dutch trading rights to Asia and the Indian and Pacific Oceans, with complete control over territories where it operated, and was a major force in Dutch colonial policy until its dissolution in 1799. The end of the sixteenth and the first half of the seventeenth century witnessed the expansion of Dutch interest not only in South-East Asia but also in the Mediterranean, the West Indies (a Dutch West India Corporation was founded in 1621), and Japan. The initial Dutch interest in the East Indies was in dominating the spice trade in competition with other European powers and local Indonesian traders, a process that was both successful and lucrative for the VOC.

After the demise of the VOC, and the strengthening position of France and Britain in South-East Asia, the Dutch took firmer and more centralised control of the region, transforming by force their former hegemony over 'a patchwork of principalities, sultanates and fiefdoms' (Marlay 1991b: 184) into a more typically colonial dominance, making use of the aristocracy of Java to exact produce such as coffee and sugar from peasant producers at artificially low prices that would facilitate greater Dutch profit. From *c*. 1830 to 1870 the Dutch introduced a cultivation system (*Cultuurstelsel*) to Java. This involved cultivators being obliged to reserve part of their land (about one-fifth) for the cultivation of targeted amounts of particular export crops and to give labour for their cultivation. The products, which were mainly sugar, tea, coffee or indigo, were paid to the Dutch administration in kind instead of rent on the land, the products being sold in Amsterdam by auction (Elson 1999: 133; Wesseling 2004: 107–8). This system in theory offered the possibility of peasant cultivators making a profit from commercial crops, and was of considerable benefit to the Dutch, but in practice the system led to rural subservience for the cultivators (Keay 2000: 449) to a point where 'the exactions became intolerable. Indonesians were driven mercilessly to grow sugar and coffee, build roads and bridges, and pay other taxes in money and labour, and the only beneficiaries were the Dutch, the co-opted native royalty, and Chinese moneylenders' (Marlay 1991b: 185). The land rent system was a continuation of British practice in Java in 1811–16, to which was added an exploitive compulsory labour element in the culture system, which operated from the 1830s and declined from the 1850s. It operated mainly on Java, but somewhat unevenly, and after the withdrawal of

Fig. 4.2 Ploughing a ricefield with water buffaloes, Java, *c.* 1880. By permission and © of Royal Netherlands Institute of South-East Asian and Caribbean Studies, Leiden, image no. 12184.

tea, pepper, indigo and tobacco from the system in 1860–4, it was ended by legislation in 1870. Wesseling shows that the 'indigenous population therefore suffered greatly under the cultivation system. Seen in a macro-economic light, it led to stagnation, because there was no incentive to innovate. It was a system of shared poverty. The native population had no access to the capital market, so that in fact two economies existed side by side, an international-European economy and an indigenous economy' (Wesseling 2004: 107).

German colonies and land policy

Germany was a late and initially reluctant colonial power, but came quickly into this role on the basis of pressure from colonisation organisations at home and concern at maintaining a powerful competition at home and overseas with rival European neighbours, together with the

prospects of commercial gain and of finding outlets for migration overseas for Germany's rapidly increasing population.

The first phase of German commercial interest in Africa, from *c.* 1847
to 1882, was mainly concerned with trade links by merchants from
major north German ports such as Hamburg and Bremen. Initial interest in South-West Africa had been generated by a merchant from Bremen,
Adolph Lüderitz, who in 1882 had requested protection from the German
Foreign Office in the event of him setting up a settlement there, somewhere in the extensive stretch of territory between Angola in the north
and the Cape Colony in the south. Britain had interests along this coast:
Walfish Bay, the site of a whaling station, had been occupied by Britain
in 1878, and the offshore guano islands were declared British in 1866
(Henderson 1993: 39).

In 1883 Lüderitz's colleague Heinrich Vogelsgang secured, by purchase
and treaty of exchange of land for weapons with a Hottentot chief, Angra
Pequeña Bay (named by its discoverer by Bartholomew Diaz in 1487) and
adjacent land for five miles in all directions, a treaty later extended to the
area between 26° S. and the Orange River. The treaty was confirmed by
the former explorer and now German Imperial Commissioner Dr Gustav
Nachtigal (Henderson 1993: 41), and the name of the territory changed
from Angra Pequeña to Lüderitz Bay in the region of Lüderitzland. The
territory was placed under German imperial protection, marking a step
forward in Germany's claim to most of South-West Africa against Britain's
interests in the region. On 7 August 1884 an official pronouncement
from the German Reich declared its annexation of the territory of Angra
Pequeña, later followed by the declaration of a protectorate of the coastal
area from the Cape Colony to Portuguese Angola: South-West Africa.
The first German governor of this protectorate was Heinrich Goering
(Wesseling 1996: 284).

This second phase of German colonial land settlement, *c.* 1883–1906,
involved greater interest, initially in South-West Africa, in the development of land for pastoral use, in broader economic development, and the
concomitant appropriation of land and indigenous labour forces in the
service of the German imperial design (Palmer 2000: 13). Trade remained
a more important factor in German West and East Africa, but in South-
West Africa from 1891, the combination of pressure from colonial interest
groups in metropolitan Germany and the assessed potential of South-West
Africa made it an early target for agricultural settlement.

The regional and social geography of South-West Africa is significant
in understanding the processes of German land appropriation in the late

nineteenth and early twentieth centuries. The three major tribal regions and groups were: Amboland in the north, populated by the Ovambo; the central region, Hereroland (Damaraland) occupied by the Herero; and Namaland (named after the Nama occupants) in the south. The Herero

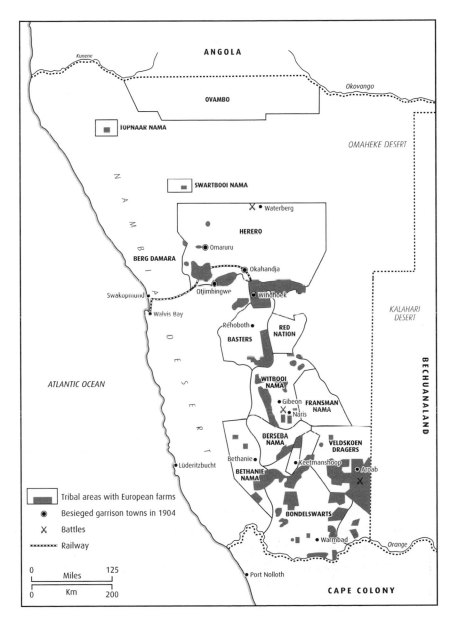

Fig. 4.3 South-west Africa: land and the Herera and Nama uprisings.
Source: Pakenham (1991: 603).
By permission of and © Weidenfeld and Nicolson, Orion Publishing Group.

and the Ovambo were Bantu-speaking people, and it has been estimated that the Herero population in the late nineteenth century was about 80,000, mainly engaged in nomadic herding of cattle, some of which had been bartered for guns (Drechsler 1986a: 39). The Nama, with a similar economy, numbered about 20,000, and, living at a more basic level of existence, were the Damara (30,000) and the San or Bushmen (3,000). Attempts at German colonisation and territorial acquisition took place against this ethnic background, in which the Nama and the Herero were constantly in conflict with each other.

The political geography of South-West Africa in 1885 included:

the territory acquired by Lüderitz which in 1885 passed into the hands of the German South West Africa Company. It comprised the coastal strip from the Orange River to Cape Frio (Walvis Bay excluded) and the hinterland of Walvis Bay. This strip was a sandy waste without any economic value, the sole purpose of Lüderitz's acquisition having been to forestall similar efforts by other colonial powers. (Drechsler 1986a: 40–1)

The other two territories of German involvement were, first, the extensive area of land placed under the German Reich's protection, where the tribes had made treaties to this effect, and, second, the area where the tribes had refused protection. The first was 'designed as a kind of supplement to Lüderitz's contracts of purchase, as a legalization of the German penetration of South West Africa', and the second was 'looked upon as a German sphere of interest by the German authorities' (Drechsler 1986a: 41). German activity and conviction of the need for a colonial territory in South-West Africa wavered in the last two decades of the nineteenth century, but in 1892 a firm decision was made in Berlin to keep the territory, and a larger military force was sent there to establish control and facilitate the appropriation of land and cattle. Theodor Leutwein, a major chief official from 1895 to 1898 and governor from 1898 to 1904, was a major agent for this purpose. He established northern and southern borders for the Herero territory in 1894 and 1895, and seized 12,000 head of cattle from the Mbandjeru (eastern Herero) in 1896–7. The question of methods of the transfer of land, held by customary tenure and partly subject to communal use rights, to potential German settlers was discussed from the early 1890s, resulting in the granting of 13,000 km² of Herero land to an English company in 1892, and the seizing of Herero land in 1894–5 for the creation of crown land. New German settlers were sold crown land and they also appropriated land from the Herero. Drechsler indicates that there was increased German settlement in South-West Africa in the later 1890s, their numbers increasing from *c.* 310 in 1891 to *c.* 2,998 in 1903, making for a total white population of 4,640, partly on account of the construction of the Swakopmund–Windhoek railway (Drechsler 1986a: 46–9).

Land and cattle were thus taken from the Herero, the Nama and others, as part of an attempt to create communities that would attract potential German settlers away from the temptation of emigration to the United States and the growing industrial cities of Germany, while at the same time enabling Germany to keep control of the territory and its economies (Palmer 2000: 13). No major policy of colonisation was, however, developed, for the initial responsibility for colonial administration was in the hands of the Colonial Office, and from 1907 the Director of Colonial Affairs, and much of it lay directly in the hands of colonial governors, remote from Berlin and government. Palmer suggests that 'German colonial administration in Africa was haphazard, slow and lacked the direction of any general colonial policy for Africa ... The powers of the governor were limited in comparison to those of the British governors' (Palmer 2000: 15). Much of the policy was determined locally and pragmatically.

In spite of this, further attempts were made to increase the number of German settlers in South-West Africa from 1903, on the basis of the large-scale expulsion of Africans from their lands. For a short time, after pressure from missionary societies, two reserves for the African population were established under legislation of 1898, one in Namaland, the other in Hereroland, but they were short-lived, being abolished after the uprisings against the Germans in 1904–7 (Drechsler 1986a: 50).

In 1906–10 a third phase of German colonial policy involved consolidation of political and military authority. Expansion of German settlement overseas continued from 1903 to 1913. From 1906 a change of colonial policy direction was experienced under the new Kolonialdirektor Dernberg, who ushered in 'a period of colonial consolidation and economic development in which larger sums of capital were invested for developments such as rail construction', and who 'enforced a new policy towards Africans: he considered them to be the most valuable colonial commodity as suppliers of raw materials and as labourers' (Palmer 2000: 17).

The annihilation by the Germans of large numbers of the African population of South-West Africa by suppression of the uprisings between 1904 and 1907 resulted in a reduction of the Herero population from 80,000 to 15,130 by the 1911 census, and of the Nama from 20,000 to 9,781, these figures also reflecting deaths in prison camps. One-third of the Damara people, who were not involved in the uprisings, were killed by German soldiers through being wrongly identified as Herero.

Drechsler (1986a: 62) has stated that this 'genocide was compounded by robbery. The uprisings had offered the German imperialists a welcome pretext for a military conquest of the territory that would settle the land issue once and for all in their favour', and by a German decree of 1905 'all of Hereroland and, a little later, Namaland were declared Crown territory. The whole of Hereroland and Namaland, with the exception only of the territory of the Berseba community, had thus passed into the possession of the German colonial rulers'. In consequence, the Herero and Nama became wage labourers, suffering from very poor health. Their numbers were supplemented by German manhunts for others of the indigenous populations who had fled to escape the wars, and they were all subject to the most inhumane treatment (Drechsler 1986b: 140).

Extension of the railway network in South-West Africa to a length of 2,104 km by 1913 meant greater prospects for German colonial settlement. Over the period *c.* 1887–1907 sufficient land for 480 farms had been sold, and an additional amount for 202 farms was sold in 1907 alone, the total number of European farms reaching 1,331 by 1913 (Drechsler, 1986b: 145). However the dream of many thousands of German settlers moving to live and farm in South-West Africa was never realised, partly on account of the amount of money needed for capital for a farm of medium size (Drechsler, 1986b: 144), with numbers of new farms declining in 1909–18. The size of the newly created land holdings varied, with the majority by 1913 being medium-sized enterprises, with 844 farms between 5,000 and 50,000 ha and 257 less than 5,000 ha, but with seven estates of more than 100,000 hectares, including those of the Rhenish and Catholic Missions. Agriculture was predominantly pastoral, involving new breeds of sheep and cattle, and ostrich farming (from 1912) (Drechsler 1986b: 144–5).

The balance of the economy was altered from about 1909 with the development of mining, including diamond mining, from which farm settlers were mainly excluded and in which the major investment and profit was made by large bank consortia and specialist diamond companies. Rich copper deposits were also exploited from about 1906 onwards, with most of the investment and profit made by large banks (Drechsler 1986b: 146–8).

German East Africa

German East Africa included a variety of environments and ethnic types. First, there was a coastal area with a hot and humid climate, populated in the late nineteenth century by developed societies resulting from the mixture over very long periods of time of Africans and Arabs. Arabs had settled along the coast and on the offshore islands such as Zanzibar, inter-marrying with Africans (Swahili), managing the trade in slaves, ivory and other commodities, and from *c.* 1850 developing plantations of sugar cane, cloves and coconuts where work was carried out by slave labour (Stoecker 1986a: 94). The major towns from which trading took place included Bagamoyo, Pangani, Tanga and Kilwa, and the nominal authority for the area was the sultanate of Zanzibar. This area was the focus of the East African slave trade which had been active early in the nineteenth century but which declined from *c.* 1873.

Significant land appropriation by Germany in this area started in 1884 when the rapacious German explorer Carl Peters was granted rights, through the company Gesellschaft für Deutsche Kolonisation, over 140,000 km^2 west of Dar es Salaam, and in 1885 a German protectorate was established (Stoecker 1986a: 95). Further land appropriation took place by Peters' com-pany (Deutsch-Östafrikanische Gessellschaft Carl Peters und Genossen) in 1885. Agreements with Britain and Portugal in 1886 established German East Africa's borders with Kenya and Mozambique. Major German com-panies and banks put up money for investment in this region, though resistance to their use of appropriated land came from Arabs and Africans, notably in 1888, with attacks by the population of the coastal region on the German ports and company land. This uprising was widespread, and undertaken by many different sections of the local populations.

Second, inland of the coastal belt was a plateau some 1,000–1,200 metres high, with environments including savannah, arid mountain regions and some tropical rainforest. To the north was Lake Victoria and mountains such as Mount Kilimanjaro, with Lakes Tanganyika and Nyasa (Malawi) to the west, and the River Ruvuma to the south. In the north-west were the kingdoms of Rwanda and Burundi, isolated by location and remote from European influence, whose minority Tutsi aristocracy, a cattle-breeding group, dominated and taxed the Hutu crop-farming people (Stoecker 1986a: 93–5).

Through military conquest and diplomatic initiative, German East Africa gradually took shape, and on 1 July 1890 its boundaries were established and agreed by the Heligoland–Zanzibar Treaty between Great Britain and Germany. Germany ceded claims to Witu, Somaliland and Uganda, conceded Zanzibar with Pemba to Britain, and obtained agreement for control of a coastal area which had been fiercely contested by the Germans through military force after the uprising of 1888. Between 1880 and 1890 the interior of German East Africa was effectively subjugated by military force, with army posts established at strategic points, including Tabora, a major trading settlement, and Ujiji, a significant point on the caravan route west from the coast (Stoecker 1986a: 102). Much of this process was carried out by a campaign of fierce military oppression and retribution, which led to the control of Burundi in 1903 and Rwanda in 1897. A consequence was the gradual movement inland from the coast of German economic interest, through the agency of companies including the Deutsch-Östafrikanische Gessellschaft. Coffee plantations were developed in the Usambara Mountains, facilitated by new roads, bridges and a railway, but the movement of coffee prices in Europe restricted their success. Other commodities developed were tobacco, coconut palms, cotton, sisal, and rubber from planted rubber trees. Coerced labour was used on the plantations. Resistance to German occupation continued, and the Maji-Maji rising of 1905, 'which was one of the most powerful anticolonial movements in the history of East Africa' (Stoecker 1986a: 112, 109), resulted in the decimation of much of the population of the region by German troops and mercenaries.

After 1905, Germany accelerated the development process in East Africa through the construction of railways and an increasing emphasis on production of raw materials for German industry and markets. African farmers living near the new railways produced crops for export, and plantations for the production of sisal, rubber and cotton were also established in regions adjacent to the railways. From the beginning of the twentieth century there was a rapid increase in plantation agriculture, with planted rubber trees gradually replacing the output of wild trees, and sisal, cotton, and coffee becoming increasingly profitable. While cultivation by Africans on smallholdings was also encouraged by the German colonial administration, this was strongly opposed by plantation owners. Progress was undoubtedly made in agricultural production in German East Africa between about 1900 and 1914, but compared poorly with agriculture in the British colony of Uganda (Stoecker 1986a: 149, 152).

The conditions for immigrant workers on the German plantations were very poor, and large numbers died from diseases such as smallpox, dysentery and tuberculosis. A death rate of 7-10 per cent and above has been estimated for plantation workers. Through the period discussed, German East Africa became 'a politically oppressed and economically dependent supplier of tropical raw materials' through military strength and other forms of coercion and suppression (Stoecker 1986a: 157, 161).

Cameroon

The chieftains of the Cameroon coast were persuaded by two German trading companies and by specious means to surrender their sovereign rights to Germany in July 1884, and German sailors landed in December 1884 to destroy villages and massacre their inhabitants (Stoecker 1986b: 28). Germany's initial influence was restricted to the coastal strip, and mainly concerned with protecting the interests of Hamburg trading companies, but early governors of this territory stirred up hatred among the indigenous people by their brutal and sadistic treatment, notably after uprisings in 1891 and 1893. This treatment provoked concerned reaction in Germany, especially by the Social Democratic Party. Steady inroads were made into the interior of Cameroon at the turn of the century, initially in the south-west for obtaining rubber, and later in the south-east, where there were extensive tropical forests for exploitation, and the north and north-east. German explorers had travelled through the north of Cameroon before 1880, and supported German claims to territorial control and rights of settlement. Cameroon continued to be an area of imperial rivalry between Germany, France and Britain, and boundary agreements in 1893 reflected political concerns rather than geographical and ethnic issues (Stoecker 1986c: 68–9).

Pressure for occupation and settlement was brought by the Deutsche Kolonialgesellschaft, which in the early 1900s took the view that the German government was moving too slowly to gain control of Cameroon. From about 1850 a significant number of German trading companies located themselves on the south and north-west coasts, and began to exploit the forest resources of large areas. The export levels from Cameroon increased rapidly between 1891 and 1906, with rubber being the most important raw material. Large plantations were established at the end of the nineteenth century, the earliest on the lower slopes of Mount Cameroon, with cocoa as the main product. As Stoecker has pointed out, 'The introduction of large-scale agricultural production by German plantation companies had far-reaching consequences for the indigenous population, primarily in western Cameroon, for it required dispossessing the local inhabitants of their land and the employment of agricultural labour' (Stoecker 1986c: 74, 72). Forcible recruitment of labour and very poor wages and working conditions made their lot unenviable.

In other areas, including the south, quick returns on capital invested in land purchase were sought and gained by companies such as the

Gesellschaft Südkamerun which was given one-fifth of the total area of Cameroon in exchange for 10 per cent of the profits being given to the German government. But real development was not what they had in mind: instead they were concerned primarily with making profits as quickly as possible. Thus, 'In fact, the purpose of the venture, which was modelled on the Belgian Congo companies in terms of structure and methods, was quick enrichment by stock exchange speculation and ruthless exploitation' (Stoecker 1986c: 75).

The pattern of exploitation, by now very familiar, was by military conquest of territory and people, followed by the organised exploitation of resources by the agents of individual trading and commercial companies. This was a kind of capitalist shifting exploitation, with companies with monopolies on economic activity and trade moving into new areas once resources had been thoroughly appropriated. The rapid acquisition of rubber and other resources was achieved by bartering guns and other artefacts for rubber, and thus reducing the time spent by local inhabitants in cultivating other crops. In turn, the price of food rose and the traders and the porters they engaged often resorted to theft and violence to obtain it (Stoecker 1986c: 77). The discontent created resulted in a number of uprisings, including that of 1904.

By 1906 most of Africa had been divided between the European colonial powers, and German policy moved towards consolidation and intensification of resource extraction from colonies. A boom in rubber prices until 1910 produced a rapid increase in the number of rubber plantations, and the development of railways facilitated tobacco and cocoa plantations. The number of plantations in Cameroon in the period 1906–13 increased from twenty-three to fifty-eight (Stoecker 1986d: 162).

The policies of individual commercial companies varied, but in their most severe form involved the resettlement of whole villages in order to locate labour in the right places. In contrast, missionary influence and German Colonial Office policy from about 1907 encouraged what was called 'native farming' in the forested areas, and the cultivation of cocoa and palm oil trees, resulting in limited success for the indigenous plantation owners. The economic boom from 1906 onwards required a much greater labour force, mainly obtained through coercion, bribery and other devious strategies.

Mortality in the labour force of some plantations has been estimated at 20–30 per cent per year, and conditions did not improve, as evidenced in accounts of contemporary witnesses, who wrote of labourers in chains and suffering from severe malnutrition. Stoecker cites the words of the

Colonial Secretary in 1913: 'It is a sorry spectacle to see villages drained of all menfolk, to watch women and children carry burdens, to find a whole people condemned to an itinerant way of life.' This exploitation furnished major profits for the European companies involved, with dividends rising for one of them from 8 per cent in 1907 to 20 per cent in 1913 (1986d: 164, 167, 168). The failure of a section of the population of Cameroon to accept German rule resulted in high rates of punishment by flogging. In all, the impact of German rule on the land and resource-use rights of the inhabitants of Cameroon was devastating, with greater effect in the forest region and less in the northern parts. Thus 'In the forest zone the existing African socio-economic and legal system showed signs of disintegrating. The colonial power began to replace it with a system fully geared to the needs of German monopoly capitalism' (Stoecker 1986d: 174).

Belgian Congo

Belgium – rather like Germany – started its life as a new nation with no aspirations to overseas colonies. Created in 1830 from the division of the former kingdom of the Netherlands, its initial economic focus was on industrial production and trade within Europe, eschewing the notion of colonies in a context of free trade, with a marked reluctance to accept the economic burdens of colonial links. Additionally, 'Belgium had no navy to protect any overseas possessions. Were it to take any bull-like steps into that international china-shop it might easily jeopardize its neutrality, and hence its very existence. Its attempt at colonisation in Guatemala in 1845 had proved a fiasco. Small wonder, then, that Belgium was an anticolonial country' (Wesseling 1996: 77).

What changed all this was the action of King Leopold II (1835–1909), whose own wish was to promote overseas exploration, trade and the acquisition of colonial territory, following the model of the Dutch in the Far East. Details of his aspirations are recited earlier in this book (Chapter 2), but in essence they amounted to an unbridled ambition for the acquisition of wealth from overseas colonies disguised as an altruistic venture to be facilitated by missionary and other philanthropic agencies (Wesseling 1996: 78–9). Areas that attracted his interest when he was duke of Brabant were in the East, including the Pacific and Indian Oceans and the China Sea, together with Borneo, New Guinea, Formosa, Tonkin, Sumatra and other places. On becoming king of Belgium, as an individual of wealth and influence, and recognising the anti-colonial stance of the Belgian people and government, he developed imperial schemes. His interest turned to Africa: the Brussels Geographical Conference of 1876, and its formulation of the International Association for the Exploration and Civilisation of the Congo, allowed some of his plenipotentiary missionaries, military personnel and explorers to force unilateral agreements on tribal chiefs, one outcome being his acquisition of the Congo Free State as a personal fiefdom. This was formally recognised by the Berlin West Africa Conference of 1884–5.

The diplomatic negotiations leading to this agreement were complex and constantly shifting, and the cartographic representations of the new state and its boundaries were uncertain at times, but a new entity was created that was to have a profound and deeply disturbing impact on its indigenous inhabitants, who played very little part in its creation. Leopold's control over the Congo Free State lasted until 1908, when he was forced by his own and other European governments to relinquish control because of deep concern at the inhuman consequences of his policy and administration (described in Chapter 2). The name of the Free State was changed to the Belgian Congo, and remained under Belgian administration until 1960. After 1908 there was a change from the gathering economy to commercial plantation activity. Major land concessions had already been made by Leopold II to Belgian companies for rights to raw materials such as rubber, but thereafter, more cautiously and with conditions attached concerning the provision of basic services for African workers, the Belgian government offered concessions to companies such as the Belgian subsidiary of the Unilever company with land rights over large areas for the commercial development of palm oil (Christopher 1984: 97–8).

Portuguese West Africa (Angola)

Portuguese involvement in the region dates from 1483, with an attempt to develop the kingdom of Kongo, but greater interest in the profits to be made from the slave trade intensified Portuguese activity in the area of the Ndongo kingdom, from the title of whose king (Ngola) the country ultimately derived its name. Military forts were established in the interior from the late sixteenth century, and a more formal system of administration developed from the mid-seventeenth century. The slave trade, fed by small-scale wars to obtain the slaves, continued into the nineteenth century, and was the major Portuguese economic activity, notwithstanding limited efforts to develop the mineral resources from the late eighteenth century, 'providing more than 80 per cent of Angola's commerce before 1832. By the time the Portuguese slave trade was abolished in 1836, over three million Africans had been exported from Angola' (Dennis 1991: 26).

Portugal secured greater control of Portuguese West Africa between the Berlin West Africa Conference of 1884–5, which recognised Portugal's claims, and 1915, by which time, after many military offensives against the indigenous populations, Portugal had gained control of the interior of the country. Intensification of white colonial settlement took place during Portugal's Republican period from 1910 to 1926.

Successful attempts had been made in 1849 and 1850 to establish white Portuguese agricultural settlement in coastal oases in southern Angola, specifically for Portuguese refugees from Brazil, with cotton as a main crop, and with the extension of military protection and settlement to the Huila Highlands between 1884 and 1886. Missionaries were also encouraged to extend their influence to areas of east and south-east Angola, but the latter region proved too difficult to colonise (Clarence-Smith 1979: 15–17).

The chartered commercial company, a device commonly used by European imperial states for colonisation and the creation of profit in Africa, was extensively used by the Portuguese. Very poor-quality land in southern Angola, for example, was given to the Companhia de Moçâmedes (Moçâmedes was a coastal trading town) in a region of strongly independent indigenous peoples, and whose only potential for profit was thought to be from mining and railway construction (Clarence-Smith 1979: 19–20).

Three phases of expansion of the Portuguese colonial nucleus in southern Angola have been identified by Clarence-Smith, determined:

on the basis of the three general criteria of the private ownership of the means of production, the employment of slave or wage labour and the predominance of production for the market. Between the 1840s and the 1860s, the ports and oases of the coastal strip were brought into production, and in the 1880s parts of the highlands were incorporated into the colonial nucleus. Finally, a few limited areas along the middle Cunene valley were annexed from the 1900s. The colonial nucleus was thus extremely restricted and discontinuous, as could be expected in a semi-arid environment with few resources. (Clarence-Smith 1979: 21)

Fishing, a small textile industry, the plantation production of cotton, foodstuffs, stock-raising (mainly by Africans) and transport and trading services were the main component parts of the region's economy, which was maintained on the basis of slave and forced labour. The appropriation of African communal land was a consistent part of Portuguese colonial development policy, with much opposition through banditry by those whose land rights were stolen. In the Huila highlands of southern Angola, for example, land was allocated to Boer trekkers from the Transvaal in the 1880s and 1890s, and in small lots to Madeirans between 1884 and 1886, with only *c.* 400 ha of communal freehold land held by Africans in the Huila Highlands in 1916 (Clarence-Smith 1979: 32–3, 44–5).

The technical and pragmatic basis on which the Portuguese government allocated land to settlers was as 'vacant' land – similar to the *terra nullius* concept elsewhere – but as the land was predominantly used for shifting cultivation and pastoralism, the distinction between 'vacant' and 'occupied' land was difficult to make and very loosely applied. Without adequate survey personnel and facilities, the policy adopted was a total rejection of the rights of indigenous people, and the granting of land to white settlers, with the consequence that 'by 1885 the Boers and the Portuguese had succeeded in driving the Nyaneka off the best lands in the northern highlands ... the settlers took all the scarce alluvial lands along the little streams of the northern highlands, where the soils and rainfall were most propitious for agriculture' (Clarence-Smith 1979: 83; 84). There was also appropriation of cattle by the new settlers in the highlands, notably the Boers, who ran cattle raids against the Nyaneka in order to replace their own cattle, which had died on account of their unsuitability to the new environment to which they had been brought.

Portuguese East Africa (Mozambique)

According to Newitt (1995: 347–8),

Although the whole 'Scramble for Africa' now appears as an irrational aberration which served no well-defined interests for any of the European powers, and can be seen as nothing more than the use of naked force to rob native Africans of their land, wealth and rights, there is no denying that, among the European scramblers, Portugal's claims to the disputed areas were far superior to those of Britain.

Portuguese East Africa – subsequently Mozambique – was part of a formerly more extensive Portuguese empire, developed after the major voyages of discovery by Portuguese navigators such as Vasco da Gama in the late fifteenth and sixteenth centuries. Trading posts were established in the late fifteenth and early sixteenth centuries along the coast of southeast Africa, and expeditions were sent to the interior to look for gold. From the early seventeenth century large estates (*prazos*) were established, under the control of white settlers (*prazeros*) who rented the land from the Portuguese state and who were expected to serve as colonial administrators. By the beginning of the nineteenth century various attempts had been made to reduce the power of the *prazos*, many of which, established along the Zambezi from the late sixteenth century, were the well-defended fiefdoms of elite Afro-Portuguese families (*muzungos*) and virtually independent of Portuguese control, and also to reduce the size of their estates. As Newitt (1995: 298ff.) has shown, the symbiotic relationship that had previously existed between the Portuguese state and the Afro-Portuguese families began to break down in the early nineteenth century, through inter-familial wars, government action, drought and famine, and changes in the external world. Thus

> While these obscure struggles, often a grotesque mixture of savagery and farce, were fought out within the cultural context of traditional Zambesi society, the world outside was rapidly changing. The explosive industrialization of Europe and the United States spread its influence until eventually the armed struggles on the Zambesi became absorbed and transformed by the global economic revolution of nineteenth-century imperialism. (Newitt 1995: 298)

There was also concern at the growing interest in the region by other European powers, including the British, Dutch and French. A major component of the region's 'economy' was the slave trade, active since at least the mid-seventeenth century and reaching maximum numbers in the 1820s, thereafter slowly declining through two official Portuguese decrees banning the trade (1836 and 1875), and through British humanitarian opposition. Notwithstanding its long interest in South-East Africa, by the time of the European 'scramble' of the 1880s Portuguese control was limited. Portugal at that time only had influence in the coastal regions and the Zambezi valley. The quasi-autonomy of the *prazero* system was effectively ended in 1888 when Portuguese military action removed the de Cruz family from its powerful position of authority, and thereafter, with some exceptions, the basis for land allocation and other economic activity was that commonly used by other European powers: the chartered merchant company. This system was also used in Portugal's other major African colony, Angola (Pollock, 1991c: 415).

The major factors affecting the economic development of Portuguese East Africa in the late nineteenth century were, as Newitt suggests: the movement of Indian capital into East Africa; British attempts to stop the slave trade and substitute a more moral kind of (free) trade; changes in the Portuguese metropolitan economy and in colonial policy; and the beginning of the South African mining economy (Newitt 1995: 317). By the 1890s the prime need was for military security and for capital investment in Portuguese East Africa. The second of these needs was met by reliance on private companies for land and mining development. New terms of reference were given to the *prazos*, differing according to whether they were in pacified or unpacified areas, and their leases were in fact largely granted to commercial companies rather than to individuals (Newitt 1995: 367). The main companies operating in Portuguese East Africa were the Moçambique Company (1891–1941) and the Niassa Company (1894–1929).

Italian colonisation

Italian colonialism and colonial settlement came later than that of France, Britain, the Netherlands and Belgium, and ran parallel with German colonialism (see Chapter 2). Italy was unified in 1870, and its attempts at colonising lands to the south across the Mediterranean (the 'fourth shore') derived in part from its struggle to become a major European power in the age of high imperialism, and to seek territories to which it could export surplus population. In 1869 the district of Assab, on the straits between the Red Sea and Gulf of Aden, was purchased as a coaling station by the Rubattino Shipping Company, and in 1882 an Italian settlement was built. In 1884–5 Italy occupied Massawa on the west coast of the Red Sea, and in 1890 these territories were designated the colony of Eritrea. Italy attempted to acquire protectorate status for Abyssinia by treaty in 1889, but was frustrated after defeat by a large well-equipped Abyssinian army at Adowa in 1896, when 6,000 Italian soldiers were killed. Italy acquired part of Somaliland by agreements with Somali chiefs in the 1880s, a lease on the Benadir ports from the sultan of Zanzibar in 1892 (conceded for payment in 1902), and various boundary agreements in relation to British Somaliland.

Renewed colonisation in Abyssinia followed Mussolini's conquest in 1935–6, which consolidated Italy's territories of Abyssinia (Ethiopia), Eritrea and Italian Somaliland into Italian East Africa. In 1911 Italy attacked the Ottoman empire territories in North Africa and by 1912 controlled the whole of Libya, the western part of which was known as Tripolitania, whose main city was Tripoli, and the larger eastern section Cyrenaica, whose capital was Benghazi. Italian consolidation was reduced during the First World War, but from 1922 the so-called *riconquista* (reconquest) of these territories heralded significant suffering, upheaval and oppression for the Libyan peoples as the interior was gradually 'pacified' by forces sometimes employing all the fearsome mechanization of modern warfare including aircraft, poison-gas, machine-guns and artillery. Yet despite the uniform intentions of Italian colonial policies, in practice the *riconquista* revealed significant geographical differentiation as the imposition of colonial authority was negotiated differently in each regional context.

This partly reflected degrees of opposition in Tripolitania from tribal groups (Atkinson 2003: 14). In Cyrenaica there was more unified opposition to the Italians by semi-nomadic groups, as a result of which subjugation of these groups by the Italians was delayed until 1932. Many members of these groups were eventually imprisoned in concentration camps from 1930 to 1932 (Atkinson 2003: 14). Italian colonisation, like that of other European powers operating overseas, was conditioned by contrasting and conflicting ideals, and was consistently opposed by those whose territory they sought to appropriate and colonise.

Colonisation began in the north of Tripolitania from 1922, using land which had been 'nationalised' on the basis that it had not been cultivated for three years – a ploy to remove land used in dry land shifting cultivation – and involved an area of 200,000 ha by 1932. Colonisation from Italy began later in Cyrenaica because of the longer period of opposition to the Italians. Christopher has shown that:

by 1940 at the outbreak of the Second World War some 375,000 ha had been obtained by Italian colonists and 3,900 families had been settled on the land. Colonisation in the 1920s had been based on private estates but these gave way to colonisation companies intent upon peasant settlement, in line with Benito Mussolini's agrarian philosophy. As a result the smaller peasant farms were situated further from Tripoli and Benghazi than the earlier estates and greater reliance was placed upon irrigation from boreholes. (Christopher 1984: 169–70)

The main crops cultivated were olives, vines and cereals.

In Eritrea, in very different climatic conditions, Italian settlement began in 1893 on the temperate plateau land near Asmara, but little land was available for state colonisation, and in spite of the immigration of nearly 6 million Italians to Eritrea between 1890 and 1905 there remained only sixty-one by 1913, and later plans for colonisation were not realised (Christopher 1984: 171).

Italian colonial involvement with Abyssinia/Ethiopia dates from 1869, with the purchase of the port of Aseb, but the defeat of the Italian army at Adowa in 1896 slowed the Italian colonial process. Ethiopia was invaded by Italy in 1935–6, with a six-year plan for settlement, infrastructure and education launched in 1937. It is estimated that by 1938 over 2,000 miles of roads had been reconstructed and that by 1939 seventy-eight new post offices had been opened, telegraph lines had been laid and extensive air network connections had been established. Settlement plans were implemented from 1938 with 600–700 colonist families from Italian Romagna and Apulia given small plots of land of between 75 and 125 acres (172 and 308 ha), but further plans were stopped by continuing local resistance to Italy's colonial presence (Townsend 1941: 141–2).

This chapter has examined the great variety of processes and outcomes of colonial land policies and practices, which were informed by a wide range of geographical, economic and social information and knowledge, of varying degrees of accuracy. In the following two chapters we describe and examine the ways in which some of that geographical knowledge was produced.

5 | Empire, exploration, and geographical knowledge

While Stanley was no saint, he was a shrewd pupil of the new press who used his formidable journalistic skills to acquire fame, freeing him in large measure from the geographical fraternity with whom he had chilly relations. But perhaps the most striking indicator of the erosion of the institutional constraints on who could become an explorer and how exploration should be conducted was evidenced with the entry of women into the fraternity. While the category of traveller had been open to women for some time, it was only around the turn of the century that women like Mary Kingsley and Gertrude Bell came to be seen as explorers. (Kennedy, 2007: 1889)

Exploration and imperialism

Geographical knowledge in various forms was both an outcome of and contribution to the processes through which the political, economic, social and cultural interests of European imperial powers interacted with those of their nascent colonies. One means by which such information was gained was the sponsorship of exploration, which – as the above quotation from Dane Kennedy's overview of British exploration in the nineteenth century shows – changed in its focus and personnel through time. Exploration is a challenging concept, having complex associations and meanings that reflect the motives and individual personalities of explorers and travellers. The accounts of their expeditions and travels help us to understand changes in the accumulation of geographical knowledge that were linked to national and institutional aspirations for overseas empires, and to contemporary scientific and belief systems. The links between exploration and empire were both direct and indirect. Dane Kennedy (2007: 1879) has suggested that exploration was a feature of European capitalist imperialism, connected to the discovery of new trade routes, markets and resources. He argues that one of the main concerns of the study of exploration should be with

how it played out in the field, shaping the perceptions and experiences of the explorers themselves and setting the stage for the subsequent assertion of Western influence and control over the lands and peoples that were being explored. There is no doubt that explorers served as an advance guard for imperial expansion – sometimes unwittingly, but often with conscious intent … By the late nineteenth century, the connection between exploration and empire was often direct and institutionalized. It was evident, for example in Henry Morton Stanley's later expeditions, which worked openly on behalf of imperial interests and resembled invading armies in their size and use of violence. (Kennedy 2007: 1890)

Kennedy also points to the rise of provincial geographical societies and the way in which the 'epistemology of exploration' contributed to metropolitan characterisation of land, people and cultures of nascent colonial territories as 'inherently alien and savage' (Kennedy 2007: 1890).

Driver (2001: 2) has also reviewed the problem of distinguishing 'between the discourses of adventurous travel and scientific exploration', suggesting that:

historians of geography ought to focus precisely on the unsettled frontier between them. During the eighteenth and nineteenth centuries, as much as the twentieth, the idea of exploration was freighted with multiple and contested meanings, associated variously with science, literature, religion, commerce and empire. The business of the scientific explorer was not always, or easily, distinguished from that of the literary *flâneur*, the missionary, the trader, or the imperial pioneer.

The last of these presumably included accounts by soldiers and military surveyors.

The term 'explorer' covers a wide variety of individuals and contexts. Images of scientific adventurers and explorers of the eighteenth, nineteenth and early twentieth centuries commonly portray individualistic, masculine, heroic, often tragic and traumatic characters, with particular styles of dress (navy or military uniform, 'safari' costume, or local dress) and equipment (scientific instruments, guns for protection and hunting, items for trading). The nineteenth-century explorer is frequently portrayed as a white male European with a pith helmet, armed with weapons to combat wild animals and human antagonists, attended by a large number of male indigenous bearers and assistants, marching in single file, and showing great courage in the face of many human and natural hazards: 'Relentlessly hunting big game or elephants, contending with mosquitoes and other nefarious insects, he never abandons his ultimate goal. By turns debonair and commanding, resolute and cautious, enthusiastic and disillusioned, he is the all-round hero, scornful above all else of deceit and irresolution. In reality explorers were much more complex figures, greatly circumscribed by the historical context' (Hugon 1993: 32).

Although most European explorers were working to instructions provided by a government ministry or a learned society, they frequently interpreted them in their own individual ways.

We now recognise, however, partly through postcolonial perspectives, that exploration and travel are much more complex and nuanced than this, and are bound up with issues of gender, culture, prejudice, scientific knowledge, geopolitics, eccentricities, opportunities, ideologies, and good or bad fortune. Gender is an important component, so that accounts of expeditions and travel by women and men are of major significance in understanding the causes and outcomes of exploration and travel. Explorers, as we will see later, could also be highly idiosyncratic and often highly eccentric personalities, loath to be tied to any broader institutional system save perhaps by the necessity of operating funds, the need to borrow instruments, and the temptation of attentive audiences, and were often vitriolic in their criticisms of other explorers and officers of scientific societies. Biographical studies are increasingly showing the variety and complexity of explorers, their journeys and their achievements. There is also recognition of apparent paradoxes, including those among the theatricalities of imperial exploration. Fabian (2000: 121) contends that:

the same men who saw their scientific mission endangered by African pomp and circumstance were in Africa as agents of an enterprise that was sold to the European public through pompous campaigns of propaganda, through exhibits and shows, and through the drama and tragedy reported in travelogues and in the press. The drama had its heroes and villains and a grand plot called *œuvre civilisatrice* ... Imperialism was a theatrical enterprise.

Motives for exploration and travel varied from the promotion of national images and scientific and commercial objectives by governments, learned societies, armies and navies, to individual curiosity. Some expeditions were more overtly scientific in purpose than others, but all were involved, in one way or another, in a search for varieties of geographical knowledge: accurate representations of the physical and human geographies of the regions and oceans through which they were conducted, mainly through maps and written accounts, together with graphic illustrations.

The means of presentation and dissemination of geographical knowledge from exploration were important. Maps, sketches, photographs and reports, for example, were some of the ways in which new knowledge from expeditions was presented, and it also formed the basis for questioning the reliability of individual explorers and their images as symbols of individual and national character. The role of indigenous people in aiding the European expeditions through provision of essential local geographical knowledge was 'to supply food and shelter, to serve as guides, translators, porters, and guards, and much more. Though the British Press tended to portray explorers as personifications of heroic individualism, they rarely accomplished their task without extensive and sustained assistance from those who were their purported objects of investigation' (Kennedy 2007: 1891–2). Explorers in East and Central Africa were highly dependent on existing supply and caravan routes, including those of slave traders; experienced wage-earning porters; and logistical caravan systems, each of which had its own pre-modern and modern trajectories. Stephen Rockel, in a detailed study of mobile labour systems in East Africa in the nineteenth century, has argued that 'The caravan system invented itself as a response to the capitalist world-market, yet it drew on pre-capitalist institutions. African cara- van operators and long-distance porters reconceptualised older ideas and invented new customs in order to act as full participants in the international economy' (Rockel 2006: 231).

These new ways of thinking about exploration have been well developed in recent years in relation to British, French, Belgian and German explor- ers (Fabian 2000; Driver 2001; Rockel 2006; Kennedy 2007). Heffernan (2001: 203) has examined what he called the 'politics and poetics of belief and disbelief' in relation to French and British ideas about Timbukto in the late eighteenth and early nineteenth centuries. His thesis is shaped around the idea of the trust in accounts of exploration and travel, the contrasts and conflicts between old and new geographical knowledge of far-off places, and the nature of the explorers themselves and of the met- ropolitan agencies, including geographical societies, by whom they were sponsored and in whose halls and journals their accounts were presented.

The problematic nature of explorers' knowledge, in relation to pre- existing knowledge of a region or place, is a key feature. Thus:

> the explorer was a rather disquieting figure to many sedentary metropolitan scientists. Most explorers were young unknown men with little or no scientific training. Their bravery and ambition were laudable but these were not the ideal qualities of the putative scientist. Eager young explorers were, almost by defini- tion, risk-takers – precisely the sort who might be tempted to fabricate evidence to increase book sales. (Heffernan 2001: 203)

Nonetheless their findings were presented, debated and published in metropolitan 'centres of calculation' such as scientific societies and muse- ums. In this particular instance, Heffernan focused on the images of Timbuktu presented and disputed in both scientific and highly personal ways by explorers and metropolitan authorities, following, as have others, the reasoning of Bruno Latour about the role of scientific controversies in our reconstruction of the processes of production of scientific knowledge, including maps (Heffernan 2001: 204–5). Heffernan analysed the representations of Timbuktu and its region that resulted from the 'Timbuktu craze', lasting from the 1770s to the 1830s. This was informed by both the science and the romanticism of the time, and by expeditions supported by the Association for Promoting the Discovery of the Interior Parts of Africa, founded in 1788. The association sponsored journeys to Timbuktu by the Scot Mungo Park, and by the Swiss Jean-Louis Burckhardt (who failed in his attempt, having died in Cairo in 1817). The political turmoil in Europe at the end of the eighteenth century and the beginning of the nineteenth transformed the contexts of exploration: 'The polite, scholarly and humanitarian view of exploration represented by the African Association now seemed almost quaint: the fading legacy of an earlier, gentler, age. A new era of total war demanded new, and correspondingly martial, forms of exploration' (Heffernan 2001: 206–7).

At the end of the eighteenth century knowledge of the lands of Africa, Asia, Indonesia, Australia and New Zealand, the scattered islands of the Pacific, and even (to a lesser extent) the interior of North America, was limited but expanding. Voyages of exploration from Europe from the late fifteenth century had opened up knowledge of the coastal regions of the major continents, and conquest and colonisation by the Spanish and Portuguese of areas of Central and South America had added considerably to that knowledge. Advances in navigation techniques and instruments and in the construction of ships (including the three-masted square rig, the construction of the caravel, and innovations in naval armament) in the late fifteenth and the sixteenth centuries added gradually to the facility for navigation and enquiry on distant seas and the coastal areas of distant lands, also stimulated by mercantilist ideas about the importance of trade for the status of individual states within Europe (Rodger 1998: 79–98).

Contacts between these newly known lands and Europe went back well before the fifteenth century. In Africa, for example, the routes of Arab merchant caravans across the Sahara, taking salt, weapons and cloth from the north to the south and gold, ivory and slaves in the opposite direction, are known from at least early medieval times, as are the accounts given by Arab explorers and travellers such as Ibn Battuta (Hugon 1993: 16). Contact with indigenous geographical knowledge in due course enhanced European perceptions, sometimes mythical and legendary in character, of the lands in which they were developing increased interest.

Eighteenth-century voyages

Major advances in European geographical knowledge characterised the
Age of Enlightenment in the eighteenth century, driven by what Stafford
described as its 'voracious appetite for facts' especially after Cook's Pacific
voyages (Stafford 1999). Withers and Livingstone (1999: 2) have described
the relationship in the following way:

In broad terms, geography's perennial fascination with the far away, with
mapping the world, with exhibiting and classifying knowledge, and with the
imposition of European ways of thinking on global realms are all recognizably
Enlightenment preoccupations. This is apparent in mathematical conceptions
of natural order, in natural theological perspectives that interpreted the world
in teleological terms; in geography as visualizing practice; in the geographical
natural histories of Buffon, Linnaeus, Zimmerman, and others; and in the
voyages and travels of explorers.

What were the contexts and outcomes of voyages of scientific discovery and other travels – significant parts of Enlightenment enquiry – for
expanding European imperial interests overseas? As with all aspects
of investigation of Enlightenment experiences, the answer is complex.
Mackay, in his study of science, exploration and empire in the period
1780–1801, pointed to two major geopolitical reasons for British interest in the South Atlantic before 1783: the concern to find a route into the
South Pacific that would not be subject to Spanish control; and the need
to have control over routes to India by sea, notably the uncertainty of the
Dutch control of the Cape of Good Hope in South Africa (Mackay 1985:
29–30). Geopolitics, including the possibility of annexing territory to the
British crown in the face of rivalry from other European states, and con-
sequentially of making full use of natural and human resources, was an
important influence. Clayton, in his study of the 'imperial fashioning' of
Vancouver Island in Canada, has suggested that the three most important
forces 'that were of general importance in the history of Western overseas
expansion [were] the West's scientific exploration of the world in the Age
of Enlightenment, capitalist practices of exchange, and the geopolitics of
nation-state rivalry'. The experiences of 'imperial fashioning', were, however, 'adapted to local terrain and gained a local texture' (Clayton 2000:
xi, xiii).

In the later eighteenth and early nineteenth centuries voyages by
British, French, Portuguese, Spanish and Dutch sailors and scientists
were undertaken across the major oceans of the world, notably the
Pacific, their main objectives being the promotion of navigation, trade

and science, and to locate a great southern continent, amenable to settlement and cultivation, envisaged by earlier geographers, and to find the western end of what was known as the North-West Passage, a strait that it was hoped would provide a sea route between the Atlantic and the Pacific. Many of these voyages were initiated and supported by European governments, through the agency of their navies, and most of the expedition commanders were naval personnel, such as James Cook. The voyages were also motivated by humanitarian sentiments: the meeting with and understanding of the cultures of indigenous peoples as part of a scientific, commercial and philosophical agenda, including the recognition of their humanity and the identification of differing orders of civilisation (Clayton 2000: 8–9).

The realisation of two of these geographical objectives was frustrated by the fact that although the Atlantic–Pacific strait did exist, it was of no practical use because of the amount of ice that prevented passage, and that a large southern continent, other than Australia, did not exist. The voyages did, however, provide substantial knowledge about the islands of the Pacific, Australia and New Zealand, the nature of the east and west coasts of the Pacific, the logistics of long-distance voyages, and the basis for settlement and colonisation of many areas by Europeans.

There were many such expeditionary voyages in this period. Jacob Roggeveen sailed to the Far East and the Pacific in 1721–2 under the aegis of the Dutch West Indies Company, including Easter Island and some of the islands of Samoa. Vitus Bering, a Dutch navigator in the Russian navy, in a voyage of 1728 located the strait, named after him, that separates the land masses of Asia and North America. Commodore John Byron was instructed by the British Admiralty to explore the South Atlantic and South Pacific, in order to locate 'any continental mass that might exist "within Latitudes convenient for navigation and in the Climates adapted to the Produce of Commodities useful in Commerce"', and undertook the voyage in 1764–5 (Beaglehole 1974: 122).

Byron annexed the Falkland Islands for the British crown, but made few important discoveries in the Pacific. His statement, prompted by sailing to the north of the Tuamotu archipelago, that there might well be a major continent or group of islands further south (Williams 1998: 556) led to the later voyages of Wallis and Carteret. Captain Samuel Wallis and Captain Philip Carteret crossed the Pacific in 1767–8, Wallis finding Tahiti and Carteret the Santa Cruz Islands, the Solomon Islands, and what he named the Carteret Strait between New Ireland and New Britain. Wallis's observation that there was a large land-mass south of Tahiti was a factor in the intentions of the following expeditions by James Cook.

Captain James Cook was a British sea captain with earlier experience of mapping the coastlines of Nova Scotia and Newfoundland. Intended initially as a scientific expedition promoted by the Royal Society, with the aid of the Admiralty, to observe the transit of the planet Venus across the southern skies in 1769, the objective of the first of Cook's three voyages (1768–71, 1772–5, and 1766–9) was amended to include the discovery of the imagined great southern continent, thus adding, as Williams has indicated, seaborne exploration to the Admiralty's responsibilities (Williams 1998: 558), though no formal plan of Pacific exploration was developed by the Admiralty. The addition of interest in new lands with new resources to the Cook expedition agenda brought into play a whole range of additional factors and concerns, not the least of which were the terms and procedures for dealing with indigenous peoples. The expeditions thus combined astronomical observations, the recording and collection of plants and animal specimens by accompanying artists, botanists and naturalists such as Joseph Banks, with the mapping of the coastlines of eastern Australia and the Torres Strait, the two islands of New Zealand and the islands of the Pacific.

On his second voyage Cook carried a copy of John Harrison's chronometer, the invention of which had massively improved the accuracy of calculating longitude while at sea (Williams 1998: 560). The consequences of the three expeditions led by Cook in terms of the effects of the acquisition and dissemination of scientific knowledge and on future colonial and imperial policy were enormous, as were the effects on the peoples of the lands that were 'discovered'. The motives for these expeditions were mixed, including imperial ambition and the development of global capitalist systems of exchange. Livingstone has asserted that:

notwithstanding the scientific achievements of Cook's seafaring ventures, his three voyages were neither conceived nor executed in an ideological vacuum. Cook, in fact, sailed under secret orders of the British Crown. His circumnavigating instructions from the royal court included the specific objective of establishing British dominion on newly discovered soil and reporting on the natural resources, both organic and inorganic, that could be exploited for Great Britain. (Livingstone 1992: 129)

Clayton (2000: 9) suggests, however, that the political and economic influences on Cook's voyages are somewhat uncertain, in the sense that there was no clearly identifiable 'imperial plan' into which they fitted, and points also to the fact that the British 'did not want Cook's voyages to become a pretext for another war with France and had no immediate plans to colonize the Pacific; they had other worries'. This does not mean, as Clayton later points out, that the Pacific had no overt geopolitical meaning for European countries; it nonetheless was a 'theatre of empire', and explorers' reports might be regarded as 'imperial allegories' (Clayton 2000: 13). Williams summarises Cook's achievements:

The observations made by Cook and his associates played an important role in astronomy, oceanography, meteorology, linguistics, and much else. In the realms of natural history the voyages were among the great collecting expeditions of any era. The amount of material brought back simply could not be assimilated by the older encyclopaedic sciences. Nowhere was this more evident than in the study of the peoples of the Pacific. It was the voyages of Cook and his contemporaries which helped to give birth in the next century to the new disciplines of ethnology and anthropology. (Williams 1998: 564)

Williams also points, as part consequence of Cook's voyages, to the subsequent development of British settlements around the Pacific rim, including those in New South Wales, Nootka Sound on the west coast of what became Vancouver Island, missionary activity in Tahiti, Tonga and the Marquesas, the expansion in trading and whaling, and the change in the administration of trade and the colonies in Britain from the Admiralty to the Home Office (Williams 1998: 564–5).

In June 1767 Wallis had sighted Tahiti, 'an encounter which was to stamp an imprint both exotic and erotic upon Europe's image of the South Sea, and when a French Expedition under Bougainville reached the island the following year reactions were even more effusive' (Williams 1998: 556). It was Wallis's reports of Tahiti and (erroneously) of a mountain peak some 70 miles to the south, mistakenly thought to be evidence of a great southern continent, together with the reports of Bougainville's expedition, that promoted Cook's first Pacific expedition. Louis-Antoine de Bougainville (1729–1811) was commissioned by the French government in 1766 to sail round the world, and became the first Frenchman to do so.

The background to his circumnavigation was the aftermath of the Seven Years War, with France drained of resources, having lost her Indian and Canadian colonial footholds, and occupying a diminished position in the European political hierarchy, all at a time when British colonialism was gaining pace. Anticipating further British territorial gains overseas, France directed her colonial policy towards the acquisition and

occupation of unsettled territories at key points on sea routes, in order to forestall some of Britain's likely colonizing moves, and to provide new bases to make up for those that had been lost. It was a policy made more urgent by the closing of Canada to French immigration and the expulsion of considerable numbers of French settlers from Acadia, part of Nova Scotia, and the destruction of their farms at the beginning of the war. (Dunmore 2002: xix)

With two ships, *La Boudeuse* and *L'Étoile,* Bougainville sailed westwards from Brest, and reached the Pacific via the Strait of Magellan, thence sailing north-west across the Pacific, reaching Tahiti in 1767 and the Tuamoto archipelago in 1768.

Dunmore has suggested that the achievements of this voyage by Bougainville impressed the general public more than they did the scientific community in France: partly because the voyage had not been conceived or supported as a scientific mission, in consequence of which no new science was expected of it by French scientific societies; and partly because of the efficacy and literary quality of Bougainville's account in stimulating the interest of the reading public (Dunmore 2002: lxx–lxxxi). Of particular interest to the educated French of this time were the accounts from the voyage to 'New Cythera' (Tahiti), presenting images of an unspoiled, idyllic paradise, inhabited by a beautiful and uninhibited people, images that resonated with Rousseau's theory of the Noble Savage, promoted in his essay of 1754 (Dunmore 2002: lvii). During their stay in Tahiti, scientists did in fact collect plant specimens and measure their longitude position, and navigation charts were made. It has been suggested, however, that it was Bougainville's exaggerated descriptions of Tahiti and its people 'that largely encouraged neo-classical myths of the noble savage and an idyllic Pacific' (Terry 1988: 153). Before leaving Tahiti, Bougainville formally took possession of it in the name of France (Taillemite 1992: 19).

There were other round-the-world voyages in the late eighteenth century that laid foundations for the acceleration of geographical knowledge in the nineteenth century. Jean-François de Galaup, comte de La Pérouse, undertook a round-the-world voyage in the years 1785–88 with the ships *Boussole* and *Astrolabe.* An expedition by the Spaniards Alejandro Malespina and José Bustamente to the Pacific from 1789 to 1794 reflected Spain's political and commercial interest in its possessions in South America and the Philippines. There were the Pacific voyages of George Vancouver, a British naval captain who had sailed with Cook on his second and third voyages, and who in April 1791 was commissioned to sail from Falmouth in England, with the ships *Discovery* and *Chatham,* to meet with a Spanish commissioner at Nootka Sound on the west coast of what would become known as Vancouver Island, in an attempt to solve a dispute between Spain and Britain over British settlement in territory claimed by Spain (Clayton 2000: 165).

Matthew Flinders, a British naval officer, charted the coasts of Australia. With George Bass, he circumnavigated Van Diemen's Land (Tasmania) in 1798 and proved that it was not part of the main Australian land mass. In the years 1801–3 he circumnavigated Australia (it was Flinders who gave the country its name) and completed the charting of its coastlines, returning to England only after a period of seven years' imprisonment by the French in Mauritius from 1803 to 1810.

Many other voyages of discovery took place in the late eighteenth and early nineteenth centuries, paving the way for further exploration of the seas and coasts around Australia and contacts with its inhabitants through the intermingling of commercial, humanitarian and geopolitical motives.

Explorations on land

In addition to the sea-based investigations outlined above, from the mid-eighteenth century onwards there were also European land-based expeditions to investigate the largely unknown geographies of a range of territories, including Africa.

Asian knowledge of Africa, with which there had long been trading links, was greater than European knowledge, although Europeans, through the literature of classical Greek and Roman civilisations, and of the conflicts between Islam and Christianity in the Mediterranean, had some understanding of the northern part of Africa. From the fifteenth century onwards, European knowledge of the coastlines of Africa and of tradable commodities, including slaves, increased with voyages of discovery en route to the Indies and the Far East, and by the settlement of the Portuguese in Ethiopia, so that by the end of the seventeenth century the outline of Africa was quite well known, though much of the interior remained a mystery. By the middle of the eighteenth century the demand for geographical information about Africa had increased, not least from the British because of the concern at the human suffering produced by the slave trade, and increasing interest in the wealth potential of trade with India and South-East Asia.

In the late eighteenth and the nineteenth century humanitarian concerns about the effects of the slave trade, and the consequences of increased contacts between Europeans and the indigenous inhabitants of Africa, India, Australia, New Zealand and the Pacific islands, the Caribbean and the Americas, 'raised questions about the ethics of economic exchange, the politics of equal rights or racial differences, and the purpose of Imperial power' (Porter 1999: 198). The intellectual arguments in Britain against slavery and the slave trade had largely been rehearsed and accepted by the 1780s, mainly in terms of slavery as a moral issue but also through questioning its economic efficacy (Porter 1999: 202). Legislation ending the slave trade was passed in Britain in the period 1805–7, and general statements about abolition were made at the Congress of Vienna in 1815 between Britain and France. But slavery continued in many colonial areas, including Africa. All these concerns led to greater focus of interest on actual or potential colonial areas.

Knowledge of the three main rivers of Africa – the Congo, the Nile and the Niger – was limited, and various government and other agencies sought to rectify this ignorance. One such society was the Association for Promoting the Discovery of the Interior Parts of Africa, founded in London in 1788. Prompted by both humanitarian and economic concerns, the twelve members of the Saturday's Club that met in a tavern off Pall Mall founded the association on 9 June 1788. Gascoigne has asserted that:

Africa had come increasingly under British gaze as a market for the growing volume of goods the Industrial Revolution made possible – particularly as the traditional pattern of trade based on slaves was under challenge from the anti-slavery movement. French exploration in Africa in the 1780s helped to give greater impetus to the establishment of the Association in 1788. (Gascoigne 1998: 179)

In July 1794 the explorer Mungo Park was engaged by the association to travel from the Gambia to Timbuktu, and he left in May 1795. Park's expedition 'settled for all time the vexed question of the Niger's direction and enlarged the bounds of Europe's knowledge of the countries of the western Sudan. It gave the association confidence to urge once again on the government the need for an active policy to develop the interior of West Africa for British commerce' (Hugon 1993: 29). Additional geographical information was brought back to England by William George Brown, who had travelled to Egypt in 1792, and returned with details of the Darfur region of the eastern Sudan (as then conceived); by Frederick Hornemann, a German explorer, who travelled inland across the Sahara from Cairo to the Fezzan; and by the Swiss traveller J. L. Burkhardt, who proposed to followed Hornemann's earlier route, but who in fact travelled in Syria, Egypt, Palestine, Arabia and Nubia from 1809 to 1815, and left geographical accounts of very high quality (Hugon 1993: 33). The members of the association decided to merge with the Royal Geographical Society, founded in 1830, because of their similar objectives.

Exploration and geographical knowledge in the nineteenth century

During the course of the nineteenth century the political, economic, humanitarian and scientific interests of governments, learned societies and missionary societies intensified, especially from mid-century onwards. The communication of the activities and outcomes of exploration also changed: increasing publicity attached to what were seen as the heroic deeds of Europeans encountering and recording uncharted areas, publicity that was extended by the printing of their accounts by book-publishers and by popular journals and (eventually) popular newspapers in Europe and the United States. There was fierce competition between the proprietors of newspapers to champion – and in some cases demean – their exploits and achievements.

Exploration became part of the culture of Britain and other colonial European powers, reinforcing not only confidence in scientific knowledge and but also changing national identities that were closely tied up with the aspirations of imperialism and colonial settlement. The links between scientific exploration, trade and imperial interests have been developed by Stafford (1999: 294), who has suggested that notwithstanding the sporadic nature of official British government support for exploration, 'the continuity of British exploration is striking, and its purpose and style remained remarkably consistent. Britain maintained a higher level of exploratory activity than any other Great Power, making the promotion and popularity of exploration a powerful indicator of the strength of Britain's expansionist drive from the 1790s to the First World War.'

There was a notable thrust in African exploration in the second half of the nineteenth century, and Stafford suggests that Africa replaced the antipodes as a main focus of exploration from the mid-nineteenth century, with the explorer combining the challenge of this unfamiliar environment with the cultural imaginations and certainties and the material imperialism of the developing European powers (Stafford 1999: 187).

At the forefront of British exploration was the Royal Geographical Society, founded in 1830 for the advancement of geographical science. It promoted exploration by providing small grants, loans of instruments, training in surveying and mapping, and advice on preparation for hazardous travels through its publication *Hints to Travellers*, first published in 1854. It also promoted a populist image of exploration through its lecture programmes at its various locations in London, with the accounts by explorers of Africa attracting large audiences. The complex relations between the Royal Geographical Society and the British imperial vision are discussed in Chapter 6 of this book, as are those of parallel societies in other European countries, including the Paris and Berlin Geographical Societies, founded in 1821 and 1828, respectively.

The range of expertise required of explorers was impressive, including skills with cartography, artistic illustration, hunting, leadership, route-planning and -finding, and scientific measurement and recording of items of natural history, climatology and location (Stafford 1999: 307). In Britain, instructions for the conduct and objectives of expeditions had usually been set by some sponsoring institution, such as the Admiralty, the Colonial Office, or (for a short time) the African Association, and then by the Royal Geographical Society. In the case of state-promoted expeditions, additional support was given through free passages on naval vessels and a range of diplomatic and consular support for approved foreign places, but was also given to 'unofficial' expeditions in remoter and unsurveyed areas (Stafford 1999: 300).

Scientific survey was at the heart of much exploration in the late eighteenth and the nineteenth centuries, so that in addition to the skills in formulating and implementing complex logistics of movement with bearers, materials, food and other supplies, through unfamiliar terrain for long periods of time, instruments appropriate for survey and measurement had to be obtained, transported safely, used and maintained. These included 'a telescope, a compass for travel and mapping, a sextant for making astronomical observations to determine latitude, chronometers to determine longitude, an artificial horizon, used in conjunction with the sextant for taking altitudes, a barometer to determine altitude by atmospheric pressure, and thermometers to record temperature and determine altitude by boiling point' (Stafford 1999: 308), together with possible additions such as survey chains, pedometers, theodolites, sounding lines, and hygrometers. There were continual problems with instruments, notably breakage and malfunction. Richard Burton's expedition to East Africa in 1857–9 was beset by problems of instrument failure and breakage:

All of the chronometers failed before the party had made much progress into the interior; most of the thermometers broke over time; other instruments were lost, stolen or stopped working owing to rough handling or harsh conditions. As a result, readings of longitude, latitude and altitude were often little more than educated guesses, marred by errors that the geographical fraternity would be quick to expose. (Kennedy 2005: 98)

Notwithstanding the many trials and tribulations accompanying scientific exploration in strange places, much was achieved through skill, persistence and ingenuity.

Driver has analysed the varied types of scientific travel by Europeans in the nineteenth century, including contrasts between 'scientific travel and literary tourism' (Driver 2001: 53) and their reflection in different instruction manuals. Some of these were issued not only by scientific societies such as the Royal Geographical Society (*Hints to Travellers*) and the Admiralty (*Manual of Scientific Enquiry*, first produced in 1849), but also by individuals, for example Francis Galton's *The Art of Travel*, published in 1855 for a wider range of users. Scientific observation presented practical problems inevitably encountered in field survey but also the problem of verification of the observations and results from a space much less controlled than a laboratory or a study (Driver 2001: 60–3, 54–5). There is also the important question of the considerable dynamic of change in the nature and purpose of expeditions and the dissemination of their findings during the course of the nineteenth century. From Britain the general trend, accelerating from the late 1870s, identified by changes in the contents of *Hints to Travellers*, was away from the key components of standardised observation techniques and records and the need for accurate scientific instruments and towards more general guides for the untrained traveller: 'By the 1860s, anxieties at the heart of the geographical establishment over the diffusion of geographical knowledge appear to have given way to a different strategy, heralded by the appearance of a second and free-standing edition of *Hints to Travellers*, explicitly addressed to the untrained gentlemanly traveller, "who, for the first time in his life, proposes to explore a wild country"' (Driver 2001: 62–3, 65). By the end of the century editions of *Hints to Travellers* were focused more on the traveller or tourist than the professional scientific expert.

Exploration in Africa

The geographical and related literature of the last decade or so indicates incontrovertibly that the writing of histories of geography is being fundamentally recast to collapse the stereotypical male image and include, inter alia, the ways in which women explorers experienced and represented the geographies of distant places, and the roles that they played in advancing imperial goals.

Mary Kingsley (1862–1900)

The *Geographical Journal* for July 1900 contained an obituary note for Mary Kingsley (Anon. 1900: 114–15), part of which reads:

We regret to record the death, announced by telegrams from Cape Town early in June, of Miss Mary Kingsley, the well-known West African traveller, who earlier this year had proceeded to the Cape, and having offered her services to the authorities at Simonstown, there contracted the illness of which she died. Devoting herself to scientific studies, she chose the West African coast lands as a field for original research in the subjects which exercised a special attraction for her, zoology and anthropology. Her work did not, therefore, lead her into any entirely unknown countries, and her contributions to geographical science were but incidental to her more definite labours in other fields. Still she did much to bring before the public a clear understanding of the nature of the West African countries, for which, in spite of many drawbacks, she continued to feel a surprising enthusiasm, her powers of observation and description rendering all she wrote unusually valuable and suggestive, although many might dissent from the particular views which she held.

This predictably patronising evaluation, presumably written by a man, considerably understates Mary Kingsley's qualities and achievements, and is not untypical of the way in which women were regarded by the establishment figures at the RGS. Women travellers and explorers contributed much to scientific knowledge of poorly known places in the nineteenth century, and continued to do so thereafter. In contrast to the social formalities attached to the behaviour of single women in their home countries, woman travellers found much greater freedom in their journeys in Asia, Africa and the Middle East, and some exhibited an almost careless attitude to physical hazards and difficulties, both environmental and human, often deriving great exhilaration from such experiences (Birkett 2004: 36–7).

Women travellers and explorers, in contrast to many of their male counterparts, rarely benefited from financial support from learned societies, including the RGS (which did not admit women to Fellowship until 1913) or newspapers and magazines, and so travelled with only modest amounts of supporting equipment and small parties of porters (Birkett 2004: 40). Expectations of equality of treatment by learned societies did, however, differ between women travellers and explorers. Mary Kingsley took the view that women had no formal place in such organisations, having the accounts of her travels read to the Scottish Geographical Society (which, ironically, had admitted women as members from its foundation in 1884) and the Liverpool Geographical Society by men. Association with radical movements such as the suffragette movement in England was rare, though overt and covert involvement and expression of opinion on other issues of the day may well have been more common. Birkett has shown that Mary Kingsley, having written an article critical of the imposition of a hut tax in Sierra Leone in the journal *The Spectator* in March 1898, was informally consulted on the matter by Joseph Chamberlain, the Colonial Secretary, and that she also spoke in her public lectures in support of British trade in Africa, but against the slave trade and the crown colony system. Her informal influence on political opinion, notably on African social, legal and economic systems, was instrumental in the development of the Fair Commerce Party – a colonial politics pressure group – and was also sustained by letter-writing on African affairs to influential players in the imperial game (Birkett 2004: 88).

Alison Blunt has also analysed Mary Kingsley's role as imperial commentator in her book *Travel, Gender and Imperialism: Mary Kingsley in West Africa*, which identifies, inter alia, some important role contrasts, for example, where

Kingsley was primarily constructed in terms of her gender subordination while at home but was able to share in racial superiority while travelling because of imperial power and authority ... Kingsley's perceptions of essential difference are undermined by her own contradictory and ambiguous subject position. This becomes clear in her personalization of both places and people, which highlights the tensions of, on the one hand, seeming anti-conquest in the femininity of her subjective identification while, on the other hand, supporting imperialism by attempting to emulate more masculine strategies of objectifying vision. (Blunt 1994: 110–11)

Mary Kingsley's travels in West Africa reflected the variety of her interests, primarily in a search for what she called 'fish and fetish', that is the natural history and customs of the regions and peoples that she experienced (Middleton 1991a: 103). Data and specimens of fish were collected for the British Museum, and her studies of fetish were for the completion of her father's work on primitive religion and customs (Huxley 1998: 7). On her journeys between 1892 and 1895 in Sierra Leone, the Gold Coast and Gabon she dressed in the clothes of a Victorian woman: Dorothy Middleton described how

she travelled through bush and swamp in a long, tight-waisted skirt and a high-necked blouse, armed with an umbrella, paying her way as a trader. Her goods consisted of cloth, tobacco and fish-hooks to be exchanged mostly for rubber ... Mary's travels in 1895 among the unpredictable Fang tribe in the interior of present day Gabon were as noteworthy as her prowess as a navigator in the tangled creeks of the Niger Delta. (Middleton 1991a: 103)

Her descriptions of places and peoples are significant, showing an acute sense of observation, and – something often lacking in male explorers – a sense of humour. One of her best-known accounts is of an encounter with a large crocodile in a mangrove swamp, and she describes the difficulties of being trapped by a falling tide in the mud of the swamp:

Of course if you really want a truly safe investment in Fame, and really care about Posterity, and Posterity's Science, you will jump over into the black batter-like, stinking slime cheered by the thought of the terrific sensation you will produce 20,000 years hence, and the care you will be taken of then by your fellow creatures, in a museum. But if you are a mere ordinary person of a retiring nature, like me, you stop in your lagoon until the tide rises again; most of your attention is directed to dealing with an 'at home' to crocodiles and mangrove flies, and the fearful stench of slime around you ... On one occasion, the last, a mighty Silurian, as *The Daily Telegraph* would call him, chose to get his front paws over the stern of my canoe, and endeavoured to improve our acquaintance. I had to retire to the bows, to keep the balance right, and fetch him a clip on the snout with a paddle, when he withdrew, and I paddled into the very middle of the lagoon, hoping that the water there was too deep for him or any of his friends to repeat the performance. (Kingsley 1998: 25)

Mary Kingsley's life ended on 3 June 1900. She had travelled to South Africa to care for Boer prisoners of war, and at the age of thirty-seven she died of typhoid fever (Blunt 1994: 54). Such was the respect in which she was held that a learned society – the African (later Royal African) Society – was founded in her honour and memory. The first article, by Alice Stopford Green, published in its journal provides a sensitive summary of her life and work, contrasting vividly with her obituary in the *Geographical Journal*, reproduced above:

No more remarkable reputation has been made in our day than that of Mary Kingsley. In 1892 she was still an unknown young woman of 30, whose life for years had been spent in a particularly arduous work of nursing a mother stricken with a dreadful illness. Practically imprisoned to the house, her heart lay in her solitary task and in study. Five years later she had become known as a traveller and explorer of extraordinary daring and endurance in the equatorial regions of West Africa; as a writer and speaker of very original gifts, who alone and single-handed was able by her genius to win the ear of the public and compel it to an interest in a subject remote and difficult; the passionate missionary to England from those obscure lands, an apostle of duty and justice. Scarce three years of this public duty had passed when at Capetown her body was laid in a torpedo boat, and with the unique honour for a woman of a military and naval funeral was carried out to be committed to the great Sea. (Green 1901: 1)

Other women explorers

Mary Kingsley was one of a number of British women who lived and travelled in West Africa in the nineteenth and early twentieth centuries. Cheryl McEwan has reviewed the contexts and writings of a number of these women, highlighting the rarity of women travelling in West Africa, and making the distinction between those who were 'travel-writers' – who travelled and wrote primarily to give accounts of their journeys and experiences – and those who were more clearly part of the imperial process – as missionaries, missionary wives, or wives of administrators (McEwan 2000: 16–17).

McEwan's study focused on seven women from different backgrounds and who fulfilled differing roles: four were colonial residents (Elizabeth Melville, Mrs Henry Grant Foote, Zélie Colville, and Constance Larymore), two (Anna Hinderer and Mary Slessor) were missionaries, and one (Mary Kingsley) was a traveller and explorer. Key themes in this important study are: 'representations of landscapes, "race", customs and women in west Africa' (McEwan 2000: 17). Important distinctions from the motives and outcomes of male travellers and imperialists are that the women travellers studied by McEwan, although clearly operating within an imperial context, did not generally engage with political or scientific debates or with the advancing of imperial claims to territory, though there were exceptions in Mary Kingsley's later pronouncements and in Mary Slessor's engagement with mission politics.

McEwan explains this general avoidance of political issues and 'quest'-focused accounts by women travellers: 'in order to emphasize their femininity and stress the credibility of their narratives, women travellers modified their texts by disclaimers and interjections of humour, or by stressing the difficulties of travel, rather than adopting the position of the adventure hero' (McEwan 2000: 19). The courage shown by women travellers in these challenging physical and cultural environments is everywhere apparent. Mary Kingsley wrote an account of meeting Mary Slessor, the missionary, in Calabar:

This very wonderful lady has been eighteen years in Calabar; for the last six or seven living entirely alone, as far as white folks go, in a clearing in the forest near to one of the principal villages of the Okÿon district. Her great abilities, both physical and intellectual, have given her among the savage tribe an unique position, and won her, from black and white alike, a profound esteem. Her knowledge of the native, his language, his ways of thought, his diseases, his difficulties, and all that is his, is extraordinary, and the amount of good that she has done, no man can estimate. (Kingsley 1998: 19)

Mary Slessor progressed in her missionary efforts from Calabar to Ikpe in the interior, where living conditions were extremely harsh.

There was increasing empowerment and facility for women to travel from the eighteenth century by improved means of transport, and a

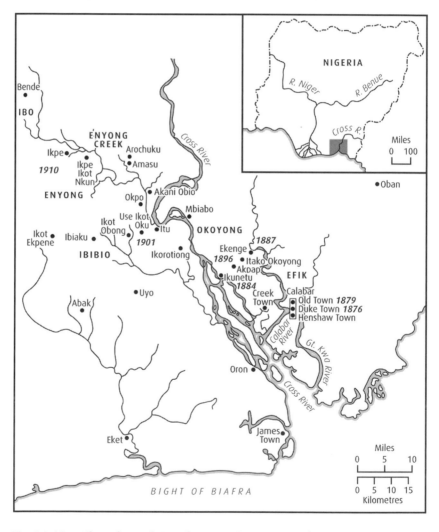

Fig. 5.1 Mary Slessor's travels into the Lower Cross region of Nigeria.
Source: McEwan (1995: 136). By permission of and © the author and Manchester University Press.

slow relaxing of the societal and cultural strictures on travel by women opened up new opportunities, notably for those with the necessary financial means. Male explorers and travellers had better opportunities to gain financial support, from scientific societies, newspapers and wealthy patrons, and were not bound by what McEwan has called 'The tensions between personal liberation and fulfilment and public and private duty' (McEwan 2000: 26).

Other highly significant factors for the women who travelled in West Africa in the nineteenth and early twentieth centuries included roles as wives of colonial officials, a wish to escape from the limiting social and family responsibility roles in which they were cast in the metropole, and, especially in Kingsley's case, being able to advance scientific knowledge. Even where some measure of escape from the conventional mores of Victorian society was possible, restrictions still applied, including that of dress. The entirely inappropriate dress style of the metropole was, almost without exception, adopted by women in the tropics notwithstanding its massive impracticability. Women such as Elizabeth Melville (wife of a colonial judge), Mrs Henry Grant Foote (wife of a colonial consul) and Constance Larymore (wife of a colonial military officer) supported their husbands' colonial objectives, and, as McEwan has shown, 'the roles of these "colonial wives" were defined by those of their husbands in West Africa; they were essentially "incorporated wives"' (McEwan 2000: 29).

The women who travelled as wives and those who were independent (and had greater opportunity to determine their own travel agendas) experienced degrees of relative freedom from their normal social contexts, mainly through travel to new places and also with the opportunities to broaden experiences and in most cases to write about them, giving an 'empowerment through text' (McEwan 2000: 42). This empowerment varied from the undoubted success of publications such as Mary Kingsley's *Travels in West Africa* to the ideas disseminated by Kingsley and in the case of other women travellers by means of letters, which were not subject to the same kind of constraints as published accounts. Mary Kingsley's publications disseminated images and ideas about Africa to large audiences, but, as McEwan (2000: 46) has indicated, the conditions of writing were quite complex: 'both imperialist and feminine discourses in nineteenth-century Britain constrained the ways in which women wrote, and the details that they were able to recount, thereby producing ambivalence and tensions within their narratives. Women travellers were caught between the conflicting narrative voices of imperialism and femininity.' This is an important point, though it is also worth questioning the assumption that there were no parallel positional constraints on men's accounts of their experiences in Africa and other places, on grounds of general metropolitan assumptions about the philosophy and practice of imperial rule and colonial development: there were 'conflicting narrative voices' of imperialism and masculinity.

The attitude of women travellers to indigenous peoples was substantially influenced by their own social status, with women such as Mary Kingsley and Mary Slessor differing from Melville, Foote, Larymore and Colvile, the second of these groups being more heavily imbued with a sense of class and race superiority, reflecting their approaches to working-class people, including servants, in Britain. Slessor and Kingsley, nonetheless, were conscious of the advantages produced by the colour of their skin and of their assumptions about their own and their country's rights to be in West Africa. The missionary Mary Slessor also, on account of her unrivalled knowledge of the Calabar region of southern Nigeria and her consequent role linking the British government with leaders in West Africa, received acknowledgement and authority from both Britain (she was Vice-Consul and magistrate for Okoyong, for example) and Africans (she was given an African name, and adopted African children) – something that would have been impossible in Britain for a woman of her background (McEwan 2000: 32, 33, 39).

The influence of women travellers in changing or negotiating policies toward indigenous peoples is significant. While some if not all were pro-imperialist in one way or another, it seems clear that there was a gathering sense of self-confidence among women travellers from Britain, notably when Kingsley, John Holt (the owner of a shipping company) and Edmund Dene Morel (the Congo reform campaigner), for example, identified themselves as a middle or 'Third Party' in between attitudes of extreme racial superiority and ethnocentrically based philanthropy (McEwan 2000: 48).

The landscape descriptions written by women travellers in West Africa, and indeed elsewhere, are complex, and differed in emphasis from one to another and from those written by men. There were, however, common elements of imitation in the contemporary writing conventions among the women travellers about imperial frontiers and ideas of wilderness and sanctuary, and deliberate orientation away from the scientific narrative perspective towards more subjective accounts. In their descriptions of West Africa in the last sixty years of the nineteenth century, women travellers varied between Paradise/Arcadian images and those describing a dark, unfathomable and dangerous region, though there was no 'singular "feminine" representation of West African environments', some being more distanced from a close personal involvement with landscape, while others were not (McEwan 2000: 87–8). McEwan concludes that this particular group of women had a significant impact on the understanding of West Africa by a broader public:

> women certainly contributed to geographical thought and knowledges at this time. Women travellers may not have 'discovered', mapped and explored 'new' territories, but they did add to the imagery constructed about the empire. Moreover, they influenced how this imagery was mapped onto the imaginations of the majority of people in Britain who did not have first-hand experience of areas of the world such as West Africa. (McEwan 2000: 215)

David Livingstone

There were many European men who went to Africa as explorers in the nineteenth and early twentieth centuries, variously motivated by interest in trade, the abolition of the slave trade, scientific goals including mapping, the advancement of their country's geopolitical ambitions, and a desire for adventure and escape. The imperial links to their explorations and expeditions were in some cases direct, in others indirect, though imperial glosses were sometimes put upon their activities by politicians and colonial administrators.

David Livingstone (1813–73) was acknowledged in his time and after his death as a famous missionary–explorer. More has been written about him and his endurance in a series of missionary and scientific explorations into north Central Africa than any other explorer before or since. He was born in Blantyre, south of Glasgow in Lanarkshire in Scotland, and while working in its cotton mills (from the age of ten) began a process of education, assisted by his family, that was to lead him to studies for a degree in medicine and theology at the Andersonian Medical School and the Theological Academy in Glasgow, and to a calling as a medical missionary. He had been influenced by his parents' religious beliefs and by an appeal for medical missionaries for China and Africa launched by a Dutch missionary, Karl Gutzlaf (Jeal, 1996: 15). In December 1840, after periods of missionary training in Essex and further medical training in London, he took his medical examinations in Glasgow, was ordained at Albion Chapel in London, and sailed to Africa under the aegis of the London Missionary Society (later the Church Missionary Sociey), arriving at Simon's Bay on 15 March 1841. His choice of South Africa as his mission field was strongly influenced by the preaching and writing of three

Fig. 5.2 Engraving of David Livingstone, 1867.
Source: Huxley (1941: 19).

LMS missionaries John Phillips, John Campbell, and Robert Moffat, especially by Moffat's book *Missionary Labours and Scenes in Southern Africa* (Jeal 1996: 18). The Cape Colony, taken from the Dutch by Britain in 1806, was seen as an important base for the colonisation of the healthier part of Southern Africa, but it was also a region of tension between the British administration and Dutch (Boer) settlers. Eventually the Boers engaged in the Great Trek north-eastwards to find land and an existence free from Britain. Livingstone travelled to Kuruman, 600 miles north of Cape Town, where Robert Moffat had an LMS mission station.

Livingstone was unimpressed by the missionary work there, and travelled on 250 miles further north-east to Mabotsa to set up a mission station, though instantly falling out with his co-founder, Roger Edwards. In January 1845 he married Mary Moffat, the daughter of Robert Moffat.

Her life with him proved to be one of courage and determination, and she suffered greatly from the demands that missionary and personal life placed upon her. Jeal has described the tribulations of the first years of her married life:

In the space of five years Mary had given birth to three children and she would shortly have a fourth, Livingstone dubbing her frequent pregnancies 'the great Irish manufactory'. Mary had been pregnant in 1850 when she accompanied Livingstone across the waterless Kalahari Desert. She lost her baby as a result and suffered partial paralysis for several months. 'The affliction', Livingstone confessed, 'causes considerable deformity, especially in smiling.' What Mrs Livingstone could have had to smile about is hard to imagine since her surviving children (aged four, three and one) had come home too weak to stand and were still suffering from the after-effects of malaria. (Jeal 1996: 29)

Mary had returned to England with their children in April 1852, just before her husband started his trans-African journey. Family life and health was something that Livingstone seems to have sacrificed in pursuit of his ambitions to open up the interior of Africa for commerce and Christianity.

Livingstone, having travelled from Cape Town to the region of the Kololo people between the Zambezi and Chobe rivers, then set out on a long journey across the continent of Africa, from the headwaters of the Zambezi to the west coast, leaving in June 1853, and travelling by canoe north-west up the Zambezi through the Barotse valley for a period of three months. Having determined that there was nowhere in the region that was free from malaria or the slave trade, he set off again from Linyati in November 1853 with twenty seven men, some oxen, a canoe, and various pieces of equipment, including a magic lantern to portray Biblical scenes, a shotgun, and the standard instruments used for determining and mapping location and altitude: sextant, thermometer, chronometer, telescope, an artificial horizon, a compass and a thermometer (Jeal 1996: 30–3; Hugon 1993: 71). He made extensive geographical observations in the course of this journey of 1,200 miles to Luanda on the Atlantic coast of Africa, during which he and his expedition suffered terrible deprivations through heat and rain, sickness, demands for payment to pass through tribal territory, and confrontations with animals and men. They arrived at Luanda on 31 May 1854, and after medical treatment returned to Linyanti, to complete Livingstone's original journey across Africa, following the Zambezi to its mouth on the Indian Ocean. He encountered the great waterfalls which he later named the Victoria Falls (the African name was Mosioatunya – 'the smoke that thunders'), crossed the Batoka

Plateau which he deemed suitable for white colonial settlement, and reached Quelimane on 25 May 1856, having completed a journey of 5,000 miles across Africa (Jeal 1996: 36).

In 1856 he returned to Britain, warmly welcomed as the first European to have crossed sub-Saharan Africa, and the identifier of the character of the vegetation, climates and landscapes of south central Africa which was previously thought to be an arid and unproductive region. He was given much recognition and many awards, including gold medals from the RGS and the Paris Geographical Society (SGP) and he became a popular hero, his book *Missionary Travels and Researches in Southern Africa*, which he wrote in 1857, selling 70,000 copies and earning substantial royalties, some of which went to his family (Jeal 1996: 37). The book was dedicated to Sir Roderick Murchison, president of the Royal Geographical Society and promoter of scientific imperialism.

He undertook a further expedition in Africa, with financial support from the RGS and the Foreign Office and tacit support from the LMS, with a publicly declared ambition to explore the headwaters of the Nile, Congo and Zambezi rivers and to evaluate the resources of the Zambezi basin, and a private intention of finding suitable territory to found an English colony in the highlands of Central Africa. Livingstone left England in March 1858 for Africa and the Zambezi expedition, accompanied by his wife and his youngest son Oswell. The other children were left in Scotland with their grandparents. Mary (who was pregnant again) and Oswell remained in Cape Town, in order to meet Mary's missionary parents in Kuruman. Her daughter was born in Kuruman in November 1858 and they later returned to Scotland. In 1861 Mary went back to Africa alone to join her husband on the Zambezi expedition, and died from malaria at Shupanga on the banks of the Zambezi on 27 April 1862 (Jeal 1996: 50). Livingstone continued with the expedition, which encountered many difficulties, including tension between the British participants, rapids, tribal warfare and famine, and he returned in 1864 with much new geographical information about the Zambezi, but no evidence of suitable sites for European settlement. In January 1865 he was invited by Murchison to lead an expedition to establish the source or sources of the River Nile, sponsored by the RGS and with geographical information as the sole aim. Livingstone agreed, but stated that he would have to add the objective of eradication of the slave trade.

The expedition started out from a location 600 miles north of the mouth of the Zambezi, aiming to head north-west from the mouth of the Rovuma River, and proceed via southern Lake Nyasa and the north of

Fig. 5.3 The meeting of Stanley and Livingstone, Ujiji, 1871. Source: Montefiore (1913: 51).

Lake Tanganyika. He located Lake Mweru and the Lualaba River which flowed out from it, which he thought to be the Nile. There were difficulties with his followers, and he had to add more, ultimately deciding to travel with Arab slave traders in order to make better progress and to understand the nature of their trade.

By 1868 illness and other difficulties forced him back to Ujiji, where he was 'found' in 1871 by Stanley, there having been no news of him in Britain for three years. He circumnavigated Lake Tanganyika with Stanley, but refused to return to England. In 1872 Livingstone resumed his geographical exploration around Lake Bangweulu, with a total company of fifty-six, including the five Africans who had accompanied him on all his journeys since 1866 (Jeal 1996: 58, 72). He reached the north-eastern shore of Lake Bengweulu in January 1873, but illness forced him to return, and on 1 May 1873 he died at a village on the River Luapula. Livingstone, in his years in Africa, had helped to fill in many of the blank spaces on European maps of that continent. His achievements were colossal. They have been summarised by Jeal:

The whole span of Livingstone's achievement was apparent then as something unique and so it still seems today: it is not simply a matter of the vast distance he tramped over, nor of the geographical discoveries he made, for his contributions to ethnology, natural history, tropical medicine and linguistics were also substantial, as were his roles as a crusader against the slave trade, a colonial theoretician and a prophet. Livingstone had always claimed that he was open-ing the way into Africa for others, and there, at last, his optimism was to prove well founded, since the events of the thirty years following his death would show that he had done exactly that – with consequences he would sometimes have applauded but more often deplored. (Jeal 1996: 74)

Livingstone, like other Victorian explorers, changed the way in which the broader populaces of Britain and other European countries saw the African world, through their lectures, publications, and the extensive newspaper reports of and debates about their achievements. Central to this new culture was the support from governments and scientific soci-eties, which gave a new legitimacy to exploration and travel and new direct discourse with politicians (Driver 1996: 135), as was the produc-tion of new maps and artistic illustrations of landscapes and peoples. Collectively, the heroic status afforded to Livingstone, Stanley and others assisted in the dissemination of images, myths and truths about Africa and the Africans (Driver 2001: 86–8), and paved the way for a more for-mal European imperialism from the mid-1880s. All this, within a context of the advance of gentlemanly capitalism, filtered through the European concept of a civilising process from superior powers: '"We come among them", Livingstone told his colleagues, "as members of a superior race and servants of a Government that desires to elevate the more degraded portions of the human family." Such a formula, symptomatic of the mid-Victorian accommodation between racism and humanitarianism, speaks volumes about the confidence and ambition of the civilizing mission' (Driver 2001: 86).

An important caveat to this is Livingstone's warning against 'the stupid prejudice against colour' (Cannizzo 1996: 141). The tone of Livingstone's accounts of his experiences in Africa differed in degree from those of other explorers, notably Stanley, and 'the playing-out of European fanta-sies of masculinity, evident in the stylised accounts of gallant escapes and perilous encounters with lions or hostile natives' (Cannizzo 1996: 175). He was somewhat less representative of this military culture than of the mis-sionary culture, which had more sensitive ways and means of interacting with indigenous cultures, though they combined in this particular man: 'Livingstone's amalgam of active heroism and religious conviction singled him out as the ultimate muscular Christian and was irresistible to the Victorian reading public', with his writing having 'quite a different tone from that of the military men, its underlying concerns being the moral reformation of Africa, the abolition of slavery and the mutual benefits that Westernisation could bring' (Cannizzo 1996: 175).

Livingstone was undoubtedly a single-minded and determined individual who did not like to be opposed, and his relations with Thomas Baines (whom he unjustifiably dismissed as artist and storekeeper from the Zambezi expedition in 1859) are evidence of this. He also had the considerable benefit of major support and promotion from Sir Roderick Murchison. Stafford has shown that 'Livingstone provided Murchison with a series of breathtaking discoveries that catapulted the RGS to a pinnacle of fame and affluence, while the President transformed the obscure missionary into one of Victorian Britain's archetypal heroes. By creating Livingstone's renown, Murchison made possible the government aid, public subscriptions, and profit from book sales which freed him to prosecute further African explorations' (Stafford 1989: 172).

Explorers and the Brussels Geographical Conference, 1876

A broader context for African exploration was that partially set by King Leopold II of Belgium in his attempt to create a massive personal empire in Central Africa, from which he correctly assumed that substantial wealth could be obtained. In 1875, aware of Livingstone's findings from

CROSSING THE LUKOJI.

[PAGE 159, Vol. II.

Fig. 5.4 V. L. Cameron crossing the Lukoji River, an eastern affluent of the Luala, Congo, in August 1875. Source: Cameron (1877: II, 159).

his expeditions in Central Africa, and in the process of receiving news of the expeditions by Stanley, who was then traversing Africa from west to east (1874–8), by V. Lovett Cameron, following the opposite route, and by the Italian-French explorer Pierre Savorgnan de Brazza's departure on his journey, King Leopold attended the conference of the Société de Géographie de Paris (SGP) in Paris. At that conference further news of exploration in Central Africa was given, and he proposed a conference, to be held in Brussels in September 1876, to consider the humanitarian needs of the populace of Central Africa and ways of advancing scientific research and realising commercial opportunities.

The title given to the conference was the Brussels Geographical Conference, and it was attended by representatives (including officers of geographical societies and explorers) of Belgium, Britain, France, Germany, Italy, Russia and Austria-Hungary. The main items on the agenda were the opening of Central Africa to the benefits of civilisa-tion, through the medium of collaborative scientific and civilising stations (*stations civilisatrices*), and the founding of an International African Association (Association Internationale Africaine – AIA). This body was to have national sub-committees, but they came to very lit-tle once the ambitions of the Belgian monarch were fully understood. The RGS refused to support the idea of the international AIA, partly on the grounds that the latter did not have constitutional authority through its charter to involve itself in political or commercial issues, and partly because the RGS preferred to steer its own course of geo-graphical exploration, which it did in this instance in the foundation of its African Exploration Fund in 1878 (Mill 1930: 122; Bridges 1963: 25–35). France and Germany did establish such committees and a small number of stations: 'As an international entity, the Association Internationale Africaine was stillborn. Very few were fooled by the word "international" – the only country to take the Association seriously was Belgium. Even so, the Belgian state did not want to shoulder responsi-bility for Leopold's African plans' (Wesseling 1996: 89). What did, how-ever, stimulate and help to realise Leopold's ambitions was the news in September 1877 that Stanley had reached the west coast of Africa. This prompted Leopold to meet Stanley to promote further exploration of the Congo in order to establish the stations proposed at the AIA meeting in Brussels in 1876.

Stanley's proposals for a further expedition to the region and for its development were rejected by the British government, but greeted with enthusiasm by Leopold. After negotiations with various financial backers, notably the Afrikaansche Handels-Vereeninging (AHV – African Trading Company) from Rotterdam, a Netherlands committee of the AIA was established in 1877, and a Comité d'Études du Haut-Congo in 1878, whose objectives were described as humanitarian, scientific and commercial (Wesseling 1996: 91). Stanley was instructed to lead an expedition to the upper Congo, where stations were to be set up and river trade opened. Stanley returned to the Congo in August 1879, but by the time his expedition started the AHV had withdrawn funding, in consequence of which the committee of the AIA was abolished, and Leopold took control of the process himself. Stanley's initial brief was to establish trade agreements with tribal chiefs for agricultural development, the building of roads and other features necessary for trade, but complications, from Brazza's next expedition, made the whole issue more territorial and political (Wesseling 1996: 92–3).

Savorgnan de Brazza (1852–1905) was born in Rome. He attended the French naval academy in 1868, but could only become an officer in the French navy after he was naturalised as a Frenchman in 1874. De Brazza was aware of Stanley's intentions, and he received support from the French committee of the AIA (after pressure by Ferdinand de Lesseps on the French navy to give him a commission), and with financial support from the ministries of education and foreign affairs, for a further expedition to the Ogouwe and the upper Congo. 'Brazza made great haste. As was his custom, he travelled light and quickly. He sailed from Europe in December 1879, left Libreville in March 1880, founded Franceville at the confluence of the Ogowe and the Passa in June, and on 10 September 1880 signed the treaty that would change the history of the Congo' (Wesseling 1996: 93). The treaty was with the local ruler or 'makoku', who by this instrument ceded his territory to French sovereignty as a French protectorate. Brazza also concluded similar treaties with chiefs for land on the right bank of the Congo near Stanley Pool in October 1880, planting the French flag and giving flags to the chiefs for flying in their villages. He met Stanley at Vivi, but concealed his territorial appropriation in the name of France.

The French government, however, would not ratify the treaties that he had signed, so Brazza returned to France in June 1882, determined to persuade it to change its mind. His achievements were applauded by the SGP and other learned societies, though he was refused further promotion by the navy (Wesseling 1993: 95, 85). The SGP published his letters, and promoted lectures by him, given to very large audiences in Paris (Lejeune 1993: 134). By late 1882 the French government changed its mind, and ratified the treaties on 22 November. In consequence of this, 'The ratification of the treaties was a clear signal that Central Africa had entered a new phase. De Brazza had, as King Leopold somewhat oddly put it, "introduced politics into the Congo."' The French Chamber, for its part, had introduced the Congo into European politics. The consequences were not slow in coming. The genie had escaped from the bottle and was to haunt Europe. In the next two years, 1883 and 1884, the Congo assumed an increasingly important place on the European diplomatic agenda (Wesseling 1996: 98–9).

Leopold II, having learned of the process of treaty-signing from Brazza, encouraged Stanley from October 1882 to use similar tactics on his behalf and on a larger scale, resulting in the signature of large numbers of treaties with many local chiefs, the use of a military force to consolidate the Belgian position in the Congo, and the foundation of Stanleyville in 1883 (Wesseling 1996: 103). Further geopolitical complications ensued with the signing of the Anglo-Portuguese Treaty of 1884 (which was never ratified by the British government), which gave Portugal control of the mouth of the Congo, thus in theory cutting off the area of the Congo basin which Leopold saw as his domain. The concept of the Congo as a free trade area was introduced by Leopold in an attempt to influence the British against the Portuguese, but temporarily aroused the concerns of the French. Eventually this complex issue was resolved at the Berlin Conference of 1884–5, where the territory was internationally recognised as the Congo Free State, France's Central African ambitions having been met by the creation of the French Congo in the area to the north of the Congo River.

This particular historical sequence of postures and tactics demonstrates the way in which the fate of a large area of Africa partly turned on the characters, ambitions, and exploration skills of two men: Brazza, an Italian who had become a naturalised Frenchman, acting primarily as an individual; and Stanley, born in Wales and brought up in the United States, whose offer of services in further investigating the commercial possibilities of the Congo basin had been rejected by the British government but eagerly accepted by King Leopold II of Belgium as part of his own territorial ambitions (which were barely concealed behind humanitarian and free trade zone claims). Stanley's motives and support will now be considered at greater length.

H. M. Stanley: hero or villain?

The life of Henry Morton Stanley (1841–1904) offers a great contrast with that of the medical missionary and explorer David Livingstone. Stanley's career as an explorer, it has been suggested,

provides a bridge between what is sometimes regarded as the golden age of exploration (*c.* 1851–78) and the era of the Scramble (*c.* 1884–91) … If the 1870s were indeed a critical turning-point in the history of European involvement in Africa, then Stanley might well be regarded as the key figure in the transition to new forms of imperialism in the closing decades of the nineteenth century. (Driver 2001: 125)

Much of Stanley's exploration in Africa, as already indicated above, was under the influence of Leopold II of Belgium, as one of what Darwin has described as 'the explorer-filibusters of whom Leopold was but a Brobdignagian example' (Darwin 1997: 634).

Stanley was born John Rowlands in Denbigh in North Wales, and having for a short while been cared for by his grandfather and then by neighbours, was sent at the age of six to the St Asaph Union Workhouse. In 1858 he went as a cabin boy on a ship sailing to New Orleans, and in the United States he was adopted by a wealthy cotton merchant, Henry Hope Stanley. H.M. Stanley, as John Rowlands had now become, fought for both sides at different stages of the American Civil War, became a war correspondent, and worked in Spain, Ethiopia, Greece and Turkey (Wesseling 1996: 82). He had several commissions from James Gordon Bennett Jr, the owner of the *New York Herald*, including the production of reports from the British military expedition against Emperor Theodore of Abyssinia in 1868, and a famous commission of 27 October 1869 to travel in Asia and then to Zanzibar, in order to mount an expedition to find David Livingstone, who had not been heard from for some time. This he succeeded in doing, at Ujiji on 10 November 1871, and the reports that he filed with the *New York Herald* 'made him an international hero, resulted in an increase in the paper's circulation, and convinced Bennett that he had indeed discovered the most effective way to create news and grab an audience' (Riffenburgh 1994: 58).

In spite of his popular reception, Stanley was disliked by his proprietor for attracting so much individual attention; by sections of the English conservative press that disliked the American press style; by the English geographical and scientific establishment, including the RGS (because he was assuming American nationality and had succeeded in finding Livingstone when an RGS expedition led by L. S. Dawson had not); because he was not a gentleman or a scientist, and because he claimed to represent Livingstone

Fig. 5.5 H. M. Stanley. Source: Montefiore (1913: frontispiece).

(Driver 1991: 146–8; Riffenburgh 1994: 60). Mill has summarised the problem: 'Stanley was not received so well by British geographers as by the public. The Council of the Society thought it incongruous and almost an impertinence that a newspaper reporter should have succeeded where a British officer, backed by the authority of the Royal Geographical Society, had failed' (Mill 1930: 114).

There were additional complications because of Stanley's attempt to represent Livingstone, particularly in the circumstance, as Stanley claimed, of Livingstone having been 'virtually abandoned by his official

Fig. 5.6 Stanley on the march to Ugogu in search of Livingstone, 1870.
Source: Montefiore (1913: 41).

sponsors' (the RGS), and of Stanley's strong criticism of John Kirk, who had been with Livingstone on his Zambezi expedition of 1858–63, and who had become British vice-consul at Zanzibar (Driver 1991: 148–9). Attempts to discredit Stanley in the public eye, however, failed, and the RGS was obliged, against the judgement of many of its prominent members, to award him its Founder's Medal in 1874 (Mill 1930: 114).

Stanley's next expedition was the Anglo-American Expedition, which lasted from 1874 to 1877, promoted by the *New York Herald* and the *Daily Telegraph*, the aim of which was to traverse Africa from east to west. This feat was accomplished in 1,002 days – though Stanley claimed that it took 999. The concept of this expedition came after Livingstone's funeral at Westminster Abbey in London in 1874, when Edward Levy-Leveson, the proprietor of the *Daily Telegraph*, agreed to a proposal by his editor Edwin Arnold 'to put up £60,000 for an expedition that not only would resolve the questions about Lake Victoria and its relation to the sources of the Nile, but that would follow the mysterious Lualaba River to its mouth, thus determining whether it would flow into the Nile, the Congo or the Niger' (Riffenburgh 1994: 64). Stanley was appointed leader of the expedition, and Gordon Bennett, the owner of the *New York Herald*, reluctantly agreed to match the sum which the *Daily Telegraph* had invested. Stanley left Zanzibar on 17 November 1874, his party including three Europeans – Frank and Edward Pocock and Edward Barker – as assistants, an African labour force of 356, together with a large quantity of stores and instruments and a collapsible boat, the *Lady Alice*, built in five sections so that it could be taken apart for cross-country travel and reassembled when water transportation became possible. They travelled to Mwanza on Lake Victoria, and after extensive sailings proved that there was only one lake, with one major outfall at Ripon Falls, the Victoria Nile. They also explored the country between Lakes Victoria and Edward, and sailed around Lake Tanganyika (Riffenburgh 1994: 65).

Stanley continued west through very difficult and dangerous country to Nyangwe on the upper reaches of the Lualaba River, the river that Livingstone had (incorrectly) thought to be a source of the Nile, but which was in fact a tributary of the Congo. They moved north-westwards in November 1876 along the Lualaba, encountering much hostility and retaliating with massive and indiscriminate firepower. Stanley followed the river to its confluence with the Congo, and named the rapids found on January 1877 the Stanley Falls, also giving his name to the large lake (Stanley Pool) found in March 1877 on the lower course of the Congo near Brazzaville (Hugon 1993: 96–7). He reached the Atlantic coast in August 1877, without his three British companions and two-thirds of his porters and labour force, who had died on the journey.

Although this major expedition had solved many of the mysteries about the rivers of Central Africa, Stanley was subject to much criticism in the British establishment and press for the ruthless way in which he had responded to opposition, in particular to his attack on the people of the Bumbire tribe on Bumbire Island in Lake Victoria in August 1875, resulting in the death of fourteen of these people in the initial confrontation, and the death of another forty-two and the wounding of a further hundred in a deliberately organised revenge attack by Stanley's followers. As Driver (2001: 132) has stated: ' What most concerned Stanley's critics was not simply the fact that he had used force; it was rather that, following a violent confrontation on the lake, he had planned an act of cold-blooded revenge, and appeared to revel in the violence that ensued', his expedition being characterised as 'exploration by warfare'.

Objections to his tactics came from humanitarian circles, including the Anti-Slavery Society, several newspapers, and some members of the RGS, partly because the RGS gave him a major public meeting followed by a dinner in his honour on his return in 1878 (Driver 2001: 136). Other problems arose from his criticism of the RGS-sponsored expedition of V. L. Cameron, who had traversed Africa from east to west in 1873–5, and had more peaceful contacts with African people, but who had turned south at the Lualaba and missed the main course of the Congo. There were also concerns about the newspapers that had sponsored his expedition, and opposition from those who sought to sustain the reputation of David Livingstone (Riffenburgh 1994: 66–7).

In 1878, Stanley was commissioned by Leopold II of Belgium, on a five-year contract, to return to the Congo for the Comité d'Études du Haut-Congo, which was later replaced by the Association Internationale du Congo. This was a newly founded organisation set up by Leopold to run the expedition and associated activities. Stanley began his work in the Lower Congo in August 1879, the intention being the construction of a road around the rapids on the lower part of the river and through the Crystal Mountains, to facilitate the construction of a railway and the carriage of steamships in parts to the upper Congo, and the establishment a series of trading, scientific and philanthropic stations (Jeal, 2007: 36–7; Driver 2004; Hochschild 1998: 53–4). Between 1879 and 1881 three of the stations had been built at Vivi, Isangila and Stanley Pool (where the station was named Leopoldville). In 1882, returning from a recuperation visit to Europe, he learned of claims by Brazza to territory on the north shore of the Congo River opposite Leopoldville, by negotiated treaty with an African chief – one of many such treaties. Stanley pressed on, and made treaties with over 450 chiefs (Hochschild, 1998: 71). Both men were caught up in the European geopolitics of the moment, though the major players resided in Europe. Stanley returned from the Congo in 1884.

Stanley's next expedition in Africa was in 1887–9, when he headed a relief expedition to find Emin Pasha. Emin Pasha was the name taken by Eduard Schnitzer, a German, when he was made governor-general of the Equatorial province of southern Sudan by the khedive. He had been stranded with the remnants of his staff and army near Lake Albert by the Mahdist uprising that had led to the fall of Khartoum. Expeditions to rescue him (and to claim territory in the headwaters of the Nile for their countries) were planned by Carl Peters, the German explorer and colonialist, by Sir William Mackinnon, the founder of the British Imperial East Africa Company, and by Stanley, who succeeded (James 1994: 280).

Predictably, Stanley returned to a mixture of celebration and severe criticism. He was welcomed by the RGS, who cast a special Stanley medal in Welsh gold in his honour and held a meeting at the Royal Albert Hall which was attended by 6,200 Fellows of the society and their guests. Bronze replicas of the medal were given to surviving African members of his expedition. A major problem, however, attached to his dealings with the infamous Tippu Tip, the Arab slave trader, the numbers killed on his expedition, his highly personalised account of his journey, and his treatment of what became known as the 'Rear Column', a group of expedition members who were sick or wounded whom he left behind on the Congo River, with tragic consequences, while he pressed ahead to make contact with Pasha (Riffenburgh 1994: 132).

What became known as the 'Congo atrocities' – his alleged use of slaves on the expedition, of floggings on the journey up the Congo, and the slaughter and destruction of people and villages en route, were highlighted by the Anti-Slavery Society and the Aborigines Protection Society, whose views were expressed at meetings and in pamphlets and books (Driver 2001: 140–1). Stanley had worked effectively for King Leopold's ambitions for Central Africa, but on completion of the Emin Pasha expedition he returned to England where he enjoyed much acclaim. He became an MP and was knighted in 1899.

The characterisation of Stanley as an explorer has taken a variety of forms and directions, ranging from the intrepid and fearless explorer to a brutal adventurer, exploiter and opportunist imperialist. Neither of these is a very subtle characterisation of a complex man, whose life and achievements are constantly being reviewed and revised as scholarship progresses. On the one hand there were the indisputable characteristics of cruelty in his treatment of African porters, the burning of villages, and links with African slave traders. On the other were his scientific discoveries, his opposition to the slave trade (to be removed by 'legitimate' trading, as Livingstone had also thought) and to the hunting and extermination of animals for sport, his criticism of racist attitudes, awareness of the lack of a legal basis for European exploration and exploitation of Africa, his courageous determination in the face of an overwhelmingly enervating physical environment and a critical Royal Geographical Society. He understood the difficulties of Central Africa, and may have had quite a humanitarian attitude to the resolution of its problems, although his liberal imperialism, says Porter, is a case of 'good (internationalist) intentions being subverted by a less scrupulous and less altruistic kind of colonialism' (Porter 2007: 9–10).

Jeal's book on Stanley (2007: 470, 472) concludes with the observation that Livingstone, in spite of his own recognised shortcomings, was oversanctified in comparison with Stanley. Jeal emphasises that:

To have been a great leader of African exploration expeditions in the anarchic last three decades of the nineteenth century required very unusual personal qualities – characteristics, in fact, that sensible, well-balanced modern men and women, leading safe lives, tend to find alarming: such as being inspired, fearless, obsessed, able to frighten, able to suffer, but also able to command love and obedience.

While Stanley was perhaps a man of extreme sentiments and ambitions, it might be worth noting that others, deemed more balanced in their attitudes and preferences, such as Halford Mackinder, one of the founding fathers of modern British geography, also exhibited extremes of behaviour while on expedition in Africa.

Stanley's perceived imperial role derived in large measure from his work for Leopold II of Belgium. At the Berlin West Africa Conference of 1884–5, he was seen as 'the leader of the International African Association in the Congo', 'the champion of Free Trade, struggling against French and Portuguese adversaries [but] in reality, he helped give birth to a state whose system of monopolies became the most vicious in African history' (Louis 2006: 89). Stanley was seen by the French as representing English interests opposed to their own imperial aspirations in the Congo, because of the rival claims to parts of the upper Congo by him and by Brazza. He played a similar role against Portuguese interest in the region. It is clear that his extensive and hard-won geographical knowledge and determination to develop peaceful links and trade in the Congo led many to see him as an influential player in this European geopolitical game:

There [in Berlin] as in England Stanley was lionized. He spoke authoritatively as one of the great explorers of the nineteenth century. One newspaper referred to him as 'himself a major power to be reckoned with', and the International Association was often identified as 'Stanley's Association'. His herculean efforts on the Congo and unsurpassed knowledge of central Africa demanded respect; when he spoke, people listened. His message can be summed up in one word: trade. (Louis 2006: 92)

It is difficult, nonetheless to produce a practical assessment of the influence of Stanley and his European contemporaries on European imperial and colonial policy, as compared, for example, with the influence of government ministers and senior civil servants. The explorers' advantage was in having first-hand knowledge of the territories and peoples involved in the colonial processes, sometimes geared to commercial and humanitarian ends, sometimes to more overt scientific investigation of the natural histories of these regions. The more famous also had the advantage of great publicity through their own lectures and publications and review by newspapers, but the publicity was not always favourable.

French explorers and expeditions

In France, the foundation of the Société de Géographie de Paris (SGP) in July 1821 epitomised the increasing national and individual requirements of members of the aristocracy, professionals, politicians and military and naval personnel for more geographical knowledge of unknown lands. A geographical society had been founded in Paris by Jean-Nicolas Buache in 1785, primarily for the production of maps, and – nearer to the African Association and in the period of the Consulate and the Empire – a short-lived Société de l'Afrique Intérieure, was established in Marseille in 1801 (Lejeune 1993: 21–2). The SGP gave advice, listed projects and gave instructions for geographical investigations, including, for example, support for the expedition proposed in 1827 by two explorers Taillefer and Peyronneau. They were proposing an expedition to Colombia, and asked the SGP for advice, which was duly given, drawing on the expertise of members. The SGP also provided instruments, general instructions and letters of commendation for consular support, and solicited support from the Ministry of the Navy on behalf of explorers and the organisers of expeditions (Lejeune 1993: 34).

In 1824 the SGP had offered a prize for a scientific description of Timbuktu, and the prize was claimed and awarded to the French explorer René Caillié who reached Timbuktu in 1828. Controversy arose at that time when John Barrow, Second Secretary to the Admiralty (and one of the founders of the Royal Geographical Society in 1830) wrote to Edme Chomard, a leading French geographer, to protest at an article by Chomard in the *Bulletin* of the SGP advancing the claim that Caillé was the first man to have reached Timbuktu and return with a scientific account. Barrow took the view that the first European to have visited Timbuktu was a Scotsman, Alexander Gordon Laing, who, responding to the SGP prize offer of 1824, had reached Timbuktu in 1826, but who had been killed on the return journey. The dispute between Chomard and Barrow continued, with Barrow using the *Quarterly Review*, in which he was a prolific geographical writer, as a vehicle for his strong criticism of the French approach to exploration, including what he deemed to be Caillié's use of disguise as a means of exploration, characteristic of 'low cunning' (Heffernan 2001: 217), in contrast to what he chose to see as Laing's virtuous character and methods. Barrow's vitriol 'was clearly inspired by the Englishman's ambition (which was about to be realized) to establish a London-based geographical society as a rival to the SGP. What better way to justify such a new venture than by whipping up anti-French feeling amongst Britain's scientific community and reading public' (Heffernan 2001: 214).

The significance of this particular case-study derives, as Heffernan has indicated, not just from national rivalries (there were, in fact, similarities in the aim of the institutions and scientific communities of both parties to boost African exploration) but also from the need for 'a much more complex reading of exploration as a means to uncover scientific truth' (Heffernan 2001: 221, 220). One seemingly paradoxical aspect of the Laing–Caillié controversy, sometimes overlooked, was the award in 1830 by the SGP of gold medals to both Caillié and the widow of Gordon Laing, in recognition of their expeditions to Timbuktw. Lejeune suggests that this is a contrary indicator to the reported French Anglophobia (and presumably British Francophobia) concerning each country's exploration of Africa (Lejeune 1993: 45).

Exploration had also been strongly supported by the French government since the seventeenth century, through the agency of the Académie Royale des Sciences, and the process continued up to and beyond the French Revolution of 1789. In the eighteenth century royalty and governments had given support to voyages of exploration, notably in the Pacific, and in 1782 Jean-Nicolas Buache had been appointed Geographer to the King (Heffernan 1994b: 21–45, 22–3). Heffernan has highlighted the intensification of state involvement with the direction and support of science after the Revolution of 1798: 'In an increasingly totalitarian atmosphere, virtually every form of research and scholarship was commandeered and directed by zealous revolutionary officials eager to establish a self-consciously rational, scientific and republican political culture ... including cartography and map-making' (Heffernan 1994b: 22–3). These continued during the Napoleonic First Empire (1804–14), when there was an intensification of training in geographical expertise, including courses in surveying and map-making at the École Polytechnique and the École des Ponts et Chaussées, laying a foundation for the continued development of the subject during the restoration monarchies of Louis XVIII (1815–24) and Charles X (1824–30), and for the foundation of the Société de Géographie de Paris in 1821.

In the period of the July Monarchy from 1830 to 1848, there was increased centralisation and control of scientific research, and two major institutions – the Comité des Travaux Historiques and the Service des Missions (the two merged in 1845, the Service becoming a sub-committee of the Comité des Travaux Historiques, and in 1874 the Service was renamed the Commission des Missions) – provided substantial support for travel and exploration (Heffernan 1994b: 23–4). The influence of the Service in support of expeditions and travels in the nineteenth and early twentieth centuries was substantial. Heffernan has highlighted the fact that 'Virtually every French major explorer and traveller of the day applied to, or was approached by, the Service. The list includes Pierre-Paul Savorgnan de Brazza, Jules-Léon Dutrueil-du-Rhins, Henri Duveyrier, Paul Flatters, Fernand Foreau, Charles de Foucauld, Auguste Pavie and Paul Soleillet' (Heffernan 1994b: 24).

Africa – a major focus of French overseas territorial and imperial interest – was a continent to which the Service allocated a large number of expeditions and travel grants, though some proposals, including that of Louis Ducouret (who strongly promoted his beliefs in the existence of unicorns near Lake Chad) for an ambitious plan for trans-Saharan and southern African journeys, were never realised. Prior to 1870, the number of applications for support for scientific missions to Africa (other than Algeria and Egypt) was small, as were those for travel to Asia and Latin America. Between 1870 and 1914, however, in the heyday of French overseas imperialism, the numbers of grants made for such journeys increased significantly, notably for work in Africa, the eastern Mediterranean, India, South-East Asia, Latin America and North America, also reflecting a change from the military-led imperialism experienced earlier in the century in North and West Africa to a more metropolitan-driven and politically influenced imperial expansion to restore and develop national honour, particularly in the aftermath of the Franco-Prussian War (Heffernan 1994b: 25–9, 34–5, 39).

The Service was not the only source of support for geographical exploration from France in the nineteenth century. The SGP continued to play an influential yet fluctuating role. The themes of French imperialism and colonialism were prominent in lectures and in the articles published in its *Bulletin*, including a significant number on Cochin China in the *Bulletin* for 1878. This was also reflected in the prominence of colonisation in the programme of the meeting of French geographical societies in Paris in 1878, and in 1881 at the International Geographical Congress in Paris (Lejeune 1993: 134–5).

Not all explorers received the unqualified support of the SGP. One notable case is that of Brazza who applied to the SGP in 1874 for support for his proposed expedition up the River Ogowe in Gabon, but was initially refused. The grounds for rejection appear to have been his age in relation to what was deemed to be such a significant mission, though the society revised its opinion and gave him support once it had realised his ability (Lejeune 1993: 133–4).

In 1875 his patron, Admiral de Montaignac, who had been made naval minister in 1874, gave him command of the expedition to what was to become, in 1886, the French colony of Gabon, his instructions being to sail up the River Ogowe, locate its source, and make links with the tribes in its upper reaches, in the hope of improving on the difficult trading conditions that were experienced with the tribes in the river's lower reaches. He arrived in November 1875, accompanied by a doctor, a quartermaster a biologist, and seventeen Senegalese. They journeyed up the River, travelling through the territory of the Bateke farmers, who traded with other groups along the River Alima, a tributary of the Congo. 'The regions he crossed appeared to be rich in desirable raw materials, especially rubber and ivory, while the natives for their part seemed keen on European products. Brazza had discovered an unknown and relatively simple access route to the Upper Congo Basin. A new future beckoned in Gabon' (Wesseling 1996: 85).

Brazza had been paid one year's salary in advance, and allowed 10,000 francs worth of credit, but the expedition lasted for three years and continued on account of funding by his mother and from his own resources, the French government having refused further support (Heffernan 1994b: 85). Brazza made two further expeditions, in 1880–1 and 1883–5, and was made Commissioner of the French Congo in April 1886, a position that he held until he was recalled in 1898 (West 1972: 143–4). His record in the French Congo was essentially one of humane and sensitive engagement with indigenous people, for which he was consistently criticised from metropolitan France and by military settlers and traders in the region. His alleged failure to support the Marchand Mission (a French attempt to establish a presence in the upper Nile that ended in the Fashoda Incident), and budget deficits were among the factors causing his removal. As West (1972: 154) puts it, the attack on him

was inspired by a group of French and Belgian capitalists, led by Leopold II, who regarded Brazza as dangerous to their plans for the Congo region. They were supported by others, in France and Africa, who had grievances against Brazza's administration. Jealous officials alleged that he was a bad administrator, that he was tired, and that he spent all his time in the bush instead of at Libreville. Traders complained that he took the Africans' side against them.

As has been shown above, he had been involved in territorial treaty-making with indigenous chieftains in the Congo, which placed him for a time at the forefront of French colonial interest in the region. He died in 1905 at Dakar. The French Congo colony became part of French Equatorial Africa in 1907.

Brazza was not the first French explorer to investigate this region: Paul du Chaillu, son of a French trader in Gabon, had explored the interior of the area in three journeys from 1855 to 1884, where he was the first European to have seen a gorilla (Newby 1975: 213). In 1839 France had set up a base on the Gabon estuary near what is now Libreville, and the naval officer Louis Edouard Bouet-Villaumez had agreed a treaty with the Mpongwe tribe for trade and protection.

The build-up of interest by the French, Belgians, English and Germans in the commercial opportunities and geopolitical value of the Gabon and Congo basins, together with a determination to eradicate the slave trade, led to an intensification of exploration, strategic settlement and political negotiation.

Other European explorers and expeditions

That there was an international interest by scientific societies in exploration is evidenced in part by the awards made by some of the European geographical societies to explorers from other countries. The RGS, for example, awarded medals in the late 1880s to European explorers of Africa, including the Germans Georg Schweinfurth and Gustav Nachtigal, and the Portuguese Major Serpa Pinto (Mill, 1930, 126–7). Details of expeditions sponsored by various European geographical societies are given in Chapter 6.

Schweinfurt and Nachtigal were but two of a number of German explorers in Africa from the 1860s. Others included Karl Mauch who explored the Zambezi from 1853 to 1872, and Gerhard Rohlfs who crossed the Sahara from Tripoli. Georg Schweinfurth (1836–1925) was a German botanist who undertook a number of expeditions in Africa, one of the earliest, 1863–6, being round the shores of the Red Sea and the territory across to the Nile, and this was followed in 1868–71 by an important expedition, sponsored by the Berlin Humboldt-Stiftung, to investigate the White Nile–Congo River watershed, when he discovered the River Welle. He lived in Cairo from 1875 to 1889, and founded a geographical society there. He was one of the first Europeans to encounter pygmies. Many of his field notes were lost in a fire, but he nonetheless published extensive scientific accounts of his travels in Africa (Allen 2004b: 206–10; Middleton 1991b: 118–19).

Gustav Nachtigal (1834–85) was a military surgeon who undertook a series of expeditions into Central Africa from North Africa, including a journey, commissioned by the King of Prussia, to take gifts to the sultan of Bornu, which started in 1869 from Tripoli. After Bornu he travelled eastwards, crossing the central Sahara through Darfur and Kordofan, eventually reaching the White Nile in 1874. A record of the journey was published with the title *Sahara und Sudan* in three volumes between 1879 and 1889 (Middleton 1991b: 119). He was subsequently sent to Tunisia as German consul-general, and to West Africa as a special commissioner, as a result of which Togoland and Cameroon were annexed by Germany (Stoecker 1986b: 28).

There were many more German and also Belgian expeditions to Central Africa. German expeditions sponsored by the Deutsche Gesellschaft zur Erforschung des äquatorialen Afrikas (German Society for the Exploration of Equatorial Africa, founded in Berlin in 1873) and ensuing institutions, included those by Pogge (1874–6), Schütt (1874–6), Buchner (1878–81), the German East African Expedition (1880–4), Pogge and Hermann Wissman (1880–3), and the German Congo Expedition (1884–6) (Fabian 2000: 283). Belgian expeditions, sponsored by the Brussels Committee of the International African Association (IAA), included the First Expedition (1877–9) by Crespel, Cambier and Dutrieux, the Second Expedition (1879) by Popelin and van Heuvel, the Third Expedition (1880–2) by Ramaeckers and Becker, the Fourth Expedition (1882–3) by Popelin, Roger and Storms, the Fifth Expedition (1883–4) and the Upper Congo Expedition (1882–5) (Fabian 2000: 283).

Fabian (2000), in his anthropological study of German and Belgian explorers in Central Africa in the late nineteenth century, has examined the range of personality types and eccentricities of these explorers. Although caught up in the commercial and political aspirations of European powers, these metropolitan rationales were frequently overpowered by personal whims, inclinations and visions, manifest in states influenced by fatigue, sickness through fever and other ailments, the use of drugs (hemp/cannabis and opiates, including the medical use of laudanum) and alcohol, sexual inclinations and practices, and violence, especially towards indigenous peoples. Some of these comprise what Fabian describes as 'the story of ecstasis in exploration': 'Myriads of causes made travellers lose control, if that is the point of searching for ecstatic elements in the production of knowledge…Still, we are entitled to imagine our explorers "drugged", most of them some of the time, and perhaps some of them most of the time' (Fabian 2000: 66–7).

The notion of explorers as tools of imperial and colonial policy has to be modified in the light of these and other complex motives and experiences, including the management of caravans of people and animals, the significance of groups rather than individuals in exploration, the identification of local polities and opposition to them, problems of communication, the management of instruments, and many acts of identification and description of objects and peoples (Fabian 2000).

The mapping and naming of places and topographic features were major tasks for explorers, and they were frequently given European names.

While they rushed (or crept) through the wilds, geographers and geographical societies in Europe were engaged in a rush to publish the latest, most up-to-date maps of travel routes and newly discovered regions of Africa. For many travellers maps became a matter of deep personal concern. Maps were a means of showing an individual's value to exploration by correcting or improving those of predecessors or competitors. (Fabian 2000: 202–3)

Some actually faked some of the data shown on maps. The German explorer Otto Schütt, in an expedition of 1878–9 sponsored by the German African Society (Afrikanischen Gesellschaft in Deutschland, founded in 1876), following an earlier expedition by P. Pogge, travelled from the west coast of Africa inland, but the details of his journey published back in Germany in 1881 contained fictitious information, a fact publicised in 1882 by the editors of the journal (*Mitteilungen der afrikanischen Gessellschaft in Deutschland*) in which they had appeared (Fabian 2000: 154–5).

The Portuguese explorer Alexandra de Serpa Pinto (1846–1900) was a soldier in the Portuguese army who was sent to Mozambique, where he was involved in the military suppression of tribal uprisings in the Lower Zambezi region and also led an expedition to study the Zambezi in 1869. In 1877 he undertook an expedition to the interior of Africa from Benguela to Lealui on the Zambezi, eventually reaching Pretoria. In 1881 he was awarded the gold medals of both the Royal Geographical Society and the Paris Geographical Society for his trans-African journey. He was made governor of Mozambique in 1889.

Exploration in Australia

As a result of the voyages of Cook, Flinders, Vancouver and French sailors and scientists in the eighteenth century, Australia's coastline was largely known and mapped by the beginning of the nineteenth century, so that further exploration, mapping and resource evaluation thereafter focused primarily on inland discoveries. As Stafford has indicated,

The focus of activity moved inland once the Blue Mountains of New South Wales were crossed in 1813. The two expeditions of 1817–18 led by John Oxley, that colony's surveyor-general, started a series of explorations by army officers such as Charles Sturt, surveyors like Thomas Mitchell, and bushmen such as Edward Eyre that revealed the broad outline of the interior by the 1860s. (Stafford 1999: 302–3)

The major expeditions in Australia in the nineteenth and early twentieth centuries were led by individuals as eccentric as those who had explored Africa. They met with harsh conditions and were sometimes destroyed by them, though they made use of aboriginal guides (Macinnis 2007). For expeditions such as these the funding and guidelines were provided by the Colonial Office, but in the 1860s the initiative transferred to the colonial governments themselves, often with strong competition between them.

The Burke and Wills expedition of 1860–1 was organised by the Royal Society of Victoria, but a metropolitan imperial influence, including that of the Colonial Office, the Admiralty and the Royal Geographical Society, together with more local influences, was evident in the Northern Australian Expedition of 1855–6, led by Charles Sturt, the assistant surveyor-general of Western Australia, and focused on the evaluation of the resources of the north coast of Australia (Stafford 1999: 303–4). Charles Napier Sturt (1795–1869) was a British soldier, commissioned in the 39th (Dorsetshire) Regiment of Foot in 1813, who had seen action in France and Quebec and a seven-year period on garrison duty in Ireland. In September 1825 his regiment was instructed to accompany convicts to Australia: they arrived at Sydney Cove in May 1827. He had taught himself surveying while on duty in France, and his proximity (as military secretary) to the Governor – Ralph Darling – facilitated an agreement in 1827 to his request to conduct an expedition into the interior of Australia 'to ascertain the level of the inland plains and to determine the supposed existence of an inland sea' (Davis 2002: xviii). The reasons for his interest in exploration included a sense that his ambition to progress away from a military role towards promotion within the colonial administration system might be advanced by this type of venture (Davis 2002: xix). The expedition lasted from November 1828 to April 1829, and 'led to such major discoveries as the Darling River and, indirectly, to the identity of many of its tributaries – the Naomi, the Gwydir, the Dumaresq, the Castlereagh, the Macquarie, and the Bogan' (Davis 2002: xix).

The second expedition started in Adelaide in August 1844 and finished in January 1846, having penetrated inland as far as the Simpson Desert before returning. One of the objectives was to locate an inland sea and the geographical centre of Australia, and to find land suitable for arable cultivation: none of these targets was reached. Nor was that of locating the imagined mountainous watershed about which Barrow wanted further geographical knowledge, though, as Davis has indicated, Sturt 'did not even realize that he had discovered a significant height of land defining the flow of waters for much of the Australian continent west of the Great Dividing Range' (Davis 2002: xxix). Although Sturt did not feel that this physically arduous expedition had successfully met its objectives, his achievements, including the identification of the arid nature of the heart of Australia, and the return of the greater number of his party, were celebrated in Australia and in London, where he was awarded the Founder's Gold Medal of the Royal Geographical Society (Davis 2002: xxix).

The expedition owed much to Sturt's personal initiative. His reports added to the geographical knowledge produced by those that had gone before, such as Flinders, Bass, John Oxley, Hamilton Hume and William Hovell, and his contemporaries Thomas Mitchell and Edward Eyre, and pointed the way for explorers who followed. He was very much a product of his times, with his surveying expertise and his discoveries on both of his major expeditions directly relevant to British endeavours to implement Edward Gibbon Wakefield's concepts of systematic colonisation in Australia. Powell has also suggested that 'it is he, more than any other individual, who deserves to be credited with defining the main arteries of the Murray–Darling Basin' (Powell 1993: 13). His dealings with the aboriginal populations that he encountered on both expeditions are significant, because he employed them as guides and emissaries (though little mention of this is made in his journal), for which they were paid in gifts. His comments in his journal largely give the impression of a humanitarian and 'unusually peaceful' approach to the aboriginal people that he encountered, including critical comment on those who had mistreated or killed them (Davis 2002: xlvii, xiv).

Davis (2002: xxx–xxxi) has characterised the man and his achievements in the following terms:

His life, like all lives, was an important one, although if it were to be measured solely by the historical and cultural benefits his Central Australian Expedition brought to civilization, Sturt's contribution would have to be considered marginal. Yet, as a nineteenth-century gentleman Sturt played an important, if amateur, role as an observer of the natural world, and his many observations about the flora and fauna of central Australia provided a significant foundation for contemporary scientific thought. Of course, Sturt's contribution to society was far more than what was offered by his 1844–46 expedition.

A later expedition was that of Robert O'Hara Burke and William John Wills in 1860-1, who tracked northwards with a dozen men across the

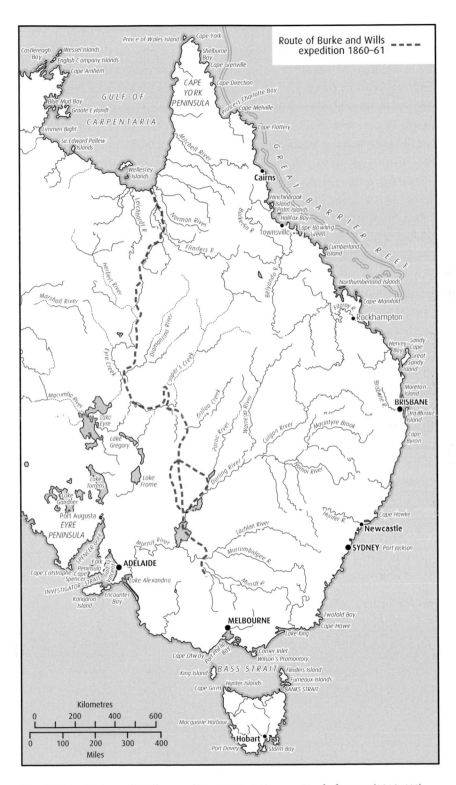

Fig. 5.7 The Burke and Wills expedition 1860–1. Source: Bartholomew (1913: 111).

arid centre of Australia, to Cooper's Creek and to the tidal section of the estuary of the Flinders River on the Gulf of Carpentaria, though they never reached the sea. They set off in August 1860 from Melbourne (where their expedition funds had been donated) with horses and camels, and stopped at their halfway point at Cooper's Creek in Queensland to set up a supply depot, with Burke, Wills, John King and Charles Gray proceeding northwards, leaving another expedition member, William Brahe, who had been instructed to wait there for three months for their return. He waited in fact for four months, but left just eight hours before they reached the depot, and as a result of diverting towards Adelaide, notwithstanding the help of food given to them by aboriginal people, Burke and Wills died, leaving King to be sustained by Aborigines until he was rescued (Allen 2004a: 332–3). Allen has suggested that 'despite the young deaths that it entailed, the Burke–Wills expedition had in many ways been successful. They had proved once and for all that there was no inland sea on the Australian continent and were the first to have crossed it from south to north' (Allen 2004a: 333).

The contributions of explorers to the geographical knowledge that informed imperial and colonial policies were substantial. Many of these explorers, notably the men, were supported by financial help and the loan of instruments, and by instructions, from a range of scientific societies and government institutions. These links are developed in the following chapter, with particular emphasis on the roles of geographical societies in the advance of imperialism and colonialism.

6 | Geographical societies and imperialism

I will not, however strong the temptation may be, enter on the interesting and much disputed controversy as to the relation between politics and Geography ... I think that I may truly say that if the modern politician requires, as indeed he does require if he is worthy of his task, to be equipped with geographical knowledge, on the other hand you geographers must admit that geography owes much to the modern politician. (Asquith 1912: 106)

These words of H. H. Asquith, the Prime Minister, were spoken at a dinner at the Royal Geographical Society and came in response to an invitation to him, in a speech by G. Curzon, the president, to acknowledge the importance of geography to politicians. Asquith clearly would not be drawn to do so, but the context of this exchange – a dinner at a major British geographical society – highlights the role that such societies played in debates on the role of geography and geographical knowledge in the business of state and empire.

A vast range of institutions had in fact developed which served and helped to promote European interests overseas in the period of high imperialism from the late nineteenth to the early twentieth century. At the outset responsibility frequently fell on the ministries for the army and navy, but gradually specialist governmental institutions developed – foreign or colonial ministries, for example – that focused more closely on imperial and colonial matters. In addition, from the early nineteenth century, a large number of scientific societies grew and expanded whose interests included the sponsoring of expeditions, recording and mapping of data, the debate of colonial issues, and in some cases propagation of colonial policies. There were large numbers of such institutions, too numerous to cover here, so the focus in this chapter will be on the roles of geographical societies and linked institutions in imperial and colonial promotion.

Institutions of course change over time, and at any given point in time may comprise kaleidoscopes of constitutional rules, organised events such as lectures, social occasions, sponsorship of expeditions, publications of journals and newsletters, dominance by particular groups and individuals, and a range of public and private debates on important and sometimes quite trivial matters. In their early days membership was often limited, by design or context, to those who belonged to social, political and military elites, and they were generally dominated by men. They served as places where new geographical information could be presented and discussed, and where it was also provided through map collections and exhibitions. They did not exist in isolation from other institutions, and there were frequently overlaps in membership.

Science and learned societies

The advancement of scientific knowledge and its dissemination to specialist and more popular audiences was a process that changed substantially in all European countries in the nineteenth and early twentieth centuries, and the groups and societies which had the production of geographical knowledge as their central concern were bound up in these changes. The evolution of societies concerned with the organisation and dissemination of scientific knowledge took a rather different path in Britain from that in France and Germany. The dissemination of both esoteric and popular knowledge occurred through the meetings and excursions of amateur clubs and the formal meetings of learned societies, via the publication of magazines, quarterlies and reviews, and for the professional scientists through publication in a growing number of specialist journals (Daunton 2005: 1–5). The attempts to spread the new knowledge from science to a wider audience were not without tension, including that experienced in geographical societies in France and Britain, for example, as will be shown later. Daunton has written of the 'epistemological sites of Victorian Britain', which 'included loose social networks; clubs or societies such as provincial literary and philosophical societies and archaeological societies, and national bodies such as the Royal Geographical Society, open to anyone (or at least any man) who cared to join and could afford the subscription; and the most exclusive, closed bodies of the elect, such as the Royal Society and the British Academy' (Daunton 2005: 10).

Contrasts with German scientific organisation and philosophy included the exclusion of the humanities in Britain from the broad concept of science and the role of research in the sciences. The presentation of papers to learned societies was controlled by influential 'gatekeepers', who had their own political and social agendas as well as scientific preferences. The British model of scientific advancement and promotion still, by the end of the nineteenth century, accommodated both full-time scientists and gifted individuals within and outside the universities, in contrast to the

German situation in which specialist scientific knowledge was largely to be found in specialist institutes and universities. In France there was a model of scientific enterprise that included the *grandes écoles* and museums, which had some parallel in the museums of South Kensington in London. Daunton, however, suggests that in Britain, in contrast to France and Germany, 'the organisation of knowledge rested on a "mixed economy" of provision and funding, with a preference for voluntarism and the market over the state whose role was to facilitate or support much more than to provide on its own initiative' (Daunton, 2005: 13, 17, 18). By the end of the nineteenth century, however, universities in Britain, including Oxford, Cambridge, Edinburgh and Glasgow, were increasingly becoming centres of specialist research and teaching. Learned societies and academic institutions in Britain were increasingly engaged with imperialism, symbolised and evidenced by the naming of Imperial College in London (formed and named to parallel research centres in Berlin), and the teaching of imperially related courses in universities, where critical anti-imperial voices could also be heard (Daunton 2005: 24–5).

Geographical knowledge and imperialism

Geography was linked overtly and covertly with imperial power, through agencies of survey and mapping – means of 'capturing' and controlling places overseas – and of cultural superimposition and modification through exploration and exploitation, and ethnological research. To these were added humanitarian objectives, including the abolition of the slave trade and the improvement of living standards. There was also some opposition by individual geographers, but rarely from geographical societies, to the imperial and colonial projects of the period. Geographical societies in many ways focused the processes of engagement between geographical knowledge and imperialism, but there were many other agents, including universities, departments of state, chambers of commerce, and scores of other learned and scientific societies, many with similar objectives to those of the geographical societies.

According to Bridges, the Royal Geographical Society and other European geographical societies were promoters of imperialism through 'infrastructures', the activities of the members and explorers who provided the cartographic information and other knowledge for the organisation and control of new overseas colonial territories, and in many cases capital through investment by individual members, facilitating the development

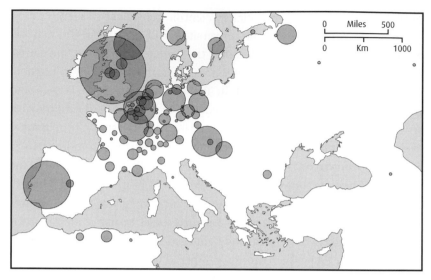

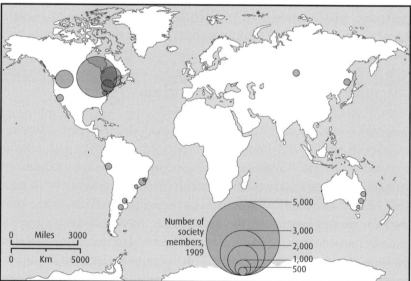

Fig. 6.1 European and non-European geographical societies in the early twentieth century. Source: Heffernan (2003: 13).
By permission of and © the author and Sage Publications.

of roads, railways, telegraphs, and administration systems (Bridges 1973, 1982). Bridges has also provided an instructive account of the positions of the various geographical societies of Europe in relation to national imperial ambitions, as evidenced in particular by their participation in and reactions to the Brussels Geographical Conference of 1876, a meeting of geographical experts on Africa (primarily explorers and representatives of the main geographical societies) convened by King Leopold II of Belgium for the purpose of giving scientific endorsement to a desired increase in European involvement in Africa: to effect a transition from the pure science of exploration and mapping to the applied science of colonialism (Bridges 1982). Delegations from the Paris, Berlin and London societies attended, led by their presidents.

One aim of the conference was the establishment of an International African Association. After the conference, the specific reactions to attempts to activate the International Association varied, but directly, and (more importantly) indirectly, the Brussels Conference seems to have served to accelerate the application of geographical expertise to colonial policy. This seems to have been particularly true in Germany, with the founding in 1876 of the Deutsches Afrikanische Gesellschaft (the German African Society) and the provision from 1878 by the state of a substantial annual sum of money for support of German expeditions to Africa (Bridges 1982: 20). A very close association developed in Germany, therefore, between geography and overseas imperialism, a process already underway in France but with a less clear link in Britain. From the point of view of the history of geography as a science, this is an important period when geographical scientific knowledge switched to a more applied emphasis.

Geographical societies in Europe

The founding of geographical societies in Europe was primarily a feature of the nineteenth century, though gatherings of citizens interested in navigation, exploration and travel date back to the eighteenth century and the geographical interests associated with science during the Enlightenment. The lack of critical and contextual histories for such organisations was noted by John K. Wright in 1957 (1957: 546), who claimed that 'no one has yet sought with any degree of scholarship and critical acumen to correlate the rise of geographical societies with larger historical events, to measure and appraise their influence, or to make comparative analysis of their functions and problems', while noting the large quantities of material available in the societies' journals and anniversary publications and in archival collections, and, in passing, the 'almost feline vitality' of geographical societies evidenced in their ability to come 'to life again after periods of torpor' (Wright 1957: 546, 548–9).

There have been major changes in the last decade or so in the theoretical and material approaches to the engagements between geographical knowledge and empire. The major starting point from a geographical point of view was Brian Hudson's paper 'The New Geography and the New Imperialism, 1870–1918' (Hudson 1977: 12–19), using Marxist and Leninist notions of imperialism, and linking geography with the new imperialism of the later nineteenth century, including militarism, the growth of European empires overseas, the economic exploitation of imperial territories, and the potent questions of race and class, contemporary theories of which were assisted by environmental determinism. This pioneer paper led, but only after a surprising interval of time, to other significant studies of the historical geographies of colonialism and imperialism in the nineteenth and twentieth centuries. Felix Driver, in a seminal paper published in 1992, reviewed the novelist Joseph Conrad's concept of a 'Geography Militant', and the ways, other than materialist, in which imperial geography was constituted, notably by culture and politics, themes further developed in the same author's book *Geography Militant* published in 2001 (Driver 1992, 2001).

The objectives of the geographical clubs and societies in Europe were primarily the promotion of travel and exploration, wherever possible through financial support and loans of instruments and equipment, the organisation of lecture programmes and social events, the publication of a wide range of geographical knowledge, and links with national and overseas geographical societies through correspondence and exchange of publications. Their membership numbers fluctuated, and the members were drawn from different social and professional groups, with military and naval personnel, politicians and government administrators, members of the aristocratic and wealthy classes, and government ministers prominent in the early days, the ranks swelling with scientists and academics as specialist science and the universities expanded towards the end of the nineteenth century. The fortunes of individual societies reflected the influence of powerful and well-connected officers, political and economic concerns, notably trade, the growth of nationalist sentiment and searches for national identity, growing competition between European states for presence overseas and, in the case of non-capital city or 'provincial' societies, a whole array of local issues, including trade opportunities.

The origins and development of societies such as the Royal Geographical Society in the nineteenth century reflected the changing contexts of national and international politics, geopolitics, commercial rivalries, major changes in cultures and lifestyles, and the redefinition of national identities. The creation of new knowledge of far-off places and peoples became a major scientific and cultural priority. This new knowledge, derived from explorations and discoveries, was extensively debated and contested both within and between European geographical societies, including the RGS, conditioned by contemporary issues such as ethnology and race, the civilising mission, and the processes of modernisation. Changes in the nature and effectiveness of transport systems and of media communication, including the development of the telegraph and the telephone, and of popular journals and newspapers, speeded the conveying of both good and tragic news, and affected the social geographies of information exchange through learned societies.

The new European geographical societies of the nineteenth and early twentieth centuries were not the only institutions to promote geography as a knowledge system that could be supportive of imperial ambition and practice: general scientific societies such as the British Association for the Advancement of Science (Withers, Finnegan and Higgit 2006: 435) and colonisation societies, for example, were also part of the complex links between the subject and imperialism.

The initial growth of European geographical societies after the foundation of the first major European geographical society – in Paris in 1821 – was slow. Geographical societies were founded in Berlin (1828), London (1830), St Petersburg (1845), Geneva (1853), Vienna (1856), Leipzig (1861), Dresden (1863), Florence (1867, moved to Rome in 1872), and Munich (1869), and by 1894 there were 84 geographical societies in Europe, out of a world total of 111 (Lejeune 1993: 85; Heffernan 1998b: 273–7). Of the 84, 30 were in France, 23 in Germany, 5 in Britain, 4 in Italy and 6 in Switzerland. Early institutional indications of the impact of European colonial activity were the founding of four geographical societies in Algeria by the end of the nineteenth century: in Oran in 1878 and Algiers in 1880. By 1914 there were many geographical societies in the countries of Europe and smaller numbers in their overseas colonies. The estimated global number of geographical societies for this date was 130. The number of members varied greatly at any given time, but a general trend was an overall increase from the 1830s to the early twentieth century. The Paris Society started with 217 founding members, with numbers declining by 1850, but by 1875 increasing to 1,353, and to 2,500 in 1885. The Berlin Gesellschaft für Erdkunde zu Berlin was founded in 1828, with 53 members, a figure that had risen to 600 in 1875 and 1,275 by 1900. The Royal Geographical Society, founded as the Geographical Society of London in 1830, with 460 Fellows (members), had increased membership to 800 in 1850, 2,400 by 1870, 3,500 by 1885 and 5,300 in 1913 (Heffernan 1998b: 275–6).

The Royal Geographical Society and British imperialism

The question of links between institutional geography and imperialism in Britain from the mid-nineteenth century onwards is one of great complexity. The Royal Geographical Society, founded in 1830, was a continuation of the African Association (founded 1788) and the Raleigh Travellers' Club (founded in 1826). In its early years, strongly influenced by the tradition of exploration coupled with scientific investigation, exemplified in the late eighteenth and early nineteenth centuries by the experiences of Captain James Cook and Joseph Banks in the Pacific and the translation of the consequent new knowledge to London, the society sought to promote geography as a science, mainly through exploration and mapping. Its aims included interests in 'collecting information, collating travellers' descriptions, producing regional surveys, or writing narratives of voyages' (Driver 2001: 36).

The Royal Geographical Society (the Geographical Society of London was its original title) had William IV (who became king on 24 June of that year) as its first patron. Before 1830, geographical issues had been debated in intellectual and social salons, including lively dining clubs, in London and elsewhere, and they, together with national governments, had given support to exploration.

The increasing complexity and contested nature of this newly developing geographical knowledge, accelerating under national and imperial influence in the eighteenth and nineteenth centuries, is an important component in the work of contemporary research on the institutions, personalities, goals, cultural contexts and outcomes associated with the development of geography and geographical societies. Driver, for example, has emphasised the hybrid nature and often contradictory objectives of a society such as the RGS, including the dynamic of negotiation and redefinition of its objectives and the evolution of 'a developing culture of exploration', a culture that 'extended well beyond the frontiers of science [which] were constantly being renegotiated and even redefined' (Driver 2001: 25).

The objectives of the proposed society, listed at the meeting of the Raleigh Travellers' Club on 24 May 1830, included the gathering and publication of new geographical information; the stocking of a geographical library, including books, maps and charts; the obtaining and provision of appropriate instruments for survey and navigation; the provision of instructions, advice, guidance and a measure of selective financial support for travellers; and the exchange of information and publications with

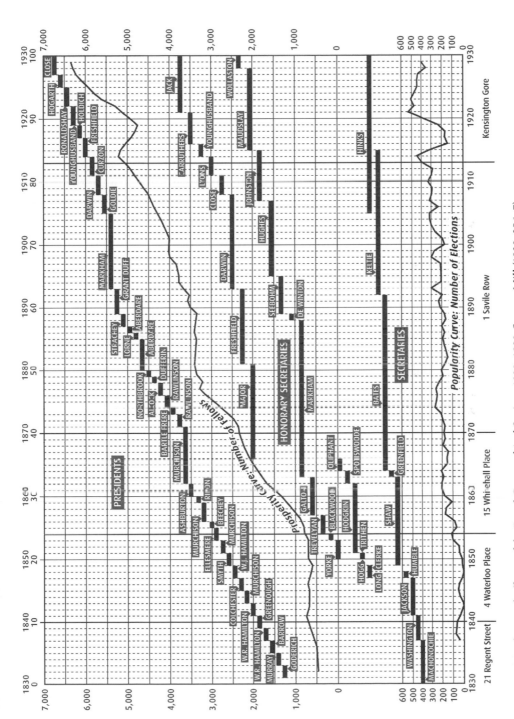

Fig. 6.2 Members and officers of the Royal Geographical Society, 1830–1930. Source: Mill (1930: 256–7).

other geographical societies and with philosophical and literary societies. Such intentions were indeed incorporated in the formal resolutions for the formation of the RGS, which received its royal charter from Queen Victoria in 1854. From the outset, as David Livingstone has indicated, the RGS was characterised by 'the imperialistic undergirding of the institution's entire project and thereby reveals that Victorian geography was intimately bound up with British expansionist policy overseas' (Livingstone 1992: 167).

The society clearly represented not just one but 'a coalition of interests', especially before 1850, and therefore might be better understood as more of 'an information exchange' than as a major centre of scientific debate (Driver 2001: 36, 7). In the second half of the nineteenth century representations of new geographical knowledge were increasingly tied in with the development of British and European imperialism, and in particular with the 'Great Game' in Central Asia and then the 'scramble' for Africa. Such interests were not solely the prerogative of the RGS, for other learned and scientific societies were caught up in the imperial rush.

Learned societies, including national and local geographical societies, are complex amalgams of formal statements of intent, charters, constitutions, rules, by-laws, premises, specialist facilities (library, map-room, reading-room, lecture-room, administrative offices and so on), the personalities of administrators, members and authors, publications, and local and national issues and events with which such societies find themselves engaged. The biographical or prosopographical aspects of a society's history are important and intriguing, especially when seen in the broader contexts of 'cultures' of the production of scientific knowledge through exploration, mapping, and debate.

The membership of the RGS was mixed in profession and interest, and included significant representation of the organs of state such as the Admiralty (John Barrow, a founder of the RGS and a second secretary at the Admiralty from 1804 to 1845), the army, the Ordnance Survey, the Admiralty Hydrographic Survey, members of other, newly founded scientific societies such as the Geological Society (1807), the Astronomical Society (1820), the Royal Asiatic Society (1823), the Zoological Society (1826), and the much older Royal Society (Driver 2001: 32).

Although relatively ineffective as a scientific society and as a focus for London society before about 1850, thereafter the RGS, under the guidance of strong presidents such as Sir Roderick Murchison, and reflecting the rapidly growing interest in science in Britain, played a more important role in the advancement of geographical science, in an increasingly imperial context, and its headquarters became an extremely fashionable venue. Even so the society, like many others, was not an organisation with a homogeneous character and membership: there were debates and conflicts of interest. Driver (2001: 26–7, 46) suggests that the RGS was an 'information exchange rather than a centre of calculation', and that by and beyond the 1870s 'the RGS was as much an *arena* as an interest group, a site where competing visions of geography were debated and put into practice'.

Unlike the major geographical societies in other European countries, and the geographical societies founded elsewhere in Britain in the late nineteenth century, the RGS does not appear to have functioned explicitly as a tool of empire, and its officers went to some lengths in its publications and debates to avoid specific reference to the political advantages of British imperial policy, even at the height of nationalist imperialist sentiments in the 1880s and 1890s. In doing so it often sheltered behind the chartered objective of being a society for the advancement of geography as a science. In contrast, its members who were politicians or civil servants working, for example, for the India Office and the Colonial Office, were closely bound up in the affairs of a developing empire, and its map room was much in demand from the military and others as a source of topographic and geostrategic information. The RGS offered an opportunity to entrepreneurs who had been economically successful overseas to meet and become part of the British establishment, and also operated as a means for career advancement for younger men through the agency of expedition and exploration (Stafford 1989: 216).

The objectives of producing and disseminating geographical information were met by support for expeditions, particularly for the production of new surveys and maps, and by the building up of the society's library, map-room and archive collections, for which financial support was given by the British government, and from 1868 the society received gifts of maps from the War Office, the India Office and the Ordnance Survey (Jones 2002). Jones (2002: 317–18), has demonstrated that notwithstanding its waves of popularity and increases in membership, 'In part, the RGS simply did not have the resources to finance large-scale expeditions', and 'Expedition finances were notoriously difficult to control, and the financial crises of the 1840s had demonstrated the dangers of uncapped expenditure. But although direct sponsorship was too expensive, the society's officers found other ways to influence the conduct of explorers', including instruction in mapping and surveying, the publication of *Hints to Travellers* from 1854 and in revised form from 1883, the establishment of an instruments committee in 1883, and the building up of the library and map collections. Annual expenditure on expeditions fluctuated, with peaks of £2,891 for the Livingstone Relief Expedition to Africa in 1872–4, £2,996 for V. L. Cameron's expedition to East Africa in 1873–7, £2,000 for A. Keith Johnston's expedition to Africa in 1877–80, £3,595 for Joseph Thompson's expedition to East Africa in 1885–7, and £8,000 to Robert Scott's *Discovery* expedition to the Antarctic in 1901–2 (Jones 2005: 329).

The most powerful of the society's presidents in the nineteenth century was Sir Roderick Murchison, who was president in 1843–5, 1851–3, and again 1862–71, and who 'exemplifies the "men of knowledge" who were most successful at mobilising and exploiting the new national scientific institutions of early nineteenth-century Britain by harmonising the diverse interests of their constituents' (Stafford 1989: 217). RGS presidents with professional and ideological links to the expanding British empire held sway until the early years of the twentieth century, when the dwindling areas of the world yet to be explored by Europeans accelerated a shift towards more scientific approaches and goals, so that the 'fashionable, political, and military factions, as well as the attendant ideologies of imperialism, racism, and environmental determinism – all of which had helped to express and justify geography's social utility during its professionalising phase – were thus gradually purged from the Society' (Stafford 1989: 219).

Other presidents of the RGS in the late nineteenth century included Sir Rutherford Alcock, Lord Aberdare (closely involved in the development of West Africa), General Sir Richard Strachey (who had served in the army in India at the time of the 1857 Uprising/Mutiny) and Sir Grant Duff (junior minister in the India Office and the Foreign Office and subsequently Lieutenant-Governor of Madras). Other major figures in the RGS closely bound up with British imperial policy included Henry Bartle Frere, Major-General Sir Henry Rawlinson, Clements Markham and Lord Curzon, Viceroy of India from 1898 to 1905.

In the early years of the twentieth century (Driver 2001: 203), the imperial interest within the RGS continued in practice to be reflected in its presidents: Sir George Goldie (a major figure in the geopolitical and commercial development of Nigeria); Sir Thomas Holdich (a military man who had been attached to the Survey of India and who became an expert on the definition of international boundaries); Francis Younghusband (who was born in India, served in the army in India, and became part of the Political Department of the Indian government); and Sir Charles Close (a royal engineer, who like Holdich had served in the Survey of India, and afterwards in tropical Africa became arbiter of international boundaries, then head of the Geographical Section of the War Office and, finally, Director-General of the Ordnance Survey) (Mill 1930: *passim*).

Imperial information links between the RGS and the military in particular are reflected in the frequency of lectures given to and published by the RGS by serving military officers (notably from India), complaints by members of the RGS Council at the failure of the War Office to agree publication of important map material and related survey findings, and in the use of the RGS map-room and library for information by government departments, conspicuously at times of crisis, including the First World War. In spite of its very close contacts with government and the War Office, the RGS was, however, very poorly represented, in contrast to the American and French delegations, at the peace conference at Versailles at the end of the First World War. It had also been very cautious (with some considerable political insight) about advancing the African survey and development proposals put forward by King Leopold of Belgium during and after the Brussels Geographical Conference of 1876.

Recent accounts of facets of the RGS in the nineteenth and early twentieth centuries, including the Antarctic expeditions to which it gave modest financial and strong moral support, have also critically examined some of the assumptions about the role of the RGS and its officers and members in the advancement of imperialism, and the extent to which the society was shaped in its priorities by imperialist ideology and practice. In a study of the ill-fated British Antarctic Expedition of 1910–13, led by Robert Scott, Jones (2003: 48) suggests that although some features of the work of the RGS, such as the training of surveyors and the mapping of unknown parts of the earth's surface, were caught up in a quest for geographical and other forms of scientific knowledge that would inform Britain's imperial development, 'the RGS was not simply an instrument of British imperial expansion. This distinctive hybrid institution generated a range of impulses, some complementary, some contradictory ... The imperial utility of geographical information varied widely, and the interests of the Society's officers and fellowship frequently diverged.' He argues that the ways in which the British nation, including the RGS, responded to the tragic outcome of the Scott expedition, for example, are more complex and nuanced than can be afforded by a simple imperialistic explanation.

Notwithstanding Britain's status as a major imperial power in 1913, the strong support of the former RGS president Sir Clements Markham for the expedition, the imperial connections of the families of the dead explorers, 'Links of Empire' posters showing the departure of the *Discovery*, the imperial rhetoric of fund-raising brochures, and the subsequent erection of public monuments in their honour and memory, the imperial construction placed on this disaster 'should not be exaggerated: most commentators did not depict the Antarctic as an outpost of empire' (Jones 2003: 213, 195).

Jones (2002: 332) claims that the reforms of the RGS in the 1870s did not have a direct causal link with the new imperialism, but the increased popular interest in empire in Britain, which was more common in the 1880s, as evidenced in statements by officers of the RGS, was 'diluted' by the greater emphasis on accurate measurement of the earth and by educational initiatives. The strongest links seems to have been through the surveying and mapping of far-off territories. As Driver (2001: 39) puts it: 'Perhaps the most important cognitive link between imperialism and science in the case of the field sciences was provided by territorial mapping, as both metaphor and practice.' To which may be added the power and influence of political and military Fellows of the RGS whose careers were inextricably linked with empire.

The 'provincial' geographical societies in Britain

In contrast to the RGS the other geographical societies in England and Scotland actively sought means to improve trade and commerce, as did many geographical societies in Europe. The Scottish Geographical Society, founded in 1884, had four branches in Edinburgh, Glasgow, Dundee and Aberdeen. The RGS had none, but near-contemporaneously with the Scottish Geographical Society (given its royal title in 1887) geographical societies were founded in Manchester (1884), Tyneside (1887), Liverpool (1891), Southampton (1897), and Hull (1909–10). The RGS was the only one not to admit women as members ('Fellows') from its foundation – a matter not remedied until 1913.

John MacKenzie (1995: 231–43) has shown that these 'provincial' societies were strongly interested in commercial aspects of empire, particularly at the time of trade depression in the late nineteenth century, and were reflective of the actions and concerns of local chambers of commerce. They were for the most part short-lived (apart from the Manchester and Scottish societies): obviously failing to keep support once the period of economic depression was over. They did, however, pursue active roles in the search for collection and dissemination of geographical knowledge, through inviting a range of speakers to their meetings, including 'heroic' explorers such as Stanley, and publishing material in journals.

Commercial geographical societies and municipal imperialism

In the late nineteenth and early twentieth centuries there was a resurgence of interest in Britain and a number of European states in the strategic and the commercial potential of their empires. With it, especially in the context of trade depression and aggressive territorial manoeuvring in Africa in the late nineteenth century, went a need for greater acquisition of geographical information and knowledge to further imperial commercial strategy and profit.

Some of the initiatives for the realisation of commercial opportunities were taken under the aegis of national and local geographical societies, working closely with local political and commercial interests, including chambers of commerce. There were in some cases important links with national government and colonial/imperial policies. This phenomenon, which had quite a short life in the late nineteenth and early twentieth centuries, has been called, for obvious reasons, 'municipal imperialism' (Laffey 1969, 1974, 1975; Schneider 1990; Heffernan 1995b; Clout 2008a; 2008b), a concept further developed below.

The British experience of commercial geography

The question of improving the trade of Britain through imperial routes and opportunities was a consistent theme of the publications of the Royal Commission on the Depression of Trade and Industry (1885–6). Appendix A of the commission's report also shows the strong feelings of British chambers of commerce and trade associations about the need for closer imperial trading links and imperial federation. The deepening concerns with the effects of the new trade tariffs of continental European countries and the United States, the crises in the Sudan and on the North-West Frontier of India, and the Berlin Conference of 1884–5 (which in effect accelerated the scramble for Africa) therefore increased these interests in commercial opportunities and the acquisition of geographical information to further this end. Thus 'in the new European struggle the fitness of the state to survive and prosper could only be achieved if the public were to be trained in an understanding of the world's resources' (MacKenzie 1995: 95).

Much of the activity in the process of gathering geographical information relevant to British metropolitan economic survival and renewal strategies focused on municipal and metropolitan chambers of commerce, as it did at the time elsewhere in industrialising Europe. For a short period from the 1880s to the early twentieth century increased efforts were made to include old and new geographical societies in Britain in this process of gathering commercially useful geographical information, and to raise interest in commercial geography. This need was also addressed, albeit for a short period, by the attempt to establish a British Commercial Geographical Society in 1884.

The RGS and commercial geography

The RGS lacked interest in commercial geography, unlike trade associations and chambers of commerce who eagerly sought commercial intelligence of a geographical nature. There were some exceptions, proved by the fact, as Driver has pointed out, that in the 1893 edition of *Hints to Travellers* J. S. Keltie advocated the putting of geographical questions about the availability of resources and the market and commercial potential of 'uncivilised or semi-civilised countries' then being explored (Driver 2001: 40–1). This is perhaps not surprising in view of Keltie's earlier visits to Britain's imperial rivals, France and Germany, in his search for best practices in the field of geographical education. In the mid- and late nineteenth century the RGS was used as a forum for people like Cameron to air their views on the necessity of replacing the slave trade in Africa with a more moral and legitimate form of commerce, hence Rotberg's assertion that in the mid- and late nineteenth century the RGS continued its role as 'the sponsor of explorers and one of the major custodians of Britain's African conscience' (Rotberg 1971: 25), but generally lacked overt enthusiasm for geographical studies of trading opportunities.

Bridges has pointed out that although discussions at the RGS about possible expeditions in the mid-nineteenth century had mentioned the identification of commercial opportunity through 'discovery' and mapping, '"the concern in this case seems to have gone no further than this sort of statement"... In 1877, the Society's Expeditions Committee said that it wished to advance geographical science "to the exclusion of any dealings with territorial and commercial undertakings"' (Bridges 1973: 222–3). Bridges contends that the main priority of the RGS was geography as science, and that it is very difficult to make a connection with its policies for exploration and the advancement of bourgeois Victorian capitalism through the careful identification and development of commercial opportunities in Africa and elsewhere. Hence:

The Society consciously shied away from non-scientific pursuits in relation to Africa after a little experience of them in relation to Leopold II's ideas. It was not, like its counterpart in Paris, a centre where those interested in schemes for overseas expansion foregathered to plan their campaigns, and it was even less like the numerous 'commercial geography' societies which, in the 1870s and 1880s sprang up in many parts of Europe including Manchester and Edinburgh. (Bridges 1973: 224)

On the other hand, it is worth noting that at a meeting at the RGS on 3 November 1884, the president of the RGS, Lord Aberdare (chairman of the United Africa Company since 1882 and of the Royal Niger Company from 1886), referred to the foundation of geographical societies in Manchester and Edinburgh in the previous month:

I am sure that I am representing your feelings in expressing our cordial hope that the societies established in such centres of intellectual and commercial activity will have a useful and brilliant career. I have watched also with great interest the attempt to found a Society of Commercial Geography in the City of London; and trust that it may be attended with the success which so useful an object deserves. (Aberdare 1884: 688)

In the discussion following the evening's paper (by Joseph Thompson, 'Through the Masai Country to Victoria Nyanza') Commander V. L. Cameron stated that:

The President had alluded to the British Commercial Geographical Society, which now had a great number of members, and he wished to thank his lordship for the kind words he had spoken about it. It had occasionally been supposed that the British Commercial Geographical Society was in opposition to the Royal Geographical Society, but it would ill become him, who owed his geographical reputation to the latter Society, to do anything against it. His object was to bring the specially commercial aspects of geography before men of business in the City, and as similar societies had been established in Germany, France, and other countries, he thought it would be advantageous to England [sic] to have one in London. (Cameron 1884: 710–11)

Cameron is referring to his attempt to form a British Commercial Geographical Society, in 1884. Cameron (1844–94), a British naval officer, was famous for having crossed Africa from east to west. His epic and hazardous journey which started from Bagamoyo in March 1873 was initially an attempt, partly funded by the RGS, to find the explorer David Livingstone. Despite Livingstone's death in May 1873, Cameron continued his travels, reaching Catumbela (north of Benguela) on the west coast in November 1875. His expedition, however, served a number of important ends, including greater knowledge of the geography and ecology of the interlacustrine region and the Congo basin, and the provision of valuable information for the anti-slavery movements (Casada 1975: 211).

Relations between the two societies were certainly not confrontational, but the token recognition that the RGS gave to the new society did not mean that it embraced commercial geography as a priority of its own. In contrast to the other geographical societies in England and Scotland, and many in Europe, the RGS tended to have only very small numbers of members who were traders and merchants. In a sample survey of 200 Fellows before 1855, the number in overseas trade was less than 5 per cent, and this proportion stayed much the same in the period 1856–76 (Bridges 1973: 224–7). MacKenzie also takes this view about the aims of the RGS: 'The provincial [geographical] societies were created as a response to the conviction that the Royal Geographical Society was neither utilitarian nor imperial enough, that the metropolis could no longer be trusted to act as a true guardian of the national interest' (MacKenzie 1995b: 95). It is obvious, therefore, that Cameron and his supporters could not expect their interest to be given priority by the RGS, and in consequence tried, in copying the European fashion, to form a society for commercial geography as a separate entity. One of the reasons for the short life of Cameron's society was that part of the role he had envisaged was played by the London Chamber of Commerce, founded in 1882, and by the Imperial Institute which was founded in London in 1887.

French geographical societies and French imperialism

The Société de Géographie de Paris was founded in 1821 by a group comprising scholars interested in ancient geographies, including Middle Eastern specialists, writers and explorers. Before the foundation of the SPG there had been a French equivalent of the British African Association – La Société de l'Afrique intérieure, founded in Marseille in 1801, which continued until about 1818 (Lejeune 1993: 22).

In the nineteenth century the SGP was poorly financed, and until the presidency of Charles Maunoir from 1860 to 1885, was unable to finance expeditions. It confined its activities mainly to lectures, publications, collections of maps, and the award of medals (Claval 1991: 130–1). French imperial activity in North and West Africa from 1830 onwards reflected more the desire to distract from domestic problems than a coherent colonial policy (Heffernan 1995b: 222). France's promotion of geography after the Franco-Prussian War of 1870–1 as a means to redress this great setback is well known, and reflected in part by the increase in members of the SGP.

The coincidence between French imperialism, the rise in membership of the SGP and the number of provincial geographical societies in France seems clear. Lejeune (1993: 82–4, 132) has highlighted the period of French expansion and consolidation as being from *c.* 1860 to *c.* 1912, with the establishment of a French protectorate over Cambodia (1863), the annexation of Tahiti (1880), protectorates over Tunisia (1881) and Annam (1881), the outcomes of the Berlin Conference (1884–5), settlement in Laos (1893), entry into Timbuktu (1894), the conquest of Madagascar (1895–6), the Franco-British Agreement on zones of influence in Africa (1899), leading to the establishment of a protectorate over Morocco (1912) and the later division of the former German colonies between Britain and France in 1919. The SGP had started in 1821 with 217 members, a figure which had only slightly been exceeded by 1864. But by 1885 there were 2,473 members, and by 1914 the number had dropped to 1,935. By 1894 there were thirty geographical societies in France, with eleven societies having been added in the 1870s and twice that number in the 1880s.

Heffernan (1995b: 222–5) has shown that promoters and practitioners of geography and history, including the SGP, were actively engaged in national educational reform, including the creation of chairs of geography in the universities, among them a chair of colonial geography at the Sorbonne. Members of the SGP were also prominent in the federation of clubs and societies which made up the Parti Colonial, a major advocate of French colonial ambition, and whose influence over national policy was facilitated by the brevity of life of the governments of the Third Republic and their focus on European and domestic policies to the exclusion of colonial issues. Many of the committees of the Parti Colonial were chaired by SGP members, but there were widely differing views about the links between the SGP, the Parti Colonial, and French imperial policy. Charles Maunoir, the secretary-general of the SGP, took the view that it was founded as a scientific society (similar arguments were produced at the Royal Geographical Society) and should have no connection with politics and imperialism. In contrast, French imperial progress was strongly advocated by commercial interests (commercial geographical societies were also being founded in Paris, provincial cities, and French colonies in the late nineteenth and early twentieth centuries) within the SGP and other French geographical societies (Heffernan, 1995b: 226).

Heffernan (1994a: 93–4) has suggested that because there was overlap between imperialism and the progress of geography as an academic subject, a view has been taken that 'European Geography was European imperialism, albeit dressed up in a slightly more academic and scholarly guise', but suggests that 'such an assessment tends to gloss over both the complex and contested nature of European imperialism, and the fierce debates and conflicts within the emerging discipline of Geography'. He develops this argument in relation to changes and debates in the SGP and beyond on the question of French imperialism. Within the SGP in the early years of the Third Republic two main groups were identifiable: those, like Maunoir, who wished to advance geography in education but keep it separate from political issues; and a second group more closely linked to French commercial and political interests.

Heffernan suggests that from about 1880 onwards there was an increasing complexity of French opinion on colonialism (by now generally accepted), and outlines five forms of geographical perspective on French imperialism in the period 1870–1920: 'utopian imperialism, cultural imperialism, economic imperialism, opportunist imperialism, and, finally, anti-imperialism' (Heffernan 1994a: 100). The second and third of these categories point to a division between the Paris-based SGP and the many provincial geographical societies in France, the former strongly advocating imperial progress as a necessary projection and confirmation of national identity and cultural superiority, the latter being much more interested in trade and monetary advantage. Anti-imperialism found few voices among geographers.

The links were complex and constantly changing, often manifest in rhetoric rather than actual impact, but in the end 'Far from weakening the moral and political force of French imperialism, the plurality of different geo-imperialist voices – the polyphony of the discourse – became itself a source of power' (Heffernan 1994a: 114). The involvement of geographers in the planning of French geopolitical tactics for the period following the war of 1914–18 was another significant link between geography and empire.

The links between geography and imperialism in France have also been explored by Soubeyron (1994), drawing on the work of Lejeune (1993) and Berdoulay (1981). Much of the energy of geographers interested in colonial development in the late nineteenth and early twentieth centuries was directed to the application of geographical methods to the practical management of the resources and peoples of French colonies. This was reflected in the publications of the SGP's *Bulletin* and in the early numbers of the journal *Annales de Géographie*, founded in 1891. The recognition of, in effect, the ending of the age of major explorations, other than polar, was reflected in the search for new goals for geography and fundamental disagreements about its proper directions, seen in what has been called the 'Battle of the *Annales*' between Marcel Dubois (first holder of a chair of colonial geography at the Sorbonne) and the regionalist Lucien Gallois.

Soubeyron contends that: 'from 1895 the change of the orientation of the journal is striking. Colonial geography is still dealt with but in the spirit of Gallois's geography. The focus is on the regional geography of the colonies, or on the influence of the environment on individuals', effecting a change of emphasis from colonial to 'tropical' geography (Soubeyron 1994: 261–2).

Municipal imperialism in France

In his review of French Imperialism Heffernan (1994a: 106) suggests,

as John Laffey has shown, in port towns like Bordeaux, Marseille and Lyon, local business communities had become increasingly aware that, regardless of the overall costs or benefits of empire to France, the local economic advantages that would accrue from increasing imperial trade were considerable. Local chambers of commerce therefore threw their full weight behind the colonial lobby, a phenomenon that Laffey refers to as 'municipal imperialism'.

The renewal of French colonial interests in the last decade of the nineteenth century was supported by the business communities of Bordeaux, Marseille and Lyon. They had problems with protectionism in the 1890s. There was much centralisation in Paris of new imperial and colonial organisations, though these had support from the provincial cities mentioned. In 1898 the Compagnie Lyonnaise Indo-Chinoise was founded, followed in 1899, by the Société Lyonnaise de Colonisation en Indo-Chine.

Schneider (1990) has also documented and analysed the links between geographical reform and 'municipal' imperialism in France in the decade 1870–80, against a background of rapid increase of geographical societies in Europe more generally (thiry-two created in this period, nine of which were in France). He showed how dissatisfaction with the more scientific approach of the Paris Geographical Society led, through the influence of *chambres syndicales*, to the establishment of a joint Commission for Commercial Geography, and to the creation of a separate commercial geographical society in Paris in 1876. The Lyon Geographical Society was established with strong commercial support in 1873, the Bordeaux Commercial Geographical Society in 1874, the Marseilles society in 1877, and there were others (Clout 2008a, 2008b).

The establishment of the new Paris society and the other provincial geographical societies with strong commercial leanings and support reflected a division of opinion not only about French imperialism, including opposition to it, but also about the balances between the scientific and applied/utilitarian functions of French geography. 'While the imperialists of the SGP tended to speak in terms of France's colonial responsibilities, those in the provincial societies looked unashamedly to the commercial profits from imperial trade. They were more unambiguously supportive of overseas conquest and of geographical research which was obviously geared towards this objective, particularly in areas of special commercial interest to the local region' (Heffernan 1994a: 107–8).

More recently Heffernan (2004: 180–97 has examined the connections between the Société de Géographie Commerciale de Paris (SCGP), founded in 1876, its subsidiary branches in Tunis, Hanoi, Constantinople, Algiers, Copenhagen and Buenos Aires, the commercial geography societies founded before 1876 in Bordeaux, Lyon, Marseille and Montpellier, and right-wing politics in interwar France, in the person of Louis Marin (1871–1960). Founded to advance the interests of French commercial enterprise across the globe, the SCGP 'offered a utilitarian and commercial prospectus that drew upon the business community for support and intellectual guidance, but spoke to a larger educated public. Solidly imperialist in origins, this form of popular commercial geography embraced representatives of all political opinions, including many on the socialist left' (Heffernan 2004: 182). Through the medium of the SCGP and other institutions, Marin engaged with and sought to promote a change in French imperial theory and practice: away from the assimilationist and republican policies of the French liberal left towards a right-wing economic imperialism linked with legal support for the racial separation of colonisers and colonised and a process of training the young colonial 'Other' populations in their own countries rather than in France. The SCGP was an arena for debate from different political perspectives, and although not a major influence on French government colonial policy between the wars it does offer a marked contrast with the kind of left-wing liberal geographical ideology developed by internationally famous human geographers in the French universities, notably the Sorbonne (Heffernan 2004: 190–3).

Portugal: the Lisbon Geographical Society

One of the most effective geographical societies as an agent and advocate of a new imperialism in the late nineteenth century was the Lisbon Geographical Society (Sociedade de Geografia de Lisboa). Founded in

1875 – much later than the geographical societies in Paris, London and Berlin – the Lisbon Society was from the outset a mouthpiece for a new kind of imperial policy, stressing the significance of trade and the economic benefit of colonies to Portugal rather than the earlier embraced ideas of moral and ideal benefits to colonisers and colonized. The new imperialists of late nineteenth-century Portugal supported 'organised exploration, government protection for shipping and trade, colonization schemes and coercive labour policies. The government was to be an active partner of commerce and banking in making Africa pay for the economic regeneration of Portugal' (Newitt 1995: 334). In this respect they had much in common with the provincial geographical societies of Britain and the commercial geographical societies of France. Their officers, notably José Barbosa du Bocage and Luciano Cordeiro (secretary of the society from 1875 to 1900), the latter involved as a geographer in the Berlin Conference of 1884–5, took a nationalist line in advocating a series of measures, including expeditions, that would counter-balance the British and French expeditions in Central Africa which had publicised the possibilities for trade and economic development. All of this was bound up with the geopolitical processes of the 'scramble for Africa'. Cordeiro, who had been the prime mover behind the foundation of the Lisbon Geographical Society, was:

> originally a man of letters being a self-made geographer for patriotic reasons, as were many other founding members. The Society included in its initial membership most of the leading public men of the day. They represented a wide scattering of scientists, politicians, journalists, army and navy men, and miscellaneous intellectuals. In 1876 it began the publication of a *Boletin* whose expenses were paid by the Ministry of the Navy and Colonies. The *Boletin* at first concentrated on Portuguese east Africa, though it published articles on other Portuguese possessions and at times delved back into the past to recount early national achievements falling under the head of historical geography. (Nowell 1982: 21)

In 1876 Cordeiro had written to the king of Portugal on behalf of the Geographical Society advocating that Portugal should commence 'an immediate, effective and energetic action in the movement for the study, geographical exploration and attempted occupation of the interior of Africa' (Nowell 1982: 22). The society had an Africa Committee, which was a major advocate of Portuguese expansion and consolidation in Central Africa.

There was a strong sense that although Portuguese traders had travelled through Central Africa before the more famous British and German explorers, there was no written account of their journeys and experiences, necessitating the promotion by the Lisbon Geographical Society of geographical and scientific expeditions in the late nineteenth and early twentieth centuries. The Lisbon Society was also particularly anxious to counter the anti-Portuguese sentiments expressed in books by British and German explorers of Central Africa. The aim was to counter the critical comments made on the links between the Portuguese traders in Africa and the slave trade, on which Britain in particular was (understandably) taking a high moral stance, supported by naval policing action along the east coast.

In addition,

For the Portuguese the most sinister aspect of the activities of these [British and German] explorers was the fact that many of them, like O'Neill, Elton and Livingstone himself, held semi-official or consular status and had to be treated as to some extent the agents of the British government. It was the hostile image generated by those writers that the Portuguese explorers and the Lisbon geographical society set out to counter. (Newitt 1995: 334–5)

In 1876 the Lisbon Geographical Society and the Portuguese Geographical Commission of the Ministry of Marine planned an expedition to open up the linking territory in Central Africa between the two major arms of Portuguese influence: Portuguese West Africa and Portuguese East Africa (Angola and Mozambique). The expedition, led by three explorers – Hermenegildo de Brito Capelo, Alexandre de Rocha Serpa Pinto, and Roberto Ivens – set off in 1877, and by 1879 Pinto had crossed Africa from west to east, with Capelo and Ivens completing their work in 1880. An outcome of this expedition was the publication of a map which portrayed the whole of central Africa as Portuguese territory, and the Lisbon Geographical Society attempted to follow up this claim by trying to raise funds from its members to establish a chain of 'civilising stations' across Central Africa. The Portuguese government and the society supported a further expedition by Capelo and Ivens, which crossed Central Africa from west to east, using old-established trading routes, in 1884 and 1885 (the years of the Berlin Conference), and also supported an expedition led by Pinto in 1885 to explore that part of the cross-Africa route from Ibo to Lake Malawi, with Pinto empowered to make treaties with chiefs in the lake area (Newitt 1995: 335–6).

Portugal had an increasing tendency to press her case for control of a large part of central Africa on grounds of historical interest and occupation, and notably in the face of the increasing interest of King Leopold II of Belgium in a kingdom based on the Congo basin. An outcome of the above expeditions was the production in 1885 of what is known as the 'rose-coloured map'. This 'showed a band of Portuguese territory stretching all the way from Angola to Mozambique and including Barotseland and the Ndebele kingdom as well as the valleys of the Kafue and Luangwa on the shores of Lake Malawi' (Newitt 1995: 341). This considerably extended the area over which Portugal had claimed sovereignty in 1880. The map, designed as an instrument of Portuguese claims, was attached to a Franco-Portuguese treaty of 1886 and a boundary convention agreed with Germany in 1886, but neither France and Germany, nor Britain, would accept the territorial implications of the rose-coloured map, preferring instead simply to agree specific boundaries between the territories which they aspired to control. The agreement which finally completed the fixing of the borders of Mozambique came in a British–Portuguese treaty of 1891, leaving Mozambique as a territory only partially implementing the ambitions encapsulated in the rose-coloured map (Newitt 1995: 343–4, 355).

Spanish geographical societies and imperialism

A year after the foundation of the Lisbon Geographical Society in 1875, a geographical society was established in Madrid. The Royal Geographical Society of Madrid (Real Sociedad Geográfica de Madrid) (RSGM) – the title adopted from 1901 when it was given the royal warrant – aimed to promote the study of geography as a science, to further its position in education, to conduct surveys and produce maps, to promote Spain's maritime and colonial interests in relation to commercial opportunity, and to arrange conferences, publications and debates on such issues. Its senior officers were closely involved with government and present at major international conferences. Francisco de Coello (1822–99), for example, who was a military engineer and secretary of the society, was present as a Spanish technical delegate at the Berlin Conference of 1884–5 (Nogué and Villanova 2002: 8).

By the time of the foundation of the RSGM Spain had only a small number of colonies: Cuba, Puerto Rico, the Philippines and colonies in Africa such as Spanish Equatorial Guinea, Spanish Morocco, Spanish Sahara, Ceuta, Melilla and Ifni, together with the Marianas, the Marshall Islands, and the Caroline and Palaos Islands in the Pacific. The Marshall Islands were transferred to Germany in 1885, Cuba became independent, Puerto Rico and the Philippines were lost to the United States at the end of the Spanish–American War of 1898, and the Carolines and Marianas Islands were sold to Germany in 1899. The loss of these territories was attributed in part to lack of adequate geographical knowledge (reminiscent of French sentiments after the Franco-Prussian War), a moral being that future colonial policies should be supported by adequate scientific survey and mapping, together with the production of knowledge of economic opportunities for trade and commerce.

García-Ramon and Nogué-Font claim that the Royal Geographical Society of Madrid's foundation

> was basic in the formulation of a new colonial policy in Northern Africa. In the Society's view and that of most of the theorists of the new colonialism, the disaster of 1898 ... could be partially attributed to the fact that Spanish society was almost entirely unaware of the geographical reality of those lands. In the absence of a widespread awareness of the economic and strategic potential of the colonies, it could hardly be expected there would be a sustained effort from Spanish society to defend them ... such a mistake should not be made again in the case of the new colonial adventure in Africa. (García-Ramon and Nogué-Font 1999: 100)

Thus at the outset the society reflected the general interest in Spain in European geopolitical designs on Africa and other overseas territories, though the real period of link between the society and Spanish colonial policy dates from the Restoration of 1875, a notable event being the Spanish Congress of Colonial and Mercantile Geography held in 1883.

There was renewed interest in Spanish colonialism from 1875, including concern at German interest in the Philippines and her other Pacific islands, and the RSGM allocated much time to debate and publications on these issues, including practical proposals for the colonisation of the Philippines by means of a private company and the use of Chinese labour for land clearing and Spanish immigrants for agricultural enterprise. These proposals were based on common assumptions about the superiority of white races over the local indigenous population. Interest in Africa was renewed, and Capel (1994: 64–5, 66) has indicated that 'Several different groups readied themselves for the race for Africa and concentrated their attention on three areas of the African continent: tropical Atlantic Africa; the Saharan coasts; and the Maghrib. Exploration, the expansion of geographical knowledge, and the ideological manipulation of spatial concepts each played a fundamental role in these undertakings.'

In 1883, the year before the start of the Berlin Conference, the RSGM sponsored a Spanish Conference on Colonial and Mercantile Geography, and during the Berlin Conference colonial matters and objectives were aired by the RSGM, with additional debate fostered by the Barcelona Society for Commercial Geography. Through the publication of commercial data and ideas about potential markets, this in turn was supported by the Spanish Society for Africanists and Colonists, which became the Spanish Society for Commercial Geography in 1885. A publication, the *Revista de Geográfia Colonial y Mercantil*, was started in 1897. The RSGM followed Spanish interest in Morocco, and sent expeditions there in 1875 and 1884 with the aid of government finance, and the government also funded expeditions into the Sahara sponsored by the Society for Commercial Geography in 1886 (Capel 1994: 70).

In 1883–6, much geographical interest was focused on the Gulf of Guinea, on account of French and German settlements there, and an expedition was sent to the Gulf of Guinea, whose objective was to 'ensure the foundation of an Hispano-African empire four times as big as Spain', but which was disguised as a scientific expedition (Capel 1994: 71, 73). The outcome was more modest on account of the contentious interests of Germany, France and Britain, and from the end of the nineteenth century the colonial interests of the RSGM were largely confined to Morocco.

Nogué and Villanova have stated that:

The SGM considered it of vital importance to be able to influence the political decisions concerning all points related to colonial intervention, and especially with regard to Morocco. The Society had easy access to the higher echelons of the administration. This was as a result of its concern for the raising of the prestige of Spain at an international level, and also because many of its members were senior civil servants or military officers. (Nogué and Villanova 2002: 7)

The society was an active machine for lobbying the Spanish government on matters related to policy for Morocco and in responding to requests for information, maps and reports on that country. The society also actively debated the broader issues of European imperial ambitions, especially those of the French, German and British in North Africa. In practice, the influence of the society on Spanish colonial ambitions in Morocco and elsewhere did not have substantive practical outcomes:

The SGM was one of the most important pro-colonial pressure groups that aspired to have Spain imitate the expansionist course set by the European powers. Without underrating the efforts of the Society, it can be stated that the results in Morocco were slight, due to both the international political situation and internal events in Spain. On an international level Spain could never compete with the big powers and there existed in the spirit of the society the mistaken conviction that colonialism was the reason for, and not the result of, the power and wealth of European countries. (Nogué and Villanova 2002: 17)

Belgian geographical societies

The Société Belge de Géographie (SBG) was founded in 1876, just before
the Brussels Geographical Conference convened by King Leopold II, and
its title was changed to Société Royale Belge de Géographie (SRBG) in
1882. Like most other European geographical societies, it initially had a
mixed membership, including senior naval and military personnel, civil
servants, industrialists, politicians and diplomats, and it promoted lectures and publications, many of them concerned with Belgian colonial
developments and ambitions. The Geographical Society of Antwerp was
also founded in 1876, and the two societies played active roles in the promotion of Belgian colonial development. In their earlier years they had
few professional geographers to draw on, and Belgian colonial policy was
substantially decided by King Leopold II himself, with the Congo organised as a personal fiefdom, but the connection between the two societies
and the king was facilitated by the high rank of their two presidents who
had easy access to the king (Nicolai 1994: 54–5). Leopold's overt intentions in convening the Brussels West Africa Conference in 1876 were to
secure scientific exploration and humanitarian development, but his private fantasies included the need for 'a slice of this magnificent African
cake' (Nicolai 1994: 53).

Both the Brussels and Antwerp geographical societies sought more
information about the world from accounts by explorers and through
the examination of maps, and also attempted to promote humanitarian
ends by opposition to the slave trade. They looked for information about
resources and trade opportunities that would be materially advantageous
to Belgium, and more generally looked for geographical knowledge to
enhance Belgium's status and influence as a relatively new nation-state,
partly through limited support of colonial policies. Nicolai (2004: 33–4,
35) suggests that 'Belgian geographers followed up and even encouraged
the progress of "L'œuvre du Congo" (the work of Congo in the sense of
"good works"), a pompous expression of the times, which denoted the
Belgian colonial occupation of Central Africa. But they contributed little on the ground.' They did not sponsor significant expeditions to the
Congo region: much of the geographical research in this area was carried
out by nationals of other countries, notably H. M. Stanley. The Brussels
Society did sponsor an Antarctic expedition in 1896. There was, however,
substantial opposition in Belgium to all colonial enterprise, including
the Congo Free State project. Some potential members with anti-colonial
views refused to join the Belgian Geographical Society, which debated the

possibility of including the advancement of colonial policy in its statutes (Nicolai 1994: 56).

The Brussels Society organised conferences on the possible resources of central Africa and their beneficial use by Belgium, and also discussions on acclimatisation of people and plants in the region. The general view was that the region could be opened for trade but that colonisation and agricultural development by Europeans was impossible. The society tried to maintain scientific interests, but by the 1890s the membership was mainly of the 'petite bourgeoisie' and junior members of the armed forces. The Antwerp Geographical Society was well supported, but its officers were not scientists but professors of the Institute of Commerce. Members of the society included some ship-owners, members of the Antwerp 'haute bourgeoisie', and many merchants (Nicolai 1994: 57–8). Both societies were given the title 'Royal' by the king in 1882. They gave modest support to geographical expeditions.

Each of the Belgian geographical societies responded somewhat differently to the international criticism of the inhumane means, including the severance of hands, used by colonial officials and trading companies operating in the Congo Free State (Belgian Congo from 1908) to punish African people for ostensible failure in rubber collection.

The Brussels-based society seems to have distanced itself in its actions and publications from other learned societies that rejected this criticism, while, in contrast, the Antwerp Society linked with others in a Federation for the Defence of Belgian Interests Abroad, founded in 1903, and published pro-Belgian colonial articles in its bulletin. One article contended that the brilliant success of the model African colony of the Belgian Congo had simply excited the jealousies of English traders and Protestant missionaries frustrated by their lack of success, sentiments supported by sections of the British and German press.

In spite of the use in the 1870s and beyond of the Belgian geographical societies as agents for the dissemination of knowledge of the geography of the Congo, in reality the role of the societies in the promotion of colonialism was quite feeble, and possibilities of strengthening their pro-colonial role were not taken up, such as a merger of the Brussels Society with the Belgian Society for Colonial Studies (La Société Belge d'Études Coloniales, founded in 1894). Nicolai suggests that the role of these two societies was quite ambiguous and relatively ineffective in relation to Belgian colonial policy in the Congo, even though Belgian geographers and other members of the geographical societies had generally supported colonial advancement (Nicolai 1994: 64).

A fortnightly journal – *Le Mouvement Géographique* – was published in Belgium from 1884 to 1922, and was a mouthpiece of scientific interest by colonial societies in and support of Belgian colonial policy, and although it never printed refutations of Belgian inhumanity to the rubber-collectors in the Congo it did publish details of the problem, while keeping its distance from the king's policies (Nicolai 1994: 61, 63–4). Ambiguity on the Congo question seems to have been an identifying feature of geographical agencies in Belgium at this time.

The Netherlands: the Royal Dutch Geographical Society

The Royal Dutch Geographical Society (Koninklijk Nederlands Aardrijkskundig Genootschap) (KNAG) was founded in 1873, but it was preceded by the Royal Institute of Linguistics, Geography and Ethnography (Kononklijk Instituut voor Taal-, Land-, en Volkenkunde) which had existed since 1851, and which had promoted research in geography. The composition of the membership was initially from professionals in the field of education, politicians (including I. D. Fransen van de Putte, the Minister for the Colonies), bankers, civil servants, military and naval personnel, and merchants, plus interested lay members (Wesseling 2004: 55; van Ginkel 1991: 153–4). The first president was Professor P. J. Veth (1814–95), professor of the geography and anthropology of the East Indies at the University of Leiden and an active and earnest promoter of Dutch colonies. The society's aim from the outset was essentially practical: to promote interest in geography as a tool for the advancement of Dutch interests in commerce, shipping, population migration and overseas colonisation, and among its activities in the late nineteenth century was the sending of expeditions to central Sumatra, Borneo and New Guinea.

The historical background to Dutch imperial policy and practice in the later nineteenth century included an inherited distinction between an inner core area of control in the Dutch East Indies that included part of Java, and the 'outer territories' which comprised the rest of the far-flung states and islands of this polity. Van der Velde shows that from 1830 to 1894 the Dutch had a policy of non-intervention in or 'abstention' from active involvement in the outer territories, but that this changed in the period from 1894 to 1914, with a period of pacification and extension of Dutch control to the outer territories, the process complicated by Dutch military involvement, including the devastating Aceh war from 1873 to 1904 (van der Velde 1995: 81).

The involvement of KNAG was a reflection of the interests of the leading members, including Veth and its first secretary, C. M. Kan, the first professor of geography at the University of Amsterdam, who lectured there on colonial geography (van der Velde 1995: 83). KNAG promoted an unsuccessful expedition to Aceh and sought support for a follow-up, blaming the failure of the first expedition on lack of necessary geographical knowledge (van der Veide 1995: 84–5). Interest was also shown in the north polar region, South Africa and the Congo River, along which there were Dutch trading posts. KNAG promoted expeditions to the Dutch West Indies and Surinam and the Dutch East Indies. To expeditions to Sumatra were added three to Borneo between 1893 and 1925, one to the Celebes in 1909–10, and ten further expeditions to Surinam in the period 1900–10 (de Pater 2001: 158).

By 1876 the society had become a vociferous and active supporter of Dutch colonial ambitions, and one concrete manifestation was the Sumatra expedition of 1877–9. The reasons for the expedition are set out in an article by P. J. Veth, the president, in a lecture given to the Royal Geographical Society in London on the evening of 10 November 1879, and published the following month in the society's *Proceedings and Transactions*:

The Dutch Geographical Society, from the date of its foundation in 1873, considered it to be, not its only, but its most important task to fill up gradually the numerous gaps still existing in our knowledge of the Indian Archipelago. As Sumatra has recently engaged much attention on account of the Acehenese war, the sudden development of agricultural industry in the East Coast Residencies, and the discovery of the coalfields of Ombilin, though nominally under the government of Netherlands India, had been left almost entirely unexplored. The Sultanate of Jambi … is watered by a fine navigable river, which has its source in our own territory, and may possibly be used for the transport of the Ombilin coal. (Veth 1879: 761–2)

The Dutch government gave some financial support, and loaned a steam launch for the expedition, and British exploration accounts, some in the possession of the Royal Geographical Society, were consulted. Most of the funding was from entrepreneurs in the Netherlands, and although there was support from the colonial administration in the East Indies, who hoped for material benefits for the colony (de Pater 2001: 135), there was also opposition to the idea of this expedition. This came from many of the resident Dutch in the East Indies, from within the Council of the Dutch Indies (notwithstanding its agreement to contribute some funding), and from the government of the interior and the army, who were opposed to extension of Dutch authority in the outer territories and to the possibility of starting another Aceh war (van der Velde 1995: 86). Much time in 1874 and 1875 was taken with obtaining permission and co-operation from the government of the East Indies in Batavia (modern Jakarta) and the Dutch Ministry of Colonial Affairs in the Hague (de Pater 2001: 155).

The task of mapping the territory of the sultanate of Djambi in the interior of Sumatra was difficult, on account of the fierce opposition of Sultan Daha who had long been actively opposed to Dutch rule. Attempts by the expedition to penetrate inland into Djambi were frustrated by a sultanate vessel, and a similar event prevented access via the Batang Hari River. Later a lack of military support thwarted the attempted access to Limun territory. The expedition largely failed in its objectives, though some useful geographical and ethnological material was collected, some by photography, and the unrest that it created in Sumatra and also in Java led to a decision from van Bosse, one of the Dutch colonial secretaries, 'to let the expedition die a natural death. In his opinion the extension of effective control should be accomplished gradually by provincial officials. "I think it would be an advantage if our provincial officials are able to act when the time is ripe and that their actions should be no longer complicated by the peregrinations of the scientific expedition of the Geographical Society"' (Van der Velde 1995: 87).

The reports of the expedition argued that although there were areas of Sumatra where the Dutch had great authority and where there was co-operation, there were also areas where Dutch authority was nominal, and where only small parties of explorers could be sent. The Sultanate of Djambi was one of a number of areas of Sumatra which retained some autonomy and which feared annexation by the Dutch, and the 'advice of the members of the expedition was to organise no more expeditions to such regions, lying in the broad zone of contact between areas that formally and in actual fact fall under Dutch authority, on the one hand, and areas where the precolonial administration still continues its relatively undisturbed and unthreatened existence' (de Pater 2001: 157).

A later expedition to New Guinea also failed through lack of support from the Dutch government and colonial ministry, in spite of the fact that other European powers, notably the British and the Germans, had close links with the island. Expeditions were not supported by the government, but they were encouraged by traders and industrialists, for example to review the tin deposits on the island of Flores. A further, largely unsuccessful expedition was sent to south-west New Guinea in 1904–5, partly driven by the acceleration of the imperial race in the region, and the advent of imperialist newcomers Japan and the United States (van der Velde 1995: 89–90). The object of climbing the Snow Mountains was not realised, though the expedition did 'discover' the mountain that was named the Wilhelmina Peak (de Pater 2001: 158). There was also a KNAG expedition to New Guinea in 1939.

In spite of the fact that the Dutch Society for the Advancement of Scientific Research in the Dutch Colonies, founded in 1890, took a strong role in Dutch colonial development, notably in Borneo, the KNAG had a role in the development of Dutch colonial policy up to the end of the nineteenth century. The role evaporated from then onwards, and scientific research became its main objective (van der Velde 1995: 90–1). The refusal of the Dutch government to supply updated information, including maps, to the KNAG, was another reason for the decline in its imperial and colonial role.

German geographical societies and imperialism

The broader context for links between geographical societies and German imperial and colonial ambitions was the newness of Germany as a nation-state – from 1871 – and its rapid industrialisation, rapidly growing population, concern about the geopolitics of Europe, and the growth of the German navy. From the time of the Berlin Conference of 1884–5 there was a debate about development of a colonial policy, opposed by some on the grounds that colonialism was an expensive and unnecessary anachronism. Bismarck himself was against it. But the combination of a growing birth rate and the need for additional food and other materials and the possible solution of overpopulation by emigration, together with the historic tradition of Prussian imperialism within central and northern Europe, plus the overseas imperialism of other European states in the late nineteenth century, caused a change of heart. New societies seeking to promote German emigration for colonisation and give advice to emigrants were founded in the first half of the nineteenth century, though few lasted after 1870. They included the Berlin Colonial Society (1844), the Society for the Protection of Emigrants (1844), the Hamburg National Colonial Society (1849) and the National Society for German Emigration, founded in Frankfurt in 1848 (Townsend 1974: 30–1). To this process of support for colonial settlement for demographic and economic reasons was added the interest of natural scientists and explorers in lands overseas, and their expeditions were promoted and sometimes modestly funded by scientific societies, including geographical societies, and scientific curiosity in Africa was stimulated by the Berlin Conference of 1884–5.

The Berlin Geographical Society (Gesellschaft für Erdkunde zu Berlin) (GEB) was the name later given to the Verein der Geographen Berlins, founded in 1828 on the initiative of the cartographer Heinrich Berghaus, with Carl Ritter as its first president, and it gave incentive and support to German exploration, especially in Africa. Its president from 1863 to 1865 was the famous African explorer Heinrich Barth, who in the middle years of the nineteenth century had travelled extensively in Central Africa, and expeditions were funded by the Karl Ritter foundation which was established in 1859 (Schelhaus and Hönsch 2001: 14).

The Berlin Geographical Society initiated the establishment of a German Society for the Exploration of Equatorial Africa in 1873, claiming that greater knowledge of the region would further advance scientific understanding and promote trade and industry. With government funding, this offshoot of the Berlin Geographical Society launched some five African expeditions before 1877, and paved the way for collaboration between aristocracy, merchants and academics in the promotion of geography as a means to advance the commercial prospects of colonies, a goal even more energetically pursued later in the century. The geographical societies of Berlin, Dresden, Halle and Leipzig, together with interested economic and commercial bodies, were instrumental in the establishment of the (short-lived) Afrikanische Gesellschaft in Deutschland (German African Society) in 1878, but after sponsorship of some expeditions to Africa, including the Loango expedition of 1873, it finished in 1899 because of lack of finance and government support (Schelhaus and Hönsch 2001: 15). 'Annexations were not yet being seriously considered, but the Society undoubtedly helped prepare the ground for Germany's transition to a policy of expansion in Africa' (Stoecker 1986e: 20). Sandner and Rössler (1994) have confirmed evidence for support from German geographers for the foundation of the German Colonial Society in 1882, though offer no evidence that there were geographers who held liberal anti-colonial convictions.

Nine new geographical societies were created in Germany in the 1870s, following unification, and by the end of the century there were twenty-one geographical societies in Germany and the German colonies, of which nine had been founded between 1871 and 1884 producing forty-two journals or periodic publications (Schneider 1990: 91). Thereafter more societies were added, reflecting Germany's growing development as a colonial power from 1884–5 in Africa, during the period of the Berlin Conference, and with the rapid extension of protection of what was to become German South-West Africa ('Lüderitzland'), and the acquisition of Togo and German East Africa

(Wesseling 1996: 111). Wesseling (1996: 1–8) suggests that in Germany 'As in other countries, the [colonial] movement could trace its origins to geographical societies and to commercial circles, especially in the Hanseatic towns.' Hamburg was a major Hanseatic town, and in 1873 it founded a geographical society (Die Geographische Gesellschaft in Hamburg, GGH).

A recent history of the Hamburg Geographical Society between 1873 and 1918 is appropriately subtitled 'Geography between Politics and Commerce' (Nordmeyer 1998). Between 1873 and 1918 the membership of the Hamburg Society's committee showed a predominance of ship-owners and businessmen, followed by schoolteachers and lecturers, and smaller numbers of natural scientists (Nordmeyer 1998: 30), and the number of articles in its journal dealing with colonial politics and Germans overseas rose from 3 (of a total of 165) in 1873–82, to 13 (141) in 1883–92, 17 (141) in 1893–1902, 19 (115) in 1903–12, and 9 (70) in 1913–18. With the exception of the period 1913–18, the great majority of articles in the journal dealt with expeditions and travels (Nordmeyer 1998: 160). Hamburg's

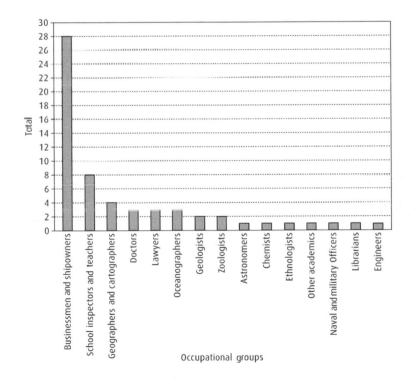

Fig. 6.3 Occupations of sixty officers of the Hamburg Geographical Society between 1873 and 1918. Source: Nordmeyer (1998: 30). By permission of the author, the Hamburg Geographical Society and Franz Steiner Verlag.

commercial interests in overseas trade had made it an important voice in German colonial policy, and led to the opening of the Colonial Institute on 1 October 1908, which subsequently became part of the university, and where a geographical seminar was organised by Siegfried Passarge. The curriculum included courses on the German colonies overseas, and expeditions were also organised.

The development of societies of commercial geography (*Handelsgeographie*) in Germany paralleled that in other European countries, and had similar origins among urban merchant communities. The year 1868 saw the foundation of the Zentralverein für Handelsgeographie und Förderung Deutscher Interessen im Auslande (Central Society for Commercial Geography and the Promotion of German Interests Abroad), initiated by the German economist Robert Jannasch and the explorer Otto Kersten, which was reorganised in 1878. It was supported by a range of people from business, geography, publishing and other professions. Its position was midway between the basic scientific geographical societies and the emigration and colonisation societies. It founded the journal *Export* in 1879, and published a geographical newsletter on world commerce and national economy. Nine branches of this society were founded. Its published aims were the study of lands of German settlement overseas and their geographical and social conditions and commercial opportunities; the collection and dissemination of information about these countries; an increase in communication between Germany and these territories; the development of trade and of naval stations; and the acquisition of colonies (Townsend 1974: 52–3).

Colonial promotion societies such as the Verein für Handelsgeographie und Kolonialpolitik (Leipzig 1879) were founded at this time. Initial German theorising about German settlement colonies came from a range of scientific institutions founded in the first half of the nineteenth century, such as the Berlin Colonial Society (1844) and the Hamburg National Colonial Society (Townsend 1974: 22–36).

From about 1871, however, there arose a more practical, commercially orientated sentiment about colonisation, and by this time Hamburg and Bremen companies had secured strong commercial bases in East and West Africa. Companies were formed to assist missionary activities in South-West Africa (1864). Hanseatic towns were also interested in the commercial opportunities of the South Pacific. There were problems with German settlers in Fiji, when it was annexed by Britain in 1874, leading to a more aggressive German policy for settlement and trade protection from 1875. A more energetic colonial commercial policy was supported by the reorganised Centralverein für Handelsgeographie, and by the Frankfurt Geographical Society, at whose meeting on 16 January 1878 a pamphlet was presented by Moldenhauer, proposing 'that all the geographical societies (branches of the old Central Association) should unite in a reorganized and co-operative effort to promote colonialism and direct emigration' (Townsend 1974: 82–3). This came to pass, having been supported by the meeting of the International Congress for Commercial Geography in Paris in 1878. The new society, with the same name, was founded in Berlin in October 1878, its purposes being 'to bring about the founding of colonies by establishing trade and naval stations' (Townsend 1974: 83).

By 1883 its membership was 3,000, and it exerted a very strong influence on developing German colonial policy. By 1880 it was one of the leading agencies for propaganda for German expansion in Morocco.

By 1880 its better known members included Walter Siemens of the electrical company, Adolf von Hansemann, head of the Disconto-Gesellschaft, Heinrich von Kusserow, Counsellor at the Foreign Office, and the explorer Gerhard Rolfs. Although the Association primarily represented the interests of companies in the Rhineland, Southern Germany, Saxony and Thuringia (who manufactured or exported finished products) and the Hanseatic shipping lines, it came increasingly to serve heavy industry and finance and assisted Krupp and Siemens with information on Morocco. (Nimschowski 1986: 130–1)

This role continued at the turn of the century, in common with other municipal geographical societies. Theobald Fischer, professor of geography at Marburg (a founding member of DKG – the German Colonial Society – chairman of the Marburg Branch of the Colonial Society, and an executive member of the Pan-German League from 1891), travelled in Morocco in 1899 and 1900, and was supported by the geographical societies in Berlin and Hamburg. His purpose was the assessment of economic potential for German development in Morocco, which he communicated through publications and lectures on his return (Stoecker and Nimchowski 1986: 231–2).

Sandner and Rössler have pointed to the openings for geography in Germany of opportunities for overseas exploration and research from the mid-1880s; the absence of geographers from anti-colonial organisations during that era; 'the transition to a resolute imperialism after Bismarck's ouster' (in 1890); and the role of geographers such as Siegfried Passarge (1866–1957) in the promotion of imperials aims and a radical form of racism (Sandner and Rössler 1994: 119–20).

Italian geographical societies and imperialism

The Italian Geographical Society (Società Geografica Italiana – SGI) was founded in Florence in 1867, and its headquarters were moved to Rome in 1871. Its earliest members were a mixture of professional men, including naval and military personnel, politicians, diplomats, scientists and those in business and commerce. There were relatively few geographers as members, comprising only 11 per cent of the membership in 1870, and 20 per cent in the early twentieth century (Gambi 1994: 76–7). The aims of the society, like others in Europe, were essentially the development and application of geography as a science. Given the composition of the membership, however, notably the preponderance of politicians, diplomats, military personnel and merchants, it was perhaps inevitable that 'this establishment constituency rendered the organization a pillar of the colonial lobby and orientated its activities towards Italy's overseas ambitions' (Atkinson 2003: 10). Expeditions from the early 1870s to the Sciotel Valley in Abyssinia, then Tunisia and Morocco, and subsequently Somaliland and Abyssinia again, mapping territory and conducting research, were intended to evaluate regional possibilities for Italian colonial settlement, for trade links and commerce, all located within a broader context of Italy's colonial ambitions (Atkinson 2003: 10; 1995: 268–9).

At the outset the few geographers involved in the SGI were more in favour of work on Italy than on regions overseas, but the politician members did not hold this view. Gambi has contended that it was politicians such as Cesare Correnti, Minister of Education to 1872 and president of the SGI from 1873 to 1879, who encouraged the society 'to become the national body which with government approval acted as the flag bearer of the colonialist lobby and directed much of the military and commercial penetration into the African interior'. The conflict of purpose of the more substantial expeditions sponsored by the SGI, such as those to the Somalian peninsula in 1891, was manifest in their rather meagre scientific output, including maps. 'Although they purportedly sought to develop scientific research, especially in East Africa, and specifically denied any other purpose, they were clearly embroiled in the web of European imperialism that spread through the continent toward the end of the nineteenth century' (Gambi 1994: 78).

The differing emphases placed by conservatives in the SGI and by more overt colonialist interests in government have been highlighted by Gambi (1994: 7–9). The rationale for a science base for the SGI's activities was advanced by a president of the society – the Marquis Francesco Nobili

Vitellesci – and Francesco Crispi, the Prime Minister. Crispi agreed only to one part of a three-part proposal for a grant to the SGI from government, namely to support expeditions to Africa, providing that it had political import and that the SGI worked with the Italian Foreign Ministry on these enterprises. The SGI became a tool of government in Italian ambitions for the colonisation of Africa, a feature helped and sustained by the very small numbers of geographers among the society's members and the large numbers of government officials, politicians and members of the armed forces. It appears that the numbers of geographers increased after the Italian acquisition of Eritrea in 1890 and of parts of Somaliland in 1891–4, and also after military defeats in Africa in 1896 and 1897.

In 1890–1914, the period of major international competition for overseas imperial expansion by the major European powers, Italy experienced opposition by younger geographers to the links between geography and colonialism. Gambi (1994: 80, 82) has suggested that 'Their hostility was either inspired by ideas spread half a century earlier by the democrats of the Risorgimento, or by socialist principles of egalitarianism expounded at the end of the nineteenth century.' The majority of Italian geographers continued to support colonial policies, however, notably for North Africa, and conspicuously in Tripolitania, Libya and Ethiopia, but the Bottego expedition to East Africa in 1897 which was funded by the SGI, together with the effects of the Italian defeat at Adua in 1896, led to a severe reaction in Italy against the SGI and exploration, an opposition which lasted until 1906 when the Italian Colonial Institute was founded with support from geographers (Atkinson 2003: 12).

The SGI returned to a central role in the Italian colonial discourse, and in 1911 'geographers provided intellectual and popular justifications for the invasion of Cyrenaica and Tripolitania. Shortly afterwards, the Society re-launched its exploration programme, but now in close collaboration with the Ministry of Foreign Affairs and with a revived focus on East Africa' (Atkinson 2003: 11). As with other European colonial powers, survey and mapping played a major role in Italian colonial policy, partly through the agency of the military Institute of Geography (Istituto Geografico Militare), founded in 1861. Surveys of Italian Somaliland were commissioned from geographers in 1913, with a brief to produce a geological map and to outline possibilities for colonial agricultural settlement (Atkinson 1995: 270). From 1914 to 1926 a more overtly political imperialism was evident in Italy, with geographers increasingly involved in the Fascist rhetoric for colonialism, in the period following the end of the First World War. This intensified from 1926 to 1943, and was partly expressed in the language of Fascist geopolitics (Gambi 1994: 86) and manifest in the pages of the journal *Geopolitica*, which was modelled on the German *Zeitschrift für Geopolitik*. As Atkinson has indicated though, '*Geopolitica*'s Africa was a continent laid open to imperial competition and the overriding force of the European powers. Africa's actual geography, its complex histories, cultures and patterns of human activities, were ignored. Rich and diverse regions were reduced to a simplistic, desocialised and largely abstract space, to be contested by the European powers' (Atkinson 1995: 290).

Symbolic approval of the work of the SGI is evidenced through Mussolini's visit in 1924, geography in the SGI having become part of the Fascist imperial process (Atkinson 2003: 13). Regional details of this process have been described and analysed by Atkinson in his study of the geographies of Italian colonialism in Libya, which involved the production of information through survey and reports, the suppression of nomadic and semi-nomadic Bedouin tribes in Cyrenaica, and their incarceration in concentration camps (Atkinson 2003: 14–15). The SGI launched eight expeditions into the Libyan Sahara from 1932 to 1936, after the Italian conquest of the territory. The report of the first expedition of 1932 provided substantial detail of the region's geography and history, situated within a discourse strong on racialist assumption about the 'inferiority' of the cultures of the Fezzan area, the concomitant 'superiority' and colonial entitlements of Italy and the Italian people to rule, and the ignoring of local indigenous knowledge (Atkinson 2003: 16–20; 23). The Italian survey and mapping of Libya parallels, at a later date, the French 'symbolic and intellectual control of Egypt and Algeria to the east and west of Libya with nineteenth-century imperial surveys' (Atkinson 2003: 24). The Italian occupation of Libya (created from the combination of Tripolitania and Cyrenaica and incorporated into Italy in 1934) ended with Italy's defeat by Allied forces in the Second World War.

Geographical societies in European colonial territories

By the end of the nineteenth and continuing into the twentieth century geographical societies, usually with some kind of link to the 'parent' societies in the metropoles, had been founded in European imperial territories. Their roles partly imitated those of the metropolitan societies, but they developed their independent agendas, conditioned by such factors as the appraisal of national and regional resource needs, their limited facilities for supporting research and exploration, and the fluctuations in their membership numbers and financial support. Because they were de facto part, or recently part, of European empires they were bound up to one degree or another with imperial agendas and events, including national European imperial rivalries.

India

The origins of modern geographical enquiry in India from the late eighteenth century have been ascribed to the need for geographical and resource knowledge by European trading companies, notably the East India Company, which had been founded in 1600, and which in the course of the late eighteenth century expanded both its influence and area of territorial control. Hence, 'The English East India Company, for its part, was quick to realize that the whole physical basis of its governance was dependent upon the geographical, geological and botanical knowledge of the areas being colonized. The colonizers fully recognized the role and importance of science in empire building' (Kumar 1997: 225).

The first geographical society established in India was the Geographical Society of Bombay, established with British initiative in 1832, and which continued in existence until 1873, when it became part of the Bombay branch of the Royal Asiatic Society of Great Britain, following a similar assimilation in 1829 by this same organisation of the Literary Society of Bombay, founded in 1804. The Bombay Geographical Society published a journal from 1837. Mill records the context of the society's existence:

in 1833, a geographical society which had been formed in the previous year at Bombay, under the auspices of the officers of the East India Company's Navy, with special reference to the exploration of Asia, wrote begging to be constituted a branch of the Royal Geographical Society, and this was done. It was arranged that similar branches should, if the demand arose, be established in other British possessions and the conditions of membership were duly formulated; but no other branch was formed, and in 1837 the Bombay Society threw off its dependence on the R.G.S. and continued its independent existence until 1873, when it entered its Nirvana as the Bombay Branch of the Royal Asiatic Society. (Mill 1930: 44)

There was then a very long gap before the foundation of the Madras Geographical Association in 1926. The first department of geography in an Indian university was at Punjab University in 1920, followed by Patna University in 1928 and Ailgarh Muslim University in 1928. Further geographical societies were founded: in Calcutta in 1933 (which became the Geographical Society of India from 1951); the Bombay Geographical

Association, founded in 1935; and the Ceylon Geographical Society, founded in 1935. The Indian Geographical Society was founded in Madras in 1926, and the Pakistan Geographical Association in 1948 (Schwartzburg 1991: 166–8).

Australia

The institutions originally involved with the acquisition, representation and dissemination of geographical knowledge in Australia were tied in with the complex processes of environmental appraisal related to settlement and economic opportunities, and thus with many aspects of British and other European imperialism. They were also inevitably linked with the changing character of the colonies in Australia, and the move towards federation. In 1830, the year of foundation of the Royal Geographical Society in London, the colonies of Australia were New South Wales (established 1788); Van Diemen's Land/Tasmania (separated from New South Wales in 1825); and Western Australia (annexed by Britain in 1829). South Australia separated from NSW in 1836; Victoria was established in 1851; and Queensland became a colony separate from New South Wales in 1859. The internal geopolitics of Australia, including the development of the individual states and the movement towards federation have been much debated, and were very much in the minds of politicians, colonial administrators and other members of the nascent Australian geographical societies.

At the outset there was no institutional template for Australian geography, as geography had not been established in Australian universities (many of the universities had not yet been founded). The existing colonial Royal Societies and later the Australasian Association for the Advancement of Science, founded in 1888, offered limited scope for geographical research and discourse. The development of land for settlement was a key theme in Australia's history, and this was reflected in the work of surveyors, climatologists and meteorologists, and explorers, some of which was discussed in the meetings and the publications of the nascent geographical societies.

Links with the Royal Geographical Society in London were frequently sought and approved by the new Australian geographical societies, but the distances between them largely limited links to the exchanges of publications and letters on a range of issues. The Australian societies seemed to relish the contacts with 'our parent society', especially when Australian geographical society members were elected Fellows of the RGS, or were awarded one of the RGS medals. The Australian geographical societies had strong links with the so-called 'provincial' societies in Britain, notably those from Tyneside, and Manchester and the Royal Scottish Geographical Society, with whom publications and correspondence were exchanged. The Australian colonies, as will shortly be seen, did, however, have their own individual and collective views on matters which were not given high priority in London.

The Geographical Society of Australasia

A meeting to organise a Geographical Society of Australasia was held in Sydney on 2 April 1883, and the society held its first formal meeting in Sydney on 22 June 1883, receiving its 'royal' title in 1886. It organised the Everill expedition to British New Guinea in 1885. The geopolitical significance of the European scramble for territory in the Pacific was shown by the large attendance (over 700) at the first meeting and by the establishment of a New Guinea Exploration Fund to facilitate an expedition to the Fly River in New Guinea (Griggs 1985: 1). At the inaugural meeting of the New South Wales branch of the Geographical Society of Australasia in 1883, it was suggested that other branches should be founded in other major cities in Australia, and the Queensland branch was founded in 1885, and continues to the present day (Griggs 1985; Butlin 2006).

Pan-Australian meetings of RGSA branches were held for several years after its foundation and records were kept, but the RGSA faded and in effect ceased to exist other than in name when the New South Wales branch stopped publishing proceedings (Aurousseau 1961: 2). The four branches were self-governing, though they did link up on matters of mutual interest, including the giving of support for Antarctic exploration. Of the original four, only the South Australian and Queensland societies survive, with the New South Wales unit having been more recently revived with a focus on teaching. The New South Wales branch, based in Sydney, had support from its colonial government but was in demise from about 1909, and in 1921 its collections were given to the Royal Australian Geographical Society. It published *Transactions and Proceedings* between 1886 and 1898.

The Victorian branch merged into the Royal Historical Society of Victoria (in Melbourne) in 1921. It had 58 members at its foundation, increasing to 121 by 1887, and one of its most distinguished members was the famous botanist and scientist Baron Sir Ferdinand von Mueller, president until he died in 1896 (Adams 1986: 21). The society supported exploration in Australia, including the expedition to Central Australia in 1889

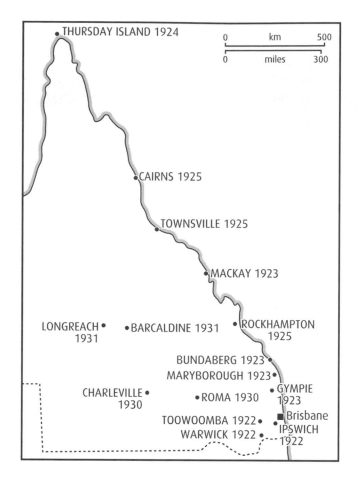

Fig. 6.4 Provincial branches of the Queensland Branch of the
Royal Geographical Society of Australasia.
Source: Griggs (1985: 57).
By permission of the Royal Queensland Geographical Society.

and the Elder expedition of 1891–2, and there were various proposals to
raise funds for Antarctic exploration. The society published *Transactions
and Proceedings*, and organised, as did all the other Australian geographical societies, lectures and social meetings.

The RGSA branch in South Australia, based in Adelaide, organised meetings, published its *Proceedings*, and sponsored expeditions, its constitution
listing its main purposes as: scientific, commercial, educational and historical (the collection of historical records of geographical interest), together
with the compilation of data on the geography of Australia (Peake-Jones
1985: 5). The first president, from 1885 to 1894, was Sir Samuel Davenport.
It supported the Elder expedition and the Calvert expedition of 1896–7, and

Fig. 6.5 Royal Geographical Society of Victoria: field excursion to J. W. Lindt's 'Hermitage' (his summer retreat) on the Black Spur at Narbethong, 1892.
By permission and © the Royal Historical Society of Victoria, Lindt Collection, S-215.002.

in its early years Peake-Jones describes it as 'an intensely loyal, patriotic and élite body: imperialist, devotedly convinced of the supremacy of the white races, and in particular of the Anglo-Saxon' (Peake-Jones 1985: 45). Western Australia never had a geographical society, probably on account of its small population and position as a crown colony without responsible government (information from Professor J. M. Cameron).

Australasia as a model of colonial science

Powell (1986) has evaluated this phase of geographical investigation in Australia in the context of the tensions between scientists in metropolitan and colonial activity, linking this with MacLeod's work on imperial science (MacLeod 1982: 1–16). Powell has suggested that geographical activity in Australia was never far removed from imperial ideologies and practices on account of engagement with early basic map-making, exploration and the development of policies for land use and rural settlement. The foundation of Australian geographical societies 'reflected the odd mixture of national and imperial sentiments which permeates so many Australian institutions' (Powell 1986: 9–11), and was illustrated by the interests of the RGSA branches in New Guinea and Antarctic exploration, for example, and also the constitutional independence of the Australian geographical societies from the Royal Geographical Society. The Australian geographical societies covered rather more limited fields of activity than the RGS in London, with the exception of exploration.

On a slightly different tack, Alan Lester has highlighted, for the cross-colonial study of humanitarian movements in the first half of the nineteenth century, the significance of new perspectives on metropolitan/ colonial core/periphery models of imperial process. He supports Dirks' insistence on seeing colonialism less as 'a process that began in the European metropole and expanded outwards', but more as 'a moment when new encounters within the world facilitated the formation of categories of metropole and colony in the first place' (Lester 2006: 230).

Heathcote has stated that exploration and resource inventory 'were high on the agendas of the geographical societies founded in the 1880s as branches of what was to become in 1886 the Royal Geographical Society of Australasia' (Heathcote 1991: 6–7). Branches of this organisation were founded in 1883 (New South Wales and Victoria) and 1885 (Queensland and South Australia), all reflecting, Heathcote suggests, the character and membership mix of the Royal Geographical Society in London.

The foundation of the (Royal) Geographical Society of Australasia in 1883, it has been suggested, owed something to imperial geopolitics. Aurousseau (1961: 1) contended that an important reason for the foundation of the RGSA was that:

The activities of France and Germany in the south-western Pacific at that time had aroused Australian vigilance. An inter-colonial conference was held in Sydney in 1883, to discuss the implications of what was happening. The abortive annexation of eastern New Guinea by Queensland took place in April 1883, only to be promptly repudiated by the United Kingdom, whereupon Germany took possession of the north-eastern part of the island. The United Kingdom then hastily took formal possession of what was left, as British New Guinea (now Papua) in October 1884.

Australian geographical societies and regional geopolitics

The geographical societies of Australia were founded at the time of high imperialism. Their concern at the geopolitical consequences of a European scramble for territory and resources in the Western Pacific led to debates on the future of Australia in the context of developing European interests in the South Pacific, the development of material and labour resources, and the promotion of expeditions for gathering more geographical information to this end. The gradual expansion of British settlement colonies in Australia and New Zealand, together with the British annexation of Fiji (which had German settlers who demanded compensation for the appropriation of their land) and the expansion of the territories of Russia and the United States to the Pacific, had meant a heightening of tension particularly between Britain, Germany and France (Henderson 1993: 66–7). By the 1880s New Guinea remained one of the larger Pacific territories that were deemed by European powers to be ripe for development.

The Dutch established trading settlements in western New Guinea in the seventeenth century, made claim to western New Guinea in 1719 and formally annexed the territory in 1895, using the meridian 141° west as the southern part of their eastern boundary, the northern section of this meridional boundary being accepted by Germany without formal accord (Dodge 1976: 177). Germany had claimed a protectorate over the north-eastern part of New Guinea and the neighbouring islands in the Bismarck archipelago in 1884. Fishers from Queensland in Australia had been exploiting pearl and bêche-de-mer resources around the islands of the Torres Strait for ten years from about 1865, but there was no great interest in the mainland of New Guinea until the 1870s. At that time Queensland became deeply concerned at German commercial activity in the region, and lobbied the British government to annexe New Guinea, together with neighbouring Melanesian islands, to offset perceived German threats to Australian security.

Frustrated by the reluctance of the British government to take action and fearful of the consequences of a German newspaper report advocating New Guinea as a site for potential German colonial settlement, Queensland annexed New Guinea at Port Moresby in 1883. It failed, however, to secure the backing of the British government, which claimed that a colony did not have the constitutional and legal powers to act in this way. Britain rapidly awoke to the dangers of lost opportunity, and in 1885 formal agreement was secured for the Dutch to control western New Guinea, the British the southern part of East New Guinea and Germany the northern part (Dodge 1976: 178; Henderson 1993: 69–70).

South Africa

The South African Geographical Society was founded in 1917, when it held its first meeting at the South African School of Mines in Johannesburg. One of the later foundations of a geographical society in the British empire, the contexts of its birth were the Great War in 1914–18, the reduction of immigrant geography teachers by the war, the existence of a country deeply divided by cultural, political and racial differences, and the enthusiasm of one individual – James Hutcheon, lecturer in geography at the School of Mines (who died only four years after the foundation of the SAGS). The society's professed purpose was 'To raise the standard of geographical education, to encourage geographical research in all its branches, and to arouse in the general public some enthusiasm in a subject which has a direct bearing on every-day life' (see Jackson, 1978: 3–12). Faithurst *et al.* (2003: 81–9) have suggested that the broad framework of the South African Geographical Society was similar to that of the Royal Geographical Society, and its main aim the promotion of education, geographical research and geography as a profession.

Only twelve years before the foundation of the Society, in 1905, South Africa had been 'a traumatised country poised uneasily between the experience of high-handed imperial domination and the beginnings of self-government and political renewal' (Dubow 2000: 70). By 1920 it was the Union of South Africa, 'a British Dominion with a population of $1\frac{1}{2}$ million whites and $5\frac{1}{2}$ million blacks. Two issues dominated the political discourse: the tussle between the English and Afrikaans white elites about South Africa's place in the British imperial sun and the relationship between the country's black and white inhabitants' (Barnard 1999: 192).

By 1920 South Africa had become a Union with four provinces, but was still part of a wider neo-imperial intention for a larger South Africa, the possibility of which was incorporated in the South Africa Act, to include Northern and Southern Rhodesia and the three protectorates Basutoland, Swaziland and Bechuanaland, together with the mandated former German South-West Africa which could make up part of an 'incomplete British–African imperial subsystem' (Barnard 1999: 192–3). The general trend in South Africa's complex politics and geopolitics from the end of the First World War to the end of the Second was increasingly towards a racist separate development policy, which was ultimately realised when the National Party 'unexpectedly edged into power in 1948'; 'apartheid became the official dogma and black–white relations, for better or worse, took a central place in South African political discourse' (Bernard 1999: 193), dominated by Afrikaner culture and politics. All aspects of life, including education, were bound up in this pernicious system.

Although lacking the support of formal geographical societies, geography was included in school curricula from 1839, and at secondary level, albeit with low status, in the Cape Colony and in all probability the other territories of Natal, the Orange Free State and Transvaal, from the mid-nineteenth century (Wesso 1994: 317–18). Thereafter the teaching of empire geography, notably in the Afrikaner territories, served to promote the ideology of the British empire, a process accelerated after the Anglo-Boer War, with geography of the British empire a key component of the draft matriculation syllabus for 1913 (Wesso 1994: 321–2).

There is no indication so far of the views of the black population on the teaching of the geographies of the British empire in the school syllabus at this time, though it is clear that the use of geography by the British to justify the Anglo-Boer War and its outcome was anathema to the Afrikaners (Wesso and Parnell 1992: 188). Wesso and Parnell (1992: 190) have suggested that the founding of the South African Geographical Society and the publication of its journal stimulated geography in South Africa, and generally helped to progress geography in tertiary education. The main influence was still British, and environmental determinism was a strong influence in the teaching of geography.

The initial membership of the society was 92 plus 13 student members. In 1919 the membership was over 200, but from 1919 to 1953 the figure ranged between 140 and 180. In 1953 it was reported that of around 160 members about 16 per cent were students, and about one-third were Afrikaans. A Cape Geographical Society was founded in 1932 as a branch of the South African Geographical Society, but it lasted for only nine years (Muller 1953: 6–7). The first patron of the Society was the Governor-General, Viscount Buxton, followed in the office by other governors-general.

The South African Geographical Society published a journal, which was almost exclusively in English: by 1953 only six articles had been published in Afrikaans, three of them between 1949 and 1953 (Muller 1953: 8) There were consistent problems in finding financial support for the journal, and in the apartheid era ethical problems were raised when in 1963 the South African Department of Education made it a condition of a grant paid to support publication that 'White and Non-White persons might not attend meetings together' (Jackson 1978: 11). The council of the society refused to accept these conditions, but the grant was nonetheless given. Similar problems and a similar response occurred in relation to a proposed geographical conference at the University of Stellenbosch in 1964, this time the objector to indiscriminate membership being the university itself. The conference was in the event sponsored by the university and the newly founded Society for Geography. Problems of accommodating the language and culture of Afrikaans-speaking South Africans led to the foundation of the Society for Geography in 1957, which promoted geography at all levels of education. It undertook some joint activities with the South African Geographical Society, and in 1994 the two societies merged to become the Society of South African Geographers. Geography developed in the South African universities from 1916.

The first chair in geography was at Stellenbosch in 1920, the holder being Piet Serton (1888–1963) from the Netherlands (Barnard 1999: 194). The early university geographers were British- or European-trained, and the subject advanced in the period 1920–60. Ideological origins continued to be reflected in school and university curricula, and after the Extension of University Act of 1959 black students had to have special permission to study at what were white universities, or studied at separate black university colleges, where they were often taught by Afrikaners, so that 'black geography students, a large proportion of which were student teachers, were confronted with a geography with strong ideological and environmental determinist undertones' (Wesso and Parnell 1992: 192).

The role of the South African Geographical Society in relation to imperial and colonial causes was implicit rather than explicit. Similar to the geographical societies of Australia, but later in date of foundation, its essence was British and the articles in its journal were largely published in English. Its main activities were the organisation of lectures, the provision of a library and map collection, organisation of local excursions and the publication of a journal. It was never involved in the promotion of major expeditions. It had a small membership, but nonetheless attempted to promote geography professionally at all levels of education and research. It was not representative of black African or Afrikaner cultures and priorities.

The founders of academic geography in South Africa saw it, according to Barnard (1999: 197–9), as a 'white man's country', adopting a position 'of the paternalistic white liberal', accepting the vision of a Little rather than a Great South Africa, with some optimism about the economic processes leading to greater fusion of communities, at least until the late 1930s when they 'began to have reservations about segregation and their optimism waned'.

This chapter has reviewed the links between geographical societies and the imperial and colonial experiences of European powers. Part of the role of geographical societies was the production of maps from field surveys by explorers and mapping agencies, and this theme will be addressed in the next chapter.

7 | The mapping of empires and colonies

It was under these conditions that I found myself attached to the Indian section of the Russo-Afghan Boundary Commission as chief survey officer... There was only one uncertainty about all this, and that was our ignorance of the country that we had to pass through, and the whereabouts of the boundary that we had to lay down. A mutual understanding about that boundary, its position in detail from end to end, could readily be arrived at by the high contracting parties in England and Russia, if maps in detail, attested by both sides, could be produced as a basis for an agreement. But there were no such maps. (Holdich 1901: 96)

As we gradually pushed our surveys right up to the Oxus, Gore and Talbot worked with the forward Russian contingent, while I kept up triangulation. All along British and Russian surveyors had worked in peace and amity together. The acerbities of political discussion, such as they were, were not for us. I found the Russian topographer ever ready to welcome any English colleague in the field of geography, and only too glad to place his little *tente d'abri* and his really excellent camp cuisine at his disposal. I acquired a taste for vodka, rye bread, and salt fish, to say nothing of caviare, which has not been weakened by time and distance. (Holdich 1901: 156).

Introduction

These extracts from the account by Colonel Sir Thomas Holdich, head of the Russo-Afghan Boundary Commission in 1884, highlight both geopolitical and personal aspects of attempts to resolve boundary questions through the creation of new geographical knowledge by survey and mapping. In his book on the Indian borderland from 1880 to 1900, Holdich gives rich detail of the mapping and defence of India's North-West Frontier and the complex logistics involved. There were many such commissions in the nineteenth and early twentieth centuries, dealing with different places and circumstances in Africa, Asia and Latin America, and geographical knowledge was a significant component part of their work.

The surveying, recording and mapping of actual or potential colonial territories was an essential part of the processes of acquisition of geographical knowledge as a basis for conquest and administration. The sequence of gathering and of output of information in map form varied according to a wide range of factors. These included the availability of local knowledge through indigenous peoples and early European travellers and settlers, the state of technical knowledge of surveying and mapping, the availability of instruments and the type and flow of instructions across an (often complex) chain of command. To these must be added the skills and effectiveness of the survey personnel, the links between field survey and production of the final map, the purpose of mapping (as a basis for taxation or for military strategy, for example) and a host of local circumstances including adverse physical and human environments and strong opposition from local people. All these have to be set against a broader background of national and international imperial and colonial policy, which was constantly changing.

The maps and mapping processes associated with European imperialism need to be approached with some circumspection. As Michael Bravo states, specifically in relation to Enlightenment cartography, but with wider application:

General pronouncements about the constitution of geography in terms of the mapping of time and space should be made cautiously. Although standardization and measurement became ideals of enlightenment geography, they were scarcely all-pervasive. If imperial cartography was actually locally circumscribed and metropolitan, it is important to identify those practices and systems of production which maintained it as a global discourse. (Bravo 1999: 230)

Quite a substantial body of theory and empirical studies has developed over the last decade or so about mapping and its significance in the imperial context from the late eighteenth century onwards. At the centre of much of the theory is the extensive work of the late Brian Harley, whose papers, published in the 1980s and early 1990s, highlighted the symbolic significance of maps. This included maps as metaphors (rather than complete, exact and accurate portrayals of landscape) for power and control, and as ambiguous indicators of highly subjective interactions between people and places which often conveyed ambiguous and contentious messages about such relations. Maps were seen by Harley as social constructs, in the way that other cultural and historical geographers have seen landscapes (Cosgrove 1984, 1999; Cosgrove and Daniels 1988). Significant elements in this ideology, frequently informed and influenced by the work of Foucault, Barthes, Derrida, Giddens and Panofsky, include (taking the titles or part-titles of some of Harley's papers) 'Texts and Contexts', 'Maps, Knowledge and Power', 'Silences and Secrecy: The Hidden Agenda of Cartography', 'Power and Legitimation in the English Geographical Atlases of the Eighteenth Century'. The map had long been, in his view, a kind of conspiracy, the product of a semi-secretive set of processes whose objective is manipulation of people and resources for strategic purposes of various kinds. Thus, in his frequently cited essay of 1988, 'Maps, Knowledge and Power', he stated: 'Yet although maps have long been central to the discourse of geography they are seldom read as "thick" texts or as a socially constructed form of knowledge' (Harley 1988: 277). His argument continues:

Maps are never value-free images; except in the narrowest Euclidian sense they are not in themselves true or false. Both in the selectivity of their content and in their styles and signs of representation maps are a way of conceiving, articulating, and structuring the human world which is biased towards, promoted by, and exerts influence upon particular sets of social relations. By accepting such premises it becomes easier to see how appropriate they are to manipulation by the powerful in society. (Harley 1988: 278)

Maps as tools of European imperialism are mentioned in the same essay, being seen both as tools of empire, in relation to initial exploration, propaganda, territorial claims, land appropriation and settlement, and as means of legitimising 'the reality of conquest and empire', evidenced in the nineteenth century in the maps produced for and during the 'scramble for Africa' and in the twentieth by the arbitrary determination and drawing of the boundaries between India and Pakistan in 1947 Hence, 'There are innumerable contexts in which maps became the currency of political "bargains", leases, partitions, sales, and treaties struck over colonial territory and, once made permanent in the image, these maps more often than not acquired the force of law in the landscape' (Harley 1988: 282–3).

These are significant ideas and challenges, and have caused many scholars to think further about the nature and meanings of maps as forms of historical evidence. They have also, as Kain and Delano-Smith have indicated, helped counter the Eurocentricity of map history and analysis, especially in the light of the major international *History of Cartography* of which Harley was a major proponent and to which he contributed. Many of his ideas about the representational power of maps have been followed by scholars researching the history of mapping in imperial contexts, 'picking up the various batons dropped by Harley in his epistemological charge through the 1980s' (Kain and Delano-Smith 2003: 409).

Harley's ideas have been subject to extensive review and critique. John Andrews, in a challenging introductory chapter, 'Meaning, Knowledge, and Power in the Map Philosophy of J. B. Harley', in the book of Harley's reprinted essays (Andrews 2001), takes issue with some of Harley's readings of map symbolism and metaphor, and with his 'cartographic philosophy'. Andrews acknowledges that Harley did not entirely reject 'positivist' aspects of maps, nor their utility as practical guides (in fact the early part of his work in cartographic history was concerned with the detailed interpretation of early county maps and Ordnance Survey maps), but focuses on Harley's engagement with aspects of maps concerned with iconic or intrinsic symbolism. He suggests that Harley's notion of the intrinsic meaning of maps requires in effect a preference for examination of the symbolic significance of 'extraneous' features, such as size, centrality, colour, script and 'silence'. The colour in which imperial territory is represented is important and revealing, and 'silences' on maps are indicative of geographical ignorance, 'negative space', and 'deliberate withholding of information' (Andrews, 2001: 14). That there are such meanings is not disputed, but Andrews suggests that there are two associated problems: essentially of meaning and message. He challenges the idea of identification of objects of intrinsic meaning by pointing to alternative readings of ethnocentric value judgements from a map, and also to the fact that the much-vaunted equatorial Mercator projection favours not Europeans but Arctic North Americans and Asians, and that the link of this projection with an ambitious overseas European imperial gaze breaks in the cases used by cartographers of non-imperial European nations such as the Swiss or the Poles (Andrews 2002: 16).

The question of the rhetorical and symbolic power of maps has also been recognised and exemplified by other scholars. Livingstone, in a discourse on the geographies of scientific exploration, contends that a map is: deceptive and distorting, because it has to represent a three-dimensional surface of the globe on a two-dimensional piece of flat paper; and has to simplify the complex physical and human data that make up the composition of the places to be mapped. The whole character of a map may be transformed by the replacing of existing place-names with European names, for example for mountains and settlements, and through colonial imagery and iconography on and at the margins of the map (Livingstone 2003: 154–5).

Omissions of evidence for indigenous settlements is also deemed to be characteristic of this mapping by imperial powers, evidenced, for example, by Captain James Cook's use, in his mapping of the coastlands of Australia, of the names of European naturalists for (re-)naming places which previously had indigenous names. Likewise, the drawing of boundaries around newly appropriated territory sometimes ignored natural features or historical territorial traditions in the determination of boundary points (which could be difficult to determine either through ignorance of local tradition or the nature of vegetation, for example dense forests), thus creating a new and artificial system of administration. Livingstone (2003: 156, 158–9) also points to the importance of the map as a mobile medium for the carrying of geographical information from remote areas to the control centres or 'centres of calculation' in the metropole.

Matthew Edney has also looked in depth at Harley's theories on the nature of maps (Edney 2005). Edney opposes the idea that Harley's initial encounter with post-structuralism was unsuccessful, seeing it more as an indicator of his 'excitement over the emergent intellectual directions' (Edney 2005: 97). Harley's experimental and innovative approaches have certainly injected further analytical power into the readings of maps and the circumstances of their creation, including the ethical questions about representations (or not) of indigenous cultures and about the use of maps in contemporary military activity in the Middle East.

Cartography in imperial and colonial practice

There has been a steady increase in the examination of colonial cartography over the last twenty years, some of it influenced by the Harley theories about maps as texts and symbols of inequitable practices of imperial power. It is now widely recognised that surveying, mapping and the dissemination of geographical information by the use and sale of maps for peaceful and military purposes was a basic component of imperialism. Tony Ballantyne, in a survey of empire, knowledge and culture, suggests that while the process of surveying and mapping was:

increasingly important within metropolitan European contexts, it was even more important in colonial possessions; it allowed not only the mapping of resources, political boundaries and urban centres pivotal to commercial relations and colonial authority, but also facilitated the ideological project of empire … maps and atlases were increasingly deployed as instruments of rule and, at an intellectual level, to order the different parts of the empire into a coherent picture of a global empire. (Ballantyne 2002: 119)

Etherington (2007: 1–2), in a recent book on the mapping of colonial Australia and South Africa, has also recognised the impact of Harley's 'new history of cartography' in providing new insights, including recognition 'that many cultures of mapping have flourished in widely separated parts of the globe, and that each deserves to be understood in its own terms rather than dismissed as primitive or unscientific'; 'that European exploration and later colonisation depended crucially on cartographic knowledge obtained from indigenous guides'; and 'that the proliferation of maps produced by colonisers erased, wrote over and displaced indigenous conceptions of space and power'.

The maps and mapping techniques used to investigate and promote the colonial territories of European powers were of different types and scales. At one level there were the sketches produced as the basic traverse surveys by explorers and administrators in the field. In contrast there were formal trigonometrical surveys. This type of survey 'was a slow, systematic, labour-intensive endeavour that could only be carried out *after* a territory was under effective colonial control, as was the case in the Great Trigonometrical Survey of India … Explorers, by contrast, generally conducted more rough-and-ready traverse surveys, which simply supplied the geographical coordinates for the routes they had taken' (Kennedy 2007: 1891). In addition there were cartograms produced by indigenous peoples, and what have been called 'fantasy maps' – maps 'created for the specific purpose of arousing interest in speculative ventures, such as colonisation schemes, or to illustrate works of fiction' (Stiebel and Etherington 2007: 41). Maps in accounts of exploration sometimes contained a mixture of two or three of these categories.

An early aspect of the interaction of cartography with colonial goals is evidenced by hydrography and chart-making. Much of the European and other investigations of far-off places in the eighteenth and nineteenth centuries had involved the mapping of coastlines and the charting of coastal waters to facilitate the safe movement of naval and merchant vessels and to promote security and trade. This was mainly a role for national navies and specialist hydrographical surveys (usually under naval control). Britain, increasingly aware of the progress in hydrographic mapping being made by, for example, the Portuguese and the Dutch, appointed an Admiralty hydrographer in 1795: Alexander Dalrymple, who held the post until 1808. The fourth Hydrographer appointed (1829–55) was Francis Beaufort, a protégé of John Barrow, Second Secretary to the Admiralty who was instrumental in the founding of the Royal Geographical Society (of which Beaufort was a Fellow) (Forbes and Hercock 2007: 23–4). Beaufort was a major hydrographer and scientist, and during his period of office he considerably increased the number of hydrographic charts available for use by naval and merchant vessels.

During the nineteenth century further hydrographic mapping was undertaken, notably on the coasts of East and West Africa, India and Australia. These surveys were enhanced by improved instrumentation, links with small-scale land surveys and written accounts by travellers and explorers. The surveys of the coasts of Australia in the nineteenth century were conducted by such hydrographers as Matthew Flinders and Philip Parker King, and some were directly undertaken with a view to land-based colonial settlements, such as those of the Swan River region in 1827 by James Stirling, a naval officer, who became a landowner and the first governor of the Swan River Colony (Forbes and Hercock 2007: 29–39).

Maps and indigenous people

Before looking at the contents, meanings and uses of European maps of colonial territories, it is necessary to pay some attention to what had gone before: that is, the representations of space and place in the indigenous/traditional societies whose territories and rights were in most cases usurped by European conquest. Maps in their modern form appear in most such societies late in the day, only from the fifteenth, sixteenth and seventeenth centuries. They had been preceded, and continued to be paralleled, by varieties of cosmographical pictograms or diagrams, many of which were ephemeral. What has been seen as a 'canonical' and Eurocentric reading of cartographic innovation in Asian, African and American traditional societies suggests that the colonial mapping as we now recognise it was an import by European explorers from the fifteenth century onwards.

Such an approach ignores mapping traditions that were already developing in such places as India, China and the Middle East and had been doing so on and off since late prehistory. It is largely from the fifteenth and sixteenth centuries that a more recognisable mapping tradition developed across the globe: Islamic mapping is evidenced from the sixteenth and seventeenth centuries, there is a Japanese world map from the fourteenth century, a Hindu globe from the fifteenth, a conspicuous increase in European and Vietnamese maps in the sixteenth and seventeenth centuries. Meso-American maps begin in the sixteenth century, as do Malaysian maps (Wood 1997: 552). Wood asserts that the rise of map-making cannot solely be attributed to the canonical progression of science in Europe (the 'rediscovery' of Ptolemy, new science, new ways of painting landscape and of managing estates, and the rise of the nation-state), and that:

> the implication that mapmaking emerges as a rationalizing tool of control dur-
> ing periods of relative prosperity in capitalist state economies is supported by
> evidence from the Habsburg, Bourbon, and Tudor realms as well. Certainly the
> aggressive use of maps in this period as tools for control of land for taxation,
> resource exploitation, and other purposes was limited neither to Europe nor its
> colonies, but was a feature of administration in the Ottoman empire, southeast
> Asian states, China and Japan as well. (Wood 1997: 553)

The non-centralised societies encountered in the processes of territorial and economic expansion had sign systems but no tradition of scripted
map-making, yet 'were intimately acquainted with the territories they
inhabited and, of course capable of making maps in any medium when
requested by traders, soldiers, missionaries, explorers or others from
expanding states' (Wood 1997: 553), and this process continued into the
nineteenth century, both as indigenous map-making and as information
provision for European administrators, traders, and map-makers.

The mapping of French colonies

There were very strong links between exploration, political and commercial ambition, and the mapping of both existing and potential French
colonial territories. There were important precedents in the eighteenth
century, notably in respect of the short-term occupation of Egypt by the
French from 1798 to 1801. Surveys were made in the period of occupation,
one outcome being 'La Carte Topographique de l'Égypte', maps published
at a scale of scale of 1:100,000, published in 1826 as part of the *Description
de l'Égypte*, a survey of the history, culture, and environment of Egypt
undertaken by the French military together with French scholars and
scientists. The *Description* (published in twenty-three volumes between
1809 and 1828) and its accompanying topographical maps have been
extensively analysed as component tools and symbols of French imperial ambition. Anne Godlewska (1995: 7) has described it as 'one of the
most appealing and remarkable published works ever to have come out of
a European imperial venture'. Edward Said allocated to it a major role in
the structure of his thesis on Orientalism (Said, 1978: 87): 'The *Description*
became the master type of all further efforts to bring the Orient closer to
Europe, thereafter to absorb it entirely and – centrally important – to can-
cel, or at least subdue and reduce, its strangeness and, in the case of Islam,

its hostility.' The forty-seven maps and related landscape sketches were published not by the Commission de la Description de l' Égypte but by the Ministère de la Guerre, because 'The maps were so effective in representation that Napoleon feared their utility to others', and because of a dispute between the civilian Commission de la Description de l'Égypte and the Depôt de la Guerre, resulting in publication only from 1826 (Godlewska 1995: 10). This symbolised new interests in the accurate scientific/geometric representation of details of topography and human settlement.

The relationship between cartography and the construction of the French and British colonial empire continued in the nineteenth century. Bassett (1994: 316–35) has reviewed some aspects of these links with reference to West Africa in the nineteenth century. He emphasises the practical uses of maps, particularly details of settlements, routes and natural resources in the advancement of empire-building, together with the uses of blank spaces and boundaries in the processes of territorial appropriation. Regnault de Lannoy de Bissy was a cartographer based in Paris in the 1880s with the Service Géographique de l'Armée, and his topographical and route maps were extensively used by explorers and soldiers in Africa, and were also exhibited at the 1899 Exposition Universelle. Bassett shows that the Congo sections of Bissy's sixty-three-sheet map of Africa at a scale of 1:2,000,000 were used at the Berlin Conference of 1884–5, and that his maps of Madagascar were used by the French army. Bissy was keenly aware of the 'civilizing and pacifying role' of France in, for example, the river basins of the upper Senegal and Niger Rivers. In his map compilations he made use of the field maps, sketches and reports of topographers linked to military expeditions, and military officers in turn relied extensively on his maps for their expeditions. Maps were also produced, for example, by Alexandre Vuillemain in 1858 in his *Nouvelle Carte Illustrée de l'Afrique*, to show the commercial potential of Africa, through representation on the map and at its margins of useful goods for trade and the locations of important colonial resources and settlements, reflecting a desire to substitute legitimate commerce for the slave trade (Bassett 1994: 317, 320, 321–2).

The use of indigenous geographical information for incorporation into the newly produced maps varied. Thus:

Use of blank spaces also resulted from disregard of indigenous geographical knowledge and from attempts by Europeans to keep their knowledge secret. The principle that only the verifiable facts should be depicted on maps ultimately came to mean that only European or European-trained explorers were reliable informants. The observations of Africans were generally rejected on the Eurocentric grounds that they were unreliable. (Bassett 1994: 322–3)

Bassett illustrates this point through examples of geographical information on the perceived course of the River Niger, particularly the rejection by the English 'armchair' geographer James McQueen in 1826 of evidence of the course of the Niger given by Sultan Bello, the sultan of Sokoto, to the English explorer Hugh Clapperton, an English naval officer engaged on an expedition to Tripolitania supported by the British government. Clapperton went south across the Sahara to Sokoto, where in 1822 he met Sultan Bello, 'and in Clapperton's presence the sultan drew the course of the river in the sand to show that it entered the Gulf [of Benin]' (Bassett 1994: 323).

Sultan Bello was a highly intelligent and deeply learned man with interests in geography, history, astronomy and theology who had produced a manuscript on the history and geography of the interior of Africa. McQueen rejected the verbal evidence of the mouth of the Niger given by Sultan Bello to Clapperton, partly because it was not drawn on the map attached to Bello's manuscript, and partly because of his view that the sultan's geographical knowledge was inaccurate and untrustworthy: only evidence produced from scientific survey by a European would be sufficient proof.

Bassett (1997: 556) has elsewhere drawn attention to the use of ephemeral maps – maps drawn with a stick in sand or on the ground by Africans to help European explorers and administrators, such as that incorrectly drawn for the explorer Charles Beke by Hádji Mohammed, a Muslim merchant, of the course of the River Gojab in Abyssinia, and the accurate map of ethnic groups in south-eastern Liberia drawn in sand for the French explorer Henri d'Ollone by a man named Toolou.

The empty spaces on Lannoy de Bissy's maps of Africa stimulated French ambitions for control and colonisation, notably in the minds of the members of the Comité de l'Afrique Française, and the consequent filling in of these empty spaces. Particular reference was made to revised maps produced for the expedition by Louis G. Binger, a military officer, 'sent by the Colonial department and the Foreign Ministry to explore and ultimately to link France's possessions between the Niger River and the Guinea coast by treaties', in the period 1887–9 (Bassett 1994: 325, 320). A map of Binger's exploration of the western Sudan, reproduced in the Parisian newspaper *Le Temps* in March 1890 showing a French zone of influence, fuelled a major diplomatic dispute with Germany in relation to an Anglo-German neutrality agreement of 1887. There are many other examples of the use of speculative boundary lines on maps of West Africa to advance the territorial claims of individual European powers, including Spanish claims south of Cape Blanc on a map of 1885, and the aspirational map of French territorial claims, focused on a proposed trans-Saharan railway, to link her empire across the Sahara from North Africa (Bassett 1994: 325, 326).

Following the Harley thesis about maps as representations of power, Bassett asserts that:

Like other forms of colonial discourse, such as speeches, books, and sermons, maps promoted the appropriation of African space under the rhetoric of commerce and civilization. Maps facilitated conquest by their accuracy and selective content. The omission of the African peoples and polities and the depiction of European settlements and place-names were central to empire-building. More than a mere reflection of conquest, maps helped to produce empire by enabling and legitimating the process of colonization. (Bassett 1994: 333)

The determination of boundaries in Africa

The Berlin West Africa conference took place between 15 November 1884 and 26 February 1885. The West Africa referred to in contemporary terminology was the area bounded by the coastline from Cape Verde to the Cape of Good Hope. The conference was convened at the request of the German chancellor, Bismarck, after consultation with the French ambassador in Berlin about the Anglo-Portuguese Treaty of 26 February 1884, by means of which Britain had recognised Portugal's sovereignty over the coast of west central Africa across the mouth of the Congo, from 8° S to 5° 12′ S (Wesseling 1996: 100). Because of the variety of territorial claims made by other European powers in this region, the treaty had caused concern, particularly to the French and Germans, and this was one of the reasons for the Conference.

The conference itself epitomised a complexity of issues engaging the major European powers at the time, including Germany's recent and sudden development of interest in overseas possessions, French concern at Britain's presence in Egypt and the outcome of French military activity in China and Indo-China (all related to the future of the government of Jules Ferry), and British concern with the Sudan and Egypt. Robinson (1988: 3) has outlined the interests represented in the preliminary discussions between Bismarck and Jules Ferry, the French Foreign Minister:

In the preparation the project served many purposes, nor was it restricted to West Africa: the plan was deeply involved in the Anglo–French quarrel over Egypt and

Anglo–German disputes over jurisdiction from Cameroon and Angra Pequeña to Fiji and New Guinea. All of these conflicts raised the question of international free trade and navigation in one form or another, and in every case, one nation feared exclusion by another. Hence the Berlin Conference has to be studied as one of a series of such negotiations. It makes little sense in isolation.

The two main sections of the conference (general principles and practical outcomes for scientific investigation and settlement) have clear significance for territorial appropriation and boundary-making and mapping in late nineteenth-century Africa. The general principles and multilateral discussions were attempts to agree on the operation of free trade and navigation in the courses, basins and mouths of the Congo, Niger and other rivers, and neutrality and free trade in the independent Congo Free State, whose existence was formally recognised by the conference. The Berlin Conference established the 'conventional Congo Basin', 'loosely defined as "all the regions watered by the Congo and its affluents, including Lake Tanganyika, with its eastern tributaries"' (Katzenellenbogen 1996: 22). This in effect comprised, by the agreement of the conference, two areas of free trade, the first from the Atlantic Ocean to the great lakes, the second from the great lakes to the Indian Ocean, the whole area designated as the 'conventional Congo Basin'.

The agreement was binding only on the signatory states, not African states (including the Sultanate of Zanzibar on the East Coast, which was a region of British interest) (Wesseling 1996: 117). Attempts were also made to try to agree the principles on which recognition of other territorial claims could be made, including that of 'effective occupation', but this was only agreed for coastal territory, and the protocol 'merely laid down that anyone taking possession of a new coastal region or setting up a protectorate over it had to notify the other signatories and to exercise a measure of effective authority. Since, however, scarcely any coastal parts remained unoccupied, in practice this proviso meant virtually nothing' (Wesseling 1996: 118).

There is some disagreement about the role of the Berlin Conference in the division of Africa between the major European imperial players. One train of thought is that the conference itself had little or nothing to do with this process, but merely facilitated, through precedents and the subsequent application of principles, the continuous process of territorial appropriation by bilateral agreement or unilateral action. Katzenellenbogen (1996: 22, 31) takes this view, supporting the idea that it was a myth that the Berlin Conference was responsible for the division of Africa among European powers. The reality of division was more idiosyncratic and unilateral, the lasting significance of the conference being the international recognition of the independent Congo Free State. He illustrates his point with reference to five examples of colonial boundary determination: the South African protectorates (Basutoland, Bechuanaland and Swaziland); the south-west border of the independent Congo Free State; the German colonies in East and South-West Africa; the boundaries of Angola and Mozambique; and the Anglo-French borders in West Africa.

Robinson (1988: 14), recognising the historiographical ambiguities of seeing the conference either as an initiator of partition or simply as a means to agree on free trade and navigation, takes the view that a number of general principles agreed at the conference, particularly concerned with free trade, were applied in Anglo-German and Franco-German agreements that were 'initiated in the lobbies of the conference and some shortly afterwards. Although many of them might have taken place in any event, the conference was largely responsible for bringing them all together to a head in Berlin.' The conference may thus be seen – from one perspective – as commercial and therefore anti-colonial, in the sense that the major European powers involved were mainly looking for commercial opportunity rather than territorial appropriation.

However, Robinson (1988: 20) is not entirely convinced by this argument, suggesting 'that the cartography under the treaty signified more than commercial enlightenment', in the sense that domestic (metropolitan) expectations did not make fine distinctions between hypothetical matters of areas of influence agreed in diplomatic treaties, whose general potential had been heralded by explorers, and the demand for real occupation and defence of colonial areas from the ambitions of other colonial powers. Once the reality of attempting to control and monopolise trade with African polities was faced, notwithstanding the initial free-trade and access principles of the conference, the territorial imperative became even stronger, particularly when European states changed their views on the need for actual occupation of their areas of commercial and strategic interest.

As Robinson (1988: 22, 25) points out, the assumptions of the Berlin Conference were almost entirely European, and related to an area which was largely unknown, despite the reports and maps of explorers such as Brazza and Stanley. Moving across a range of interpretations of the effects of the Berlin Conference, Robinson concurs with a view that 'The probability is therefore that the intervention of the Concert at Berlin set off the partition of tropical Africa as a whole into spheres of influence ... To make pre-emptive cartography necessary on such a scale, the future of Central Africa had to be drawn into the working of grand diplomacy'.

Foeken (1995) has examined some thirteen theories to explain the processes and outcomes of the Brussels Conference of 1876 and the Berlin Conference of 1884–5 for the partition of Africa among European powers. The principal types of explanation are listed as economic, political, elite and local circumstances, and he relates them to a four-stage chronology of the partition of Africa (1875–9; 1879–82; 1883–4; and 1884–5). He concludes, not surprisingly, that 'each theory contains elements which, for a certain actor and at a certain moment, may have been decisive in the process of decision making. However, no one theory can be considered as the whole truth. Political decisions are seldom based on one consideration, but it is always difficult to determine the relative weight of the various alternatives' (Foeken 1995: 98).

The one certainty in most of this is the general lack of concern for indigenous rights of resource-use and territory, but a relevant test of the theory about the precise role and intent of the Berlin Conference is the sequence of dates at which specific boundaries were designated (and ultimately mapped and fixed on the ground) for African states under European hegemony. This is not clear-cut: the diplomatic exchanges on recognition of the general and specific boundaries of European spheres of influence frequently took time. Wesseling (1996: 128) instances the 249 boundary treaties concerned with territory in West Africa signed by the British and French between 1882 and 1905. The basis of agreement was often an outline treaty, later to be confirmed by the recommendations, surveys and border markings of boundary commissions. Many of the claims to territory made in the mid- and late nineteenth century were made in considerable geographical ignorance:

The treaties had been framed in very general terms and showed that those responsible for them knew very little about the geography of the area. Frontiers were fixed in accordance with the course or aspect of rivers and mountains, or at least that was the general idea. The picture on the ground was different. As Lord Salisbury put it in his famous sally, 'we have been giving away mountains and rivers and lakes to each other, only hindered by the small impediment that we never knew exactly where the mountains and rivers actually were'. Sometimes the mountains and rivers turned out not to exist. If still less was known about the area, the boundaries were fixed according to degrees of longitude and latitude. (Wesseling, 1996: 128)

Unheard voices

The Berlin Conference of 1884–5 was a European affair whose main purpose was to review and resolve European influences in Africa. At no stage were the African voices heard. Representatives were present from Britain, Germany, France, the Habsburg empire, Belgium, Denmark, Spain, Portugal, Italy, the Netherlands, Russia, the United States and the Ottoman empire. There were practical difficulties of including in the assembly a very wide range of representative monarchs and leaders, yet the material advancement of Africa was part of the deliberations in Berlin, and African representatives could have been found.

Gann (1988: 32) cites Sir Edward Malet, the British ambassador in Berlin, speaking in November 1884: 'I cannot forget that the natives are not represented amongst us, and that the decisions of the Conference will, nevertheless, have extreme importance for them.' The impact of the conference on the resolution and determination of boundaries for African states under European hegemony is not entirely clear, but some basic issues need to be addressed, particularly about African concepts of boundary relative to those of Europeans. One obvious paradox is that African knowledge of spaces of local political and economic activity was infinitely more detailed and accurate than that of European powers, yet the Europeans were happy to draw lines on maps over areas of which they had limited geographical knowledge, while African need for and use of precise boundaries was limited and thus rarely manifest. Nugent suggests that in the pre-colonial period Africans did not lack a sense of territoriality, 'merely that political space was mapped mentally rather than cartographically' (Nugent 1996: 36), and that the difference during the colonial period was that African states operated on a different set of assumptions from those of the European nation-state.

He suggests four areas of difference. The first is that whereas modern European states were used to discrete spaces marked by boundaries, with the whole of a region or continent completely sub divided into political units, African practice was more an arrangement of centres of power and influence surrounded by unappropriated territory. Second, the fixed nature of European boundaries contrasted with the fluid or oscillating nature of African boundaries, responding to ecological change, especially variations in rainfall. Third, in respect of the links between state and people, there was a contrast between European states and the relative stability of linked populations and the frequency of floating – often nomadic – populations in some West African states. Fourth, contrasts existed between the assumed absolute sovereignty of European states and the 'tributary provinces and the metropole' of African polities (Nugent 1996: 39–41).

Arbitrary boundary determination in Africa

What were the consequences of this for the rulers and inhabitants of African polities? An immediate answer might be that colonially superimposed boundaries would for the most part be artificial. Nugent indicates that 44 per cent of African political boundaries comprised astronomical lines (meridian parallels), 30 per cent were mathematical lines, that is arcs or curves, and only 265 related to geographical features (Nugent 1996: 41–2), but alludes to the important processes of adjustment of arbitrary boundaries in several phases, sometimes to include known African chiefdom boundaries. In the case of the boundary between northern Nigeria and current Niger, there were at least three phases of boundary-drawing and revision: the first in 1890, consequent on an Anglo-French treaty, and 'agreed upon before the two powers had established a physical presence in the areas concerned. Since it had to be concluded in the midst of profound ignorance, it is not too surprising that this boundary line was crudely defined. The agreement established a straight line between Say on the River Niger and Barruwa on Lake Chad.' Subsequent changes were made in 1898 and between 1904 and 1906, to make use of 'pre-colonial frontiers and to take account of local trade routes' (Nugent 1996: 42–4). Changes were also made to the boundary between the Gold Coast (Ghana) and Togo, originally set by Britain and Germany, and revised when the area was partitioned by Britain and France after the First World War, using geographical features such as rivers, with adjustments to correct anomalies (that divided tribes) continuing until 1929, the whole process avoiding the arbitrary use of straight-line borders. Nugent suggests an interesting general principle, namely, 'that the more often boundary questions were reopened, the greater was the likelihood that indigenous lines of demarcation would displace the notorious astronomical and mathematical lines' (Nugent 1996: 46).

Much of the work in boundary adjustment was made by boundary commissions and it would be helpful to have some statistical measure of the number of boundaries in Africa – and indeed elsewhere – that were changed through the colonial period by re-negotiation, and of the role of Africans and indigenous peoples elsewhere in the presentation of requests for change. The propriety and efficacy of border commissioners varied enormously.

Lord Curzon, in the text of his Romanes lecture on 'Frontiers' at the University of Oxford in 1907 (Curzon 1907), encapsulated much contemporary thinking at the beginning of the twentieth century on the broad issue of international frontiers and boundaries, including the work of the boundary commissions which had been an important piece of machinery for establishing frontiers and boundaries since the eighteenth century. The process ideally requires that:

local surveys or reconnaissances, where one or the other has been found, precede the discussions of the statesmen. Small committees of officials are frequently appointed in advance to consider the geographical, topographical, and ethnological evidence that is forthcoming, and to construct a tentative line for their respective governments; this, after much debate, is embodied in a treaty, which provides for the appointment of Commissioners to demarcate the line upon the spot and submit it for ratification by the principals. Geographical knowledge thus precedes or is made the foundation of the labours of statesmen, instead of supervening at a later date to cover them with ridicule or reduce their findings to a nullity. I do not say that absurd mistakes and blunders are not committed. I could, if I had the leisure, construct a notable and melancholy list. But the tendency is unquestionably in the direction of greater precision both of knowledge and language. (Curzon 1907: 21)

He indicated that some latitude was allowed to the commissioners for departures from the treaty for practical matters 'of mutual concession'. His comments on the use of local geographical knowledge were not untypical of the time:

where native agents are admitted, usually in a subordinate and advisory capacity, they are apt to interpret their functions as justifying an exceptional measure of vacillation, obstruction, and every form of delay. Any one who has had experience of demarcation of the frontiers of Persia and Afghanistan will recall the prodigies that are capable of being performed in these directions. (Curzon 1907: 23)

Some glimpses from the life of a boundary commissioner are to be found in an account of Stewart Gore-Browne's work from 1911 to 1914 on the Anglo-Belgian Boundary Commission for Northern Rhodesia (implementing a vague agreement between Britain and King Leopold II of Belgium). This is cited in a biography by Christina Lamb (2000) entitled *The Africa House*:

The Anglo-Belgian Boundary Commission had been something of a disappointment, too, though [Gore-Browne] had revelled in the outdoor life and the hunting. It was all *far too bureaucratic and tied up with the petty egos of other officers.* Within three months Captain Everett, the second-in-command, was eaten by a lion, *a most ill-omened start.* Major Gillam, who headed the Commission, spent most of his time in a haze of whisky and kept issuing and rescinding orders ... The work marking out the border had been *damnably slow.* The 1894 agreement between Britain and Belgium's king Leopold was vague, simply stating that the border was to run southwards from Lake Bangweulu to its junction with the watershed separating the Congo and Zambezi rivers, following this line for 550 miles till it reached the Portuguese frontier. (Lamb 2000: 11)

Gore-Browne attributed the slowness of the process to the vagueness with which the King of Italy – the initial arbiter – had outlined the boundaries, to the lack of good instruments for survey, the weather, smoke from fields being burnt before planting, and the rough terrain. He regretted the failure of the commission to take account of tribal borders. The end of the commission's work was on New Year's Day of 1914, when they met with the Anglo-Portuguese Commission for the designation of the border between Northern Rhodesia and Angola: '*Another few parcels of Africa squared off on the map*, Gore-Browne wrote in his diary' (Lamb 2000: 11).

A consequence of the division of Africa into, in effect, European-dominated polities in the nineteenth and earlier twentieth centuries, is the 'permeability' of the boundaries thus established (Griffiths 1996: 68–84). One of the severe criticisms of the outcomes of the Berlin Conference of 1884–5 is that the resulting international boundaries divided cultural areas and tribes. One figure cited by Griffiths is that '103 international boundaries in Africa cut through a total of 131 cultural areas, some of which are partitioned by more than one boundary'. These boundaries, however, are frequently ignored by people moving within a cultural area and by nomadic peoples, and that borders are not always clearly marked, so that there will always be an element of permeability (Griffiths 1996: 74, 81).

In his preface to a study of two territorial disputes from southern Africa in the late nineteenth century, Seligmann (1995: 173) outlines difficulties arising from boundaries that were agreed on the basis of diplomatic exchanges in Europe not corresponding with the data and details on maps actually drawn in the territories involved. One area of dispute was the British/German colonial border between German South-West Africa and British Bechuanaland. For the designation of the boundary between the two territories in the vicinity of Rietfontein and Olifants Kloof, 'the partitioning of territory as defined by treaty and the marking of a frontier as determined and mapped locally were found to be at variance' (Seligman 1995: 173). The issue arose from a claim by the Wittbooi Hottentots, who were fighting against German troops in the area, to have their 'belligerent status' recognised by adjacent British colonies. The issue was raised with the British Foreign Office, but dropped after its diplomats in Berlin had

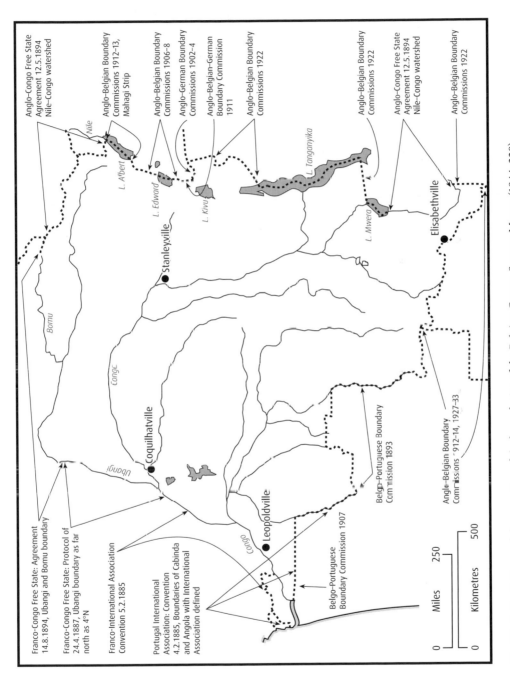

Franco-Congo Free State: Agreement
14.8.1894, Ubangi and Bomu boundary

Franco-Congo Free State: Protocol of
24.4.1887, Ubangi boundary as far
north as 4°N

Franco-International Association
Convention 5.2.1885

Portugal International
Association: Convention
4.2.1885, Boundaries of Cabinda
and Angola with International
Association defined

Anglo-Congo Free State
Agreement 12.5.1894
Nile-Congo watershed

Anglo-Belgian Boundary
Commissions 1912–13,
Mahagi Strip

Anglo-Belgian Boundary
Commissions 1906–8

Anglo-German Boundary
Commissions 1902–4

Anglo-Belgian–German
Boundary Commission
1911

Anglo-Belgian Boundary
Commissions 1922

Anglo-Belgian Boundary
Commissions 1922

Anglo-Congo Free State
Agreement 12.5.1894
Nile-Congo watershed

Anglo-Belgian Boundary
Commissions 1922

Nile

L. Albert

L. Edward

L. Kivu

L. Tanganyika

L. Mweru

Bomu

Congo

Ubangi

Congo

Stanleyville

Coquilhatville

Leopoldville

Elisabethville

Belgo-Portuguese Boundary
Commission 1893

Anglo-Belgian Boundary
Commissions 1912–14, 1927–33

Belgo-Portuguese
Boundary Commission 1907

Miles   250   500

0

Kilometres

0

Fig. 7.1 Delimitation and demarcation of the boundaries of the Belgian Congo. Source: Mason (1944: 220).

been provided by the Reich Colonial Division with a map from Richard Kiepert's series of five maps of German colonies, produced in 1892 and bound as the *Deutscher Kolonial Atlas*. The Wittbooi claim was rejected by the British Foreign Office, but a series of disputes arose thereafter over the determination of the boundary between the two hegemonies, partly influenced by different methods of survey, and the border was not agreed finally until the late 1890s.

The mapping of India

British commercial interest in India dates back to the beginning of the seventeenth century, with the granting of a charter to the East India Company in 1600, whose initial aim was to compete with Portugal in the Indonesian spice trade. One outcome was the establishment of a base in western India in Surat, whose port was Gujarat. By mid-century trade had increased in a range of commodities, including cotton and silk cloths. By the mid-eighteenth century the main East India Company trading centres were Calcutta, Bombay and Madras, marking the beginning of British imperial influence in India, and in the last forty years of that century British control expanded in southern India and in the Ganges valley. The process of expansion of British power in India continued in the nineteenth century, and by 1885 Britain directly controlled much of northern, north-western, western and eastern India, the remaining parts surviving as Indian states under British rule. It was at the end of the eighteenth century that a major survey was initiated that in many respects epitomised the links between knowledge and imperial power: the Great Trigonometrical Survey of India.

Prior to the initiation of the Great Trigonometrical Survey of India in 1802, India had a long tradition of various forms of mapping, dating back to late prehistoric times, in the form of 'map-like graffiti', map symbolisations and sculpted bas relief cosmologies. In the Moghul period from 1526 to 1857, various forms of globe and astrolabe were made, mainly in the north-west and in an 'Islamicate' tradition, and Hindu cosmographic globes and planispheric maps were made in this period. Regional maps, route maps, maps of towns and fortifications, sometimes with topographic features such as hills and watercourses, derive from the eighteenth and nineteenth centuries (Schwartzberg 1997: 572–3, 1992: 295–509). Bayly also, in his analysis of the links between information – including geographical

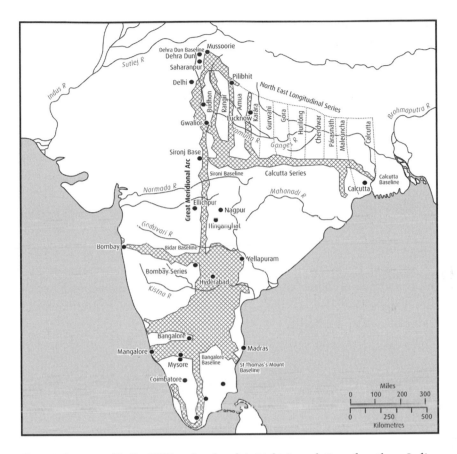

Fig. 7.2 Surveys of India: William Lambton's initial triangulation of southern India (1799–1817) and the arcs of the Great Trigonometric Survey of India, completed by 1843. Source: Edney (1997: 20). By permission of and © University of Chicago Press.

knowledge – and empire in late eighteenth- and in nineteenth-century India, contrasts the geographical knowledge that came from the Puranas (ancient Sanskrit texts of legends and genealogies) with the more scientific geographies, based on Enlightenment reasoning and collection of scientific data, that were used by the British to correct what they saw as 'wild conceptions' that could be countered by the distribution of globes (Bayly 1996: 301). Indian scholars attempted to accommodate these ancient concepts with the newer ideas about the location of places, linking traditional geographical myths with European realities. There was a tradition of mapmaking in India, with route maps, world maps and some larger-scale maps known and created under the Mughal emperors, and such maps were used in the early stage of conquest.

The Great Trigonometrical Survey of India

The origins of the Great Survey lie in the work of the surveyors who were appointed by the East India Company. Edney (1997) has produced a seminal account of the contexts and texts of maps and mapping in India in the eighteenth and nineteenth centuries. He has demonstrated, inter alia, that the basis of all mapping was the existing process of information acquisition and management by the states of South Asia and the East India Company, and re-asserted Bayly's notion that the success or failure of states and institutions depended on their use and control of information.

From 1765 there was an increase in the need for and use of maps in civil and military administration: 'The character of British mapmaking in India was defined by a four-way competition between the need for geographical information, the availability of labour to undertake the necessary surveys, the availability of money to pay for the surveys, and the adherence to cultural expectations for making as comprehensive and as accurate maps as possible' (Edney 1997: 161).

William Lambton is the surveyor credited with the establishment of the Great Trigonometrical Survey of India: he was appointed as brigade major to the 33rd Foot Regiment, embarking for Mysore in the Madras Presidency and sailing from Calcutta in 1798 to take part in the Fourth Anglo-Mysore War, which resulted in British control in 1799, with Lambton charged with new surveys of the territory. At this time he developed the idea for a geographic survey and geodesic triangulation of southern India. This ultimately led to the triangulation of the whole of India, though Edney points out that this larger ambition was not Lambton's initial intention (Edney 1997: 179).

After surveys of Mysore, Lambton's survey of the arc of the meridian 78° longitude began on 10 April 1802, and started the measurement of a degree of latitude by means of a 7.5 mile (12 km) base line at St Thomas Mount in Madras. This was then continued by triangulation to the Mysore plateau, with a second longitudinal base line measured in 1804 near Bangalore, which was continued across the peninsula, and subsequently extended as an arc of the meridian 78° longitude. It provided the basis for the subsequent triangulation of the whole of India.

The conditions in which Lambton and his surveyors and successors worked were inevitably beset with difficulties of terrain, climate, ecology, relations with local inhabitants, and the instruments used. Keay has described the problems encountered by the surveyors when they continued the survey across the Western Ghats and down to the shores of the

Arabian Sea. The Ghats 'represented the Survey's first mountain challenge. The dense forests and choked ravines of the Ghats were even more impenetrable than the Kistna-Godavari jungles which would so impress George Everest; and their moist malarial climate, at its worst in the post-monsoon period when Lambton made his final push, was deemed even more lethal' (Keay 2000b: 57).

By 1815 Lambton had triangulated the southern part of India south of the River Krishna (Kistna). In 1818, he was joined by Captain George Everest, who had recently been involved in surveys in Java, and his survey project was given the title of the Great Trigonometrical Survey of India. The survey continued northwards, though Lambton died in 1823, at the age of 70, before the project was complete. George Everest, who was made Surveyor General of India in 1830, took over the task, which was finished in 1841, including the extension of the great arc to the Himalayas, whose highest peak was named after him.

Edney has claimed that the Great Trigonometrical Survey was constructed by the British 'as a public works which could not be undertaken by the Indians themselves, but which was as concrete and as necessary as irrigation canals and military roads for pulling together, improving, and defining India and its inhabitants. And the spatial significance of the trigonometrical surveys was *inscribed* into the maps the British produced. They defined India' (Edney 1997: 319–20). He also suggested that this was a contested enterprise, in that the control of surveillance was never total: there were inconsistencies and disagreements within the East India Company; there was resistance from Indian people themselves; and the linguistic distance between Indian and British restricted control. Problems with local opposition arose partly from the use of flags by the surveyors, from the amount of labour that they had to recruit from local populations, from an endemic concern that the production of greater knowledge of Indian places would almost certainly increase the amount of revenue from land, and from failure to use local names of natural features, including those of rivers (Edney 1997: 326, 328, 331).

This line of thinking has been followed by Tickell (2004: 20) who examined the reports, field journals and letters associated with the Great Trigonometrical Survey in a context of 'the wider production of colonized space as a process of agnostic negotiation between colonizer and colonized'. Exploring the received wisdom of the idea of the map as a form of colonial control, and Edney's qualification of the idea, particularly in relation to 'the discursive, flexible quality of the imperial map', Tickell instances the search by Lambton, in the area near Tanjore in southern India, for vantage points from which survey sightings might be taken. Many of these were temples, and they required delicacy and diplomacy to negotiate their use as survey sights. Everest, working in Bengal and the Deccan plains, had to construct cairns and build more substantial towers for observations, which acquired symbolic and superstitious character in the minds of local people, resulting in their destruction. Tickell also cites 'Indigenous strategies of mistranslation' that exemplify this discourse: citing Ramanuajan's story of the naming of a bridge over the Coom River as Hamilton Bridge, and its ultimate translation as Barber's Bridge, on account of Hamilton being pronounced *Amittan* in Tamil, and the word *Ammattan* in Tamil meaning 'barber' (Tickell 2004: 22–3, 26).

An additional example is the attribution by local people of spiritual/ miraculous significance to Everest's survey sites and instruments. Contrasting with these masculinist imperial gazes is the account of the experiences of survey expeditions in the diary of Honria Lawrence, the wife of one of the survey officers. This 'works at a remove from the more technical business of the cartographic survey, and her narrative often shifts uneasily between amateur ethnography, forms of the picturesque, and the recording of botanical details', and her sensitivity to the contrasts between indigenous and European cultures. Tickell concludes that the imperial project was more nuanced than models of monolithic discourse would suggest, so that 'the cartographic notions plotted out in this paper also challenge the axiomatic intellectual autonomy of the colonial, and remind us that Indian "meanings" were always, inescapably, part of the Imperial text' (Tickell 2004: 27, 28, 30).

We may also need to remind ourselves that local labour and Indian expertise might not always have been unwillingly dragged into the cartographic conspiracies of the British. Trained Indian surveyors ('pundits') were highly valued, employed for example in the Abyssinia campaign in the late nineteenth century, and awarded medals by the Royal Geographical Society.

Other visual representations of imperial landscapes and peoples

Representation of imperial and colonial 'other' peoples and landscapes was a highly significant part of the geographical experiences evidenced by a great range of visualisations of empire in the later nineteenth and early twentieth centuries – what Jeremy Foster has called:

> processes that have to do with the imaginative and discursive appropriation of geographical space … The form of discourse most often associated with this process involves production and circulation of *visual* images of the shared territory. Smoothing out the world's inconsistencies, aberrations and contradictions, and privileging that which is picturable over that which is not, such imagery offers a confirmation of nationhood, and renders a national territory visible to all through reproduction and circulation. (Foster 2003b: 657–8)

The picturing and presentation of images from overseas territories to the metropole and within the territories themselves took a variety of forms: exhibitions, museums, photographs, living exhibits, including zoos, films, paintings, prints, postcards, plays and operas. Space does not permit analysis here of these rich sources, on which there is an impressive and productive literature. Imperial and colonial exhibitions have been extensively covered by Hoffenburg (2001), Jennings (2005), Aldrich (1996), Clout (2005), MacKenzie (1984), Woodham (1989), McKay (2004), Ewans (2003) and Stanard (2005).

There are insightful reviews of the history and uses of photography in colonial contexts by Ryan (1995, 1997), Schwartz and Ryan (2003), Falconer (2001), Blunt (2003), Killingray and Roberts (1989), Ranger (2001), Quanchi 2006, Gardner and Philp (2006), Foster 2003a, 2003b), and Osborne (2003).

This chapter has focused on the cartographic representations of places and spaces of empires and colonies and the topographic and cultural meanings that can be read from them. The next chapter looks at another aspect of the cultures of imperialism and colonialism: the geographies of the 'civilising mission'.

No doubt, the Dreaming as a whole might take on such qualities of the sublime, but its landscape is the landscape of the everyday, which the young Romanticist's mountains are not. It is a landscape of *things* – animals, plants, rocks, streams – *unseparated* in the spiritual and physical presences. That is to say, the knowledge of their spiritual nature cannot be separated from the knowledge of them as practical, material things – in many cases, what modern Western society would understand as commodities. It was an alive landscape with which the human, as part of it, needed to negotiate. (Kenny 2007: 155–6)

Introduction

The Dreaming was part of the cosmology of a young aboriginal Australian – Nathanael Pepper – living in the Wimmera region of what is now Victoria in the mid-nineteenth century, whose life was changed by the presence of European missionaries and settlers. The complex interaction between the two cultures and their respective cosmologies, detailed later in this chapter, identifies some of the imperial and colonial processes which engaged European powers and their target populations in the nineteenth and twentieth centuries, and which were neither neutral nor unaffected by tensions between these cultures. It is clear that many of the attempts made to impose European cultural forms and systems on what were frequently deemed to be inferior cultures involved coercion of one kind or another, but the processes involved were complex. They cannot be explained simply in terms of a European cultural system being unilaterally imposed on passive indigenous peoples. European powers were consciously and subconsciously promoting what is called a 'civilising mission' or 'mission civilisatrice': the engagement of a complex set of values and prejudices with indigenous cultural ideas and practices in the hopes of material and spiritual improvement. The processes were, however, multi-directional, interactive and mutually informing.

Postcolonial theory among other things emphasises and gives priority to the experiences of the 'response side of the equation: how it was understood, interpreted, reshaped or employed, or rejected' (Dunch 2002: 303–4, 306), and potentially helps us to understand the complexity of and evidence for indigenous interactions and agency, not least the real difficulty of characterising pre-colonial cultures and societies. There is a need to review the image promoted by Europeans of the perceived backwardness of many indigenous societies. Fabian (2000: 165), writing about German and Belgian explorers in Africa in the nineteenth century, asks if we can

begin to dismantle the myth of modernity's march into central African savagery? Expeditions, at once symbolizing and enacting the march, did not proceed from open civilization through mixed regions toward closed savagery. In their wish to participate in what we would later call the world system, some African populations – among them most of those the explorers met – were just about as far removed from savagery and modernity as the European nations the explorers represented.

Fabian states that Africans had sophisticated political units and traded in a world market, and he highlights the contrasting 'savagery' of the conduct of many European expeditions.

Concepts of the civilising mission varied between and within European imperial powers. Kelly (2006: 134) claims that in France, for example:

The civilising mission was therefore both a guiding aspiration of the colonial enterprise and a framework for criticism of its actual implementation. It acted both as the presentational device that allowed France to show its imperial activities in the best possible light, and also as a yardstick by which its failings were measured. It was inseparable from the universalist republican enterprise, which could be taken to place a duty on France to extend the benefits of civilisation in which its leaders passionately believed.

Under imperialist and colonial systems, cultural interactions were iterative processes. Stoler and Cooper (1997: 1) assert that: 'Europe's colonies were never empty spaces to be made over in Europe's image or fashioned in its interests; nor, indeed, were European states self-contained entities that at one point projected themselves overseas. Europe was made by its imperial projects, as much as colonial encounters were shaped by conflicts within Europe itself.' We should accept, therefore, that much of the interaction between cultures and traditions in greatly varying colonial contexts was and is in effect the outcome of complex 'negotiations' between local agents, individuals, or groups who respond to challenges to existing local belief systems by seeking, consciously or otherwise, to reach some sort of valid accommodation more satisfactory than a confrontational position.

It can be argued that the whole imperial/colonial/indigenous engagement process was determined more by local circumstance or confrontation than by general policy edicts from afar. Admittedly the colonisers and imperial promoters in the field were to varying degrees influenced and funded by metropolitan policies and agencies, but the actual implementation of those policies on the ground was a transforming process, for many practical and some ideological reasons. An important aspect of understanding the interlinking of European cultures with local cultures of belief is the historical depth and persistence of many of the latter. Another significant aspect of cultural changes through religious systems is their dynamic: some new religions persist through time, others do not, some exist peacefully alongside pre-existing belief systems, and others do not.

Race and empire

In the period under consideration these basic premises were underpinned by quasi-scientific anthropological theories, including those developed in the growing knowledge areas of anthropology and ethnology. Aligned with natural theology, the concept of acclimatisation and polygenism, geographical writings emphasised the links between climate, race, and moral precepts and behaviour: 'The idea that climate had stamped its indelible mark on racial constitution, not just physiologically, but psychologically and morally, was a motif that was both deep and lasting in English-speaking geography' (Livingstone 1994: 140).

Enlightenment notions of the influence of natural environments on the cultures and life characteristics of different groups (races) had fed into an adapted form of Darwinism ('Social Darwinism') or scientific racism that was used to account for perceived actual and potential differentials of development, and to a notion that 'the expansive, imperial "races" of Europe and the European settler communities in the Americas benefited from unique climatic and environmental circumstances, it was claimed, and that these advantages had created energetic, expansive civilizations. The very different climates and environments of the colonial periphery had created inferior societies and weaker civilizations in need of an ordering and benign European presence' (Heffernan 2003: 14). Reformation and management of both people and environments could make for improvement, using assumed superior European technical knowledge and moral precepts. Climate, it was thought, could also restrict the potential of places for white settlement, and affect the behaviour of European colonists, with tropical environments seen as impossible places for Europeans to settle, and of which moral laxity for Europeans temporarily resident was a by-product. The mixing of races was also a main concern for colonial policy-makers, apologists and enumerators, though assumptions of moral laxity and a weakening of survival rates were countered by discourses around the advantages of racial mixture.

Such racist ideas were questioned by contemporary radical and some-times anarchist perspectives, and it has been argued that there was great dissonance between racist theory and a broader contemporary concept that racism was 'at odds with an underlying or universal moral feel-ing; there was an implicit sense, even at the time, that colonialism was a negative or shameful venture' (Heffernan 2003: 15). The uncertainty of metropolitan thinkers about this and other aspects of colonial theory and practice is encapsulated in Alice Stopford Green's tribute to Mary Kingsley, published in 1901:

In the hurry of conquest we have as yet no scientific study of the necessary condi-tions of tropical existence, the economic and domestic problems, the real relations of white and black races, and what principles of Science and Statecraft should gov-ern the policy of a dominant power in Africa. People in England who were think-ing of Africa at all in the brief and accidental intervals that the English Public and Parliament have to give to such things, were chiefly occupied in speculating generally how to keep European hands off and to broaden the vast dominions of the Empire so as to give the British public all the glory and none of the expense. 'Armed with absolutely no definite policy, they drift along with some nebulous sort of notion in their heads about "elevating the African in the plane of civilization".' (The last sentence is a quotation from Mary Kingsley.) (Green, 1901: 10)

Current thinking on these issues is not only highly critical of these rac-ist concepts but also emphasises the greater variety of local difference in the attitudes of colonist and coloniser, countering the idea that 'colonial-ism was monolithic, uncontested and efficacious' (Thomas 1994: 12). We are also reminded by Stoler and Cooper of the complexities of the motives, processes and outcomes in attempts to link colonial knowledge and power, recognising that, for example:

categories of 'caste' in India and 'tribe' in Africa were in part colonial constructs, efforts to render fluid and confusing social and political relationships into catego-ries sufficiently static and reified and thereby useful to colonial understanding and control. But they could not be simply colonial categories: their elaboration required the knowledge of elders or pandits who were sought to manipulate the creation of knowledge for their own purposes. (Stoler and Cooper 1997: 11)

The complexity of these issues has to be acknowledged. It is necessary to heed the cautionary advice of, for example, McCaskie (2004: 167) writing on cultural encounters between Britain and Africa in the nineteenth century, where the 'leitmotif is a tangled knot of realities and representations', in the form of 'an ever evolving cultural hybrid in which imagined, willed, and contingent acts are densely interwoven'.

The imperial and colonial experiences of European states and their agents, and, equally important, of those indigenous peoples who were affected by them, were never static, both in terms of changes in human actions and in changing physical environments. A major concern was acclimatisation of plants, animals and peoples, notably in the tropical regions. Identification of areas of white settlement was difficult, partly through failure to understand what seemed at first sight to be familiar and manageable landscapes and ecological systems, and also failure to comprehend indigenous land-use and landownership systems. A key feature of European environmental concern was the cause of high death rates in the tropics, particularly of European military personnel, who were exposed to a range of fevers including malaria (a natural prophylactic to which – cinchona – was known, cultivated in India and the Dutch East Indies, for example, but which was not chemically analysed or widely available until much later). Another problem was the slow realisation that the process of moving indigenous peoples away from their home areas, particularly troops or construction workers on large capital projects such as railway and canal construction, could produce very high rates of debilitation and death.

What has been called the 'moral climate' of the settlement and labour force debates from the mid-nineteenth to nearly the mid-twentieth century was based partly on relative ignorance of tropical diseases and their prevention, and partly on unexamined prejudices about the capacities of various people to work in tropical climates. The debates and publications on white settlement and labour, notably in the tropics, was initially burdened by physiological misunderstanding and also, notably in Australia, by the development of a whites-only policy (for a 'white Australia') and, in an equally misguided way, of racial discrimination through apartheid in South Africa. The theme of acclimatisation is dealt with at greater length in Chapter 9 of this book.

Religion and imperialism

Österhammel (1997: 95) has outlined several permutations and effects of the meetings or clashes of religious cultures within colonial contexts. One is the facilitating of a process of transition to an indigenous church based on the 'new' religion: in the case of Protestant Christian missionary work in Africa a relatively early and continuing 'self-Christianization and transition to indigenous churches' developed, and paved the way for decolonisation. A different process and outcome of engagement between European-based missions and African people resulted in the 'stimulations of non-Christian counter-movements, that is the transfusion of Christian elements into different religions such as Hinduism in India'. Not all existing religions in colonial territories were susceptible to Christian influence, however. Islam, for example, had its own dynamic and policies of expansion, which effectively resisted Christian proselytisation (Österhammel 1997: 98, 99–100).

The spread of European imperial power in the nineteenth and early twentieth centuries continued and sometimes built on a base established as far back as the sixteenth and seventeenth centuries, notably by Roman Catholic missionaries, including Jesuits from Spain and Portugal. The general trajectory of missionary work in the period of high imperialism is not difficult to identify, though it must be recognised that in both early modern and modern periods there were missions operating outside of formal empire. There are, however, several basic concepts that need to be reviewed, before a wider narrative can be attempted.

The meanings of religion

The first question is about the associated meanings of the term 'religion'. Western religious traditions embrace concepts and systems of private, personal belief that are generally regarded as separate from the more public culture of politics, this separation deriving from historical dispute in northern Europe in the eighteenth century and the later separation of church and state. King (2005: 284) asserts that 'Modern notions of religion reflect Christian theological assumptions, in particular the preoccupation with orthodoxy and truth (rather than practice and forms of life) and with a canon of authorized scriptures as the location of the true essence of religion.' These have wrongly, in King's view, been also identified, through the imperial process and beyond, with Asian religions such as Hinduism and Buddhism, and also with Islam, within which politics and religious form are much more closely intermingled. The Christian model cannot be superimposed on these other religious belief systems and cultures. This issue takes us further into the realm of the Orientalist study of Islam, and the view of some Islamist scholars that it is impossible for Islam to be studied sympathetically from a perspective of Western scholarship, though there are counter-arguments about this constituting a kind of 'Occidentalism' (King 2005: 284–5).

A second major challenge is the identification of religions by origin and scales of activity, a process that is also complex and beset with difficulty. One of the reasons for this is the heterogeneous nature of all religious systems, and their dynamics: they develop and change through time and in differing socio-political and cultural environments. A basic classification will have to suffice, for reasons of brevity. A fundamental distinction can be made between tribal systems that incorporate elements of local or regional tradition, belief and practice, ethnic religions that are closely linked to a national culture, and universal or global religions that seek to expand, such as Christianity, Islam and types of Buddhism.

The first of these is characterised by such elements as 'belief in spirits, supernatural forces, gods and cults, witchcraft, sorcery, sacrifices, rituals, taboos, veneration of ancestors, and ceremonies of rites of passage such as naming ceremonies, initiation rites and customs associated with deaths and burials' (Opoku 1990a: 217), and was widespread in the pre-colonial period in Africa, Asia, North and South America, and the Pacific. The second type does not usually seek to expand and make converts, and examples of broader-based forms, Park indicates, are 'Judaism, Shintoism, Hinduism and the Chinese moral-religious system (embracing Confucianism and Taoism) which mainly dominate one particular national culture' (Park 2005: 440).

Religion and the civilising mission

A traditional model or 'master-narrative' of the role of European and other missions in the development of empire has incorporated the ideas that missions were part of empire, collusive with metropolitan governments and with commercial interests in the tripartite role of Christianity, commerce and civilisation. Etherington and Maxwell (2004: 194) claim that: 'The explosive expansion of Christianity in Africa and Asia during the last two centuries constitutes one of the most remarkable cultural transformations in human history. Because it coincided with the spread of European economic and political hegemony, it tends to be taken for granted as a reflex of imperialism.'

Recent qualifications to this idea of missionary works as reflexes of European imperialism, however, include the recognition of Christian proselytising activities before and after British and European imperial processes in the modern period; the fact that much of this work happened outside of imperial territory, and that some of the work within imperial bounds was carried out by non-Europeans, notably North Americans; the changing nature of missionary activity from a small to an institutional scale; and the greater recognition of the roles of indigenous peoples as agents in the spread of new, often hybrid, religious ideas and practices (Etherington and Maxwell 2004; Martin 2006). Maps, at least of the Christian world, 'rarely coincided with the contours of formal empire' so that missions sometimes pre-dated imperial rule or were located in territories under the control of another European power (Etherington 1999: 303). Missionaries were, it is now thought, not 'junior partners in the project of imperial overrule... [but] ... the missionaries, who aimed to replace indigenous cultures with European "civilization" and who frequently allied themselves with native governments, nevertheless transmitted a religion which native peoples turned to their own purposes: spiritual, economic and political'. The role of African Christians and cosmologies has also been underestimated by the view that 'Christianity in sub-Saharan Africa has been merely the ideological superstructure of Western capitalism' (Etherington 1999: 309).

One important conclusion from an overview of missionary work in India during the British Raj points to the uncertain position about the relations of mission and empire:

there can be no easy summary of the relations between missions and colonialism. Hitherto there has been too much emphasis on linkages and too little attention paid to indigenous agency, impacts of conversion, reactions to conversion (or to counter-conversion), and indigenous movements. Much of what happened still lies hidden from the gaze of historians. Furthermore, profound tensions existed between the imperial system and established religion of any sort. (Frykenberg 2005: 129)

The conventional image of a mission as a source of conversion for non-white indigenous peoples has also to be qualified by the recognition that much of the funding for work by British Anglican, Presbyterian and Methodist missions in British colonies in the nineteenth century was provided for work among white settlers (Etherington 1999: 303). Alternative exegeses of the mission narrative emphasise clearer gender perspectives, the iterative–negotiative relationships between missions, missionaries and their target populations, the processes of proselytisation by preaching and printing, and by institutional channels.

Global trends and contexts

The interactions of religious belief systems with European imperialism in the nineteenth and twentieth centuries have to be viewed in the broader context of major trends and changes in both global and local religions. The nineteenth and early twentieth centuries witnessed substantial expansion in most major religions, partly through greater association with rapidly developing ideologies of nationalism and the character of the nation state (both within and beyond Europe), and partly through the social influences of industrialisation, together with the greater availability of the printed word, including religious texts. The main interactions with organised religion were with Hinduism, Buddhism, Sikhism, Islam, Christianity and Judaism, whose basic tenets and histories are briefly summarised below.

Hinduism

Hinduism is exceptional in this 'ethnic' group in that it originated in north-west India, in the Punjab, but later expanded eastwards and southwards, and ultimately beyond India, through the migration of indentured labour, to other areas including Africa, the Caribbean and Fiji and other Pacific islands (Park 2005: 445). To describe Hinduism as a single religion is, however, misleading. Many commentators have highlighted the pluralistic nature of 'Hinduism' (itself a Western term), in that it had no single founder, 'has no prophets, no set creed, and no particular institutional structure. It emphasises the right way of living (*dharma*) rather than a set of doctrines, and thus embraces diverse religious beliefs and practices. There are significant variations between different regions of India, and even from village to village. There are differences in the deities worshipped, the scriptures used, and the festivals observed' (Goring 1992: 218). Hinduism is very closely tied to the land: elements of the earth are revered as sacred, including mountains, trees, and rivers (notably the Ganges), and is also characterised by castes – marriage groups ranked hierarchically, with the Brahmins at the top and 'untouchables' or 'outcastes' at the bottom (Chapman 2000: 34–6). In its many forms it closely interacted with European imperialism, conspicuously in India, from the eighteenth century onwards.

Buddhism

Buddhism was of a much later foundation than Hinduism, based on the teachings of Buddha (Siddhartha Gautama) and the law of *karma*, incorporating the notion of progress to *nirvana*, and spread from the border of the Ganges plain into other parts of India, including Ceylon, in late prehistoric and early historic times, and thence via missionaries to China, South-East Asia, Tibet, Korea and Japan, and Mongolia. It eventually shrank within its originating core area (Park 2005: 446). In India and South-East Asia in particular it was involved in interaction with European imperialism.

Sikhism

Sikhism is a smaller religious culture, which developed in the Punjab at the end of the fifteenth century, around the guidance of the Guru Nanak, and included parts of Islam and Hinduism, with the Punjabi language and culture and several sacred scriptures at the centre. After the British annexation of the Punjab in 1849, Sikhism spread to other parts of India by the migration of Sikh traders and Sikh soldiers in the British army, and thence to parts of South-East Asia, Australia, New Zealand, Fiji and East Africa, with further dispersal after the Second World War (Park 2005: 446).

Islam

Islam began in Arabia in the seventh century, founded by the prophet Mohammed, born in Mecca *c.* 570. Obedience is made to the will of God (Allah), revealed through the Koran (Quran). Islam spread from Arabia to western Europe, North, West, East and South Africa, India and South-East Asia, partly by force of arms, partly along major trade routes from Arabia to Central Asia and China and across the Sahara Desert, and partly by relocation diffusion (Park 2005: 449). By the time of the high imperialism of the later nineteenth century it had become a major world religion, and in many areas interacted with colonial ideologies and other religions.

Christianity

Christianity was born in Jerusalem with the death of Jesus Christ, and spread slowly via disciples, then preachers and missionaries, to the eastern Mediterranean, Egypt, Gaza, Malta and Rome, thence to western Europe, and subsequently North and South America, Africa, parts of India, China, Japan, South-East Asia and the Pacific islands (Park 2005: 447–8). In its many forms and divisions it was a major component of the cultural interactions of European imperialism with indigenous cultures and religions,

Fig. 8.1 Annual gathering to prayer, Jama Masjid mosque, Delhi, *c.* 1902/10.
By permission of and © Cambridge University Library, RCSPC – Y3022QR-R-184.

and with other major religions such as Islam in the later nineteenth and the twentieth centuries.

Judaism

Judaism is a very old culture and belief system that spread, initially by forced dispersal in the Roman era, from Palestine in the Middle East to areas of southern, western and eastern Europe and subsequently to many other parts of the world. It did not have the same scale of interaction with high imperialism as Islam, Hinduism and Christianity, save for the experiences under League of Nations mandates for Palestine.

Patterns of expansion of religions

The role of missionary activity in the development of European/indigenous engagements and discourses is complex. Major questions and problems attach both to the identification of broader global and regional patterns of expansion of religious belief systems, and also to the characterisation of the roles and impacts of individual missionaries and missionary societies, and the interactions between colonisers and colonised. Dunch (2002: 307) critically targets the older model of missionaries who were 'routinely portrayed in both literature and scholarship as narrow-minded chauvinists whose presence and preaching destroyed indigenous cultures and opened the way for the extension of colonial rule'. He is also critical of the notion that missionary roles are closely linked with official and assumingly co-ordinated imperial government policies for the political, economic and cultural development of colonies, arguing that the majority of missionary societies had few if any links with metropolitan government and its representatives in the colonies, or with colonial traders and economic interests.

None of this adds up to an argument that missionaries in the colonies and imperial territories could not in some way have been informal agents of cultural imperialism: they could, but saw their role more as adherents and advocates of a form of superior 'civilisation'. The role of indigenous targets of missionary ideologies and practices in the discourse should be more strongly emphasised, even in cases where they were ineffective: competing claims about the practical utility and symbolism of such features as rain-making, ploughs, clothing, buildings, time and language were the subjects of dialogue on both sides (Dunch, 2002: 308, 310, 311). They must also be situated in the much wider contexts of the contemporary changes that were being experienced in a modernising metropolitan Western world, including secular rationalism and Christian attempts to counter it. In terms of these broadening global trends and transformations, Bayly (2004: 330) has argued convincingly that, contrary to much contemporary opinion in the nineteenth (and twentieth) century that religion was dramatically declining in influence, the experience was quite different. 'In reality, the great religions staged a remarkable resurgence after 1815. In the process, they transformed themselves and the societies within which they worked.' The outreach of these religions widened in the era of European imperialism, often experiencing internal revision and compromise with secular trends in order to promote a more confident and greater external influence over the populations of both the rapidly industrialising regions of Europe and Africa, parts of Asia, the Pacific and the Americas.

The revival and character of major religions on a global scale in the nineteenth century after 1815 were influenced by competition. Bayly (2004: 330) asserts that 'It has always been clear that Judaism, Islam, Hinduism, and Buddhism reformulated themselves partly in response to vigorous missionary assault from Christians in the age of empires. Within the Christian world, even Roman Catholicism was forced to reevaluate its doctrines and practices in the early nineteenth century in reaction to the growing secular power of Protestants and their imperialist evangelization.' Bayly (2004: 331) also highlights the significance of both the spread of Islam in energising Christian response and the internal struggles within Islam 'on the fringes, in places such as northern Nigeria, the Sudan, and the Dutch East Indies, which fed back into and revivified the organization and theology of the centre'. Competition between belief systems made for the iterative transfer of ideas and practices within and between religious groups, as did the spread of more authoritative and formalised structures for the major religions of Asia. The clarification of both the essences of doctrine and the establishment of stronger authority aided the rapid geographical expansion of the major religions, initially at home (through variants of 'missions' to the poor) and then overseas.

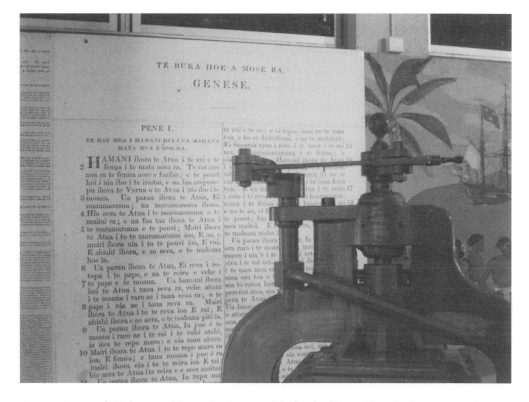

Fig. 8.2 Image of a Tahitian Bible (the beginning of the book of Genesis) and printing press, Musée de Tahiti et des Îles, Papeete, Tahiti. Photo © R. A. Butlin.

Fig. 8.3 Église Évangélique de Polynesie Française (Evangelical Church of French Polynesia), Papeete, Tahiti. A Protestant church originally founded by the London Missionary Society, and built on the site of a church established in 1818.
Photo © R. A. Butlin.

Also significant was the expansion of religions through new technologies that facilitated easier travel and better medical provisions, improving the possibilities for residence in equatorial and tropical environments, and also accelerating the spread of printed texts, including biblical translations into indigenous languages, and evangelical tracts. 'Religious literature was at the forefront of the print revolution as it expanded beyond the European, American, Chinese and Japanese elites. Religious instruction became more widely institutionalized, with the expansion of mosque schools, Hindu and Buddhist temple schools, and Christian Sunday schools' (Bayly 2004: 333, 335).

The expansion of major religions, notably Christianity and Islam, was assisted in circumstances where the belief systems targeted for conversion had similar concepts of divinity to those of the proselytising religion, and also by the indigenous reinterpretation of what until then had been geographically and culturally restricted tenets of faith.

Gender, missionary activity and the imperial gaze

Gender is an important aspect of all processes of imperial advance and retreat, and thus of any analysis of missionary activities and their effects. By the end of the nineteenth century many of the main European- (and American-)based missionary societies were well established, and promoted their belief systems through direct proselytisation and through education for biblical literacy and practical skills. At the height of the European imperial presence overseas much of the opportunity and burden of missionary work was carried out by women: a factor almost without exception common to all the European imperial and colonising powers. While women's work as missionaries has been rather underplayed in historical literature, there is a growing body of work in the field of the history of religion and missiology, and in the contexts of postcolonial and feminist theory.

In a review of the literature on women and cultural exchanges in the British empire, Grimshaw and Sherlock highlight scholarship that provides accounts of women in the mission fields in the contexts of cultural exchanges and conflicts between men and women and different ethnic groups (Grimshaw and Sherlock 2005: 177–8). Mission women have been linked by revisionist historians to the imperial project and therefore have been seen as part of a process of interference with and change in indigenous cultures. Their agency in the modernisation of their own position is now recognised, with greater autonomy and freedom of choice provided through mission activity overseas, especially in the later nineteenth century when more women went into the mission fields. Those who went as wives of missionaries were burdened with many domestic, marital, family, missionary and educational roles, and by problems of health through childbearing and disease, but opportunities did occur for running mission stations, through the periodic absence of missionary husbands, and for the gendered division of labour to be narrowed and the way opened for the employment of women as missionaries themselves (Grimshaw and Sherlock 2005: 182–3).

Women missionaries could access places and communities not accessible to men, including the zenana (domestic and work spaces for Muslim and Hindu women) of India (Grimshaw and Sherlock 2005: 184–5). The distinction of roles between men and women missionaries gradually reduced, and the rules for the selection of women for the mission fields were revised, for example at the Edinburgh missionary conference of 1910, though the status of women missionaries, some of whom had been ordained or made deaconesses in their churches, was more restricted at home than overseas.

Of equal interest have been studies of 'how indigenous women might respond [in leadership positions in their churches] to and resist the interventions of white missionary women … adapting knowledges that were

Fig. 8.4 Baptist Mission, Pallabella, Congo *c.* 1880/90.
By permission of and © the Royal Geographical Society Picture Collection, RGS S0005845.

useful to them and rejecting those that were not ... the outcomes of the missionary enterprise for indigenous women have varied with the nature of colonialism in each region and the dynamics of power between colonizers and colonized' (Grimshaw and Sherlock 2005: 189).

The above comments mainly apply to Protestant missions of various kinds, and additional difficulty attended the work and lives of missionary nuns, whose roles were constrained by the rules of their orders, including restriction of movement and financial and institutional subordination to male clerical superiors, though with measures of freedom coming through the foundation of specialist orders and later autonomy on financial and institutional matters.

Much of the work on the interaction between women and imperial missionary activities has focused on the diffusion of aspects of domesticity for indigenous women which were emphasised in European teaching and training, placing emphasis on reproduction, nurture and practical household skills (Adams 2006). Adams, however, has drawn attention to much wider goals than domesticity that were introduced and negotiated between the external agency of missions and other institutions in Africa and African women. In her detailed study of the British southern Cameroons in the period from 1922 to 1961, Adams shows how the British administration, in addition to focusing on domestic skills, especially towards the end of the period of colonial rule, also tried to provide wider opportunities for women, including better education, opportunities for travel, and wider participation in public life, a reflection in part of the increase in the number of women colonial officers. A conspicuous development towards the end of the colonial period was the recognition of the roles of women and women's associations of a non-political character, such as corn mill societies, and the Women's Corona Society (which undertook philanthropic and welfare work). Adams shows that the agency of Cameroonian women in their interaction with the British administration was mediated by class differences, so that 'the corn mill societies were directed at grassroots women, while the Women's Corona Society sought out educated, elite Cameroonian women', and that 'Cameroonian women instrumentally rejected and incorporated elements of colonial practice and selectively incorporated certain gender discourse into their post-colonial activities' (Adams 2006: 15).

Although France had few women explorers of the new lands of empire, there were significant numbers of French women involved in the teaching and medical missions that existed in many places before the formal establishment of French control. Patricia Lorcin has cited the cases of the foundation by the Sisters of Saint-Joseph de l'Apparition of

one of the oldest schools for girls in Tunis in 1843, four decades before Tunisia was declared a French protectorate. In Algeria, in 1870, Cardinal Charles-Martial Lavigerie established the order of the Sœurs Blanches (White Sisters), eleven months after he founded that of the Pères Blancs (White Fathers). These orders were created just prior to the civilian administration, under whose aegis the settler colony came into its own. From Algeria the two orders fanned out and attained importance in Sub-Saharan Africa. (Lorcin 2004: 300)

The spread of European Christian missions

Significant ideas have developed around the relative conceptions of time, space and place between Western and indigenous peoples in the context of missionary activity (and indeed more broadly of imperialism). Ranger quotes a Native American theologian, George Tinker, whose sentiment was that a different kind of Christianity was necessary rather than impossible for Native North Americans: 'The issue is not whether time or space is missing in one culture or the other, but which is dominant. Of course Native Americans have a temporal awareness, but it is subordinate to our sense of place. Likewise, the Western tradition has a spatial awareness, but lacks the priority of the temporal' (Ranger 2002: 261).

It cannot always be assumed that missionary activity as part of an imperial dynamic was conditioned by a single national or imperial influence. Missionary societies from across Europe often collaborated quite soon after their foundation (Porter 2005: 48–9). During the course of the nineteenth century, however, the detached position which missionary societies had taken in their relations with imperial governments and commercial agencies gradually changed. In Britain, closer links were made by the evangelical missionary societies with government colonial policy and commerce, largely as a matter of practical necessity rather than collaborative ideology, for these were useful channels by which their own particular goals might be reached. This was not, of course, a one-sided relationship: missionaries often had an earlier significant presence in colonial territories than the metropolitan governments, who depended on them for the initial promotion of their 'civilising mission'.

Many new missionary societies had been founded in Britain and Europe in the late eighteenth and early to mid-nineteenth century, including the Methodist Missionary Society (1786), the London Missionary Society

(1795), the Church Missionary Society (1799), the British and Foreign Bible Society (1804), the Berlin Missionary Society (1824), the Swiss Basel Mission (1815), and parallel institutions in Denmark, France, Sweden and Norway. The Bible had been translated into about 520 different languages by the end of the nineteenth century, and spiritual and practical knowledge was spread through religious ceremony, teaching in schools, medical missions and hospitals, agricultural and horticultural projects, printing and publishing ventures, industrial schools, and the teaching and learning of handicrafts. By the end of the nineteenth century many women had become missionaries, and there was parallel recruitment of indigenous people as pastors and lay workers.

Missionary impact overseas was strong in regions of high density but poor populations, such as Hindu societies beset by famine, land problems and debt in late nineteenth-century India, challenging local beliefs, habits and customs. European soldiers, administrators, settlers and missionaries promoting and following the course of European imperialism were also faced with belief systems other than Christianity. In North, West and East Africa there were significant Islamic populations, and the Islamic faith was conspicuous and growing elsewhere, in parts of India and in the Dutch East Indies. In India there were Hindu and Sikh populations, and there was a great variety of indigenous belief systems in all parts of the European empires.

Christian ideologies engaged with existing belief systems in many different ways, and contributed much, through education and practical skills, to the development of national identities and independence movements. Christianity, civilisation and commerce were seen as the increasingly linked aims of colonisation in the second half of the nineteenth century, though the exact permutations differed by national origin, through time, and by place. The attempts at dissemination of a great variety of Christian denominational thinking and practice to those territories appropriated and colonised by European powers in the nineteenth and twentieth centuries were part of the broader *mission civilisatrice*. At one extreme, there can be no doubt that in some cultures and geographical locations, including early mission stations in south-west Australia, there was deemed to be a direct link between civilisation and Christianity. As Brock (2000: 171) states: 'Christianity could not be attained until the indigenous peoples wore European clothes, lived in nuclear monogamous families, worked regular hours, and received rewards for their labour, preferably as wages. Education was also essential for the civilizing process.' Attempts by indigenous peoples to accommodate the new and old cultures by some mingling of belief systems was not often approved by the expatriate missionaries, though it undoubtedly did happen, often under the influence of indigenous converts.

A detailed study by Robert Kenny of the tensions experienced by Nathanael (his Christian baptismal name) Pepper, of the Wotjobaluk aboriginal people of the Wimmera region in the north-west of the colony of Victoria in Australia, who converted to Christianity at the Moravian Ebenezer Mission in 1860, provides a good example. In his book *The Lamb Enters the Dreaming: Nathanael Pepper and the Ruptured World* (Kenny 2007), he shows the complexity of two very different cultures – aboriginal and European – and the dynamics of their internal and external interactions, including both conflict and understanding. Thomas Mitchell, the government surveyor for New South Wales, came to the region in 1836 to explore and survey the land and estimate its potential for the grazing of cattle, horses and sheep. He praised the land highly, but he had traversed the region in the winter, and Kenny suggests that he

might not have been so praising of the land if he had come in summer. Here, it is not the winters that are barren but the summers, when the plants lie dead or dormant under the dry heat. Here, autumn comes like a minor spring: the bush flowers at first rains, new growth sprouts from the trees, and colour overthrows the dead ochre. The lushness continues through winter, albeit with diminished vigour, until the full spring breaks. But at spring's end, it dries again, and the colour dies. Wildlife stay close to the remaining waterholes and streams. (Kenny 2007: 163–4)

Settlers came with horses and cattle to Wimmera in 1842, and slightly later with sheep. The cosmologies of Europeans and aboriginal Australians differed greatly, and informed relations between the two groups. Many of the aboriginal people fled at the sight of new people, who with their cattle and sheep presented images immensely different from 'life in a world where kangaroos, wallabies, emus, echidnas, possums, wombats, snakes, and lizards were the most visible things... Onto this ground enter bullocks, men on horseback, massive carts, and herds of sheep' (Kenny 2007: 167). These animals were seen, as kangaroos and other species had been for aboriginal peoples, as totemic symbols linked to the culture of the newcomers. As totems or symbols they were targets for attack by the aboriginal peoples, attacks which brought strong punitive retaliation by the settlers. Disease, including epidemics of smallpox and tuberculosis, also devastated the aboriginal Australians, after the arrival of settlers in this region in the 1840s. Nathanael Pepper became a Christian through the missionaries of the Ebenezer Mission, who strove to advance and protect his people, but his life epitomises the internal struggles between aboriginal and European cosmologies, the latter linked in part to social Darwinism, and attempts to promote Christianity through indigenous converts. Pepper's life was short: he was thirty-six when he died of tuberculosis (something that he had for most of his life). In this pioneer study Kenny sensitively identifies and evaluates the many complex changes ensuing from the meeting between these two cultures in a colonial context: 'Nathanael Pepper's conversion functioned within a realm of suffering, but what he and his people in the Wimmera suffered from was not the result of missionisation or Christianity but of colonisation ... Colonisation was not a product of an imperialist ideology but of opportunism and greed' (Kenny 2007: 339).

Christianity and its Bible-based teaching was part of the colonial project, not only in its general association with the timing and location of imperial advance and colonial settlement but also in specific issues of religious ideology and practice. Adamo (2007: 22), in a postcolonial critique of Western missionary engagement in Africa, examines the ways in which 'African biblical studies, especially the Psalter, have also been colonized in various ways'. He uses a categorisation of these colonial biblical interpretations proposed by R. S. Sugirtharajah, which includes the inculcation of European cultures; the encroachment of alien values; the displacement of local culture; biblical analogies in support of European conquest; the textualisation of belief; and the historicisation of faith (Sugirtharajah 2001: 61–73). To this he adds in a contemporary setting the continuing presence of colonial thought in theological colleges and seminaries in Africa, where 'our curriculum betrays us as still being slaves to the tradition of western biblical scholarship', a process also promoted in theological institutions outside Africa that are attended by African biblical scholars. He feels that a process of decolonisation of the Psalter for Africans needs to take place in these institutions. African cultural hermeneutics entail the use of African comparative, evaluative, Africa-and-the-African-in-the-Bible, the Bible as power, African bibliographical, and reading with the ordinary people approaches' (Adamo 2007: 23, 24, 228).

In spite of the promotion of Christian religion together with commerce and wider moral secular issues, there were also difficulties for proselytisation from the mid-nineteenth century, for example after the Indian Uprising/Mutiny of 1857, the rebellion/uprising in the West Indies in 1865, and the fizzling out of Livingstone's attempts to bring both Christianity and commerce to Central and East Africa (Porter 2005: 53–4). Strategies were changed, focusing more on 'faith missions' and interaction with indigenous peoples in situ, quite often in very remote areas, accompanied by a weakening of metropolitan influence on missionary society policy, and an infusion of pre-millennial philosophy (Porter 2005: 54–5). This produced change from the Enlightenment-rooted ideas which underpinned notions of linking Christianity with commerce and the advent of peace and prosperity, and replaced them with a more apocalyptic prospect for the world and the consequent need for widespread repentance.

Commerce and the civilising mission

There were, as we have already seen, links between the attempts to advance Christian beliefs and the development of commerce, opened up by the 'discoveries' of explorers such as David Livingstone during the middle and later nineteenth century, through explorers' real or anticipated discovery of a variety of agricultural and industrial raw materials in colonial territories. Gründer has claimed that the Protestant world took as a model the programme of David Livingstone (1817–73) for linking Christianity and commerce, with an emphasis on the need to replace the iniquitous slave trade with a moral and legitimate trade, and that this precept was strongly influential on missionary thinking for a long time (Gründer 1988: 85). Gründer asserts that the Christianity and commerce maxim, in the form of 'humanitarian idealism, philanthropism, and "free" trade' was in part the outcome of the emancipation brought by the Industrial Revolution and the French Revolution. He is speaking mainly about the middle classes, notably the British Protestants who had founded the modern missionary movements, which had also influenced missionary activity from continental Europe and North America. His idea is that this freedom, characterised by the 'transition from a bureaucratic to a constitutional-liberal state', allowed a new 'bourgeois individualism' that could support action independent of the state, including the promotion of missionary activities in the interior parts of Africa. Livingstone's travels in East and Central Africa set off new missionary activity, just as H. M. Stanley's arrival at the Lower Congo in August 1877 also initiated a renewed focus on missionary activity in West and Central Africa, and also induced new commercial and territorial interests by European states (Gründer 1988: 85–6).

Christian missions in India

The relationships between Christian missions in India and the formal imperial network in which they operated were complicated, for the commitment of the British Raj to the support of the elites of different cultures and belief systems negated easy access by missions to the Indian populace. When access was formally permitted in the Renewal Act for the East India Company in 1813 the effects were contrary to expectation, in that Christian attempts at conversion succeeded in achieving the opposite: a strengthening and revision of major Indian religions and the rise of nationalistic sentiment, to be contrasted with the greater success of Christian proselytisation in areas of weak imperial authority (Frykenberg 2005: 107).

Missionary impact was seen as a contributing factor to the Uprising/ Mutiny of 1857, and suspicion about the role of missions remained after the abolition of the East India Company in 1858. Frykenberg has suggested that European and other missionary activity was most effective in areas outside the direct control of the Raj, with northward progress being made from bases in the south. Early activity by Danish missionaries had been experienced from 1706, but major missionary advance came in the nineteenth century, so that by its end high conversion rates among tribal people were being recorded in Assam in the north-east. In the period *c.* 1840–80, 'some of the most dramatic religious changes occurred in forested mountains around the territorial edges of Empire and in the interior wilderness areas of the interior', much of it promoted by indigenous Christians, backed up by logistical, training, and text printing support from American Baptists, Welsh Presbyterians and others, so that 'The intellectual and ideological roots owed at least as much to the American Midwest, Halle, and Herrnhut as to the British Isles'. Of particular note was the case of the Naga people of the Naga Hills region, whose adoption of Christianity was initiated by an Assamese Baptist, but mainly implemented by male and female indigenous pastors and teachers, securing a cultural and religious foundation whose effects stretched well into the twentieth century (Frykenberg 2005: 112, 115–16). Another sector of success was among people of low status.

In spite of the notable impacts of indigenous Christians, the formal opening of India to missionaries from outside the subcontinent nonetheless brought in a large additional number of missionaries, who were by and large not greatly effective in initiating new ideological or social movements, but who were successful in creating such institutions as schools and hospitals, as well as interdenominational rivalry. The question of caste was significant in the dealings of missionaries with Indian people. Initial support for caste separation at worship events by the Anglican Bishop Reginald Heber was reversed by another bishop in 1834, resulting in serious strictures against and punishments of Indian Christians who refused to abandon caste segregation (Frykenberg 2005: 120).

The history of Roman Catholicism in India includes a period of difficulty from 1773 to the early 1830s, in which there was only a low level of activity, but which changed from the 1830s with the establishment of new apostolic vicariates in Madras, Bombay, Calcutta and Ceylon, the Coromandel Coast and Pondicherry and Madurai; the restoration of the Jesuits (suppressed in 1773); the assumption of control over all Catholics in India by Pope Gregory XVI, and the creation of a Catholic hierarchy for India in 1886. Catholic emancipation in Britain by mid-century and migration to various parts of the British empire led to a greater Catholic presence in India and elsewhere, so that 'Catholic institutions and missionaries within the Indian Empire, like other Catholic institutions and missionaries, flourished as never before. Having no illusions or pretensions to being part of the establishment, either ecclesiastical or imperial, they could carry on with their programme beneath the radar of official sensitivities' (Frykenberg 2005: 125–6).

The Punjab was a 'missionary frontier' region of India where the conflict of religions and cultures between Hindu, Muslim and Sikh already existed, and was further exacerbated by the incoming of British and American Christian missionaries. By the 1840s the majority of foreign missionaries in India were women, and 'Universal claims clashed with local dilemmas of gender, race and imperial privilege', advancing challenges to existing institutions and customs and uncertainties about the future. Because the religious affiliations of Indians were tied very closely to complex cultural and historical nexuses, religion itself was never going to solve the problem of 'dual identity' for those Indians who received an 'external' religion. The issues and clashes between cultures and religions, as Frykenberg puts it, 'were more than religious or theological. They were cultural, political and psychological' (2005: 129). He suggests that 'the works of missionaries – agents belonging to hundreds of missionary societies from overseas – rarely benefitted from colonialism. Pre-colonial, non-colonial, and anti-colonial missionaries, taken together, outnumbered colonial missionaries' (Frykenberg 2005: 129).

The Salvation Army

The experience of the Salvation Army is particularly interesting, both as an opponent of colonialism and in its spiritual and material activities.

Cox, in his study of missionary history in the Punjab, has shown that the Salvation Army evangelists who went to India from Britain in the nineteenth century initially tried to overcome cultural differences by adopting local customs of dress and lifestyles. This was based on a view that the officers of the Salvation Army 'had in their own minds a clear sense of the difference between the Empire of Christ and the Empire of Britain' and 'were not there to promote a western way of life but to put the love of God into action through service' (Cox 2002: 234), first in large cities and thereafter in the countryside.

The organisation was founded in London as the East London Christian Revival Society by William Booth, and its name changed to the Salvation Army in 1878, accompanied by the change to a military style of uniform. In 1882 Commissioner Booth-Tucker initiated the Army's work in India, and although their activities at first were not favoured by British officials, eventually there was an accommodation of differences, and joint projects with officials, including work with 'criminal tribes' (Tolen 1991: 114–15). The Salvation Army was particularly active in the Punjab in the late nineteenth and early twentieth centuries, with numbers of Salvation soldiers there rising from 3,236 in 1900 to 18,000 in 1911, the Army's character in the region being distinguished 'by its opportunism, by its egalitarianism with respect to gender and race, and by the working-class background of its European missionaries', the last of these 'testimony to a Salvationist willingness to avoid the snobbery, professionalism, and bureaucratic clericalism that characterized male Anglican and Presbyterian missionaries' (Cox 2002: 235–6). This was reflected in their extensive use of women as leaders in missions, together with Indian men and women, an indication of the balanced gender and the anti-racist positions taken by the Army, which was more markedly anti-racist in practice than other British missionary societies.

The Army uniform, initially including white, but later red, jackets, was worn by all adherents, and extensive use was made of music, pageant and spectacle, including fireworks, processions, open-air meetings and cinema, to attract attention and promote their cause (Cox 2005: 238). Institutions which they introduced in their territories of operation mirrored many of those in Britain, so that 'Leper colonies, hospitals, homes for women, boys' industrial homes, beggars' homes, vagrants' colonies, dispensaries, orphans' homes, village schools, and boarding schools were just some of the institutions established in order to transform the nature of life on the subcontinent' (Tolen 1991: 116).

The Salvation Army was involved in the attempted reform of 'criminal tribes' (groups of Indians, who, in the context of colonial ideas about caste and metropolitan practices of social control, had been deemed 'criminal tribesmen' by legislation in 1871 and 1911) starting in 1908, when Commissioner Booth-Tucker agreed that the Army would take over a reformatory in the United Provinces. The reform of these 'criminal tribes' was partly farmed out by presidency governments to missionary societies, who set up reformatory settlements, and the Salvation Army played a prominent role in this process (Tolen 1991: 114). The purpose of the reformatory was to change the 'habitus' of individuals and communities, partly through changes in modes of dress and adornment, standards of hygiene, regulation of time and work habits, and 'induction into the processes of commodity production and the conventions of selling one's bodily activity as labor for a wage. This initiation took place in factories, workshops and industrial schools under the supervision of Salvation Army officers. External markets were established for the sale of leather-work, silk products, carpets, mats and other commodities produced in the reformatories' (Tolen 1991: 118). The Bible was also a major symbol of reform, together with other forms of written word, which enabled transformation to free status through the issue of a certificate of good conduct.

In India the resilience and roots of existing religions, notably Hinduism and Islam, meant that the missionary efforts at conversion were not greatly effective. It has been suggested that the energies of these religions were directed, in the face of Christian attempts at conversion, towards internal change and reform, such as improvements in education among Hindus in Bengal, together with searches for the finding and reinterpreting of old Hindu texts and customs, with similar researches into Quranic traditions by Muslim teachers in the Punjab and eastern Bengal in the period 1760–1860 alongside the use of Christian texts to highlight the inadequacy of Christian scriptural writings and traditions (Porter 1996: 210–11). These admixtures may well have increased senses of Indian community identities, and also encouraged opposition to colonial administrations.

One of the many interesting features of Christianity in India, especially in the nineteenth and early twentieth centuries, was its link with an increasing sense of national identity. Christians were a small percentage of the population in 1881 (about 0.73 per cent), and their numbers grew slightly, to 2.4 per cent in 1951, four years after India's independence (Oddie 2001: 348). There was an uneven spread of Indian Christians across the country, there being more in the south than the north, and in some areas of north and central India they were fearful of being overwhelmed by Hinduism, with this sense of vulnerability informing their attitudes to nationalist movements (Oddie 2001: 348–50).

The Indian Christian population was heterogeneous because of caste systems, degrees of literacy, and the types of environment in which they lived (the majority being poor rural peasants). Nonetheless, there were a few with mission education who saw the value of a clearer development of national identity, a need for greater recognition of Indian tradition, and rejection of British racial discrimination and the British administrative yoke.

Oddie cites examples of Indian Christians who, in all denominations, were discriminated against by refusal to grant them equal status with their British counterparts, a process which strengthened their feelings about India's national identity, and led, through demands for change and greater freedom of opportunity, to involvement with nationalist movements. This was not a simple process, for it led to tensions within the nationalist movement between Christians on the one hand and Hindus, Muslims and others, for the reason that Indian converts to Christianity were regarded in effect as Europeans, and not representative of Indian culture and tradition. A counter to this was the move to indigenise forms of worship, which was not greatly successful, and the development of the *ashram* movement, notably from 1921 to 1947, which emphasised and promoted the role of religion in communities and the establishment of practical aids to everyday living in those communities, which was much more successful (Oddie 2001: 351–2, 354).

Imperial power and cultural change in Africa

Missions in Africa

Missionary activity in Africa accelerated from the 1840s. There was no conspicuous evidence of an increase in the rate of conversions, but there was significant progress in the translation of the New Testament, hymn-books, prayer-books and other important pieces of relevant literature into local languages.

By the middle of the nineteenth century the Protestant missionary movement had developed strongly from its late eighteenth-century British and German origins. The German Missionary Society was founded in 1815, later changing its title to the Basel Evangelical Missionary Society, and it trained missionaries for other societies from 1816, including British and Dutch, and established its own mission centres in the Gold Coast (1828), India (1834), Cameroon (1886), Borneo (1921) and Nigeria (1951). Other missionary societies were founded in Germany, in Berlin, Leipzig and

Bremen. By the mid-nineteenth century, most main Christian denominations in Europe were active in the mission fields (Hastings 1994: 245), but were mainly funded through lay initiative. By the later nineteenth century the missionary movement was inevitably caught up with the advance of European imperial expansion, though in early phases of missionary work there was only a weak link with imperial ambition, partly because many of the missionaries came from the Free Churches and lower classes. Even the upper-class evangelicals who were politically active and who founded the Church Missionary Society (CMS) were not inclined to become missionaries. Initially the CMS recruited missionaries from Germany (the Lutheran church). At mid-century,

the missionary movement was a singularly non-denominational function of international Protestantism of a rather lay and individualistic sort. Its most characteristic organ in the early period was undoubtedly the London Missionary Society, and nearly all the LMS's ablest men were Scots. If the LMS sent out a Dutchman as its pioneer to the Cape, or Philip, Moffat, and Livingstone, all Scotsmen, if the CMS sent out a succession of German Lutherans, it was all one. (Hastings 1994: 246–7)

The movement gradually became more widespread, and was caught up in European imperial and colonial ambitions. Major changes from the 1840s included realisation of the necessity for a 'native agency', recognition for a more coherent theory of mission, the impact of a high death rate among missionaries, especially from the 1841 Niger expedition, and divisions resulting from representation of larger numbers of denominations in the mission fields, including a stronger Catholic presence. In Lyons the (Roman Catholic) Society for the Propagation of the Faith was founded in 1822, to give financial support to missions, and in the same city in 1856 was founded the Society of African Missions, which became active in West Africa, notably Dahomey (Hastings 1994: 247, 249).

A very influential agent in the development of missions in Africa was David Livingstone, the missionary and explorer. His frustration at the ineffectiveness of the existing missions in southern Africa, at the lack of encouragement of 'native agency', and at the brutalities of Boers towards Africans, was linked to his vision of gradually converting Africans to Christianity, leading to the growth of a civilised African society through legitimate trade and commerce (as opposed to the illegitimate slave trade). He became 'a British consul, a professional explorer, an anti-slave propagandist, but, above all, a sort of honorary patron and guide to the missionary world generally' (Hastings, 1994: 251).

When he returned to Africa in 1857–8, on his Zambesi expedition, he founded two new mission stations and the Universities Mission to Central Africa, but neither of these was successful. He did, however, increase metropolitan awareness of the spiritual and commercial potential of Central Africa, and the need to wipe out the iniquitous slave trade through humanitarian endeavour and legitimate commercial activity. He died in Africa in 1873 (Hastings 1994: 251–3).

There had been Roman Catholic missionary work in West Africa and the Kingdom of the Congo from the fifteenth to the eighteenth century, mainly by the Portuguese, but this influence had disappeared by the early nineteenth century (Gründer 1988). Catholic missionary activity in West and Central Africa had diminished through the opposition effected by Enlightenment thinking and the French Revolution, so that missionary planning at the beginning of the nineteenth century had to be based on very large areas. Enthusiasm was generated among the few Catholic missionaries in western and West-Central Africa by the convening of the Brussels West Africa Conference by King Leopold II of Belgium in 1876, but not for Bishop Charles M. A. Lavigerie (1825–92) whose ambitions were expressed through his foundation of the White Fathers in Algiers in 1868.

In the context of the Brussels Conference and King Leopold's proposal for the establishment of an International African Association, Lavigerie suggested that the Catholic church should undertake exploration and settlement as well as missionary work, as other European denominations were doing, leading to the development of the notion of a Christian kingdom in Central Africa. This 'missionary strategy … to encircle Muslim Central Africa in a pincer-movement from the north' (Gründer 1988: 89–90) was in fact strongly resisted by the Muslims, and required increased European Christian missionary activity in East and West Africa.

Other factors driving Lavigerie were a desire to keep ahead of Protestant missionary activities and to assist in France's nationalist ambitions for greater influence and glory, though these in his view were always to be secondary to the religious activities of his missionaries. Lavigerie envisaged an active role for the Catholic church in French imperialism, also sustaining a vision of the restoration of a Christian empire in North Africa, including Algeria and Tunisia – the former home of St Augustine (Lorcin 2004: 300; Aldrich 1996: 129). His title of 'Archbishop of Algiers and Carthage, Primate of Africa', is indicative of what he thought to be the contexts and purpose of his work. His territorial authority included West and Central Africa, and his concerns, allied to the spread of Christianity,

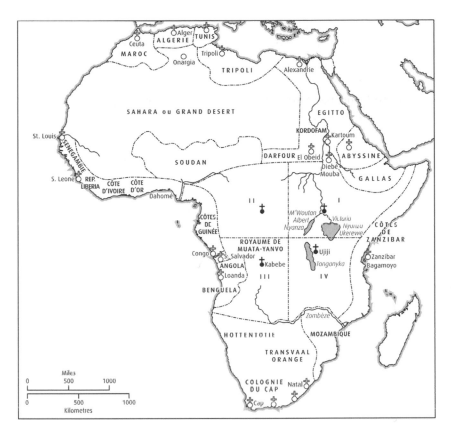

Fig. 8.5 Lavigerie's Africa: plans for Roman Catholic church administration in Central Africa. Source: Gründer (1988: 90). By permission of the German Historical Institute, London.

were the abolition of the slave trade and advancement of human rights (Wesseling 2004: 64). A map incorporating Lavigerie's religious geostrategies gives a clear impression of his ambitions.

After the Berlin Conference of 1884–5, European missionary activity in Africa was more energetic and increasingly widespread. Although missions had existed in Africa before the main European attempts at dominance and colonisation occurred, later in the century much of their activity mirrored the increasing geostrategic interests and presence of European power. Britain, though reluctant to commit herself to an extensive policy of territorial annexation (with the exception perhaps of the strategically important Cape and Suez), largely on grounds of cost, was stimulated to further colonial action in Africa by the ambitions of France, Germany, Belgium, Portugal and Italy, and by obvious opportunities for economic gain, through the goldfields of South Africa, for example. The factor that other European powers had in common was a desire to thwart British aspirations to global dominance through an increased presence in Africa.

Geopolitical issues notwithstanding, most of the governments of the European states were very reluctant to commit major expenditure to their colonies (Hastings describes it as 'a cheap and feeble colonialism'), relying instead on trading companies and missionary societies to achieve their economic and cultural ends. In this way the missionary societies and their representatives in the mission field were caught up in the colonial project, though by no means always in a conformist and supportive role.

In some cases there was, however, quite a close link between the pre-colonial presence of missionaries and their support for metropolitan policies of territorial annexation. The German Rhine Missionary Society (Deutsche Rheinische Missionsgesellschaft) had been active since 1842 in Namibia, and consistently advocated its formal annexation by Prussia. British Protestant societies (part of the established church) were also supportive of colonial protectorates, essentially to keep out missions from other European countries, as in the case of the CMS in Uganda, where it successfully campaigned for the retention of the Imperial British East Africa Company (Hastings 1994: 411–12). Changes in controlling authority also caused changes in missionary activity.

Both Protestant and Catholic missions assisted German forces during the anti-colonial movements in East Africa in 1888–9, and 'Many missionaries co-operated on principle with the administration and the military, some even with German firms; others were occasionally to be found taking the part of the Africans against officials and plantation owners, but were careful not to indulge in "unpatriotic" criticism of the colonial system as such' (Stoecker 1986a: 108). By 1914, there is evidence of the reward given to those societies that had supported the German troops in their suppression of the great uprisings in German South-West Africa of 1907–14. Among the seven largest landowners in South-West Africa were the Rhenish Mission with 140,000 hectares and the Catholic Mission with 130,000 hectares (Drechsler 1986b: 144).

Civilising mission and relations with existing religions: Islam in Africa

A distinction can be made between what might be termed Arab Africa and Black Africa. In Black Africa there was more Islamic contact with indigenous primal religions, and greater accommodation between Christianity and indigenous peoples, including a willingness to translate key texts of the Bible into local languages.

With the intensification of European involvement in Africa in the late nineteenth and early twentieth centuries, and the steady advances of Islam in West and East Africa in that period, there were differing interactions between Islam and the colonising states. Hastings (1994: 405–8) suggests that on the whole the interactions of Islam with the British, French and Germans in Africa were positive: generally

all three nations recognized how powerful Islam already was in areas they wished to control, and the last thing they wanted to do was to provoke a Muslim-inspired anti-colonial movement...Experience in India and elsewhere had long trained British administrators to treat Islamic susceptibilities, particularly where rulers were Muslims, with quite special sensitivity. The role of the Sultan of Zanzibar in the east and the sultans of northern Nigeria in the west was here of primary importance in shaping the British attitude to African Islam on both sides of the continent. (Hastings 1994: 406–7)

There was more tension between Belgians and Portuguese and Islam in Africa, reflecting close links in these two states between the state and missionary endeavour.

Religion and culture systems in South-East Asia

The history of indigenous and introduced religions in South-East Asia is both complex and dynamic, and only a few salient characteristics and developments can be considered here. A prime feature is the way in which religion in various forms guided and informed decisions from both the urban and the rural areas, notably the latter. 'Once implanted in Southeast Asia, the universalizing faiths become localized as Thai, Filipino, Vietnamese, or whatever. Core doctrines entered into play with older local preoccupations, such as ancestor worship, invulnerability, magic, healing, worship of village and mountain spirits, and ideas of power' (Ileto 1994: 194).

Islam was introduced to the region from the seventh century AD by Muslim traders from India, Persia and southern Arabia who were active in the harbours and ports of the region. It expanded

like a slow, giant wave, starting from northern Sumatra as early as the thirteenth century and reaching Borneo and the Southern Philippines in the sixteenth century A.D. In 1300, the kingdom of Pasai at the northern tip of Sumatra had become Muslim; the first Muslim graveyards in East Java date to the same period. In 1500 Islamic polities could be found throughout Sumatra, Java, Sulawesi, and the Moluccas. Later the coastal areas of Kalimantan and the islands of Sulu, Mindanao, and Palawan joined the Islamic world. (Houben 2003: 153)

Islamic South-East Asia was affected by the expanding European colonial system from the sixteenth century, and by the main colonial era of the later nineteenth and early twentieth centuries most of the region was under European influence. Christianity had been introduced by the Spanish to the Philippines, by the Dutch to their East Indies colonies, and ultimately by the British and French to their areas of colonial influence. Christian missionaries were active in Vietnam, especially after the French took control, and parts of the Dutch East Indies, but Christianity made little progress in strongly Buddhist or Islamic areas, including Burma and Malaya. Other traditions encountered by European imperial powers in South-East Asia were Confucianism and Taoism, both originally rooted in China.

The interactions between introduced religions and their links with indigenous peoples and cultural systems were complex and ever-changing. Although there are major differences between Christianity, Islam and Buddhism, they had in common the fact that they were often used as bases for strong resistance to colonial power. Ileto states that 'Despite the differences in doctrinal content between, say, Thai Buddhism and Filipino Christianity, the religio-political terrains in which they operated were very similar, leading to striking regularities in the style of anti-colonial resistance throughout Southeast Asia' (Ileto 1994: 195). The processes involved were in many cases continuations of opposition to centralising political tendencies within the region over a long period of time. It is interesting that in the case of Vietnam, whose culture was based on a mixture of Confucianism, Taoism and Buddhism, attempts to centralise and integrate all elements of Vietnamese society were through the promotion of Confucian ideals, though this was strongly resisted, and resulted in widespread uprisings: 305 between 1802 and 1840 (Ileto 1994: 199). As elsewhere in European colonial areas, local customs were frequently incorporated into the larger religious systems, both for the creation of a more acceptable cultural and belief system and as bases for anti-authority and anti-colonial movements.

Changes within the wider worlds of the major religions also had their impact in South-East Asia, including the ways in which the increased number of pilgrims travelling to Mecca in the second half of the nineteenth century (because of greater wealth and easier travel once the Suez

Canal was opened in 1869) were exposed to radical movements within Islam. They brought back the desire for a stricter orthodoxy that would promote opposition to the Dutch in Java and Sumatra, where the existing official Islamic polity was seen as being in a poor state and in need of strong opposition from the perspective of reformist Islam. Islam was not the only basis for opposition to the Dutch colonial presence on Java, for example, for there were other secular movements with a similar aim (Ileto 1994: 206, 220–1).

Local agency in religious missions

The 'model' of the conversion to Christianity of Africans, Asians, Australian Aborigines, Maoris and the First Nation peoples of North America by well-intentioned European priests and lay missionaries in the period of high imperialism, and as part of the European civilising mission, has now been modified extensively, in rather the same way that our notions of 'heroic' European explorers opening up uncharted and unmapped parts of Africa and Australia, for example, has also changed. The major new factor is the recognition that religious promotion, like exploration, would have been impossible without the highly significant agency of local indigenous people: 'the "victory" of more orthodox forms of belief and of colonizing religion, notably Christianity and Islam, was nowhere achieved without the agency of local people' and succeeded in Africa in the nineteenth century 'only where it worked with the grain of social change in Africa itself' and similarly elsewhere where it adapted to local cultural priorities and changes (Bayly 2004: 335). The complex negotiations and engagements between indigenous believers and leaders and the metropolitan-funded missionaries were the realities of the formation of local religious and cultural beliefs. The same was true of the contemporary spread of Islam, in South and South-East Asia for example, where it succeeded through the creation of bonds of trust in trade and migrant peoples (Bayly 2004: 335).

Indigenous interaction with and agency for new European-initiated religious missionary movements was a complex process. Rather than initiating a direct and total acceptance of, for example, European-based Christianity, by indigenous peoples, the arrival of missionaries set in train at least a three-way process, involving the route from Europe to the indigene, their response, and consequent attempts by both principal parties to accommodate the tenets of the other's faith and culture. Peggy Brock

(2000) has captured this complexity in her analysis of 'first' encounters between missions and indigenous peoples in British Columbia and south-west Australia.

Much depended here and elsewhere on the economic activities of the target populations, some of them mobile, others more sedentary with settlements in villages. Conventional missionary practice, for the most part imitating life in Europe, was to locate in settlements where churches and schools could be established. Major challenges were presented by pastoral and nomadic societies, where a more itinerant mode was needed. Brock has shown that although settlements were generally needed as a base for European missionaries, a more itinerant mission could be offered by indigenous evangelists, and occasionally by some European sects, travelling for example along the coast and rivers of British Columbia to attend those involved in hunting, fishing and mining. Initially there were no aboriginal villages in south-west Australia from which missionaries could operate, but by mid-century mission stations and monasteries formed a focus for missionary activity, and a refuge for aboriginal people from Australia's increasingly colonising society and from the risks of children being sent far afield for schooling (Brock 2000: 168, 171).

Humanitarian components of the civilising mission

While the many negative aspects of colonialism have been researched and analysed, more recently there has developed a mode of analysis that looks at more positive aspects of colonialism, including humanitarian and philanthropic motives and outcomes. Lambert and Lester, for example, have outlined the possibilities for such an approach in their work on geographies of colonial philanthropy in the British empire in the eighteenth and nineteenth centuries (Lambert and Lester 2004: 320–41; see also Lester 2001; Lester 2004).

The essence of the Lambert and Lester thesis is that 'Imperialism was, and is, about far more than simple domination of other people in distant lands. It entails such domination, but has always also entailed idealist and "progressive" agendas for intervention in the interests of colonized subjects' (Lambert and Lester 2004: 320). They contend and demonstrate that there was much debate of utopian/philanthropic issues, including aspects of land appropriation and treatment of indigenous peoples, along and across *networks* of imperial communication, and that such debates took place across what in effect were global spaces, and also more locally within colonial spaces. The debates were iterative and 'co-constitutive', and are exemplified through, for example, 'the abolition of the slave trade and then of slavery itself in the Caribbean, the Cape Colony and the rest of the British empire; the "opening up" of India to Christian evangelization; and the appointment of "Protectors" and return or reservation of land to safeguard indigenous peoples from British settlers in the Cape, Australia, New Zealand, and British North America' (Lambert and Lester 2004: 321–3).

British philanthropists were motivated in their concern for humanitarian issues abroad by linked problems of inequity, poverty, and discrimination at home. The dissemination of anti-slavery opinion was facilitated by the already well-developed networks of circulation of 'capital, labour and commodities', and drew together agencies such as abolitionist, philanthropic and missionary societies. 'Thus was a vast and disparate array of fragmentary knowledge and impression moulded into colonial philanthropic discourses that embraced the entire imperial expanse.' The contentions and actions were not, of course, just one-way, and they were opposed by various groups of West Indian planters for whom continuation of the slave trade and slavery was deemed essential, who equally used 'circuits of communication and imagination' for their particular purposes (Lambert and Lester 2004: 324, 326). Webs of conceptualisation, communication and action often overlapped, but some, notably those based on metropolitan governmental nodes, were more extensive than those of, say, isolated missionaries in Africa, India or Australasia.

Education systems in the European colonies

An accurate balance-sheet of educational achievement under colonialism is difficult to produce. While it is clear that basic education was provided under religious (including missionary) and secular agency in many colonial territories, and progress was made in basic practical skills, its very provision carried long-lasting ideological and cultural effects, such as the use of an alien metropolitan language and other links to European cultures, and a general neglect, at least until after the First World War, of secondary and higher education. Other difficulties accrued from the use of European curricula and textbooks, the creation of an educated elite that adopted European rather than local cultural stances, the weakening of traditional local religious beliefs and cultures, and suppression of the roles of women (Opoku 1990b: 336–7). Writing on Africa, Opoku is also of the opinion that 'it is not that colonialism did not do anything positive for Africa, but that, given its opportunities and resources and the power and influence it wielded at the time, it could and should have done far more than it did', including for education.

Part of the perceived civilising mission was a great variety of attempts to improve the practical and in some instances the basic literary skills of indigenous peoples. The main focus of the European agencies involved in the process varied from one state and institution to another. The basic agencies were schools, which

> were the foremost mediators of these [colonial] cultural values. They were run partly by missionaries and partly by the state. Some educational institutions were non-missionary private schools. France preferred a public instructional system, while Great Britain, Belgium, and Germany let the missions run the schools, providing only subsidies. Since education was not usually a priority for colonial politics, local variants were all of different types. (Österhammel 1997: 100)

Colonial educational processes were, like most other aspects of the 'civilising mission', caught up in the interactions between the wider policies of the imperialists and local practices (Madeira 2005: 57). A major feature of colonial educational and religious systems was the debate over appropriate languages to be used: that is, local colloquial languages or the language of the coloniser. Use of the metropolitan language would certainly facilitate communication at certain levels, but it was also feared that it would expose indigenous peoples to dangerous revolutionary ideas. The use of local languages was a major concern and policy of missionaries in their endeavours to promote Christianity, and also to facilitate, through translation, local knowledge of the Bible and the inculcation of further practical skills. Approaches to indigenous language and educational systems varied, with Quran schools being prohibited in some Islamic regions such as Algeria and allowed in others such as Malaya (Österhammel 1997: 101).

The basic choice for colonial powers in their creation of goals for education in colonial territories was whether to focus on the education of an elite that would provide a skilled administrative labour force and perhaps political support, or on the education of a larger part of the population (Wesseling 2004: 60). In many cases the means of instruction of the administrative elite was in the European language, with mass education, where it developed, being in local languages. In the case of India, the main choice was – in terms of government support – Anglicisation of an Indian elite and instruction through the English language, though there was education at a lower level and without government support in Hindi and Bengali, and there were also Muslim and missionary schools.

In a historiographical review of British imperial educational concepts and agency in India, Whitehead has outlined the contrasting views on education at the beginning of the nineteenth century: the Orientalist view, seeking to promote indigenous cultures and languages; the missionary view, highly critical of Indian practices such as sati and the caste system, and seeking to improve Indian society; and the Utilitarian view that sought reform of Indian society through science and technology and via European ideas of justice and progress (Whitehead, 2005a: 318). Attempts to develop and shape an education policy in India during the period of East India Company rule were inconsistent, and the 1857 Uprising/Mutiny ended the company's role in India and ushered in the need for new thinking. This took place along the lines of market forces, the dynamic of supply and demand varying regionally, so that the possibility of an overall policy was remote. There was considerable expansion in British-based education in India later in the nineteenth century, but it was mainly aimed at improving the quality of secondary and tertiary education (even though the needs of primary education were much greater) and for which there was a demand from white-collar workers to support the complex administrative systems (Whitehead 2005a: 320). The problem of primary schooling, in village schools in particular, related to the lack of money for payment of a fee, the operation of the Hindu caste system which did not encourage upper classes to take an interest in the education of the lower, and the Hindu and Muslim traditions that gave low priority to the education of girls.

The emphasis by the British on a Western/European style of education and at higher levels (even though they recognised the importance of trying to create and support village primary education, which was opposed by the rural populace and by Hindus) meant that it had very little influence on the mass of the population, whose education, where it existed, was through Islamic, Hindu and Bengali schools and Christian missionary schools. The latter had less British government support than in Africa, on account of the concern about opposition from Hindus and Muslims to attempted conversions. Education became the responsibility of elected Indian provincial governments in 1921, after a period in which efforts were made to adapt educational provision to local conditions, reflected in the report of the Royal Commission into Decentralization in India of 1909 (Whitehead 2005a: 323–4).

In Africa, British colonial educational policy also varied, with much of it based on pragmatism rather than general principle. In places such as the

Sudan and northern Nigeria, where there was a very strong Islamic presence, governors played down the Christian missionary school ambitions, though missionary educational provision overall had a major effect on primary education in Africa, with support from the British government. The challenges facing British administrators and policy-makers of education in colonial South Africa were not dissimilar from those posed elsewhere in the British empire, notably India, in respect of the role of education for indigenous peoples. As late as 1938, H. S. Scott, once director of education in Kenya, writing about 'The content of native education' in South Africa in his section on education in W. M. Hailey's *An African Survey*, outlined the difficulty.

The problem of native education is peculiar because the circumstances of an undeveloped race are different from those of a homogeneous and relatively static modern community. In such a community, the chief function of education is to maintain the continuity of culture by transmitting to successive generations not only accumulated knowledge but acquired standards of value and conduct; in Africa education is, and is intended to be, an instrument of change. (Scott 1938: 1207)

It would be wrong to assume, however, that there was a simple Africa–British dichotomy in discourse about education in Africa, for there was clearly disagreement within Britain over education in the colonies, evidenced by the concern of both metropolitan and Africa-based educationalists at the perceived apathy of the Colonial Office on this matter, and also the influence of African initiative in seeking European-style education for the purpose of material advancement (Whitehead 2005b: 444–5). Whitehead has argued that the British government was very late (the 1920s) in its attempts to produce a consistent general policy for education in Africa, and this is confirmed by Scott in Hailey's *African Survey*, where he outlines the main tenets of this policy. They were the adaptation of policies to indigenous tradition; training leaders in local communities; the achievement of better standards of living; with the 'greatest importance to be attached to religious teaching and moral instruction. The most effective method of training character was considered to be the residential school' (Scott 1938: 1229–30).

The policy recognised the fact that most schooling was provided by missions, and that these were supported by grant aid. The significance of indigenous languages for instruction at primary level was also accepted, but with the very strong proviso that English must be used for higher levels and for technical schools. The prime agency for primary and secondary schools would be the missions, with government responsible for higher and technical instruction, with some help from the missions.

Within the British empire the educational policy of mission schools varied greatly, mainly according to local conditions and customs. In general terms it was the European missionaries themselves who took responsibility for education, as against the widespread use of indigenous pastors for conveying the Christian message. This type of education provision was remarkably original, bettering in some cases the inadequate provision for education in parts of Europe. In the colonial territories British missions provided education free of charge, and encouraged the education of both boys and girls in co-educational boarding schools. In sub-Saharan Africa there were problems with the education of girls and women, a negative cultural feature of African society which related to control and tradition, and sometimes Anglican missions in Bantu-speaking Africa paid in cattle for girls to attend school (Etherington 2005: 263).

In other parts of the British empire missionary education was welcomed, for example in the colonies in the South Pacific. In Australia and Canada the migrations of indigenous peoples led to attempts at stabilisation through the founding of mission settlements. In Australia this process had sinister racial undertones. Etherington (2005: 264) suggests that the

Canadian Schools hoped that their students would return to their own people as adults and act as emissaries of 'Christian civilization'. Australian schools had a more sinister character. State policy made them a dumping ground for Aboriginal children of mixed descent, whose descendants, it was hoped, would eventually lose all visible traces of 'coloured' ancestry. Most of those children – the so-called 'stolen generations' – never saw their mothers again.

Attempts in India in the early nineteenth century to provide a government-initiated education scheme, including the teaching of English for the purpose of training junior administrators, were supplemented by Christian mission schools doing the same, and adding, despite protest from Islamic and Hindu societies, instruction about Christianity. In the British empire as a whole there were great variations in elementary school teaching. One of the most difficult factors in the missionary education of indigenous children was that of race: the direct or indirect discrimination against indigenous young people by attaching conditions to government grants that limited the extent of 'improvement', on grounds of an assumed limited potential, to manual work of one kind or another, and by (contradictory) criticism of missionary education for its potential to facilitate insurrection. Racism and discrimination were part of this conceptual package, conspicuously in British territories in South and East Africa (Etherington 2005: 271).

Education in the French colonies

Initial French provision in the early nineteenth century came through support for mission-based education, but progress to mid-century was slow, partly because of the seeming lack of vision about the role of education in the French *mission civilisatrice* (Scott 1938: 1261–2). A principal concept governing France's relations to her overseas territories was 'assimilation' – a 'policy aimed, in bureaucratic terms, to make colonies little overseas Frances and perhaps, in the fullness of time, to turn Africans, Asians and islanders into French men and women of a different colour' (Aldrich 1996: 110). In practice, as with other European empires at the time, this was more difficult to achieve, because of the enormous variety of cultures and environments that the French encountered, and the policy was changed to a wider concept of 'association' by the early years of the twentieth century.

Education policies were developed and adapted to particular needs and circumstances. Early provision for education in the French colonies, in addition to the local provisions that already existed, for example in Muslim schools, had been made by missionaries, and further provision was made through government-sponsored state schools, reflecting in part the increasing separation of church and state in France, which climaxed in the early years of the twentieth century (Aldrich 1996: 225) with the passing of the enabling law on 9 December 1905. One of the consequences was that missionary schools had to give instruction in French and to promote loyalty to France, and their teachers had to have the same qualifications as teachers in the secular government schools.

The use of the metropolitan language was part of the assimilation policy of the French in their colonies, partly for fusing cultural traditions and partly for the training and control of indigenous administrators. Nonetheless there were occasions when, in the schools in Hanoi for example, classical Chinese was permitted as a substitute study for Latin and Greek (Österhammel 1997: 101). The matter of language in education is part of a bigger issue of assimilation of colonial peoples into a centralised metropolitan culture as against a laissez-faire policy. There are ideological bases for these contrasting colonial philosophies. Assimilation for

France was linked to basic egalitarian ideas that derived from the French Revolution and the abolition of slavery, and a wish for centralised control of colonial territories. In the British case, emphasis on cultural adaptation and use of local customs and organisations in their colonial polities reflected a more limited interest in overseas expansion (Clignet and Foster 1964: 191–2).

Clignet and Foster, and more recently Madeira, have pointed out that although France has been categorised as an assimilator, and Britain an advocate of indirect rule and the use of local political structures in the colonial system, the distinction is inaccurate. This is because there are instances of both Britain and France adopting, for certain of their colonial areas in Africa, the policies associated with the other, and it is interesting to note how Portuguese colonial educational policy drew on both of these (Madeira 2005: 36). In parts of Africa and India controlled by Britain, 'the fragmentation of traditional political authorities made indirect rule impracticable. Where traditional political unity did not exist, it was often necessary to impose unity by direct administration' (Clignet and Foster 1964: 192). Equally, although Algeria under French hegemony was part of a centralised assimilation process, other parts of French Africa, such as Morocco and Tunisia, had degrees of autonomy, as did the kingdom of Moro Naba in Upper Volta and the kingdom of Sanwi in the Ivory Coast, both of them French protectorates in the nineteenth century (Clignet and Foster 1964: 191).

Belgian and Portuguese colonial education policy

The education policy of the Belgian government for the Belgian Congo relied enormously on missionary provision, both Catholic and Protestant, particularly for the education of the indigenous peoples. The terrible atrocities in the Congo region, when it was a part of the personal fiefdom of Leopold II, led to the transfer of power of this territory to the Belgian government in 1908. There had been Catholic and Protestant missionaries in what had been the Congo Free State, with the balance of favour allocated to Roman Catholic orders after a 1906 concordat for missions in the Free State between Leopold II and the Vatican. The policy followed by the Belgian government after 1908 was one of reliance, more than in British colonies, on religious orders. By 1941 there were 5,252 subsidised mission schools for Africans in the Congo, six state schools for Africans, and three for European children (Mason 1944: 235). Among the main missionary groups were the Christian Brothers, the White Fathers and Sisters, the Marist Brothers, the Salesian Fathers and the English Baptist Missionary Society. Scott (1938: 1271) highlights the French–Belgian contrast in colonial education provision: 'it may be said here that the Belgian policy assigns to the African a different cultural future from that envisaged by the French; it looks less to his association with European civilization than to his fuller development within the range of his own economic and social environment'. It differed also in that the teaching of Belgian languages, especially Flemish, was only required for Congolese who were likely to have contact with Europeans; otherwise local languages were the mode of instruction.

In Portuguese colonies in Africa the main language of instruction was Portuguese, and the general policy of education was similar to that of France. Portugal as a colonial power was forced by the activities of other European countries in Africa, by consequent treaties of agreement from 1884 to 1891, and by internal social and political changes, to intensify her effective occupation of territories in Africa, and concede rights for establishing missionary stations. Madeira shows how 'three main themes dominated the colonial educational discourse: assimilation of the indigenous population to the Portuguese culture; the creation of an indigenous working force through practical education; and the nationalization of the indigenous population through the civilizing mission of the Portuguese towards the primitive peoples' (Madeira 2005: 47), a combination of the assimilationist and indirect rule colonial policies of the British and the French, though support of the civilising mission by the Catholic church in respect of colonial education actually reversed the anticipated roles of church and state, notably in Mozambique. A broader and yet equally important point raised by Madeira concerns the fractures between ideal metropolitan educational ambitions for the British, French and Portuguese colonies and local implementation. Global and local debates on colonial education were 'open to contestation and reshaping' within and between the colonial hegemonies of European states, and involved a 'power–knowledge discourse aimed at constructing colonial subjects as individuals, enabling them to imagine themselves as belonging to a particular cultural polity' (Madeira 2005: 34, 56).

German colonial education

The German colonial experience in Africa was short-lived, and the policy for education in two of her colonies – German South-West Africa and

German East Africa – shows elements of the pragmatism and adjustment evidenced in British and Belgian colonies, and variation between colonies according to historical and demographic circumstances. The essential difference between these two German colonies derived from the relative proportions of white European (mainly German) settlers in each. The end product at the time of Germany's loss of these colonies at the end of the First World War was a well-trained and literate African workforce in German East Africa, where there had been a larger number of European settlers, on which subsequent administrative and labour force structures could be based, and in the case of South-West Africa a remaining high degree of illiteracy (Cohen 1993: 115–34).

German South-West Africa became a colonial territory by annexation in 1884. Education for indigenous people was in the hands of a number of missionary societies, including the Rhenish Missionary Society (whose work in the region had started in 1842), and who worked among the Nama and Herero peoples, and the Finnish Missionary Society whose work began in 1870 among the Ovambo people in the north. In 1888, 1896 and 1910, Catholic missions were established among the Nama, Herero and Okavango respectively. These missions were the only providers of education for indigenous people, and promoted Christianity as a main objective through the teaching of sufficient literary skills for their pupils to read the Bible and other religious literature. Practical skills were also taught, with different emphases for young men and young girls. The large-scale appropriation of indigenous land resulted in a major immigration by white settlers, and the demand for a black or mixed-race workforce. Although the individual missions had virtually sole control of the education system, there being almost no state provision by Germany and no overall mission policy, they 'contributed to this settler ideal of cultivating black labour by the kind of education they gave to the indigenous peoples... [and] deculturalised the people and imbued them with western norms and values, believing them to be superior, and thereby severing the local populations from their traditional African culture, history and identity' (Cohen 1993: 117–18).

A range of basic academic and practical skills was taught by the Rhenish Mission, over a schooling period of four to six years, through the medium of the local language, and oral German was also taught, in contrast to the Finnish Mission which did not teach German. By 1912 the Rhenish Mission had thirty-five schools, and the Finnish Mission had thirty-nine (Cohen 1993: 119–20). Separate provision was made for mixed-race students. Cohen summarises the missionary provision of education in South-West Africa: 'elementary teaching was didactic and mechanistic, with an emphasis on rote learning. In this it did not differ greatly from most elementary schooling in Europe, where the three R's formed the basis of instruction, together with some history and geography and needlework for girls and various handicraft skills for boys' (Cohen 1993: 122), though there was some teaching about the local environment. By 1918 the total number of mission schools was 115. State grants were made to mission schools from about 1902, on the proviso that they teach the German language.

There was much better provision for the education of white children. German East Africa, in spite of being the largest of Germany's colonies in Africa, had a smaller white population (4,866 in 1912) than South-West Africa (14,816), partly on account of the perception that East Africa's tropical climate was less favourable to white settlement, and partly because of the land appropriation policy in South-West Africa. In German East Africa there were existing Islamic schools, to which were added missionary schools from the mid-nineteenth century and then government schools from 1891, with these two latter types differing in objective, the missionary schools (operated by three English and two French missions) providing religious and basic skills education, but increasingly focused on the needs of commerce and colonial administration. The government schools were adaptations of German primary schools, and at the insistence of the local governor, who was sensitive to the possibility of a conflict of national loyalty through mission training, set up schools that would create loyalty to Germany and provide junior civil servants. In missionary schools the languages employed were local vernacular and some German and Swahili, while in the German schools teaching was in Swahili, though German was also taught (Cohen 1993: 128–30). The outcome was a contrast between German South-West and East Africa, with the indigenous peoples in East Africa having been much better equipped for a post-German future than those of South-West Africa, for whom only meagre and inadequate educational provision had been made.

It will be obvious from what has been said above that a main issue of colonial systems in Africa and elsewhere was that of the education of indigenous people. One of the major criticisms of the assimilation policies in Africa was:

that they attempted to engage the interest of the pupil in matters which lay outside the needs and experiences of African life. The history and geography which he was taught were often those of Europe; the teaching of literature tended to confine itself to the grammar and syntax of a European language; there were at least some instances in which the pupil was taught the botany of European, not African, plants … it could not be said to be the type of education most adapted to help the African to make the most of his environment. (Scott 1938: 1279–80)

Metropolitan images

Although much work remains to be done on the representation of images of colonial territories in school activities and texts in Europe, some seminal publications show what might be possible. Teresa Ploszajska, for example, has argued and shown that imperial representations in school geography books in Britain at the height of imperial activity formed a significant part of the broader body of pedagogic imperial propaganda (Ploszajska 1999, 2000; Maddrell 1996). In textbook representations of Australian environments and peoples, for example, pupils learned of the barren and hostile nature of much of the Australian environment, and within a 'racialised framework of understanding, Australian aborigines were almost invariably compared unfavourably with the non-white populations of all other British imperial territories. Individually and collectively, the texts presented an almost entirely unequivocal narrative of a people they judged to be the world's most savage, uncivilised, dirty, and barbaric' (Ploszajska 2000: 130), compared with model images of hard-working white settlers. This kind of distorted image was characteristic of other school geography texts in Britain and other European countries, and these very texts were often exported without modification for use by indigenous children in the colonies to accommodate local understanding and culture, a feature that continued, shamefully, at least into the 1950s.

In this chapter we have reviewed significant questions about the 'civilising mission', especially about religious belief systems. Many of these incorporated concepts of nature and the symbolism of places, topographic features, plants and animals. In the following chapter we look specifically at the complex interactions between people and their physical environments within the imperial and colonial contexts.

In any discussion of the geographic structures of the Bengal countryside, rivers come first. This immediately qualifies the common notion of historians of the *longue durée* that geographic structures are constants. Nothing is really permanent in the deltas of the great rivers; there is little that endures. In rural Bengal – a land of torrential monsoon rains, warm and humid air, catastrophic cyclones and tumultuous earthquakes – the mighty tributaries of the Ganga carried away vast tracts in their sweep until they themselves were obliterated and lost their identities in newer, stronger, currents. It was probably the transparent transience of their physical environment that inculcated in the peasants of Bengal a spirit of resignation and renunciation. (Bose 1993: 9)

Introduction

Sugata Bose opens his classic study *Peasant Labour and Colonial Capital: Rural Bengal since 1770* with a chapter on ecology and demography, from which the above quotation is taken, and in which he places clear emphasis on the natural environments and their influences on the peasants of Bengal, especially the repeated changes of course of its rivers. This is partly conditioned, as it needs to be, by qualifying comments on the role of human agency, notably where it has 'shown a little less ability in harnessing the forces of geography than in aggravating their destructive consequences' through the obstacles to river channels and drainage systems by embankments for roads and railways (Bose 1993: 13).

One of the major aspects of human–environmental interaction in the colonial territories of European imperial powers, as shown in the above example, was the influence of natural hazards, including floods, volcanic activity and earthquakes, drought and famine, desiccation, soil erosion, climatic variation and change, and various biological hazards including insect-borne diseases. Much of the European colonial world, being in tropical or sub-tropical environments, was highly susceptible to such hazards, some of them infrequent, some more frequent. The interactions of indigenous and colonial populations with the enormously varied physical environments of territories subject to imperial power and colonial settlement have received increased attention over the last twenty years or so, and there is an extensive theoretical and empirical literature on complex human–environment links, much of it in writings on the history of geographical thought and also in the growing field of environmental history (Williams 1994; McNeill 2003; Baker 2003: 72–108; Powell 2000; Simmons 1993; Proctor 1998). It is nigh impossible to draw up a balance-sheet of losses and gains, but human populations did learn to adjust to and recover from even debilitating and destructive climatic events. Stuart Lane has also recently reminded us, that 'It is well-established that – because of spatially differentiated access to resources, including power and wealth, ability to act, or agency – the same hazard does not have the same impact everywhere. There are templates of historical-geographical inequalities that condition how people cope with hazard and risk' (Lane 2008: 67). The emphasis in this chapter will be on human agency, response to the challenges of both normal and exceptional environmental conditions, and the ways in which environments were conditioned by technology, ideology, and social and political developments, including attempts at conservation.

In the imperial contexts of the late nineteenth and early twentieth centuries, one perspective, articulated by the German geographer Ernst Friedrich in 1904, 'suggested that European global expansion and resource gathering for basic needs were based on an exploitive and destructive economy, or *Raubwirtschaft*, that had destroyed the flora, fauna and soils over vast areas' (Williams 1998: 277). Concern by British colonial administrators about the potential and actual deterioration of the hydrological environments of India and the habitats and fauna of British Africa, for example, was an ironic preface to the continuation of such exploitation on a large scale, notwithstanding the early attempts at conservation.

Approaches to environmental issues

Mackenzie has labelled as 'apocalyptic' the strong sentiments, expressed by scholars in the 1970s and 1980s, about the effects of imperial and colonial developments on environmental transformation and degradation, citing inter alia A. Crosby's book *Ecological Imperialism* (Crosby 1986). Crosby gives an account of a campaign of global imperialism, of 'organisms of all sorts being marshalled, consciously and unconsciously, for such a campaign ... These events were promoted by economics, aesthetics, sport, nostalgia, or simply absent-mindedness and inefficiency' (MacKenzie 1997: 219). MacKenzie includes in this apocalyptic group works that contrast European-created environmental damage with an assumed innocence of links between indigenous peoples and their environments – what he terms visions of 'Merrie Africa', Merrie Australia' and 'Merrie India', which are part of a 'dramatic counter-progressivism' that 'views world history as one long free fall, with imperialism as its global accelerator' (MacKenzie 1997: 220). In similar cautionary vein (and in the same book of essays) David Lowenthal argued that the evaluation of the role of indigenous peoples in environmental interaction as unfalteringly positive ('stewards blessed with inherent environmental wisdom') needs to be revised: 'Just as indigenes changed their environments more radically than settlers realized, so too they not infrequently wrought environmental havoc. No culture has a monopoly on ecological sanctity... To view indigenes as incapable of harm is as dehumanizing as earlier notions that they could do no good. Romantic primitivism jeopardizes realistic rapport with the environment' (Lowenthal 1997: 234).

MacKenzie contrasts the apocalyptic views with 'Neo-Whiggism' (which emphasises progress in bourgeois environmental ideas and practices by Europeans in imperial contexts from the seventeenth century onwards), and both this and the apocalyptic school are thought to

ascribe too much power to empire. The British Empire, vast and apparently despotic as it seemed, was in reality a ramshackle conglomerate, very far from the all-seeing, all-powerful monolith envisaged by Edward Said and his discourse theorists. It was decentralized and highly heterogeneous, bearing within it many different types of rule as well as social, economic and racial systems. What is more, its influence was felt in distinct parts of the globe over very different time-spans. (MacKenzie 1997: 222)

MacKenzie's third and fourth categories of empire/ecology types are 'the longer perspective school', which is mainly concerned with work on Africa, with fragile and marginal environments, and which sees the history of modern imperial influences as 'but one phase in much longer cycles of environmental ups and downs', of which indigenous people were cognisant, and a 'fully integrated school', which 'often deals with constructions of nature as well as the supposed realities. It also attempts to set environmental issues into their full economic, political and cultural contexts', and is at its best when incorporating trans-national perspectives (MacKenzie 1997: 222, 224). The fully integrated school of thought provides most of the underpinnings of the following parts of this chapter.

Science and colonial environments

It may be helpful to look briefly at the wider question of links between science (and the history of science) and colonialism. This is a subject with an extensive literature. Vessuri (1994: 181) has described colonial science from the end of the eighteenth century as an important tool of colonial resource extraction:

By the end of the eighteenth century, agricultural and mineral sciences were employed more systematically to exploit the resources of the colonies. New soil conditions, surveying, pests, weather conditions, transportation, and communication required scientific inputs. Economic and geobotany acquired enormous importance. Every new plant was scrutinized for its use as food, fibre, timber, dye, or medicine. Among their central tasks, professional botanists sought the best techniques for transplanting commercially viable species from one part of the world to another. Their technical work was closely linked to the establishment of plantation economies on conquered land, as reflected in the history of sugar, cocoa, coffee, tea, rubber, quinine and sisal. These activities were best carried out on institutional locations *in situ*. There was a proliferation of institutions from the last quarter of the nineteenth century onwards in many different latitudes. Botanic gardens consciously served the state as well as science, and shared the mercantilist and nationalist spirit of the times.

In the nineteenth century natural history museums also grew in number, as did various types of colonial institutes and museums nearer the end of the century. At this time schools and institutes of tropical medicine also developed, mainly but not exclusively in metropolitan settings. The pace of introduction of universities to the education systems of colonial territories varied widely, progressing quite slowly in the colonies of Portugal but more quickly in those of Spain, with acceleration in the efficacy of the systems after the achievement of independence of Spanish colonies in Latin America in the nineteenth century (Vessuri 1994: 182–4).

In Australia, in spite of government support for research and the creation of universities from the 1850s to 1914, the expatriate professors, mainly from England, and the institutions themselves contributed little to the advancement of practical science, on account of the small population of Australia, the colonial economies, and 'an emerging egalitarian and anti-intellectual tradition more intense than in North America' (Vessuri 1994: 184–5). This is a highly contestable notion, for much serious applied work was carried out by colonial and state institutions in Australia, and by gifted individuals working for them, a thesis extensively reviewed and researched by Joseph Powell, notably in connection with the historical geographies of water management in Australia. Thus:

Too many 'centre' and 'periphery' designs are stale promotions for an overused resort. Conventional analyses of Australia's imperial connection undervalue important reciprocities, impressive evidence of local initiative, and productive interchange with other settler societies. Furthermore, notwithstanding the seemingly ubiquitous influence of investment flows and the bonding relationships of high science within the British sphere, Australia's colonists also relied on their own vernacular brands of science and on a negotiation of diverse relationships with a wider world. (Powell 1997: 102)

The space within which scientific activity took place was contested, characterised by Bourdieu, Latour and others as 'a space where struggles for the monopoly of the scientific authority or credit take place' (Gaillard 1994: 205). Notions of peaceful co-existence between local and metropolitan science, conspicuous in areas of European settlement, also need to be accommodated, as do the multiplicity of processes and outcomes involved in the interaction not only between metropole and colony, but within, between and beyond the colonial territories of different European powers. The whole question of the spatial location of imperial science is now the subject of interesting revision, with older models being substituted by more complex interactive models of description and application. Livingstone, for example, has argued that there is a geography of science, in the sense that although science is seen as a universal and not a localised phenomenon, and scientists and others have underplayed possible outcomes of the locations of scientific ideas and experiments, there are significant spatial aspects to the practice of science.

Livingstone believes 'that there are questions of fundamental importance to be asked about *all* the spaces of scientific enquiry. What excites my interest, therefore, is the attempt to determine the significance for science of sites where experiments are constructed, the places where knowledge is generated, the localities where investigation is carried out' (Livingstone 2003: 3). A key aspect of this theme is what Livingstone calls 'movements of science' – the ways in which ideas and practices are disseminated and modified in transit across space and on arrival in new locations, citing as examples the movement of species of animals and people, specimens of plants, technical equipment and techniques, including those of mapping and survey, the links between scientific societies, and the characterisation of zoo-geographical regions, by Darwin and Wallace, for example (Livingstone 2003: 135–86).

These observations are relevant and helpful to an understanding of the diffusion, interaction, modification and rewriting of scientific episodes and experiences in colonial and imperial situations. Lester has argued, in the context of a 'new' imperial history, that the growing sophistication of theories based on metropole–colonial links 'is founded on an awareness that these interactions were components of much more extensive networks connecting multiple colonial and metropolitan, as well as extra-imperial sites' (Lester 2006: 231).

David Arnold, reviewing the changing historiography of colonial/ imperial science, highlighted the change from generalities about an assumed domination of a European technology diffused to imperial places to a more subtle analysis in which technology is seen 'as a cultural space in which various forms of interaction and exchange, of mimesis and reversal, became historically possible. The history of technology thus becomes less an investigation of origins and inventions (a history that has long privileged Europe) than an enquiry into uses, meanings and effects' (Arnold 2005: 87). He does not dispute the 'physical clout and ideological force' of new European ideas and 'heroic' technologies of, for example, irrigation systems and railways in the European colonies, notably from the late nineteenth and early twentieth centuries, but wonders how much they affected local populations, in contrast to 'the humbler technologies of the sewing machine, typewriter or bicycle', suggesting that 'All was not sudden change. While some pre-existing technologies clearly were rapidly displaced, many older ones quietly continued or evolved symbiotically'. He points to the historical multiplicity of centres of technical innovation in addition to Europe, and to the need to see colonies as places of technological innovation (Arnold 2005: 92, 98).

Woodland and forests

There was no major natural resource in European imperial spaces whose use was not contested or negotiated from a pre-existing use-base, and forests and woodland ecologies loom large in these discourses. The attempts by European foresters and officials to use, renew and conserve these resources took place in environmental conditions very different from those at home, and attempts at superimposing European principles and practice were frequently opposed by local people whose rights and customs of forest and woodland use, notably in tropical and monsoon conditions, differed substantially in physical composition and social context from those evolved in temperate climates. Polarised distinctions between European and local forestry use and practice may also be exaggerated, in view of the sometimes positive practical interaction of ideas, notwithstanding ideologically opposed knowledges and positions (Arnold 2005: 95–6).

In all the territories of the modern European empires there is evidence over long periods of time of gathering, hunting, shifting cultivation, tree planting, management by fire, and links with regional trading economies. Products continued to be gathered, used and sold after the advent of colonial rule: in parts of South-East Asia, for example, '"forest" or "jungle" products remained important for revenues, employment, and use, including rattans, fruit, bamboos, natural latexes, gums, resins, birds' nests, incense woods, camphor, meat, skins, animal organs, feathers, and living wildlife', the most valuable timbers including teak and *ramin* (Peluso and Vandergeest 2001: 767). They were not pristine ecological sources linked to utopian indigenous societies, the truth being, as Michael Williams puts it, that 'long before the supposed Eden was spoiled by the grasping, exploitative European invaders, shifting cultivators and peasant agriculturalists were chopping, burning and grazing their forests, changing them to cropland and grassland' (Williams 2003: 336).

India's woods and forests

A major area where both opposition and positive exchange of ideas and practices were experienced in woodland and forest management was India. The 'natural' resources of India, including its forests and woodlands, were part of a wider interest of British imperialists in the more extensive exploitation of formally and informally controlled tropical territories, notably in Africa and Asia, and in changing the customs and legal systems by which they were regulated. Improved technical knowledge and transportation systems (including the railway) facilitated and accelerated the rate of exploitation and management of local populations over long periods of time, eliminating their systems of shifting cultivation, hunting and gathering by clearing land for plantation agriculture and extracting valuable timber such as teak for commercial markets.

After the Indian Uprising/Mutiny of 1857, the abolition of the East India Company and the adoption of the role of governance of India by the British crown, there was an increasing tendency to maximise revenue through the commercial management and exploitation of resources, based on a principle of sole individual or institutional rights, and uses and ownership of land, in contrast to existing local custom and tradition, including

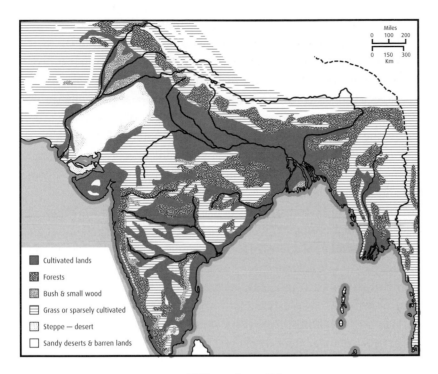

Fig. 9.1 India: vegetation. Source: Wilmot (1914: 77).

Legend:
- Cultivated lands
- Forests
- Bush & small wood
- Grass or sparsely cultivated
- Steppe — desert
- Sandy deserts & barren lands

shifting cultivation, or *jhum*. In their work on state forestry and conflict in British India, Guha and Gadgil (1989: 172) state that: 'In essence, state monopoly and its commercial exploitation of the forest ran contrary to the subsistence ethics of the peasant. To adapt a contrast first developed by E. P. Thompson in his study of the eighteenth-century food riot, if the customary use of forest rested on a moral economy of provision, scientific forestry rested squarely on a political economy of profit.'

This conflict was not just a product of new British policies for forest management in India after 1857. As Williams (1997: 175) has shown, the intense exploitation of woodlands started well before 1857: 'in the Muslim overlordship areas of the north and west, pasturing and forest exploitation had been severe' and in the south-west 'shifting cultivation existed side by side with permanent agricultural settlement' while in other areas large landowners strongly influenced forest-use practice.

At the heart of much of the conflict between indigenous peoples and colonial powers and their local representatives was a fundamental disagreement on the premises and practicalities of the rights of use of land and forest resources. The essence of colonial or imperial forest management policy from, say, the middle of the nineteenth century onwards, was that a modernising state should foster the abandonment of what were seen as wasteful land-use systems by indigenous peoples, particularly in the form of shifting cultivation, and promote more rational, commercially orientated systems, which would give higher production and better commercial prospects, together with increased tax revenue. A consequence was the increasing erosion of forest areas (and also loss of subsistence arable land) by the development of commercial monocultural plantations by Europeans, notably for the production of tea and coffee, cotton and sugar cane. The two systems, in the eyes of the modernist administrators, could not be allowed to co-exist.

Against this, traditional systems of use provided, at least in theory, not only for a rational ecologically balanced use of trees and timber, but also for a vital use of other products of wooded environments – leaves, nuts and woodland pasturage, for example. This is an important general theme, not only in British imperial territory, such as India, but in the overseas territories of such countries as Germany and France. Among others, Rajan (1998) has highlighted this contrast, which he ascribes to the policies of modern forest management developed in Germany from the eighteenth century and in France from the early nineteenth century, both of which were influential on British imperial forestry policies. In France:

As in Germany earlier, forests began to be regarded as a territory special to the economic vitality of the country as a whole and a legitimate subject for state intervention... The purpose of forestry was to serve the economic and especially industrial needs of the national economy. In keeping with the German tradition French foresters sought to convert all forested lands into commercially viable monocultural forests... The system had no place for local forest inhabitants in forest management. Local knowledge systems were consequently discredited and replaced with an approach that was based on long-term biological cycles that suited the nation's economic, and especially, industrial needs. (Rajan 1998: 342)

This mapped on to the character of British forest management in India from 1850 onwards, with the establishment of the Indian Forest Service, staffed initially by foresters who had been trained either in the French forestry school at Nancy or in various forestry schools in Germany (Rajan 1998: 343). Williams estimates that in South and South-East Asia in the period 1850–1920 'crops increased from 78 million to 119 million ha (net change of 41 million ha), forests and woodland declined by 33 million ha, and grasslands declined by a net 8 million ha', the decline in forested area in India in this period being the outcome of railway expansion, an increase in population of 236 million, and the commercialisation of agriculture (Williams 2003: 355, 357).

A Forest Department was founded in India in 1864, and relevant forest management legislation introduced in 1865. There is an interesting connection between the essentially conservationist policies of the Indian Forest Service and the ideas of the American George Perkins Marsh on environmental degradation by human agency and the need for conservation measures, as, for example, expressed in his book *Man and Nature* (Rajan 1998: 350). A new administrative control was thus placed over forests and forest-use policy in India, which by the end of the nineteenth century controlled one-fifth of its land area (Williams 2003: 366). Forest Acts – in 1865 and 1878 – gave greater power to the Indian Forestry Service, and the few districts not covered by these Acts had similar authority by 1890 through their own official legislation. Power was given to foresters not only over preserved and protected forests, but also over village and communally managed forests and woodland, in the latter case resulting in a wholesale condemnation of grazing of animals in forests, an attitude of ecological moral superiority towards such use, and the conviction that more education had to be given to local communities about their proper use of this resource (Rajan 1998: 352), in respect of the use of wood for construction purposes by villagers, together with their customary use rights over pasturing, the gathering of fruits and nuts, and the taking of game. This inevitably led to conflicts between the technocrat foresters, local forest-use customs, and other agencies of government (Williams 1997: 178; Rajan 1988: 361).

Accounts of the historical use of forests and woods in India are beginning to include aspects of positive interaction between local and colonial use systems. One example is provided by Mahesh Rangarajan's (1998) study of forest management in India's Central Provinces between 1850 and 1930. In the Central Provinces control of large forest areas was partly vested in the private forestry areas of land agents and land tax collectors, the forests containing mixed deciduous forests including *sal* (*Shorea robusta*) and teak (*Tectona grandis*) (Rangarajan 1998: 576–7). Conservation measures were adopted in the mid-nineteenth century, though there were concerns that over-rigorous protection would drive away local tribal people who depended on forest use rights. Measures were, however, taken to preserve these use rights. There was also concern at the exploitation of timber by individuals stimulated by markets for railway sleepers, though this process in turn encouraged further conservation.

South-East Asia

The political economies of resource exploitation in South-East Asia raised interesting issues about collaboration with and resistance to colonial powers by indigenous entrepreneurs. Important features in this evaluation include the nature of the distribution of resources and also the roles of local elites. There was, for example, a marked contrast between Java and Burma in the degrees of the focus of resistance and nationalist movements on forests: 'a more overtly repressive [Dutch] colonial regime than in Burma meant that the Javanese lacked a public forum in which to voice resource and other grievances' (Bryant 1998: 47), which was reflected in the involvement of timber merchants in nationalist movements in Burma but not in Java. In the case of Burma in the late nineteenth and early twentieth centuries there was co-operation between the British colonial regime and the Burmese middle classes in the development of forest and other resources, even though the Burmese were critical of the British preference for non-Burmese business enterprises. This was a feature partially replicated in the Philippines under Spanish and then American rule (after 1898) by the indigenous owners of plantations and sugar refineries (Bryant 1998: 48).

The 'genealogies' of the differences between colonial powers, and their discourses within colonial territories, between the promoters of what they have called 'political forests' (state-designated forests) and the conservers of customary rights in Indonesia, Malaysia and Thailand, specifically in Java, Dutch Borneo, the Malay States, Sarawak and Siam, have been highlighted by Nancy Peluso and Peter Vandergeest (2001). They use Foucault's tripartite division of governmentality, involving population, political economy and apparatuses of security, and highlight two significant forest practices – the creation of special institutions for forest control and 'the codification or definition of people's rights of access to political forests' – both incorporating aspects of territorial and resource or species control (Peluso and Vandergeest 2001: 765).

The forests of this region had been extensively used for a long time before the period of high colonialism for subsistence and trade purposes, but the advent of the Dutch and the English as colonial powers ushered in new methods of production such as plantations for the cultivation of rubber, tobacco, coffee, sugar and tea, for example, and new systems of resource governance, specifically administration of political forests and scientific services. Appropriation of the legal control of land and resources was a basic process, though it varied in chronology: it occurred much later in Dutch Borneo than in the Malay States and Java. There was much disagreement about the concept of 'state forest'. The nature of regional forest ecologies was also important, including the concentration and dispersion of valuable tree species, together with the markets in which they were sold, as was the location of forests in relation to road and sea links and to centres of administration and government. Teak from the Java forests was extensively 'used in domestic colonial industries and for construction, most teak in Siam was exported, providing an important supplement to rice export earnings' (Peluso and Vandergeest 2001: 767–9). There was a very much lower percentage of areas of forest in Java, but within forest areas larger percentages (17–32 per cent) in State Reserved Forest in Java, Federated Malay States and Kedah in the late 1920s to the early 1930s than in Siam, Dutch Borneo and Sarawak (0–1 per cent). There were stronger links to commercialisation and industrialisation in Java and the Malay states, and Java had higher rural population densities than other islands or regions in South-East Asia (Peluso and Vandergeest 2001: 770–2).

Fig. 9.2 Clearance of forest for coffee plantation, Baret, Sumatra, *c.* 1880.
By permission of and © KITLV 3334, Leiden, Netherlands.

A question that vexed colonial administrators was the extent and nature of use rights over village land, a feature difficult to identify because of the general lack of survey, though in Java village maps were produced by the Topographical Survey to show taxable fields (after land rent surveys were conducted from 1907 to 1920) and use rights were also identified by default after the mapping of forests or agricultural land. In Kalimantan/ Dutch Borneo, where Dutch control was consolidated in the late nineteenth century, attempts at forest law legislation came late, and their form and the responsibility for payment for the survey and the mapping of forest land was much debated and disputed, a consequence being 'the failure of the colonial foresters to establish a centralized political forest in Dutch Borneo under colonialism' (Peluso and Vandergeest 2001: 776–7).

Forest use and management in Africa

A common theme in the history of human agency and environmental change in Africa is conflict and collaboration over the use of trees and forests that followed European colonisation, involving, as elsewhere, different interpretations of customary use and attempted innovations through European scientific forestry from the late nineteenth century onwards. Karen Brown has succinctly summarised some of the key features of this interaction in Africa. They include a tendency for colonial forestry and agricultural officers to blame Africans for land and resource degradation, then to use this as a prop for land appropriation and scientific management policies; the clash of cultures, which led to physical opposition from indigenous people because of Europeans' ignorance of the physical and spiritual significance of resource-use practices; the ecological and economic rationale of European silviculture; the foundation of official forest departments and the demarcation of reserves; the extent of collaboration between indigenous and colonial forest users; and the variety of the geographical, social, ecological and economic impacts of colonialism (Brown 2003: 343–56).

The governor of Nigeria and scientists in the Cape in the mid-nineteenth century had expressed concern at the rate of loss of forests: in Nigeria through the collection of rubber and in the Cape for timber and land for agriculture and pasture. Fears of a reduction in rainfall, and of deforestation and soil erosion, were attributed to indigenous practice in the Cape and Nigeria, for example, but also to commercial logging and to mining, as in Zimbabwe, and through the actions of poor white woodcutter populations in the Cape (Brown 2003: 346). Forest departments were established and state forests demarcated and regulated in Africa by the British, French and Germans between 1880 and 1920, with more added in the interwar period in Northern Rhodesia (Zambia), and Tanganyika (Tanzania). The extent to which the colonial powers could act in forestry management and use depended partly on the character of imperial and local power. In Nigeria, where indirect rule through local leaders operated, 'African leaders were able to negotiate far greater communal control over natural resource allocation', as also happened in Zimbabwe, where the 'economically influential commercial logging companies could often evade strict regulations', in contrast to South Africa, where there was more intervention (Brown 2003: 347).

Resistance to the regulation of forest use was quite common, even in parts of South Africa where internal disagreements between colonial administrators frustrated attempts at control, and it was also effective in Kenya in the 1950s during the Mau Mau uprising, expressed in 'incendiarism, or the selected burning of trees, as well as the illegal occupation of forests by people and livestock, the poaching of game, the destruction of boundary fences or assaults on colonial officials and headmen who collaborated with them' (Brown 2003: 349). Reforestation was actually a part of the land management strategies of some African communities, exemplified inter alia by the preservation and planting of trees in forest islands in a forest–savannah transition zone by the people of the Kissidougou district of the French colony of Guinea (but misunderstood by French colonial officials as being evidence of the decimation of formerly more extensive forest); by the indigenous soil stabilisation policies of the Soto in Lesotho; and by the preservation of fruit trees by the Ovambo from Namibia (Brown 2003: 352).

Williams has suggested that the ignorance of colonial officials of the ecological sensitivity of indigenous practices, including shifting agriculture, was particularly pronounced in the tropical forests and savannahs of West Africa, and draws further attention to the work of Fairhead and Leach in Guinea, which was extended to much of West Africa's forest belt, leading to their startling conclusion that 'views on deforestation have been unilineal and have obscured more complex histories. The extent of the forest in the past has been grossly exaggerated, thus making any diminution appear even greater' (Williams 2003: 405; Fairhead and Leach 1995).

In the German colonies in Africa the conservation of environmental resources, including the management of forest and woodland, was part of broader strategies of control of many aspects of colonial life and livelihood in the late nineteenth and early twentieth centuries. Regulations to protect trees and bushes were introduced around Windhoek in South-West Africa by 1894, partly as an outcome of the criticism of indigenous and colonial woodland destruction (*Waldfrevel*, or sins against the forest) by the botanist Hans Schinz, and by 1900 these regulations had been extended to cover the whole country (Rollins 1993). They were further extended in the first decade of the twentieth century by the establishment of nurseries and forest research stations.

A review of forest resources was undertaken at the same time in German East Africa, with conservation measures recommended, including the protection of river bank forests from erosion, something that had already been instigated in Cameroon by 1900 (Rollins 1993: 194). Three wildlife reserves were also established in South-West Africa by 1907 in recognition of the need to protect both the environment and its inhabitants, including the San Bush people, so that 'sensitivities to the local environment thus seem to have been highly compatible with a genuine respect for native cultures'. Other reserves were established in East Africa in 1908, and more in Togo and Cameroon in 1913 (Rollins 1993: 195). The seeming altruism of these decisions is, however, contested by Rollins, who points out that voices advocating the sympathetic treatment of indigenous peoples were rare in Wilhelmine Germany, and that 'The uniform enthusiasm for these measures gives one pause. When even the German Colonial Society begins to push for nature reserves, it is hard to banish the suspicion that these seemingly neutral efforts to help the environment were in fact active components of the imperial programme' (Rollins 1993: 195). Rollins shows the similarity with British colonial practice for nature reserves, which could be read as devices for de-populating regions of troublesome people. Rollins contends that in a broader context these assumptions about German superiority over African people were part of a process of self-identification, based on a national sensitivity, through the concept of *Heimat*, to land and environment – a creed that was adopted even by Social Democrats. This process may be seen as a kind of 'environmental chauvinism', which was not only experienced in German colonies in Africa, Asia and the Pacific, but also in other European colonial areas, and which blamed local people for environmental damage and offered scientific solutions to environmental management as replacements for earlier religious and philosophical underpinnings (Rollins 1993: 197; 201).

Australia, New Zealand and Canada

The temperate latitude colonies of Britain experienced major changes in vegetation, including forests, long before the period of high imperialism from *c.* 1880 onwards. Reasons included the felling of trees for commercial sale at home and overseas, the use of timber for the construction of houses, fences, ships and utensils, and the clearing of forest and woodland for agriculture. Concern among the countries of the British empire between the two world wars addressed, through the British empire forestry conferences, the need for more adequate timber provision.

Australia and New Zealand had both been occupied by indigenous populations long before the coming of European settlers and administrators from the late eighteenth century. Aboriginal clearance of the forests and scrublands of Australia reflected both the densities of population and the variations in ecological geography. The components, pattern and gradations of forest across physiographic zones at the time of the first European settlement have been characterised by Williams (2003: 328):

Australia's dense eucalypt forests are located in the humid areas in the extreme southern and eastern portions of the continent. As rainfall decreases inland large trees give way to open savannah forest, which in turn merge into scrubby trees, often the distinctive mallee vegetation – multiple-stemmed, drought-resistant eucalypts with massive lignotuber roots. Beyond that again lay mulga scrub and grassland, and finally stony and sandy deserts.

Williams estimates the extent of tree cover before settlement at about 238 to 244 million hectares, of which 30 million was suitable for timber exploitation and for clearing for agriculture, with an average of 36 per cent modification since 1789, derived from varying percentages such as 69 for Victoria and 32 for Western Australia, and indicative of the more complex 'biographies of individual forests' (Williams 2003: 328–30). The rest of the tree-covered area, though not suitable for commercial timber, was nonetheless usable for domestic purposes. The greater part of Australian forests was hardwood, with a small percentage only of the eucalypt trees usable for commercial timber, including such species as jarrah, karri, blackbutt, spotted gum, Cypress pine, messymate stringbark and mountain ash (Williams 1988: 116).

Local aboriginal impact on Australian forests was marked, especially by the use of burning, which may have been responsible for the destruction of rainforest in favour of the drought-tolerating dry sclerophyll forest, and perhaps for the creation of grassland from open woodland (Heathcote 1975: 56). Attempts to use nineteenth-century explorers' accounts of the burning of trees and other vegetation in the Kimberley region show that the practice existed, but there is ambivalence about some of the accounts which are not clear about the types of fire recorded (e.g. signal or camp fires as opposed to vegetation fires) (Vigilante 2001).

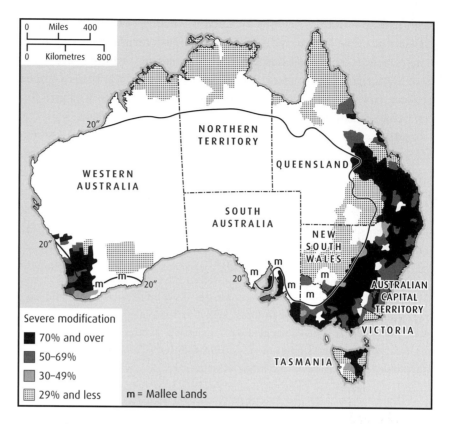

Fig. 9.3 The modification of Australian vegetation since 1780. Source: Williams (2003: 330). By permission of and © the University of Chicago Press.

More dramatic was the massive impact of European settlement on the felling of trees for timber and the clearing of woodland for agriculture and pastoral purposes. Williams (2003: 330) estimates that some 87.6 million ha of woodland were cleared in Australia between 1750 and 1920, using various methods including ringbarking and firing, with stumps left or taken out later, and conspicuously affecting the 'brutal and complete' clearing of the rain and wet sclerophyll forests and the 'Big Scrub' areas of semi-tropical rainforest across the New South Wales–Queensland border, about 4 million ha in extent (Williams 1998: 118). Of this, 'between 1880 and 1910, over 2.8 million ha had been cleared for dairying, sugarcane growing, and lumber' (Williams, 2003: 331).

Elsewhere, the purpose of woodland clearance was the creation of grassland for pastoral farming, including dairying, with cattle and sheep, and for wheat cultivation, stimulated by growing urban markets within Australia, the development of railways, and technological innovations such as the refrigerator, the cream separator and the milk-testing machine. By the end of the nineteenth century forest conservation had been introduced in all states, and in some re-afforestation had commenced, as in South Australia and New South Wales (Williams 1998: 119–22, 125), though Powell suggests that 'By 1901, forest management in the newly federated states was still laced with good intentions and largely innocent of hard design' (Powell 1988a: 39). Progress in Australian forestry was made in the first forty years of the twentieth century – the outcome of the

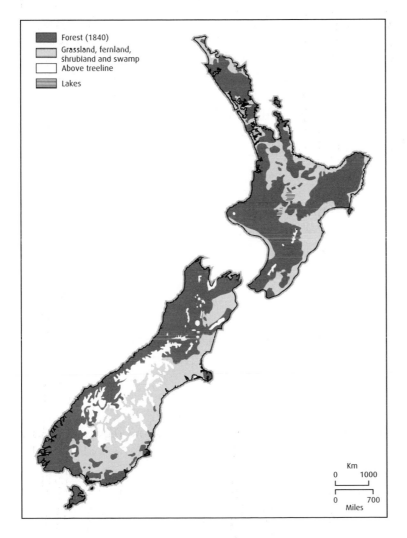

Fig. 9.4 New Zealand forest and other vegetation, *c.* 1840.
Sources: Wynn (2002: 104); © Oxford University Press, Melbourne;
Plate 12 – the forest *c.* 1840 – in McGibbon (1997). By permission of and
© David Bateman, Auckland, New Zealand.

energies of a small number of advocates and practitioners and facilitated by forestry conferences in the major cities between 1911 and 1924, which 'displayed comparable historical perceptions, including the articulation of British-style ambitions for national and imperial self-sufficiency. The need for federal initiatives and co-ordination were also popular themes' (Powell 1988a: 161). The process of developing forestry policies was also linked with the British empire forestry conferences held between 1920 and 1947 (see below).

The trees of New Zealand had been affected by long periods of modification by Maori people. As elsewhere, the impact of pre-European populations varied with different regional ecologies. Evidence for deforestation by the use of fire appears to date back to AD 1300–1400, and points to a late colonisation by groups from Polynesia. The vegetation complexes that they found essentially showed a north-west/south-east, or windward and leeward, division, the former distinguished by the prevalence of dense, humid forest, based on volcanic soils in the north, and with very large trees such as rimu and kauri. In the south-east 'there was a more open forest dominated by mataī, kahikatea, and tōtara, with beech forest in the mountains and at the eastern edges. In a few districts, such as the Canterbury Plains and inland Otago, there was a low forest of toatoa, kānuka, and kōwhai around open basins covered in light scrub and tussock' (Andersen 2002: 27).

The use of fire, for moa-hunting or for clearance for cultivation, was less effective in the more humid windward forest than the drier leeward province, with the forests of the eastern part of the South Island substantially reduced between 1300 and 1450 AD, together with part of the east coast of the North Island, in each case leaving extensive tussock grassland, and a reduction to scrub and fern ecologies in parts of the windward province. A basic characteristic of New Zealand trees was their slow rate of re-growth after burning and the absence from the forests of food sources for people (Anderson 2002: 31). European settlement had a major impact, with a reduction of the forest from 50 per cent of the land area to about 25 per cent between 1840 and 1900, notably from 1890 to 1900 when the clearing was mainly for pastoral farming for sheep and dairy production (Williams 2003: 332).

The significance of wood for New Zealand's rapidly developing European (Pakeha) population has been emphasised by Graeme Wynn: 'Nineteenth-century New Zealand was a wooden world. Its citizens' very existence rested upon the forest's bounty' (Wynn 2002: 105). Wood was used for house-building, firewood, the building of bridges and roads, fencing, and the manufacture of furniture and implements, and by 1911 New Zealand had 411 sawmills employing over 7,000 people. Kauri (*Agathis australis*) forests were a major target for cutting, with the rate increasing until the early twentieth century, whereafter it declined, but the consequence was its near elimination (Wynn 2002: 106–7). The kauri is a very large tree, and provided both timber and a resin or gum for industrial processes.

Exploitation of kauri forest, notably north and east of Auckland in the North Island, accelerated from the 1860s, facilitated by steam-powered hauling and sawing machinery and contributing to the growth of Auckland and of the frontier settlement of North Auckland and the Coromandel Peninsula. 'From the early 1870s to the 1910s sawmilling was the largest source of employment in Auckland province, with 3500 or so employed in 1906 for example. In addition, several thousand people worked the gumfields either full- or part-time' (MacKay 1997: 48). In the same period there was also massive clearance of bush in the lower North Island, described by Michael Roche as 'the biggest such clearance in the country's history and one that was questioned, if at all, more for its too rapid destruction of a valuable resource than for the process itself' (Roche 1997: 47). The process was aided by rail transport and by crown encouragement to acquire title by lease or sale.

The main agents for forest removal were settlers and farmers. Concerns at the rate of forest removal in New Zealand, and consequences such as rapid soil erosion, had been expressed since the 1840s, but forms of restraint and conservation began with the issuing of timber licences in 1849, and a New Zealand Forests Act of 1874. Forest reserves were established under the 1877 Land Act, and further steps were taken for state forests and reserves with the State Forests Act of 1886. The concern for this important resource and for New Zealand's environment was, interestingly, conditioned by events and experiences elsewhere, including the work of George Perkins Marsh and the Forest Conservancy in India (Wynn 2002: 114, 116).

Conservation continued in New Zealand in the early twentieth century. Roche has shown that there were 'significant conservation episodes between the 1920s and the 1950s', initially on crown land and later on private land from the early 1940s (Roche 2002: 183). Reduction in the over-exploitation of the forests of New Zealand was achieved by the use of: timber export controls from 1918 to 1922; exotic afforestation; the creation of a state forest service in 1921; and a National Forest Inventory in 1921–3. The government increased its involvement as an agent in forest regulation and management, including that of indigenous forests, and took various steps including enactments to promote soil and water conservation. These had parallels in Australia and the United States, with 'game management being less significant in New Zealand than in the United States, and deforestation and forest management being comparatively more important than in Australia' (Roche 2002: 197).

Canada was a colony with vast stands of forest and woodland, notably the boreal coniferous forest that makes up about one-third of Canada's land surface and over two-thirds of its forested area, comprising a 1000 km wide belt across Canada from the Yukon in the north-west to Newfoundland and Labrador in the east. To the north is the northern tundra, and to the south 'the montane and sub-alpine forests of British Columbia, the grasslands of the Prairie Provinces, and the Great Lakes–St Lawrence forests of Ontario and Quebec' (see http://atlas.nrcan.gc.ca/site/english/maps/environment/forest). The boreal forests were the homes of both sedentary and nomadic indigenous peoples.

During the nineteenth century there was extensive felling and clearing of boreal forest in Canada, much of it for export to Britain, Europe and the United States. The uses for trees, sawn lumber and square timber were many and varied. Trees for ships' masts for the Royal Navy were felled and cut in the Maritime Provinces and St Lawrence valley, together with lumber – mainly in the form of planks or boards – processed in sawmills, and axe-hewn square timber for export to Britain, where the demand was substantially increased during the Napoleonic Wars (Wynn 2006).

From the 1830s there was an expansion in the timber trade with Britain and the United States, the major species being pine, with a rapid extension of the industry in eastern British North America between 1810 and 1850, and with the advent of railways extending the areas of lumber production to the west and the north. Forest exploitation was regulated in the 1820s in New Brunswick and Upper and Lower Canada, and licences were employed to restrict illegal use. Increased mechanisation, access and entrepreneurial scale were characteristic of the later nineteenth century, and a major lumber industry had started in British Colombia on the west coast from *c.* 1850, using the Douglas fir and red cedar, and selling initially to markets around the Pacific (Wynn 2006).

A major factor in the deforestation of British North America/Canada was the growth in demand for wood exports to Britain and the United States. Wynn (2007: 205) points to the dramatic increase in demand: a 500 per cent increase in wood exports to Britain between 1850 and 1870; an increase from 22 per cent by value of its exported wood products to the United States in 1850 to nearly 42 per cent by 1870, and exports from Canada to the United State 'climbed more than threefold (in value) from the depression-induced trough of 1879, to a nineteenth-century peak in excess of $15 million in 1896'. The increase in deforestation was aided by major advances in technology, including transport and the application of steam-power to sawmills (Wynn, 2007: 207).

Forest and woodland were also cleared for agricultural land. In the period from *c.* 1910 to 1940, a new, boreal frontier opened to farm settlement across the width of Canada, in effect, as John Wood (2006: 39) states, 'a transition from one kind of agricultural frontier to a fundamentally different one, from prairie/parkland to naturally wooded land, comparable with the reverse transition from the eastern woodland to the prairie two generations earlier, and requiring different skills and farming techniques'. A somewhat idealistic notion was held by government officials about the potential of the boreal forest land for frontier settlement. They overlooked the use rights of indigenous First Nations peoples and held disparaging views of Ukrainian and other eastern European settlers. Enticements to settle included propaganda promoting western regions from the federal government, provincial government incentives, the northward extension of railways in Ontario, and the Catholic church sought to advance a Christian perspective of socio-economic order through its Union Catholique des Cultivateurs in Québec (Wood 2006: 41, 42). The settlers' perceptions were partly influenced by the notion that the amount of land available for settlement was rapidly reducing, and were also linked to an ignorance of the harshness of the conditions, including the 'coldness and unpredictability' (Wood 2006: 44) of the weather, the poor podsol soils, alfisols in the west, and wet histosols at the margins. The failure rate of new settlement was high, exceptions including the settlement of the Peace River region of Alberta extending later into British Columbia (Wood 2006: 51).

British empire forestry conferences

Concerns within the British empire about environmental degradation, mainly through deforestation, had been expressed and acted on in India since 1855, though general concern among European states about its effects on climate dated back to the seventeenth century. Barton maintains that 'Only in the British Empire did a multi-use forestry programme first solve the tensions between laissez-faire notions and the need for far-sighted state management of resources' (Barton 2001: 543; 2002), and that this concern was then routed via Africa and Australasia to Canada, the

United States and other parts of the world. This singular thesis, based on a perspective of officials and imperial policies, is open to dispute, on grounds of underestimating earlier research, the examples chosen, and a limited coverage of the contemporary literature (Powell 2004).

These discourses of forestry and environmental best practice have been reviewed by Powell in his study of the British empire forestry conferences (Powell 2007). Meetings were held in London in 1920 and 1947, Canada in 1923, Australia and New Zealand in 1928, and South Africa in 1935, but no meetings were held in Africa or India. They were motivated by the shortage of timber after the First World War, and the concern for a resource and geopolitical counter-balance to the growing power of Germany and the United States, and evidenced in British ideas for an Imperial Forestry School based in Britain, though this was not supported by the Dominions (Powell 2007: 9). The Canadian conference of 1923 raised, among other topics, the long-running question of shifting cultivation in Africa and Asia, from which there were few representatives at the conference.

The Australasian tour of 1928 provided an opportunity to experience different types of woodland, and for further discussion about the links between deforestation, climate and soil erosion (Powell 2007: 13, 17). The series as a whole provided a valuable forum for discussion, and also highlighted common and individual concerns of an ecological and geopolitical turn. Powell concludes that '"Empire forestry" would be unfairly portrayed as a quixotic quest. It could scarcely be claimed that other imperial projects – for example immigration and settlement, trade, and communications – were in comparison unalloyed successes. But they must have seemed rather more tangible and accessible, less open-ended, and arguably more susceptible to stable configurations in time and space' (Powell 2007: 26).

Water use and management

Water is everywhere a vital necessity for the existence of humans, animals and plants, especially in areas of shortage and variability of supply, and its influence is a result of human activity and climatic fluctuations. The history of water use and management encompasses a very long period of time.

The water management systems of the European colonial territories in the nineteenth and twentieth centuries evidenced both continuity and innovation: continuity with ancient systems, and innovation through technological advances in engineering and in forms of capital investment and labour management and exploitation. They also illustrate the complex constraints placed by the colonial powers on the existing political ecologies of water use by means of changes in land tenure, land taxation, unsympathetic attitudes to pre-existing systems and restrictions on expenditure. Technological innovation was not always on a large scale: water supply was enhanced by quite small technologies such as windpumps in arid areas of Australia, for example. Nor was technical advance in water management always beneficial: it could result in waterlogged soils and the production of conditions conducive to malaria. The absence or excess of water supplies was a major contribution to the incidence of famine and flood and the marginality of human life.

It is necessary to bear in mind that water is not an independent 'given'. Mosse reminds us that 'water resources are never simply there, but are produced, used, and given meaning by shifting social and political relationships'. He also draws attention to Sivaramakrishnan's 'caution against recent theorizing in environmental history' and 'the emphasis of cultural geography on representations, especially the inherent instability of meaning [which] is often taken to the point of making nature epiphenomenal or passive, a text, a spectacle, icon, or theatrical production' (Mosse 2003: 3).

Irrigation systems in India

Much of the history of irrigation works in India can be reviewed, according to Mosse, under two headings: engineering and management paradigms. The first, characteristic of much colonial thinking, saw irrigation as 'a mathematically modelled system which can be engineered to maximize water control'. The second, the management model, focuses more on human behaviour, especially efficient use of water resources. Both of these approaches, however, pay insufficient attention to significant social and political processes (Mosse 2003: 20).

India has a long history of water management, including dry land irrigation and the management of wetland in the form of paddy-fields. Indications of sophisticated water-management systems from prehistoric times survive, in the Indus valley, for example. More generally there is historical evidence in rice-growing areas and elsewhere of wells, water storage cisterns and reservoirs, and in some lowland areas there are very old barrage and canal systems. These historical legacies, especially the larger schemes, largely fell into disuse in the second half of the eighteenth century through political and military conflict, but in the early nineteenth century

the Military Engineers of the East India Company began to take a strong interest in the restoration of some of these older works. This was not as incongruous as it seems: much that was taught to military engineers of the period concerned fortifications, with massive stone abutments and revetments, in short building skills allied to those now required. Starting in the 1820s in the Western and Eastern Jumna in the North-West Province near Delhi canals were repaired and renovated. In the 1830s in Madras Major Arthur Cotton redeveloped the Grand Anicut (Barrage) on the Kaveri (Cauvery) and its distributaries, and then later the Krishna–Godavari delta as well. (Chapman 2000: 107–8)

The history of water provision and management in India closely reflects aspects of its geography, especially its climate. Some areas receive very high amounts of rainfall, and others very small amounts, and the reliability as well as the quantity of rainfall is a crucial factor. Thus there are some areas where irrigation makes agriculture possible by providing much more water than is naturally available, others where irrigation is designed to even out water availability in circumstances of profound variation in the yearly amounts produced by the monsoon from June to October. Headrick summarises the conditions:

Irrigation, then, serves two purposes: to water lands like Sind and much of the Punjab, where agriculture would otherwise be impossible; and to provide water to vulnerable regions where the average rainfall is adequate (250 to 2,000 millimetres), but the climate is often subject to droughts. These regions include the Gangetic plain and much of the Deccan, in other words two-thirds of the continent. (Headrick 1998: 172)

There are major differences in the flow of water through rivers in different parts of India, notably the Himalayan snow-melt-fed Indus and Ganges, and the rain-fed waters of the rivers of the Deccan, and also in the effects of topography on the potential for irrigation.

There were two traditional indigenous methods of water and irrigation provision in India – wells and tanks – before the main engineering development of barrages and canals in the second half of the nineteenth century. Wells had been sunk down to about 50 feet/15 m, and were known as 'spring' wells when dug in clay (these are more common), and 'percolation' wells when dug in sand. Various types of lining and tapping of water were used, and many wells had a short life. In the Punjab wells were generally dug very deep, requiring masonry walls to shore them up. Wells for irrigation were exempt from the taxes levied on other types of irrigation method. The means of lifting water from a well also differed: one means was by a leather bag connected to a lever on a post; another used a rope and pulley, with the water lifted by bullocks walking on an inclined plane whose length was the depth of the well; a third type is the Persian wheel, involving an endless chain on which are fastened large numbers of water buckets and which was worked by bullocks (Carrier 1928: 125).

Carrier stated that 'The system of well irrigation extends mainly over that part of the United Provinces lying between the Ganges and Gogra rivers, and it is said that three-eighths of the artificial watering of India is carried out in the Indo-Gangetic Plain and by these methods. There is also some well irrigation in Madras and Bombay', the main crops in these regions being poppies (for opium) and wheat and rice (Carrier 1928: 125). In *c.* 1914 the area of India irrigated by wells was estimated at 13 million acres (5,261,100 ha), and the average area fed by water from wells at between 3–12 acres (1.21–5.26 ha). Many of the wells were temporary, and the work involved in their construction and feeding the water to the land was tedious and difficult (Cotton 1914: 127).

Tanks – artificial reservoirs – were the second type of indigenous water extraction for irrigation used in India, but were less widespread, being

Fig. 9.5 Irrigation in the Central Provinces, India, *c.* 1904.
By permission of and © the Royal Geographical Society Picture Collection S000274.

characteristic mainly of the Deccan and Madras, and of the states of Hyderabad and Mysore, the latter with about 20,000 tanks in 1914 (Carrier 1928: 126). They comprised a variety of forms and sizes, ranging from large lakes (formed by damming a river), chains of pools of water drawn off from a river, or simply an excavated depression, common in Bengal. These were also sometimes temporary features, mainly on account of silt-ing. The estimated area of land in India for which irrigation was provided by tanks *c.* 1914 was 8 million acres (3,237,600 ha) (Cotton 1914: 127). Ceylon was also a major area of irrigation by tanks, the use of which dates back to late prehistory. Some were extremely large (4,425 acres/1791 ha, and 22 feet/6.7 m deep) (Carrier 1928: 127).

Mosse (2003) has studied historic village tank systems in Tamil Nadu in South India as physical resources with strong reference to their sym-bolic significance through social structures, status, caste and prestige. His work challenges the idea that pre-colonial water management systems operated as sustainable systems which were fractured by colonial state interference, leading to severe environmental degradation through the alienation of village community rights of use and management of water. The tank system itself in this region was a product of state action from the sixteenth to the eighteenth century, with use rights for water and land given by Maravar kings, by political patronage and caste dominance, to various groups, including chieftains, temples and the headmen of villages. The royal endowment system continued through the time of British colo-nial rule, but maintenance of irrigation systems was given by the British to the *zamindars* (middlemen), who failed to provide adequate incentives for irrigation system maintenance, and it was this that contributed to the decay of the system rather than the removal of communal authority by the colonial power.

A third type of irrigation system was the use of canals and barrages. Inundation canals are the older form, in which seasonal floodwater from rivers is collected by canals, built at right angles to a river. The disadvan-tage is that such systems do not provide year-round water for irrigation, and they may also suffer from rapid deposition of silt, and fluctuations in the amount of mountain snow-melt and in the timing of the floods. Such a system was characteristic of the Punjab and the lower part of the Indus plain, and canal systems date back to well before the British annexation of these regions. Prior to British control the inundation canal systems of irri-gation in the Indus basin were organised and expanded by the indigenous Indian states (Gilmartin 1995: 215). A second version of canal irrigation was that involving the construction of some sort of dam, barrage, *anicut* or weir to hold back water, thus making it available throughout the year via distributory 'perennial' canals. The means of holding back the irrigation water from rivers varied according to local physiography and soils.

Although generally associated with the use of modern engineering techniques, small dam systems had long been used in Mughal India in the valleys of the Baglan region in the Sahyadri mountains, in South Bihar, and in the Tamil Nadu area of southern India, indicating 'that small-dam systems flourished mainly in piedmont areas where rainfall was less and the rivers often dried up or dwindled to a trickle during the dry season. The dams not only fed canals but also created reservoirs in which water could be stored during the dry months of the year' (Hardiman 1995: 188). An interesting aspect of the small-dam systems of the Sahyadris is that, against the Wittfogel thesis (that centrally organised large-scale irrigation systems predominated in the distant past and were a significant basis of despotism), 'small-dam systems of irrigation [also] existed in the past which were sustained over long periods of time. Although they depended on state support, at the village level they were controlled and managed by communities' (Hardiman 1995: 188, 209). A the other end of the scale were the many large projects, involving dams and extensive channelling of water for irrigation, that formed a major component of the British colonial policy for agricultural development in India from the 1860s through to the 1920s.

The history of irrigation systems in India under British control, especially after 1858, is closely tied to the greatly increased and more direct role taken by the British government of India in matters of 'works of internal improvement'. A large-scale irrigation scheme in India, as Chapman has asserted, became from *c.* 1860 onwards 'a political statement first and foremost. It is also of course an economic statement of costs and revenues, and a technological artefact of good or bad design. The acquisition of land, the methods of revenue raising, the distribution of water, all take place *given* the nature of the political system. The political system here [in India] was British imperial hegemony' (Chapman 2000: 116). The context of his remarks is an account of the British influence on the development of the Five Rivers irrigation scheme in the Punjab from *c.* 1850 to 1910, which connected, via new canals, the major river arteries of the region.

The intensification of British involvement in India in the nineteenth century, initially through the East India Company and more directly after 1857, led to a series of major efforts to finance, design and promote large capital works, including railway networks and water management systems. It would be too easy to see these as simply a triumph of Western

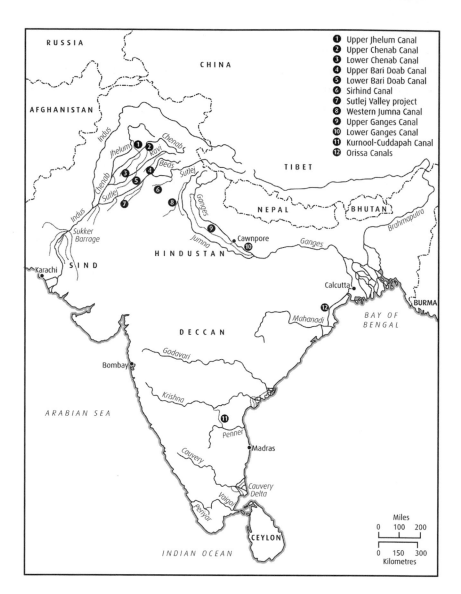

Fig. 9.6 Irrigation canals in India to 1942.
Source: Headrick (1988: 174). By permission of and © Oxford University Press.

capitalism and technical skill, not least because the outcomes may be disputed. On the one hand it has been argued, for example, that the British-developed canal irrigation and water transport networks in India were major achievements, facilitating increases in agricultural production, and making for a measure of provision against frequent famines.

Against this is the contention that the resulting agricultural productivity was limited. The restoration of older works by the British East India

Company in the early nineteenth century, such as the Eastern and Western Jumna Canals and the Delhi Canal, had some positive effects, but they also brought problems: a lack of control of water flow and therefore water-logging and salinisation of soils, and malaria; problems with silting; and a wide range of problems of administration, including the comprehension of water- and land-use rights (Hardiman 1995: 175). Finance for these projects was a recurring difficulty, but the advantages of irrigation systems were shown in the differential rates of agricultural production during the severe famine of 1837–8, which persuaded the East India Company to invest further in irrigation structures, including an improvement of old barrage structures on the Cauvery Delta in the Madras Presidency and the addition of a masonry dam. A massive scheme to irrigate the Rorkee plateau between the Jumna and the Ganges was agreed by the East India Company in 1841, but complicated by disagreements about its primary purpose: for irrigation or for the improvement of navigation. The limited training of the engineers involved was partly solved by periods of study of practical hydraulics back in Britain and observation of hydraulic works in Italy.

The construction of the key Ganges Canal in the North-West Provinces was completed in 1854 (Hardiman 1995: 177). The project was realised at very great cost, and the shortage of skilled surveyors resulted in the construction in 1848 of Roorkee College, now a university, for the specialist training of irrigation engineers (Chapman 2000: 109). With further debilitating famines in the period 1832–41, attention was focused on the use of the water of the rivers Godavari and Krishna flowing eastwards from the Western Ghats to the Bay of Bengal, and a Godavari irrigation project was begun in 1846, followed by the Krishna Delta project in 1851. By 1890–1 the Godavari project irrigated an area of 283,000 ha, and the Krishna Delta scheme about 150,000 ha (Hardiman 1995: 180).

There was a conspicuous humanitarian element in the planning of some of these large irrigation systems in India. One of the constant preoccupations of European imperial governments in the later nineteenth and earlier twentieth centuries was the cost of empire, and this was particularly true of the British and India. Attention was paid to estimating the financial returns against costs of irrigation projects, and their efficacy in increasing agricultural productivity and saving lives during times of famine. Sir Arthur Cotton, lecturing in Manchester in 1866 at a Social Science Congress, made clear that he felt that a government had a Christian duty to construct irrigation systems to protect and promote life: 'But what shall we say to the loss of our character as a Christian Government from our having so neglected both to execute those works that can alone prevent these famines, and also to prepare for each famine when it was imminent?' This sentiment was supported by Florence Nightingale (Chapman 2000: 111). Cotton took the view that with the necessary involvement of what he saw as superior British engineering talent, the solution to India's problems of inadequate production and distribution of food lay in the construction of railways and large-scale canals that could be used for both transport and irrigation.

The perceived success of British irrigation engineering in India was a matter of considerable interest in other parts of the empire, exemplified by the Australian Alfred Deakin, formerly Minister of Public Works and Water Supply in Victoria and subsequently Prime Minister of Australia, who visited India in 1890–1 and produced a book *Irrigated India: An Australian view of India and Ceylon. Their Irrigation and Agriculture*, published in 1893 (Chapman 2000: 112; Powell 1976). Deakin (1856–1919) travelled widely in search of best practices in irrigation, and also visited California, Mexico, Ontario, Italy and Egypt to extend his knowledge of different practices, and published accounts of *Irrigation in Western America, so far as it has relation to the circumstances in Victoria* (1885), and *Irrigation in Egypt and Italy* (1887).

There remained, notwithstanding the schemes developed in the 1880s, large areas of India which had little or no irrigation, tragically demonstrated by the major famine of 1876–8. The Indian Famine Commission report of 1881 recommended two main types of infrastructural strategy ('protective works') that would assist in combating famines in the future. These were railways and irrigation schemes, and one of these was a large irrigation project – the Periyar Project in southern India which involved the construction of a large dam across the Periyar River in Travancore and a tunnel through the Western Ghats to the Vaigai River in Madurai, for the purpose of using water from the rainfall of the Ghats for the irrigation of the much drier area to the east. The project was completed in 1895 (Hardiman 1995: 189).

Colonially promoted irrigation systems focused on the production of commercial crops, and were less efficient in productivity than fully working traditional systems, which also minimised risks of salinity and malaria. Colonial investment in irrigation was a fraction of that in railways, and colonial irrigation systems, while yielding small profits for investors, singularly failed to alleviate the massive starvation that accompanied the famines of the late nineteenth century, so that, for example, the '420,000 square miles devastated by the 1899–1900 drought, mostly in the Bombay Presidency and the Central Provinces, contrasted with the less than 100,000 acres of canal-irrigated farmland in the same area' (Davis 2002: 334).

The effects of the devastating famines in the years from 1899 to 1903 highlighted the need for further provision against such events, and a report was commissioned by Lord Curzon, the Viceroy of India, on the use of irrigation schemes as protection against famine. The report of 1903 showed how small were the areas of India irrigated from canals, minor government works and privately owned springs, wells and tanks. Several major irrigation schemes were put in hand as a consequence of the report. These included the Triple Canals Project, which was designed to irrigate the area between the Ravi and Sutlej rivers in north-west India, begun in 1905 and eventually finished during the First World War. The improvement of irrigation schemes accelerated after the war, by the use of such technical innovations as the tube well, involving pumping the water to the surface by electric or diesel engines, and this period also saw an increase in the scale of irrigation projects, for example the Sukkur barrage on the Indus and the Sutlej Valley Project (Hardiman 1995: 192–4).

The class and ethnic contexts of the development of large-scale irrigation works by the British, using formal mathematical and environmental models of such large river basins as the Indus, are significant. Gilmartin has advanced the powerful argument that the model of market rationality used by the British, involving the efficient use of water from major engineered irrigation systems to master both environment and indigenous peoples in the interests of political control and profit, was of no advantage, indeed was disadvantageous, to the majority of the Indian population, and led to continuing problems of environmental degradation. These people were treated as part of the managed environment, thus creating a two-part system:

with a system of rational environmental control operating on one side, and a world of indigenous, customary and kin-based community organization operating on the other. Even as indigenous communities were rigidly excluded from influence over the main, scientific irrigating system, their domination over the disposal of water 'beyond the outlet' was largely accepted as an inevitable fact of colonial irrigation. Indeed, such communities came to be viewed as part of the natural environment, to be 'controlled and guided, led and regulated', like Punjab's rivers, by 'scientific' administration, rather than as allies of government in a common project of rational environmental domination. (Gilmartin 1995: 227)

The decline of traditional tank and channel water use in colonial South Bihar has been attributed to new revenue systems introduced by the colonial administration: 'In particular, by facilitating and encouraging a shift from "produce" to "fixed" and then to cash rents, the colonial administration invariably upset an entire rhythm of procedures, protocols and duties between tenants and landlords over the question of the maintenance and servicing of the ahar-pine [tank-channel] network' (D'Souza 2006: 623).

The consequences, as anyone who has, for example, studied the history of land drainage in Western Europe and elsewhere would predict, were consistent failures of co-operation by villagers and local communities in the vital processes of maintaining the systems, conspicuously not keeping the irrigation watercourses free and clear of impediment, with consequent problems of silting and waterlogging. The nature of the efficiency of the local management of irrigation systems and of the land that they watered varied considerably over the very large areas of the major river systems such as that of the Indus, reflecting differing cultures and hierarchical/social balances and aspirations for local power, but parts of the community side of the maintenance system must have worked reasonably well.

Local organisation of irrigation management was not always, however, compatible with the British scientific and administrative model, causing conflict between the officials of the Irrigation Department and the 'networks of clientage and kinship relations' that operated at local level, leading ultimately to efforts 'to define new indigenous models of community coterminous with new state models of environment' (Gilmartin 1995: 231, 233). The financial costs of major irrigation schemes in India, such as the Sarda Canal, constructed in the 1920s, were high, but the environmental consequences of this and other projects were also massive, as measured in terms of waterlogging, salinisation and the increase in malaria. 'In 1928 the first section of the Sarda Canal was opened to the sound of imperial trumpets. The huge tracts of saline-alkali waste- and semi-wasteland which today surround the central and lower reaches of the canal have regrettably vindicated the talukdars [local cultivators from Oudh who had objected to the scheme in a petition in 1872] in their opposition' (Whitcombe 1995: 258). Similar problems were also experienced with the other large canal projects of British India – the Western Jumna Canal, the Ganges Canal, the Bari Doab Canal, and the Sukkur (Lloyd barrage).

As Headrick has shown, irrigation schemes in India were less well known and understood and thus attracted less interest from the British administrators in India than the railways. Railways provided speedy movement of troops and lucrative markets for British industrialists, so that irrigation attracted significantly less financial support, and it was not until the 1930s that investment in irrigation matched that of the railway systems (Headrick 1988: 195). The colonial experiments with irrigation technology and application in India, however, not only provided for the needs of the people of India but also served as sources of innovation for other schemes in other parts of the British empire, including Australia.

Water management in Australia

The arid and semi-arid environments of Australia posed substantial problems for British settlers, but fewer problems to the aboriginal peoples who had inhabited Australia long before Captain Cook landed at Botany Bay in 1788. The gradual penetration of settlement inland from the early coastal settlements required improved technical knowledge of ways of watering the dryland landscape to render it fit for cultivation, pastoral farming and mining activities. The experiences resulted in varied and often pragmatic responses, but by the late nineteenth century knowledge of advanced irrigation systems from other parts of the British empire, and from California and Italy, was informing Australian thinking about environmental amelioration.

Powell (1997) has outlined and substantiated a chronological sequence for the history of water management in Australia. The main periods that he suggests are: first, the era of 'empiricists and synthesizers', from 1788 to 1880; second, the era of 'irrigationists and sanitarians' from 1880 to 1900; third, that of 'science, technology and organizational reform', from 1900 to 1950. The period 1788–1880 was also characterised by the initial appraisal and realisation of farming opportunities by squatters and farmers through the mapping of river systems and through the use of small dams, wells and waterholes.

Early mining activities, such as the gold rushes in Victoria, promoted questions and disputes about rights of access to and use of water, and resulted in legislation to confirm community rights, partly influenced by Californian experience. Thus:

The role of miners from California in devising ingenious cross-country water transfers is generally acknowledged and, in so far as they were already familiar with American furores over water rights, it is reasonable to suppose that their lively presence was also noticeable in these Victorian disputations. Water rights took on greater significance during the introduction of government-sponsored irrigation schemes in south-eastern Australia and on the South Island of New Zealand. (Powell 1997: 103–4)

Hunting and conservation

One of the (mainly masculine) preoccupations of European colonial societies overseas was the hunting of game for sport. This contrasted with the
mainly subsistence hunting of animals by indigenous populations.

Sometimes the two came into conflict. The elimination of large numbers of animals through hunting for sport eventually led to the promotion
of a range of conservation measures.

A masculinity perspective is common in the imperial literature on
hunting. Woollacott has characterised it as follows:

A hypermasculine cultural figure, closely linked to that of the explorer, was the big
game hunter. Big game hunters who had their heyday in the later nineteenth and
early twentieth centuries, were privileged and often powerful EuroAmerican men
who went to Africa and India to pursue, conquer and possess animals that were
considered both dangerous and exotic. By bringing home their trophies, big game
hunters established a proprietorial relationship with the colonies and their fauna.
At the same time, they asserted their own race-based superiority: the superiority of
their skills and weapons, and their virility or masculinity. (Woollacott 2006: 71)

Fig. 9.7 Aboriginal hunting camp, Murray River, *c.* 1888/9.
By permission of and © Cambridge University Library RCSPC-Y308A-089.

MacKenzie, in his important study of hunting and conservation in imperial contexts, pointed to the links between big game hunting, bravado and masculinity, and between hunting, the natural world, conservation and the culture of imperialism:

Changing approaches to hunting constitute an important theme in human history. The pursuit and killing of animals has invariably developed ideological overtones and both literature and the pictorial arts have tended to stress the mythic, courtly and martial rather than the purely practical aspects of the chase. Many European hunters in the nineteenth century were aware of this tradition and turned hunting into a symbolic activity of global dominance. Thus hunting became part of the culture of imperialism. (Mackenzie 1988: ix)

Hunting was not gender-specific: the notion that hunting was a male prerogative

is essentially a perception of the nineteenth and twentieth centuries, linked with the severe separation of masculine and feminine worlds in that period, and to the valuation of the Hunt as the promoter of supposedly distinctive male virtues. In many hunting and gathering societies any tendency to a sexual division of labour was overridden by the demands made by the chase upon sheer numbers of human participants. (MacKenzie 1988: 21)

This European culture of hunting animals transferred gender and culture preference and prejudice from metropole to colony, though there were exceptional women who were determined to succeed in hunting big game in the colonies. Mckenzie (2005: 546) has shown how processes of masculinisation of the moral values of hunting in later Victorian Britain 'were transmitted and assimilated by Victorian and Edwardian middle-class men, and in turn, shaped the attitudes and responses of Edwardian women'. The ritual of 'blooding' young men at their first kill in field sports was an essential part and caste mark of a curious masculine indoctrination and affirmation, and similar ritual practices were adopted in imperial contexts, with the killing of game seen as a necessary 'moral instruction' and means of character development (Mckenzie 2005: 546–7).

Mckenzie states that:

Although the *Encyclopaedia of Sport* (1911) suggested that there were not many sports from which women were now excluded, it insisted that sports such as cycling and lawn-tennis were more *appropriate* for ladies than shooting. Big-game hunting therefore   particularly its more dangerous forms such as alligator shooting – and other 'unfeminine' practices such as badger-digging were properly undertaken by men. They masculinized men; they unfeminized women.

In spite of this 'patronizing parochialism' (Mckenzie 2005: 548) there were some women who engaged in big-game and other forms of hunting. Mckenzie cites publications such as Catherine Nina Jenkins' *Sport and Travel in both Tibets* (1909), Agnes Herbert's *Two Dianas in Somaliland* (1908) and Isabel Savory's *Sportswoman in India* (1900), each in their own way challenging masculinist assumptions about the gender-specificity of the chase. Savory travelled alone in India and Africa 'in search of sport and adventure. In India she enjoyed tiger shooting in the Deccan, the thrill of which had "not been worked" from a woman's perspective, and contributed to a growing awareness, by some men at least, of women's capacities in hunting and shooting' (Mckenzie 2005: 549–50).

Notwithstanding these exceptional cases, opportunities for training women in the use of weapons were restricted, their participation in hunts of various kinds was generally limited, and the type of hunting conditioned the possibilities of women's involvement. Thus, as Mckenzie indicates, women were increasingly involved in hunting on horseback with hounds, a sport favoured in the British colonies, including India, in the later Victorian period:

By the late Victorian period, women were chasing the fox in some numbers in established hunts. What were the reasons for the change? Arguably, it reflected wider social changes in gender relationships influenced by an upsurge in female confidence due to increased opportunities for education and employment. An ancillary reason was the unprecedented interest in natural history field clubs and the study of natural history by women. (Mckenzie 2005: 553)

Negative male attitudes persisted (and doubtless persist now) to women's involvement in hunting, but gradually pioneer women initiated invasions of this restricted practice and made a niche for themselves which slowly pointed the way forward to greater equality.

Hunting of wild game by European men also provided an opportunity for asserting their dominance over nature and indigenous peoples (who themselves had been and continued to be hunted, like animals, in colonial territories), and for the translation of this activity back to the metropoles in the form of stuffed hunting trophies and skins for use as rugs. In colonial places the devastation of wildlife was frequently dramatic. Elephants, lions, tigers, rhinoceros, gorillas, buffalo and other animals were slaughtered in large numbers.

Ivory was a major commodity of trade, revenue and 'imperial subsidy' in Central and East Africa, with East Africa 'the world's greatest source of ivory' (MacKenzie, 1988: 148, 151). It had been a commodity in European–African trade since the sixteenth century, and was linked with

Fig. 9.8 Porters with elephant tusks, Uganda c. 1906/11.
By permission of and © Cambridge University Library RCSPC – Fisher Y3045C   036.

the slave trade of East Africa, but became a major international commercial commodity in the nineteenth and early twentieth centuries. It provided raw material for a wide variety of objects in the industrialising countries of Europe and North America – jewellery, miniature carvings, piano keys, cutlery handles, billiard balls – and the elephant populations declined dramatically as a result. Christopher states that 'by 1891 Zanzibar accounted for three-quarters of the world's supply [of ivory]. In the second half of the nineteenth century the quantity passing through Zanzibar rarely fell below 200 tons per annum. The number of elephants killed must have amounted to an astounding 40,000–60,000 per annum, clearly a rate that could not be maintained indefinitely' (Christopher 1984: 89).

In East Africa, in addition to private hunters, district officials supplemented their own income from the hunting of elephants and the sale of ivory tusks. Hunting also provided significant quantities of animal hides, meat and trophies for hunters, and had provided meat, materials for crafts and trade, a basis of symbolic ritual and a means of protection for a long time for indigenous peoples (MacKenzie 1988: 149, 155–6).

The extensive shooting of animals in Africa prompted moves to initiate game reserves. Edward North Buxton, who had previously acted against the enclosure of Epping Forest north of London for conservation reasons, and who hunted in Africa in the early years of the twentieth century, noted the substantial reduction of large mammals such as antelope, lions, elephants, rhinoceros and hippopotamus through overhunting by bloodthirsty Europeans and others (Prendergast and Adams 2003: 252). Buxton became president of the Society for the Preservation of the (Wild) Fauna of the Empire, which was instrumental in the advocacy of game reserves and national parks, notably in Africa (MacKenzie 1988: 211–13; Beinart and Hughes 2007: 291). The situation was not dissimilar in other European colonial territories elsewhere in Africa. MacKenzie has shown in his comprehensive study of hunting and conservation that ivory-hunting by Europeans, sometimes with the assistance of Africans, was, for example, extensive in the Belgian Congo and in French Equatorial Africa, especially between the First World War and the later 1920s, partly on account of liberal game laws, and partly because of the very large areas that could not be policed (MacKenzie 1988: 154).

A hunter named Dugald Campbell was active in French and Belgian territory in Africa up to the 1920s, and in spite of Belgian publicity for the promotion of national parks,

the Congo continued to offer opportunities akin to those of the late nineteenth century. The river Congo provided ready access to vast reserves for the big-game hunter. Campbell observed the assault of traders upon the rare gorilla population of the north-eastern equatorial forests and published a photograph of nine gorilla heads laid out on a hunter's table. A Belgian newspaper printed a photograph of a big-game hunter proudly displaying twenty-one hippo heads. (MacKenzie, 1988: 154)

The centrality of the Belgian Congo to other European colonial territories made it a focus for European hunters.

The regions of extinct volcanoes such as Virunga and Grands Lacs in the western part of the Congo attracted British, Belgian and German explorers and hunters, and there were many myths about the people and animals that lived there. King William of Sweden, on a Swedish zoological expedition 'among pygmies and gorillas' to Central Africa in 1921, shot a gorilla, but sought to initiate a reserve area at Kivu for the conservation of flora and fauna and of the environment more generally (Schuylenbergh 2005: 155, 156). The American naturalist and taxidermist Carl Akeley, on an expedition to Kivu from the American Museum of Natural History in New York, advocated the creation of a gorilla sanctuary for the preservation of the mountain gorilla (*Gorilla beringei*).

The nature of hunting in imperial territories varied according to the history of settlement, the varieties of fauna, the nature of the topography and terrain, the cultures of the hunters and of indigenous peoples, and the methods and weapons of the chase. From a British perspective, hunting in India was mainly a sport, offering recreation and social contact, together with useful links to local people and regions, though it also fulfilled the roles of defence of people, stock and crops against wild animals, and sometimes the provision of meat. The British combined both Indian Mughal hunting traditions with those of lower-caste peoples, and added their own traditions of fox-hunting and fishing, using a range of hunting weaponry, both ancient and modern. The cultivated plains with their deer, antelopes, wild pig and wildfowl differed in topography and fauna from the forest regions with their wild buffalo, bison, deer and carnivorous animals (MacKenzie 1988: 168–70).

The three main animals hunted in India were the tiger, the elephant and the pig. The tiger was a challenging and dangerous animal, which killed large numbers of people and livestock, and provided good hunting sport, magnificent heads and skins for trophies, and was a source of many dramatic hunting tales. The hunting of tigers for sport was often by Europeans on the backs of elephants, though with Indian people on foot acting as beaters. Very large numbers of tigers were killed, and the population was reduced, with the tiger becoming an endangered species by the 1930s when the first efforts at conservation were made. Elephants were not hunted or shot in the numbers experienced in Africa, as there were fewer Indian elephants and they were less valuable as a source of ivory. Nonetheless concern at the diminution of numbers by the 1870s secured the first moves towards protection and conservation in Madras in 1873, and the whole of India in 1879 (MacKenzie 1988: 179–83). Other sports included pig-sticking from horseback, and the imported and modified fox-hunt, each of which had their own cultures, means and ends.

It is difficult to quantify the effect of hunting on the ecologies and environments of imperial territories. Beinart, in a review concerned primarily with MacKenzie's 1988 book *The Empire of Nature*, questions the extent to which the agency for decline in game numbers and environmental degradation in southern and central Africa rested 'with imperial hunters, with settlers, or with Africans enmeshed in the nets of colonialism' (Beinart 1990: 162). Acknowledging the need for pre-colonial African societies to protect themselves from dangerous wild animals, plus their need for meat and items for trade, and the impressions of the complex motives for big-game hunting left in the accounts of European hunters from the late nineteenth and early twentieth centuries, Beinart argues for a wider perspective for big-game hunting in Africa. He suggests that 'we should hesitate before allowing these hunters to occupy the centre stage. They were men with literary skills, publicists from a confident culture writing for a hungry market; some appropriated enormous prowess for themselves and their technology. Like African chiefs they were perhaps laying down claims to possession through demarcating their hunting ground: conjuring the empire as estate' (Beinart 1990: 166–7).

Beinart contends that the efficacy of imperial hunters was not the only cause of reduction in wild animal populations, for there had been substantial loss of game in southern Africa by the early twentieth century, some of which was due to African Griqua and Boer farmers and the 'unintended' consequences of imperial occupation, such as the spread of rinderpest to wild animals and the shooting of predators by farmers to protect their livestock and crops. The thesis that Africans were more sensitised to and in control of their environments has to be tempered by a recognition that the dynamics of those environments, partly through 'natural' disasters, was equally important, and that regions differed in their experience of environmental change. Europeans tended to blame environmental degradation on indigenous peoples in Africa, India and elsewhere – a reflection of the Europeans' self-perceived superior status and sensitivity to environs. The effects of hunting by colonial personnel and the broader effects of a colonial economy on the environments of colonial territories reflected 'complex historical interaction between people, indigenous vegetation and animals, markets, new beasts, new diseases and new crops. Empire could bring depletion of game; it could also trigger loss of environmental control which increased the range of habitats for some wild animals' (Beinart 1990: 169–71, 172).

Concerns about overkill by imperialists and indigenous peoples led in the early twentieth century to a greater concern for conservation of species and habitat, as shown above in the case of the Belgian Congo. Part of the supporting explanation of this is perhaps a change in metropolitan societies to a more sympathetic attitude to animals (even though they were still being killed in domestic hunts and stalks), and also a change of mind by the imperial hunters, transformed into 'penitent butchers' (Beinart 1990: 175) who sought, partly out of self-interest, to preserve levels of game animals in owned properties and on game reserves, and to obviate illegal hunting and poaching by indigenous peoples and poor whites. Another important factor was the increase in scientific knowledge of the flora and fauna of imperial territories, and consequent 'new conservationist discourses in the nineteenth century which influenced colonial bureaucracies and colonial legislation. By the turn of the twentieth century, legal regulation of hunting, game and forests was well established; early game reserves had been demarcated' (Beinart 1990: 177), but this did not signify a promotion of conservation by imperial governments over the needs of economic exploitation and political control, nor an even spread of such conservation spaces.

Jepson and Whittaker (2002) have linked modern trends in wildlife preservation in Indonesia with the origins of the conservation movements in the United States of America and Europe in the nineteenth and early twentieth centuries, which had derived in part from concerns by hunters about the reduction in game numbers and also from an increasing interest in natural history. These American and European elites had taken the opportunity to display their hunting skills by prowess in the field in the American West and in Africa, and by exhibiting their hunting trophies. In the later nineteenth century there was also concern at the massive diminution or eradication of animal species such as the bison of the Great Plains and the larger animals of Africa, together with the rapid deforestation of the Great Lakes region in the United States (Jepson and Whittaker 2002: 132–3). The Society for the Preservation of the Wild Fauna of the Empire, founded in London in 1903, was a significant event in the history of wildlife conservation movements in Europe and the United States. Concern over the severe reduction in numbers of game animals in South Africa had produced Acts for game preservation in the Cape in 1866, which were widened to include the whole of the British South African territories in 1891, the establishment of the Sabie game reserve in the Transvaal in 1892, the encouragement of the establishment of game reserves in Africa by the Foreign Office, and parallel developments in German East Africa (Prendergast and Adams 2003: 252).

There were continuing trans-European attempts to secure preservation of wildlife both in the metropoles and in the colonial territories, notably the International Consultative Commission for the Protection of Nature, established in 1913, which together with other European committees and the US Boone and Crockett Club helped to create, inter alia, the King Albert National Park in the Belgian Congo in 1925 for the preservation of the gorilla population (Jepson and Whittaker 2002: 140). In 1933 a conference on African wildlife was convened in London. This 'marked international agreement on protected areas (national parks and sanctuaries) as the primary goal for achieving wildlife preservation. This was a major shift in British government policy, which thirty years earlier was resolute on the game law system and until 1931 considered national parks premature in British colonies' (Jepson and and Whittaker 2002: 142). It was followed in 1947 by the establishment of the International Union for Nature Protection.

Jepson and Whittaker have outlined the history of fauna preservation in the Netherlands Indies, stimulus coming early in the nineteenth century from the governor of Java, from Sir Stamford Raffles, and from Carl Reinwardt, director of the Royal Cabinet of Natural History, through the establishment of a Natural History Commission, and by a Netherlands Indies Association for Nature Protection (NIANP) (1912). 'Hunting and species legislation was introduced to the Netherlands Indies in 1909, an action that reflects international support for such policies among colonial governments following the 1900 convention' (Jepson and Whittaker 2002: 147). The NIANP campaigned for the establishment of forty-two small game reserves between 1912 and 1922, and a policy of wildlife sanctuaries was agreed in 1930. Jepson and Whittaker suggest that there was a significant 'flow of conservationist ideas into the Netherlands Indies from Europe and North America and that the movement was metropolitan and international in character. This perspective helps explain the timing of conservation events in the Netherlands Indies, in particular why attempts to establish nature reserves in 1886 and 1887 failed, and why hunting was not regulated until 1909' (Jepson and Whittaker 2002: 151–2, 153). Whether these movements were exclusively for the benefit of Europeans, however, or whether there was at least a measure of recognition of indigenous land-use rights, including hunting of game for subsistence purposes and practices, is not clear.

There were parallel developments by other European countries. In France, concerns for deforestation and perceived consequent climatic change in the French colonies of the West Indies fed through to concerns about the possible consequences of environmental deterioration for 'the survival of European civilization. Indeed, many authors feared that this degradation might result in Europe suffering the fate of the great civilizations of the ancient world' (Ford 2004: 188). Significant developments included the establishment of thirteen national parks in Algeria between 1923 and 1937 and ten *réserves naturelles* in Madagascar from 1927. Response to the broader European initiatives outlined above was made by the creation of *réserves naturelles intégrales* – departures from the American idea of national parks in that they 'were areas that would be protected from any form of hunting, fishing or exploitation. They were to exclude human presence of any kind', were conceived as counters to the deterioration of the environment and the consequent decline of civilisation, and were established in Algeria, Madagascar and West Africa (Ford 2004: 196).

French Indo-China, according to a wartime book produced in 1943,

offers hunting equal in standard to that of India or parts of Africa. Among the best hunting grounds are the plateaux of Lang Bian and Darlac. The chief game animals are elephants, tigers, leopards, Gaur and Bantang, several species of deer, and wild boars. In suitable country all are plentiful. The French residents indulge in much shooting, especially of deer, from motor cars. The most popular method is to travel quietly by night along the roads that pass through jungle country, spotting the animals with headlights. The tiger and leopard are shot from ambush, with the help of a decoy; wild oxen are usually stalked. (Darby 1943: 90–1)

The same source refers to a law of 1917 dividing Lang Bian into three districts for the purpose of hunting: preserved (no shooting without a special licence); protected (shooting prohibited at all times apart from small animals in the winter); and free.

In the Belgian Congo by 1944 there were national parks or sanctuaries, from which hunting was almost entirely banned, such as the Parc National Albert, mainly a sanctuary for gorilla and okapi, the Parc National de la Kagera, and the Parc National de la Garamba, a shelter for the white rhinoceros. In addition there were general game reserves and elephant reserves. Protected species outside the reserves, on account of their rarity or functions as destroyers of pests, included:

the rhinoceros, giraffe, gorilla, chimpanzee, certain monkeys, zebra, okapi, various antelopes, pangolin, egret, stork, shoe-bill, crested crane, owl, vulture, ibis, flamingo, heron, nightjar, and insectivorous birds. Except in the total reserves, lions, leopards, hyenas, hunting-dogs, baboons, birds of prey (but not vultures and owls), crocodiles, pythons and poisonous snakes, jackals, servals, wild cats and other small carnivorous animals, otters and warthogs may be killed at any time. (Mason 1944: 113–14)

How this actually worked in practice, however, and the extent to which both Europeans and indigenous people felt bound by these restrictions, is difficult to discern.

Acclimatisation and its institutions

A major aspect of the European imperial experience was the complicated discussion of the influence of climate and culture on acclimatisation and settlement. This focused on the evaluation of the possibilities for European settlement and labour in the tropical and equatorial regions of their empires, together with assessment, through theory and practice, of the ability of certain animals and plants to survive and prosper in such places, and the reverse possibility of growing tropical plants in temperate latitudes. Interest in acclimatisation goes back at least to the late eighteenth century, and it developed as a subject in a number of disciplines, including geography, where its implications, including those of health and disease for settlement of Europeans in alien climatic regions overseas, reached a high point in the 1930s (Livingstone 1987) with a number of major publications on the subject. These included two special publications by the American Geographical Society – *The Pioneer Fringe* (1931) and *White Settlers in the Tropics* (1939).

Anderson has pointed to the significance of the nineteenth century as 'a century of acclimatization', when, 'as never before, Europeans mobilized the natural world to their economic and cultural advantage … In an age when the colonial powers were intervening in the world's human order, acclimatization provided a way for scientists to intervene in its natural order' (Anderson 1992: 135–57).

The topic exercised the minds and practices of the medical professions, which sought to understand tropical diseases and hazards, and to provide advice on prophylactic measures, including affusions, purgatives and stimulants – advice which 'ranged from observations on dress, exercise and sleep, to comments on the virtues of bathing, the benefits or evils of alcohol, and the conduct of "the passions"' (Livingstone 1987: 361). Acclimatisation of plants and animals was a major feature of debates by agriculturalists, botanists and biologists in the spaces and journals of learned scientific societies, including geographical societies such as the Royal Geographical Society. Geographical expertise, such as that of the British geographers E. G. Ravenstein and Clements Markham, was included in special medical treatises and conferences (Livingstone 1987: 363).

Debates on acclimatisation were reflected in the 'moral discourses of climate' (Livingstone 1994), the large numbers of acclimatisation societies that developed in Europe and America in the late nineteenth and early twentieth centuries, and the development of botanical gardens for the propagation and diffusion of aesthetically and commercially significant plants (Livingstone 1987, 1992: 232–41; Bell 1996). Livingstone's observation that 'Geographical discussion of climatic matters throughout the nineteenth, and well into the twentieth century were profoundly implicated in the imperial drama and were frequently cast in the diagnostic language of ethnic judgement' is significant, and well exemplified in relation to 'anthropo-climatology and white acclimatization' (Livingstone 1994: 133, 137).

A theme frequently addressed by nineteenth- and early twentieth-century climatologists, geographers, ethnologists and anthropologists, together with politicians and administrators (who sought to evaluate the development and profit-making potential of their overseas colonies) was the link between climate and human potential. Generally speaking, there were many who felt, often with very little background knowledge, that because of the climates in which they lived indigenous peoples lacked any inherent potential for cultural, economic and political self-advancement, and that any attempts to promote these objectives would fail. Similes and metaphors ascribing to such peoples the characteristics of animals were common.

There was a distinct change in attitude from the late eighteenth to the mid-nineteenth century on the question of European adaptability to unfamiliar climates, notably those of the tropics. In the late eighteenth century, adaptation or 'seasoning' by Europeans was thought possible, but by the mid-nineteenth century a more pessimistic view was developing. It was thought that whereas animals could slowly adapt to tropical climates, white people could not, with the degeneration of physical, mental and even moral fibre being the most likely outcomes. Edmond has pointed out the irony of this change against the gradual reduction of mortality, through medical and other knowledge, of European residents, including troops, in the tropics at this time (Edmond 2005: 176–7). The increasing contact between Europeans and indigenous peoples heightened the perceived contrast between racial types, originally thought to have been strongly influenced by climatic difference. This idea changed with the advent of germ theory, and 'led many scientists to the conviction that germs rather than the sun, heat and moisture were the primary constraints upon tropical colonization' (Bell 1993: 329).

Tropical medicine, which appeared as a subject in the major European universities from the end of the nineteenth century, focused on the pathogens that most affected Europeans in the tropics and less on the European diseases that had devastating effects on indigenous peoples, and was thus a metropolitan and imperial pro-European construct or emphasis, linked also with a fear of the invasion of temperate regions, including Europe, by dangerous tropical pathogens brought by immigrants (Edmond 2005: 181).

The 'growing belief that the tropics were dangerous fever nests, probably uninhabitable by Europeans for any prolonged period, greatly complicated the fact of their increasing economic and imperial importance for Europe and the United States' (Edmond 2005: 176–7). A further complication was that the trend from climatic explanations for differences in health between Europeans and those of the 'Other' world of the tropics – towards a greater reliance on germ theory – ushered in the application not only of new science but also a new range of moral assessments of climatic and environmental factors by means of which potential for white settlement could be judged. These in themselves were highly complex (Bell 1993: 329; Livingstone 1991, 1994: 133). Complexities included the perceived special vulnerability of women and children to tropical environments, the need to have places of retreat to higher altitudes (hill-stations) within and beyond the imperial tropics for Europeans during very hot seasons, the development of special types of clothing, and broader issues about the need for emigration from overpopulated European countries, and the extension of European settlement frontiers.

Specialist agencies for the study and debate of acclimatisation were founded, including the Société Zoologique et Botanique d'Acclimatation, established in Paris in 1854, the Akklimatisations-Verein in Berlin (1838), the Comité d'Acclimatation de l'Algérie (1859), the Acclimatisation Society of Great Britain and the Ornithological Society of London (1860), the Royal Zoological and Acclimatisation Society of Victoria (Melbourne, 1861), the Società di Acclimatazione (Palermo, Sicily, 1861) and others in the United States (Livingstone 1987: 363–40; Lever 1992: 193–4); the Nelson Acclimatisation Society (New Zealand, 1863), the American Acclimatisation Society (New York, 1871), and the Society for the Acclimatisation of Foreign Birds (Cambridge, Massachusetts, *c.* 1873). Many of the thirty-seven acclimatisation societies listed by Lever (1992) were in the British colonies of Australia, Tasmania and New Zealand, but there were many more in other imperial territories, including those of France (Osborne 2000: 135–51).

Acclimatisation societies in Europe and beyond had their own dynamics and chronologies, and were also subject to varying degrees of opposition. They were primarily associated, as were other institutions such as geographical societies, with the period of high imperialism and opportunities for European settlement and political and economic benefit through trade. Osborne has suggested that acclimatisation 'was especially prominent during eras of economic protectionism, when tariffs favoured new ventures such as llama culture and the cultivation of vanilla beans' in such places as Australasia and Algeria, and also caused the modification of legal structures in colonies such as New Zealand for the protection of acclimatised fish, game birds and fauna (Osborne 2000: 142).

Initial evidence in support of the claim that white Europeans could not work in the tropics came from medical statistics, particularly the higher death rates of European troops and administrators from tropical diseases, and the seeming direct effects of tropical climate on the body, with anthropologists such as W. Z. Ripley and geographers such as E. G. Ravenstein taking the impossibility of settling tropical regions with Europeans as axiomatic (Livingstone 1987: 372). What Livingstone has called 'differential racial acclimatisation' – the possibility of white settlement in the tropics – had its supporters, including the Edinburgh scientist Robert Felkin whose knowledge of Africa and of tropical diseases led him to the views, given in 1886 and 1891, that 'acclimatisation potential varied from one ethnic group to another; that coastal swamplands were especially harmful to northern Europeans since they were the breeding ground for miasmic fever; that racial purity needed to be maintained if acclimatisation was to have any chance of success' (Livingstone 1987: 376–7).

The main objectives of the French Société Zoologique et Botanique d'Acclimatation were 'the introduction, acclimatisation, and domestication of animals, whether useful or ornamental. The perfecting and multiplication of races newly introduced or domesticated. The introduction and cultivation of useful vegetables' (Lever 1992: 4). The society was also responsible for the development of innovative agricultural and horticultural crops in Algeria, which from 1859 had its own acclimatisation society (Lever 1992: 9–10). The Paris Society had commissions and committees, including one on Algeria, and members of this permanent commission advised the French government on agriculture and settlement in Algeria, sometimes embracing rather far-fetched proposals, with the experimental *jardin d'essai* in Algiers acting as a colonial laboratory, which included research on 'useful organisms including ostriches, Chinese yams, bamboo, and cochineal beetles' (Osborne 2000: 144–5). Botanical gardens in Algeria also acted as places of experiment.

Additional branches of the Paris acclimatisation society were founded in the French colonies at Cayenne, Réunion, Martinique and Guadaloupe, and the movement of plants and animals between them and the metropole was aided by the French navy (Osborne 2000: 145). In contrast to France, where the Paris acclimatisation society had played a pioneer role in the introduction of offshoot societies to its colonial territories, some British colonial territories had been ahead of the metropolis. From the late eighteenth century, exotic animal species and plants were imported into Australasia, including the highly significant Spanish merino sheep as the basis of the growing Australian wool industry, imported some sixty years before the funding of acclimatisation societies in Australia (Osborne 2000: 146, 148).

These acclimatisation societies were obviously part of the broader application of European science to European imperial goals, and as such reflected European ideas about agriculture and development, but they achieved limited success, partly on account of imperfect knowledge and science, partly because of their roles as reinforcers of nationalist and imperial goals, including, in the case of Algeria, the desire to restore the country to its perceived fertility in Roman times (Osborne 2000: 150). By the same token, although a balance-sheet of the effects of the introduction of exotic species by colonial acclimatisation societies has yet to be produced, and accepting that imported species did cause great difficulty, some advocates claim that the importation of deer, fox, rabbit and prickly pear to Australia – major threats to Australian agriculture – cannot be blamed on the activities of acclimatisation societies. Thus 'it is likely that – except for Europeans themselves – indigenous species, rather than acclimatized exotic organisms, were much more disruptive to European-style agriculture in areas like the forests of eastern Australia' (Osborne 2000: 141, 142). The societies also, for the most part, took little account of indigenous practices.

Botanical gardens

One of the significant features of European imperialism, heightening during the late eighteenth and nineteenth centuries, was the transfer of plants from one part of the empire to another. This may be seen as part of a much wider set of processes and ideas about human agency and environmental influences, including climate, which influenced the diffusion of resources and peoples in an imperial context. One of the major agencies for such transfers was the botanical garden – an important part of the imperial ecological armoury.

Much has been written about botanical gardens – especially Kew Gardens in London – as significant institutional agencies, with emphasis on imperial centrality, the ideas and influence of individual directors and the importance of royal patronage, against a background of technical improvements in the means of facilitating the transport of plants, notably Wardian cases, and high levels of botanical knowledge (Brockway 1979; Drayton, 2000; Beinart and Middleton 2004).

Botanical gardens are part of a broader context of historical concerns about human effects on the environment, means for improvement, and, in the imperial context, means for the discovery, evaluation, propagation and commercial production of plants. This had profound scientific but also cultural implications, not least the benefit of new crops and commodities for the well-being of the world, or, as Drayton (2000: 232) puts it, 'Modern imperialism, however much it served to prosecute the private interests of elements of powerful nations, always identified itself with this sacred work of expanding the scope of world trade.' Richard Grove has shown the antiquity of attempts to master and control the products of nature for the benefit of humans and their environs, dating back at least to the organisation of botanical knowledge collected on voyages of discovery in the fifteenth and sixteenth centuries into botanic, medical and acclimatisation gardens from the late fifteenth century, notably by the Dutch and Portuguese, and the incorporation of plans for botanical gardens from early Arabic botanical texts (Grove 1995, 1996).

This trajectory continued through government involvement in the development of Renaissance physic and botanical gardens of France, the Netherlands, Britain, Germany and northern Italy. Its modern form came from the Enlightenment, and symbolised scientific, aesthetic and spiritual interests, in sites where plants could be produced for medical purposes and had clear symbolic links to the re-creation of an earthly paradise like the Garden of Eden (Grove 1996: 124; Prest 1981; Withers 1999; Johnson 2006: 44). Grove has also drawn attention to the significance of Indian caste systems in the development of imperial European knowledge of South Asia (Grove 1996: 128).

In the nineteenth century there was a rapid expansion in the number of botanical gardens, consonant with the exchange of plants that would facilitate the practical development and commercial goals and improve the aesthetic quality of both metropolitan and overseas landscapes. The increasing involvement of the European state with environmental management and conservation and imperial expansion, requiring a strong alliance with natural science, notably botany (Drayton 2000: 235), was also a relevant process. Johnson states that:

Overseas empires provided a vehicle and sites for the development of networks of plant exchange, and the gardens themselves acted as spaces for the reciprocal representation and circulation of knowledge between empire and home. Between 1837 and 1901 there were at least 378 botanical gardens across the globe. Britain had the largest network, peaking at well over a hundred overseas gardens and twenty-one at home in Britain and Ireland. (Johnson 2006: 45; McCracken 1997: 2–3, 16–19).

This expansion was particularly remarkable during the reign of Queen Victoria (1837–1901), with an increase from eight to over one hundred gardens, half of which were in India, Australia and New Zealand (Osborne 2000: 145; McCracken 1997: 17–19). The early development of botanical gardens in the British empire owed much to the influence of Kew Gardens, especially under the influence of Joseph Banks between 1722 and 1820, and particularly through the materials collected by the plant hunters that he sent overseas, and later by William Hooker, who became director in 1841, and his son Joseph. The colonial botanical gardens could never be of sufficient size to display examples of all the exotic plants of empire, and instead showed samples on a quasi-cartographic basis (Johnson 2006: 45).

Each of the British colonies has its own history of development of botanical gardens and similar institutions. India, notwithstanding its size, had few official botanical gardens. Calcutta, Ootacamund, Saharanpur and Peradeniya in Ceylon were noted in 1883, with agri-horticultural gardens in Calcutta, Balasore, Lucknow, Chittagong, in Burma at Rangoon and Mulmein, and gardens on the estates of Indian princes (McCracken 1997: 29–30). Even though important new work came from the botanical gardens, such as tea-growing and the acclimatisation of flowers and vegetables, McCracken suggests that its contribution was much less than that envisaged by Kew, this in turn explained by the very low ratio of imperial botanical gardens to the total population, and the fact that such a relatively low percentage of the population lived in towns and cities, urban settlements being the favoured sites for botanical gardens in Britain and elsewhere (McCracken 1997: 24–5).

In contrast, the botanical and related gardens established in Australia were more successful, this being mainly (at least from a European perspective) a land of British colonial settlement, in which the population was mainly located in towns and cities and whose municipal wealth had been boosted by the discovery and winning of gold in the mid-nineteenth century. Highly successful botanical gardens were established in three of the Australian colonies in the Victorian period at Sydney, Adelaide and Melbourne, and there were other successful gardens at Brisbane, Port Darwin and Hobart, together with nine municipal gardens also in significant population centres (McCracken 1997: 30–1). The balance-sheet of successes of the botanical gardens of the British empire, in the sense of facilitating the introduction of crops and plants

Fig. 9.9 Kirstenbosch National Botanical Garden, Cape Town, founded in 1913. Photo © R. A. Butlin.

('economics') profitable to colonial settlers and the metropole, was not impressive. This was partly on account of the tendency of colonial farmers to favour monopoly crops and to move quickly from one to another in the hope of obtaining higher yields and profits, but with greater success at the introduction of secondary crops at the end of the nineteenth century (McCracken 1997: 132–3).

McCracken contends that 'the lure of monoculture was often very great. Thus we find Ceylon agriculture dominated by spices, then coffee, then cinchona, and finally tea. Time and again curators built nurseries of tens of thousands of young economics only to find local farmers apathetic about trying new crops.' This evaluation of the low rate of success of these botanical gardens owes much to what might be seen as artificially pessimistic annual reports by curators, who were 'keen to create the impression that their gardens were in the forefront of economic botany', even though they may have had few species of 'economics' to offer. There were successes, mainly in the propagation and promotion of sugar cane, coffee, tea, rubber and forest trees (McCracken 1997: 133, 135, 137).

Dutch botanical gardens

The Dutch made extensive use of their East Indies domain to apply science to the improvement of tropical agricultural production. This link had deep roots, in that the botanical garden at Leiden, founded in 1593, was a major point of initial contact for botanical knowledge and plant diffusion with South and later South-East Asia, particularly for the Dutch empire. A major and much later overseas colonial botanical garden was the one created from 1817 on Java at Buitenzorg, now Borgor, on Mount Salak, 58 km from the capital Batavia, in response to a proposal by Dr K. Reinwart, who had just been appointed 'director of agricultural establishments, arts and science for the Netherlands East Indies' (Headrick 1988: 219), and who collected very large numbers of tropical plant species in the period 1817–22 and had successfully imported and promoted such commercial crops as tea, cinnamon, cacao and tobacco. His successor, a gardener rather than a scientist, obtained and disseminated the high-yielding cinchona which became a very important commercial and export crop. Buitenzorg was upgraded by the Dutch government in 1870 to a major agricultural experimental station, which flourished in the period 1877 to 1911, partly on account of the construction of a visitors' laboratory in 1884 to facilitate links with science elsewhere. Although about one hundred Indonesians were employed on the site, none was able to develop as scientists. Scientific experiment and plant development was also achieved by a number of plantation research centres, and Headrick contends that in consequence 'the Netherlands East Indies had the most complete and best organized botanical and agricultural research network in the tropics' (Headrick 1998: 219–22).

French botanical gardens

The history and character of the French development of botanical gardens and experimental stations were different from those of the British, Dutch and Germans. Headrick (1998: 222) suggests that whereas the botanical gardens of the Dutch and British were closely linked to the needs of empire, the major French institutions were more closely geared to the needs, culture and politics of the metropolis, evidenced by the Jardin des Plantes in Paris. The Jardin des Plantes had its origins in a royal medicinal plant garden founded in 1626, but underwent a change of name (Jardin Royal des Plantes) and a widening of scientific function in 1718. A further change took place after the French Revolution in the name of the garden to the Jardin des Plantes, and the specimen collections, laboratory and other facilities were given the name of the Muséum National d'Histoire Naturelle (Hepper 1986: 299). Although plant collectors were sent to many parts of the world to add specimens to French collections and gardens, economic botany was not part of its function, so that in the second half of the nineteenth century, it 'retained its dedication to descriptive natural science and taxonomy long after other institutions had shifted their focus toward experimental biology. As a result, it did not keep up with the science faculty of the University of Paris or, in botany, with Kew' (Headrick 1998: 223, 224).

Responses to the botanic transfer needs of the growing French overseas empire mainly came later, from the 1880s, when the need for a new role was advocated by the director of the botanical garden at Montpellier, and exemplified by the initiative in seed and plant transfers to and from French tropical colonies by Maxime Cornu, professor of culture at the Muséum in Paris. Stimulus had been provided by the Société Zoologique d'Acclimatation established in 1854, and attempts had been made to introduce exotic commercial crops such as coffee and spices to Algeria. One of the main means of experimenting with and transferring plants was the experimental garden (*jardin d'essai*). A *jardin d'essai* was opened in Algiers, two years after the French invasion of 1830, and an initial success was the Australian eucalyptus tree. By 1860 its director Auguste Hardy claimed that 'the whole of colonization is a vast deed of acclimatization' (Osborne 2000: 136). The French consistently experimented with the acclimatisation of tropical crops in Algiers, partly to try to develop cane sugar, coffee, exotic spices and fruit to replace the supplies lost with the independence of St Domingue in the West Indies.

Interest in the acclimatisation of tropical crops was accelerated in France and its colonies by the report of a commission which had visited this type of garden in Germany, Britain and Belgium, and which suggested Kew and Berlin botanical gardens as models. A decree of 28 January 1899 established a *jardin d'essai* in the Bois de Vincennes in Paris, directed by Jean Dybowski for the Ministry of Colonies (Headrick 1998: 225). The Geographical Chronicle section of *Annales de Géographie* of 15 January 1899 reports the decree as a recommendation of the commission which 'c'est déclarée à l'unanimité en faveur de la création d'un jardin colonial métropolitain, sur le modèle de ceux de Kew et de Berlin'. This new garden was soon active and effective in spreading seeds and plants to similar gardens around the French empire. Freidberg has shown in a seminal study of the historical geography of food in Burkina Faso that:

By the turn of the century, more modest experimental gardens (*jardins d'essai*) were multiplying across France's expanding colonial empire in West and Central Africa. Although modelled after *jardins d'essai* in France, the African sites typically doubled as *potagers* (kitchen gardens) for local colonial officials, and their diverse crop mix included vegetables that the officials themselves habitually ate in France, such as *haricot vert*. These were not considered luxuries, but rather dietary necessities in places where local vegetation seemed strange and savage. (Friedberg 2003: 449)

Nonetheless, experimental botanical gardens in the French empire never operated on the same scale as those of their European colonial rivals, a fact attributed by Headrick to the lateness of the second French colonial empire (apart from Algeria) and the consequent lack of settlers and investors, together with the geographical factors of poverty of resources and populations, though there were exceptions, notably in Libreville in Gabon and Saigon in French Indo-China (Headrick 1998: 227–8). Yet there is a seeming paradox in that the period after 1870 was also a time when French science was increasingly influenced by the growing colonial lobby, was more closely linked with the development of specialist units within the universities, and was becoming less of an amateur interest (Heffernan 1994b, 21–45).

Major studies of botanical gardens, though shedding much light on their history, character and influence, nonetheless have to be evaluated against other complementary processes, including the influence of colonial estate-owners and forestry authorities, and the significance of non-institutional and informal agencies. Settlers evolved their own intermediate, non-professional botanical intelligence and technology that informed their decisions about which exotics were useful and desirable – and how they could be grown in a hostile environment (Beinart and Middleton 2004: 13). Beinart and Middleton illustrate the significance of informal agency in the process of transfer with reference to the spread of field crops (prickly pear, maize, manioc, sweet potatoes) in the south of Madagascar before botanical gardens were introduced, and point also to the significance of seeds carried by frontier European settlers to, for example, America and South Africa. They also raise the interesting question of the difference between informal agency and the unintentional spread of plants (and animals), and of the chronology and reasons for acceptance or rejection of plant transfers. They give examples of indigenous resistance to official attempts to introduce cash crops, for example in Mozambique to the cultivation of cotton, on grounds of intensification of labour or loss of labour and land, and the consequent unreliability of food supply, and the preference for older familiar species of maize in Kenya over the varieties introduced by colonial officials. On the other hand, there is clear evidence of the adoption by Africans over a long period of time of American species of cultivars (Beinart and Middleton 2004: 13–20).

It is also worth adding that despite their best endeavours, the attempted spread, for example of medicinally prophylactic plants via botanical gardens, could go astray, sometimes because of the poor specimens collected by plant-hunters. A good example is that of the British attempt to obtain and diffuse the cinchona tree, a historically known species whose bark countered the effects of malaria. The story is well documented (Honigsbaum 2001; Williams 1962: 431–42).

In this chapter we have reviewed a range of themes about human–environmental links and changes in European territories, including deforestation, the management of water resources, the hunting and conservation of game, and the use of botanical gardens for plant dissemination. In the next chapter we look in more detail at the ways in which some of the new imperial routes and communications systems facilitated the movement of ideas, goods and people.

10 | The arteries of empire: transport and communications

While the railways were expanding in this dramatic fashion, a network of telegraph lines was being strung equally fast across the length and breadth of Northern Nigeria, despite large stretches often disappearing whenever the local inhabitants needed to renew their personal ornaments and fishing hooks with the much prized copper wire the government had so kindly made available to them. However, whatever temporary setbacks there may have been, this process of extending land communications, which also included the construction of laterite surfaced roads, plus the introduction by John Holt & Company (Liverpool) Limited of a small river fleet, reduced so considerably the government's dependence on its own fleet that in due course it was able to withdraw from its role as a public carrier and limit its marine department's activities to the more technical requirements of ensuring safe navigation. (Baker 1996: 214)

Introduction

Geoffrey Baker's account of the development of communication networks in Nigeria in the period 1900–14 in his history of the Royal Niger Company, from which the above quotation is an extract, highlights the significance of roads, railways, water routes and the telegraph to a developing British colony. European imperialism had a profound effect on the geography of transport, communications and production systems of the countries which came under European control. Headrick (1988: 5–6) developed the theory that advances in European science and technology in the eighteenth and nineteenth centuries strongly influenced the economic and commercial growth of the leading European states in that period, and was also responsible for the speed and extent of European imperial control and development overseas. Through the development of steam-powered and iron- and steel-clad ships, improvements in weapons, communications (by cable and telegraph) and means of combating tropical diseases, tools were introduced by means of which 'Europeans brought about the shift in global relations we call the new imperialism'. Headrick's thesis is not entirely about technology: he is careful to point out that these new means of eroding the power of distance and the restrictions of topography, of increasing substantially the rates of industrial production, and of control through the weapons of armies and navies, were paralleled by substantial cultural impacts, not least the acceleration of involvement in global systems of power and incorporation, and desires for improved national systems of transport by sea.

Beyond the history of the technical achievements of transport and communications systems within the imperial context is the wider question of speed, modernity and the time–space compression from the late nineteenth century onwards (Kern 1983). Technologically and culturally facilitated speed had deep implications for economic change and development, but 'speed also had multiple other attractions and connotations in the modern era. It was promoted for reasons of military control in colonial discourses and glorified in revolutionary rhetoric to speed up the utopian promises of the new society to come. In the United States speed was even endorsed as a personal moral virtue' (Simonsen 2005: 100–1).

Roads and empire

All the territories that came under European imperial influence had long-existing transport networks, including complex systems of roads and routes used for the transport of people and goods, including the routes used by nomadic peoples. Although water transport by sea and river was more efficient than overland transport, there were large parts of many of the countries and regions that came under European imperial influence that lacked a suitable navigable river network, and therefore were dependent on the use of animals or porters along extensive caravan routes. In Asia there were many historic caravan routes that conveyed goods across difficult terrain and hostile environments, the longest of these, the Silk Road, stretching from the Middle East across to China. Most of the trans-Asiatic routes started from Baghdad, and there were links to cities in India such as Lahore, Delhi, Jodhpur, Agra, Surat, Ahmedabad and Burhanpur (Chaudhuri 1985: 169). There were also many caravan routes across the Sahara Desert.

Existing routes for movement of people, animals and goods were caught up in the complex processes of imperialism and colonialism. Rockel, in his study of the movement of caravan labour in nineteenth-century East Africa, has shown that 'travel by foot was the only possible means of transportation in nearly all of precolonial East Africa ... the main axis of

East African commerce was along the foot tracks of the central caravan route, stretching over 950 miles through Tanzania' (Rockell, 2006: 4). The thousands of caravan porters who moved along these routes were vital to regional trade, to the spread of the Christian and Muslim religions, to the interactions of isolated communities, and to European colonisation (Rockell 2006: 4). Although the system of porterage had developed in a pre-capitalist context, 'East African porters developed a transitional form of wage labour shaped by indigenous precapitalist labour norms but closely linked to merchant capital and the global economy', as 'a fully fledged *African* response to the world economic system' (Rockell 2006: 6–7).

Larger-scale road systems were constructed in imperial territories to speed the movement of goods and people (especially troops), exemplified by the frontier roads that were constructed and extended by the British in India, Canada and South Africa (Christopher 1988: 47–8). In mid-nineteenth-century Canada, however, the road network, as evidenced in a travel census in 1848 for Nova Scotia, New Brunswick and Canada East (Quebec), shows how important were the short arteries of transport such as roads, cart tracks and bridle paths. Mackinnon's study of this census shows how the pre-railway

domestic economy operated: via a network of great roads and bye roads, maintained by statute labour and at public expense. While many of these roads were little more than rough cart tracks and bridle paths, often described in disparaging terms by visitors and colonial officials, they were adequate for the demands of small, colonial economies dependent on small-scale mixed farming, domestic production, and employment in the staple trades. (Mackinnon 2003: 19–20)

New roads were constructed in the British empire as feeder roads to railways and, from the beginning of the twentieth century, roads of better quality were constructed for use by motorised vehicles. The Germans constructed roads as part of an integrated transport system in Togo (Christopher 1984: 82). Christopher (1988: 48–9) also points to the fact that 'road construction led to a boom in mass movements in tropical colonies where the bicycle provided a means of transport for people previously without even baggage animals'.

River systems of colonial territories

While discussions of the development and consequences of networks of transport and communication in imperial contexts tend to emphasise innovations such as railways, we must also keep in mind the continuing significance of historic modes and means of transport such as roads and river routes. In all the areas of European imperial interest, including those with small colonial populations and those which were developed as settlement colonies, there was a long history of the use of rivers and natural lakes as lines of communication and sources of water for the survival of people and animals. They were sources of various kinds of food, including fish, initially used by indigenous peoples and thereafter also by immigrants. They offered ways into extensive continental interiors for early explorers, and later provided routes for naval and commercial vessels in the processes of advancing power and control. They were often thought to be important routes for the exploitation of the commercial potential of the basins that they served, but navigational obstacles, especially on rivers like the Congo, often frustrated the dreams and aspirations of the European administrators, explorers and metropolitan investors. Rivers were not, of course, constant and predictable in their flow, being subject to drought and flood.

The Mekong River, for example, became, at least for a short period in the course of French expansion in South-East Asia in the nineteenth century, the focus of utopian dreams about a river route to China from the Mekong Delta. A French scientific and commercial expedition – the Mekong Exploration Commission – supported by the Ministry of Marine in Paris, attempted between 1866 and 1868 to navigate the Mekong upstream from Saigon, the expedition being led by Commandant E.-M. L. de G. Doudart de Lagrée, with the naval officer Francis Garnier as his deputy.

The geopolitical purpose of the expedition is clearly characterised by Keay:

The river could do for Saigon what the Yangtze was doing for Shanghai or what the Mississippi might have done for the former French possession of New Orleans. As a highway of commerce with the markets of inland China, and as a slipway for extracting the minerals and forest produce of the intervening lands, it would furnish an entrée into continental Asia, so redeeming the fortunes of the struggling colony in Saigon and endowing France with the potential for an eastern empire of its own. (Keay 2005a: 290; 2005b)

The outcome was in some respects negative: the river was not navigable by steamboats with shallow draught for commercial purposes, on account of the many rapids in its course, notably those above Kratié and the substantial Khon Falls. The expedition did, however, reach and cross the Chinese frontier into Yunnan in 1868, where Lagrée died, and the survivors then found the headwaters of the Red River, which offered a realistic shipping route into and out of China, with Hanoi as the key port city (Keay 2005a: 301–4). An attempt to promote and consolidate French control in the north – in Tonkin – was made in 1873 with an attack on Hanoi from the sea by a small French expeditionary force, but the force was routed, and attempts to regain French control only recurred in 1882–3, with advances into Tonkin, and the bringing of Annam under French protection. A continuing effort was made to review the navigability of the Mekong as a trading route within Indo-China, with many attempts made to create routes through the rapids south of the Khon Falls, using steam vessels.

Similar difficulties were faced by explorers in Africa looking for routes to the interior. Although rivers such as the Niger were navigable over much of their length and attracted the attention of early European commercial and territorial interests, many were not, on account of rapids and waterfalls, as the missionary and explorer David Livingstone found in 1858 in his expedition along the lower Zambezi, notably when he came across the Kebrasa Rapids (Christopher 1984: 73–4). The upper reaches of rivers such as the Nile and the Congo were found to be navigable, and prefabricated steamboats were used by European companies on the upper Congo, the Nile, and Lake Chad. In the case of the Congo Free State, the upper Congo was the central artery in the exploitation of resources, and was linked by railways which bypassed some of the difficult rapids, with Leopoldville, which was founded as a base by Stanley in 1882, and which became a very large port. The French used the upper Niger and the Senegal for transport, as, to a lesser extent, did the British on the upper Nile and Lake Victoria. The arid parts of North and South Africa did not have river systems that could be used for transport, because of low flow and shallow draught, and South Africa's resources were developed more by road, railway and sea transport (Christopher 1984: 74).

The main rivers of India had a long history of use as transport arteries. Chaudhuri states that the Indus and the Ganges had long witnessed the carriage of trade goods on river boats to the Indian Ocean, though movement was dependent on the seasonality of water flow, the rivers being low in the dry and cold season of the year when much less water was released by the Himalayan glaciers. The water levels rose in the monsoon season, and facilitated river transport. 'Huge, flat-bottomed boats were used to carry all sorts of heavy goods, and in Bengal the inland waterways provided the main means of commercial transportation. There were other rivers in India, South East Asia, and China which had a comparable role: the Godivari and the Krishna, the Mekong in Indo-China, the Yangtze in China' (Chaudhuri 1985: 167). In India and Burma the major rivers were important links in the trading and transportation systems, including the Irrawaddy which 'was navigable for some 1,650 kilometres above Rangoon and the trade and passenger service on this prime artery was dominated by the Irrawaddy Flotilla Company throughout the colonial period. Similarly the Brahmaputra provided the main means of access to Assam from Calcutta' (Christopher 1988: 47).

Sail-based trading routes: the Indian Ocean and the South China Sea

While much of the history of transport change in the era of high imperialism is related to technical changes in propulsion and in ship design, the persistence of earlier forms of boats and trade networks must also be acknowledged. Bose, in his account of the Indian Ocean and its littoral territories in the ages of high imperialism and anti-colonial nationalism, reminds us that:

one needs to be careful not to write out of history the dogged resistance of sailing communities in the Arab and Malay worlds, even while acknowledging the dominance that European shipping came to exercise in the waters of the Indian Ocean. The Arab dhow and Malay *prahu* boats, with all they represent, had a much longer afterlife than is commonly supposed. (Bose 2006: 28)

Gilbert in his study of dhows and the colonial economy of Zanzibar from 1860 to 1970 shows the weakness of theories that reduce the significance of dhow-based trading around the Indian Ocean in and beyond the colonial era on the basis of a modernity represented only by steam-powered vessels. His view is that 'steamers did not replace dhows during the colonial era. Rather the two reached an uncomfortable accommodation, wherein both economies continued to function in the same geographical area, each mostly confined to and defined by its own commodities, means of transport, and organization, but with few points of contact and often intense conflict between the two' (Gilbert 2004: 6). Dhows, subject to climatic regimes, notably the monsoon, carried commodities such as 'salt, dried shark, dates, mangrove poles, grain, coconuts, carpets, ghee, rose-water and suchlike' and were seen by colonial officials, partly on the grounds of their historic association with the slave trade, as anti-modern, particularly as blocks to the modernisation of the clove industry, but were useful as carriers of the commodities mentioned above (Gilbert 2006: 6). There were differences in the geographies of areas in which dhows and steamships operated, the former mainly in the western Indian Ocean, southern Arabia, the Red Sea and the Persian Gulf, the latter in trade to the Atlantic and Bombay (Gilbert 2006: 7).

There were also symbolic contrasts between steamships (including naval vessels), which were seen as tools of colonial modernity and control, and the dhows, seen as 'native vessels', reflective of a different type of economy including the slave trade. This distinction resulted in differential classifications between the dhows, generally under 500 tons, which were subject to search and seizure by naval vessels, and steam-powered ships that were generally over 500 tons and not subject to this process. A change in the basis of this distinction was made 'in the Brussels Treaty of 1892, which basically declared that a native vessel was either a vessel commanded and manned by "natives" or a vessel which had the appearance of a native vessel', a definition not ended until 1921 (Gilbert 2006: 135). Dhows enjoyed some advantages, in that they paid lower fees because they made less use of port infrastructure.

Cleary's detailed study of trading patterns in Borneo in the nineteenth century has demonstrated the complex interactions between indigenous and colonial trading and production systems and the persistence of traditional routes. Increasing European interest in Borneo in the nineteenth century, with the establishment of the British state of Sarawak and of North Borneo, and the continued Dutch control of Kalimantan (Borneo), added another layer to the existing trading pattern of the collection by indigenous groups of exotic products from the interior, which were then sent downriver by merchants to the coastal ports, whence they were sold into regional or international markets by Chinese or Malay traders (Cleary 1997: 29–45).

The significance of the shipping routes along Borneo's north-west coast in the South China Sea increased in the colonial context, with particular reference to trade with China through Hong Kong and the search for coaling stations for steamships along the coast of Borneo. To the trade in luxury 'exotic' products and 'jungle products' gathered by indigenous peoples from the interior there was added the colonial dimension ('colonial products'), through the familiar agency of the chartered company, for example the 'new products that would prove attractive to the European market. The encouragement of trade in sawn timber, precious metals, minerals (coal, and at the end of the century, oil), tobacco and rubber were to become the aims of the North Borneo Chartered Company or the Dutch administration in Kalimantan'. The outcome was an increase in the exports of the various Borneo states from 1860 to 1940, as well as imports of foodstuffs, opium, fabrics and industrial products, mostly coming from Britain via Singapore, and whose cyclical variation reflected the demands for infrastructural innovations such as railways, especially in Sarawak and north Borneo (Cleary 1997: 32, 37–8).

Cleary concludes that the traditional gathering of jungle products, including birds' nests and rattan canes, was sustained and accelerated by the colonial presence, and that the modern export staple sector, mainly involving minerals, was 'by contrast, slow and muted' in its development. He makes an important point also about the linkages of traditional economies with colonial exports, in the sense that even the commodities most eagerly sought as export staples such as tobacco, rubber or timber were complemented by the indigenously gathered 'jungle rubber', 'native tobacco', various types of cane, and other forest products. With reference to Wallerstein's models of the historical development of the world economy, Cleary contends that 'the metropolitan core could not, at will, simply crank the resource-rich periphery into life. The process of resource exploitation, and the articulation of indigenous and colonial production systems, depended on the local state, on geographical location and on both local and external investment decisions' (Cleary 1997: 44).

Ships, seaways and imperialism

The basis of European links with the far reaches of what were to become their empires and colonies had been from the fifteenth century the use of sailing ships of various kinds to link the metropoles with Africa, Asia, North and South America, and ultimately with Australia, New Zealand and the islands of the Pacific Ocean. The beginning of the seventeenth century saw the founding of major national companies for trade with the Indies, East and West, and other parts of the world, and extensions of geographical knowledge of the islands of the South Pacific and southern Australia.

The scientific voyages of the eighteenth century by Samuel Wallis; James Cook; Louis-Antoine, comte de Bougainville; Jean-François de Galaup, comte de la Pérouse; Alejandro Malaspina; José Bustamente and others in the Pacific created new knowledge of the region and new skills in marine charting and navigation. Navigation had been much improved with the development of a sophisticated chronometer and increases in the size and speed of merchant and naval sailing vessels, to which were gradually added from the late eighteenth century the application of steam power to propulsion and the use of iron, later steel, for cladding and then for construction. The availability of the new technology, however, did not bring about the immediate demise of sailing ships, for until the opening of the Suez Canal in 1869 much of the trade with India and the Far East was carried out by large sailing ships, including the large East Indiamen of the Dutch and English East India Companies. The great tea-clipper *Cutty Sark*, launched in 1869, was initially engaged in the tea trade from China and India, and even after the impact of the Suez Canal it continued as an important vessel in the wool trade from Australia. Similar vessels continued to operate in the nitrate trade from South America until the opening of the Panama Canal.

The pattern of shipping that had developed from the second decade of the nineteenth century was one linked to market capitalism and the notion of free trade, all bound up in a growing global trading system. The history of sea transport to and from the European colonies generally involved the gradual building up of trade links by smaller merchant companies from the colonial states, followed by consolidation at a later date into larger companies. The Peninsular and Oriental Company started in 1834 as the Peninsular Steam Navigation Company, sailing from Britain to the Iberian peninsula. Later, as the Peninsular and Oriental line in 1837, it carried mail to Gibraltar, Malta and Alexandria, and by 1842 it was carrying mail from Suez to Ceylon, Madras and Calcutta. Thereafter it stretched its activities eastwards to Penang, Singapore, Hong Kong and Shanghai, and later to Bombay, Sydney and Yokohama. In 1914 it merged with the British India Steam Navigation Company, which had started as the Calcutta and Burmah Steam Navigation Company, founded in 1856 as a small carrier, but which expanded to cover the conveyance of freight and people over much of South and East Asia and to Australia (Headrick 1988: 39–40).

Merchant shipowners from Hamburg and Bremen began such a process from the time of the lifting of the Napoleonic blockade in 1813, and initially German ships were used, after the further removal of obstructive British legislation to free trade between 1822 and 1854, to carry cargo on charter from English, Dutch and Chinese merchants. From 1850 to *c.* 1880 German ships carried on coastal trading in South and East Asia, and increased trade with West Africa, frequently financed by British banks (Stoecker 1986e: 12–13). German mercantile shipping from the Hanseatic ports became part of a large British international trading process, and relied to a degree – in the days before Germany had a formal colonial

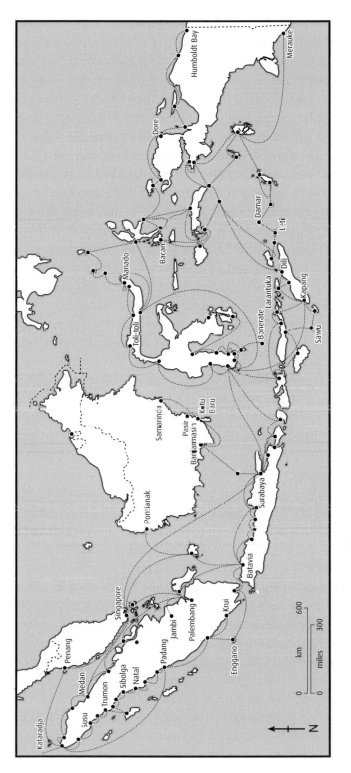

Fig. 10.1 Regular steamship services of the Koninklijke Paketvaart Maatschappij (KPM) in the Netherlands Indies in 1891.
Source: Cribb (2000: 141). By permission of and © Taylor and Francis Books UK.

policy – on protection by British colonial administrators and gunboats (Headrick 1988: 14).

The advancement and maintenance of Dutch economic and strategic interests in South-East Asia were facilitated by the award by the Dutch government in 1888 of contracts for regular mail and cargo services in the Netherlands Indies to the Koninklijk Paketvaart Maatschappij (KPM), a private steamer company, which linked many parts of the region (Cribb 2000: 141).

Steam power was introduced to merchant and naval vessels in the early nineteenth century, initially in the form of paddle steamers of various types and designs, but they were overtaken by the development of the steam-powered propeller. Where they did remain active for a long time, in the form of shallow-draught sternwheelers, was in such areas as Africa, India, Australia and North America, where they were used both commercially and as naval vessels in shallow coastal waters or rivers. Steam and sail power were used together on merchant, and conspicuously on naval, vessels for some time after the application of steam to the propulsion of ships: navies, including the British, maintained this mixture longer than was really necessary, on account of conservative views of change and training, and most naval powers only abandoned sailing ships after 1880–90.

The advent of steam propulsion could only be of use to European imperial powers where, in the first instance, supplies of fuel, wood and then coal could be made available at critical refuelling points in a long voyage. At a later stage oil was a more effective and more transportable means of firing ships' boilers, requiring less crew labour than ships powered by coal-fired boilers. The experimental introduction of oil to ships occurred in the 1860s, and Russian ships had adopted the system by the 1880s, with other nations following. Britain converted to oil firing navy ships after the end of the First World War, and acquired oilfields in the Middle East for this purpose (Hugill 1993: 134).

Great technical strides forward were made during the late nineteenth and early twentieth centuries in the design and building of both naval and merchant ships, including reduction of hull displacement (for using the Suez and Panama Canals), and merchant ships were affected by the increasing lightness of construction materials for ships and ships' boilers, and of the turbine engine, together with the use of oil (Hugill 1993: 134–5). Naval ships had different requirements. Hugill (1993: 135, 137) has shown that the range of a warship needed to be about three times that of a commercial vessel, relying (once they had fuel-powered propulsion) on secure supply depots, which is why sail power was maintained for warships long

Fig. 10.2 Arrival of KPM ship *Reael* at Jakarta, 1893.
By permission of and © KITLV Leiden, KITV 11702.

after it had been abandoned by merchant ships. Nonetheless, the development of a global range of coaling stations, conspicuously by the British, as well as in-voyage refuelling, facilitated the wider distribution of navy vessels. British coaling stations were established in the Falkland Islands, South Africa, Vancouver Island, Singapore, Hong Kong, Hawaii, Samoa and the Philippines. In addition naval dockyards were located and developed at what were deemed to be strategic points around the world. British naval dockyards were founded in the West Indies, Canada, Australia, India, Saint Helena, Gibraltar, Malta, Aden, Simonstown in South Africa, and Singapore in the Far East.

Their commercial counterparts were entrepôt trading stations, initially small groups of trading posts which gradually increased in size according to changes in the volume and character of the commodities traded. Some of these, such as Singapore, Sydney, Calcutta, Batavia, Alexandria, Cape Town and Bombay, became major colonial port cities, carrying a range of imperial and administrative functions, and in some, such as Port Said,

Karachi, Dakar, Hong Kong and Singapore, completely new port facilities were constructed (Christopher 1988: 73–8; Headrick 1988: 32).

Speed and sailing times

The outcome of these major technical changes in shipping was greater speed for both merchant and naval ships. The time taken in the eighteenth century for large sailing ships to travel from London to Calcutta had been between five to eight months, but by the 1830s this had been reduced by steam propulsion to a month for mail, and by the 1840s to the same time for passengers and freight, a figure further reduced to two weeks by 1914 (Headrick 1988: 20). The time of a voyage by sea from Amsterdam to the Dutch colony of Java had been a whole year in the seventeenth century, reducing to three or four months in the 1850s and one month by 1900. A further consequence for merchant ships was the possibility, with shorter voyage times, of carrying a wider range of cargoes than the luxury items that had characterised their early voyages in the seventeenth and eighteenth centuries, and at lower cost.

In addition to improvements in the speed of movement and the regularity of services, which enabled the profitable transport of commodities such as jute, mineral ores, coal, wool and petroleum, technical changes from the 1880s such as refrigeration facilitated the transport of meat and dairy products to Europe from Australia and New Zealand (Headrick 1988: 22). More specialist shipping companies developed from the 1830s and 1840s starting with the transport of mail, a process heavily subsidised by national governments, sometimes via the purses of the colonial territories. More than one-third of the annual payment of one million pounds to British mail shipping lines came from colonial funds, with India having to pay for half the loss on the P&O Company's contracts (Headrick 1988: 37).

Cartels or 'conferences' of European shipping companies were formed to offset fluctuations in business and prices and to a degree the competition from tramp freighters. By 1911 there were some fourteen major shipping companies, mainly the outcomes of mergers of smaller companies, thirteen of them operating from Europe, six of which (Peninsular and Oriental, British India, Blue Funnel Line, the French company Messageries Maritimes and the German companies Hamburg-Amerika line and Norddeutscher Lloyd) were active in South and East Asia, and two (Union Castle and Elder Dempster) in Africa. Headrick has indicated that smaller German shipping companies, such as the Woermann Line, were used to carry on the trade with Germany's poorer colonies such as

Togo, Cameroon and German South-West Africa, to which was added the Hamburg-Bremen-Afrika line and the Deutsch Ost-Afrika line before the First World War (Headrick 1988: 39, 42).

The Suez Canal

In the late nineteenth and early twentieth centuries the distance and time taken to travel by sea between European metropoles and distant colonies was dramatically reduced by the application of modern capitalist finance and engineering technology (and the use of large numbers of overworked and exploited labourers) and by the construction of major canals capable of carrying ocean-going vessels that linked the Pacific with the Atlantic Ocean and the Indian Ocean with the Mediterranean. The first of these was the Suez Canal, completed in 1869.

Fig. 10.3 Entrance to the Suez Canal from Port Said, 1888.
By permission of and © Cambridge University Library, RSPC-Y308A-002.

In its modern form the idea of such a canal had in part evolved from the utopian ideas of the Saint-Simonians in France – the name given to a group of thinkers and activists with radical socialist beliefs, based in Paris in the 1820s and 1830s, who claimed that modern technology, including the development of canals, railways and other innovative forms of communication, could help link the cultures of Europe with those of Africa and Asia (Heffernan 1994a: 101). The leader of the Saint-Simonians, Prosper Enfantin, following the earlier ideas of Claude Henri de Rouvroy (who died in 1825) about such a canal, 'spent three fruitless years between 1833 and 1836 in and around Cairo trying to persuade anyone who would listen of the need for a canal link between the Red Sea and the Mediterranean. Whilst in Egypt, Enfantin met and greatly impressed Ferdinand de Lesseps, the young French pro-consul in the region' (Heffernan 1994a: 101). In 1854, the Vicomte Ferdinand de Lesseps (later president of the Société de Géographie de Paris, from 1881 to 1890) raised the idea of a French project for the canal with his friend Prince Mohammed Said, Viceroy to the sultan of Turkey, who agreed, on very generous terms, to the proposed canal company. In the same year an Egyptian company – La Compagnie Universelle du Canal Maritime de Suez – was created to manage the construction of the new canal and undertake its operation for ninty-nine years.

The initiative for the construction of the Suez Canal had come from France, anxious to extend control in the Middle East, especially Egypt, with support from Egypt (wishing to escape from Ottoman empire hegemony) and opposition from Britain. The design and much of the capital came from France, and the labour was almost entirely Egyptian.

The shares in the Suez Canal Company were at first held mainly by French and Egyptian investors, but the Egyptian shares were purchased by the British government in 1875. The construction of the Suez Canal started in 1859, and it opened on 17 November 1869, having a length of 101 miles (163 km). It was a major factor in the compression of the time and space of maritime links between Europe and the Middle East, South and South-East Asia, the Far East and the Antipodes. The distance reductions were particularly dramatic: London to Bombay via the Cape was 19,755 km, but via the canal it was 11,619 km, a distance reduction of 41 per cent, with a 29 per cent reduction from London to Singapore, and a 26 per cent reduction from London to Hong Kong (Headrick 1988: 26).

The cost in Egyptian life in its construction was enormous – about 20,000 Egyptian labourers died in the process. This was part of a much larger process of the acquisition, capture and control of large numbers of bodies as a consequence of a major capitalist production project, with the 'creation and management of large bodies of migrant workers, to build and maintain the new structures being laid in place across the Egyptian countryside – roads, railways, canals, dams, bridges, telegraphs and ports. Larger projects such as the Suez Canal required the movement and supervision of tens of thousands of men' (Mitchell 1988: 96).

The opening of the Suez Canal was a dramatic affair, symbolising, according to Ismail Pasha, the khedive of Egypt, the re-orientation of Egypt from Africa towards Europe, and characterised by much pomp and circumstance, including a performance of the opera *Aïda*, based on an idea by the archaeologist and Egyptologist Auguste Mariette and composed by Giuseppe Verdi. Against this, it must be borne in mind that the canal 'was also a massive financial burden for the Egyptian people whose taxes and labour assisted its completion. Ismail Pasha's political designs bankrupted his country and jeopardized its future' (Carter 1999: 113).

At its opening the Suez Canal did not immediately solve the problem of very long journeys for ships sailing from Europe to Asia, as its depth was insufficient for the largest steamships, and sailing on the canal was only allowed in hours of daylight, but gradual deepening and the use of electric light on ships increased the numbers using the canal (Headrick 1988: 26–7). Britain was the main user of the canal, her ships making up 80 per cent of the traffic in the 1880s, and staying at over 60 per cent until the 1930s.

The Panama Canal

The Panama Canal, completed in 1914, was also a project in which de Lesseps was involved. The idea of a canal across the isthmus of Panama linking the Atlantic and Pacific oceans was developed at a conference in Paris in 1879, and de Lesseps, famous for his involvement in the successful Suez Canal, was given charge of the project through a new company – the Compagnie Universelle du Canal Interocéanique. The choice of the isthmus of Panama was partly determined by an earlier agreement in 1846 whereby an American diplomat, under the Monroe Doctrine, secured from Colombia exclusive rights of transit across the isthmus for the United States, and this, stimulated by the Californian gold rushes of 1850, initiated the building of a Panama railway across the isthmus, which had been completed by a New York company in 1855.

In 1880 the French company was in being, and in 1881 it began the construction of the canal along the line of the Panama railway. There were serious difficulties from the outset in raising capital for the Panama Canal project, and major environmental hazards were experienced. As with the Suez Canal, the cost in loss of life among labourers was huge: some 22,000, mainly West Indian workers, had died on the project by 1889, when the managing company was liquidated, and de Lesseps and his son were charged in France with fraud and mismanagement. They were found guilty and the son was imprisoned for a year (Frenkel 1992: 145). The environmental hazards included yellow fever and malaria, and the hardness of the rock from which the canal was being excavated. A new French company (Compagnie Nouvelle du Canal du Panama) was established to complete the work, which it was unable to do, and the project was ultimately transferred to the United States after long debate on the choice of Nicaragua or Panama as the route for the new canal, reviewed by two separate US canal commissions. The context of American geopolitics during the presidency of Theodore Roosevelt was one of greater focus on processes of modernisation at home and a clear policy in which 'successive administrations sent marines and gunboats throughout the Caribbean and Central America to enforce a pro-U.S. political order sympathetic to marauding corporations and bankers, in one instance even establishing a whole new country for the purpose, Panama' (Smith 2003: 84).

The Spooner Bill of 1902 gave the US president $40 million for the purchase of the New Canal Company from France and enabled him to start the negotiation of a treaty with Colombia – a formidable task, only resolved after Panama declared its independence from Colombia and after the ratification of the Hay–Bunau–Varilla Treaty in 1903 and 1904. This treaty gave the USA control of a zone ten miles wide along the canal, in return for a payment in cash and a promised annual rent, with Panama in theory retaining sovereignty over the canal area with the exception of police and judicial control by the USA (Frenkel 1992: 146). Processes, including better medical knowledge of fever, were set in train to eliminate malaria and yellow fever from the canal route. A series of American engineers proceeded with the work, starting in 1904, and the canal was completed in August 1914. It was used by 2,000 ships per year during the First World War, the figure increasing to 5,000 after the war.

The construction of the canal involved difficult geopolitical and engineering issues, but like its forerunner the Suez Canal it facilitated the advance of imperial power, including that of the United States. The proposal for the construction of the Panama Canal, however, had its critics within the United States, who argued that the country should not be an imperial power; that imperialism frustrated processes of free trade

(Frenkel 1992: 145, 147–8); and that there was preferential treatment of white workers, who had higher salaries paid in American dollars, based on the gold standard, as opposed to the lower salaries of the West Indian workers paid in Panama currency which was backed by the silver standard. This discrimination was also reflected in the settlement geography of the zone, where three types were recognised: American 'gold towns', West Indian 'silver towns' and the Latin American cities of Panama, the gold towns being direct imitations of American ones and where little Spanish was spoken.

In a recent publication, Matthew Parker has emphasised the opposition to the construction of the canal, mainly on geopolitical grounds, when concerns were voiced about:

> the change in the status quo that such a radical altering of the geography of the world would usher in. The Americans, in particular, were fiercely opposed to a foreign power controlling any transcontinental waterway. The French attempt would bring heavy criticism of the 'over-optimism' of its promoter, Ferdinand de Lesseps, and its failure would see his ruin and disgrace, as well as financial and political disaster for France. The American project was even more controversial, entailing at its inception the murky activities of political lobbyists and a vivid demonstration of a new kind of United States, casting off its historical aversion to imperialism and aggression on the international stage. (Parker 2007: xviii–xix)

Naval vessels and imperial power

Changes in naval vessel design were on the whole slower than those for merchant vessels, but from about the middle of the nineteenth century the navies of the major European powers, plus those of Russia and Japan, increased the use of iron in construction, and then of steel, from about 1875–80. Other important innovations included the propeller, the compound and other sophisticated forms of steam engine, the steam turbine and the progressive sophistication of the power and range of armaments. The Luppis-Whitehead self-propelled torpedo was first produced in England in 1867, and by the late 1870s was widely used. Specialist torpedo boats were also adopted by many navies in the period 1880–90. The development of guns with swivelling turrets changed the nature of naval manoeuvres, and with the building and use of large battleships with heavy armament and cruisers with varied armament in the late nineteenth and early twentieth centuries there was much debate about their strategic use.

Each European nation with a navy of its own varied the use of larger battleships, lighter cruisers and torpedo boats to suit different areas of naval action. Britain, for example, while giving her navy a global role, including protection for her colonies and trade routes, nonetheless constantly campaigned for a greater contribution to imperial defence from the colonies themselves. By 1907 Britain had all of its battleships, most of its armoured cruisers and two-thirds of its unarmed cruisers in European waters in the seas around Europe, with only small numbers of cruisers and destroyers in squadrons elsewhere: thirteen in the China squadron, nine in the Australian, five in the East Indian, three in the Cape of Good Hope squadron, three in the North American, and three in the West Indian (O'Brien 2001: 155–6).

Changes in the balance of naval power in imperial advancement and defence came in the later nineteenth century with the rapid division of Africa, South-East Asia and many of the Pacific islands between European imperial states, and with the growing imperialism of Japan and the United States. Britain remained the major global naval power until the end of the century, but only by balancing different requirements: 'While the empire was based on the battle fleet there had to be a balance between forces protecting British commercial interests in the wider world, and the battle fleet in home waters and the Mediterranean' (Lambert 1995: 162). This balance was further influenced by the changing position of Britain's European rivals, by changing technology, and by the desire of British governments to minimise naval and military expenditure.

Sea power was used in the advancement of British interests in and trade with China, notably in the opium wars from 1839 and the occupation of Hong Kong in 1841. Britain effectively exercised a combination of sea and military power, including the strategic and troop resources of India, which enabled them 'to annexe Burma, occupy Aden, and dominate the Persian Gulf. Sea power was critical to imperial development, the more so when armies could be moved by sea, and steamships opened up the great rivers of the world' (Lambert 1995: 180–1). The operation of small gunboats in river estuaries in parts of the British empire or other areas of imperial interest was a key part of imperial security and of efforts to stamp out the slave trade from Africa. In Nigeria, for example, in the course of the quest by Britain and France for preferential status for trading with indigenous groups and for strategic commercial bases, in addition to local treaties of friendship, bribery, and legal systems for the protection of British and French settlements, various types of gunboat were used to suppress local resistance to foreign hegemony and to the abolition of the slave trade.

Local naval engagement was also experienced elsewhere in the European imperial realms. In South-East Asia from about 1840, the Dutch, British and (later) Spanish navies were active in the suppression of piracy (in collaboration with local chiefs), slave-raiding and slave-trading: 'where treaties and blandishments were ineffective, search-and-destroy missions followed. British and Dutch gunboats moved from the Straits of Melaka to the Riau archipelago and the coasts of Borneo. Later in the century, Spanish squadrons finally succeeded in reducing the Sulu strongholds to ruins' (Trocki 1999: 98). The Dutch navy, like those of the British and French, had played a significant role, in collaboration with Dutch colonial armies, in the establishment of Dutch authority in Indonesia in the nineteenth century. Having realised by 1814 that the presence of a small number of Dutch naval vessels in the region would be inadequate to police the seas of Indonesia, to stamp out piracy and to move troops from one strategic point to another, a local 'Indisch' navy – of the colonial Dutch government in Batavia – was created in 1816 to fulfil a range of civil and military purposes, and it continued in existence until 1962 (Moor 1998: 106).

The development of railways and railway networks

The application of steam power to land-based locomotion in Western Europe in the early nineteenth century presaged a major revolution in the speed, efficiency, reliability and productivity of land transport for goods and passengers, an innovation that was to spread quite quickly in Europe and to other areas of the world during the nineteenth century.

The advantages of a railway system of transport had been known since its early use in England: the Stockton and Darlington railway, built for carrying coal, was completed in 1825 and the Liverpool and Manchester railway, the first to be built for passenger traffic, was in use from 1829. These were quickly followed by developments of railway transportation in the United States, Belgium and France. The railways in the United States ran over much longer distances than those in Britain, and by 1840 the length of track in the USA was twice that in Britain, and by 1860 three times the length (Hugill 1993: 173). By the end of the century large distances were covered by railways in the developed economies of states such as Britain, the USA and Russia: the first transcontinental link was completed in the USA in 1869, and in Russia in 1901 with the trans-Siberian link.

Railways were more reliable than other means of transport that were dependent on a satisfactory state of roads, trackways and rivers, subject in many countries to climatic and other physical disturbances. Financially railways were a risk, in that investment was always based on the hope of expansion in traffic and a sound financial return. They required enormous fixed capital costs, together with the necessary financial institutions such as banks, capital markets and railway companies for their creation and continuation. Another major requirement was land in large quantities, and with legal rights of use mainly allocated to the railway owners. They required highly specialised personnel to run the trains, wagons and carriages, an industrial base for manufacture, and fuel for locomotion. Their reach was much wider than the actual lines that they initiated and promoted.

Railways played an important role in European imperialism. In the British empire the transportation of bulk commodity agricultural products such as grain in Canada was made cheaper and more viable by the railway, which also opened up areas of cotton and jute production in India, connecting them with mills in Bombay and Calcutta, and facilitated wool and wheat production in Australia, and a range of commodities in New Zealand (Fieldhouse 1996: 117). Initially there was a slow rate of return to investors, on the grounds that railway construction was slow and in every sense laborious, and in some areas of the world speculative risk was high on account of particular environmental and cultural factors. Because of the size of investment required to construct and operate railways in imperial territories, the metropolitan states were often required to put up capital or guarantee investments and rates of interest. As Fieldhouse (1996: 117) has indicated, the British settlement colonies made them 'the largest source of political patronage available to poverty-stricken colonial politicians. Borrowing in Britain for the construction of a railway, whether state or privately owned, caused money to flow into an economy, enabling politicians to provide employment and enrich their supporters with contracts or sub-contracts.'

Land was also needed in large quantities for the tracks, stations, yards and other physical necessities of railway operation, but this fixed asset was supplemented by a wider and more flexible geographical basis of sources of finance, labour, political control and manufacture (Headrick 1988: 49–53). Complex difficulties of construction, operation and maintenance were experienced during the nineteenth and early twentieth centuries.

The development of the Indian railway system

The development of what became one of the largest railway systems in the world began in India in 1850, seven years before the Indian Uprising/ Mutiny. The history and geography of Indian railway development is quite exceptional, in respect of its size, density and cost; the fact that it was not tied to a local or national industrial economy at the zenith of railway growth; and India's colonial status. As Kerr states: 'No railways operated in India in 1850. Twenty-five years later India had an extensive network of trunk lines. Fifty years later, in 1900, trains steamed through most parts of India along railways whose trunk and branch lines extended over 25,000 miles of track. Railways, to paraphrase Theroux, had come to possess India and to make her hugeness graspable' (Kerr 1997: 1).

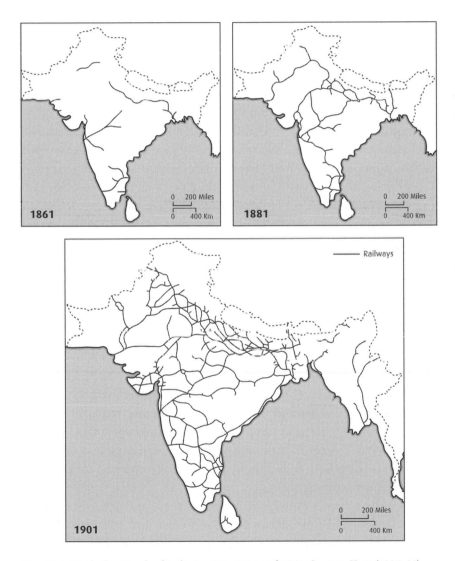

Fig. 10.4 The rail network of India in 1861, 1891 and 1901. Source: Kerr (1997: 39). By permission of and © Oxford University Press India, New Delhi.

The origins of the intense phase of railway-building in India in the second half of the nineteenth century lay in the efforts, from 1841, of a number of British engineers, notably Rowland Macdonald Stephenson, to persuade the East India Company to agree to support the building of railways. Stephenson was initially unsuccessful, but nonetheless sailed to India in 1844 to survey a potential route from Calcutta to Delhi and to press the case for Indian railways. He highlighted commercial and military reasons for their construction, and others emphasised what might be termed the potential modernising and civilising impact of railways on Indian people. Scottish and Lancashire cotton manufacturers were also very interested in a means of speeding up the transfer of raw cotton from production areas of the Deccan to ports in India such as Bombay.

Further pressure, as Headrick (1988: 59–60) has indicated, was put on the board of the East India Company to agree to requests for railway-building by such agencies as the P&O shipping line, city bankers, newspapers and journals, and midland industrialists. In 1849 the court of directors of the East India Company finally agreed, and the East India Railway Company (EIR) and Great Indian Peninsula Railway Company (GIPR) were founded, with complex conditions included in their contracts about capital, returns to shareholders, sale of the railways, and the allocation of free land and services by the state (Headrick 1988: 61). After an initial delay, the influence of the marquis of Dalhousie, governor of India from 1848 to 1856 and formerly president of the British Board of Trade, with close connections to railway matters, was brought to bear. 'In the Indian case the railways began as a colonial project and remained "colonial" until 1947. Dalhousie, a top-level colonial official, delineated a colonial railway system whose benefits to the colonial connection had to be represented to other Britons. The author and the audience were British' (Kerr 2003: 300). He wrote a minute to the court of the East India Company on 20 April 1853, drawing attention to the five-fold increase that railways would produce in the speed of moving military strength about the country. He also wrote of the economic benefits in language very similar to that of the contemporary European explorers of Africa, who were seeking both to eliminate the trade in slaves and to substitute more legitimate commerce.

The construction of railways in India was thus seen, at least by British imperialists, as much more than a vital economic and military necessity: railways were part of the process of the civilising mission. After Dalhousie, writers such as Sir Bartle Frere, governor of the Bombay Presidency (and later a president of the Royal Geographical Society) also emphasised the civilising and social effects of the railways. A major consideration and priority would be the linking of the Presidency cities of Calcutta, Madras and Bombay, and the North-West Province around Delhi.

Financing the railways was a problem. British investors had to be convinced that their money would yield reasonable returns through investment in a system in India whose physical environs and political contexts were problematic. This difficulty was partly obviated by a Railway Guarantee Scheme, agreed in 1849, through which the East India Company guaranteed a rate of return of 5 per cent to investors, the vast majority of whom were in Britain. The physical conditions in India meant that the cost of railway construction and maintenance was high, and the railways were not financially profitable until the twentieth century.

In 1850–1 construction of two lines began. The first was in Bengal, 121 miles (195 km) in length, running north-west from Howrah (on the opposite bank of the Hooghly River from Calcutta) to the town of Raniganj in the coalfields of Burdwan: this was opened in 1855, though shorter lengths had previously been in use. Another line, 35 miles (56 km) long, was constructed eastwards from Bombay to the edge of the Western Ghats (Kerr 1997: 26–7): this was the first of the two to be opened – in 1853 – though again shorter lengths of the route had previously been operational. After ten years of railway construction, though initially slowed by disagreements between the East India Company's resident engineers and the government's consulting engineers (mainly army officers), a significant length had been constructed.

In addition to extending the EIR and the GIPR systems, in the period 1853–71 a number of main trunk line railways were constructed, including lines from Calcutta to Delhi, Bombay to Allahabad, and Bombay to Madras. There were 20 miles (32 km) of railway in India in 1853. By 1860 there were 838 miles (1,348 km) of operating railway track and services, and in the following year 1,587 miles (2,522 km), giving an idea of the speed of construction (Kerr 1997: 38, 41). By 1880 there were 8,995 miles (14,476 km) of railway, 23,627 miles (38,023 km) in 1900, and 30,572 miles (49,200 km) in 1910. Not all of this spectacular growth was of new lines and routes: there was some double-tracking, which had reached 1,474 miles (2,372 km) by 1900. Major nodes, including workshops, were also significant features of the railway landscapes of India.

The logistics of railway construction in India were complex, not least because of the absence of heavy industry, requiring the large-scale importation of rails, engines and other equipment from Britain. Kerr (1997: 22) estimated that 'By the close of 1863, 2,764,781 tons of railway material – rails, sleepers, locomotives etc. – valued at £15,128,856, had been sent in 3571 ships from Britain to India ... Each mile of railway built in India through the 1860s required, on average, a separate ship carrying some 600 tons of material from Britain', and then inland transportation to the sites of railway construction – another major logistical challenge.

In addition to the railways constructed in the areas of India controlled by Britain, from 1870 the Indian Princely States also began construction initiatives, first from Hyderabad, that linked in with the British systems. The combination of different agencies for railway construction made for a system that was highly heterogeneous in character. Gauges included a broad standard gauge (the earliest), a 5 foot 6 inches gauge, a metre gauge, narrow gauges of 2 foot and 2 foot 6 inches in hills regions and Princely States, and others. A similar complexity was evident in the number of administrative bodies: in 1905 there were state railways (15,000 miles/24,140 km), guarantee scheme railways (7,000 miles/11,265 km), native state railways (3,500 miles/5,632 km), non-guarantee scheme railways (1,400 miles/2,253 km) and those run by non-assisted companies (1,300 miles/2,092 km) (Chapman 2000: 99–100).

Political protests and uprisings in India slowed the construction of railways, especially in the late 1850s, mainly in the north of the country, notably the Santhal uprising of 1856 and the Uprising/Mutiny of 1857–8. The Santhal uprising was in part motivated by the activities of the European railway builders in the Rajmahal hills, and 'was brutally suppressed by British-led troops. Heroism with bows and arrows and axes was no match for the firearms of the sepoys, as the death toll of some 20,000 Santhals attested' (Kerr, 1997: 35–7). The Indian Uprising/Mutiny slowed railway construction, principally on the routes of the EIR, but also acted as a spur to further railway-building after the event for strategic reasons. The broad question of the security of the British Raj was important, as was the deep concern for the military protection of specific features of the system such as tracks, bridges, stations and tunnels. Railway construction had significant ecological effects, through both the building of embankments that interfered with natural drainage channels, creating malarial water-filled hollows, and the enormous amount of wood taken from Indian forests for use as sleepers and, for a while from the 1850s to the 1870s, as fuel, before coal production became sufficient. It has been argued that another negative impact of the railways was the stimulus of commercial agriculture to the detriment of the rural poor (Chapman 2000: 104).

Physical obstacles and human cost

There were many physical obstacles to the completion of what became the fourth-largest railway system in the world by 1900. Some of these related to the physical geography of parts of India, including the Western Ghats, the hills and mountains of the north, and the swamps and rivers of Bengal. Major engineering feats included the crossing of the Western Ghats to reach the cotton-producing region of the Deccan plateau. This involved a line that climbed 1,821 feet (555 m) in 15 miles (24 km), and the creation of fifteen tunnels with a combined length of 12,000 feet (3,658 m). The Siliguri–Darjeeling Railway, finished in 1878, had a 2 foot gauge. It climbed into the Himalayan foothills from Siliguri at 398 feet above sea level to a summit altitude of 7,407 feet in less than 50 miles (80 km), with gradients of up to 1:19, and using many loops. It carried passengers up to the hill stations, together with tea and rice. In addition to the hill railways, other engineering feats included the construction of major bridges over the large rivers to withstand normal and monsoon flooding across wide flood-plains, such as the 3,064 m, 93-span bridge over the Ganges at Patna (1900), and the Landsdowne bridge over the Indus at Sukkar (1889) (Christopher 1988: 55).

Another major factor was the labour force – both for track and physical plant construction and maintenance and for the general running of the system, linking back to a very complex logistical means of overseeing and supervising which started with the politicians, investors and administrators in Britain, and fed down to administrators and various kinds of supervisory engineers in India (Kerr 1997: 25). Kerr has estimated that the number of labourers employed in railway construction in India increased from 180,601 in 1859 to 221,253 in 1900, and this did not include those involved in reconstruction. Most of these were unskilled, from low-caste groups, and included women and children. Earth-working castes and tribes became a vital part of the construction process (Kerr 1997: 189–92).

The conditions under which the railway labourers worked were hazardous, exposing them to accident and death, diseases such as cholera, malaria, pneumonia and typhoid fever. They were also oppressed and given poor wages, to which they would sometimes respond with collective protest. But,

Physical obstacles and worker resistance notwithstanding, India did have the world's fourth largest railway network by the early twentieth century; a network built by Indian labour, under British direction. Management succeeded. The civil engineers of Victorian Britain had one of their greatest accomplishments, though many among them died on the job. Indians, however, did most of the dying, and most of the work. (Kerr 1997: 195)

Segregation was evident in the provision by railway companies in India of separate company housing for Europeans and some Eurasians in enclaves in urban areas, the only form, according to Arnold, of white colonisation in colonial India (Kerr 2001: 55).

The railways had beneficial effects. They offered a speedy way of moving food in times of famine. There were serious famines in Orissa in 1865, and the United Provinces (Uttar Pradesh) in 1868–70, partly alleviated by the movement of food by rail. In 1880 a Famine Commission stated that India required at least an additional 20,000 miles (32,186 km) of railway, 5,000 (8,046 km) of these for famine relief (Chapman 2000: 99; Kerr 1997: 43). The railways provided for greater mixing of social and religious groups, and helped in the development of the Indian coalfields and commercial agriculture, much of it for overseas markets.

The benefits and disadvantages of this phase in the historical geography of the development of India's railway system are difficult to establish in any detail, but its broader facets include the construction of a more rapid and expeditious means of movement of people and goods within India and to and from points of export (and import), an achievement purchased through investment of money largely by British investors under advantageously guaranteed rates. People transported more rapidly by rail included British and Indian troops being moved to points of conflict, including the North-West Frontier, but also ordinary Indians, who, mainly travelling in the poor conditions of third-class carriages, made up the bulk of railway passengers.

The railways facilitated greater British control of India, but in the last analysis they also greatly assisted communications between different people in different parts of the country, and thus the acceleration of a new national consciousness that would eventually throw off the colonial yoke (Kerr 2003: 307).

The symbolic pride in the development of railways in India was marked by the architectural style of some of the major stations. The Victoria terminus in Bombay, opened in 1887 on Queen Victoria's Jubilee Day, 'was built of Italian marble in a blend of Gothic, Indo-Saracenic, and Venetian styles, with a dome copied from Westminster Abbey. Other stations of that period imitated everything from Roman baths and Alpine chalets to Mogul tombs' (Headrick 1988: 74). Further symbols of imperial provenance include the names of stations on the Nilgiri mountain railway in

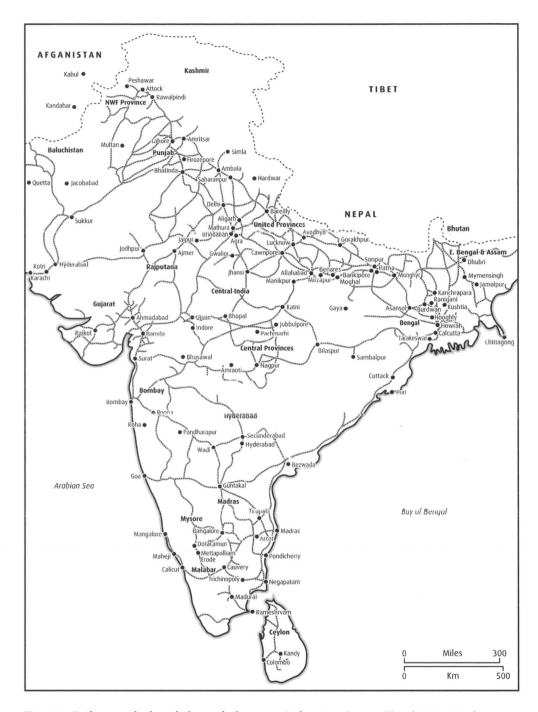

Fig. 10.5 Railways and selected places of pilgrimage, India, 1931. Source: Kerr (2003: 308–9). By permission of and © Oxford University Press India, New Delhi.

South India en route to the hill stations of Konoor and Ooty (Ootacamund), many of which – including 'Allderly, Hillgrove, Runnymeade, Wellington, Lovedale – and their modest but English-looking buildings echoed the comfort and quiet of far-off, rural, England: both signified the attempted recreation of home away from home' (Kerr 2003: 293).

The construction of the moral and economic balance-sheets of the advantages and disadvantages of the building of railways in India is highly complex. Kerr, in his introduction to a collection of essays on the subject, has drawn attention to the varying current opinions on a whole range of related topics. One key question is the role of railways in the shaping and making of modern India, with contrasting views seen from, on the one hand, 'triumphalist' writings from imperialist perspectives. These focus on the beneficial effects of railways on the making of modern India, seen as a direct outcome of British control and capital investment. On the other hand, there is the powerful idea, evidenced in the writing of Mahatma Gandhi (even though he, like other nationalists, used the railways to travel to promote their cause), that railways 'propagate evil' through British control, and the notion of later postcolonial commentators that the British influence on railway-building and management was disadvantageous to India (Kerr 2001: 8).

These 'ameliorist' and 'immiserationist' schools both have much to support them. The railways created national markets, for example in foodstuffs, and stimulated local markets for agricultural products. They provided employment for a very large number of labourers and administrators, they accelerated urbanisation, and 'if the railways shaped cityscapes, they reshaped landscapes and mindscapes' (Kerr 2001: 8, 10), through a wide array of engineering constructions, through the transport of pilgrims and tourists, through the alleviation of famine and through the facilitation of a growth of nationalism (Kerr 2001: 11). They also brought environmental problems, such as a reduction in forests and the interruption of water-courses, creating stagnant water and malarial breeding-grounds. And the railway itself was a means of transmitting diseases. The lateness or absence of railways in some regions of India affected levels of development.

Railways in South-East Asia

British and French imperialist dreams and achievements were reflected in the history of railway conception and building in this extensive and diverse region from the late nineteenth century. There were thoughts about the possibility of a British rail route from Moulmein in Burma to

Simao in Yunnan – the 'overland to China' – from the 1860s to the 1880s, and a French consul in 1885 proposed the construction of a railway from Haiphong to Mandalay. Neither of these came to fruition, but the first railway in the region was built by the British from Rangoon to Toungoo and opened in 1885. This was one of a series of transport innovations, including improved roads and navigation, introduced by the British to Burma.

The Indian experience contrasts substantially, for reasons of geography, with developments elsewhere in South and South-East Asia. The Dutch in the Netherlands East Indies did not start railway construction until 1864, in spite of plans for railways from the 1840s, with the beginning of a railway built by the Netherlands Indies Railway Company on Java from Semarang to Yogyakarta in the Princely States, whose construction was completed in 1873. Wesseling (2004: 30–1) states that:

> By the end of the 1870s a total of 300 kilometres of railway lines were in use on Java , while on Sumatra there were 245 kilometres of state railways and 122 kilometres of private lines. Of course the situation in the Netherlands-Antilles was not comparable to that of British India, because India was a subcontinent, while the Netherlands-Indies was an island kingdom where shipping connections were of paramount importance. In French Indochina, where developments ran nearly parallel to those in the Netherlands-Indies, there were 2,056 kilometres of railways in use in 1914.

Railways in Africa

The development of railways in Africa was, not surprisingly, uneven and episodic, varying with the chronology of changing European interests and investments in the nineteenth and early twentieth centuries. The traditional means of transport, by porterage, cart, and river, were extremely slow in comparison with the railway and steam-powered river transport – both by this time part of the rapidly advancing industrial economies of Britain, Germany, France and the United States.

Many of the new railway lines in Africa in the late nineteenth century were built by governments 'chiefly for strategic reasons, but their economic impact was even more profound, for they frequently cut transport costs by 90 to 95 per cent, restructured trading systems, released labour, and provided outlets for inland commodity production, thereby creating distinctively colonial economies' (Iliffe 1995: 205–6). They also influenced the expansion of ports such as Dar es Salaam, Mombasa, Dakar and Conakry, and the decline of others not connected by railways into the interior. They initiated and facilitated the development of major mineral sources in the Witwatersrand, South-West Africa, Southern Rhodesia, Angola, Asante, Tunisia and central Nigeria. They were also influential in the development of European settlement and various kinds of commercial agriculture in areas such as Southern Rhodesia, Swaziland, southern Nyasaland, South-West Africa, the highlands of Kenya, Algeria, Tunisia, the plains of Morocco, and German East Africa, while also stimulating indigenous agricultural production geared to the market needs of European settlers.

In purely economic terms, many parts of Africa were totally unsuited for railway communication, partly because of the highly uneven distribution of population, and partly on account of extremely difficult environmental conditions. The monetary and labour costs of railway construction were particularly high, and extreme hardships were suffered by the Africans who formed the majority of the labour force engaged in their construction (Christopher 1984: 75).

A broad pattern of financing railways in Africa was support from either governments or private investors, but many failed to make profits for their investors and were then given government subsidy or taken over by the government. The effect of the railways was not always beneficial to existing long-established trading systems. The trans-Saharan trade link between Hausaland and Tripoli, operated by Tuareg desert traders, was badly affected by the progress of the railway northwards from the coast of Nigeria to Kano, built in part to expand the cotton production of the north, and was a contributing factor in the Tuareg revolt in 1916 (Iliffe 1995: 204). The construction of the railway from Dar es Salaam on the east coast of Africa to Kigoma on Lake Tanganyika effected a major reduction in the number of caravan porters who left Bagamoyo to travel inland, from 43,880 in 1900 to 193 in 1912.

The historical geography of railway development in Africa produced a pattern of higher density in the Maghrib of North Africa and in South Africa, moderate development in the Sudan and Nigeria and in other mineral-rich areas of Central and southern Africa. Many of the railway routes constructed in Africa had a political purpose, reflected in the pattern of railways in French West Africa, for example, where links from interior to port were frequently conditioned by the colonial boundaries that had been or were in the process of being established. This resulted in a series of almost parallel routes linking the hinterlands of French territories to coastal ports at Dakar, Conakry, Abidjan, Lomé and Cotonou, but these were never linked together – a contrast with the railway system developed in British-controlled Nigeria (Curtin 1995: 462).

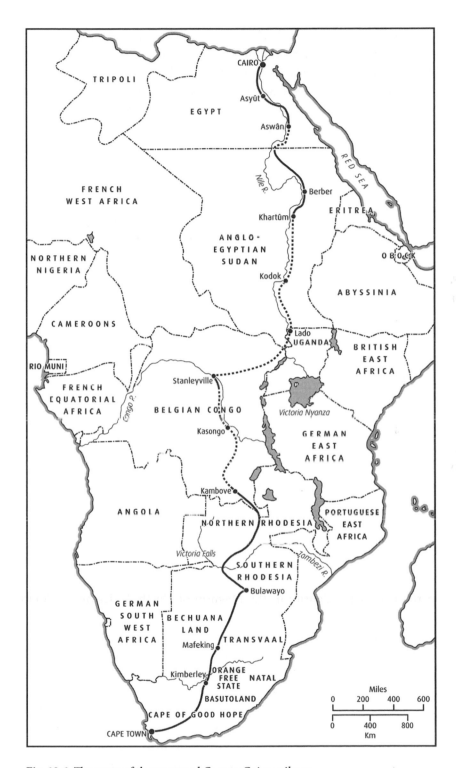

Fig. 10.6 The route of the proposed Cape to Cairo railway.
Source: Bartholomew (1913: 119).

The late nineteenth and early twentieth centuries were times of great – if impractical – European colonial visions about trans-African railways, in some cases linking to European systems. The main proposals were for railways from the Cape to Cairo (British, largely the idea of Cecil Rhodes); and a French plan for a trans-Saharan railway, to link Algeria in North Africa with French territory in West Africa and even further south to the Congo and west to the Sudan (Christopher 1984: 76–7).

The Cape-to-Cairo project started well, with connections northwards from the Cape of Good Hope, and by 1910, partly through the energies of the British South Africa Company, links had been made to Elizabethville in the Belgian Congo, but further links were thought to be uneconomic and the idea was never fully realised. Similar frustration was experienced in the uncompleted project for a French trans-Saharan railway, envisaged at one stage as part of a French colonial link from Dunkirk to Brazzaville, but the links between French territories in West and North Africa were never made. The idea of a trans-Saharan rail link was first propose by French explorers in the mid-nineteenth century, and taken forward by a plan published in 1875 to develop such a route for the purposes of completely controlling Algeria, its commercial development, and the elimination of the slave trade. Three surveys were undertaken, the third – a mission led by Paul-Xavier Flatter – ended in the killing of most of its members by Touaregs in 1881.

The idea of a trans-Saharan railway was revived in the 1890s by a strong colonial lobby in Paris and by increasing Franco-British rivalry, and a line was proposed from the Mediterranean coast to Colomb-Béchar, then to In-tassit in the Sahara, thence splitting into two lines, one to Ségou, Bamako and possibly Senegal in French West Africa, the other via Niamey or Ouagadougou either to the Congo or to the Gulf of Guinea in French Equatorial Africa (Aldrich 1996: 174–5). A survey mission was sent out in 1898, but nothing happened before the First World War, and in spite of frequent resurrections of the idea through the 1930s to the 1950s this idealistic dream was never brought to fruition.

The sequence of railway development in Africa is that the earliest developments – in North and South Africa – were conditioned by economic expansion, and later phases of construction were experienced in the tropical colonies for movement of crops and minerals to areas of processing or to the exporting ports. In North Africa the main influence on railway construction was the need of European coastal settlements for means to transport agricultural produce. By 1911 there were 3,337 km of railways in Algeria, and 1,800 km in Tunisia. Other large colonial railway systems in Africa by that time were those of French West Africa (four separate systems with a total length of 2,457 km), German South-West Africa (2,372 km), and South Africa (11,225 km) (Christopher 1984: 77).

In South Africa the construction of railways began in the second half of the nineteenth century, when rapidly increasing industrial and agricultural sectors of the economy and the speed of urban development required better transport systems than those provided by ox-wagons, in spite of road improvement in the first part of the century. There were major problems of cost and speed of transport in connecting the coastal ports such as Durban with the interior, including the slowness to exploit mineral resources, such as the copper deposits in the Transkei and Namaqualand and the coal resources of Natal (Christopher 1976: 174–5).

The first lines in South Africa were short lines to Durban from its port (1860) and from Cape Town to Stellenbosch, Wynberg and Wellington (1860–4), both bought by the governments of the Cape and Natal. Later, the discovery and development of diamond mines at Kimberley in the late 1860s prompted a need for railway construction to this location 600 miles inland from Port Elizabeth, and lines were constructed to Cape Town, Port Elizabeth and East London, the Cape Town link being completed in 1885. Greater acceleration in railway construction was stimulated by the discovery of the Witwatersrand goldfields in 1886, resulting in lines being built from Witwatersrand to the Cape and the Natal ports and also to Lourenço Marques (this line built because the Transvaal government wished to have a port outlet and link that was not controlled by Britain). These lines were constructed between 1887 and 1895 (Christopher 1976: 177–8). There was further development to the north, partly stimulated by the British notion of a Cape-to-Cairo railway, with lines constructed from Kimberley to Bulawayo (1897), from the Mozambique coastal port of Beira to Salisbury (1899), and from Bulawayo and Salisbury to the Victoria Falls (1902, 1904). A link to the Congo border was completed in 1909.

There was further intensification of railway networks after the Anglo-Boer War. Christopher explains that:

In the years 1901–1915 an average of over 400 miles of line was opened in each year, more than doubling the total length of track in the subcontinent. In this period a major programme of branch-line construction was undertaken to link mines, towns, irrigation schemes and developing agricultural regions to the main-line system, while in much of the area south of the Witwatersrand, lines were built to link up established agricultural zones. (Christopher 1976: 179–80)

In French Equatorial Africa a major project that was actually completed was the Congo–Océan railway, built to link the interior from Stanley Pool at Brazzaville on the River Congo to Pont-Noire, a port on the coast, the line running entirely through French colonial territory. This project was conceived in the 1890s, but the beginning of construction was delayed until 1921, and it was not completed until 1934. A rail link, on which French goods had been carried, had been built in the Congo Independent State in the 1890s from Matadi to Stanley Pool, a route that was improved further by 1930, but French national pride, colonial ambition and related strategic concerns led to the building of the wholly uneconomic Congo–Océan railway (Curtin 1995: 462–3).

The cost of building this line, measured in human misery, was very high, partly because of the need to bring in labourers from savannah lands to the north in Chad and Ubangi-Shari to work in heavily forested highland regions crossed by the railway route. 'From 1921 to 1932, some 127,250 men worked on the Congo–Océan railway, about one in ten men in the AEF. Approximately 16,000 died on the job. At the coastal end of the line, where work was hardest and labourers came from furthest away, a fifth of all workers died' (Aldrich 1996: 176). Medical care improved in the last few years of construction. The cost of construction was estimated at over one billion francs. It had few positive effects on the economy of this sparsely populated region, and the inordinately high cost remained a burden to later generations in the AEF in the form of taxes (Curtin 1995: 463).

In German South-West Africa railway-building was rapid in the late nineteenth century. The financing of railways in the German colonies in Africa was initially left to private enterprise, with rates of interest guaranteed by government, but early in the twentieth century, after a visit to German East Africa and South-West Africa, Bernhard Dernburg, director of the Colonial Section of the German Foreign Office and then Secretary of State (from May 1907) with responsibility for the new Colonial Office, persuaded the Reichstag to fund the construction of new lines in South-West Africa and East Africa, and to take over the financing of the privately financed line from Dar es Salaam to Morogo (Henderson 1993: 102–3).

Some small railway lines to serve the copper mines in the north of South-West Africa had begun in 1885, and in 1897 the Colonial Section of the Foreign Office agreed to build a state railway project linking the port of Swakopmund to Windhoek, the capital (a distance of 383 km) in order to obviate the effects of the rinderpest outbreak of 1897 and to facilitate the movements of German troops. The line was finished in 1902, and further lines were built, including the Otavi railway linking Swakopmund to Otavi, Tsumeb and Otavi and Grootfontein, completed by 1906, and a southern line from the port city of Lüderitz to Keetmanshoop by 1909, with the two systems connected as a loop by 1912. These routes were also instrumental in giving access to inland pastoral lands around Windhoek (Christopher 1976: 79).

In German East Africa railway lines were constructed from Dar es Salaam to Lake Tanganyika (completed in 1914) with a branch line to Lake Victoria. In the protectorate of British East Africa a railway was constructed from Mombasa at the coast inland to Kisumu on Lake Victoria, motivated by British political concern to have control of the Nile headwaters and also by a determination to eliminate the active slave trade in the region. It was begun in 1895 and completed in 1901 and cut the time of a journey from two months to two days and the cost of freight transport by about one-tenth. It also stimulated cotton production in Uganda and white settlement in Kenya.

In the Belgian Congo, external links through the slave trade and later more legitimate commerce had necessitated better links between the interior and the coast or between mines and the rail networks of other colonial powers. Thus short railways were used to bypass difficult sections of major rivers, and a link was made with the South African railway system and the Katanga copper mines. Construction of a railway between Leopoldville on the southern shore of Stanley Pool on the River Congo and Matadi on the Congo some 100 miles to the south-west was begun in 1890 and completed in 1898, under the aegis of the Compagnie du Chemin de Fer du Congo which had been set up in 1889 and granted a concession from the Belgian government to construct the Matadi to Leopoldville single-track railway. As with all railway constructions in tropical Africa in the nineteenth century, the work was very difficult, and initially made extraordinarily slow progress. It was constructed at high cost: from 1889 to 1891 it is estimated that 900 of the employed workers died, and the financial cost by the time of completion was 60 million francs (Mason 1944: 457–63). Initially the railway was built with a narrow gauge, incorporating steep gradients and tight curves, but the gauge was subsequently widened and the route straightened.

Other railways built in the Belgian Congo include the Boma–Tshela line, which took from 1898 to 1935 to be completed; and the Stanleyville–Ponthierville, Kindu–Albertville railway originally in three sections but later in two, started in 1902 by a Belgian company with the purpose of linking the Congo River system with the lakes of Central Africa, the critical link being that between Kabalo on the Lukuga with Albertville on Lake Tanganyika. The Stanleyville–Ponthierville section was completed in 1902, the Kindu to Kongolo section between 1906 and 1910, and the final section to Albertville (formerly Kalime) by 1915 (Mason 1944: 467). A line was also constructed between 1923 and 1937 between Aketi and Mungbere, with branch lines to Bondo and Titule, to tap the trade westwards from the eastern part of the Belgian Congo that might be directed east and northwards towards the Nile (Mason 1944: 485).

Railways in New Zealand

Railways in New Zealand, as in many other European colonies, were originally funded by private companies, but the difficulties of construction in such a challenging physical environment led to them coming under the control of the state. An early account of railway development suggested that:

> in general the railways were treated more as a factor in development than as a revenue-producing institution. Thus profits tended to be low, and did not meet the interest on capital expenditure. But New Zealanders were content to pay the price, preferring low rates to increased profits. As an adjunct to railway management the State has acquired, and operates, coal mines, maintains repair shops, and builds locomotives. (Kearnshaw 1925: 265)

Forty-six miles of railway had been built in New Zealand before 1870.

The gold mining boom from 1861 to 1871, and the major agricultural revolution immediately afterwards, encouraged the development of railways, and this was also facilitated by the allocation of £10 million of British capital to a public works programme that included road, railway and telegraphic communications construction, land purchase, and water supply to the goldfields. This was initially intended to help settle the Maori problem on the North Island, but most of the money was in fact spent on the South Island. This financial input increased the total length of railways in New Zealand to 1,287 miles (2,071 km) by 1881, two-thirds of which was in the South Island. The major route ran from Waipara to Bluff along the east coast. 'Branch lines fingered inland to tap the goldfields, to bring out the fine Merino wool from the high country stations, the wheat from the plains and downlands, and to distribute the bituminous West Coast coal and foreign goods brought in through the ports at

Fig. 10.7 Flinders Street Station, Melbourne, Australia. The main centre for Melbourne's suburban rail network. Built between 1905 and 1910 to a design by Fawcett and Ashworth. Photo © R. A. Butlin.

Lyttleton and Port Chalmers' (Cumberland and Whitelaw 1970: 39, 44). In spite of extensions of the railways from Auckland to Te Awamutu, from Wellington to Masterton, from Hawera to New Plymouth and Waitara and Ormondville to Napier, the system remained fragmented, and connection between Auckland and Wellington was not made until early in the twentieth century.

Telegraphs and telecommunications

A major contribution to the very substantial speeding up of information about empire and colonies and other related matters, such as political, military and trade intelligence, was the development of a worldwide network of telegraph cables from the 1840s onwards by the major European world powers and by the United States. The postal systems that preceded and continued in parallel with them were very slow until the development of air transport. The geopolitical and geostrategic connotations of the development of the telegraph, telephone, radio and radar have been extensively reviewed by Hugill (1999) and Headrick (1988), and only an outline of their development and implications can be included here.

The telegraph had profound effects on the shrinkage of imperial distances in the nineteenth and early twentieth centuries, and on the competitive geostrategic and material edges of European powers. It facilitated the rapid flow of information for both commercial and political ends, giving greater access to and control over prices and trade flow and reducing the possibilities for local decision-making and action independent of metropolitan authority. This innovation 'led to a greater degree of metropolitan control over trade as the major wholesale firms and banks were able to replace the smaller colonial concerns and achieve a high degree of commercial dominance in the colonies' (Christopher 1984: 71).

Hugill (1999: 21) shows that 'Britain led in global submarine technology by the late 1860s and in wireless telegraphy after 1900, though the lead belonged alternately to Britain and America until the early 1920s, when Britain moved ahead through the switch to higher-frequency, short-wave radio.' Germany had been a slow starter, and relied on imported technology in the later nineteenth century. Telegraphy has distant historical origins, but the electric telegraph was a child of the 1830s and 1840s, and by

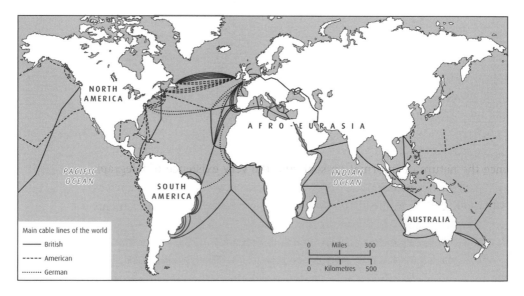

Fig. 10.8 American, British, and German submarine cables 1911.
Source: Hugill (1999: 44); by permission of and © Johns Hopkins University Press.

the late nineteenth century there had developed a worldwide network of submarine cables, largely built by Britain and with Britain at its centre. The evolution of telegraph technology progressed through various stages of efficiency, with high-speed lines being developed between 1894 and 1910 (Hugill 1999: 28–9).

Imperial telegraph systems comprised the inter-colonial links by submarine cable and the internal land links that connected remoter and often politically sensitive frontier regions with urban control centres. A cable to India was successfully laid in 1870, spurred by the events of the Indian Uprising/Mutiny of 1857, and the completion of cable links to South Africa were stimulated by such events as the Zulu War of 1879. By the end of the nineteenth century Britain had cable links to most of its colonies, and in 1929 the British overseas lines were combined in the Cable and Wireless Company, whose telegraph cables made up more than half of the world's submarine cable length (Christopher 1988: 64). In regions such as West Africa there was much duplication of cable routes by competing countries such as Britain, France and Germany (Headrick 1988: 106–8).

Early French attempts to link with its North Africa colonies by cable were undertaken by British technologists, but France laid her own cables in the last two decades of the nineteenth century and the first decade of the twentieth, expanding to the rest of her colonies through British cables, reflecting the different attitudes of the two governments to the cost of colonies (Headrick 1988: 111–13).

After a slow start, Germany gradually built up connections to her colonies, mainly those in West and South-West Africa. The effects of the telegraph on the efficiency of communications between metropole and colony and between colonies were varied. On the one hand speed of communication rapidly increased, but the quality of information transmitted was in the hands of civil servants and colonial officers, who could strongly influence the nature of information sent, and the very existence of telegraph systems heightened the rivalry between colonial powers in regions such as West Africa, though the effects on world trade and on labour movements were profound (Headrick 1988: 107, 110).

Radio communication to imperial bases developed from *c.* 1912, and facilities were constructed by all the European powers, with major coverage being provided in the 1920s and 1930s. Extended global telephone networks also developed during this period with improving technologies, including shortwave transmissions.

Air transport and routes

One of the most significant technical innovations for communication with and protection of empire was the aeroplane. Attempts by humans to fly in machine-propelled aircraft date from the early twentieth century, with the achievements of the Wright brothers in the United States in 1903 and 1905, and their flight in France in 1908. Geopolitical conditions in Europe, especially the First World War, advanced the use of aircraft for military purposes. A series of money prizes was offered by the English newspaper the *Daily Mail* for significant flights, one for the first English Channel crossing (won by Blériot in 1909) and then for transatlantic flight (won by Alcock and Brown in 1919 for a flight from St John's in Newfoundland to Clifden in Ireland), and this promoted further interest not only in what were to become conventional aircraft but also in flying boats and airships (Hugill 1993: 251–2). The airship had a short career between 1852 and 1937. Zeppelin constructed airships that were used, ineffectively, for

Fig. 10.9 Passengers embarking on an Imperial Airways plane at Malakal, Sudan, with young African observers, *c.* 1930.
By permission of and © Royal Geographical Society Picture Collection, S0010330.

military purposes in the First World War, and airships were transferred to Britain, France, Italy, Belgium and Japan by way of war reparations. Major fatal accidents in 1910 and 1931 heralded the end to this form of transport, which in any case was being overtaken by the aeroplane (Hugill 1993: 260, 262).

The advance of aircraft as a means of communication and control in the period of and after the First World War had profound significance for the advance and maintenance of European overseas imperial influence. It

> was part of the process of global modernization that began in the nineteenth century... From its invention in 1903, the heavier-than-air flying machine moved relatively slowly to the centre stage of technological wonders, but once it did reach that point, around 1909, it held its symbolic hegemony through until the Second World War... The aeroplane did not simply relativise space by further shortening travel time and distances, rather flying was a new visual representation and appropriation of space. (Simonsen 2005: 102)

The aeroplane became, as Edmonds has stated, both a symbol of modernity and a practical means of transport and communication, and also 'a new area of endeavour in which technological developments had to fit in with political realities... Communications were the glue that made the British Empire possible' (Edmonds 1999: 91).

Aircraft design and production were stimulated by the First World War, with the production of smaller combat aircraft and larger bomber aircraft, such as the German Riezenflug, built at Staaken near Berlin by the Zeppelin company. In effect, as Hugill (1993: 253, 255) shows: 'By 1919 in Germany, the essentials of aircraft structure had been worked out and aerodynamic theory had developed scientifically. Pioneering use had been made of airplanes to carry passengers and mail in the United States. The Germans had begun to use the airplane as a strategic bomber, and the British were about to do the same at war's end.'

The effect of air power on geopolitical thinking varied between individual imperial countries. In Britain, H. J. Mackinder in his famous 1904 paper to the Royal Geographical Society, 'The Geographical Pivot of History', failed, as Leo Amery (one of the commentators on his paper) suggested, to take full account of the potential of air power for global balances of power in the future (Butlin 2005: 42). Even in his later publication, *Democratic Ideals and Reality* (1919), he still failed to acknowledge the full geopolitical and economic significance of air power for the future (Hugill 2005: 110). Elsewhere in Britain, the United States and Europe, there was a greater appreciation of the potential of air power as a means of moving people and goods, of defending territory at home and overseas, and of supporting warfare on land and at sea (Hugill 2005: 118–20), and major developments occurred in the design, building and use of aircraft between the First and Second World Wars.

The British Royal Air Force was created in 1918 (previously it had been part of the army), and by 1919 the use of aircraft had become an important component of British activity in the Middle East. The use of aircraft for commercial purposes began with flights across the English Channel, initially through government-subsidised privately owned companies, but in 1924 the merger of a number of private companies, with a government subsidy and government-nominated directors, formed Imperial Airways, a company whose purpose was service to the British empire (Porter 1991b: 163).

The demise of the airship led to the advance of the long-range flying boat, which dominated commercial connections between Europe and her empires, and between the United States and her growing empire, between 1914 and 1939. The hulls of flying boats were initially constructed of wood, but Germany led the way in the construction of metal hulls, and Britain, the United States and Japan followed (Hugill 1993: 263–4). Flying boats were used extensively in the Caribbean, the Atlantic and Pacific coasts of the USA and in South America, and trans-Pacific routes were developed by Pan Am. For Pan Am and Imperial Airways, the choice of routes for carrying passengers, freight and mail was determined by both commercial and strategic considerations (Hugill 1993: 263–5). Large flying boats themselves had difficulties, not least on account of the weight effects of having to strengthen their hulls to protect against landing in rough seas, and by the end of the Second World War they had been overtaken by advances in the design and production of aeroplanes operating from land bases (and from aircraft carriers).

Imperial Airways operated on European routes from London from 1924 to 1927, but then started the development of longer-distance routes with a service between Cairo and Basra. Subsequent expansion included routes to Karachi, Delhi and Jodhpur, connections south from Cairo, which reached Cape Town in 1932, and with connections to Calcutta, Rangoon and Singapore in 1933, Australia in 1934 (with Quantas Empire Airways), Hong Kong in 1935, and Khartoum and Kano in 1936, in which year the imperial network from London was complete, having been delayed by connection problems between London and Europe, especially Italy (Pirie 2004: 63).

Imperial Airways gave up many of the European routes before the Second World War, being unable to compete with more heavily subsidised

European airlines, and by 1938 became almost entirely dependent on routes to the empire, with British Airways having been established separately as a European carrier. In that year its passenger and freight-carrying routes stretched over 25,000 miles (40,233 km), but it was not the only carrier used to, from and within imperial territories, for national carriers had developed which covered Canada (never served directly by Imperial Airways), Australia, India and South Africa, for example (Pirie 2004: 64–5).

There had been recognition of the potential for air transport to link people and goods from around European empires from the early 1920s. The logistical advantages for bringing together via air transport states-men from the metropole with those from the outer peripheries of empire, for example Australia and New Zealand, was recognised at an Imperial Conference in London in 1926, but regular air mail services between Britain and Australia only started in 1934 (followed by passenger serv-ices in 1935), the delay influenced by the use of a monopoly airline by the British government, the level of technology, and the anticipated potential of the airship (Edmonds 1999: 92).

A combination of the influence of other British agencies such as the Foreign Office, the Air Ministry and the Post Office, together with Imperial Airways' comparative inefficiency of operation, delayed progress, and there were diplomatic difficulties over the use of routes. In October 1934 a proposal was made for an Empire Air Mail Scheme, involving the use of large flying boats carrying mail and people, to operate a first-class mail service at reasonable cost and to improve links between the countries of the British empire, with a service to Australia proposed to start in 1937 (Edmonds 1999: 94–5, 101). Disagreement between Britain and Australia over the cost of air mail, the involvement of Australia's domestic carrier Quantas Empire Airways, and the type of aircraft to be used, particularly from Singapore to Australia, delayed the introduction of the scheme until August 1938.

From quite early times in aviation history there was competition on long-haul routes as well as short-haul European routes. With the develop-ment of longer-range aircraft the competition for business in the Far East and Australia grew stronger. The Dutch airline KLM, founded in 1919, competed strongly on the routes to the farthest parts of the Dutch empires, and was joined in 1928 by its sister airline KNILM (Royal Dutch Indies Airlines). KLM started a passenger service from Amsterdam to Batavia (Jakarta) in Indonesia in October 1931. These airlines were in competition with Imperial Airways, which enjoyed the advantage of Britain's refusal of overfly rights on some imperial routes and of trust agreements with other airlines that handicapped the Dutch airlines' business.

In Germany, the heavily subsidised national company Deutsche Luft Hansa (Lufthansa from 1933), formed in 1926 from a merger of two companies, operated Junkers and Dornier aircraft over a large number of routes, including one to China from 1930. France had established an airmail service between Casablanca and Fez in Morocco in 1911, and from 1918 the company Lignes Aeriennes Latecoere (named after its founder), operating from Toulouse, gradually expanded to cover western coastal North Africa, Dakar, and ultimately Brazil. The Belgian airline Sabena (Société Anonyme Belge d'Exploitation de la Navigation Aérienne) was created in 1923 by the Belgian government, the colony of the Belgian Congo, and a small company (Sneta) that had operated air services in the Belgian Congo from 1920. Sabena managed the services from Belgium to the Congo, onward to Broken Hill in Northern Rhodesia and to Madagascar, and also internal flights within the Congo.

The effect of air transport of people and goods on the geographies of European imperialism was far-reaching. Colonial administrators could travel to and from the metropole and within colonial territories in much less time than before. Much still depended, however, on transport by road, rail and water, which in many parts of the empire remained very slow, tedious and dangerous. The coming of effective aviation also affected the strategic support of empire. Aircraft were used in the Italian War of 1911–12 and the Balkan Wars in 1912–13, and, together with airships, extensively in the First World War (with over 100 aircraft used by the combatant powers), initially for reconnaissance but later for aerial combat, strafing and bombing of military and civilian targets, and supporting military action on the ground (Black 2002: 150–1).

In the aftermath of the war and the arrival of new colonial obligations for Britain and France in the League of Nations mandated territories of Palestine, Transjordan, Iraq, Lebanon and Syria, air power was deployed widely, frequently against major nationalist uprisings, and was similarly employed in older colonies. In the British case, the use of air power was more than a strategic innovation: it was also an attempt to police colonial territories more cheaply than by employing large numbers of troops on the ground, though frequently the two were combined. Clayton has indicated that 'The control of the Empire and repression of insurrection was secured by new technology without which the British might have been forced to abandon several areas, including part of the Middle East. Foremost was the use of air power for reconnaissance, supply and attack. The bombing of dissidents, at times ruthless, ensured British authority at immense savings of manpower' (Clayton 1999: 290).

Aircraft and heavy bombing were used in the suppression of a revolt led by the tribal leader Mohammed bin Abdullah Hassan in British Somaliland in 1919–20, and provided for the RAF chief of staff, Air Marshall Trenchard, evidence of the capability of a combination of air power, armoured car groups, and local troops in Mesopotamia (Corum 2000: 61; Omissi 1990). A major uprising against the British administration took place in 1920, stimulated by broken promises of self-government to Arabs and Kurds, and was suppressed only with the aid of nearly 30,000 ground troops (mostly from the Indian army) and four RAF squadrons. Thereafter military control of Iraq was left in the hands of four RAF armoured car companies, eight RAF squadrons, and 15,000 locally recruited Iraq levies and police (Corum 2000: 65).

In 1922 the RAF was given military responsibility for Iraq, and bombing was continually used in retaliation for uprisings, as it was in other parts of the British empire such as Aden and the North-West Frontier of India (Corum 2000: 62–3). The policy of using air power to replace military garrisons, and its intended effects, were clearly stated by an RAF officer, Wing Commander J. A. Chamier, in 1921:

the Air Force must, if called upon to administer punishment, do it with all its might and in the proper manner. One objective must be selected – preferably the most inaccessible village of the most prominent tribe which it is desired to punish. All available aircraft must be collected ... The attack with bombs and machine guns must be relentless and unremitting and carried on continuously by day and night, on houses, inhabitants, crops, and cattle ... This sounds brutal, I know, but it must be made brutal to start with. The threat alone in the future will prove efficacious if the lesson is once properly learnt. (cited by Corum 2000: 66)

Such tactics provoked metropolitan opponents, and in 1924 the Labour government in Britain commented critically on these methods, an argument countered by the RAF in terms of the supposed humanitarian aspects of air control, including warning villages of raids unless they conformed to demands. The War Ministry also expressed concern at the bombing of women and children, which was an unconvincing protest when seen in the light of the destructive tactics of military expeditions on the ground. Air power was not just used in the suppression of rebellion: it was also used to punish communities that did not pay taxes (Corum 2000: 66, 68). Air power was not, of course, always a successful tactic for the colonial powers, as camouflage and movement at night were tactics successfully adopted by indigenous combatants. The North-West Frontier Province of India and Aden were two of the most active locations for the RAF in its colonial role. The French extensively deployed aircraft in campaigns against the tribesmen involved in the Druze revolt in Syria in 1925–7, and in Morocco in the 1920s (Corum 2000: 69).

The many means and modes of transport that both facilitated and resisted imperial control and colonial influence by European states also had a strong influence on the development of urban networks and individual towns and cities. We turn to this urbanisation theme in the following chapter.

the administration did issue [in Brazzaville] a draconian decree which imposed restrictions on drumming, affecting not only recreational dancing but also funeral rights and the celebrations for the end of mourning known as *matanga*. Not only was 'drumming and noisy dancing' limited in time and space, that is to hours prescribed by the administration and on the outskirts of the town, but Africans had to give advance notice and pay a fee, which was particularly resented, since it was set at a rate that was difficult for workers to meet. (Martin 1995: 37)

Imperial and colonial urbanisation

The extract above from a section on 'segregating space' from Phyllis Martin's study of leisure and society in colonial Brazzaville in French Equatorial Africa refers to a decree issued by the French administration in 1904 which tried to address one of the consequences of the segregation of Europeans and Africans in the town. Such cultural conflicts were part of the tensions endemic in the character of many colonial towns and cities, but the processes by which they were identified and expressed were complex and dynamic – something that will be further explored later in this chapter.

Urbanisation in a wide variety of forms was a significant geographical feature of the regions which experienced European imperial and colonial influence both before and during the period of high imperialism in the late nineteenth and early twentieth centuries. Most of the territories involved had deep roots of urban development, including Africa, India, and South-East Asia, though others had only experienced the growth of urban settlements after European colonisation from the eighteenth century onwards, such as Australia and New Zealand. Formal planning of new parts of old towns was part of the imperial process, and ideas about the planning of urban form and function moved within and between imperial networks. Of course, colonial towns and cities were more than built physical environments: a crucial component was their complex and often changing cultural mixes and social structures, reflective of very different cultural trajectories and ideologies which not infrequently led to tensions and conflict.

General theories of colonial urban development are not plentiful. Early theories tended to focus on the economic, social, political and topographical influences on urban morphology, using dual models of the division of colonial cities into a colonial/European sector and a 'native' or indigenous sector. Anthony King's work on colonial urban development is helpful, through focusing on both European and local influence, situated in the operation of a global economy, on the planning and development of colonial towns and cities (King 1976; 1999: 99–118; Driver and Gilbert 1999: 1–20). More emphasis is now being given to theory, social structures and the situated ideologies of non-Europeans, linked to the physical fabric of built environments, and to cultural interaction. Progress has also been made on the effects of imperialism and colonialism on the cities of the metropolitan countries, including building design.

Brenda Yeoh, in the preface to her important study of colonial Singapore, *Contesting Space in Colonial Singapore* (2003: 2), outlines three key components of colonial urbanism. These are, first, their 'racial, cultural, social, and religious pluralism'; second, their social structuring, which was radically different from Western industrial or pre-industrial urban social structures, and with race as a major component; and, third, 'the concentration of the social, economic and political power in the hands of the colonizers, often a racially distinct group'. In this major historical study of the power relations and built environment of Singapore, Yeoh (2003: 10) seeks 'to move beyond looking at the colonial city as a product of inexorably dominant forces to examining the contemporary social meanings of its built environment as transformed by social, political, and economic conflicts between different groups with different claims on the city'.

Yeoh (2003: 9) proposes a conceptual model that provides for 'the insertion of conflict and collision, negotiation and dialogue, between colonizer and the colonized in shaping the urban landscape', by means – insofar as the data and records will allow – of a focus on the daily lives and routines of different groups of inhabitants. It re-empowers those individuals and groups who hitherto have largely been regarded as an underclass, upon whom the designs and whims of colonial policy-makers have been imposed, but who in practice strongly influenced both the maintenance of traditional structures and also their modification.

While colonial authority exercised a 'cultural hegemony' which incorporated European cultural ideologies about health and disease and their promotion and elimination, other ethnic communities and sub-groups had effective counter-strategies, born of their own cultures and practices, which could and did change or delay colonial impact. Hence:

The Chinese who came to Nanyang, for example, brought with them an entire array of organizations such as clan and dialect associations, trade guilds, temples dedicated to a panoply of Chinese deities, and secret societies which provided the institutional structures within which social, cultural, religious, and recreational activities were performed. Through these institutions, Chinese groups had access to a certain range of services which supported immigrant life such as the provision of medical care, job protection, education, entertainment, and facilities which catered to the observance of the rites of passage without recourse to the colonial host society. These organizations also provided convenient institutional focus points for the consolidation of power and the organization of counter strategies to confront whatever means of control imposed by the colonists. (Yeoh, 2003: 14–15)

Measures used to counter or renegotiate colonial control strategies ranged from overt opposition, including strikes, to more passive resistance through delaying tactics and the exploitation of legal loopholes, strategies that were open to and used by individuals as well as groups.

Among the important elements of the urban role of colonial Singapore, established on Singapore Island as a significant hub for British trade in South-East Asia in 1819, were its port and entrepot functions and focus for a large immigrant labour force from the Malay archipelago, India and China. The hegemony of the British was carried out by an administrative municipal authority and the use of the army and navy, linked to Victorian ideologies of control and civilisation. Victorian metropolitan notions of the management of sanitation and health, including problems of disease and the need for the creation and maintenance of a well-planned city, for example, were central to British ideology and policy in Singapore.

These major objectives, however, were opposed both in ideology and in practice by other ethnic groups. The cultural traditions of Asian immigrants included particular practices, for example, for avoiding European municipal disease control by keeping victims of infectious diseases at home (rather than transferring them to quarantine in isolation hospitals, as the British required), the burial of the dead in private burial (as opposed to municipal) grounds, and the use of verandas (covered walkways in front of tenements or shop houses) for trading by Asian shopkeepers and for cultural activities. There were riots against the municipal authorities in 1888 when they attempted veranda clearance under a British ordinance that empowered removal of what were deemed to be obstructions to movement (Yeoh 2000: 152–7). These examples of the contesting of use rights of public, private and sacred spaces in Singapore illustrate, in the scholarly detail provided by Yeoh, that the processes of modification of components of the built and other environments of this particular colonial city did not reflect simply the effects of a dominant colonial authority on powerless groups of Asian immigrants. Singapore was, rather, 'an area characterized by conflict and compromise because those vested with formal power to control the built environment and those who lived in and used it entertained differing interpretations and perspectives on health and disease, on order and disorder, and ultimately, on what constituted the effective management of life and death in an urban context' (Yeoh 2003: 312).

Urban life and development in colonial Africa

African urban development has deep roots, and urbanism had flourished and in some cases gone from many areas before the Europeans arrived in the sixteenth and seventeenth centuries. Major urban growth had taken place in the navigable lower Nile valley in prehistory in the Egyptian and Nubian kingdoms, evidenced by such cities as Thebes, Memphis and Meroe, and towns and cities were developed along the north coast of Africa (the Maghrib) by the Phoenicians from the twelfth century BC, including Leptis, Oea (Tripoli) and the great city of Carthage, destroyed by the Romans in AD 146. In the Horn of Africa Aksum was a major trading city, and there were many trading urban settlements in tropical Africa, notably on the middle Niger, in the forest region of West Africa, in the Great Lakes region, along the East African coast and in the Zambezi valley (Anderson and Rathbone 2000: 2). Many of the towns of the Maghrib were walled, sited near water sources, and traded across the Sahara, and these were sites for the growth of Islam, which had spread westwards from Arabia in the seventh century AD.

The plateau regions of Central Africa contained major historic urban sites such as Great Zimbabwe. The coastal exploration and settlement of Africa from Spain and Portugal around the coasts of Africa from the fifteenth century revealed prosperous towns on the coast of East Africa, and of West and West-Central Africa (Anderson and Rathbone 2000: 3–4). The European presence in towns in Africa was generally insignificant, at least numerically, before the nineteenth century, but with the gradual intensification of European interest in Africa from early in that century, the numbers of Europeans in towns increased. The ending of the slave trade ushered in new commercial relations and orientations, with greater success accruing, for example, to towns on the coast of West Africa that became involved in the trading through European companies of commodities such as vegetable oils and cocoa, giving advantage to such places as Dakar, Freetown, Accra and Lagos. The largest towns in Africa were along the coast of West Africa, but there were also important towns in eastern and southern Africa, including Ethiopia, the coastal towns of the Indian Ocean such as Mombasa, Bagamoyo and Zanzibar, with smaller towns like Ujiji inland (Anderson and Rathbone 2000: 5–6).

Brazzaville

Two of the main urban centres resulting from French and Belgian colonial penetration of central Africa were Brazzaville and Leopoldville, located on opposite sides of what had been called Stanley Pool – a section of the River Congo which expands to lake size after it emerges from a narrow river corridor upstream. The great breadth of the Congo River was described by the companions of H. M. Stanley, who witnessed this phenomenon on 12 March 1877, as a 'pool' and it was named Stanley Pool. Its logistical significance lay in the fact that river transport below the Pool was impossible, on account of a series of cataracts and rapids between the Pool and the Congo estuary. Historically the Pool therefore was the point of transshipment at which goods from the interior directed towards the coast and Atlantic trade had to be transferred to porters who carried them along trails to the Congo estuary. As Martin has explained, to the French explorer Léon Guiral, who arrived at the Pool in 1882, and to other Frenchmen who reached there in the late nineteenth century, the potential for a river port was apparent, the location summarised by Martin as follows:

Through the remarkable configurations of the river, the region had huge economic significance. Upstream was the gateway to hundreds of kilometres of waterways; 1,300 kilometres of navigable water separated Brazzaville from Bangui on the Ubangi river, or a boat could travel 1,700 kilometres to Stanley Falls (Kisingani) on the great Congo bend. Tributaries on the right bank such as the Sanga, Alima and Likuala-Mossaka, which lay in future French territory, were all major arteries of African trade. (Martin 1995: 13–14)

This had been the site of trading links well before the arrival of the Europeans, notably for the substantial trade in slaves and ivory operated by Loango traders, and the Pool was also an important market focus for regional food products and artefacts.

H. M. Stanley, returning to the Pool in 1881 as representative of King Leopold of the Belgians, and in connection with the development of the Congo region through Leopold's International African Association, acquired a site on the south side of the Pool, and there established the basis of the town of Leopoldville. A small river port, named Brazzaville after the French explorer and administrator, was established by the French on the north side of the Pool by 1884, at a point where there were also two African settlements, named after the Tio chiefs Mfoa and Mpila, comprising mainly loose clusters of trading houses. The wealth potential of these settlements through trade was recognised in the region, but with the arrival of the French their wealth declined for the rest of the nineteenth century (Martin 1995: 16).

In the last two decades of the nineteenth century there was little recognisable urban development on the Brazzaville site, for it was mainly a point of acquisition of porters and supplies for the large French expeditions moving to and from the interior, though by the beginning of the twentieth century there were sizeable African populations in the town, who had mainly migrated in from elsewhere in response to a series of labour requirements and opportunities presented by French companies and administrators. The African population of Brazzaville has been estimated at about 5,000 by 1900, increasing to about 10,000 by 1913 and 15,000 by 1931 (Martin 1995: 28).

The social geography of Brazzaville reflected, initially in a minor way, the segregationist tendencies of the French, indeed of most Europeans in colonial towns. The French presence was marked by the houses of the administrators, the barracks, the mission station of the Holy Ghost Fathers, separated from a mixture of African workers' houses. There was no evidence of formal town planning. Formal segregation ensued after Brazzaville replaced Libreville as the capital of French Congo in 1904 and became the capital of French Equatorial Africa in 1909, when town improvements were approved and funded, with commune status being granted in 1911. The formal planning of the town incorporated key concerns about 'prestige, health policies, the cultural incompatibility of Europeans and Africans, and law and order' (Martin 1995: 32–4).

Relations between Africans and Europeans deteriorated because of a series of food shortages for African workers, resulting from the collapse of the pre-colonial food production system in the face of the capitalist system which, as it turned out, could not accommodate the food requirements of the growing urban population. This led to food riots by Africans, which peaked in 1911. In consequence strong measures were taken to design and control African settlements at Bacongo and Poto-Poto through greater and more systematic surveillance, planned layouts which facilitated military control, and a system of subsidiary management by local chiefs. So, in a relatively short period of time, a small settlement on the banks of the Congo had been radically changed by the marginalisation of the pre-colonial economy of the Tio people by the capitalist economy and the cultural reforming tendencies of European missionaries, administrators, soldiers and companies, who were seen as local and foreign elites, and who 'aided the creation of identities shaped by new boundaries of space, language and class', not least the increased distances that African men and women were obliged, through the new planned and socially segregated layout, to walk to their places of work (Martin 1995: 43–4).

The creation of a distinct kind of urban ethnic geography continued during the twentieth century up to the time of independence, evidenced both through the intensification of identity of the African populations with particular areas of the city, such as Bacongo and Poto-Poto, and also by attempts by the French to control the urban leisure of Africans in order to create greater stability and reduction of threat to the white European population. This was a process, as Martin points out, that was being reproduced over most of Francophone Africa. The First World War created a new dynamic in Brazzaville, with the movement of troops defending the frontier with German Cameroon, and after its conclusion with the coming and going of labourers working on the construction of the Congo–Océan railway in the period 1921–34, and the further segregationist urban designs of the interwar period (Martin 1995: 96–7, 53).

Segregation in French and British colonial cities

Studies by Curtin (1985: 594–613) and Goerg (1998: 1–31), for example, of the location and relocation of European and African populations in various African colonies have shown that attempts to relocate Europeans in urban areas reflected changing notions of medical knowledge derived both from racial and medical policies, and urban re-design. Historical analysis of African towns in the 1980s suggested that there was a difference in segregation policies between the French and the British, the former encouraging population mixing and the latter residential segregation, but with a change at the beginning of the twentieth century to 'a new segregative policy', evidenced in Goerg's study of Conakry in French Guinea and Freetown in Sierra Leone, demonstrating 'the same discourse of separation. Both the French and English used the hygiene paradigm to enforce a clear division between so-called races and ethnic groups and to make these categories visible in everyday life' (Goerg 1998: 2, 3).

Curtin had suggested that the process, developed in India, of establishing 'hill stations' for European officials and military personnel at high altitudes to avoid the high summer heat was imitated when discovery was made towards the end of the nineteenth century of the links between malarial parasites and mosquitoes. Initially it was thought that the risk to Europeans of being affected by malaria was tied to the false assumption that it was highest in proximity to African children up to the age of five (Curtin 1985: 598–9).

Printed instructions about solutions to the malaria problem were drawn up at the Liverpool School of Tropical Medicine and issued in 1900 by the British Colonial Office, advocating eradication of mosquitoes, protection against mosquito bites by increasing ventilation in houses, and segregation of Europeans from Africans. Curtin (1985: 599) points out that the implementation of these rules was varied. In Freetown in Sierra Leone a new European suburb – 'Hill Station' – was constructed above the town between 1902 and 1904, in which Africans were allowed to work in the daytime but not to stay there at night. This became a contested strategy, for Freetown had an active and articulate African middle class that objected to the confiscation of land for the new site, to the segregation that was involved, and to the opportunity costs of the funds used in construction. An irony was that the segregated Europeans were found to be as vulnerable to malaria as anyone else.

In Bathurst – a town in Gambia that had not experienced segregation before – plans were laid for a health segregation of Europeans in 1911, but the plan was opposed and never implemented. Similar opposition and the wisdom of the governor also prevented a similar scheme in Accra in the Gold Coast, and there was a similar outcome in Lagos in Nigeria (Curtin 1985: 601, 603). The forcible removal of Africans away from the seafront at Duala, involving loss of land and prime sites for trade and business, was planned by the German colonial authorities in Cameroon in 1910, and this was opposed by African middle-class entrepreneurs and European missionaries. In German East Africa stronger attempts were made to solve the malaria problem through mosquito eradication and more active administration of quinine, but even here there were calls for segregation (Curtin 1985: 607–8).

Curtin identified similar variations linking hygiene and health with attempted segregation in French African cities, citing Saint Louis in

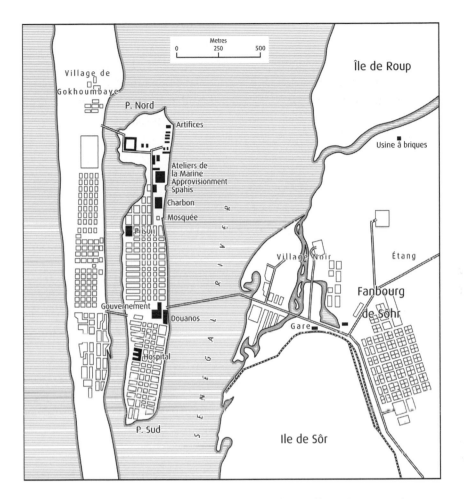

Fig. 11.1 St Louis, Senegal, *c.* 1900. Source: *Atlas Colonial Illustré* (*c.* 1900: 99).

Senegal as an example of a historical city that resisted segregation, but seeing Dakar, in spite of African opposition, as a city where an attempt was made to expel Africans to an external medina during a plague event of 1914.

He concluded that 'some form of racial, social, or cultural segregation triumphed everywhere in colonial Africa – most fully in South Africa, Rhodesia and elsewhere in the Belgian Congo – but with a different mixture of racial, medical and social justification in each case' (Curtin 1985: 612), with the Belgians, as in Leopoldville, as 'the most thorough practitioners', and the migratory labourers' compounds in the industrial areas of the Witwatersrand another strong example. Goerg contends that her study of separatist European quarter policies in the cities of Conakry and Freetown have broader replications elsewhere in Africa in the period up

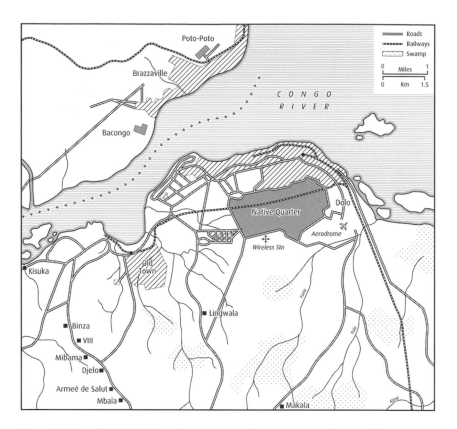

Fig. 11.2 Leopoldville, Belgian Congo, *c.* 1940. Source: Mason (1944: 325).

to the beginning of the First World War: 'despite what seems to be a radical theoretical opposition between the French and British approaches, most cities in Africa became characterized by sharp contrasts, between the "white city" and African districts or so-called "villages"' (Goerg 1998: 25–6).

The ideas about separation of indigenous people from expatriate populations in European colonies also reflected concepts and legislation of spatial social engineering in the metropolitan countries, most particularly as applied to the poorer working-class populations of their larger cities. In addition, some colonies offered opportunities to architects and urban planners to implement ideas on urban modernity for which openings at home were not plentiful. In a study of architecture and urbanism in French colonial policy from 1900 to 1930, Wright has shown how administrators in French colonies such as Indochina, Madagascar and Morocco used urban culture and design both 'in efforts to make colonialism more popular among Europeans and more tolerable to colonised peoples' (Wright

1987: 291). The experiments with urban design in these countries tried to accommodate both indigenous and immigrant French settlers, for

> colonial officials needed policies that could effectively quell the possibility of social unrest and encourage economic development; they required homes and workplaces for French settlers and for the indigenous populations drawn to the new colonial metropolises; and most of all the political system provided policy makers with a degree of authority for carrying out their plans that simply did not exist in Paris, Marseille or Lille. (Wright 1997: 326)

Applications of avant-garde modernism in what were regarded as laboratories (*champs d'éxperience*) for experiment were subject to fewer constraints than in the metropole, and administrators such as Hubert Lyautey in Morocco produced regulations intended to be conducive to improved design, experiment, economic advancement, social security and political stability, and also to more urban conservation, reflecting the new ideology of *association*. Wright (1987: 300–3) shows how Lyautey's concept was applied between 1912 and 1925 in Morocco, through the preservation of historic buildings and antiquities (via the influence of a former student of the École des Beaux Arts) and the construction of modern *villages nouvelles* adjacent to but separated from the existing city by a *cordon sanitaire*. This was demonstrated by the designs for Fez, Marrakesh and Meknes by the architect Henri Prost, and in Casablanca. Major Arab population growth up to the First World War, together with attempts at health and sanitation improvement and cultural image, also led to the design and building of new settlements.

Algeria

Algeria experienced a long and complex interaction with the French metropole, between ethnic and socio-economic groups, and between various French settler presences. Prochaska has argued that it is necessary to see French settlers in Algeria as a separate group from the temporary colonial administrators, the military, and the like, and that the *pieds noirs* have a distinct history, identity and role in colonialism that links the more material aspects (settlement and infrastructural developments) of colonisation (Prochaska 1990a: 6–11). Different from a plural society, in which sub-groups existed but with little in common and where generally a dual economy (bazaar as against firm-centred) obtains, 'in settler colonies the settlers constitute a third group. It is not simply the existence of settlers which makes a difference, but rather the implications and consequences which result from their presence that is significant', one of the most significant consequences being the strength of their interaction with the decolonisation process, producing a 'three-sided conflict...which explains why decolonisation is so much more violent in settler colonies such as Algeria, Kenya, and Rhodesia-Zimbabwe than elsewhere' (Prochaska 1990a: 9, 10–11).

Algeria's colonial cities like many elsewhere in the modern European colonial realm were characterised by the interaction between distinct groups of colonisers and colonised, by political control, by increasing control (through development of commerce, railways and steamships) of their hinterland, by contrasting morphologies and styles, and by distinct municipal facilities such as sanitation, water supply, and land use. Components of newer colonial cities would include:

a Western-style central business district, a corresponding indigenous and stranger retailing district, residential neighbourhoods segregated along class and ethnic or racial lines, and military and police quarters (forts, cantonments, barracks). The divers manner in which these sectors of the colonial city are combined to create quite differently-looking cities should not obscure the fact that they are essentially variations on the same basic colonial forms. (Prochaska 1990a: 11, 18–19)

The coastal port city of Annaba – previously Hippo Regius under the Romans, the home of St Augustine, and renamed Bône under French rule – was controlled before the French invasion in 1830 by a Turkish Bey from Constantine, a city inland to the south-west. Thereafter it was under French control, with buildings and adjacent lands appropriated, and resources such as cork oak forests exploited, together with the iron ore, initially from the Edough Mountains/Bône plain junction, and later from the Ouenza Mountains, with phosphates from the Tebessa Mountains to the south. On the eve of the French conquest the city had a pre-colonial form: it was walled, with six gates, and an irregular layout, with the main square at the centre, on the south side of which was the Salah Bey mosque, with another major mosque – the Sidi Bou Merouane mosque – on the east. There was a synagogue near the west gate, and a casbah or fort to the north, outside the walls. Cemeteries – Muslim, European and Jewish – were all outside the city walls, and in the areas adjacent to the walls were orchards and cultivated gardens (Prochaska 1990a: 77, 36).

French occupation of the city included the takeover of buildings abandoned by the inhabitants during the French invasion, and the demolition of others. When Algerian inhabitants returned to occupy these buildings, many of which had been appropriated by the French army, they were forced to sell them at nominal prices to European military officers and speculators or other local entrepreneurs, before leaving the city, and thus creating a significant majority population of Europeans (Prochaska 1990a: 64). The poor quality of the city's living conditions, in addition to periodic outbreaks of cholera and typhus, together with endemic malaria, kept the rate of natural population increase low until the late 1860s, the actual increases in population occurring through immigration.

From about 1870 Bône grew through an expansion of its regional and port roles as a funnel for the export of raw materials to France and the import of manufactured goods. Phosphates and iron ore formed a significant part of its trade. Railways were built and the port improved to accelerate this colonial export–import function, with the port improvements running well over estimated costs (Prochaska 1990a: 113). The city was significant for its ethnic separations, with Europeans occupying the better houses and others such as Jews, Arabs and Berbers the lower-quality housing. The development of a new city and suburbs (a common feature of urban design in France's colonies) to the west of the old city created a new built and social environment (Prochaska 1990b: 510–13). The French urban planning of the new city had all the hallmarks of colonialism, with French street names, French boulevards with trees, and a French town hall or *mairie*.

In the period 1881–1901 'the total population of the old city remained virtually stationary, but nearly 3,000 Europeans left and some 2,000 Algerians moved in. During this period the new city and the Colonne Randon [a working-class area named after a French general and developed from about 1859] added about 4,000 Europeans apiece' (Prochaska 1990a: 157–60). A large number of Algerians also lived on the outskirts of the city, and most of the small Jewish population remained in the old city, though by 1911 some had moved to the wealthier new city. By 1920 this city was a

settler colonial society in which the European colonizers outnumber the Algerian colonized two to one. A French colony in which the Italians, Spanish, and Maltese are as numerous as the French, and form colonies within the colony. A French colonial society created largely by naturalizing Jews and Europeans. A colonial society stratified along lines of race and class, and typified by residential segregation, vertical occupational stratification, functional occupational specialization, plus unequal pay for equal work. It all fits together. (Prochaska 1990a: 177–8)

Similar residential patterns were experienced in the colonial city of Algiers, for as late in the colonial period as 1954 the configuration comprised a European core, within which was located the pre-colonial Algerian casbah, with the majority of Algerians in the outer zone. The Algerian

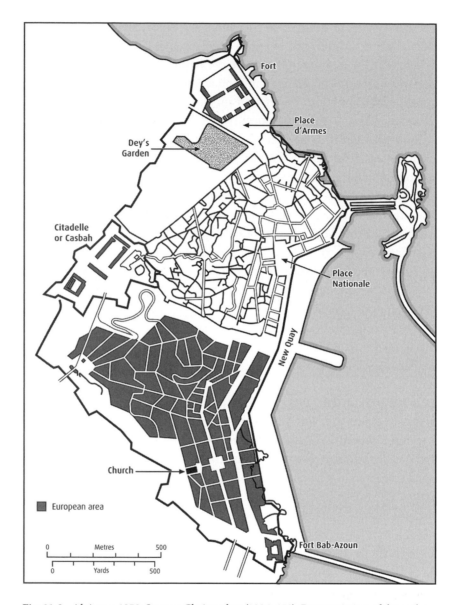

Fig. 11.3. Algiers *c.* 1850. Source: Christopher (1984: 178). By permission of the author.

population, of which large numbers were only employed part-time in domestic and labouring roles, lived in poor conditions, including the *bidonvilles* and hutted camps in the outer zone (Eichler 1977: 7).

Our understanding of segregation in European colonial cities, however, is gradually being refined by a departure from the simpler dualistic idea of colonial and indigenous quarters in such cities, towards a more nuanced view that accommodates more interaction between groups. Stephen Legg,

Fig. 11.4 Algiers , *c.* 1890. Source: *Atlas Colonial Illustré* (*c.* 1900: 24).

for example, in a recent study of the historical geographies of Delhi's urban development, has suggested that this dual-cities hypothesis 'does not always reflect the intermingling of the two societies, nor the various types of spatial formations by which the colonisers attempted to order the native cities outside of which they dwelled' (Legg 2007: 216).

Segregation in the towns and cities of South Africa

Christopher (1994: 35) dates the beginning of formal urban separation between races in South Africa to the abolition of slavery in 1834 and the consequent migration of black Africans to the towns. He instances the creation of a separate suburb for the 'charges' of the London Missionary Society in Port Elizabeth in 1834, and the regulations by the Cape colonial government for separate locations near to white towns for non-white urban dwellers, and this practice was widespread in the Eastern Cape in the second half of the nineteenth century, though not in the Cape Colony or Natal.

Separation of black and coloured people (as they were classified) was characteristic of the Orange Free State in the later nineteenth century and the Transvaal after 1900. Separate compounds for mine labourers were introduced to combat diamond smuggling in the Kimberley area, but the same practice was also adopted in gold and coal mining. By the creation of the Union of South Africa in 1910 the overall position was that 'a wide variety of urban policies relating to the indigenous populations were in force, in contrast to the reasonably uniform rural reserve policies. The attempt to introduce national uniformity was only undertaken in the 1920s, as a result of the accelerated migrations of Blacks into the towns and the consequent competition between Black and White workers', and formal regulations requiring the separation of populations were introduced by the Natives (Urban Areas) Act of 1923, which was continuously revised up to the major consolidation of legislation in 1945 (Christopher 1994: 37–8).

A policy of urban apartheid had thus been applied from 1910, and was enhanced by discriminatory developments in state housing after 1918. Discrimination against the Indian urban populations was part of the colonial history of South Africa, accelerating in the later nineteenth and early twentieth centuries, with further discriminatory legislation increasing up to 1948 (Christopher 1994: 39–42). The levels of discrimination did vary up to the period of introduction of a national apartheid policy in the late 1940s and early 1950s, with the greatest indices of discrimination shown for the black population.

The election of the National Party to government in 1948 intensified the policies of separate rights, including residence rights, for whites and non-whites, ushering in one of the most inhumane and brutal regimes experienced in a colonial context, and which continued until the early 1990s. Hence 'Separation was to be introduced at all inter-personal levels ranging from separate park benches for Whites and other people to separate independent states for members of the various defined populations groups', a policy that was begun in 1950 by the Minister of Native Affairs, H. F. Verwoerd, and further means for urban residential and workplace discrimination were introduced in the Population Registration Act and Group Areas Act of 1950 (Christopher 1994: 65).

The consequences of apartheid for the populations of South Africa and for South Africa's standing in the world community are well known, but its application, in the form of pass laws, large-scale transfers of black population, segregation of residence and work and leisure places, and a range of additional personal discriminations, was strongly contested, and also resulted in tension between the ethnic groups which were the targets of white discrimination. Tensions were manifest in the 1959 and 1960 riots in Durban, the killing of sixty-nine black people in Sharpeville in the southern Transvaal on 21 March 1960, the banning of the African National Congress, and the arrest and imprisonment of its officers in 1963, the riots against the compulsory use of Afrikaans in black schools in Soweto and other towns in the Witwatersrand, resulting in 575 deaths, of which half were in Soweto. Boycotts and protests intensified from 1985 to 1990, and states of emergency were declared. Detention without trial had been introduced by the South African government in 1960 following the Soweto protests, and it is estimated that 'in the course of the period from 1960 to 1990 78,000 people were detained without trial. One of the notable features of this legislation was the virtually unlimited power exerted by the Security Police over the detainees, and the consequent number of deaths in detention' (Christopher 1994: 161–5, 170).

South Africa also exported its colonial persecutions and discrimination policies to South-West Africa (Namibia), over which it had a League of Nations mandate after 1919, and it opposed transfer of trusteeship to the United Nations in 1945. The mandate was revoked by the United Nations in 1966. The name of the country was changed to Namibia, and preparation was made for its independence. Apartheid laws had been applied by South Africa since 1948, and a number of 'homelands' were created. Major challenges to South African authority started with violent opposition to forced removals to the external neighbourhoods of Windhoek in 1959, and accelerated with the foundation of the South-West African People's Organisation (SWAPO), which started an armed insurrection in 1966. Namibia became independent in 1990, after a period of intervention by South Africa against insurgencies in Angola, Mozambique and Namibia itself (Christopher 1990: 180, 184–8).

Urban India

The region covered by the city of Delhi witnessed the flowering of no fewer than nine different urban settlements, from the city of Indraprastha in the seventh century BC to the modern decolonised city of Delhi. The contrast between Old and New Delhi is significant in both morphological and symbolic terms, the one signifying an ancient culture with particular urban traditions, the other an intrusively spectacular piece of urban design resonant of colonial modernity (Chatterjee and Kenny 1999: 72). New Delhi was one of a large number of British colonial cities that epitomised the hegemonic and cultural attitudes of the colonisers to the colonised, including the physical separation made between the areas in which the two groups lived, a contrast greatly emphasised by the planning and construction of New Delhi between 1911 and the early 1930s. There also developed a third, hybrid, element of urban culture and form – an outcome of the contacts between the two cultures.

Old Delhi (Shahjahanabad) was built from 1658 by Shah Jahan ('King of the World'), one of the great Mughal emperors, whose ambitions were frequently signified and realised in buildings. Old Delhi was built to replace Agra as the capital of the Mughal empire. The great Red Fort and the large Jama Masjid mosque (Friday mosque) were major constructions, but this was in fact 'a whole new city with professional thoroughfares, bazaars, caravanserais, shaded waterways, spacious squares and massive stone walls. "The new walls were punctuated with twenty-seven towers and eleven gates enclosing some 6,400 acres; about 400,000 people lived within them'" (Keay 2000a: 335).

This large capital city sustained its cultural and administrative vitality between 1638 and 1761, but declined rapidly after being sacked by the Persians in 1739, with a consequent loss of status and wealth. From 1803 the city was controlled by British residents for the East India Company.

Fig. 11.5 The Red Fort, Delhi, initially constructed 1639–48. Photo © R. A. Butlin.

In the nineteenth century the principal urban centres for British India were the port cities of Calcutta, Bombay and Madras, which conformed in their physical and social segregation patterns to the 'norm' of British colonial cities, whereas Delhi experienced a greater social and economic intermixture of populations in the period up to 1857: 'The city's European, Hindu and Muslim elites interacted in various activities, including literary and academic events, and participated in certain commercial ventures such as the organization of the Delhi Bank' (Chatterjee and Kenny 1999: 78). After the Uprising/Mutiny of 1857, for which Delhi was a major centre, the authority and rights of the East India Company were removed in a proclamation of 1858 and taken over by the British crown. Concern at the causes of the Uprising/Mutiny led to a more cautious and sensitive approach to Indian customs and traditions, while at the same time effecting strong military control. After 1858 British policies towards north Indian cities, notably those like Delhi and Lucknow which had been focal points of the Uprising/Mutiny, took the form of tighter control of the built environment, notably in regard to what have been described as 'three themes: safety, sanitation, and loyalty ... Safe, sanitized, and loyal cities, delineated by colonial urban policies, contributed to the larger imperial objectives of constituting authority and order in Indian society' (Chatterjee and Kenny 1999: 80).

Major changes were made to the structure and morphology of Delhi, one-third of which was demolished. The British forced most of the Muslim and Hindi populations to leave the city, and reconstituted the Royal Palace as a military fort, clearing areas around it to provide clear fields of fire for guns. Around the walls of the palace a zone was created from which housing and agriculture were banned, and the military cantonment was brought back within the city walls (King 1976: 210–11). Within the cantonment there was segregation of British and Indian troops, while British civilians were moved out of the walled city to the 'Civil Station' to the north, characterised by wide streets, good water supplies, drainage and sanitation, and lower densities of population, in contrast to the character and facilities of the older, Indian, part of the city. A key component of colonial cultural use of urban and rural residential space in colonised India was the bungalow or bungalow complex, a part of the built environment of cities in India with a strong European presence. King describes its main features:

The typical bungalow consists of a low, one-storey, spacious building, internally divided into separate living, dining and bedrooms, the latter with attached rooms for bathing. A veranda, forming an integral part of the structure, or alternatively, attached to the outside walls, surrounds all or part of the building. The bungalow is invariably situated in a large walled or otherwise demarcated 'compound' with generally one main exit to the road on which it is situated. For much of the period under discussion, the kitchen, as well as servants' quarters, stabling and room for carriage or car, are separated from and placed at the rear of the bungalow. (King, 1976: 125)

Bungalows and their complexes were located either in rural areas, in the case of plantations for tea or rubber, for example, or outside indigenous settlement areas and providing residences for colonial administrators, or in the civil station or military cantonment of urban areas. The explanations of bungalow complexes must go wider than their actual sites, in the sense that they reflect a series of assumptions about values inherent in colonial cultures, including an elevated position where possible for reasons of drainage and sanitation and provision of fresh air, a site away from indigenous settlement areas, and the provision of a favourable prospect or outlook. Space for bungalows and their compounds was plentifully available in colonial India, and labour for their construction and service readily and cheaply available. Climatic factors, notably the heat, were countered by the provision of open ground around the bungalow, together with the planting at its edge of trees for shade, which had also been thought to be protective of malaria. The layout of bungalows and compounds provided for greater social interaction between residents and for demarcations of space, the compounds usually being bordered by a low wall, hedge or high bank. The conceptual model of the bungalow and its compound reflects the complex European colonial societies in India, and to a degree the underpinning metropolitan culture, in contrast to the cultural concepts reflected in indigenous urban settlement areas (King 1976: 134–5, 144, 155).

The city walls of old Delhi had been breached by the coming of railways, and eight railways entered the city between 1862 and 1906. Delhi's three elements of cantonment, civil station and 'native city' were characteristic elements of many British colonial cities.

New Delhi

These colonial urban trends towards a safer, more effectively sanitised and loyal Delhi were further accelerated by the decision of the British in 1911 to change the imperial capital of India from Calcutta to Delhi, and specifically to a new site adjacent to the old city which would be named New Delhi. Calcutta was geographically peripheral to India as a whole, and the arrival of many new technologies such as the railway, telegraph, telephone, and better printing facilities favoured the adoption of a more central capital city. In the first instance a temporary capital was constructed between 1911 and 1921, on a site within the Civil Lines, where a local circuit house was converted to a 'Government House', a new Secretariat was constructed, and new bungalows and hotels were built to accommodate the growing colonial bureaucracy (King 1976: 231–4).

The decision to locate the new national capital at Delhi had much to do with its ancient tradition as a major centre for earlier Indian dynasties, its central position advantaged by the advance of the Indian railway system, and the link in 1890 with Simla, the hill station to the north which became the 'hot weather capital'. Factors that determined the layout of New Delhi included the decision to site Government House on the highest point of the 'Ridge'. Modernist concepts of town planning, including those of the garden city, were used, so that:

the creation of New Delhi incorporated contemporary western town planning concepts with colonial grandeur. Grand central vistas, ubiquitous gardens at traffic intersections and along squares and circles, and wide tree-lined roads dominated the landscape of New Delhi. Bungalows on large individual plots and open green spaces interspersed between socially segregated areas – housing government officials according to the Government's 'Warrant of Precedent' were intrinsic features of the imperial capital. (Chatterjee and Kenny 1999: 85)

The policy to move the capital of India from Calcutta to Delhi was announced by King George V at the Delhi Coronation Durbar in December 1911. Hitherto the government of India, under the control of the Viceroy, had spent the four winter months at Calcutta, and the rest of the year at Simla, the hill station in the Punjab. Delhi's climate was thought to be healthier, and the city was more central for the governing of India, although the climate in summer was very hot, and a retreat to Simla was still necessary. Early in 1912 the Secretary of State for India, Lord Crewe, asked the president of the Royal Institute of British Architects to suggest three experts to advise on the site and planning for the new capital. The experts appointed were Edwin Lutyens, John Brodie (Liverpool's City Engineer), and Captain George Swinton (chairman of London County Council). A site on a ridge at Raisina, south-west of old Delhi, was chosen after considerable search and review, and the process of designing and building the new city began. This took much time and was beset with differences of view between Lutyens, the Viceroy Lord Hardinge, and Herbert Baker, who was brought in as collaborator with Lutyens (Lutyens 1991).

The architectural styles of the new city had been a matter of considerable thought, debate and disagreement, reflecting not only the particular architectural tastes of the main agents in design, including the Viceroy, but also egocentric ambitions, seen for example in Lutyens' insistence on being the sole designer for the central buildings of the new city.

Lutyens and Baker had other current imperial urban projects in train, notably in South Africa. Lutyens designed the Johannesburg Art Gallery between 1911 and 1940, and Baker, who had worked in the Cape Colony since 1892, and had moved to Johannesburg in 1902, designed the major official office complex – the massive Union Buildings – across a large site in Pretoria for the government of the newly unified South Africa between 1910 and 1913 (Stamp 2004; Abramson 2004; Etherington 2007). Lutyens' principal construction in New Delhi was the Viceroy's House (Rashtrapati Bhavan), constructed as an acropolis at the top of Raisina Hill, with the intention that it should be entirely visible from below, but Lutyens' intention was frustrated by the gradient to the top which, when the Secretariat

Fig. 11.6 Rajpath, New Delhi. Wide street and imperial buildings, part of the Lutyens/Baker design for New Delhi. Photo © R. A. Butlin.

buildings designed by Baker were completed, obscured the view of the portico of the Viceroy's House from below. The house itself incorporated many stylistic elements, including classical European, Mughal, Hindu and Buddhist. The house was not completed until after the First World War, and was first occupied in 1929. Baker designed the two Secretariat buildings, which faced each other across the King's Way leading up to Government House, and also a new massive circular legislative building to the north-east. These two architects were part of a wider group including Robert Toy Russell, who designed many of the houses and bungalows; Henry Medd, designer of two churches; and Arthur Shoosmith, the architect of the Garrison Church (Stamp 2004).

The layout at New Delhi was a hexagon, with the residence of the Viceroy at the centre, from which three axes ran out to the city's main mosque, the Muslim tomb of Safdar Jang, and the earlier Delhi site at Indraprastha. King (1976: 238) has suggested that the plan was influenced both by earlier designs for cities in Europe, such as Karlsruhe and Versailles, and also by

Fig. 11.7 India Gate: the triumphal stone arch at the eastern end of Rajpath, New Delhi. An All-India war memorial, commemorating the 90,000 Indian soldiers who died in the First World War, the North-West Frontier military activities and the Afghan action of 1919. Photo © R. A. Butlin.

nineteenth-century Western town plan models for industrial populations. The plot was divided into hexagonal grids, which were variously allocated on the basis of functional need and highly stratified social divisions. King (1976: 244) suggests that to meet residential requirements:

Five basic types of area were created: one for 'gazetted officers', mainly though not entirely European, the second for European 'clerks'; a third was set aside for indigenous 'clerks' and lower-ranking officials, and a fourth, for members of the indigenous elite, the nobility of the 'native states'. The fifth area was 'non-official' space, occupied by those with insufficient rank or status to qualify for a place within the Imperial City.

The names given to places in New Delhi directly reflected colonial precepts and hierarchy. The principal streets were named after British royalty and other major figures associated with the British colonial presence in India, such as Hastings and Clive, while in a series of gradations outwards from the centre the nomenclature was chosen from an array of names of indigenous rulers, governors-general or Viceroys, and then in functional, non-personal terms ('Race Course Road, Park Road') (King 1976: 246–7).

The cantonment was laid out in a grid-square pattern with distance between the barracks of Indian and British troops, and with the officers' residential areas built at much lower densities. As far as civil requirements were concerned, King has suggested that among the important factors was a series of technological constructions, including the need to consider the implications of the telephone, bicycle, motor car, cinematograph, radio and aeroplane, determining in different ways the scale of planning of the new city, including the width of roads and the locations of administrative buildings, an airport, cinemas and radio stations. 'In this sense, New Delhi, both in its functioning as well as its lay-out, represented a dependent, technological appendage of a Western industrial estate. Without this technology it could function only by substituting manpower for tasks designed for machine' (King 1976: 236–7).

The population densities of the old and new cities reflected the great contrast in history and culture, with the old city having a density of approximately 50,000 people per square mile, and the new city about 1,970 per square mile. Formal and conceptual distinction was made by the British between the new and the old cities, the new city deemed representative of an assumed colonial cultural superiority, the old city seen as symptomatic of the faults of the Mughal empires, including architectural tradition, and a reminder of the 'slums' of industrial England. These perspectives were reinforced by the perceptions of the designers of New Delhi (located well to the south of the old city), especially Edwin Lutyens, that the new city should be conspicuously separate from the old, with few transport links and the protection of the old city wall maintained. Hence:

Preservation of the city wall and the open space via legal controls emerged as an important issue for the authorities in New Delhi. The historic wall served as a 'picturesque screen' hiding the slums of old Delhi; the open space between the two cities sanitized and separated New Delhi from what was referred to as the 'disease and rats of the old city'. (Chaterjee and Kenny 1999: 85–6)

The difficulties of the conditions in the old city were recognised, but action on proposals for amelioration was very slow in forthcoming.

The religious and educational needs of the populace were met through spatial allocations of sites that reflected the colonial hierarchy, with Christian churches at or near the centre, and Hindu temples, mosques, indigenous Christian churches and Hindu and Muslim cemeteries at the periphery. Economic and social and sporting functions of the city, such as markets, shops, hotels and clubs, and facilities for tennis, cricket and golf, also reflected this dual personality (King 1976: 253, 255–63).

So far the historical geography of New Delhi has been reviewed largely from the perspective of colonial ideas and plans. There remains, however, the question of the ways in which Indian people interacted with plans both for New Delhi and also for the old city. Parallel to the transfer of the capital from Calcutta to New Delhi, the British colonial government also attempted to control and improve the environmental conditions in the old city.

The methods used included the focus of the Delhi Improvement Trust on poor living conditions and high population densities. The Delhi Improvement Trust was founded in 1937, the outcome of a report by A. P. Hume in 1936 on the relief of the 'congestion' in Delhi, whose main recommendation was the reduction of the city's population by 100,000. This was highlighted in a further report of 1938 which spoke of the need to alleviate slum conditions which had challenged and defeated the city authorities for a period of twelve years or more, since 'The effect of unhealthy conditions of life is demonstrated by the statistics of tuberculosis, infant mortality and enteric fever' (Chatterjee and Kenny, 1999: 87). The main concern was about the areas of southern Old Delhi nearest to the site of New Delhi, as much because of the proximity of such very poor conditions and the likelihood of protests to the sanitised model settlement that was being constructed, rather than a deep humanitarian concern for the conditions of the poor.

One of the complex challenges to the controllers of the old city was that of sewage disposal, including the removal of night soil, and in the late nineteenth and early twentieth centuries the clearing of this inevitable but noisome product was a growing problem. Underpinning the thinking of colonial city administrators was the scarcity of revenue to fund modern sewerage systems, and the colonialist notion that indigenous peoples were incapable of adopting innovative systems. The lack of adequate water supply in the old city prevented the application of modern water-based sewage technology. Prashad contends that:

In elite areas of Euro-America and in colonial enclaves, urban municipalities installed technical innovations, such as sewage lines and running water. The existence of technological practices, however, does not ensure their universal application. To the bourgeoisie of Europe, the development of the notions of hygiene came to be linked with culture rather than with technological advance... In the colonial context, the problem of producing an immaculate city was resolved by making use of manual labour in native areas a 'natural' phenomenon and by attributing to it lower standards of hygiene. (Prashad 2001: 117)

A partial solution to this major problem involved attempts at combining old technology – the manual labour of the street sweeper – with modern forms of transport, such as motorised lorries and a light tramway, to remove the sewage to the outside of the city, and even further away. Refuse railway trains were also used to move sewage from outside the city to dumping grounds about ten miles away. The cost was always a factor, and New Delhi was seen as a drain on financial resources that might otherwise have gone to improve sanitation in the old city. There were protests by local elites to this effect in August 1935, one contention being that 'All the congestion, insanitation and disease in Delhi today, were due to the advent of the Government of India to Delhi from Calcutta' (Prashad 2001: 131).

The natural ecological use of street sewage for manuring the land outside the city of Old Delhi changed in the early nineteenth century, with a marked reduction in the number of rural villages in the hinterland. Various schemes were brought in to render the sewage less harmful and make it more readily available for fertiliser, including the development from 1894 of an experimental trenching farm to the south of Delhi (Prashad 2001: 139) and a sewage farm at Kilokri from 1933.

Sanitary landfills had also been developed around Delhi since the mid-nineteenth century. From 1936, a technology that had been known since the 1880s – incineration – was brought into use in an attempt to solve the problem of refuse. The system, however, as Prashad has concluded:

> was governed not by machines, but by labour. The refuse was removed by sweepers as quickly as possible, using carts and lorries. They then either buried the refuse in sanitary landfills or dumped the refuse in water courses ... The sanitation system survived only through a greater intensification of labour and a creative use of the environment. The labour process, far from holding back development, enabled the system to survive. Without that creative flexibility there would be no sanitation system at all. (Prashad 2001: 155)

What, though, of the lives and livelihoods of the street sweepers themselves? They had their own geographies of location and operation, and of hazard, but we seem to know little about them.

Using a range of critical theory developed initially by Foucault, Stephen Legg has recently provided an important and seminal account of the development of spatial manifestations of aspects of governmentality in Delhi. He focuses on residential, policing and improvement landscapes and their interactions, within broader national, imperial and other international frameworks of information flow and influence, with the reconstruction of Old Delhi and the construction of New Delhi. He reads New Delhi as a 'space of sovereignty', a product of an undemocratic transfer of a capital city, as an aesthetic symbol (for the British) of 'peaceful domination' of Indians, and as a major influence on colonial urban historiography, and strongly asserts that 'As a space of colonial violence and display, or a site of nationalist resistance, mobilisation or functionalism, Old Delhi has been distanced and silenced. It is chained to a binary that depicts it as subordinate, Old and Other, against the powerful, New, colonial self of the capital' (Legg 2007: 29). He offers new ways of looking at the historical geographies of major colonial cities, and this work will doubtless be followed by other studies, using a combination of theoretical analysis and empirical substance. In an earlier study of women's roles in India in promoting nationalist aspirations through their roles in the home, he has also suggested that, even in the strong colonial context, 'In nineteenth-century India, the British were not the only group cultivating a "modernizing regime" and thus not the only group to struggle with concepts of gender and sexuality' (Legg 2003: 11).

Health regulation and sexuality in colonial cities

Much attention has been paid by researchers in recent years to the question of attempts at the regulation of prostitution, especially in urban areas, in European imperial contexts. Regulation in Europe began in the France of Napoleon, starting in Paris early in the nineteenth century, and expanded from regulations for the military to those for the whole population, and was followed by similar regulations in Russia, the Netherlands, and Great Britain up to the mid-nineteenth century. Limoncelli suggests that the movements for regulation were 'actively promoted by coalitions of military administrators, medical doctors and conservative politicians, often with the tacit approval of the dominant religious organizations. These supporters assumed that men were not able to be continent. They therefore sought to control the contexts within which men would have sexual relations' (Limoncelli 2006: 35–6).

Geographical perspectives on the histories of prostitution have been added, for example, by Howell and by Kumar, through analysis of regulation of prostitution in the territories of the British empire (Howell 2000, 2004, 2005; Kumar 2005). An early work by Hyam (1988) highlighted the significance of opportunities for heterosexual and homosexual gratification, particularly with exotic partners, as both 'an incentive for colonial service and a consolation for its hardships and deprivations' (Woollacott 2006: 89) and also their influences on the spread of venereal diseases, especially syphilis. Critiques of this thesis have pointed, among other things, to its narrow (white, European, male) perspectives and its underestimation of racism, force and rape, and the economic and social underpinnings of prostitution (Woollacott 2006: 89). Howell echoes this critique when he writes that 'Prostitution regulation has rightly come to be recognised as a critical prop of imperial rule, vital not only to the campaign against venereal diseases but in a wider sense to the maintenance of racial and sexual privileges upon which colonial authority depended' (Howell 2005: 176). Following in part the work of Levine (2003) on prostitution in Hong Kong, the Straits Settlements, Queensland and India, and its differences from processes and conditions in Britain, Howell demonstrates that the regulation of prostitution varied between the overseas territories of the British empire. In the 'near' empire territories of the Mediterranean, the basis of regulation was 'ethnic exclusions, national identities, sovereign claims, rather than the racial categories adopted in the far-flung territories' (Howell 2005: 178–9). This was different from the policy in Ireland. His map of the dates of introduction of regulationist legislation for prostitution in Britain and the British empire shows that after Gibraltar *c.* 1800, the later nineteenth-century chronological sequence starts with Hong Kong (1857), followed by Malta and the Ionian Islands (1861), India (1864), Great Britain and Ireland (1864–9), Ontario, Quebec and St Helena (1865),

Jamaica and Ceylon (1867), Barbados, the Cape Colony and Queensland (1868), Trinidad and New Zealand (1869), the Straits Settlements (1870), Labuan (1877), Victoria (1878), Tasmania (1879), and Fiji in 1882 (Howell 2005: 178), though many of these were subsequently amended or supplemented.

The regulation measures in Hong Kong, a colony and military base of considerable strategic importance, were much more intense, intrusive and strict than those in Britain. They were also racist and segregating in that separate brothels were licensed for European and Chinese men, registration and medical examination were restricted to sex workers who served European men, and reflected different cultural attitudes to the medical examination of women. These regulations were paralleled by other measures of control and surveillance to minimise the vulnerability of the colony to an undermining of imperial authority (Howell 2005: 180–1). Later developments varied these local geographies of prostitution, including a classification of Chinese and European or foreign clientele brothels into three classes, which partly ran counter to the earlier racial basis of segregation (Howell, 2005: 184).

Viewing the Hong Kong experiences of regulation in a wider imperial perspective, Howell (2005: 186, 191) contends that they were indicative of a British government practice of allowing high degrees of autonomy to colonial administrators, and in this case justifying regulation of prostitution ' because it was a response to local, but also to specifically *Chinese* conditions'. Nonetheless, he argues that this degree of autonomy was not consonant with an overall British imperial policy of regulation of prostitution, in contrast to the actions and ideologies of those who were prominent in the repeal of the British Contagious Diseases Act in 1888, which also brought about the repeal of the related Hong Kong legislation. Their views and actions were symptomatic of a 'repeal vision, produced by international and empire-wide humanitarian networks', and which 'authorized a geography of the British imperial system, in which colonial sites lost their specificity in their connections to each other and to the metropolis'.

Kumar (2005: 156) offers an important perspective that prostitutes in both rural and urban areas in India in the nineteenth century were not simply the recipients of official imperial disapproval and regulation, but were active in asserting their own rights and 'despite being victims of tradition, patriarchy and colonial order', 'were able to carve out spaces for resistance based on their agency'. He emphasises the differences in cultural contexts, especially British and Indian, in which prostitution was understood, and argues that its regulation in India was not just a British imperial construct but something that long pre-dated British rule. The colonial discourses on the subject polarised masculine and feminine identities, created politicised and 'racialized sexual politics of gendered control', notably in the period 1860–90, and were interlinked with particular medical perceptions and knowledge, including public health policy. New features of prostitution under the British colonial order included a wider social range of women sex workers and of clients, and new systems of control (Kumar 2005: 156–7, 158).

The perception of prostitutes in pre-colonial India as a functional group among many others influenced their designation as 'criminals' in colonial times. There was thought to be a need for further regulation, even though forms of regulation had existed in India since late prehistoric times, with different status being accorded to women involved in religious ceremonies and in courtesan contexts. In colonial times there was a transition from middle-class to lower-class women prostitutes, and an increase in their numbers at times of economic or social disorder, such as famine. There was specific legal regulation through the Cantonment Acts of 1864 and 1880, relating to the military, and the Contagious Diseases Act of 1868 for civilians. Lock hospitals, first founded in England in 1747 for the treatment of venereal disease, and which succeeded the leprosy hospitals, were part of the imperial strategy for combating these diseases. They were introduced to military cantonments in India in 1805 through the influence of East India Company army officers, but although the lock hospital system was abolished in 1830, it was reintroduced in the 1840s and 1850s (Kumar 2005: 162–3, 166). The Contagious Diseases Act of 1868 was applied to India as to other British colonies, and made very strong provision for the registration, inspection and regulation of prostitutes, and their confinement to specific places, including regulated brothels or *chaklas* established in the military cantonments. Kumar (2005: 170) argues that, notwithstanding the many and varied attempts at control of prostitution in imperial India, 'the prostitutes retained an immense capacity for agency and constantly subverted the colonial designs of regulation and control of their activities', including forms of costume, use of marriage-related names, and operation outside the zones of supervision.

Of equal interest and significance were the national and internationally linked voluntary associations and movements for the abolition of the regulation of prostitution, which started in Britain and spread internationally from the 1870s. They campaigned against the regulatory models that had spread from European countries to their colonies, and which included the licensing of brothels and registration of prostitutes, together with compulsory medical examination of the women (Limoncelli 2006: 31–2). The abolitionists took the view that the regulation of prostitution betokened double standards for men and for women, and exploited women ruthlessly and insensitively (Limoncelli 2006: 37, 42, 44).

The chronology of abolition differed between European countries: in France in 1899, Germany in 1898, and the Netherlands in 1913, for example. All brothels in the Netherlands had been abolished by 1911, and the registration of prostitutes by 1913, with abolition in the Dutch East Indies in 1910. The early success in the Netherlands is attributed by Limoncelli to the existence and support of other socially reforming organisations concerned with the advancement of women's rights and religious reform. The later abolitionist achievements in France and Germany were attributable to the lack or later development of such movements.

Cities in British settler colonies

Australia, New Zealand, Canada and South Africa were the largest areas of settler colonies in the British empire. As populations grew, so did the urban network. The locations and processes of allocating land and designing the layouts of towns and cities in settler colonies were linked to a web of imperial influences and processes, including the appointments of governors-general for individual territories, the appointment of surveyors with consequences for urban planning, trans-imperial discourses of design and layout, and the complex influences of land speculators, investors and of national and international economic, political and social factors.

Australia

With the exception of Sydney, Australian cities were mainly products of the nineteenth century, and were founded and grew at a time of major technical improvements in transport and construction, stimulating rapid and strong suburban growth, linked to expanding international trade (Williams 1974: 420). In many respects, urban development in Australia was different from that in other settler colonies. Although the contexts of capitalist world development, inputs of overseas (notably British) capital, people and technology are relevant and important, the role of government in this developing capitalist society, especially in the field of land allocation, was a crucial factor shaping Australia's urban history. Daly has suggested that 'Australia thus became *such* a highly urbanised society because of the particular interplay of local, social, economic and political forces and the critical role of government' (Daly 1988: 45).

Much of the rapid development in the later nineteenth century was stimulated by land and housing markets profoundly affected by property dealings supported by overseas capital at times of high levels of immigration, conditioning cycles of boom and depression, and the appearance of distinct ethnic clusters in the cities. In the period 1880–93, 66 per cent of Australia's new capital came from Britain; £50 million of British capital was invested in Victoria in the late 1880s; and British deposits made to Australian banks at 3.5 to 5 per cent could be reinvested at 7 to 10 per cent (Daly 1988: 42, 44).

In Australia the main sites of early major urban development were coastal – Sydney (1788), Perth (1829), Melbourne (1835) – or near-coastal – Adelaide (1836), for example. Melbourne was founded by white settlers from Van Diemen's Land in 1835 as a small village settlement, initially without official approval but confirmed in 1837 by the governor of New

Fig. 11.8 The Royal Exhibition Museum, Melbourne, built for the International Exhibition of 1880, and used as the site of the first Australian parliament from 1901 and the Victoria state parliament from 1901 to 1927. Photo © R. A. Butlin.

South Wales, in whose territory it was at that time located, and it was named after Lord Melbourne, the British Prime Minister. A grid-plan layout was drafted, based on historical usages in the English enclosure movements and the American rectangular survey, but it was modified to fit with local physiography. It comprised, as did Adelaide, a central core of town land for business and commerce, an area of park lands for public use, and an outer belt of suburban lands (Powell 1970: 37). Within the city provision was made for very wide streets, and the sale of urban land plots by auction began in mid-1837.

Melbourne benefited from the Victoria gold rush beginning in 1851, and its population increased from 97,000 in 1850 to 126,000 in 1861, 268,000 in 1881, and 473,000 by 1891, by which time it was the thirtieth-largest city in the world and the seventh-largest in the British empire (Briggs 1968: 278; Daly 1988: 42). Speculation in land, the gold rush, and capital investment from Britain (attracted by high interest rates) were among the factors encouraging growth, and Melbourne expanded at a rapid rate, enjoying boom conditions in the 1880s. Low-density housing expanded into the suburbs, and the central commercial area developed modern facilities.

Briggs neatly captures the conditions:

The Melbourne boom reached its height in 1888. By then the city had been provided with its first electric light, with telephones, with new suburban railways, with cable trams ... with lavish new shops, complete with hydraulic lifts, with busy highly decorated arcades, with new theatres, hotels and restaurants, and with dozens of opulent new mansions in the suburbs, particularly in the fashionable suburb of Toorak. (Briggs 1968: 288)

Not everyone in Melbourne was rich enough to afford such opulent mansions, but the standard and design of housing for those further down the income scale was good, and extensive use was made of cast-iron in decoration. The depression of the early 1890s was characterised by the bankruptcies of banks, businesses and land companies, often in cases of financial fraud, by the drying up of British capital investment, and by a fall in wool prices. Not surprisingly, one effect was the development in Melbourne, in other cities, and the country more broadly, of strong nationalist sentiments. The Sydney newspaper *The Bulletin* 'began to serve as the chief instrument of a new kind of aggressive Australian nationalism, preaching the cause of labour, attacking the obsolete social distinctions and hierarchies of England, encouraging the emergence of a new group of Australian "nationalist" writers interested in Australian people and in Australian landscapes, and, above all, proclaiming distinctive Australian values' (Briggs 1968: 292). The depression of the early 1890s resulted in a reduction in the population of Melbourne, but urban fortunes revived and there was further suburban development up to and beyond the First World War.

The design and layout of the city of Adelaide, planned and founded in 1837 by the Surveyor-General William Light, showed at its instigation many influences from actual and conceptual notions of the character and form of an ideal city, including perhaps William Penn's Philadelphia; an idea for the town of Azilia in Georgia (which was never built); Savannah; Granville Sharp's idealised concept of 1794 for new townships in colonies such Upper Canada; and some utopian ideas for town layouts in industrialising Britain, including those of Robert Owen (Williams 1974: 389–97). Like Melbourne, the choice of site for Adelaide was controversial, and reflected the experience and personality of the Surveyor-General of South Australia, William Light (1786–1839).

Light's career was bound up in the networks of the British empire. He was born in Malaya, educated in England, travelled in India with the Indian army, served in the cavalry in the Peninsular War, travelled in Europe and Egypt, and was eventually appointed Surveyor-General of South Australia with a commission from the governor to explore South Australia's coasts and determine a site for its first settlement. He determined the location near the east coast of the Gulf of St Vincent, and inland from the swamp lands on the coast. His choice of site for the capital city of South Australia was much criticised, and he was also pressured by orders to survey a large area around the site with inadequate labour, technology and finance. He ultimately resigned, in poor health, in 1838, and died in 1839 (Williams 2004). Williams has concluded that in respect of his choice of site 'Time has vindicated him entirely – his was an excellent site, and in the modern city of Adelaide the separation of port and industry from the central business and administrative district has proved a great advantage', though he attributes the idea of the layout plan to Matthew Hill (Williams 2004).

In fact the three-part composition (the town lands or city, parklands, and outer suburban lands), mentioned above for Melbourne, was more strictly adhered to in Adelaide. The plentiful supply of land in the town lands and the high prices paid led to much vacant land in the centre and the location of poorer people in the outer parklands. The population of Adelaide's urban area increased from 6,107 in 1843 to 35,380 by 1861. This growth, together with that of public transport systems, notably tramways, was reflected in the greater heterogeneity of types of employment and activity, suburban growth of differing character, and more distinct zones within the city area of south Adelaide (Williams 1974: 404).

Change was also evident in the gradual movement from building construction in mud and wood to brick, stone and concrete, the latter characteristic of the city and 'superior suburbs'. Suburban growth continued into and beyond the early twentieth century, the population of Adelaide's suburbs increasing from 17,077 in 1861 to 102,163 in 1901. The total population of Adelaide increased from 163,000 in 1901 to 350,000 in 1941 (Williams 1974: 404, 410, 420, 425).

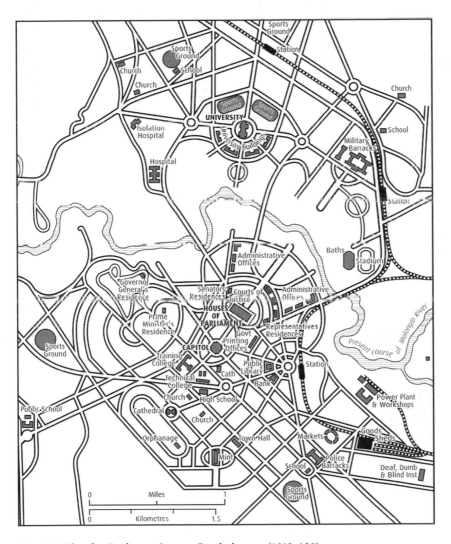

Fig. 11.9 Plan for Canberra. Source: Bartholomew (1913: 130).

Sydney is the oldest of Australia's major cities, having been founded in 1788 on a site on the southern shore of Port Jackson chosen for a colony of convicts transported from England, and which was already the territory of groups of aboriginal people. It expanded beyond the convict settlement site, conspicuously after 1868 when the transportation of convicts ended and when free emigration to Australia was encouraged, so that its population grew from 54,000 in 1851 to 400,000 by 1900, and to one million by the late 1920s.

Canberra, the capital city of Australia, came into being as a consequence of the federation of the six Australian colonies into the Commonwealth of Australia on 1 January 1901, and the need to locate, design and build a capital city on Commonwealth territory. A congress to discuss the development of the new capital city was held in May 1901 in Melbourne, and it was agreed that the design for the capital would be chosen on the basis of a competition. Fifteen possible sites in New South Wales were visited in 1902 and 1903, and initially the site of Dalgety was chosen, but this was then rejected because it was thought to be too far from Sydney, and the Yass-Canberra site was chosen in 1908. This comprised an area of 1,015 square miles (262,884 ha). The call for entries for an international design competition was made in 1911, but there was concern at the announcement that the final decision would be made not by professional peers in architecture and planning but by a politician – the Minister for Home Affairs, and also that the competition would be open to entries from beyond Australia and the British empire. One hundred and thirty-seven entries were evaluated by a panel of judges, reduced to shortlists of forty-six and then eleven. The winner was Walter Burley Griffin, an unknown American from Chicago, who had worked with Frank Lloyd Wright, and whose entry had been jointly produced with his wife Marion Mahoney Griffin. Vernon has stated that the winning entry by the Griffins 'was distinguished by its sensitive response to the site's physical features, especially in its rugged landforms and watercourse. This attribute proved paramount to their design's success. Organized on a cross-axial scheme, the plan fused geometric reason with picturesque naturalism. When negotiating the fit of their geometric template with the actual site, the couple opted to venerate existing landforms' (Vernon 2007: 168).

The focus was the Capital Hill, originally intended as the site of a Capitol building, but now the location of the Parliament Building, from whence radiated a series of major avenues and near which were the institutions of government. To the north was another centre, the London Circuit, a focus for civic and commercial institutions (Christopher 1988: 100–1). The layout symbolised the Australian Federation. Its plan and architecture also reflected aspects of the Garden City movement, which had originated in England, and also the City Beautiful Movement, together with clear influences from Frank Lloyd Wright and the Prairie style.

Vernon argues that 'the Griffins fashioned Australia's new national, cultural history from its ancient natural history – as demonstrated by the design significance they accorded to the physical features of the site ... the coincidental compatibility of the Griffins' approach with imperial technique likely contributed to their design's embrace by the empire's Australian dominion', though there was no reference in plan or buildings to aboriginal tradition (Vernon 2007: 170–1), a fact partly redeemed by naming the city Canberra. The real and symbolic American influence on the design of Canberra was modified by William Holford, an English town planner, who was employed in 1957 and who 're-colonised the Australian capital with a picturesque aesthetic, recasting Canberra's die as British, if not imperial' (Vernon 2007: 178).

Dutch colonial cities

The urban network of the former Dutch East Indies had deep historical roots, with cities on Java and Sumatra dating from the eighth century AD, and cities such as Demak, Benten, Aceh, Surabaya and Makasar were major Islamic centres in the pre-European period, and experienced reorganisation of form and structure following the Dutch colonisation of the East Indies in the sixteenth and seventeenth centuries (Ford 1993: 376). By the beginning of the eighteenth century, coastal cities such as

Jakarta, Semarang, and Surabaya each had central areas modelled after ideal Dutch port cities, complete with canals, city walls, cathedrals and townhouse architecture. Interior towns such as Bogor and Bandung, on the other hand, were designed as highland resorts with large estates and gardens ... In each case European, especially Dutch, ideal landscapes were imposed on alien cultural and physical environments. Those aesthetic features led to problems as the cities grew. For example the canals of Jakarta quickly became sluggish, malaria-infested disamenities rather than Dutch-style open spaces, and the city became famous for its rich variety of diseases. (Ford 1993: 376)

A strong Chinese immigration followed, and segregated communities developed. By the late eighteenth century the swampy environs and silting canals of the major Dutch cities, including Batavia, together with the unwholesome smells that came from deposits of debris, led to attempts to relocate the European sectors to adjacent higher ground. In Batavia a new settlement, linked by a new road, was developed to the south of the older city in an area known as Weltevreden, which was progressively laid out in a geometrical form, with the old city, whose walls and fortifications were demolished, becoming a port district, and by the 1850s having the overall plan of an hourglass, and a population of 70,000 (Ford 1993: 377). The change of site was characteristic of a distinctive European perception of a different environment, including the idea that houses and streets were too closely spaced for a healthy environment, and the proximity of Chinese cemeteries to the old city was also deemed unsanitary and undesirable (Cobban 1985: 307).

Cobban (1985: 309) indicates that:

By the end of the nineteenth century the morphology of the old town of Batavia differed very much from its characteristics during the previous two centuries. Features that had made the settlement unique among Asian cities and colonial capitals had gone. Successive administrations had filled in the interior canals to convert them to streets; the fort and most of the outer and inner canals on either side of the wall had been razed. New structures like the Court of Justice had arisen on the town-hall square.

Dutch influence on its major colonial city was thus maintained into the nineteenth and early twentieth centuries, in form, function and level of segregation. Indigenous inhabitants and Chinese populations maintained a separate geographical location.

Colonial towns and cities in the Philippines

In the Philippines, a Spanish colony until the Treaty of Paris at the end of the Spanish-American War (1899–1902) which gave the country to the United States, population clusters – small trading ports – pre-dated the Spanish colonisation from 1565. Manila was designated as a *cuidad* or city in 1571, with further *cuidades* established at Cebu (Santismo Nombre de Jesus), Naga (Nueva Caceres), and Lallo (Nueva Segovia), and towns (*villas*) at Aravelo and Fernandia (Doeppers 1972: 773). These towns and cities were characterised by the familiar Spanish colonial urban elements of formal layout and segregation of ethnic groups (Spanish at the centre, Filipinos and Chinese at the periphery), and their evolution followed a sequence of takeovers of indigenous cities and a focus on coastal sites for trading opportunities, and later on inland sites along trade routes. Large churches in the cities indicated the strong process of attempted proselytisation of Filipinos to the Catholic faith, including the Muslims of the lowland areas (Doeppers 1972: 773). Urban layout reflected the principles and experiences of early Spanish colonisation in Mexico: 'In Mexican *reducciones* a grid pattern was surveyed and lots assigned for the residences and gardens of the resettled. A central church was chosen and rectangular plaza laid out facing it. A house was built for the friar and [a] network of tributary villages established' (Doeppers 1972: 776).

Manila rapidly became the largest urban community in the Philippines, and maintained its predominance thereafter, particularly in the nineteenth century, after a new phase of economic change and expansion, including the development of new agricultural land, and the country opening up to trade in a world market, especially with Britain and the United States. Manila grew to a population of 190,000 by 1903, and retained its historical importance as a primate city in its region. Its port functions were increased, and it became a major centre for Filipino, Spanish, Chinese, British and American entrepreneurs. It 'remained the chief place of business not only because it was the centre for credit but because it was the hub of information as well. Transoceanic vessels and, later, cables served as the lifelines of news about world prices and demand for Philippine commodities, while the railroad and telegraph lines brought in crop information speedily from outlying districts in Luzon' (Larkin 1982: 618). The second city was Iloilo, with a population of about 25–20,000 in 1903, followed by Cebu, with a population of about 20,000 in 1903. Their growth had been stimulated by the opening of trade and particularly the export of sugar from the sugar-growing estates.

Imperial cities in Europe

Global interaction between metropole and colony was at least a two-way process, shown in the imperial architecture and symbolic displays and events of cities such as London, Paris, Brussels, Rome, Berlin, Madrid, Lisbon, Amsterdam, Seville, Glasgow and Marseilles. Driver and Gilbert have argued that imperialism links strongly with the 'cultural history of the modern European metropolis', an influence and interaction reflected in landscape designs, buildings and monuments, in written texts, maps, and performance spaces, and in contrasts between European imperial cities, and the ways in which 'the nature of that relationship was defined partly in relation to European as much to non-European "others"' (Driver and Gilbert 1999: 3–9).

The monumental symbolism of empire and attitudes is amply illustrated by the Albert Memorial in London and the Vittorio Emanuele II monument in Rome. The Albert Memorial was built (1872–6) to a design by Sir Gilbert Scott, as a tribute to Prince Albert, the Prince Consort, who died in 1861. It is one of London's most conspicuous symbols of empire and incorporates groups of statues reflecting the extensive and varied regions within the British empire and its cultures and science.

The Vittorio Emanuele II monument is a memorial to the king of Italy who died in 1878, a testimony to the long imperial history of the city of Rome, and in some senses a pointer to the fascist imperial building and landscaping that was to follow. It was 'designed to be a highly rhetorical symbol whose message of unity and rebirth was directed at all Italy, and whose very location declared a blatant connection between the national altar of modern Italy and the classical empire once founded on the same hill' (Atkinson, Cosgrove and Notaro 1999: 53).

The buildings and public spaces of London, especially the City, reflected its role as the metropolitan centre of the British empire through architectural styles and celebratory gatherings. Iain Black has shown how the rebuilding of the Bank of England building between 1919 and 1939 was explicitly designed by Herbert Baker (a major agent in imperial town planning, notably New Delhi) 'within a series of imaginative geographies of empire. Baker, designing within a consciously imperial classical tradition, left inscriptions of empire on all aspects of the Bank's rebuilding, from the general plan to the smallest details of sculptural and allegorical work on the facades and interiors' (Black 1999: 111).

In this chapter we have examined various facets of imperial and colonial urbanism. These were linked to systems of economic development, including agricultural and industrial production systems and the recruitment and management of labour forces. Some aspects of these systems are reviewed in the following chapter.

Even when a colony was not primarily acquired for economic reasons, extensive effects on the economy of the region in question were inevitable. The establishment of colonial rule was one of the most important means of acquiring natural resources and human labour to foster intercontinental trade, which accelerated during the early modern periods. The economic effects of colonialism on the periphery varied vastly by time and place: West Africa differed greatly from East Africa, as did Sumatra from Java. (Österhammel 1997: 71)

This quotation from Jürgen Österhammel's overview of the basic features of colonialism reminds us that the territories of European colonies in the late nineteenth and early twentieth centuries found themselves increasingly incorporated into global economies and resource use systems, many dominated by metropolitan centres far removed from the areas of production. Some of the colonial areas had long been linked to trans-oceanic trading systems, such as the sugar producing regions of the West Indies and South America, and the spice islands of South-East Asia. Growing populations and increasing industrialisation in Europe created greater demands for foodstuffs and luxuries, and the need for overseas markets for industrial produce.

The colonial production and trading systems were linked to fluctuating markets and thus subject to major depressions in demand and profits. They were also subject to changes in metropolitan government policies, notably in attitudes to and the practice of free trade and to processes of imperial preference and policy-making. Larger amounts of capital for investment were generated, but the amounts invested in the European colonies varied between countries. Ferguson shows, for example, that 'by 1914 the gross nominal value of Britain's stock of capital invested abroad was £3.8 billion, between two-fifths and a half of all foreign-owned assets. That was more than double French overseas investment and more than three times the German figure' and much of it went to the United States, Russia, and other European countries, British capital being more widely dispersed, with high investment in the United States, white settler colonies, and lesser amounts in Asia, Latin America and Africa (Ferguson 2003: 242).

The geographies of Britain's expanding capital investment overseas did not neatly coincide with her formal empire, evidenced by investment in the countries of Latin America. Wherever they were, and whatever imperial system they operated in, the production systems in the European colonies changed dramatically from the second half of the nineteenth century through the period of high imperialism, partly through the development of more intense capital investment and exploitive trading systems. While investment in commercial agriculture in European overseas territories increased in the nineteenth and twentieth centuries, subsistence or near-subsistence rural economies characterised very large areas, though many of them were affected by growing commercial pressure to increase production for markets and to surrender land for plantations.

Colonial agricultural systems in the nineteenth and early twentieth centuries

The agricultural systems encountered, and in some cases supported and promoted, by colonial powers during the period of high imperialism varied according to local historical tradition, imperial and local policy and the strong influences of the environment, including climate. Morag Bell (1986: 72) asserts that in Africa:

it is clear that the types of political, administrative and economic structures established under colonialism and imposed upon the newly integrated African societies differed markedly between regions of the continent, between individual countries, and within different parts of each country. For example, a dominant feature of West African colonial experience was that the principal factor in agricultural production, land, remained under African ownership while European capital concentrated on trading activities. By contrast much of East, Central and Southern Africa was dominated by European-owned estates or plantations while the distribution of foreign-owned mining concerns extended from Sierra Leone and Mauritania to the Congo and Northern and Southern Rhodesia.

There were substantial variations in landholding and land-use practices across the European colonies, some of which have already been considered in Chapter 4. In this chapter we again look briefly at indigenous agricultural systems and at the plantation economies which were supported by European investment in Africa, South-East Asia and India and then move on to aspects of mining and industrial development.

Indigenous agricultural systems

At any given point in the late nineteenth and early twentieth centuries a significant part of agriculture in the colonial territories of European states was indigenous in origin and character. On the verge of being caught up in a global system of trade and commerce, mainly through commodities that would feed the raw material requirements of European industries and contribute to the feeding of their populations, a primary objective

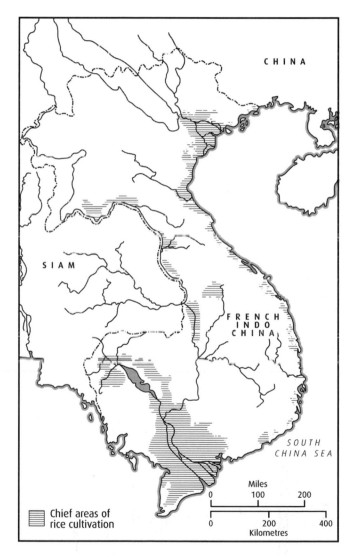

Fig. 12.1 Rice-growing in Indo-China, *c.* 1940.
Source: Darby (1943: 263).

of agriculture was to feed indigenous people and to provide them with a basis for regional trading and barter. The advent of a more extractive kind of colonial policy, tied in with a developing world system of demand, supply and trade, frequently allied indigenous agricultural systems with the gathering of natural commodities such as rubber, before the impact of heavier capital investment from the European metropoles led to a more specialised production of the same commodity in plantations. The forces for change included the demand for industrial raw materials such as rubber, timber and cotton, and the objective of satisfying consumer tastes and demands for such commodities as spices, coffee, tea, sugar and tobacco. Colonial impact on the rural economies and social systems of regions within the European hegemonies varied, partly in relation to the presence or absence of significant white settlement, and the particular goals of the colonial economy, but it was frequently fed by ignorance of indigenous land-use rights and practices (see Chapter 4).

In South and South-East Asia the dominant production systems of commodities such as rice that were essential parts of the indigenous subsistence economies did not easily accommodate a colonial export economy, nor did indigenous codes of land-use rights and ownership systems. The same was true of many parts of Africa, Australia and New Zealand and many island systems of the Pacific. Change in use rights and control of production became an essential part of the colonial economy (especially when land was an essential guarantor for the raising of investment capital) as did cadastral mapping and the introduction of systems of taxation to cover the high costs of colonial administration (Cleary and Eaton 1996: 35).

The new exploiting systems of land use also required a very different labour system. Cleary and Eaton have characterised the traditional use rights and systems of South-East Asia as

complex systems, circumscribed by a range of customs and obligations whose development reflected social, political, demographic, and geographical conditions. In areas of extensive shifting cultivation – the northern highlands of Thailand, Borneo, the Outer Islands of the Dutch East Indies – use rights were often carefully circumscribed by social custom and communal pressures. Rights of disposal were rare and, in any case, vested in the community rather than the individual, and a range of subsidiary rights overlay the fabric of use. The agricultural calendar, dictated by both environmental conditions and social custom, likewise complicated the apparently simple nature of land clearing and utilization. (Cleary and Eaton 1996: 37)

The systems involved in the production of rice were complicated, both physically and socially, and included control of water-use rights. Shifting cultivation (clearing of land from forest, followed by cultivation and then a fallow period) has long been, and in remoter places remains, a major component of the rural production system in South-East Asia, and includes some systems for the cultivation of rice. Cleary and Eaton have described the distribution and operation of shifting cultivation by the Dayak peoples in Sarawak, its environmental impact varying particularly with the length of the fallow period. The greatest persistence of customary land tenure and use rights in South-East Asia is in Papua New Guinea, where Cleary and Eaton estimate that 97 per cent of the country was still operated under traditional tenurial and use systems at the very end of the twentieth century (Cleary and Eaton 1996: 52–7).

Indigenous subsistence agriculture and European-controlled commercial agriculture, including plantations, might be seen as the main components of colonial rural production systems, but there were many indigenous production systems that gradually adapted to production for markets. As Curtin (1995a: 450) has indicated:

Recent studies in agricultural history, however, tend to show that African farmers were not unthinking traditionalists. Their knowledge of local conditions and suitable techniques was far better than that of the European 'experts' who came to give them advice about what to plant and how to take care of it. They were usually willing to change, even anxious to change, if they could see the possibility of substantial profit at small risk.

Curtin cites as examples of 'agricultural change on African initiative' the expansion of peanut-growing in Senegal and the Gambia and the growing of cocoa in the Gold Coast in the nineteenth century (Curtin 1995a: 453–6).

Plantation agriculture

Plantations had a long history in the conquest of tropical regions by European powers and agencies from the sixteenth century onwards, and, until the abolition of the slave trade, operated on the basis of the most heinous appropriation and cruel use of slave labourers. The reintroduction of plantation agriculture into many European colonial territories in the nineteenth and twentieth centuries during the gradual eradication of slavery was a continuation, in slightly different form, of the exploitation of poor labourers. It was also symptomatic of the exposure of the world outside the metropolitan hearths of Europe to change to a more fully fledged advance of global capitalist relations of production, a system 'which was relatively capital-intensive, privately financed, corporately managed and technologically advanced. Its most common manifestation was the modern plantation, a system of production which was the symbol and the direct result of intrusive high colonialism' (Elson 1999: 154).

The management and finance of these plantations was usually though not exclusively in the hands of European or North American enterprises, and normally reflected actual or perceived demands from the industrialising countries of the world for food or industrial raw materials. The introduction of plantation agriculture was in some cases dramatic and swift, but in others a more gradual change was experienced under the influence of commercialisation. Bose has suggested three phases in the history of plantations for Bengal in India: the first an increased scale of accumulation, giving rise to managerial farming and plantations; the second involving subsistence commercialisation, wherein 'poor peasants driven by their concerns of securing basic subsistence in a context of demographic and social pressures turned to the cultivation of high value and labour-intensive cash crops in an attempt to eke out a larger gross income from their diminishing smallholdings', exemplified by the production of jute on smallholdings in East Bengal in the late nineteenth and early twentieth centuries; the third an investment of merchant capital but without major changes in landholding, such as the production of indigo in West Bengal in the early nineteenth century (Bose 1993: 41–2).

There was also the case of further development of commercial crops on peasant holdings following the introduction of special crops to plantations, evidenced by the growing of tea on peasant smallholdings in South India, Ceylon, and the Dutch East Indies, and of rubber in Malaya and Sumatra after their introduction on estates and plantations in those regions. In some other areas, such as the cotton-growing areas of Uganda, production was more successful on indigenous land than it was on the lands of white European settlers (Christopher 1988: 184). The situation in Uganda was that few Europeans had settled there by the beginning of the twentieth century, and this, plus the guarantee of land rights to Africans in 1900, led to a significant increase in the growing and export of cotton – by a factor of seven between 1908 and 1914, mainly by 'a mass of small producers who still grew their own food: those in Buganda and Busoga led the way, but by 1914 much cotton was coming from Teso' (Roberts 1986: 655–6).

Plantations in Africa

In the course of the nineteenth century, during the period of the scramble for Africa and similar competitive geostrategic scrambles for territorial control elsewhere in the world, the earliest capitalist use of natural resources, apart from minerals, was through the gathering of naturally occurring products such as rubber, hardwood timber, various animal products including ivory and skins, and the produce of the oil palm. The oil palm, notably in West Africa and the Congo basin, had been used for a long time, but as other trees were increasingly cut down for timber, the oil palm was allowed to expand its area and its product was increasingly used and traded locally:

from West Africa, supplying material for soap, lubricants and lighting fuel to distant markets, [the oil palm] had suffered growing competition from both vegetable and mineral substitutes in the latter part of the nineteenth century; but against that, the chemists had found ways of making it eligible in the form of margarine, and this demand gave economic value to the kernel as well as the pericarp. (Wrigley 1986: 97)

The oil palm was cultivated elsewhere in Africa, notably the Belgian Congo, demonstrating in part the possible commercial cultivation for export of trees and plants that grew in Africa and which had naturally advantageous properties such as oil, strong fibres and complex chemicals that developed because of the strong sunlight and afforded a basis for chemicals and flavours, evidenced in their use for 'edible and inedible oils, for textile and rope materials and for those frequent small doses of nicotine, caffeine, and theobromine without which the stresses of industrial life would have been harder to endure' (Wrigley 1986: 97–8). The coconut palm, sesame, sisal hemp and the groundnut may be added to this list. Wrigley argues, however, that these plants grown and used in Africa offered no natural advantage in export markets, in comparison with other tropical and sub-tropical regions, apart from a low-cost labour force. He also shows that the real comparative advantages accrued to tree products such as cloves, grown in and near Zanzibar, tea in the Kenya highlands, and coffee and cocoa.

Coffee was collected from native forest species in equatorial Africa, notably around Lake Victoria, in Angola, and in the Ivory Coast, with mountain coffee found in parts of the East African uplands. Wrigley has shown that there was in effect a choice in the agricultural policies of colonial governments: either to leave production to African smallholders working to their own small scale and pace, or to invest capital and look for larger-scale, better-organised units of production. He contends that the distinguishing factor in this kind of decision was not necessarily the advantage of agriculture with high capital investment, but the potential advantages that derived from the scale of processing the plants grown, such as tea, sugar, sisal and tobacco: these 'were strong candidates for the plantation mode, because harvesting and processing needed to be closely linked' (Wrigley 1986: 103–4). Cotton could be and was grown on African smallholdings, for example in the Sudan, as well as groundnuts (before 1947), and cocoa, and even mountain coffee to an extent.

In Africa the main components of plantation agriculture and management were the familiar ones of adequate land, land-use rights and capital together with an adequate labour force and the technology for processing the crops grown, where required, and adequate means of transport to processing points and to ports for export. Christopher has suggested that, in contrast to South-East Asia, it was much more difficult in Africa to obtain the necessary ingredients and conditions for plantation development. The reasons included inadequate supplies of labour, except where forms of coercion were possible, and the difficulty of obtaining land concessions because, in the case of the British colonies, of opposition by British administrations to plantations and to concessions of indigenous land rights. In West Africa they were 'exceptionally zealous in their defence of African land rights' (Christopher 1984: 99).

There was early development of plantations for growing sugar cane in Natal, where there was major white European settlement, from the late 1830s, by use of overseas labour, including Indian indentured labourers from 1860 to 1911. The initial size of the plantations was small – about 100–250 ha, but the size increased by the end of the century.

In other parts of Africa small plantations were also developed, mainly from the 1890s, but not on the plantation scales of South-East Asia and Central America, and with stronger colonial control, so that crops such as cotton, groundnuts, coffee, tea and sisal were grown in areas where African production was deliberately restricted and where African rights of land use and occupation were ignored or distorted (Christopher 1984: 99, 102). Both the German and the French governments, however, were active in encouraging plantations in their colonial territories.

Plantations in German colonies

The Germans encouraged plantations, as a device for colonial exploitation and control, in Cameroon and German East Africa. The earliest German plantations in Cameroon were set up in the last years of the nineteenth century, promoted by colonial officials in Cameroon and in Berlin, and by the explorer Eugen Zintgraff and the agriculturalist Ferdinand Wohltmann. The first major plantation company in Cameroon was the Westafrikanische Pflanzungsgesellschaft Victoria, founded in 1897. It had 2.5 million marks in capital and had acquired 20,000 ha of low-cost plantation land by 1904, with an additional 16,000 ha owned by subsidiary companies. Two other plantation companies were added: the Westafrikanische Pflanzungsgesellschaft Bibundi in 1897, initially with 6,000 ha but growing rapidly from that base, and the Molive-Pflanzungsgesellschaft in 1899 of about 14,000 ha. There was particular emphasis on the growing of cocoa on the slopes of Mount Cameroon, and the plantations were started on land that had been appropriated from its African owners, and worked with forcibly recruited labour, in very poor conditions, as described by a deputy governor in 1900: 'these people lead a wretched existence. They are poorly paid, and partly in the form of worthless goods at that. Their diet is unsuitable, and they are ill-housed and treated in the most savage fashion. This is how matters are on average. So you will no longer find anyone who is willing to work in the plantations' (Stoecker 1986c: 74–5).

The cavalier disregard of the German government and colonial authorities for the land rights of the Africans was further evidenced in 1898 when one-fifth of the Cameroon (81,597 km^2) was awarded to the Gesellschaft Südkamerun, a consortium financed by German and Belgian investment, for a 10 per cent return of profits to the government. Stoecker has indicated that the members of the Gesellschaft Südkamerun 'had no intention whatsoever of developing the 8 million hectares handed over to them on a major scale. In fact the purpose of the venture, which was modelled on the Belgian Congo companies in terms of structure and methods, was quick enrichment by stock exchange speculation and ruthless exploitation' (Stoecker 1986c: 75). The populations of these appropriated concessionary lands were subdued by military force (but not without resistance, both locally and by criticism within the German government), and the resources of the land were quickly removed for profit. The number of plantations in Cameroon increased in the period 1906 to 1913 from twenty-three to fifty-eight, the newer estates mainly producing rubber, tobacco and bananas. Although some land was reserved for the local population (so that a labour force could be secured) most of the land on the slopes of Mount Cameroon, for example, was appropriated by and for German companies (Stoecker 1986d: 162).

The opening-up of the interior of German East Africa, following the suppression of the Maji-Maji uprising in 1905–6, was partly determined by the building of railways from Tanga to Mombo (the Usambara line) in 1905 and the Dar es Salaam line completed in 1907, which facilitated the development of a colonial economy and the transport of commercial crops for export. The plantations were worked by forced African labourers at very low wages and in very poor conditions. Major plantations were established for the growing of sisal, rubber and cotton (Stoecker 1986f: 149). Small coffee plantations were part of the exploitative mechanisms established by German companies in German East Africa, notably in the Usumbara Mountains, but these were not very successful. Major plantations for coffee were successfully established on the slopes of Mount Kilimanjaro and in the Moshi district, and in the Bukoba district in the north-west.

The control of finance for these German plantations was in the hands of the Deutsch-Ostafrikanische Gesellschaft (DOAG): 'Operating either directly or through subsidiaries of its own, it held a virtual monopoly in key areas of German East Africa's colonial economy. Together with the trading firms closely linked with it, the company controlled the purchase of export products from both African smallholders and European plantations' (Stoecker 1986f: 153).

There were, as in the colonies of other European powers, contrasts in agricultural productivity and success within the French empire in Africa. One of the least successful was French Equatorial Africa, where a main instrument of promotion of commerce was the granting of rather anachronistic territorial concessions from 1899 to forty French and other European companies for an annual rent and a contribution to infrastructural costs, in return for which they were granted monopolies on the trading of rubber and ivory and freedom to work the land for thirty years, after which it was intimated that they would be given the land (Aldrich 1996: 192–3). By the end of the thirty-year period only eight of these companies survived, and there was a record of very poor treatment of their African workforces.

Plantations in South-East Asia

The plantation became a major part of the colonial life and landscape of South-East Asia in the nineteenth and twentieth centuries, with effects on land rights and production systems. The major differences between indigenous agricultural systems and plantations were the scale of plantation operation, the way in which plantations were organised, their control by foreign administrators and technicians, their specialisation in individual crops and their focus on export markets. This was, of course, true of plantations in most parts of the colonial world. In South-East Asia there were variations in the terms on which land was granted to planta- tion enterprises, though the basic factor was the appropriation of land, by alienation via crown grants or long-term leases, as in the Dutch East Indies after the Basic Agrarian Act of 1870 (Cleary and Eaton 1996: 80).

A forerunner of plantation agriculture was the monopoly spice trade, followed by the creation of plantations for the production of sugar and coffee, and aided by the establishment of the culture system in the nine- teenth century, which involved a system wherein 'peasants were compelled to cultivate government-owned export crops on a fifth of their land, or to work sixty-six days a year on government estates or projects such as roads or irrigation systems. Much of the *sawah* [wet rice cultivation] area was used for sugar, while the more accessible and fertile highlands were taken over by coffee plantations' (Cleary and Eaton 1996: 7, 8–9). The culture system was replaced after 1870 by corporate plantations, and their intro- duction brought with it new crops such as sugar, tobacco, rubber, coffee, cocoa and palm oil, and although efforts were made, partly via a sophis- ticated land registration system like the Torrens system in Australia, to protect indigenous land rights, they were not always successful, especially in areas of major population increase such as Java.

The nature and scale of plantations varied greatly. The frontier region plantations in South-East Asia produced a major transformation from what was seen as under-utilised wilderness to very large-scale plantations of sugar cane, rubber, palm oil and tobacco, such as those established by the French in the grey and red lands to the west and north-west of Saigon. This increased the area under rubber trees to 90,000 acres (36,421 ha) by 1929, and in the remoter islands of the Netherlands East Indies by the developments of plantations for the production of sisal, rubber, palm oil, tobacco and tea. Rubber plantations in Malaya and sugar plantations in the Philippines used Chinese and other labourers. Recruitment of labour, of necessity from outside the production regions, was characteristic of frontier plantations. Profitability depended substantially on satisfactory recruitment and maintenance of a labour force, for the preparation and cultivation of land, which could be carefully controlled and whose costs could be kept low. Different systems applied in areas that were already cul- tivated, under rice for example, and Elson has demonstrated the transition in Java from the use of part-time seasonal labour for sugar production, on what had been wet rice land, for processing in advanced-technology Dutch sugar mills, to the more familiar corporate model in the 1880s after depression and crop disease (Elson 1999: 155–6).

The recruitment and control of labourers from distant places was a continuing problem in many parts of South-East Asia. Elson shows that the large reserves of labour in Vietnam were in the lowlands of Tonkin and Annam; Chinese and Indian workers were used in the plantations in Malaya; Javanese from the centre and north-east were used in Sumatra. These were mainly young men, sometimes with families, and sometimes young women who were recruited for labour and forced into prostitution. Their work and lives were generally difficult, with only low wages being paid:

what little disposable income remained men often spent on gambling and prostitutes; systematic indebtedness was a useful means for plantation managers to manage their workforces. With appalling conditions, disease was rampant and death never far away; in 1927 in Cochinchina, one in twenty plantation workers died, and local death rates were often much higher than that. This was double the overall mortality rate for the colony, and among a population of workers supposedly in the prime of life. (Elson 1999: 157)

Netherlands State 'Coolie Ordinances' of 1880, 1884, and 1893 assisted the plantation owners to subjugate the workers, though inevitably some of them retaliated physically against this suppression and brutality, and also demonstrated their opposition by desertion.

A consequence of the application of capital-intensive and monocultural plantation methods in South-East Asia was population increase, mainly but not exclusively through immigration, notably in Java where the population increased from 3.5 million in *c.* 1800 to 40.9 million by 1930, and in Malaya, whose population increased from 250,000 in 1800 to 3.8 million by 1931, with similar rates of increase in the Philippines and Burma. There is much debate about the contribution of natural population increase to these swelling figures in South-East Asia in the late nineteenth and early twentieth centuries, particularly around the roles of reduced mortality and increased fertility. Elson favours the influence of 'a significant reduction in mortality, possibly augmented by a small increase in fertility resulting from more settled and regular times', more sophisticated analysis being prevented by lack of suitable demographic data (Elson 1999: 158, 160).

Plantations in French Indo-China

Plantation agriculture was extensive in the French colonial empire. As in other European colonial territories, materials such as rubber were first exploited by use of indigenous labour to collect wild rubber in areas over which French companies had been granted concessions, and then larger areas of land were offered, supposedly open for exploitation and free of indigenous land-use rights. A French Commission on Colonial Concessions was established in 1898 to promote a large allocation of land for plantations in the colonies of French Congo, French West Africa, Madagascar and French Indo-China. The amounts of land given over to plantations varied, with the largest concessions in the French Congo, Madagascar and French Indo-China and smaller concessions in French West Africa.

French Indo-China was perhaps the most agriculturally productive part of the French overseas empire. Like other European colonial regions, its full exploitation was attendant on the development of increased capital input and an improved transport system, but it had a productive soil for commercial agricultural products grown on plantations, a large potential labour force and adequate finance from the Banque de l'Indochine. Rice and maize were major crops in the colonial economy. The area of rice cultivated doubled in the first three decades of the twentieth century, much of which went to Hong Kong and China, and there was also a substantial increase in the production of maize, largely because of increased demand from France.

Rubber was a major plantation product in Indo-China, described by Aldrich as 'an economic sector to itself' (Aldrich 1996: 189), the plant having been first imported to the region in 1897, with the most rapid acceleration in the rubber plantation area in the 1920s, the area increasing from 29,000 ha in 1921 to 127,000 in 1927, of which 98,000 ha were in Cochin China, 27,000 ha in Cambodia, and 1,700 ha in Annam. Rubber, as Aldrich states,

emerged as a quintessentially colonial primary product destined for metropolitan markets, produced by native labourers working in harsh conditions on plantations owned by Europeans in a pattern of proprietorship showing distinct traits of monopoly control. A third of the 1005 plantations totalled more than 40 hectares and represented 94 per cent of the total area planted in rubber; 27 companies owned over two-thirds of total hectarage planted in rubber. Rubber accounted for most of Indo-China's exports in the 1930s; most went to France. (Aldrich 1996: 189, 190)

The major areas of rubber plantation in Vietnam were in the region of the grey and red soil areas north and north-west of Saigon. The largest of the French rubber plantation companies was the Société financière de Caoutchoucs, which also operated in Sumatra and Malaya (Darby 1943: 297). Much of the investment from France was speculative, but dividends were handsome. In Vietnam the workforce largely comprised indentured labourers from the north, and the same was true of rubber plantations in Cambodia (Elson 1999: 155). In contrast, coffee plantations in French Indo-China were far less successful: the first such plantation was developed in 1888 in the hill country around the Tonkin Delta, but the poor soils were soon exhausted and revived only with the application of animal manure in a linked animal-husbandry system. Further development of coffee plantations further south on the red soils of central and south Annam occurred in the 1930s. In the year 1937–8 there was a plantation area of *c*. 13,000 ha, producing 1,500 tons of coffee (Darby 1943: 299–300).

Rubber plantations in Malaya

As with other colonial plantation products, the production of rubber generally in the colonial world combined the ingredients of European technical expertise and European and Chinese entrepreneurial capital, linked to world market demand and the use of local and immigrant labour forces. Increase in demand came after the invention of the rubber tyre by John Dunlop in 1888, and the development of the automobile industry in North America, leading to high prices for rubber. Malaya shared in the rubber boom, the rubber plant *Hevea brasiliensis* having been introduced in 1877 and grown in plantations from 1895, replacing the native wild rubber that had hitherto supplied the market and whose production globally reached a peak in 1910–12 (Headrick 1988: 244).

Rubber was grown in plantations cleared from forest land that had been granted to Europeans and Chinese entrepreneurs, and was worked by immigrant labour from South India and China. Investment was a medium-term matter, as it took about six or seven years from planting to the first harvesting of latex from the plants, so that the major investors in the period from 1905 onwards included both small and very large companies, including Malay Peninsula (Johore) Rubber Concessions Ltd, which had 20,000 ha. The overall area of *Hevea* rubber plantations expanded rapidly, 'from 2,400 hectares in 1900 to 219,000 in 1910, and over 900,000 after 1920. By 1910 *heveas* had displaced all other export crops and occupied 62 per cent of the cultivated land of the Federated Malay States.' Malaya suffered, as other rubber-producing regions did, from the world depression of the 1930s, but demand picked up again, and productivity was enhanced with the adoption of new types of rubber plant produced by Dutch and other scientists working in South-East Asia through grafting, artificial pollination, and selection (Headrick 1988: 246–7).

Plantations in the Dutch East Indies

In the Dutch East Indies plantations were a major part of the colonial economy from the late nineteenth century. They grew tobacco, rubber, palm oil, tea and sisal, and had first developed in the remote and thinly populated frontier areas of the outer islands, including eastern coastal Sumatra, and they were serviced by large numbers of indentured labourers, initially from China and later from Java. Sugar plantations in the Philippines developed in the Negros region from the late nineteenth century, replacing the smallholder sugar production complexes near Luzon (Elson 1999: 155). The Java sugar industry developed not in a remote frontier zone but in the heavily populated areas of north, central and eastern Java, where 'the industry was based on hiring peasant wet-rice land for cane growing for periods ranging from three to (after 1918) $2\frac{1}{2}$ years', and using for labour the peasant landholders who grew other crops for themselves in between the growing seasons for cane.

The scale of production of sugar cane increased dramatically in the first thirty years of the twentieth century, with intensive capital investment (Elson 1999: 156). Headrick has shown that the growth of sugar cane in Java reflects two key aspects of its processing and propagation: 'the industrialization of cane processing in the nineteenth century, and the biotechnical revolution of the plant itself in the twentieth' (Headrick 1988: 238). The technological changes came largely from Europe, and included the changes in processing facilitated by steam engines and steel machines, and the transport of sugar cane from plantation to processing factory (replacing the older mills) by railway, and they radically changed the economic and human geography of sugar production from cane.

Prior to the adoption of modern technology, sugar had been rather inefficiently produced in Java on Chinese-owned estates, but the introduction of new machinery by European planter–entrepreneurs, together with the use of either seasonal labour or a symbiotic relationship with rice-growing under what later became known as the cultivation system effected major changes. The depletion of the sugar cane on Java by the sereh disease from 1884 resulted in the transfer of sugar plantations to large corporations, such as the Dutch Maatshcappij ter Exploitatie der Pamanoekan Indische Handelsbank (the estates later purchased in 1910 by the Anglo-Dutch Plantations of Java, Ltd), together with investment in fertilisers, new varieties of sugar cane, and new systems of propagation (Headrick 1988: 219, 239–41).

From the late 1880s onwards there was active experimentation with the breeding of new species of sugar cane in the Dutch East and West

Indies, resulting ultimately in the hybrid species 2878-POJ which was more resistant to disease and at the same time gave higher yields, increasing sugar cane output not only in the Caribbean, notably in Cuba, but also in Java, where the 2878-POJ species had become dominant by 1930, giving yields 20 per cent higher than before, and influencing the greater concentration of the sugar-producing industry (Headrick 1988: 240–1; Galloway 2005: 1–23).

In Java the land-use and social connotations of the modernisation of sugar production were that production involved inter-rotation with different crops, including rice, and a hierarchical management and labour structure, dominated by small numbers of European managers and technicians, but worked primarily by Javanese labourers, 300 of them full-time and up to 5,000 part-time. But sugar as a world trade commodity was vulnerable to changes in demand, and in the mid-1930s sugar demand dropped with the Depression, leading to a 50 per cent reduction of the area under sugar in Java, and a massive reduction in income so that, in Headrick's words: 'The sugar symbiosis, based on the most scientific form of agriculture and the most efficient colonial administration the world had ever seen, crumbled, leaving behind a large population of poor farmers crowded on a small island' (Headrick 1988: 242, 243).

Tea plantations in India and Ceylon

Change in taste in Western Europe was the major factor in the initiation of tea plantations in India and Ceylon. The increase in purchasing power in Britain, for example, increased dramatically in the second half of the nineteenth century and with it the demand for tropical products, including tea and sugar. Courtenay provides the following figures: 'Whereas in 1850 the average British per capita consumption of tea was 1.86 lbs. per annum, in 1875 the figures were 4.43 lbs. of tea and 59.35 lbs. of sugar, and in 1900, 6.07 lbs. of tea and 85.53 lbs. of sugar' (Courtenay 1969: 33). The origin of tea plantations in India was in the early nineteenth century, with the awareness of tea-growing by Singpho hill people in the north-eastern Assam valley and the realisation of greater potential for production in that area, the loss of monopoly of the tea trade with China by the East India Company in 1833, and the need for a replacement supply (Courtenay 1969: 37). Sir Joseph Banks had from 1788 advocated the propagation and distribution of tea plants via the botanical gardens at Calcutta and Saharanpur in India, but it was only after 1851, when Joseph Fortune returned from China with tea plant seeds from Shanghai, which were given to the

Calcutta botanical gardens for dissemination, that tea was grown commercially in India (McCracken 1997: 139).

The Assam Company for growing tea in that region was formed in 1839, incorporating a number of small experimental estates, to which varieties of Chinese tea plants had been brought, and in 1841 tea covered 2,638 acres (1,067 ha), producing 10,712 lbs (Courtenay 1969: 38). Tea plantations were established at Darjeeling (where higher-quality tea was grown), at altitudes of over 3,000 feet in the Himalayan foothills, and later in the Nilgiri and Wynaad Hills in South India, where they replaced coffee-growing, and there was further expansion in Assam (Christopher 1988: 180–1). Tea-planting was later developed in Ceylon, which specialized in high-quality tea.

The labour forces for the tea plantations were mainly imported from other regions of India, though initially the tea gardeners of Assam included many Chinese, changing to indentured Indian labour after the Chinese were deemed to be unsatisfactory. In Darjeeling, Nepalese labour was used from about 1850, and the expansion of tea-growing into the Jalpaiguri Duars in Bengal, after annexation from Bhutan, was accelerated by government land grants and by use of low-cost tribal labour from Bihar which in the late nineteenth century was suffering from famine, loss of land rights and rebellion (Bose 1993: 95–6). The payment in the Jalpaiguri tea plantations varied according to the tasks allocated: plucking, and pruning or hoeing, the labour force being at the bottom of a four-tier hierarchical organisation – management, staff, sub-staff and labour.

Labour conditions in the tea plantations or 'gardens' were very poor. Chapman has graphically characterised conditions in Assam: 'In the 1860s European planters were encouraged to develop new tea "gardens", a grimly euphemistic expression given the horrific conditions in which the labour force was kept. The labourers were mostly recruited from lower castes and tribes from poor areas of Chota Nagpur and the Deccan, and transported in appalling conditions to be given little shelter, medical help or food' (Chapman 2000: 119).

The ethical questions and related reformist ideologies surrounding the exploitation of labour and the general effects of monopoly capitalism in British colonies, including tea plantations in Ceylon and palm oil plantations in West Africa, were for a time addressed inter alia by the egalitarian and philanthropic institution the Co-operative Wholesale Society, in its 'seemingly incongruous involvement in colonial systems of production and trade of a movement espousing equity and mutuality', which included the purchase of tea estates in India and Ceylon and co-operative ventures in the production of palm oil in West Africa (Purvis 2004: 153). Although limited in practical achievement, these ventures in the early twentieth century 'reveal a continuing determination to maintain a stake in colonial trade to serve the interests of co-operative consumers at home' and in practice extend 'the domestic contest between co-operation and private capitalism' (Purvis, 2004: 162). The movement of tea to major ports of India, especially in the north-east, was a problem. Initially the main route was the River Brahmaputra, on which there was a paddle steamer service to Calcutta, and links by short railways to the Brahmaputra were built in the 1880s (Courtenay 1993: 39).

In Ceylon the demise of the coffee crop, because of the *Hemiteia* fungal leaf disease in the 1860s, and the mismanagement of many of the coffee plantations, led to an increase in the growing of tea, which had been introduced in 1828. Attempts to introduce cinchona were unsuccessful, partly because of overproduction in the world market, and there was a dramatic increase in the area of tea-planting from 2,000 acres in 1876 to 100,000 acres in 1886 (McCracken 1997: 138). A Tamil labour force for the Ceylon plantations was imported from South India, and the movement of crop and labour was facilitated by the smallness of the island and by the pre-existing port and railway infrastructure established for coffee production (Courtenay 1993: 41).

Regions of European settlement and farming

While much attention needs necessarily to be paid to the consequences of European colonial investment in monopoly agriculture, such as large-scale plantations, in the tropics and sub-tropics, and where Europeans were a minority, there were also many areas where, because of the perceived low density of the indigenous population, large numbers of settlers could be granted land under many different conditions. The circumstances of what frequently was the expropriation of what was inaccurately perceived as 'waste' land from indigenous communities has been outlined in Chapter 4, but must constantly be borne in mind when analysing areas of large-scale European settlement.

Canada was a major recipient of migrants from both Europe and the United States in the nineteenth century. There had been migration of British loyalists after the American Revolution, and also to escape slavery in the United States, and there are estimated to have been 40,000 black migrants to Canada by 1860, with additional streams of immigrants, notably from China, to provide part of the labour force for railway-building. From 1895 to 1914 there were large numbers of immigrants from southern and eastern Europe, and there was further official encouragement of immigration from Britain from 1932. The population of Canada increased from 3.6 million in 1871 to 10.3 million in 1931 (Castles and Miller 1993: 52), but the indigenous population fell. Martin contends that 'For Canada's indigenous peoples, the nineteenth century was a disaster. They had constituted at least one-fifth of the population in 1815 but by 1911 their total numbers halved to just over 100,000, barely 1 per cent of Canada's total... The titles of legislation, such as the Gradual Civilisation Act (1857) or the Indian Advancement Act (1884), are memorials to failure' (Martin 1999: 533).

The settlement and rural production systems that had developed in Canada reflected differing cultures and historical change, evidenced in the French seigneurial land system with its very long plots laid out with a river as a base, the British Maritime Province system with irregular blocks of land, the systematic and geometric layouts of early nineteenth-century settlements and fields in the township system of Ontario, and the rectangular survey system, similar to the American system, that characterised the layout of settlements and farmsteads in the Prairie Provinces (Christopher 1988: 194–5). The nature of the farming systems and priorities adopted varied with environmental circumstances and economic and commercial opportunity, and the time taken, especially in wooded areas, for clearance of trees. The 'clearance of the land was thus a long, drawn-out process, and the semi-sufficient stage was retained for a considerable time in remote areas. Only on the grasslands could large-scale cropping begin almost immediately after occupation, resulting in often spectacular advances in settlement, but equally disastrous retreats' (Christopher 1988: 199) .

Land was a significant component influencing much of the modern rural and indeed urban development of Australia in the nineteenth and twentieth centuries. The theoretical basis of land allocation in the late 1820s and early 1830s was the Wakefieldian doctrine, mainly applied to South Australia, but there was also evidence of adjustment of these theoretical concepts to meet the environmental realities. Thus, as Powell has shown, by the mid-nineteenth century there were two types of land settlement, the one small-scale, carefully ordered, and near the coast, the other pastoral, based on the insecure use rights of squatters, who had grazing licences and then leases, and covering vast areas of territory (Powell 1988b: 17). Large numbers of land acts were passed in the Australian colonies between

1860 and 1890, many focused on the concept of the small, 'yeoman' type of farm, but with many variations, notably where arable farming was combined with the grazing of livestock, thus requiring larger holdings. This problem was solved pragmatically at this time, so that ' "family-farming" in the Australian mould, replete with fragmented parcels and complicated partnerships and any number of subleasing and sharing arrangements, recorded a shaky but unmistakable advance' (Powell 1988b: 17).

From the 1870s easier access to unallocated land was facilitated for pioneer farmers, which, together with the improvement of communications, refrigeration, irrigation, the hybridisation of plants such as wheat, and livestock breeding, led to a change, as Powell sees it, 'towards *land management* from earlier aggressive sorties into *land development*' (Powell 1988b: 17). The policy of 'Closer Settlement' was developed from the 1880s, implemented by the encouragement of voluntary sub-division and taxation incentives for privately owned land, and government sub-division and settlement of crown lands and of repurchased lands (Powell 1988a: 44–5). This process facilitated the allocation of land to a greater number of people in the context of a landownership pattern dominated by a small number of owners and the frustrations of aspiring rural settlers, but also of the continuing contestation of grazers. The rights details of land tenure and attached rights at regional and colony scales is too complex to be reviewed here, but it should be noted that there were differences at given points in time between colonies (or states as they were to become after Federation in 1901). Weaver has pointed out, for example, the novelty of Queensland's land allocation policy from 1884, aimed at dealing with the predominance of large estate owners and sugar growers, in which land leasing was substituted for land alienation through exclusive ownership (Weaver 2003: 319).

The range of tenures and their significance for individual states in 1901, in many ways reflecting their individual histories and policies of settlement, has been exemplified by Powell in a table of types of land tenure in 1901 (Powell 1988b: 19). This shows Queensland as having the highest amount of leased/licensed public land (65.3 per cent), followed closely by New South Wales (64 per cent), with a drop to South Australia (35.2 per cent), Northern Territory (33.6 per cent), Victoria (30.4 per cent), and thence to Western Australia (15.6 per cent) and Tasmania (33.6 per cent). The largest percentage of alienated private land was in Victoria (35.7 per cent), followed by Tasmania (27.5 per cent), with New South Wales having 10.9 per cent of public land in the process of alienation. The lease was an important agent of land management, in that it allowed regulation and money-raising on crown lands, and the retention of the right of dispossession if more intensive agricultural settlement became possible (Christopher 1988: 206). Larger commercial units, however, could bargain successfully for use rights for extensive sheep and cattle stations.

A combination of increasing home and overseas demand for cereals, meat and dairy products stimulated agricultural productivity in Australia in the nineteenth century. There were of course market and environmental fluctuations, affecting supply and demand, but at the same time international trade in wheat was facilitated by the repeal of the British Corn Laws in 1846, by increasing demand for Australian produce as a result of the disruption of trade by war in European supplies of grain to Britain, the improvement in telegraph communication, the greater speed and larger size of ships, the opening of the Suez Canal in 1869, and with the refrigeration of ships' holds from the 1880s (Heathcote 1975: 105–60). Between 1850 and 1914 the better soils of the south-east and the east coast supported wheat, dairy farming and sugar production, but by the 1880s the ploughed grasslands and savannah woodlands were settled, and the farming frontier moved to arid shrublands, with the problems of clearing mallee and acacia scrubs solved by technical inventions such as the grapnel, rollers, and stump-jump ploughs (Heathcote 1975: 107). The merino sheep was introduced to Australia in the early nineteenth century, and by the last decade of the century, after large sheep runs had been purchased and improved with irrigation systems, the exports of wool from Australia comprised half of the value of that country's exports, there being some 106 million sheep by 1893 (Fieldhouse 1996: 128).

A major feature of European colonial policy was the creation of reserve lands in which to confine indigenous peoples, in policies of separation of settlement and economic activity, frequently in regions poor in natural resources. This system was extensively developed in Canada and Australia (and in the independent United States), and also in East and South Africa, where reserves served as a tool for separate development. Conversely, in areas deemed suitable for European settlement, lands were reserved for them, such as in the 'white highlands' of Kenya, where land that had been part of the territory of the Masai and Kikuyu peoples was allocated to European settlers from the early twentieth century.

The effectiveness of this settlement policy was less than is sometimes projected by images of a luxurious and indolent lifestyle, at least of the aristocratic settlers. Lonsdale has pointed out that:

Black and white interests were similarly matched in Kenya, despite the apparent supremacy of its settlers, whose pioneers arrived after 1902. Their overbearing politics masked underlying weakness. There were never more than 2,000

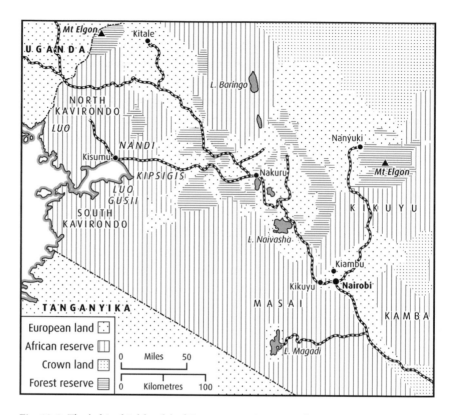

Fig. 12.2 The 'white highlands' of Kenya, 1935. Source: Roberts (1986: vii).
By permission of and © Cambridge University Press.

farmfamilies before 1940, a minority of the white population ... private family
farms in Kenya's cool highlands, as distinct from lowland company plantations
of sisal or upland coffee or tea estates, were no better bet for recovering the £6m
spent on railway and conquest. (Lonsdale 1999: 533–4)

Mining

The discovery and exploitation of precious minerals in European imperial
territories is a major theme in the history of metropolitan–colonial links
in the nineteenth and twentieth centuries. They added to the incentives
for migration of miners and speculators from Europe to the colonies and
also between colonies. Individual desire for making quick fortunes was
an incentive, and mineral riches also offered a profitable means of payment for infrastructural development through railways, roads, ports and
various other kinds of communication (Fieldhouse 1996: 134–5). Not all

mineral discoveries were substantial or profitable, and an added complication was the fluctuation on world markets of the price of the commodity,
making investment highly speculative for both metropolitan and colonial
investors and local entrepreneurs. Mineral extraction and processing
became major parts of the economies and geographies of the white settler
colonies, including Canada and Australia, and remain so at the present
day, giving rise to disputes over the mineral rights in territories controlled
by indigenous peoples. There is no space in this book, however, for these
to be included.

The incidence and development of precious metal resources were dependent of course on patterns of past geological activity and the history of human
settlement in particular regions. They were also partly dependent on the history of indigenous knowledge. The use of these resources was influenced in
part by earlier indigenous knowledge and practice, and they were soon conditioned by the fluctuations in demand and price on world markets. Capital
investment in the mining of sub-surface commodities such as gold and diamonds was very high, and the range of necessary activities associated with
their extraction and processing brought many changes in population, living
conditions, and landscapes. There were, however, other, 'democratic' forms
of gold-winning – alluvial gold, for example, was obtained through panning
the sediments carried and deposited by rivers.

The mining of gold

One of the most dramatic instigators of migration and intensive mining
activity was gold, a commodity highly valued from prehistoric times, and
one which attracted increasing attention in the nineteenth and twentieth
centuries, both as a medium of exchange and as the basis for many forms
of personal decoration.

The second half of the nineteenth century embraced the greatest mining migrations in world history, when dreams of bonanza lured thousands of gold and silver seekers to the far corners of the earth – to California in 1849, to Australia and
British Columbia in the 1850s, to Colorado for gold in 1859 through 1865 and for
silver in the 1870s, and to New Zealand for gold in the same decades. (Dumett
1998: 9)

This later extended to the Kolar fields in India, the Transvaal in 1886–95,
and other regions in Russia and North America.

The gold rushes of the later nineteenth century might be seen as a more
practical and profitable outcome of the much earlier expectations of the

perceived and legendary mineral riches of the new worlds as seen from the Ages of Discovery onwards. Other common factors in this modern phase of gold mining included the almost continuous sequence of gold and other precious metal mining from the 1850s, the transmigration between sites of miners from Cornwall and other parts of England, from North America and from Australia (Dumett 1998: 11).

Another factor was the role played by major metropolitan cities in the financing, promotion and organisation of the mining of precious metals. London, for example, provided the mechanism and driving force for the issuing of shares (by the London Stock Exchange) for many overseas mining enterprises in the 1870s and 1880s, tapping into the need for higher rates of interest than could be provided by domestic investment. It was also a centre of expertise in the technology and management of mining enterprises which fed out to the entrepreneurial mining companies in Africa, Australia and New Zealand, and North and South America, and was bound up with the trend for gold to be used as a security base for national currencies, the Bank of England being required to maintain a gold holding of at least 25 per cent of issued banknotes. This meant that there was a continuous need to find new sources of gold to support the gold standard basis of the currencies of major capitalist states (Dumett 1998: 10).

Gold rushes in Australia and New Zealand

The earliest gold 'rushes' within the British empire were in Australia. Early discoveries of gold were made in the 1840s, but the Californian gold rush of 1849 stimulated further interest in Australia, leading to the gold rushes near Bathurst in New South Wales and in the region around the towns of Ballarat and Bendigo in central Victoria, both starting in 1851. These early discoveries were of alluvial gold, which required less capital investment than sub-surface gold, and activity then moved to deeper mining from clay and rock, which required more equipment and capital (Hughes and Phillips 2001: 150). W. Bate has described the nature and social effects of alluvial gold mining around Ballarat and Bendigo in Victoria. In the period from 1851 to 1861, he estimates that 400,000 migrants were attracted there, of which three-quarters were British and Irish, with some coming from California. By 1871 the population of the gold towns of Victoria was 145,978, and of New South Wales 7,624 (Bate, 2001: 20). Apart from the immediate economic effects, alluvial gold also promoted profound social change. Although the region had previously prospered from commercial capitalism based on pastoral farming,

gold was the key. As the lubricator of world trade during the period of great industrial and commercial expansion, it was in such demand that its price remained stable and high. It was, moreover, currency. People and whole communities who dug it gained capital and freed themselves from the expensive borrowing and outside control. It spelt freedom and supplied a social energy rarely enjoyed elsewhere. Alluvial gold was the democratic mineral. Because nature had processed it, no middleman could get between the digger and his winnings. (Bate 2001: 7–8)

From the late 1850s another phase of gold mining developed, through deep-shaft mining in quartz deposits in the Ballarat–Bendigo region and elsewhere in the colony of Victoria. The third phase, in the late nineteenth and early twentieth centuries involved hydraulic mining or sluicing – the removal of sediment from hillsides and creek flats with high-pressure hoses, the sediment being flushed into ponds, whence gold was filtered out. To this was added dredging, introduced from New Zealand in 1899 (Garden 2001: 29–30, 40–1).

For their time the Victorian goldfields ranked high on the list of producers: Hughes and Phillips have stated that Ballarat and Bendigo were two of the largest producers in the world, with 2 per cent of the world's production up to the start of the twenty-first century. Their main period of production was from *c.* 1851 to 1910, reaching a peak in the mid-1850s, thereafter being more dependent on gold from quartz veins, and with a later minor upturn in production in 1900, but rapid decline from 1909 and near cessation in 1920 (Hughes and Phillips 2001: 133–5).

The local and global effects of gold mining in Victoria were substantial. Population migration to the goldfields, already mentioned above, was a significant factor in the increase in the population of Victoria from 73,000 in 1851 to 540,000 in 1861. The Californian and Victorian gold rushes

precipitated global migration at a rate and scale rarely seen. This was mainly from Great Britain and Ireland (more than 80 per cent of the Victorian population in 1857), and also to a lesser extent from China (13 per cent in 1857) where political events had caused an economic downturn in a coastal region. The remainder were mostly Germans, with smaller numbers of Americans and French. (Hughes and Phillips 2001: 148–9)

The additional migrants did not, except early in the 1850s, find direct employment in the goldfields, but were employed in various servicing capacities.

The overall effects of the gold rushes on the societies, economies and landscapes of Victoria were profound. They stimulated an increase in population, including the numbers in service professions such as store-keepers and doctors, and those involved in missionary and other religious work, together with the assertion of a strong trades union movement. In spite of the opportunities given to the miners, the gulf between them and the local and colonial administrators was too great to be resolved other than by protest, which at times was extremely vigorous (Bate 2001: 25). Towns flourished with house-buying investment, and there was a major benefit for Melbourne, though some of the smaller settlements did not last for long. A new communications infrastructure was created, and modifications to natural drainage and to ecological systems, including the removal of much of the native flora and fauna, comprised a kind of negative ecological imperialism. The environmental consequences were

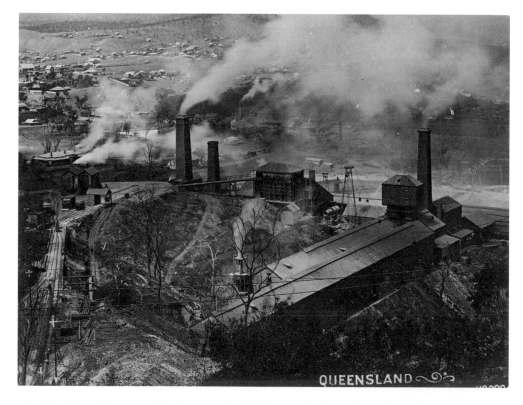

Fig. 12.3 Mount Morgan gold mine complex, Rockhampton, Queensland, Australia, *c.* 1910. This view is of the central portion of the mine complex, 24 miles/38.6 km from Rockhampton. The mine was discovered in 1882. There was also an important copper mine on this site. By permission of and © Cambridge University Library RCSPC-Fisher-Y30850–040.

landscapes that bore the ugly scars of a variety of intrusive and disruptive mining technologies, which were only partially disguised by subsequent vegetation growth (Garden 2001: 35).

Further gold discoveries in Australia were made in Queensland and in Kalgoorie in Western Australia, developed in the 1880s, with the Kalgoorie deposits requiring deep mining techniques and substantial investment capital for machinery and processing. Heavy capital investment was also required in the later phase of mineral exploitation in New South Wales, via the Broken Hill Proprietary Company (Fieldhouse 1996: 137).

In New Zealand gold was discovered on the North Island in the hills of the Coromandel peninsula in 1852, but exploitation was prevented by the hostility of the Maoris, and gold was not won here until 1862. A goldfield was opened at Collingwood, Nelson, in 1857, with little immediate return. Gold was discovered in the Tuapeka valley, Otago, South Island in June 1861,

and by the end of December that year 187,696 ounces of gold had been produced at Tuapeka. The population of Otago had increased in six months from 12,000 to 30,000. This heralded the gold rushes of New Zealand and in the ten years 1861 to 1871 the European population of the country increased two and a half times, from 99,000 to 256,000. From 1862 to 1870 gold comprised 50 to 70 per cent of the value of New Zealand exports, and in the decade following it contributed 20 to 40 per cent annually. (Cumberland and Whitelaw 1970: 35)

Further gold rushes followed in 1864 at Westland and in 1867 at the Thames quartz field on Waihi and the Coromandel peninsula. The three main goldfields were Hauraki (North Island), West Coast, and Otago (South Island), the last of these mainly an alluvial field. The West Coast fields had alluvial as well as quartz reef gold, and the Hauraki field was mainly a quartz-based goldfield (McKinnon 1997: 43–4).

The effects of these various gold rushes were profound, in terms of increases in population, the opening-up of relatively unknown parts of the country, and their short- and long-term impact on landscapes. Techniques for winning the gold had clear impacts on landscapes, from the use of picks and shovels to the damming of streams, the use of hydraulic mining, and the use, from *c.* 1863, of the modern gold dredge, to which steam power was applied from the 1880s. The industry attracted many Chinese labourers, as it had in Australia. The main urban beneficiary of the gold strikes in the South Island was Dunedin, whose population of 6,349 in 1861 had swelled dramatically to 15,790 in 1864, and 45,000 in 1881 (Cumberland and Whitelaw 1970: 36).

Mining in Africa

The rich and extensive metallic and precious minerals, notably gold, copper, diamonds and tin, in Africa's ancient rocks that had been mined by indigenous peoples using basic methods and used for the production of a range of tools and ornaments over a long period of time were subject to the intense pressures of the world economy during the period of high colonisation from the 1880s onwards. Exposure of Africa for the second time to the world capitalist economy (the first being the slave trade) induced not only the winning and smelting of metallic ores and the mining of diamonds but also the regulation of market supply, for example of diamonds, by companies such as De Beers in South Africa. It has been said that diamonds 'had initiated the economic revolution in southern Africa, but gold carried it much further' (Wrigley 1986: 89). There were, of course, wider implications than this for the discovery of gold, diamonds and other minerals, particularly for the development of more effective imperial control.

South Africa

The discovery of diamonds and then gold in South Africa in the 1860s and 1880s had profound effects on the political geography of the region, for by 'raising the prospect of a self-sustaining, and even organically expanding economy within a united southern African whole – in other words a configuration – the discoveries made the independent Boer and African republics of the interior seem much more significant thorns in the side of the British colonial administration than they had previously appeared'. The British saw here an opportunity, with the discovery of diamonds, for reducing its commitment, for a more logical integration of labour force and mining areas, and for an easier flow of the labour force across Boer republics to the mines (Lester 1998: 43–4).

Diamonds for use in developed countries as personal adornment and for industrial purposes were extracted and processed in considerable quantities from 1867, when they were found at Kimberley. After 1908 diamonds were found in South-West Africa, so that by 1910 half of the world's diamonds came from South Africa (Walshe 1986: 545). Diamonds were first located in the alluvial terraces of the Harts and Vaal rivers, and this discovery in 1867 drew a large number of diggers to the area, estimated as 10,000 in the Kimberley area by February 1871 (Christopher 1976: 161). Dry digging began from about 1870, and in 1871 diamonds were found on a site of what was to become the great Kimberley mine (Pollock and

Agnew 1963: 171). The site of the Kimberley mine had 400 claims, each one over a very small area, but these were consolidated, and in 1888 control of the diamond industry was in the hands of De Beers Consolidated. There was strong disagreement between the British, the Griqua people and the Orange Free State about sovereignty over the diamond fields, and the British government annexed the territory and allocated it nominally to the Griqua people as the Crown Colony of Griqualand West in 1871 (Christopher 1976: 161). The Transvaal was annexed in 1877.

Christopher has quantified the effects of diamond mining on the economy of the Cape: diamond exports increased from a quarter of the colony's exports in 1872 to over one-half by 1877, and the money created supported major projects such as buildings and railways. Other effects included the growth of the town of Kimberley, transformed from a mining camp settlement around the major mine site or 'Big Hole', to a town with a population of *c.* 20,000 in 1877 (Christopher 1976: 161–3, 164). The social geography of the town was also transformed, with the addition of *c.* 10,000 African mine labourers by about 1875 and the development of compounds organised by the mining company for male African labourers. Outside the Cape, diamonds were also worked in the Orange Free State and the Transvaal.

A major European impact on the landscape and society of southern Africa through heavily capitalised mining of gold took place in the Transvaal. Gold had been discovered there in 1852 and in Tati in Bechuanaland in 1866–7, but major development only followed its discovery in the Witwatersrand region of the eastern Transvaal in 1868. Initial working of alluvial gold occurred near Lyndenburg in 1872, and in 1875 in the De Kaap valley to the north of the town of Barberton. A gold rush, involving some 1,500 miners/diggers, mainly winning alluvial gold, took place around Pilgrims Rest from 1873 to 1877 (Christopher 1973: 166). It was followed by the discovery of more valuable sites in the eastern Transvaal in 1882. The biggest gold rush at this time took place in the Witwatersrand from 1886, with the rapid purchase by diamond magnates such as Cecil Rhodes of the farmland on and beneath which gold was located (Pollock and Agnew 1963: 178).

The technology required for winning the gold from these major subterranean deposits was complex and capital-intensive. The total value of gold mined in the Transvaal increased from £6,010 in 1885 to £1.5 million in 1898, and after the Anglo-Boer War reached £37.4 million in 1913 (Christopher 1976: 169).

Immediately before the major gold discoveries, the Transvaal, had suffered financially through the vicissitudes of the annexation by the British in 1877, and the regaining of independence by the Boers in 1881, but rapid change followed the discovery of gold, including the immigration of large numbers of miners and supporting service populations and the establishment of a rapidly growing urban network, including the town of Johannesburg, which by 1892 had a population of *c.* 80,000, and by 1896 102,000 (Pollock and Agnew 1963: 181). Notwithstanding the Transvaal government's initial provision for the layout of only a small town, Johannesburg might have grown even more rapidly but for the delay until 1894 of the proof of existence of valuable gold deposits deep below the land surface, and the tensions produced by the conflict of political and other interests between Britain and the Boers. The population of the Transvaal increased from 30,000 in 1872 to 119,000 in 1890, and the populations of the Orange Free State and Natal more than doubled in the same period (Christopher 1976: 167).

A major outcome of the growth of gold mining was a substantial increase in the unskilled male African labour force, paid at very low rates. Pollock and Agnew estimated that before the Anglo-Boer War there were 100,000 Africans employed in the Rand gold mines, and after the end of the war 50,000 Chinese labourers were brought in to swell the size of the workforce. For political reasons, however, they had all been repatriated by 1910, by which time the size of the African labour force had increased to over 100,000 (Pollock and Agnew 1963: 186) and the European mining workforce was about 24,000.

The recruitment and management of the African labour force and the minimising of wage levels was in the hands of the Chamber of Mines, the Witwatersrand Native Labour Association and the Native Recruiting Corporation, which drew heavily on Mozambique for labour (Christopher 1984: 113). The migrant African workers were almost entirely male, living in workers' compounds set up by the main mining corporations. The effect on their families and the communities from which they had come was profound. The industrialisation and urbanisation of the Witwatersrand in the late nineteenth and the first half of the twentieth century, together with the political tensions that resulted in the Anglo-Boer War and its aftermath, intensified trends begun in the eighteenth century. As Lester (1996: 72) states,

The ideological legacies of the eighteenth century – the assumption of exclusive white access to power, land and wealth, and the expectation of service from cheap black labourers – were made tangible in space through industrialization and urbanization in the nineteenth century ... Afrikaners, meanwhile, had responded to the uneven material and ideological consequences of the closing of the frontier, and the penetration of British capitalism and imperialism, with the development of an ethnic particularism.

Diamonds in South-West Africa

At the end of a vicious German campaign of ethnocide, including the attempted extermination of the Herero people, diamonds were discovered in South-West Africa in 1908 and 1909 in river gravels near Lüderitz, and by 1913 their total export value was *c.* £2 million. Labour for mining the diamonds was obtained through forced labour of the Ovambo people, through treaties with their chiefs, and 'Conveniently for the Germans, the Ovambo were already impoverished by drought, flood and locusts, and by 1910 several thousand Ovambo were going south each year to work for a spell in the mines or on the railways; "temporary" shortages were made up by recruiting from the Cape' (Walshe 1986: 558–9).

Mining in West Africa

The Gold Coast

There had been a long tradition of mining gold in the Gold Coast – the very name is symbolic – before the period of European colonial exploitation. This dates back to before the arrival of Portuguese merchants and voyagers in the sixteenth and seventeenth centuries. The *sikifado* – gold miners – played very significant roles in the history of the Akan people, in that gold was an indication of wealth and a medium for exchange, and underpinned state formation in all the major kingdoms. Indigenous production was maintained even beyond the advent of European technological and capital-based mining. Indigenous mining took three forms: panning along alluvial rivers and in their estuaries, mainly carried out by women and children; shallow-pit surface mining by men, women and children; and deep-shaft mining for reef gold, this only in the dry season, carried out by men, but with family support. Gold mining was a valuable supplement to agricultural production, carried out in the period from January to April when there was less need for agricultural activity (Dumett 1998: 41, 51, 83).

Mechanised gold mining with European input of capital and technical expertise lasted from 1877 to the early twentieth century. There was a gold rush from 1877 to 1885, following the engagement of British troops in the Sixth Asante War (1873–4). British government reluctance to promote speculative investment, and its greater interest in maintaining adequate defence and security of other economic interests, facilitated in part an African gold rush by African miners – mainly Nzeman – from other regions into the gold-rich areas of Tarkwa and Aboso from about 1875 to 1880. There thus co-existed two pre-colonial modes of production, one in agriculture, the other in mining. European mining activity started in 1877, with an Englishman taking a concession for mining of the known reef gold of the Tarkwa Ridge, though earlier interest had been shown by some Dutch miners and by M. J. Bonnat, a Frenchman who had persuaded a group of French investors to buy concessions and make a survey in 1877 (Dumett 1998: 89, 91–2). An African Gold Coast mining company was established by Bonnat's French merchants and a group of investors from Liverpool who sent out a party in 1878 to investigate reef gold possibilities, but the problem of flooding of shaft mines proved to be insuperable without adequate pumping equipment. Subsequent attempts by African promoters and further European efforts produced only modest quantities of gold, but by 1888 only six mining companies were active in the region, the main thrust of new licensed activity not coming until the Anglo-Boer War, when general South African gold production fell.

Mining interests in the Congo

Recognition of the mineral deposits of the Belgian Congo and neighbouring Northern Rhodesia ('The Copper Belt') came early in the history of European colonial interest, but the resources were initially thought to be poor and isolated. Copper had been used by Africans for decoration and adornment, for wire, for weapons and for various utensils for a very long time, and was won via small shallow open-cast mines, the malachite ore being smelted in clay furnaces fired by charcoal. Larger-scale exploitation through investment of European capital and expertise was stimulated by demand from industrialising Europe (Headrick 1988: 269–70). The Union Minière du Haut-Katanga was founded in 1906 with 10 per cent of the company owned by the Belgian bank the Société Générale de Belgique au Congo (the major holding in UMHK was by the British company Tanganyika Concessions Limited, founded by Robert Williams in 1899 for prospecting in Northern Rhodesia), with formal rights for eighty-four years for the winning and working of copper and also with rights for tin. C. C. Wrigley has outlined the context of the early capitalist working of copper in this region, stating that its output 'came overwhelmingly from the great metalliferous region around the Congo–Zambezi watershed, straddling the border between British and Belgian territory. The anciently worked deposits lay on the Belgian side of the line, and it was here that capitalist production started, the first exports beginning in 1911 as soon as there was a rail connection to the sea' (Wrigley 1986: 91–2).

There were major logistical difficulties: the copper deposits were located 2,000 km from the coast, and 10,000 km from European markets (Vantemsche 2005: 83–91). Prospecting after the granting of the concession in 1906 immediately revealed the presence of many ore deposits with high yields of copper, but a major problem, as Headrick has stated, 'was getting equipment in and copper out. At the time the nearest railroad was at Broken Hill in Northern Rhodesia. When Prince Albert, heir to the Belgian throne, visited the Congo in 1908, he took a steamer to Cape Town and a train to Broken Hill, and then travelled the last 500 kilometers on foot and by bicycle' (Headrick 1988: 271). A rail link between Broken Hill and the Congo border was made in 1909, and to Elisabethville in 1910.

The process of commercial working began in 1911, with a steady increase in production to 1930, accompanied by progressive development of related railway systems and technical facilities such as smelters. In the Katanga copper area, basic furnace smelting of copper was used at first near Elisabethville, but replaced by a more efficient water-jacketed smelter with the coming of the rail link, while different chemical and industrial processing means were used from the 1920s in the Panda–Jadotville area. Progressive innovations in processing and smelting technology included the gravity concentrator, flotation, leaching and electrolysis. In addition to the major problems of transport of copper to export markets, there was also a major problem of skilled and unskilled labour. At the outset not enough skilled engineers could be recruited from Belgium, so numbers were supplemented by recruiting from America, South Africa, Northern and Southern Rhodesia, and Britain, but not without fear of an excessive British presence and its possible implications for control (Headrick, 1988: 271, 273, 275).

From c. 1911 to 1918, African labour for the winning of ore by pick and shovel had to be brought in, on one-year contracts, from a wide area, including Rhodesia, the Lower Congo and Ruanda–Urundi, as the population of the mining areas was very thinly scattered. Later, from the late 1920s, because skilled labour was difficult to obtain at a time of increasing mechanisation of the industry, a 'stabilisation' system was introduced for recruiting Africans (on three-year contracts) and their families and providing training for skilled technical activities, under a highly paternalistic regime (Headrick 1988: 275).

Production of copper in the 1920s made the Belgian Congo the third-largest producer in the world, after the United States and Chile, and for a short time the Union Minière was the largest copper-producing company in the world. Depression followed in the 1930s, but production totals regained their former heights in 1939 and 1940. The main areas of production were in the south-east, around Elisabethville, a central mining area near Jadotville, and in the west around Ruwe (Mason 1944: 402–3).

A consequence of the increased exploitation of minerals in the Belgian Congo was urban expansion, notably of Elisabethville, whose population had reached 33,400 in 1929, including 3,500 Europeans, with one-third of the African inhabitants in mining and similar compounds, one-third in a separate indigenous quarter, and the rest in the European section. The population of the town decreased during the depression, but built up again after about 1937, reaching a total of 219,000 in 1960 (Christopher 1984: 117–18).

Tin in Malaya

The use of tin as an alloy and as a plating of steel for tin cans increased in the later nineteenth century and after the depletion of tin from Cornwall after 1871. Malaya became the major supplier in the growing world market. The cassiterite ore from which tin is produced had been mined in Malaya by local agriculturalists on a part-time basis over a long period of time, but with increased demand in the later nineteenth century entrepreneurial skills and labour were provided by Chinese immigrants, and rice farmers from Kwangtung with hydraulic skills, particularly in the Malayan tin regions of Perak and Selangor. Mining was open-cast, with water used to concentrate the ore in sluice boxes, before smelting in small clay-built smelters, and working conditions for the miners were very bad (Headrick 1988: 261–2). With British rule in the former territory of the East India Company and the Straits Settlements from 1858, the output of tin increased to 50,000 tons in 1895, having been 6,000 tons in 1871, the output before 1874 produced entirely by Chinese workers.

The role of local Malay chiefs in brokering the production of tin through their political authority transferred to Straits investors who

dealt directly with Chinese mine operators who assumed virtually complete control of the tin fields. Apart from their technological skills in mining, dredging and smelting, the dominance of tin-mining by the Chinese merchants and mine-owners was a function of superior business practices, socially lubricated capital and marketing networks, and their ability, through wealth and the strategic use of clan organizations and secret societies, to recruit and control ever larger numbers of cheap indentured labourers from southern China. (Elson 1999: 143–4)

From the 1880s a number of European companies became increasingly involved in tin production, still using Chinese labour, though they had nearly all failed by the mid-1890s. A transition occurred from the 1890s from the Chinese-based surface-deposit mining to deeper mining by European companies, via hydraulic hoses, bucket dredges, and the instigation of what are thought by some to have been better business methods that facilitated efficiency and the raising of capital for these more expensive mining techniques. Whether this transition was largely instigated as a preferential and selective process by the new British colonial power, or was simply a reflection of advantageous business methods, is a matter of debate, though it is clear that legislation did create higher Chinese labour costs, greater difficulties for dumping spoil, greater control of water supplies and of the licensing of mining sites, and thus discriminated in effect against the smaller-scale Chinese mining activities (Headrick 1988: 263, 266–8).

Mineral extraction and processing in India

The historical geography of the production of iron and steel from Indian raw materials contrasts with that of many other metallurgical endeavours in other colonial territories, in so far, as Headrick (1988: 260) asserts, that 'European investors showed no interest in it. Colonial administrators were mildly interested for fiscal and military reasons but lacked the technical and managerial competence to succeed. So it was the Indians who seized the opportunity to build a modern steel industry.'

India had a long tradition of artisan and industrial skills, used in basic iron-making, evident before the advent of the British in the seventeenth century. Iron was made, frequently by agrarian nomadic groups, by smelting the ore in primitive furnaces fuelled by charcoal. Basic iron-smelting techniques were still in use in the nineteenth century, and Headrick has described the way in which 'twenty men operating a furnace could make 50 to 100 kilograms of raw iron per day. In the early 1850s the average iron furnace in the Birbhum district of Bengal produced 24 tons of wrought iron per year; elsewhere, the average production per furnace may have been around 5 or 6 tons' (Headrick 1988: 279). In the nineteenth century metallurgical technology and productivity in India was sufficient to meet the needs for basic tools and hardware and the military need for weapons, but not the demand for rails for the rail system that grew very rapidly from 1853, a demand that was not met from Indian production until about 1918, the greater part being met by imports mainly from Britain, with the remainder from Belgium.

Unsuccessful attempts were made in the 1830s and 1850s to develop ironworks using various types of European technology, and from 1855 to 1879 the Indian government attempted to develop a domestic iron industry, still using charcoal, to offset the costs of developing a railway system, but this too was unsuccessful. The alternative use of coke from coal was considered, for there were known coalfields, including the Raniganj field north of Calcutta. The poor quality of the Indian coal was offset by the low labour costs of production, so that there was an increase in annual coal output in India from 100,000 tons in the late 1850s to 16 million tons in 1914 (Headrick 1988: 277–9, 282, 284). The successful development of iron production awaited the sale of the Bengal Iron Works by the government of India to a Calcutta managing agency in 1889, and an agreement to purchase 10,000 tons of iron for a period of ten years, but only at a discounted rate in order to counter the opposition of British iron producers. By 1914 the company was producing 72,000 tons per annum.

The history of steel production in India is essentially one of Indian initiative, taken by J. M. Tata, a cotton industry magnate, and a geologist, P. N. Bose. Tata, having been refused permission to mine iron ore deposits and to have a British guarantee of purchase of the products of his proposed steel mill, travelled to Britain, Germany and the United States to study production methods, and returned to India in 1902, handing the steel production plan to his son. Bose was an employee of the Geological Survey of India who had studied in London. In a report of 1887 he described the existence of rich haematite iron ore in the Raipur district, though without nearby coal for smelting, but after leaving the GSI he found a major rich deposit in Orissa at Gurumaishini Hill, a fact he communicated to the Tata family.

Government aid from 1905 by way of the guaranteed purchase of 20,000 tons of steel rails for ten years, together with railway connections, led to the construction of the Tata iron and steel works. Increasing competition for Indian markets for steel from Belgium and Germany accelerated the British government's support for the Tata Iron and Steel Company project at Sakchi near Jamshedpur, which first produced steel in 1912, and which benefited substantially from the demands of the First World War (Headrick 1988: 287–91).

Industrial production

The period of high imperialism witnessed many changes in industrial production in the metropolitan countries, but less in the colonies, and in certain areas, including textile production, there was increased competition. Lacking for the most part markets, finance and technology for modern industrial production, the European colonies, apart from those of predominantly white settlement, depended for a whole range of industrial products, including the component parts of railway systems, on the heavy engineering and other mechanised industries of their imperial controllers. Where there were existing industries, competition and prosperity were thwarted to a degree by imperial powers controlling the trading of colonial industrial produce, such as textiles from India to Britain, both by free trade policies and by a refusal to allow India to protect her textile industry by tariffs until such time as it could successfully trade against competition. Similar policies were followed in Dutch and French colonies. Nonetheless nascent industries did develop, such as the low-quality and low-cost textile production in India initiated by both British and Indian entrepreneurs, so that 'India in 1895 had a substantial number of power looms concentrated in the cities of Bombay and Ahmedabad. Bengal supported a large, though mainly foreign-owned, jute-processing industry' (Bayly 2004: 182). Various policies to encourage local industry in India were introduced in the late nineteenth century: 'In the 1880s, Lord Ripon's policy of favouring local manufacturers for government purchases stimulated a whole range of industries and culminated in the development of a state-operated iron and steel plant' (Cain and Hopkins 1993: 343). In French Indo-China there was extensive mining activity, mainly of coal and tin, and, in spite of concern at competition with French manufactured goods, there were local industries making cloth, mills for husking and bleaching rice, and the production of cement and consumer goods such as paper and matches (Aldrich 1996: 191).

Small-scale industry, in the form of crafts, the repair of appliances and the manufacture of domestic and agricultural goods and utensils, was widespread across most European colonies, conspicuously in towns and cities but present in most centres of population.

In parts of the British empire, the modernisation of production systems was opposed by colonial administrators, as in West Africa, where 'the colonial officials were generally hostile to modern industry because it was inconsistent with their model of a society based on an autonomous rural peasantry' (Fieldhouse 1996: 138–9).

Notwithstanding the efficacy of imperial systems of protection of domestic industry, it is also true that lack of industrial development in the overseas territories related partly to lack of demand and low local incomes, making investment in modern industry too risky a venture, because, in many cases, of higher costs of production (Fieldhouse 1996: 141).

13 | The endings of empire: decolonisation

The naked truth of decolonisation evokes for us the searing bullets and bloodstained knives which emanate from it. For if the last shall be first, this will only come to pass after a murderous and decisive struggle between the two protagonists. That affirmed intention to place the last at the head of things, and to make them climb at a pace (too quickly, some say) the well known steps which characterize an organized society, can only triumph if we use all means to turn the scale, including, of course, that of violence. (Fanon 2001: 28)

The above extract from Frantz Fanon's powerful book about the effects of French colonisation in Algeria (*The Wretched of the Earth*) highlights one aspect – the brutality – of processes leading to decolonisation of European colonies. With some notable exceptions, particularly of Dutch, Belgian, Portuguese and parts of the French imperial territories, Europe's overseas empires rapidly declined in the middle decades of the twentieth century, many after great trauma and loss of life. One major factor was the acceleration of nationalist aspirations, movements and protests from within colonial territories. Another was the consistent opposition to European colonialism by the USA from the end of the First World War, especially at the Paris Peace Conference at Versailles in 1919, which continued during and after the Second World War (notwithstanding the United States' own continuing imperial history). A 'metropolitan' influence on decolonisation was the unacceptable financial and administrative cost of maintaining and policing an overseas presence, not least after the enormous depredations of the Second World War and the emergence of a new world political, economic and social order. The effects of the Cold War between the West and the Soviet Union and its allies did, however, have the effect of prolonging the French and then the American presence in Indo-China, notably and catastrophically in Vietnam, Laos and Cambodia.

Decolonisation

The term decolonisation covers a variety of circumstances and processes. Darwin has suggested that there are at least four possible definitions. The first is a legal transfer of authority, with the end of colonial rule and the creation of an independent state. A second definition involves the treating of 'decolonisation as a mere formality: a piece of constitutional fol-de-rol whose purpose was as often to preserve Imperial influence as to end it ... independence was no more than a collaborative bargain' (Darwin 1999: 542–3), but as Darwin indicates such a definition ignores the substance of a country's change to independence. A third possibility is a more radical definition, which pays more attention to decolonisation as part of a process of breakdown of colonial rule and to an even wider phenomenon, a 'global colonial order', characterised by a particular division of labour and resources. Darwin, on the basis of the above reasoning, defines decolonisation, fourth, 'as the more or less complete overthrow of this structure of institutions and ideas between 1945 and the mid-1960s, and its replacement by a "post-colonial order" whose first phase ended in 1990' (Darwin 1999: 544), a working definition employed in this chapter.

The process of 'decolonisation' (a phrase of the 1930s but with increasing currency in the 1950s and 1960s) (Chamberlain 1999: 2) had earlier origins, with the loss of Britain's thirteen colonies in North America in 1783, France's loss of New France in 1759–60, and the independence from Spain and Portugal in the period 1808–26 of eleven of their territories in South and Central America. There was also the progress to political self-government in the nineteenth and early twentieth centuries of Canada, Australia, New Zealand, and South Africa, all former parts of the British empire. These earlier experiences, including those of what were essentially regarded as colonies of white settlement (notwithstanding the existence of indigenous peoples), contributed by precedent to nationalist and independence aspirations, notably in Asia and Africa, in the twentieth century.

The first major territory to achieve independence within the British empire following the Second World War was India and Pakistan, and this in turn was used as a precedent for independence movements in Africa and East Asia. The fact that decolonisation of most European overseas territories occurred within a short space of time, however, indicates that, as Darwin has argued, it must be viewed in a wider context of systemic failure, a feature of which was the rejection by the people of regions and countries under colonial control 'of the global colonial order of *c.* 1880–1960' (Darwin 1999: 554).

Darwin rejects two theories of British decolonisation: 'planned obsolescence' – the idea that independence had for a long time been a deliberate part of British policy; and an alternative 'neo-colonialist' notion that British decolonisation was a spin-off from changes in the nature of international capitalism – a 'conspiracy of commercial interests'. He suggests that an understanding of the history (perhaps it should be histories) of decolonisation 'requires the careful fusion of three "sub-historiographies": the domestic politics of decline; the tectonic shifts of relative power, wealth and legitimacy at the international level; and the colonial (or semi-colonial) politics of locality, province and nation'. The third of these may be the most difficult, notwithstanding the strength of the 'subaltern studies' arguments, for the obvious reason that materials for the identification and partial reconstruction of the experiences of the 'archivally voiceless or disinherited' are rare, and also that such a perspective may too easily be lost in a welter of postmodernist theoretical writing that is only loosely connected to grounded colonial experience (Darwin 1999: 545, 552, 556).

India and Pakistan

The processes leading to the independence of the Indian subcontinent from British imperial governance were complex and had harrowing and lasting outcomes. The historical record is that the Indian Independence Act of 1947 divided the Indian subcontinent into two political entities, India and Pakistan. After referenda smaller relics of the French colonial presence in India were merged with India between 1949 and 1956, and the Portuguese were deprived by India of their territories of Goa, Diu and Daman in 1961. Parallel to the Indian independence movement, Ceylon (Sri Lanka from 1972) achieved independence from Britain in 1948, through the efforts of Buddhists and the secular activities of the Ceylon National Congress, founded in 1919, and the Sri Lankan Tamils (Marlay 1991c).

The history of independence movements in the subcontinent covers a century or more, but the final push to independence was achieved in an astonishingly short time. Various attempts had been made during the nineteenth century to accelerate the removal of the British, the most dramatic being the Uprising/Mutiny of 1857. Its causes are reasonably well known, and its effect on British policy was immediate and far-reaching, including the taking of direct power of administration (formerly in the hands of the East India Company, which was abolished). The protest by Indian soldiers in the Bengal army against the infringement of Muslim and Hindu religious taboos by greasing with pig and cow fat the rifle cartridges which were to be used in new percussion small arms, a practice introduced in the 1840s, also fed other grievances that had been building for some time. The Bengal army in 1857 comprised seventy-four regiments, of which fifty-four became involved in the Mutiny or Uprising against the British. David has argued that the main causes of the Mutiny derived, in fact, from the inadequacies of the seniority system of promotion for Indian soldiers and officers in the Bengal army which 'deprived the commanding officer of an important power to reward, thereby reducing his authority over his men; it frustrated ambitious and talented sepoys who had to wait in line for promotion; and it produced old, inefficient and often bitter officers who had no worthwhile occupation. These last two groups may hold the key to the mutiny' (David 2003: 32). Another factor was the poor education and training of many British officers, and the increasing boredom in their daily lives, coupled with a distancing between British officers and Indian troops or sepoys, partly fostered by the decline in the language skills of the officers. Reading and spoken knowledge of Hindustani and Persian had been required of British officers since 1837, but by the time of the Uprising/Mutiny many had abandoned this requirement, understanding, as David indicates, that 'as far as their career prospects were concerned, patronage was far more important than a knowledge of native languages', misunderstandings often leading to the court-martialling of Indians because they had failed to understand what the officers were instructing them to do (David 2003: 40).

The consequence of these and other failings in army administration led to a position where:

By 1857 the Bengal Army was ripe for mutiny. Its infantry regiments, in particular contained a significant proportion of malcontents who were seeking an end to British rule. They were, by definition, ambitious men drawn from a complete cross-section of army ranks. Their aim was to replace their British employers with a native government that would, at the very least, provide greater career opportunities and increased pay. (David 2003: 45)

The Uprising/Mutiny started on 10 May 1857 and the rebels marched to Delhi. It spread rapidly from Bengal southwards across the Gangetic Plain into central India, where it was supported not only by Indian troops but also by civilians. Major focal points in the historical record and imagination were the sieges of Delhi, Lucknow and Cawnpore. The whole history of the process is marked with sequences of horrific massacres and retributive punishments. It ended in 1858, but it was not until 8 July 1859 that peace was restored in India.

There are various readings of the causes and consequences of this action of 1857. It can be seen as a reaction against the effects of British authority, including land taxation, and attempts at reform and modernisation. Washbrook has re-examined this explanation in relation to nineteenth-century pre-Mutiny Indian economy and society, and concluded that the main intentional and coincidental effects of British rule in India at this time

were less to transport British civilization to the East than to construct there a society founded on the perpetuation of 'Oriental' difference, as Edward Said puts it. India became a subordinate agricultural colony under the dominance of metropolitan, Industrial Britain; its basic cultural institutions were disempowered and 'fixed' in unchanging traditional forms; its 'civil society' was subject to the suzerainty of a military despotic state. British rule before the Mutiny may be credited with having fundamentally changed Indian society. (Washbrook 1999: 399)

Anglicised Westernisation accelerated in Lord Dalhousie's period as Governor-General of India (1846–56), manifest in his changes in property rights, including those of the *ryotwari* settlements in Madras and Bombay, his reform of the army, his opposition to caste and to the privileges of Bhumihars and Rajputs, his promotion of Western education, Christianity, mass education, universities, and his criticism of Hinduism and Islam. Washbrook (1999: 417–19) points out that Dalhousie's influence was more than a reflection of a strong personality: it was equally a reflection of the contemporary circumstances of a deficient East India Company army and world depression in the 1840s, of changing technologies such as steamships, railways and telegraphs, together with increases in the number of Europeans working in India.

Washbrook sees one of the main reasons for the Uprising/Mutiny as the 'way in which Dalhousie's eager Westernizing policies rubbed up against the sets of vested interests built up under the previous neo-Orientalizing Raj', including the abolition of privileges for the high-caste members of the Bengal army, the annexation of the kingdom of Oudh in 1856, and the revisions that threatened the property rights of peasants. Thus 'The contradictions of British rule – caught between inventing an Oriental society and abolishing it – were manifest in many of the complex patterns of revolt witnessed in 1857' (Washbrook 1999: 418–19).

The effects of the Uprising/Mutiny on the journey to Indian independence were mixed. On the one hand, direct rule from Britain was imposed, and various reforms made to the organisation and composition of the Indian and the Presidency armies. A rapid increase in the extent and speed of modern communications such as the railway and telegraph systems also facilitated the rapid movement of troops and the acquisition and dissemination of intelligence, to quell potential mutiny. On the other hand, some earlier reform processes were abolished, including the further annexation of Indian states. Treaties with India's 500 princes, who had for the most part been loyal to Britain during the Mutiny/Uprising, were confirmed, as were the rights of landlords, and there was a significant reduction in missionary activity (Keay 2000a: 446–7). The historic fact of the Uprising/Mutiny was a facet of the movement of India towards independence from imperial rule.

After 1857–9 various factors affected further movement towards independence. These included the education of a Hindu elite exposed to British ideas of ideal polities and self-government; the 'diaspora' of Indian indentured labour across the world – a part consequence of the gradual abolition of slave labour and the slave trade in British and other colonies, and consequent exposure to alternative systems of government and of human rights; the geographical and cultural separation of the increasing number of British families in India from the Indian population, fostering resentment at lack of recognition of Hindu, Muslim and Sikh traditions and cultures; and the invasion of Indian markets by goods produced in industrialising Britain, which undermined Indian domestic industries and created massive unemployment.

An early institutional move towards independence came from the founding of the Indian National Congress in 1885 by nationalists with different views of the ways of achieving independence, but with the common goals of social reform and greater representation. Some minor progress was made through the Act of 1888 introduced by Lord Dufferin and the Lansdowne Act of 1892, both providing for local councils that were intended to inform and consult with the British administration, but the British did not take sufficient heed of what they were hearing from these indigenous agencies. Further steps toward independent self-government were provided by the 1909 Government of India Act, a consequence of the division by the Viceroy Lord Curzon of the province of Bengal, resulting in anti-British Hindu sentiment in Bengal. The new Act moved India further towards self-government by 'increasing the number of non-official members elected to the provincial and central legislatures, allowing discussion on the Indian budget, and providing for the admission of Indians to the Viceroy's Executive Council and the Council of India in London' (Kaminsky 1991: 302–3).

The Act was also a divisive influence, providing as it did for a separate Muslim electorate, which was a concern for the majority Hindu population of the country. India fought with Britain in the First World War, and many

Indian troops were killed. In 1916 a pact was agreed between the Indian National Congress and the All-India Muslim League, which included provision in principle for separate electorates and for greater devolution for the Provinces, which in practice would be beneficial for the Muslims, who were in a minority overall but a majority in particular regions, notably the Punjab, Sind, and Bengal. At the end of the war Mohandas K. Gandhi (the 'Mahatma' or Great Soul) advocated non-violent protest against the British control of India. The punitive Rowlatt Act of 1919 against civil rights and insurgency created large-scale unrest, worsened by the outcome of police firing on protestors in Amritsar in the Punjab, on the orders of the British General Dyer. Three hundred and seventy-nine people were killed, and 1,208 injured, including women and children. Chapman describes this event as 'the kind of incident which, like Sharpeville, years later in South Africa, or Tiananmen Square in Beijing, simultaneously demonstrated the power of the State and yet demolished its legitimacy' (Chapman 2000: 140).

Part of the background to the processes of independence in the 1940s was Britain's changing relationship with India and with the rest of the world. There were some fears that an independent India, especially one without formal contact through membership of the Commonwealth, might be more vulnerable to Russian influence (a reminder of the 'Great Game' fears of the mid-nineteenth century), though India's intention to join the Commonwealth tended to allay such concerns. Britain was no longer as strongly linked to India by trade and investment: Brown indicates that 'British exports to India declined dramatically after the First World War from two-thirds of India's imports in 1914 to 8 percent in the 1940s: investment in India also flagged', and balances of payments also changed (Brown 1999: 440, 443). The efficacy of the Indian Civil Service also gradually weakened from the First World War onwards.

It would be wrong to assume that from the 1880s onwards the ambitions of India's different major groupings for independence were clear and internally uncontested. Judith Brown, among others, has pointed to the changes within the Muslim League, for example. An initial concept of Muslim independence being achieved in an area of northern India, operating within an overall federal system, changed to the idea of a physically separate state. Similarly, there were differences of opinion between the two major figures of the Indian National Congress, Gandhi and Nehru. Brown writes that:

The dilemma for Indians who consciously spoke the language of national demand was that nations, whether in Europe, Asia, or elsewhere, are not natural communities of affection and identity though they often draw on a range of pre-existing and deep-rooted linkages. They are to an extent 'created', 'constructed', and 'invented' in hearts and minds and in terms of organized structures. Congress leaders struggled with interwoven issues inherent in constructing a nation out of rich and often contradictory diversity. They wrestled with the definition of Indian national identity and the relation of linguistic, social and religious differences to such a potentially overarching unity. (Brown 1999: 440–1)

Brown characterises Nehru's ideas of Indian national identity as reflective of 'Western, secular terms', affording equal opportunity for all inhabitants of a newly independent state, whereas Gandhi wished to retain an 'orientalist' and religious concept of India that recognised the enormous historic diversity of religions and cultures (Brown 1999: 441). Overall, it also had to be recognised that any national aspirations were almost entirely determined by a privileged elite, and did not for the most part incorporate the wishes of significant numbers of women, for example, or of people from lower-caste groups.

Gandhi was imprisoned in 1922, and on release continued the campaign for independence. Again in 1930 he led a symbolic breach of the British monopoly of salt production at the Gulf of Cambay, leading to the outbreak of riots, bombings, assassinations and sabotage (Kaminsky 1991: 303). Twenty-seven thousand Indian nationalists were imprisoned by the British, and at the same time there were major conflicts between Hindus and Muslims, the latter seeking separate political status, an idea dating from the prescient promotion of the Pakistan National Movement by C. Rahmat Ali in the mid-1930s. Greater representation (from 7 million to 30 million people entitled to vote), transfer of more power to the Provinces and the notion of a federal structure were granted in a Government of India Act of 1935 (Chapman 2000: 144–5), but in 1937 the Muslim League formally sought the creation of a Muslim state separate from that of the Hindu and other populations of India, a position formally declared by its leader Mohammed Ali Jinnah at Lahore in 1940.

The declaration of war against Germany and Italy in 1938 on behalf of India by the Viceroy Lord Linlithgow, without seeking the support of the national legislature, was strongly criticised by the Indian National Congress, and further protests were made, of such a kind and extent that the British promised independence after the end of the war. Thus in 1947 the Indian Independence Act was passed which provided for the partition of India into two independent states – a Hindu-majority India and a Muslim-majority Pakistan, the latter to comprise Muslim majority areas in the west and the east of India (Kaminsky 1991: 304). Pakistan was a new name; as Chapman puts it: 'an artifice, using P for Punjab, A for the

Afghan Province (meaning the North-West Frontier Province), K for Kashmir and S for Sind and taking the-stan from Baluchistan. This was the land it claimed' (Chapman 2000: 151).

The events leading to and immediately succeeding the partition of India in August 1947 were confused and traumatic, partly reflecting the speed with which the British moved to secure India's and Pakistan's independence at the end of the Second World War. Britain's financial position at the end of the war and the election of a Labour government (committed to social and economic reforms at home, and abdication of colonial responsibilities overseas), together with riots in Calcutta, East Bengal, Bihar, the Ganges valley and the Punjab (Chapman 2000: 162) in August 1946, speeded the process.

One of the consequences of British anxiety to be rid of India was the very short time given to Lord Mountbatten, the new Viceroy, to negotiate the processes of independence, and, with the assistance of a lawyer – Sir Cyril Radcliffe – to propose and determine new boundaries and details of population transfer between the two new states. There were also profound national and regional differences of opinion and intent between various factions in the movement to independence, which changed, for the Muslims, from what in principle had been a Congress goal of 'Quit India' to one of 'Divide and Quit'. A wide variety of options had been reviewed before 1947, including the addition of regions to the existing provinces and states, and a river basins scheme for a federal India (Chapman 2000: 147, 163–8). Notwithstanding differences within the Indian National Congress about partition, Mountbatten presented a plan for the separation of India into two states –India and Pakistan- and the outline plans were accepted in London and India at the end of May and the beginning of June 1947, with the deadline for implementation set for 14 August 1947.

The geographical contexts and boundary outcomes of partition

The defining and identification of newly constituted political entities on the grounds of boundaries had always posed problems for European colonial powers. In Africa, in the nineteenth century when precise geographical knowledge was lacking, arbitrary lines were roughly drawn on maps, which then had to be determined in the field by joint boundary commissions. The problem in India was different. India had been well mapped in the nineteenth and early twentieth centuries, and there was census data available which might be used in establishing religious and other demographic distributions of population. The 1941 census was the demographic database for the decisions on partition. The problem here was twofold: accommodating the varying expectations of different religious groups, and thus determining the best fit to the demographic distributions, notably of Muslim and Hindu; and also the astonishingly short time in which the task was carried out. A major problem that was not faced up to was the distribution of non-Muslim and non-Hindu minorities, including Sikhs, who were primarily to be found in the Punjab, and who wished to remain in India. On 20 February 1947 Britain had declared its intention of leaving India by June 1948: in fact, India and Pakistan became independent in August 1947.

Two boundary commissions were established for Punjab and Bengal (with Assam), the two regions through which the new state boundaries would be drawn. The commissions had the same chairman – Sir Cyril Radcliffe, an outstanding English barrister – and comprised two nominees each from the Congress and the Muslim League – senior provincial high court judges from the Hindu and Muslim communities. An earlier proposal from Jinnah that the commissions be composed of senior law lords from the English House of Lords was opposed by Mountbatten 'on the grounds that most Law Lords were elderly people who could not sustain the sweltering heat of the Indian Summer' (Cheema 2000: 5). Radcliffe had no prior experience of India, his appointment being justified on the grounds that he would come to this work without prejudice. The process of determining the new boundaries across Bengal and Punjab was complex. Public hearings were held by each of the commissions, which Radcliffe did not attend, preferring instead to receive daily summaries. These public meetings allowed for the presentation of the cases of the significant religious groups, notably Hindu, Muslim and Sikh. Because of the balance of interests, the final decision was left to Radcliffe, who had made his mind up by 8 August, paying particular attention to the religious affinity factor, but he did not make the award public until 17 August (Cheema 2000: 6). One of the outcomes was the inclusion of Calcutta in India, in spite of the fact that its hinterland had a Muslim majority (the city itself did not). One option for decisions in marginal cases was the use of the referendum, but Mountbatten opposed this procedure other than in the case of the North-West Frontier Province.

There remained a period of about six weeks in which the new boundaries could be determined. The assumptions were that boundaries would be drawn in such a way as to accommodate the distributions of majority groups in these regions, but that other factors, including irrigation and drainage systems, would also be taken into consideration. There were many uncertainties, including the consequences of Mountbatten's insistence on a forty-eight-hour delay between Independence and the publication of the awards, and the inability to anticipate whether the princely states on the border regions would opt to stay in India or go to Pakistan (Cheema 2000: 175).

Preliminaries to the meetings of the boundary commissions included meetings of the provincial assemblies of Bengal and Punjab to decide whether or not the provinces should be divided, with the not surprising outcome of Hindu majority regions in favour of partition and Muslim majority areas against it (Cheema 2000: 5). Radcliffe met the Bengali Commission in Calcutta between 10 and 12 July, then travelled to the Punjab, making a return visit to Bengal early in August (Ilahi 2003: 80). The awards were announced on 17 August. For Bengal,

the Award gave West Bengal an area of 28,000 square miles, containing a population of 21.19 million people of which nearly 5.3 million (or 29%) were Muslims. East Bengal got 49,000 square miles for a population of 39.11 million, of which 29.1% (11.4 million) were Hindus. West Bengal got 36.36% of the land to accommodate some 35.14% of the people, while East Bengal got 63.6% of the land to accommodate 64.85% of the population. (Chatterji 1999: 213)

West Bengal, including Calcutta, remained as part of India, while East Bengal became part of Pakistan. Not surprisingly there were very many disagreements with the details of this particular part of the Radcliffe Commission's award, but there were also broader problems, including lack of access for many people to the published award, leading to rumours and killings, and also problems of definition and demarcation of the borders.

The use of boundaries between administrative units posed difficulties, especially when the administrative boundaries were not marked on the ground, necessitating resort to substitute settlement and survey maps which were inaccurate and out of date. Similarly, the efficacy of river channels as boundaries partly depended on whether the rivers flowed for the whole year (mainly those fed by Himalayan meltwaters) or whether they dried up for part of the year. Flooding also affected the use of river channels as borders, and channels also changed their courses. There was no

guarantee that Bengal's volatile rivers would stick to the course that they were following at the time of partition. In January 1948, a police officer reported that the River Ichhamati, which defined the boundary between Khulna and the 24 Parganas, had taken a new course sixteen miles south of Hasnabad … Radcliffe had not given any thought to the possibility of rivers changing course; a serious lapse in a province whose rivers were notoriously wayward. (Chatterji 1999: 222–3)

Changes included the frequent creation, between old and new courses, of sandbars or *chars* whose positions were of strategic significance, and whose size sometimes allowed them to become sites for whole new settlements. Air surveys were not considered as a tool for looking at potential boundary locations (Chatterji 1999: 222–4).

A boundary award in such heavily populated territories was always going to create severe difficulties. As Chatterji (1999: 225) states:

The border cut a channel several hundred miles long, mostly through settled agricultural land. The Bengal countryside was a dense patchwork of small and large holdings, rights over which were shared in a variety of ways … The line which severed this landscape was bound to disrupt every aspect of existence for the rural community, criminalizing the routine and customary transactions by which it survived. It separated the peasant's homestead from the plot he sharecropped in the last season and the peasant-proprietor from his holding. It cut creditors off from debtors; landlord from tenants.

There were additional and predictable problems related to the movement of livestock along and across the new borders, to the fragmentation and abolition of fishing rights, to loss of access to markets and to urban services, including hospitals, with disruptions of transport systems, including railways, and the disruption of family networks. Smuggling became a new economic option, and large areas became militarised because of their proximity to an international border (Chatterji 1999: 225ff.).

There were similar consequences of drawing the new India–Pakistan borders in the Punjab, together with the great and continuing problem of Kashmir. One of the most contentious parts of the award was the allocation of the larger part of the district of Gurdaspur, with a Muslim majority, to India, which had the effect of providing a land link between the Princely State of Jammu and Kashmir and India, a link of which India later took advantage by improving the road from Gurdaspur to the Sialkot to Srinagar road via the Banihal Pass (Chapman 2000: 179). Disturbances in this state occurred in the summer of 1947, leading to the presence by early 1948 of Indian and Pakistani troops in Kashmir. A United Nations resolution of April 1948 required a plebiscite, but this was rejected, though a ceasefire was agreed in January 1949, and since then the territory has been disputed, with frequent military combat across a high-altitude and disputed ceasefire Line of Control, first conceived by the UN in 1972. Kashmir is in effect divided into two parts, one administered by Pakistan, the other by India (Chapman 2000: 198–9).

Additional difficulties posed by the Punjab division related to water use rights. The Punjab is watered and drained by five major rivers – the Indus,

Jhelum, Chenab, Ravi and Sutlej, with the Sutlej primarily on the Indian side of the border. An extensive canal irrigation network, developed over a long period of time but enhanced during the British Raj, linked the rivers, but was disrupted by the boundary award from which India gained greater advantage. As Cheema (2000: 14) shows:

Not only Radcliffe decided to give Muslim majority areas to India disregarding the basic principle employed for the division of Punjab, he also gave to India two very important headworks which fed canals in West Punjab. Both the Madhopur headworks on river Ravi and Ferozpur headworks on the Sutlej river controlling the Upper Bari Doab and Dipalpur canals in West Punjab and Easter Grey canal which irrigated also parts of Bahawalpur were given to India … Radcliffe was assured by his Indian as well as Pakistani colleagues that the existing arrangements for sharing of water would be respected … Following the dissolution of the Arbitral Tribunal (which was set up to deal with the disputed cases) on 1st April 1948, India immediately stopped, without any prior warning, the flow of waters in Central Bari Doab and Dipalpur canals causing extreme hardships for thousands of Pakistani cultivators.

The human consequences of partition

The immediate aftermath of partition was not only the creation of two new political entities in three locations (India and East and West Pakistan), but also a lengthy period of human misery and deprivation. Almost inevitably, minority groups were left on the 'wrong' side of the new borders between India and Pakistan, with horrific consequences. The new India had a population of which 11 per cent was Muslim, while East Pakistan had a 30 per cent non-Muslim population. Minority groups near borders were subject to massive violent persecution and loss of life, and enormous migrations took place, with minority groups seeking greater security in new homelands (Chapman 2000: 191–2). Estimates for the scale of these tragedies vary, but a minimum figure for loss of life is 250,000, the maximum 1 million, and for migration within and from Bengal and the Punjab 12 million in late 1947 to early 1948, rising to 15 million by 1950.

The balance of scholarly opinion is that Bengal, partly on account of earlier measures taken by the Viceroy Lord Curzon, and later through the influence of Ghandi in the wake of the killings in Calcutta of 1946 (he had threatened to fast to death if the killing did not stop), made the transition relatively peacefully, though inter-religious conflicts, notably in Delhi, led to more killings. There was a major two-way population migration, and economic consequences for the mills of Calcutta and in the loss of Calcutta for East Bengal (Keay 2000a: 506).

In the Punjab, with stronger military traditions in most Muslim, Hindu and Sikh communities, Muslim League opposition early in 1947 to a Sikh/Congress/Unionist Party coalition administration created civil disturbance and much urban bloodshed, and 5,000 people were killed. Complications over the disruption of Sikh communities in Bengal by the new borders led to further migrations and loss of life, with the overall death total being somewhere between 200,000 and a million (Keay 2000a: 508). The estimated number of people involved in migration as a result of partition was about 10 million.

Sixty years after the creation of these new separate states in the subcontinent, it is still difficult to give a comprehensive explanation of the processes by which they were created. Nationalist aspiration, in many different forms, was obviously a contributing factor, as were changes to the old imperial regime in India which began in the late nineteenth and early twentieth centuries. Brown has argued that the 'precipitate end' of British India 'was caused by pressure of war rather than by nationalist demand or liberal Imperial design' (Brown, 1999: 445), but these last two processes were undoubtedly influential in many different ways.

In the end this dreadful historical era should be marked not so much by the names of the principal actors such as Jinnah, Gandhi, Mountbatten and Radcliffe but by the memory of the many unknown people who died as a consequence of partition. Keay writes of death in the Punjab in the following way:

But as with the famine, the earlier killings in Bengal and Bihar, and other such 'upsurges', the names of the victims were unrecorded, their numbers uncounted. Unprepared and overwhelmed, neither of the new nations could do more than feed the living. Meanwhile Mountbatten, 'determined to keep clear of the whole business', as he put it, had washed his hands of the Panjab and headed for the hills. The history-makers looked the other way. (Keay 2000a: 508)

The extensive and complex consequences of partition, not least the loss of human life, should not be underestimated. The speed with which the British abandoned India was a major factor, as was the speedy and unsophisticated nature of the determination of boundaries, together with the changing positions of political groupings and the deep fears and suspicions of one community for another. There are, however, alternative ways of seeing the events and the aftermath of partition. Cyanendra Pandey, for example, has argued that while there is 'a pressing need to recognize the enormity of the event called Partition, and the universality, the obscenity and the unacceptability of the violence … accounts of violence … contribute significantly to the making of new subjectivities, new versions of self and other, new communities and new histories' (Pandey 2003: 175–6).

Ceylon

The circumstances of the independence of Ceylon in 1948 are very different from those of India and Pakistan, specifically, and in some senses ironically (compared with that country's later history), in relation to the smooth and non-violent transfer of power in February 1948. Ashton has stated that

> Especially important from a British viewpoint was the regional context, in which the transfer of power in Ceylon was peaceful, orderly, and negotiated by consent. The communal violence which cast such a long shadow over the transfers of power on the Indian subcontinent was entirely absent in Ceylon. Equally, Ceylon did not, as did Burma, commence its independence hovering on the brink of civil war ... In short, not only was Ceylon viewed as a 'model' colony, it was also viewed as the model for others to follow. (Ashton 1999: 447)

The reasons advanced by Ashton for the smoother transition to independence in Ceylon include a recognition of the potential efficacy of moderation and co operation with and by the colonial power; its smaller size; the Westernised nature of Ceylon's elites, which were at the same time less politicised than their equivalents in India; economic development, especially the plantation economies, of the nineteenth century; and the rivalry between Sinhalese and Tamil elites. Ceylon (Sri Lanka) was, however, caught up in ethnic violence from the 1980s, which continues to the present.

Burma and Malaya

Burma had been occupied by the Japanese army since 1942, and after a long and difficult series of military campaigns was won back in 1944–5, at which point the Burmese and the British each took the view, for different reasons, that Burma should not continue as a British colony, and independence came early in 1948. Malaya had a more important role than Burma in the British empire, on grounds of its strategic position and resources such as rubber and tin. Like Burma the Straits Settlements, the Federated Malay States and the Unfederated Malay States were invaded by Japan in the Second World War, at the end of which these three units, with the exception of Singapore (which became a crown colony) were combined into the Malaya Union, and then the Federation of Malaya in 1948. After a communist uprising in the early 1950s, the new state of Malaysia, comprising the Federation of Malaya, Singapore, Sarawak and Sabah was created in 1963, and this became independent in 1965, although Singapore seceded from it in the same year (Olson 1991e: 384–5).

Africa

It is generally agreed that there were three major phases of independence in Africa after the end of the Second World War. The first involved mainly North Africa, where (apart from Egypt in 1922 and Algeria in 1962) all countries became independent between 1951 and 1956. The second sequence incorporated thirty countries across Central, Saharan and tropical Africa. Their independence was achieved mainly in the 1960s. The third sequence, about a decade later than the second, mainly involved Portuguese colonies – Mozambique and Angola – and Southern Rhodesia, South Africa having acquired Dominion status in 1910 and de facto independence in 1927. The former Southern Rhodesia became independent as Zimbabwe in 1980.

The European withdrawal from control over many parts of Africa can be attributed to a number of causes and interactions. The Second World War left European powers in a position of gratitude to many of their colonies for supplying troops and materials. At the same time the shifting balance of world power to the United States and the Soviet Union meant – as neither of these powers had African colonies – that Africa was less important as a geopolitical fulcrum. Another factor was the move away from the racist and patronising attitudes and language that had been typical of the late nineteenth and early twentieth centuries. The cost of maintaining a presence in these countries was also a consideration, as was the growing representation of former European colonies in the General Assembly of the United Nations.

Independence movements within the African colonial territories ranged from peaceful advocacy and protests to the fiercest and bloodiest of guerrilla warfare campaigns. From the outset of European colonial rule there had been resistance to alien control – sometimes known as 'primary resistance' – but Curtin suggests that this was generally a spent force by the First World War, being replaced in the period between the wars by a miscellany of processes, including the activity of political groups such as the West African National Congress and the South African National

Congress, including both peaceful and more violent protests (Curtin 1995b: 515–16).

Common ideologies, often based on religious beliefs, such as Islam and some breakaway Christian sects, informed some of the resistance movements, for example in North Africa, Nyasaland and the Lower Congo, while women's protests against alien control in south-west Nigeria in 1929–30 (the Aba women's war) served a similar purpose, starting in 1925 with singing and dancing their protests, but then in 1929 a series of riots against native courts and stores set up by the British were initiated.

In the largest confrontation, more than 10,000 women converged on an administrative centre, their faces covered with blue paint, fern-covered sticks in their hands symbolizing unity and danger. In this case the soldiers fired, killing more than fifty women. The government then made an effort to allay some of their grievances, and the movement died down, though the women remained bitter far into the next decade. (Curtin 1995b: 515–16)

Linked economic interests, sometimes through the agency of trade unions, also played a role, as did the complex actions based on shared senses of ethnic and cultural identity at a variety of geographical scales. Ethnic identity was used as a tool for manipulation of indigenous peoples by colonial powers, but was used by indigenous groups to advance their claims for greater autonomy. It also served in some cases to delay full autonomy and to create major difficulties after independence.

Political parties played a primary role in the movement of African territories to independence. These parties, Curtin (1995b: 520) contends, were sometimes based on European models. The links between ethnic groups and political parties varied: sometimes, as in Nigeria, directly reflecting language groupings – Ibo, Yoruba and Hausa   but in other cases involving a heterogeneous assembly of people from different ethnic and cultural traditions. Although political parties had existed in northern and southern Africa since the nineteenth century, and continued in existence through the period of high imperialism from the 1880s to the 1920s, the main advance in their role as advocates of independence came after the end of the Second World War. In Africa the war 'served as a major catalyst of the independence movements. It sometimes hardened attitudes, sometimes modified them, but everywhere it sharpened the aspirations for further social, economic, and political change and brought into the open aspirations that had been building since before the First World War' (Curtin 1995b: 521), mainly by the broadening of appeal beyond the indigenous elite to the less privileged parts of the countries' populations.

Decolonisation in British Africa

Decolonisation took place in British colonial Africa between 1957 (Gold Coast/Ghana) and 1964 (Northern Rhodesia/Zambia and Nyasaland/ Malawi). There was a difference of chronology of independence in settler colonies such as Kenya and Southern Rhodesia, and those colonies where white settlers and administrators were a small minority – principally the West African colonies plus Uganda, Tanganyika and Zanzibar. The Gold Coast (Ghana) achieved independence in 1957, the first British African colony to do so, but only after considerable internal conflict. The sequence of independence of other British African colonies is shown in Fig. 13.1.

Fig. 13.1. Africa in 1998: independence dates.
Source: Chamberlain (1999: xi). By permission of and © Blackwell Publishers.

Areas of white settlement, including Kenya and Southern Rhodesia, experienced greater resistance to independence by these settlers at the same time as indigenous struggles to promote independence and the ending of European priorities for resources, notably land. In Kenya from 1952 to 1955, for example, there were violent conflicts between Mau Mau rebels and the British settlers and army, a factor leading to independence in 1963 (Chamberlain 1999: 49–52).

The Portuguese in Africa

Angola and Mozambique were the two principal Portuguese colonies in Africa. The Salazar government had been in power in Portugal since 1932, and from 1951 to *c.* 1971 encouraged white settlement in the colonies, notably Angola. This led to increasing conflict between coloniser and colonised, partly on grounds of competition for employment (Chamberlain, 1999: 90–1). Chamberlain has argued that 'In the Portuguese empire, even more than the French, the end came in full-scale war. Salazar had gambled everything on making metropolitan Portugal, itself a poor country, the centre of a rich empire … In the end the colonies destroyed, not saved, the regime which Salazar had so carefully built up' (Chamberlain, 1999: 91). After much conflict with great loss of life, Guinea-Bissau became independent in 1974, and Mozambique and Angola in 1975.

The French in Africa: North Africa, West and Central Africa and Madagascar

The experiences of French colonies in their search for independence were very different from those, say, of the territories of the British empire in Africa. The weakening of French imperial power accelerated after the end of the First World War, with the migration of large numbers of black Africans to neighbouring British colonies to escape compulsory labour service, for example in public works or on European plantations, and also payment of tax. Other frustrations with French colonial economic, cultural and educational policy meant that 'By 1939 France had forfeited much of the loyalty which her imperial subjects had shown during the First World War. Once the Second World War had shattered her power and prestige, she lost her Empire as well' (Andrew and Kanya-Forstner 1981: 247). It has been claimed that French popular opinion on colonialism returned to a state of apathy after the First World War, in spite of the acceleration of schoolroom imperial propaganda through texts on history and geography after about 1925, and the popularity of colonial expositions, for example in 1931, and an increase in the interwar period of French foreign investment in her empire. Investment increased, but the trade balance was affected by the Great Depression, so that 'By 1938 France's annual balance of trade deficit with the Empire stood at 4 milliard francs' (Andrew and Kanya-Forstner 1981: 248–9).

French policies for her colonial empire were as complex as the rapid changes of government in the later years of the Third Republic (1871–1940). There were always tensions between republican ideals and the conduct of empire, not least in the practical failure to grant full equality of status to imperial subject peoples linked to ideologies of the civilising mission and a greater France. Instead, there was promotion of a system of racial and political oppression, evidenced by anti-conscription riots in French West Africa and French Indo-China during the First World War, by interwar army uprisings in Syria, Morocco, Indo-China and French Equatorial Africa, and the failure by France to give equal democratic, social and economic rights to colonial troops when the First World War ended (Thomas 2005; Conklin 1997). The policy choice between assimilation or association with indigenous peoples in France's colonies between the wars was made in favour of the second of these, notwithstanding some minor gestures towards assimilation.

Prompted initially by the Russian revolution of 1917, and by the publication of Lenin's book *Imperialism: The Highest Stage of Capitalism*, anti-colonialist ideologies spread out from Russia to other countries, including France. In the 1930s the need for both colonial and European appeasement was heightened by fear of Russian ideological and territorial expansion (Andrew and Kanya-Forstner 1981: 249). The French Communist Party's position on colonialism was, however, as Aldrich has suggested, ambivalent. He notes that 'The tumult of interwar Europe – marked by rise of the radical right and the effects of the Depression – projected Marxist theory and Communist practice as a legitimate alternative to capitalism, bankrupt western democracy, fascism and racism' (Aldrich 1996: 268).

Between the two world wars there were nationalist protests in French colonial territories, such as Tunisia in the mid-1930s, Morocco in the early and mid-1930s, and a continuation of nationalist sentiments in Algeria. Fascist colonial expansion was evidenced by the invasion of Ethiopia by Italy in 1935, which added to the growing tension between European states (Aldrich 1996: 272–3).

In the Second World War France lost control, during the Vichy regime, of her African, Asian (notably Indo-China) and some of her Pacific colonies, and contact with empire was disrupted by the military campaigns between Britain, America, Japan, Germany and Italy. In spite of the opportunities to do so, France was reluctant to cede independence to her colonies after the Second World War, and suffered through her willingness to mount military campaigns to retain colonial territory, often at tremendous human and economic cost, notably in Indo-China and Algeria. A conference of French colonial administrators in 1944 made the position clear: no independent self-government for colonies, though some measure of indigenous participation was envisaged. In 1946 representatives of the colonies were able, at the drafting stage of the constitution of the Fourth Republic, and in the context of association with the Socialist, Communist and Christian Socialist parties, to influence changes in the status of colonial populations. These included the ending of forced labour and the granting of French citizenship – though without rights that were equal to those in the metropolis and to overseas French settlers (Aldrich 1996: 280–1).

In 1946, four of the older colonies – Martinique, Guadaloupe, Guyane and Réunion – were made *départements*, and an Economic and Social Development Fund was established to assist the colonies. The French Union, established by the constitution of the Fourth Republic, included statements on the equal rights of the citizens of French overseas territories, and a tripartite division between the metropole, overseas *départements* and associated territories and states. The ideals of the Fourth Republic's constitution for overseas indigenous populations, however, were not matched in reality by any significant improvement in their rights, the power still resting with metropolitan France and with European settlers in the colonies.

Opinion across the world, notably in the United States and the Soviet Union, the United Nations and China, moved against colonialism in the aftermath of the Second World War, though public opinion in France was in favour of colonial retention (Aldrich 1996: 283). Militant independence movements in three French colonies – Sétif in northern Algeria in 1945, Indo-China and Madagascar in 1947 – led the way to a disruption of French colonial policy and to the independence of a number of these territories.

The uprisings at Sétif in Algeria and in the regions of Mananjary and Manakara, which eventually spread to about 16 per cent of Madagascar, were brutally suppressed by French forces, with great loss of life and the suppression of pro-independence political parties, such as the Mouvement Démocratique de la Rénovation Malgache (MDRM). Madagascar had been administered by the Vichy regime during the Second World War, then occupied by Britain in 1942–3, and by the Free French from 1943. The 1947 uprising was suppressed, but pressure for independence continued, and after reforms by the French in 1956, the Malagasy Republic came into existence in October 1958 as an autonomous state within the French Community, and it obtained full independence in June 1960.

Algeria

Algeria was a highly enigmatic and much troubled part of the French colonial world from the time of the French invasion in 1830 to the granting of independence in July 1962. In the nineteenth century guerrilla warfare against the French occupants was constant. It has been estimated that the numbers of French immigrants had increased from 27,000 in 1841 to 75,000 in 1845, and to about 300,000 by 1860 (Marsot 1991b: 10). The total of all European immigrants, including those from Spain, Malta, Italy and Germany, has been estimated as 7,812 in 1833, 23,023 in 1840 and 76,668 by 1844 (Heffernan 1989: 380). By 1871 Algeria had been divided into three *départements* – Algiers, Oran and Constantine – represented in the Chamber of Deputies in Paris by Europeans or elite Algerians.

It has been argued that some of the origins of modern Algerian nationalism lie in the interwar period, not just in anti-French activity in Algeria itself, but also in mainland France, notably in Paris. It has been estimated that 1931 was the year in which the Algerian population in France was about 123,000. In 1929 there were about 4,000 Algerians in France who belonged to the party Étoile Nord-Africain (ENA) founded in Paris in July 1926 with support from the Parti Communiste Français and which, together with the Parti du Peuple Algérien (PPA) founded in 1937, was the platform for Algerian nationalist representation in the interwar period. The ENA had a chequered history, being dissolved twice by the French government, the second time in 1937, just a year after it had withdrawn its support for the Front Populaire. Aissaoui has suggested that the nationalist aims of both parties were shaped by ethnic and racist discourses:

This ethnic identity was posited as a means of countering the colonial narrative which aimed to divide the North African Muslim population among ethnic lines (that is, between 'Arabs' and 'Berbers') ... Both the ENA and P.P.A.'s ethnonational claims were grounded in religion and history. Islam was constructed as a high culture capable of mobilizing North Africans around the movement's nationalist agenda, and as the foundation of a once great Arabo-Islamic culture that their nationalist project aimed to restore. (Aissaoui 2003: 188–9)

He also argues that racism perniciously permeated all aspects of Maghribis' lives – it 'epitomized all the forms of oppression that they were subjected to, and informed the way in which militants within those movements mobilized or should mobilize'. Their contacts went beyond Algeria, reaching to black and Annamese nationalists within France, Moroccans, Tunisians and Palestinians outside France. The diasporic experience of North Africans in Algeria, forced to migrate as poorly paid labourers to France because of taxation and land alienation to Europeans, was the basis of the attempts by the ENA to activate and educate them in the cause of independence for their homeland.

The violent uprising of May 1945 and its suppression by the French army, using scorched earth tactics, marked the renewal of a struggle for independence, accelerated by the insurrection of 1 November 1954, which marked the beginning of the Algerian war which lasted for eight years. The nationalists (FLN) were assisted by Morocco and Tunisia and the broader Arab world. France had a major military presence in Algeria (about 500,000 troops) facing a much smaller number of guerrillas, and by the end of the war the numbers of people killed are estimated as 300,000 Algerians and 21,000 Europeans (Marsot 1991b: 10–11) . Events in Algeria were closely linked to the politics of metropolitan France, and caused the collapse of the Fourth Republic in 1958 after an insurrection of settlers and army officers ('pieds noirs'), but efforts at appeasement by General de Gaulle were unsuccessful, and after further French military revolts and right-wing terrorist activity a ceasefire was negotiated in March 1962, followed by a referendum and a declaration of independence in July 1962 (Marsot 1991b: 11).

During the course of the Algerian war, French public opinion was divided, intellectuals supporting the rebellion, and right-wing supporters, including former army officers, very much taking against it partly in fear of the possibility of a communist regime. A continuing aspect of French colonisation policy in Algeria was the forced settlement or re-settlement of poor people from France, and during the 1950s of Algerians themselves, in new controlled and planned settlements. In the mid-nineteenth century there had been attempts to solve concerns in France about the likely political and social consequences of the growth in rural–urban migration by encouraging both migration to Algeria from other European countries and the removal of large numbers of the unemployed from Paris to Algeria. Late in 1848 some 14,000 people were selected to travel to forty-two new colonial settlements in Algeria, some of the sites unfit for agriculture and some appropriated from the Arab and Berber inhabitants. They would be under military rule for a year, and have a grid-plan layout.

The nature, design and names of the *colonies* were therefore deliberately selected to demonstrate the power of the French military authorities over both the European *colons* and the indigenous population … most informed observers saw through the rhetoric and recognized the scheme for what it was. The Parisian *colons* were being resettled, not as colonial pioneers but as potential threats to political order within the city. (Heffernan 1989: 385–6)

Changes of metropolitan policy, the poor conditions in which the new settlers found themselves, and the unsympathetic nature of the local military administrators, led to revolt, return migration, and cholera and typhoid epidemics. Heffernan contends, however, that:

despite the agony of these earlier years, the former *colonies agricoles* all survived as villages and many recovered to become large and prosperous centres of European commercial and political hegemony during the Second Empire and Third Republic. Indeed, during the era of colonial myth-making which began towards the end of the nineteenth century, the former *colonies* became the symbols of an heroic pioneering spirit which demonstrated the continuity of the French presence in North Africa and provided a kind of vindication for colonial rule. (Heffernan 1989: 397–9, 403)

This forcible resettlement of the indigenous populations of Algeria was wide-ranging and traumatic. As Sutton and Lawless have stated: 'Of all the hardships to which Algerian rural society was subjected between 1954 and 1961 none was more brutal than, nor had such far-reaching consequences as, the massive regrouping of the rural population by the French army, partly to protect it but also to prevent it from actively assisting the guerrillas' (Sutton and Lawless 1978: 332).

French West Africa and French Equatorial Africa

By 1938 France had two large groups of colonial territories in West and Equatorial Africa, together with two mandated territories – Togoland and Cameroon. Cameroon was part of a former German colony allocated to France by the League of Nations at the end of the First World War. Togo was also former German territory, which in this case was divided between Britain and France at the end of the First World War, with mandates from the League of Nations in 1922. French West Africa was a very large area extending some 2,000 miles (3,219 km) inland from the Atlantic Ocean to Lake Chad, and was administered by the French from 1895 to 1958, with Dakar as its capital. It comprised Mauretania, Senegal, Guinea, the Ivory Coast, Dahomey, French Sudan, French Guinea, Upper Volta and Niger.

French Equatorial Africa included Chad, Gabon, Middle Congo and Ubangi-Shari, comprising an area of 967,000 square miles (2,503,563 km²) stretching from the Atlantic Ocean to the south Sahara region of Central Africa, having its capital at Brazzaville. French West Africa was a coherent block of African colonial territory, but French Equatorial Africa was not – it was the product of French exploration and initiatives from 1843 to 1908, which produced what Wilson has described as 'a territorial monstrosity, five times the size of France, stretching from five degrees south of the Equator to twenty-three degrees north and from the savannahs of the south to the Sahara Desert. Such ecological diversity was matched by the variety of France's subjects … it took five months to reach Chad from France by way of Libreville and Loango' (Wilson 1977: 126).

The progress to independence from France of these two large African colonial territories mainly took place in the period of and after the Second World War. French Equatorial Africa had opposed association with the Vichy government and had allied with the Free French and General de Gaulle. Important factors contributing to the ultimate independence of French colonies in sub-Saharan Africa included 'increasing literacy and education, the militancy of trade unions, and institutional opportunities for political participation afforded by the Fourth Republic. Charismatic Western-educated leaders also began to establish political parties; usually based on cities, they gradually widened their base to the African masses' (Aldrich 1996: 298–9).

In 1946 the constitution of the new Fourth Republic gave overseas *département* status to Chad, Gabon, Middle Congo and Ubangi-Shari. In the same year nationalist parties were formed, and this together with the debacle at Dien Bien Phu in 1954 in Indo China, the rebellion in Algeria in 1954, and the outline law (*loi cadre*) of 1956 in France giving wider representation in the colonies, led to the dissolution of the federation of French Equatorial Africa and the independence of the four states within the French Community in 1958 (Chamberlain 1999: 76; Cherkaoui 1991a: 230).

Despite religious conflicts in Chad in September 1958 between Muslims, Christians and animists, and the experience of major inflation, the population of Chad voted for autonomy in a referendum, and the federation of French Equatorial Africa was dissolved. Full independence for Chad (in June 1960) followed an unsuccessful attempt to restore the federation of French Equatorial Africa. Gabon also voted for full independence in 1960 (Low 1991: 124), as did Middle Congo (which became the People's Republic of Congo, and Ubangi-Shari (which became the Central African Republic).

The process of independence for the countries of French West Africa was equally swift. Of the eight territories, which in 1956 had also become part of a federation in the French Union, and had also been given wider rights of suffrage with the advent of the French Fifth Republic in 1958, Guinea became independent in 1958, and the remaining territories at various dates in 1960 (Hartwig 1991b: 235–6). The movements to independence in French West Africa accelerated after the start of the Fifth Republic in 1958. The ceremonial celebrations of the birth of the French Community in July 1959 were followed two months later by requests from French-controlled African states for transfer of authority from France. In 1960 all the territories of French West Africa, comprising Senegal, Mauretania, Mali, Upper Volta (Burkina Faso), Niger, the Côte d'Ivoire, and Dahomey (Benin), together with four states of French Equatorial Africa and Cameroon, Togo and Madagascar, all became fully independent (Aldrich 1996: 303).

Belgium in Africa

The Congo Free State was established in the Congo basin following the Berlin West Africa Conference of 1885. At the outset in effect a personal fiefdom of King Leopold II, the horrors of Belgian exploitation of Congolese natural resources, notably wild rubber and ivory, and the dreadful treatment of the forced labourers, led to major international protest movements, and the transfer of power to the Belgian state in September 1908, and a change of name to the Belgian Congo. Strong concern at the atrocities was voiced in Britain by the Aborigines' Protection Society in 1896, and similar criticism was voiced in the House of Commons in London on 20 May 1903.

A report in 1904 by Roger Casement, the British consul in the Congo, detailed the horrors of the exploitation of the labour force, and his report was followed by the establishment of the Congo Reform Association by E. D. Morel. Similar protest and reform groups were established in France and Germany, and there was equal concern in the USA where Samuel Clements (Mark Twain) wrote extensively in protest. So great was international concern that Leopold himself sent a committee of inquiry that reported late in 1905, and it confirmed what was already known. As Wesseling (2004: 169) has asserted,

The damage inflicted on the Free State was enormous. According to the most authoritative estimates, the population of the Congo was halved in the years between 1880–1920, dropping from 20 million to 10 million. Wholesale massacres were the most spectacular cause of this decline in population ... More people died before the famines that occurred as whole population groups fled before the advance of the Free State's soldiers and even greater numbers died of disease.

The change to the Belgian Congo under the control of the Belgian government – the Congo was its first colonial possession – did not immediately improve labour conditions, as forced labour continued through the agency of plantation and railway companies, and the decline in revenues from rubber, gold and copper led to the introduction of a hut tax in 1910 (Wesseling 2004: 169). On the eve of the First World War new economic impetus had been provided by development of a new palm oil industry, and of the Katanga copper resources. Although the Belgian Congo was neutral according to the Berlin Act, it was bound up with the French in the conflict against German troops on the Cameroon border, and also, together with the British, on the west shore of Lake Tanganyika. By the end of the war Belgium had occupied Ruanda and Urundi, and was resentful of the allocation of all of former German East Africa to Britain by the Paris Peace Conference at Versailles. After further negotiation, Belgium was given mandates for the two territories.

The development of the Belgian Congo after the First World War was taxed by the continuing problems of over-exploitation of the indigenous labour force, and failure to re-invest much of the profit made by European companies into the Belgian Congo. Attempts were made in the 1930s to remedy the situation by restricting the amount of labour used by foreign enterprises, and limits were placed on the distances over which labour could be recruited. Nonetheless, there were uprisings by indigenous populations in the interwar period, and a fiercely suppressed Kivu rebellion occurred between 1919 and 1923, but nationalist movements continued before and after the Second World War (Ratliff 1991: 50). In spite of Belgian attempts to keep contemporary African anti-colonial sentiments out of the Congo, further protests occurred, notably in Leopoldville in January 1959, in consequence of which independence was agreed, and was achieved in June 1960.

Spanish decolonisation

In the period 1950–76 Spain moved to freer trading in world markets, earning more foreign currency through trade and emigrant workers' remittances, and thus diminished the role of overseas colonies in her economic system. The colonies in turn moved to a developmental perspective, enjoying economic prosperity through aid and improvement programmes that were paralleled by movements towards independence. This was a phase where there was 'a spurt of "developmental late capitalism", not dissimilar to the "second colonial occupation" experienced by British and French colonies in Africa...Economic growth propelled by state planning went together with crash programmes in the fields of education and health, which had been sadly neglected for many years' (Clarence-Smith 1991: 71).

A pragmatic process of decolonisation was begun by Franco to decrease Spanish postwar international isolation, beginning with the northern and southern zones of the Morocco protectorate in 1956 and 1958 respectively, followed by Equatorial Guinea in 1968 and the western Sahara and Mauretania in 1976, leaving Ceuta, Melilla and the Canary Islands as the remainder of a once much larger Spanish colonial presence.

Decolonisation in the Dutch East Indies

The Dutch East Indies – which became Indonesia – was an extensive, complex and diverse geographical, cultural and political entity, into which the Dutch were bound initially by the activities of the Dutch East India Company (Vereenigde Oost-Indische Compagnie or VOC) from the end of the sixteenth century. The company had quasi-sovereign powers, including the rights to negotiate treaties with indigenous polities and to claim territory for the Dutch. The diverse character of the Indonesian archipelago has been outlined by Wesseling (2004: 102):

The Indonesian archipelago comprises many thousands of islands, some of which – Sumatra and Borneo – are very large, while others are extremely small. There are also groups of islands, such as the Lesser Sunda Islands and the Moluccas. The whole of Indonesia lies in the tropics, but the physical geography of the country is very diverse. There are volcanic islands such as Java (large parts of which are suitable for *sawah* rice cultivation), as well as impenetrable forests on Borneo. There is also enormous cultural diversity.

The archipelago was an important crossroads of international trading routes for a range of both valuable commodities such as pepper and spices and items such as rice and fish. The initial basis of Dutch power was Batavia (modern Jakarta) on Java, but by the eighteenth century the Dutch controlled the whole of the East Indies apart from a small British settlement in southern Sumatra and Portuguese Timor. By the end of the eighteenth century, during which Dutch power and economic profit had waned, the VOC was dissolved, and control vested in a Dutch Committee

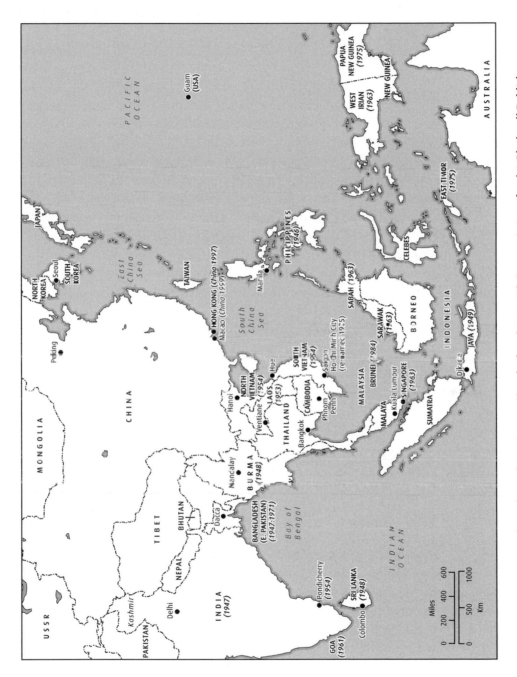

Fig. 13.2 Asia in 1980: independence dates. Source: Chamberlain (1999: xiii). By permission of and © Blackwell Publishers.

for the Affairs of East Indian Trade and Possessions. In the eighteenth century the fortunes of the region reflected power struggles in Europe, with French control of the Netherlands placing it in the war against Britain, and in 1811 Britain took over the East Indies, a situation further changed in 1814 when Britain returned the East Indies to the Netherlands. Dutch focus in the early nineteenth century was principally in Java, and the outbreak of the Java war – a series of regional rebellions – in 1825 compounded economic and political difficulties, and resulted in great loss of life, estimated at 15,000 among the Netherlands–Indies army and 200,000 Javanese (Wesseling 2004: 106).

In 1830 the Dutch introduced a 'cultivation system' (*kultursystem*). The system distorted the nature and exploitation of the labour force. It removed any incentive to improve agricultural production, and was a cause of famine in central Java in 1849–50. Unrest in Java and criticism of the system in the Netherlands led to its partial dissolution in the years from 1860 to 1864, but in the second half of the nineteenth century insurrection continued in Sumatra, Borneo, the Celebes, Bali and other places, resulting in part in reforms – the so-called 'Ethical Policy' early in the twentieth century (Marlay 1991b: 185).

These developments were taking place against a background of gradual Dutch consolidation and extension of its East Indies empire, initiated by the Aceh war that lasted from 1873 to 1903. The context of the long and bloody Aceh war was the opposition by this powerful independent state in north Sumatra to a Dutch–British agreement of 1871 which allowed the Dutch to control Aceh in exchange for the surrender of small Dutch territories in West Africa (on the Gold Coast) to Britain, and the invasion of Aceh by the Dutch in 1873 to forestall a possible American–Aceh treaty.

The process of extension and consolidation of the Dutch empire in Indonesia involved treaty negotiations with other European powers which seemed to be looking to extend their own empires in the region and the subsequent appropriation of power from indigenous rulers. Major developments included border agreements with Britain on Borneo, with Portugal on Timor, and with the British on New Guinea in 1895, the border with former German territory being agreed with Australia after the end of the First World War.

National movements began in Java in 1908, through students at the indigenous doctors' training school, the Budi Utomo group, campaigning for social justice, followed by the Indonesian party (1912, mainly Indo-European) and the Sarekat Islam (also 1912) which by 1919 had 500,000 members. The Indonesian Social Democrat Organisation was founded in 1914, 'which developed in a radical-revolutionary direction under the leadership of the Dutch Marxist and professional revolutionary, Henk Sneevliet' (Wesseling 2004: 220). The occupation by the Japanese (1942–5) stimulated nationalist movements both by guerrilla activity and by the encouragement of nationalist groups by the Japanese, and a consequence was the declaration of independence in Batavia in August 1945, and of the republic of Java and Sumatra in 1946. But only after the intervention of the Security Council of the United Nations in 1947, and after continued fighting between the Indonesians and the Dutch, did the Dutch recognise the Indonesian Republic in 1949, to which was added western New Guinea in 1963 (Chamberlain 1999: 84–6).

French Indo-China

Opposition to the French in Indo-China intensified in the early twentieth century, stimulated by nationalist developments in India, the peasant revolt of 1908, the Chinese nationalist revolution of 1911, the formation of a Vietnamese Parti Constitutionaliste in 1917, the refusal by the French for a Vietnamese council (leading to an embrace of communism in the interwar period), and revolts led by the revolutionary group the Tahnh-Niên Hôi organised by Ho Chi Minh (Chamberlain, 1999: 79). The decolonisation movement in French Indo-China involved not only the French and the Vietnamese, but also the Americans who were active in attempts to counter communist (especially Russian and Chinese) influence in parts of the world where there was deemed to be an American strategic interest at stake.

The region was occupied by the Japanese during the Second World War, but at its end in 1945 the Vietminh Front seized Hanoi and declared independence. French troops returned in 1946, intent on regaining North Vietnam from the Vietminh, but the situation worsened to include Laos and Cambodia, and in 1954 French troops surrendered at Dien Bien Phu (Chamberlain 1999: 78–80). Although Laos became independent in 1949 and Cambodia in 1953, they continued to be bound in regional conflagration after the USA was drawn into the 'defence' of Indo-China in 1965 and started the bombing of North Vietnam (earlier determined by the seventeenth parallel). American air and ground forces were involved until 1973, when they were withdrawn by President Nixon. In the eight-year conflict, 'more than 55,000 American soldiers were killed; the Vietnamese dead, both north and south, totalled well in excess of half

a million' (Chamberlain 1999: 82–3). In May 1975 South Vietnam surrendered to the north, and the Socialist Republic of Vietnam came into
being in 1976.

The decolonisation of the Pacific islands

Aldrich (2000: 173–91) has drawn attention to the lack of scholarly interest in the processes of decolonisation of the Pacific islands in the years
following the Second World War, because of greater interest in the process
in Africa and Asia. Key features of decolonisation in the Pacific islands
were its later occurrence than elsewhere (essentially 1962 to the mid-
1990s); the lack of nationalist militancy; and the apparent reluctance of
the indigenous populations to disengage from controlling colonial power,
and of colonial powers to give up their Pacific island territories. Early
independence for Pacific polities was also discouraged by the small size of
many of the islands, by cultural heterogeneity, the presence of significant
numbers of immigrants, for example in Fiji, and by the weak development
of political structures (Aldrich 2000: 175–6).

Examples of some of these constraining factors are the geographical
spread of the population of French Polynesia, where in 1961 'the 84,551
inhabitants … lived in five island groups extending over an area greater in
size than Western Europe', the cultural heterogeneity of Melanesia, where
'Over seven hundred and fifty languages were spoken in PNG [Papua
and New Guinea], some one hundred and twenty in the New Hebrides',
and the fact that in most of the Pacific territories Europeans controlled
the administration and the economy of islands and island groups where
they had a significant numerical presence, such as Fiji, PNG and French
Polynesia. Smaller numbers elsewhere also had a disproportionate influence (Aldrich 2000: 175–6).

British policy in practice meant the appointment of non-elected
Europeans to legislative and administrative bodies, with little opportunity
for indigenous peoples to have the franchise and thus to elect their own representatives. France was a different case, as the French had clear views about
the links between colonies and the metropole, involving the election of representatives from the Pacific island territories both to local councils and for
a while (1956–8) to the French parliament, so that 'provisions for citizenship, representation in parliament, and elections with universal suffrage set
French territories apart. Policy-makers reasoned that these arrangements
satisfactorily restructured the relationship between overseas territories

and the metropolis. Moves for independence or self-government were to be combated as subversive' (Aldrich 2000: 176).

Residual colonial perceptions of indigenous peoples, in the Pacific and other regions of European imperialism, as being culturally and intellectually unfit for self-government, and lacking in formal education and appropriate institutions for the advancement of independence, sustained the dependency philosophy. The main planks of the policy of Britain, France and other European states, and the United States were for slow economic and political development, and improvements in education and health services. In spite of periodic uprisings against colonial rulers in the 1920s and 1930s, for example in Western Samoa, there seemed to be little nationalist ambition on the part of indigenous populations for independence. Two exceptions were in French colonies: the formation of the multi-race Union Calédonienne in the 1950s, which sought greater representation and better living standards, though not independence; and, second, in French Polynesia, through the advocacy of a Tahitian – Pouvana'a a Oopa – for greater autonomy, and later in 1958 for independence. Initially this was unsuccessful, and Pouvana'a a Oopa was removed from the political scene, but his initiatives stimulated later independence movements (Aldrich: 2000: 177).

American views of the potential of incorporating Hawaii as a constituent state fluctuated, but concern with racial issues held back this process until 1959. In other small island polities of the Pacific independence was opposed by vested economic interests, especially mining corporations, and national military concerns, including nuclear weapons testing, and it was not until the late 1960s and 1970s that decolonisation occurred in Oceania. Western Samoa became independent in 1962, Nauru in 1962, Tonga and Fiji in 1970, the Ellice and Gilbert Islands in 1978 and 1979, and the Solomon Islands in 1978. The last British Pacific territory to become independent was the New Hebrides (1978, Vanuatu in 1980), where the process was complicated by the existence, since 1906, of a joint English and French jurisdiction. Papua New Guinea, which was an Australian United Nations Trusteeship from the end of the Second World War, moved gradually to autonomy in 1951 and 1964, through the establishment of a legislative council and then a house of assembly, finally achieving independence in 1975.

The process of progress toward autonomy varied between colonial powers. A number of French colonies retained and further developed links with metropolitan France. Wallis and Futuna are volcanic islands, about 110 miles (177 km) apart, at the western limit of Polynesia, west of Western

Samoa and north-west of Tonga. In 1962 they agreed an arrangement for French citizenship and right of residence in France and New Caledonia, together with parliamentary representation. French Polynesia experienced a varied suite of political ambitions by indigenous peoples, and a measure of autonomy, short of full independence, was granted in 1984, with France retaining responsibility for 'external relations, immigration, currency, defence, justice and the police – a considerable list of attributions – but the local assembly handles other administration' (Aldrich 2000: 182).

The progress of New Caledonia to independence – not yet achieved – has been difficult, the process involving violent conflicts between loyalists and pro-independence supporters from 1984, heightening in 1988. From 1998 the expectation was that there would be gradual progress to sovereignty by 2013–18. Aldrich (2000: 182–3) contends that the movement towards independence has been more contentious in French territories and largely unsuccessful, because 'Extremely high subsidies and other aid from Paris, citizenship and rights of abode throughout France have convinced many (including the numerous "settlers" and expatriates) to reject independence'. Aldrich's conclusion about aspirations to or disinclinations for independence in Oceania is that the postwar experiences of the colonial powers – Britain, France, the United States, Australia and New Zealand, and to a much lesser extent Chile (Easter Island) – were not as urgent or divisive as those in India, Indonesia and Algeria, so that 'With the possible exception of the Netherlands in New Guinea, no colonial country has been thwarted in achieving its aims: Britain to withdraw from Oceania, Australia and New Zealand to wind up the colonial era in measured fashion, France and the United States to retain some control of territories. In Oceania, decolonisation has marked a victory for the old colonial powers' (Aldrich 2000: 188).

14 | Conclusion

The dynamics of the widely differing European imperial and colonial links overseas, and the diverse reflections of those links in the metropoles themselves, from the period of high imperialism in the late nineteenth and early twentieth centuries, are complex and not easy to unravel. Imperial ambitions and realisations were not for the most part accurate projections and fulfilments of carefully thought out national or international geostrategic master plans, nor were they largely historical accidents (the 'fit of absence of mind' thesis); more often they were the products of pragmatic interactions between regional and national processes within colonial progenitor states (and the adjustments made to suit local conditions and cultures), and used to resolve developing local tensions within colonised territories and on a larger scale between colonising powers.

The agencies of imperial and colonial projection included individual politicians, political parties, government ministries (whose goals and structures were constantly changing), perceptive liberals and racist conservatives, despotic monarchs, religious groups, and ambitious scientists, explorers, travellers, and military and naval officers, merchants and entrepreneurial capitalists, together with a wide range of institutions including learned scientific societies, colonisation and acclimatisation societies, utopian environmentalists, trading companies, and highly idiosyncratic (and frequently unbalanced) individuals. The historiographical record until comparatively recently had foregrounded the roles of men, but work in a postcolonial context has now partly redressed this imbalance by examining in detail the various roles of women and wider gender and sexuality issues in imperial and colonial contexts.

One of the exciting developments in the study of the geographies and histories of imperialism and colonialism in recent times has been an expansion in the range of explanatory theories and ideas, often changing or adapting existing theories and ideologies. For the geographer the centrality of space and place – part of its conceptual and empirical armoury over a long period of time – has been retained in studies of the historical geographies of imperialism and colonialism, but with added insights through postcolonial theory. In consequence new questions have been asked, for example, about the production of geographical knowledge that informed imperial ambition, including maps, and about the key questions of the roles of indigenous peoples and of gender roles, notably of women. Additionally aspects of geopolitics and of rural and urban interactions, commercial incentives, population trends and compositions, means of travel and communication, institutions, and concepts of civilising missions have also been addressed. The concept of scale is important for the geographer in particular, as is the acknowledgement that small-scale, highly localised analyses of colonial experiences and negotiations of individuals and groups are as significant as processes operating at increasingly global scales.

An extremely important aspect of newer research and publication has also been the increased emphasis placed on the active roles in discourses and interactions of indigenous peoples in colonial places. There is an increasing and careful evaluation of the substantial exploitation and appropriation of such people, their rights and their resources, and the record is quite dramatic and disturbing, in South and South-West Africa and Australia, for example. On the other hand, increasing attention is being paid to the use that was made of indigenous knowledge to facilitate European exploration, mapping and settlement – sometimes formal acknowledged, but frequently not. The nature and extent of the indigenous contributions to the production and modification of colonial development was strongly conditioned by a range of factors, including the specific environmental and administrative structures at the times of attempted colonisation. It is clear, however, that the role of indigenous people was crucial in determining the course of empire and colony, notably through their local authority and knowledge, which allowed part retention of earlier administrative structures and cultures. Colonialism also re-made the national identity of metropolitan countries such as Britain and France.

The processes of European colonialism and de-colonisation from the late nineteenth to the mid-twentieth century must also be seen in the much wider context of the history of empires in the world as a whole in the modern period. At the beginning of the period of imperial renewal studied here, for example, there existed a still extensive Habsburg empire, Chinese empire, Ottoman empire (which diminished at the end of the First World War) and Russian empire, and new empires, notably American and Japanese, were coming into being. The new European empires and colonies had been preceded by a host of others, some of which, in the form of the Mughal empire in India and smaller polities in Africa, for example, had been targets for negotiation by Europeans when new colonial relationships were being forged. The differences between the new and the older empires included the fact that the older empires lasted much longer than the modern:

> while the new ones, such as the African colonies of the French, British and Belgians, lasted only decades. At first glance, the new empires had more effective technological and organizational means of exerting and maintaining power. The striking aspect of these comparisons is the extent to which 'modern' European states in Africa did not exercise such power. Colonial rule was empire on the cheap (Cooper 2005: 156)

Cooper suggests that the 'ambiguous relationship of imperialism and capitalism over time' led to the uneven developments that facilitated European imperial activity during the period of high imperialism, and that this was also bound up with the complex development of the European nation-state, including France at the time of the Third Republic, supporting a colonialism of progress based on the maxim of liberty, equality and fraternity (Cooper 2005: 172).

The main actors in the European political stage on the eve of the wave of new imperialism in the late nineteenth century were not yet, however, all nation-states. It was a world 'of empires, old and would-be. It was precisely the fact that the important actors were very few in number and thought in supranational terms that turned the changing pattern of economic interaction into a Scramble' (Cooper 2005: 182). It was also an opportunity for personal aggrandisement through colonial projects, as evidenced by the ambitions for Central Africa of the Belgian monarch Leopold II, and of Cecil Rhodes.

An important question is the significance of European imperial and colonial activity for the modern period. Postcolonial discourse has shown that the new geographies and conditions associated with European imperial activity in a globalising economic, political and social environment were not unique and may have been overemphasised. Darwin (2007: 14) argues that in the aftermath of discourses set in train by work such as that of Edward Said, which:

> was part of a great sea change, a conscious attempt to 'decentre' Europe or even to 'provincialize' it ... Above all, perhaps, the European path to the modern world should no longer be treated as natural or 'normal', the standard against which historical change in other parts of the world should always be measured. Europeans have forged their own kind of modernity, but there were other modernities – indeed many, modern modernities.

Cooper has reviewed the concept of modernity as applied in this context, and argued that in spite of limitations it should be used with greater sensitivity to different analytical approaches and critiques of representation, and to provide 'a focus on process and causation in the past and on choice, political organization, responsibility, and account-ability in the future' (Cooper 2005: 149). Darwin concludes that there are many examples, including much of Asia (except India) China, Japan, and Middle Eurasia, where European power was ineffective, and which moved gradually into political and economic modernities of their own, recognising some of the advantages of the Western model of modernity, but not its imperial and capitalist processes, and that the late nineteenth century – the zenith of European imperialism – was also a time of great resistance to imperial processes (Darwin 2007: 499–500). At the same time he attributes to European states a major role in global transform-ation, by 'the global exchange of manufactures, raw materials and food-stuffs, in huge volumes and values, with the accompanying flows of people and money', together with the spread of European imperial and colonial systems over substantial areas of the globe (Darwin 2007: 15). The rela-tive significance of European high imperialism is clearly under review, and will be further helped by additional detailed studies, from different regional perspectives, of other empires and polities with which European states and institutions were engaged.

In addition to the enhancement of domestic economies by trade with overseas possessions, the policies, cultural assumptions and forms of sci-entific and more general knowledge of European powers influenced their thinking about the cultures and capabilities of indigenous peoples. For the most part this may be characterised as an assumption of racial superior-ity, highlighting the assumed physical, mental and uncivilized inferiority of Other peoples, supported by pseudo-scientific theories about climatic determinism, social Darwinism, and capabilities for work and culture (the 'moral economy' of climate). This civilising mission, as it became known, translated in different ways to local circumstances, but ranged from the most extreme form of racism – people regarded as animals to be treated brutally and destroyed where necessary – to much more humanitarian recognition of human rights and potential. Thomas (1994: 190) thus sug-gests 'that modern colonial discourses have represented native peoples in a number of ways: as heathens but potential Christians, as savages to be wished away, as primitives defined through the negation of modernity and as distinct "races" or "cultures" possessing particular natures'.

In the nineteenth century there had been awareness of the fragility of cultural assumptions about indigenous peoples and cultures, and the negative consequences of colonialism for them. This led, among other things, to the creation in 1835 of an Aborigines Select Committee by the British parliament, the production of a report in 1837 and the formation in 1837 of a British and Foreign Aborigines Protection Society.

The Society aimed 'to assist in protecting the defenceless and promoting the advancement of the Uncivilized tribes' by guiding colonial policy through the materials and the mobilization of 'popular opinion' ... Such trans-imperial institutional humanitarianism would continue through the remainder of the nineteenth and into the twentieth centuries, intervening critically, if not always particularly powerfully, in British colonial affairs. (Lester 2005: 71)

Generalisations on this issue, however, require critique, qualification, and more empirical investigation. Stoler and Cooper's (1997) 'rethinking a research agenda' of the links between metropole and colony is extremely helpful, highlighting, inter alia, what they call 'ambiguities of difference', including:

that the otherness of colonised persons was neither inherent nor stable; his or her difference had to be defined or maintained ... social boundaries that were at one point clear would not necessarily remain so. In pursuing a 'civilizing mission' designed to make colonised populations into disciplined agriculturalists or workers and obedient subjects of a bureaucratic state, colonial states opened up a discourse on the question of how much 'civilizing' would promote their projects and what sort of political consequences 'too much civilizing' would have in store. (Stoler and Cooper 1997: 7)

They also highlight the different outcomes envisoned from their civilising missions by Dutch, English and French colonialists, and the processes of negotiations and modification of those outcomes by indigenous colonial populations.

In the Philippines as much as in Africa, people heard what Christian missionaries had to say but scrambled the message – sometimes finding in the mission community something valuable and meaningful to them, sometimes using their mission education to gain secular advantage, sometimes insisting that their conversion should entitle them to run the religious organization themselves, and sometimes dismantling both doctrine and organization to build a religious edifice or even a revolutionary movement that was wholly new, neither the Christianity of Europe nor a recognizable variant of local religious practices. (Stoler and Cooper 1997: 7)

The links between the production of geographical and other forms of knowledge and the advancement of imperial policy and colonial practice have been considerably refined and advanced by studies, for example, of the collection of census material and of survey and mapping. These both had practical ends, not always altruistic, including the assessment of liability for tax on land and other property, and of the ethnic compositions of given populations, for purposes of control. However, a 'conspiratorial' perspective – data collection as a means of surveillance – can be over-emphasised at the expense again of wider understanding of more subtle interactions between subject and object in the various processes of knowledge production. The roles and experiences of individual administrators, census enumerators and surveyed people are most important and should be further reviewed in relation to available empirical data. This is also true of power and control perspectives of mapping and surveying, requiring necessary recognition to be given and information incorporated about the nature of the country surveyed, the available technologies used, the negative effects of the processes of surveying on local communities, compromises effected on the drafting table, and the uses to which maps were put. There are excellent examples of the possibilities of cartographic history on this sort of basis, including Edney's (1997) important study of the mapping of India.

The scientific societies and the general contexts of the production of scientific knowledge in the metropole and colony during the nineteenth and twentieth centuries need to be further investigated, both in respect of the roles of energetic individual explorers and administrators, and of local people in the colonies, for example, and we need to know more about the complicated links between the scientific institutions and scientists of metropole and colony. Scientific knowledge, it has been argued, reflected an imperial hierarchy, with scientific work in Australia, for example, closely tied for recognition and promotion to the scientific societies, notably the Royal Society, in London. The early nineteenth century witnessed the birth of a whole range of scientific societies in Europe, including the geographical societies of Paris, Berlin and London, and they further proliferated during the rest of the century. The question of the links between the production of geographical knowledge and imperialism has been well covered (Bell, Butlin and Heffernan 1995; Godlewska and Smith 1994; Driver 2001), but it is interesting to note Stoler and Cooper's observation (1997: 14) that:

While the disciplines of geography and anthropology helped to make the expanding world intelligible and manageable, the relationship of disciplinary knowledge and colonial rule was an ambiguous one. Geography brought the same conceit of science to domestic state building – making terrain, roads, sites of possible military conflicts, and resources knowable quantities – as to overseas ventures. But it would be more accurate to say that geographers' ways of looking at the world were shaped in the same historical process as state expansionism, rather than that the discipline grew up to serve the colonising state ... Moreover, geographers and other social scientists disagreed among themselves.

This is most certainly true, though perhaps needs to be qualified by the recognition that from at least the early modern period there were different kinds of geography and that they related quite differently to imperial and colonial policy in and between different European states. In Britain, as has been shown in Chapter 6, geography, exemplified at least by the Royal Geographical Society, had a coincidental relationship with imperialism, in the sense that although it did not directly influence policy as a scientific institution, it promoted the production and dissemination of knowledge useful for that purpose through supporting and training for expeditions, loaning survey instruments, arranging and publishing lectures by explorers, maintaining collections of maps, books and photographs, and having the power and connections of individual members, including statesmen and military personnel.

This contrasted with the 'provincial' geographical societies in Britain, whose strong commercial membership led to closer direct ties to colonial promotion, especially of trade. Similar societies to these – societies of commercial geography – were common in other European states, including Germany and France, whose main geographical society (Paris) had very close links with the French government and colonial policy. Geography only developed as a significant university discipline in Britain from the late nineteenth century, and in the twentieth century was only slowly included as a participant in major colonial research projects (Butlin 2003).

Geographical theory and practice has informed this book in content and in the variety of geographical scales of examples used, ranging from large-scale global to small-scale local. They have been incorporated to aid the identification and examination of imperial and colonial interactions, including population change and movement, land appropriation, geopolitical chronologies and spaces, geography as scientific knowledge, visual representations of colonial places and peoples, cultural perceptions and changes, trade and transport, urbanisation processes and changing environments. Most of these have strong links with geography as it is generally understood, but the concepts and practices of modern geography continue to change, and with them there occurs an expansion in the range of data and other sources employed, and in our bases for understanding. A key aspect of much relevant work on imperialism and colonialism by historical geographers has been the intensive investigation of archive sources, particularly for the gifted linguist, though many more remain to be examined. Photography, paintings, sketches and other visual material is now very much a part of the range of historical sources used by geographers in their research, critically evaluated in relevant contexts.

The analysis of colonial towns and cities, while still for example presenting and analysing variations in urban form and basic demographic contrasts, now incorporates more sophisticated ways of looking at the cultural origins, characteristics and interactions of different culture groups and the tensions generated by conflict of tradition and purpose, and at the complex ideas, negotiations, institutions and policies that underpin the understanding of the social and built environments of Singapore, Delhi, Brazzaville and Bône, for example. The historical geography of individual buildings, streets and monuments, and their symbolic reflection of ideologies of empire, is another significant area of research, on which progress is being helped by broader concepts of landscape, notably landscape as text capable of multiple interpretations rather than invariable given fact.

Movement and exchanges between parts of empires were important factors in maintaining contact, debate and control. The technological revolutions that produced steam-powered railway engines, factory machines, steamships, drainage pumps, refrigerated ships, cables, telegraphs, telephones, wirelesses and more effective armaments facilitated the more rapid movement of people, goods and information, and thus closer connection. These did not just favour the metropolitan states, for they also provided means of communication, movement and action for those who were opposed to imperialism and who sought to end it by means peaceful and violent. Inter-colonial linkages are also significant factors in our attempts to understand imperial processes of the movements of knowledge and its translation into action. These include a range of humanitarian concerns that linked parts of the British empire, together with conferences that attempted to co-ordinate and promote empire-wide policies for resources, including forests, and for economic planning.

One of the great strengths of geographical analyses of imperial and colonial processes and interactions lies in the broad area of environment and environmental change. This is not just a question of recording human-induced changes from a variety of archival and field sources, but also appraising and evaluating the impacts of longer-term climatic change, such as the El Niño Southern Oscillation and its effects on climate and famine. Major studies of issues such as the historical geography of resource management have been extensively undertaken, by Williams (2003) on forest clearance and management and by Powell (1976, 1993, 2000), for example, on water management in Australia, supported by a wide range of maps. The study and mapping of such phenomena is not the sole prerogative of the geographer, and much valuable work is being undertaken by historians and ecologists of the dynamics of human–environment relations in colonial contexts, generally under the umbrella heading of environmental history.

Key features of environmental history have been successfully incorporated into national historical atlases, including the *New Zealand Historical Atlas* and the *Historical Atlas of Canada*, and it would be helpful to see more collaborative work of this kind, perhaps even an attempt to map a wide range of historical environmental phenomena at global scales. The historical dynamics of environmental change, including the erosion of soils, changes in river and irrigation systems, changing ecosystems, land drainage, and changes in technologies and in policies of environmental management, including wildlife conservation, would add much, when mapped, to our understanding of these phenomena.

Traditionally historical geographies of imperialism have stressed territorial aspirations and disputes, including the negotiation and designation of boundaries, a matter of great importance in Africa, for example, where the speed of European territorial aggrandisement in the late nineteenth and early twentieth centuries almost always outran European geographical knowledge, leading to complex inter-state border commissions (usually of military personnel) charged with the agreement and determination of colonial boundaries. Beyond this, however, there is now a growing body of work by geographers which is concerned with the geopolitics and ideologies of imperialism, and the complex processes that led to ambitions to acquire and control overseas territories, and the interactions between coloniser and colonised (Blunt and McEwan 2002). This has in part been influenced by critical concern about renewed manifestations of European (and American) imperialism in Indo-China, and more recently in Palestine, Iraq and Afghanistan. Gregory, in his powerful book *The Colonial Present*, has argued that untenable Western imaginary geographies of the Middle East have continually underpinned geopolitical stances and unjustified atrocities, and confined us to 'the treadmill of the colonial present', to escape from which 'it will be necessary to explore other spatializations and other topologies, and to turn our imaginative geographies into geographical imaginations that can enlarge and enhance our sense of the world and enable us to situate ourselves within it with care, concern, and humility', and to realise and respect truths other than our own within the reality of continuing 'disagreements, conflicts and even enemies' (Gregory 2004: 262).

Recent celebrations of the sixtieth anniversary of the independence of India and Pakistan from British colonial rule in 1947, with the re-examination of cause and consequences, are potent reminders of what was and was not achieved, particularly the awful human consequences of the speed of the British determination of boundaries and withdrawal. The broader issues of the consequences of colonialism for other territories, in Africa for example, with their seemingly endemic problems of political and economic instability, cannot be reviewed here, but they provide continuing necessity for reflection on the causes and consequences of Europe's high imperialism from the late nineteenth century.

References

Aberdare, Lord 1884 'Address on the Opening of the Session 1884–5', *Proceedings of the Royal Geographical Society*, VI, 688–90.

Abramson, D. M. 2004 'Baker, Sir Herbert (1862–1946)', in H. C. Matthews and B. Harrison (eds.), *Oxford Dictionary of National Biography*, Oxford: Oxford University Press.

Adamo, D. T. 2007 'Decolonizing the Psalter in Africa', *Black Theology*, 5, 1, 20–38.

Adams, J. D. 1986 'Frontiers of History and Geography', *Victorian Historical Journal*, 57, 1, 17–27.

Adams, M. 2006 'Colonial Policies and Women's Participation in Public Life: The Case of British Southern Cameroons', *African Studies Quarterly*, 8, 3 [online at: http://web.africa.ufl.edu/asq/v3/v8i3a1.htm].

Aissaoui, R. 2003 '"Nous voulons chercher le bâillon et briser nos chaînes": Racism, Colonialism and Universalism in the Discourse of Algerian Nationalists in France between the Wars', *French History*, 17, 2, 186–209.

Ajayi, A. D. F. and Crowder, M. 1985 *Historical Atlas of Africa*, London: Longman.

Aldrich, R. 1990 *The French Presence in the South Pacific 1842–1940*, London: Macmillan.

  1996 *Greater France. A History of French Overseas Expansion*, London: Macmillan.

  2000 'The Decolonisation of the Pacific Islands', *Itinerario*, 24, 173–91.

Allen, B. 2004a 'William John Wills 1834–61', in B. Allen (ed.), *The Faber Book of Exploration*, London: Faber and Faber, 332–43.

  2004b 'Georg August Schweinfurth', in B. Allen (ed.), *The Faber Book of Exploration*, London: Faber and Faber, 206–10.

Anderson, A. 2002 'A Fragile Plenty. Pre-European Maori and the New Zealand Environment', in E. Pawson and T. Brooking (eds.), *Environmental Histories of New Zealand*, Melbourne: Oxford University Press, 19–34.

Anderson, B. 1991 *Imagined Communities*, New York: Verso.

Anderson, D. M. and Rathbone, R. 2000 'Urban Africa. Histories in the Making', in D. M. Anderson and R. Rathbone (eds.), *Africa's Urban Past*, Oxford: James Curry, 1–17.

Anderson, W. 1992 'Climates of Opinion: Acclimatization in Nineteenth-Century France and England', *Victorian Studies*, 35, 135–57.

Andrade, E. Jr, 1991 'Spanish-American War', in J.S. Olsen (ed.), *Historical Dictionary of European Imperialism*, Westport, CT: Greenwood Press, 576–8.

Andrew, C.M. and Kanya-Forstner, A.S. 1981 *France Overseas. The Great War and the Climax of French Imperial Expansion*, London: Thames and Hudson.

Andrews, J.H. 2001 'Introduction: Meaning, Knowledge, and Power in the Map Philosophy of J.B. Harley', in J.B. Harley, *The New Nature of Maps. Essays in the History of Cartography*, ed. P. Laxton, Baltimore, MD: Johns Hopkins University Press, 1–32.

2008 'Using and Making Maps', *Journal of Historical Geography*, 1, 144–7.

Angell, N. 1910 *The Great Illusion*, London: Heinemann.

1938 *The Great Illusion – Now*, Harmondsworth: Penguin.

Anon. 1900 'Obituary. Miss Mary H. Kingsley', *Geographical Journal*, 16, 1, 114–15.

Arnold, D. 1988 *Famine. Social Crisis and Historical Change*, Oxford: Blackwell.

1993 'Social Crisis and Epidemic Disease in the Famines of Nineteenth-Century India', *Social History of Medicine*, 6, 3, 385–404.

2005 'Europe, Technology, and Colonialism in the 20th Century', *History and Technology*, 21, 1, 85–106.

Ascherson, N. 1999 *The King Incorporated. Leopold the Second and the Congo*, London: Granta Books, 2nd edn.

Ashton, S.R. 1999 'Ceylon', in J.M. Brown and W. Roger Louis (eds.), *The Oxford History of the British Empire*, vol. IV: *The Twentieth Century*, Oxford: Oxford University Press, 447–64.

Asquith, H.H. 1912 'Speech at the Annual Dinner of the RGS', *Geographical Journal*, 40, 105–8.

Atkinson, D. 1995 'Geopolitics, Cartography and Geographical Knowledge: Envisioning Africa from Fascist Italy', in M. Bell, R.A. Butlin and M.J. Heffernan (eds.), *Geography and Imperialism 1820–1940*, Manchester: Manchester University Press, 265–97.

2003 'Geographical Knowledge and Scientific Survey in the Construction of Italian Libya', *Modern Italy*, 8, 1, 9–29.

Atkinson, D., Cosgrove, D. and Notaro, A. 1999 'Empire in Rome: Shaping and Remembering an Imperial City, 1870–1911', in F. Driver and D. Gilbert (eds.), *Imperial Cities*, Manchester: Manchester University Press, 40–63.

Atlas Colonial Illustré c. 1900 Paris: Librairie Larousse.

Aurousseau, M. 1961 *Notes on Geographical Associations Formed in Australia*, Sydney.

Bailey, A. 2005 *Making Population Geography*, London: Hodder.

Baines, D. 1994 'European Emigration, 1815–1930: Looking at the Emigration Decision Again', *Economic History Review* new series, 47, 3, 525–44.

Baker, A.R.H. 2003 *Geography and History. Bridging the Divide*, Cambridge: Cambridge University Press.

2005 'Writing Geography, Making History: D. W. Meinig's Geographical Perspective on the History of America', *Journal of Historical Geography*, 31, 634–46.

2007 'Classifying Geographical History', *Professional Geographer* 59, 3, 344–56.

Baker, G. L. 1996 *Trade Winds on the Niger. The Saga of the Royal Niger Company 1830–1971*, London: Radcliffe Press.

Ballantyne, T. 2002 'Empire, Knowledge and Culture: From Proto-Globalization to Modern Globalization', in A. G. Hopkins (ed.), *Globalization in World History*, London: Pimlico, 115–40.

Barnard, W. S. 1999 'Encountering Adamastor: South African Founding Geographers and their Regional Geographies', in A. Buttimer, S. D. Brunn and U. Wardenga (eds.), *Text and Image. Social Construction of Regional Knowledges*, Leipzig: Institut für Länderkunde, 192–204.

Bartholomew, J. G. 1913 *A Literary and Historical Atlas of Africa and Australia*, London: Dent.

Barton, G. 2001 'Empire Forestry and the Origins of Environmentalism', *Journal of Historical Geography*, 27, 4, 529–52.

2002 *Empire Forestry and the Origins of Environmentalism*, Cambridge: Cambridge University Press.

Basalla, G. 1967 'The Spread of Western Science', *Science*, 156, 616–22.

Bassett, T. J. 1994 'Cartography and Empire Building in Nineteenth-Century West Africa', *Geographical Review*, 84, 3, 316–35.

1997 'Maps and Mapmaking in Africa', in H. Selin (ed.), *Encyclopaedia of the History of Science, Technology, and Medicine in Non-Western Cultures*, Dordrecht: Kluwer, 554–7.

Bassin, M. 1999 *Imperial Visions. Nationalist Imagination and the Geographical Expansion in the Russian Far East, 1840–1865*, Cambridge: Cambridge University Press.

Bate, W. 2001 'Gold, Social Energiser and Definer', *Victorian Historical Journal*, special issue on 'Victoria, 150 Years of Gold', 72, 1–2, 7–27.

Bayly, C. A. 1996 *Empire and Information: Intelligence Gathering and Social Communication in India, 1780–1870*, Cambridge: Cambridge University Press.

1999 'The Second British Empire', in R. W. Winks (ed.), *The Oxford History of the British Empire*, vol. V: *Historiography*, Oxford: Oxford University Press, 54–72.

2004 *The Birth of the Modern World*, Oxford: Blackwell.

Beaglehole, J. C. 1974 *The Life of Captain James Cook*, Stanford, CA: Stanford University Press.

Beaujot, R. 1998 *Immigration and Canadian Demographics: State of the Research*, Ottawa: Strategic Planning and Research, 2–3.

Beinart, W. 1990 'Empire, Hunting and Ecological Change in Southern and Central Africa', *Past and Present*, 128, 162–86.

Beinart, W. and Hughes, L. 2007 *Environment and Empire*, Oxford: Oxford University Press.

Beinart, W. and Middleton, K. 2004 'Plant Transfers in Historical Perspective: A Review Article', *Environment and History*, 10, 3–29.

Bell, M. 1986 *Contemporary Africa*, London: Longman.

1993 '"The Pestilence that Walketh in Darkness". Imperial Health, Gender and Images of South Africa c. 1880–1910', *Transactions, Institute of British Geographers* new series, 18, 327–41.

1998 'Reshaping Boundaries: International Ethics and Environmental Consciousness in the Early Twentieth Century', *Transactions, Institute of British Geographers* new series, 23, 151–75.

Benton, L. 1999 'Colonial Law and Cultural Difference: Jurisdictional Politics and the Formation of the Colonial State', *Comparative Studies of Society and History*, 41, 3, 563–88.

2002 *Law and Colonial Cultures. Legal Regimes in World History, 1400–1900*, Cambridge: Cambridge University Press.

Berdoulay, V. 1981 *La formation de l'École française de Géographie*, Paris: Bibliothèque Nationale (CHTS).

Birkett, D. 2004 *Off the Beaten Track: Three Centuries of Women Travellers*, London: National Portrait Gallery.

Black, I. 1999 'Imperial Visions: Rebuilding the Bank of England, 1919–39', in F. Driver and D. Gilbert (eds.), *Imperial Cities. Landscape, Display and Identity*, Manchester: Manchester University Press, 96–113.

Black, J. 2002 *Warfare in the Western World 1882–1975*, Chesham: Acumen.

Blaut, J. M. 1993 *The Colonizer's Model of the World*, New York: Guildford Press.

2000 *Eight Eurocentric Historians*, New York: Guildford Press.

Blum, A. 2002 'Resistance to Identity Categorization', in D. I. Kertzer and D. Arel (eds.), *Census and Identity: The Politics of Race, Ethnicity and Language in National Censuses*, Cambridge: Cambridge University Press, 121–47.

Blunt, A. 1994 *Travel, Gender and Imperialism: Mary Kingsley in West Africa*, London: Guildford Press.

2003 'Home and Empire: Photographs of British Families in the Lucknow Album, 1856–57', in J. M. Schwartz and J. R. Ryan (eds.), *Picturing Place. Photography and the Geographical Imagination*, London: I. B. Tauris, 243–60.

2005 'Colonialism/Postcolonialism', in D. Atkinson, P. Jackson, D. Sibley, and N. Washbourne (eds.), *Cultural Geography. A Critical Dictionary of Key Concepts*, London: I. B. Tauris, 175–81.

Blunt, A. and McEwan, C. 2002 'Introduction', in A. Blunt and C. McEwan (eds.), *Postcolonial Geographies*, London: Continuum, 1–6.

Boomgaard, P. 2002 'From Subsistence Crises to Business Cycle Depressions, Indonesia 1800–1940', *Itinerario*, 3, 4, 35–49.

Booth, A. 2008 'The Economic Development of Southeast Asia in the Colonial Era: c. 1870–1942', *History Compass*, 6, 1, 25–53.

Bose, S. 1993 *Peasant Labour and Colonial Capital: Rural Bengal since 1770, The New Cambridge History of India*, vol. III 2, Cambridge: Cambridge University Press.

2006 *A Hundred Horizons. The Indian Ocean in the Age of Global Empire*, Cambridge, MA: Harvard University Press.

Bosma, U. 2007 'Beyond the Atlantic: Connecting Migration and World History in the Age of Imperialism, 1840–1940', *International Review of Social History*, 52, 116–23.

Bravo, M. T. 1999 'Ethnographic Navigation and the Geographical Gift', in D. N. Livingstone and C. W. J. Withers (eds.), *Geography and Enlightenment*, Chicago: University of Chicago Press, 199–235.

Brayshay, M. and Cleary, M. 2002 'Editorial: Shaping Colonial and Imperial Landscapes', *Landscape Research*, 27, 1, 5–10.

Brett, M. 1986 'The Maghrib', in A. D. Roberts (ed.), *The Cambridge History of Africa*, vol. VII: *From 1905 to 1940*, Cambridge: Cambridge University Press 267–328.

Bridges, R. C. 1963 'The RGS and the African Exploration Fund, 1876–80', *Geographical Journal*, 129, 1, 25–35.

1973 'Europeans and East Africans in the Age of Exploration', *Geographical Journal*, 142, 220–32.

1982 'The Historical Role of British Explorers in East Africa', *Terrae Incognitae*, 14, 1–21.

Briggs, A. 1968 *Victorian Cities*, Harmondsworth: Pelican Books.

Brock, P. 2000 'Mission Encounters in the Colonial World: British Columbia and South-West Australia', *Journal of Religious History*, 24, 159–79.

Brockway, L. 1979 *Science and Colonial Expansion: The Role of the British Royal Botanic Gardens*, London: Academic Press.

Brown, J. M. 1999 'India', in J. M. Brown and W. Roger Louis (eds.), *The Oxford History of the British Empire*, vol. IV: *The Twentieth Century*, Oxford: Oxford University Press, 440–1.

Brown, K. 2003 '"Trees, Forests, and Communities": Some Historiographic Approaches to Environmental History in Africa', *Area*, 35, 4, 343–56.

Bryant, R. L. 1998 'Resource Politics in Colonial South-East Asia: A Conceptual Analysis', in V. T. King (ed.), *Environmental Challenges in South-East Asia*, Richmond: Curzon, 27–52.

Butlin, R. A. 1993 *Historical Geography: Through the Gates of Space and Time*, London: Arnold.

1995 'Historical Geographies of the British Empire, c. 1887–1925', in M. Bell, R. A. Butlin and M. J. Heffernan (eds.), *Geography and Imperialism 1820–1940*, Manchester: Manchester University Press, 151–88.

2002 'The Bits of the Map Formerly Coloured Red: *The Oxford History of the British Empire*, Vols III–V', *Journal of Historical Geography*, 28, 1, 118–24.

2003 'British Geographical Representations of Imperialism and Colonial Development in the Early and Mid-Twentieth Century', in D. Gilbert, D. Matless and B. Short (eds.), *Geographies of British Modernity*, Oxford: Blackwell, 229–49.

2005 'The Pivot and Imperial Defence Policy', in B. W. Blouet (ed.), *Global Geostrategy: Mackinder and the Defence of the West*, London: Frank Cass, 36–54.

2006 '"Geography – Imperial and Local"; The Work of the Royal Geographical Society of Australasia (Queensland Branch) 1885–1945', in I. R. W. Childs and B. J. Hudson (eds.), *Queensland Geographical Perspectives*, Milton: Royal Geographical Society of Queensland, 217–41.

Cain, P. J. 2007 'Capitalism, Aristocracy and Empire: Some "Classical" Theories of Imperialism Revisited', *Journal of Imperial and Commonwealth History*, 35, 1, 25–47.

Cain, P. J. and Hopkins, A. G. 1993 *British Imperialism: Innovation and Expansion 1688–1914*, Harlow: Longman.

Caldwell, J. C. 1990 'The Social Repercussions of Colonial Rule: Demographic Aspects', in A. A. Boahen (ed.), *General History of Africa* vol. VII: *Africa under Colonial Domination 1880–1935*, abridged edn, Paris: UNESCO, 200–7.

Caldwell, J. C. and Ruzica, L. T. 1978 'The Australian Fertility Transition: An Analysis', *Population and Development Review*, 4, 10, 81–103.

Cameron, V. L. 1877 *Across Africa*, 2 vols., London: Daldy, Isbister and Co.

1884 'Comments on J. Thompson's Paper on "The Masai Country"', *Proceedings of the Royal Geographical Society*, 6, 710–11.

Cannadine, D. 2001 *Ornamentalism*, London: Penguin Press.

Cannizzo, J. 1996 'Dr Livingstone Collects', in J. MacKenzie (ed.), *David Livingstone and the Victorian Encounter with Africa*, London: National Portrait Gallery, 139–68.

Capel, H. 1994 'The Imperial Dream: Geography and the Spanish Empire in the Nineteenth Century', in A. Godlewska and N. Smith (eds.), *Geography and Empire*, Oxford: Blackwell, 58–73.

Carrier, E. H. 1928 *The Thirsty Earth: A Study in Irrigation*, London: Christophers.

Carter, M. 1999 'Spectacular Suez: The Gala Opening of the Suez Canal, 1869', in B. Harlow and M. Carter (eds.), *Imperialism and Orientalism. A Documentary Sourcebook*, London: Blackwell, 100–65.

Casada, J. A. 1975 'Verney Lovett Cameron: A Centenary Appreciation', *Geographical Journal*, 141, 203–15.

Castles, S. and Miller, M. J. 1993 *The Age of Migration: International Population Movements in the Modern World*, London: Macmillan.

Castree, N. 2006 'David Harvey's Symptomatic Silence', *Historical Materialism*, 14, 4, 35–57.

Çelik, Z. 1997 *Urban Forms and Colonial Confrontations*, Berkeley: University of California Press.

Chamberlain, M. E. 1999 *De-colonization*, 2nd edn, Oxford: Blackwell.

Chapman, G. P. 2000 *The Geopolitics of South Asia from Early Empires to India, Pakistan and Bangladesh*, Aldershot: Ashgate.

Chatterjee, S. and Kenny, J. T. 1999 'Creating a New Capital: Colonial Discourse and the Decolonization of Delhi', *Historical Geography*, 27, 73–98.

Chatterji, J. 1999 'The Fashioning of a Frontier: The Radcliffe Line and Bengal's Border Landscape', *Modern Asian Studies*, 33, 1, 185–242.

Chaudhuri, K. N. 1985 *Trade and Civilisation in the Indian Ocean. An Economic History from the Rise of Islam to 1750*, Cambridge: Cambridge University Press.

Cheema, P. I. 2000 *The Politics of the Punjab Boundary Award*, Working Paper No. 1, Heidelberg Papers in South Asian and Comparative Politics, Heidelberg: South Asia Institute.

Cherkaoui, S. El M. 1991a 'French Equatorial Africa', in J. S. Olson (ed.), *Historical Dictionary of European Imperialism*, Westport, CT: Greenwood Press, 228–30.

1991b 'Djibouti', in J. S. Olson (ed.), *Historical Dictionary of European Imperialism*, Westport, CT: Greenwood Press, 175–6.

Childs, P. and Williams, R. J. P. 1997 *An Introduction to Postcolonial Theory*, New York: Prentice Hall.

Christopher, A. J. 1976 *Southern Africa*, Folkestone: Dawson.

1984 *Colonial Africa*, London: Croom Helm.

1988 *The British Empire at its Zenith*, London: Croom Helm.

1992 'Ethnicity, Community and the Census in Mauritius, 1830–1990', *Geographical Journal*, 158, 1, 57–74.

1994 *The Atlas of Apartheid*, London: Routledge.

1999 *The Atlas of States. Global Change 1900–2000*, Chichester: John Wiley.

2001 *The Atlas of Changing South Africa*, 2nd edn, London: Routledge.

2005 'Race and the Census in the Commonwealth', *Population, Space and Place*, 11, 103–18.

2008 'The Quest for a Census of the British Empire c. 1840–1940', *Journal of Historical Geography*, 34, 268–85.

Clarence-Smith, W. G. 1979 *Slaves, Peasants and Capitalists in Southern Angola 1840–1926*, Cambridge: Cambridge University Press.

1991 'The Economic Dynamics of Spanish Colonialism in the Nineteenth and Twentieth Centuries', *Itinerario*, 15, 1, 71–90.

Claval, P. 1991 'Paris Geographical Society', in G. Dunbar (ed.), *Modern Geography: An Encyclopedic Survey*, London: St James Press, 130–1.

Clayton, A. 1999 '"Deceptive Might": Imperial Defence and Security, 1900–1968', in J. M. Brown and W. R. Louis (eds.), *The Oxford History of the British*

Empire, vol. IV: *The Twentieth Century*, Oxford: Oxford University Press, 280–305.

Clayton, D. 2000 *Islands of Truth: The Imperial Fashioning of Vancouver Island*, Vancouver: University of British Columbia Press.

2008 'Colonising Cartographies', *Journal of Historical Geography*, 1, 157–62.

Cleary, M. C. 1997 'From Hornbills to Oil? Patterns of Indigenous and European Trade in Colonial Borneo', *Journal of Historical Geography*, 23, 1, 29–45.

2003 'Land Codes and the State in French Cochinchina c.1900–1940', *Journal of Historical Geography*, 29, 3, 356–75.

Cleary, M. C. and Eaton, P. 1996 *Tradition and Reform: Land Tenure and Rural Development in South-East Asia*, Oxford: Oxford University Press.

Clignet, R. P. and Foster, P. J. 1964 'French and British Colonial Education in Africa', *Comparative Education Review*, 8, 2, 191–8.

Clout, H. D. 2005 'Geographers in their Ivory Tower: Academic Geography and Popular Geography in Paris 1931', *Geografiska Annaler*, series B, 87, 1, 15–29.

2008a 'Popular Geographies and Scholarly Geographies in Provincial France: The Société Normande de Géographie, 1879–1937', *Journal of Historical Geography*, 34, 24–47.

2008b 'Popular Geographies in a French City Port: The Experience of the Le Havre Society of Commercial Geography, 1884–1948', *Scottish Geographical Journal*, 124, 1, 33–77.

Cobban, J. L. 1985 'The Ephemeral Historic District in Jakarta', *Geographical Review*, 75, 3, 300–18.

Cohen, C. 1993 '"The Natives Must First Become Good Workmen". Formal Educational Provision in German South West and East Africa Compared', *Journal of Southern African Studies*, 19, 1, 115–34.

Cohen, R. 1995 'Prologue', in *The Cambridge Survey of World Migration*, Cambridge: Cambridge University Press, 1–2.

Cohn, B. S. 1984 'The Census, Social Structure and Objectification in South Asia', reprinted (1990) in B. S. Cohn, *An Anthropologist among the Historians and Other Essays*, New Delhi: Oxford University Press, 224–54.

1996 'Introduction', in *Colonialism and its Forms of Knowledge: The British in India*, Princeton, NJ: Princeton University Press.

Coleman, D. 2003 'Mass Migration and Population Change', *Verlag für Sozialwissenschaften, Wiesbaden, Zeitschrift für Bevölkerungswissenschaft*, 28, 2–4, 719–51.

Conklin, A. 1997 *A Mission to Civilize: The Republican Idea of Empire in France and West Africa 1895–1930*, Stanford, CA: Stanford University Press.

Constantine, S. 1999 'Migrants and Settlers', in J. M. Brown and W. R. Louis (eds.), *The Oxford History of the British Empire*, vol. IV: *The Twentieth Century*, Oxford: Oxford University Press, 163–87.

Cooper, F. 2005 *Colonialism in Question*, Berkeley: University of California Press.

Cooper, F. and Stoler, L. (eds.) 1997 *Tensions of Empire: Colonial Cultures in a Bourgeois World*, Berkeley: University of California Press.

Coquery-Vidrovitch, C. 1988 *Africa: Endurance and Change South of the Sahara*, Berkeley: University of California Press.

1990 'The Colonial Economy of the Former French, Belgian and Portuguese Zones, 1914–35', in A. Adu Boahen (ed.), *General History of Africa*, vol. VII: *Africa under Colonial Domination 1880–1935*, abridged edn, Paris: UNESCO, 162–72.

Corum, J. S. 2000 'The Myth of Air Control: Reassessing the History', *Aerospace Power Journal*, 14, 4, 61–77.

Cosgrove, D. E. 1984 *Social Formation and Symbolic Landscape*, London: Croom Helm.

(ed.) 1999 *Mappings*, London: Reaktion Books.

2008 *Geography and Vision. Seeing, Imagining and Representing the World*, London: I. B. Tauris.

Cosgrove, D. E. and Daniels, S. (eds.) 1988 *The Iconography of Landscape: Essays on the Symbolic Representation, Design and Use of Past Environments*, Cambridge: Cambridge University Press.

Cotton, J. S. 1914 'Agriculture', in A. J. Herbertson and O. J. R. Howarth (eds.), *The Oxford Survey of the British Empire: Asia*, Oxford: Clarendon Press, 113–37.

Courtenay, P. P. 1969 *Plantation Agriculture*, London: Bell.

Courville, S. 2000 *Le Québec: Genèses et mutations du territoire. Synthèse de géographie historique*, Québec: Les Presses de l'Université Laval.

2001 'The Colonial Dream. Empire, Quebec and Colonial Discourse in the Nineteenth Century', in I. S. Black and R. A. Butlin (eds.), *Place, Culture and Identity. Essays in Historical Geography in Honour of Alan R. H. Baker*, Québec: Les Presses de l'Université Laval, 289–309.

2002 *Emigration, colonisation et propagande. Du rêve américain au rêve colonial*, Québec: Éditions MultiMondes.

Cox, J. 2002 *Imperial Fault Lines. Christianity and Colonial Power in India, 1818–1940*, Stanford, CA: Stanford University Press.

Cribb, R. 2000 *Historical Atlas of Indonesia*, London: Curzon.

Crosby, A. W. 1972 *The Columbian Exchange: Biological and Cultural Consequences of 1492*, Westport, CT: Greenwood.

1986 *Ecological Imperialism: The Biological Expansion of Europe, 900–1900*, Cambridge: Cambridge University Press.

Crush, J. 1986 'Swazi Migrant Workers and the Witwatersrand Gold Mines 1886–1920', *Journal of Historical Geography*, 12, 1, 27–40.

Cumberland, K. B. and Whitelaw, J. S. 1970 *The World's Landscapes*, vol. V: *New Zealand*, London: Longman.

Curtin, P. D. 1985 'Medical Knowledge and Urban Planning in Tropical Africa', *American Historical Review*, 90, 3, 594–613.

1989 *Death by Migration: Europe's Encounter with the Tropical World in the Nineteenth Century*, Cambridge: Cambridge University Press.

1995a 'The Colonial Economy', in P. Curtin, S. Feierman, L. Thompson, and J. Vansina, *African History: From Earliest Times to Independence*, 2nd edn, London: Longman, 446–68.

1995b 'African Resistance and the Liquidation of European Empire', in P. Curtin, S. Feierman, L. Thompson and J. Vansina, *African History: From Earliest Times to Independence*, 2nd edn, London: Longman, 513–30.

1998 *Disease and Empire: The Health of European Troops in the Conquest of Africa*, Cambridge: Cambridge University Press.

Curzon, G. N. 1893 'Journeys in French Indo-China (Tongking, Annam, Cochin China, Cambodia)', *Geographical Journal*, 2, 2, 97–111.

1907 *Frontiers*, Oxford: Oxford University Press.

Daly, M. T. 1988 'The Australian City: Development in an Open World', in R. L. Heathcote (ed.), *The Australian Experience*, Melbourne: Longman Cheshire, 37–54.

Dalziel, R. W. 1999 'Southern Islands: New Zealand and Polynesia', in A. Porter (ed.), *The Oxford History of the British Empire*, vol. III: *The Nineteenth Century*, Oxford: Oxford University Press, 573–96.

Damodaran, V. 1998 'Famine in a Forest Tract: Ecological Change and the Causes of the 1897 Famine in Chota Nagpur, Northern India', in R. H. Grove, V. Damodaran and S. Singh (eds.), *Nature and the Orient*, Delhi: Oxford University Press, 853–90.

Darby, H. C. (ed.) 1943 *Indo-China*, Geographical Handbook Series, Naval Intelligence Division, Cambridge: Cambridge University Press.

Darwin, J. 1997 'Imperialism and the Victorians: The Dynamics of Territorial Expansion', *English Historical Review*, 112, 447, 614–42.

1999 'De-colonization and the End of Empire', in R. W. Winks (ed.), *The Oxford History of the British Empire*, vol. V: *Historiography*, Oxford: Oxford University Press, 542–4.

2007 *After Tamerlane. The Global History of Empire since 1405*, London: Penguin/Allen Lane.

Daunton, M. 2005 'Introduction', in M. Daunton (ed.), *The Organization of Knowledge in Victorian Britain*, Oxford: British Academy/Oxford University Press, 1–29.

David, S. 2003 *The Indian Mutiny*, London: Penguin Books.

Davis, M. 2002 *Late Victorian Holocausts. El Niño Famines and the Making of the Third World*, London: Verso.

Davis, R. C. (ed.) 2002 *The Central Australian Expedition 1844–1846: The Journals of Charles Sturt*, London: Hakluyt Society.

Dennis, M. 1991 'Angola', in J.S. Olson (ed.), *Historical Dictionary of European Imperialism*, Westport, CT: Greenwood Press, 25–7.

Dodge, E.S. 1976 *Islands and Empires*, Oxford: Oxford University Press.

Dodgshon, R.A. 1987 *The European Past. Social Evolution and Spatial Order*, London: Macmillan.

1998 *Society in Time and Space. A Geographical Perspective on Change*, Cambridge: Cambridge University Press.

Doeppers, D.F. 1972 'The Development of Philippine Cities before 1900', *Journal of Asian Studies*, 4, 31, 769–92.

Drayton, R. 2000 *Nature's Government. Science, Imperial Britain, and the 'Improvement' of the World*, New Haven, CT: Yale University Press.

Drechsler, H. 1986a 'South West Africa 1885–1907', in H. Stoecker (ed.), *German Imperialism in Africa*, London: C. Hurst, 39–61.

1986b 'South West Africa 1907–1914', in H. Stoecker (ed.), *German Imperialism in Africa*, London: C. Hurst, 136–47.

Driver, F. 1991 'Stanley and his Critics: Geography, Exploration and Empire', *Past and Present*, 133, 134–66.

1992 'Geography's Empire: Histories of Geographical Knowledge', *Environment and Planning, Series D, Society and Space*, 10, 23–40.

1996 'David Livingstone and the Culture of Exploration in Mid-Victorian Britain', in J. MacKenzie (ed.), *David Livingstone and the Victorian Encounter with Africa*, London: National Portrait Gallery, 109–38.

2001 *Geography Militant. Cultures of Exploration and Empire*, Oxford: Blackwell.

2004 'Henry Morton Stanley 1841–1904', *Oxford Dictionary of National Biography*, Oxford: Oxford University Press, available at: http://0-www.oxforddnb.com/articles/36/36247.

Driver, F. and Gilbert, D. 1999 'Imperial Cities: Overlapping Territories, Intertwined Histories', in F. Driver and D. Gilbert (eds.), *Imperial Cities*, Manchester: Manchester University Press, 1–20.

Driver, F. and Martins, L. 2005 'Views and Visions of the Tropical World', in F. Driver and L. Martins (eds.), *Tropical Visions in an Age of Empire*, Chicago: University of Chicago Press, 3–20.

D'Souza, R. 2006 'Water in British India: The Making of a "Colonial Hydrology"', *History Compass*, 4, 4, 621–8.

Dubow, S. 2000 'A Commonwealth of Science: The British Association in South Africa, 1905 and 1929', in S. Dubow (ed.), *Science and Society in Southern Africa*, Manchester: Manchester University Press, 66–99.

Dumett, R.E. 1998 *El Dorado in West Africa: The Gold-Mining Frontier, African Labor, and Colonial Capitalism in the Gold Coast, 1875–1900*, Athens: Ohio University Press.

Dunch, R. 2002 'Beyond Cultural Imperialism: Cultural Theory, Christian Missions and Colonial Modernity', *History and Theory*, 41, 3, 301–25.

Dunmore, J. (ed.) 2002 *The Pacific Journal of Louis-Antoine de Bougainville 1767–1768*, London: Hakluyt Society.

Dyson, T. 1991a 'On the Demography of South Asian Famines, Part I', *Population Studies*, 45, 5–25.

1991b 'On the Demography of South Asian Famines, Part II', *Population Studies*, 45, 279–97.

Eardley-Wilmot, S. 1914 'Vegetation, Forestry and Fauna', in A. J. Herbertson and O. J. R. Howarth (eds.), *The Oxford Survey of the British Empire: Asia*, Oxford: Oxford University Press, 76–112.

Edmond, R. 2005 'Returning Fears: Tropical Disease and the Metropolis', in F. Driver and L. Martins (eds.), *Tropical Visions in an Age of Empire*, Chicago: University of Chicago Press, 175–94.

2006 *Leprosy and Empire. A Medical and Cultural History*, Cambridge: Cambridge University Press.

Edmonds, L. 1999 'Australia, Britain and the Empire Air Mail Scheme, 1934–38', *Journal of Transport History* 20, 2, 91–106.

Edney, M. H. 1997 *Mapping an Empire: The Geographical Construction of British India, 1765–1843*, Chicago: University of Chicago Press.

2005 *The Origins and Development of J. B. Harley's Cartographic Theories*, *Cartographica*, monograph 54, 40, 1–2.

Eichler, G. 1977 'From Colonialism to National Independence: Algiers' Social Ecology', *Geojournal* 1, 5, 5–12.

Elson, R. E. 1999 'International Commerce, the State and Society: Economic and Social Change', in N. Tarling (ed.), *The Cambridge History of Southeast Asia*, vol. II: part 2, Cambridge: Cambridge University Press, 127–91.

Emmer, P. C. 1997 'European Expansion and Unfree Labour: An Introduction', *Itinerario*, 21, 1, 9–15.

Etemad, B. 1998 'Europe and Migration after Decolonisation', *Journal of European Economic History*, 26, 3, 457–70.

Etherington, N. 1999 'Missions and Empire', *Oxford History of the British Empire*, vol. V: *Historiography*, Oxford: Oxford University Press, 303–14.

2005 'Education and Medicine', in N. Etherington (ed.), *Missions and Empire*, Oxford History of the British Empire Companion Series, Oxford: Oxford University Press, 261–84.

(ed.) 2007 *Mapping Colonial Conquest: Australia and South Africa*, Perth: University of Western Australia Press.

Etherington, N. and Maxwell, D. 2004 'Missions and Empire', *Journal of Religion in Africa*, 34, 1–2, 195–9.

Ewans, M. 2003 'Belgium and the Colonial Experience', *Journal of Contemporary European Studies*, 11, 2, 167–80.

Fabian, J. 2000 *Out of Our Minds. Reason and Madness in the Exploration of Central Africa*, Berkeley: University of California Press.

Fairhead, J. and Leach, M. 1995 'Reading Forest History Backwards', *Environment and History*, 1, 55–91.

Faithurst, U. J., Davies, R. J., Fox, R. C., Goldschlagg, P., Ramutsindela, M., Bob, U. and Khosa, M. M. 2003 'Geography: The State of the Discipline in South Africa (2000–2001)', *South African Geographical Journal*, 85, 2, 81–9.

Falconer, J. 2001 *India: Pioneering Photographers 1850–1900*, London: British Library and the Howard and Jane Ricketts Collection.

Fanon, F. 2001 *The Wretched of the Earth*, London: Penguin Classics reprint.

Ferguson, N. 2003 *Empire: How Britain Made the World*, London: Allen Lane.

Fieldhouse, D. K. 1982 *The Colonial Empires. A Comparative Survey from the Eighteenth Century*, 2nd edn, Basingstoke: Macmillan.

1996 'For Richer, For Poorer', in P. J. Marshall (ed.), *The Cambridge Illustrated History of the British Empire*, Cambridge: Cambridge University Press, 108–46.

Finlay, R. J. 1995 'The Rise and Fall of Popular Imperialism in Scotland', *Scottish Geographical Magazine*, 111, 1, 13–21.

Flint, J. E. 1960 *Sir George Goldie and the Making of Nigeria*, Oxford: Oxford University Press.

1999 'Britain and the Scramble for Africa', in R. W. Winks (ed.), *The Oxford History of the British Empire*, vol. V: *Historiography*, Oxford: Oxford University Press, 450–62.

Foeken, D. 1995 'On the Causes of the Partition of Central Africa, 1875–85', *Political Geography*, 14, 1, 80–100.

Forbes, V. L. and Hercock, M. 2007 'Charting the Way to Empire: The Hydrographic Office', in N. Etherington (ed.), *Mapping Colonial Conquest: Australia and South Africa*, Perth: University of Western Australia Press, 11–40.

Ford, C. 2004 'Nature, Culture and Conservation in France and her Colonies 1840–1940', *Past and Present*, 183, 173–98.

Ford, L. R. 1993 'A Model of Indonesian City Structure', *Geographical Review*, 83, 4, 374–96.

Forsyth, D. S. 1995 'Imperialism and National Identity in Nineteenth Century Scotland', *Scottish Geographical Magazine*, 113, 1, 6–12.

Foster, J. 2003a 'Capturing and Losing the "Lie of the Land": Railway Photography and Colonial Nationalism in Early Twentieth-Century South Africa', in J. M. Schwartz and J. R. Ryan (eds.), *Picturing Place. Photography and the Geographical Imagination*, London: I. B. Tauris, 141–61.

2003b '"Land of Contrasts" or "Home We Have Always Known"?: The SAR&H and the Imaginary Geography of White South African Nationhood, 1910–1930', *Journal of Southern African Studies*, 29, 3, 657–80.

Foucault, M. 1997 *Discipline and Punish: The Birth of the Prison*, Harmondsworth: Penguin.

Frenkel, S. 1992 'Geography, Empire, and Environmental Determinism: The Case of Panama', *Geographical Review*, 32, 2, 143–53.

Friedberg, S. 2003 'French Beans for the Masses: A Modern Historical Geography of Food in Burkina Faso', *Journal of Historical Geography*, 29, 3, 445–63.

Frykenberg, R. E. 2005 'Christian Missions and the Raj', in N. Etherington (ed.), *Missions and Empire*, Oxford: Oxford University Press, 107–31.

Gaillard, J. 1994 'The Behaviour of Scientists and Scientific Communities', in J.-J. Salomon, F. R. Sagasti and C. Sachs-Jeantet (eds.), *The Uncertain Quest. Science, Technology and Development*, Tokyo: United Nations University Press, 201–36.

Gale, F. 1969 'A Changing Aboriginal Population', in F. Gale and G. H. Lawton (eds.), *Settlement and Encounter: Geographical Studies Presented to Sir Grenfell Price*, Melbourne: Oxford University Press, 65–88.

Galloway, J. 2005 'The Modernization of Sugar Production in Southeast Asia, 1880–1940', *Geographical Review*, 95, 1, 1–23.

Gambi, L. 1994 'Geography and Imperialism in Italy: From the Unity of the Nation to the "New" Roman Empire', in A. Godlewska and N. Smith (eds.), *Geography and Empire*, Oxford: Blackwell, 74–91.

Gann, L. H. 1988 'The Berlin Conference and the Humanitarian Conscience' in S. Förster, W. J. Mommsen and R. Robinson (eds.), *Bismarck, Europe and Africa: The Berlin Africa Conference 1884–5 and the Onset of Partition*, London: German Historical Institute and Oxford University Press, 321–31.

García-Ramon, M. D. and Nogué-Font, J. 1999 'Spanish Colonial Policy in Morocco and its Impact on Regional Monographs', in A. Buttimer, S. D. Brunn and U. Wardenga (eds.), *Text and Image. Social Construction of Regional Knowledges*, Leipzig: Institut für Länderkunde, 100–10.

Garden, D. 2001 'Cataclyst or Cataclysm. Gold Mining and the Environment', *Victorian Historical Journal*, special issue on 'Victoria, 150 Years of Gold', 72, 1–2, 28–44.

Gardner, H. and Philp, J. 2006 'Photography and Christian Mission. George Brown's Images of the New Britain Mission 1875–80', *Journal of Pacific History*, 41, 2, 175–90.

Gascoigne, J. 1998 *Science in the Service of Empire; Joseph Banks, the British State and the Uses of Science in the Age of Revolution*, Cambridge: Cambridge University Press.

Gellner, E. 1983 *Nations and Nationalism*, Oxford: Oxford University Press.
    1993 'The Mightier Pen? Edward Said and the Double Standards of Inside-Out Colonialism', *Times Literary Supplement*, 19 February, 3–4.

Gilbert, E. 2004 *Dhows and the Colonial Economy of Zanzibar 1860–1970*, Oxford: James Curry.

Gillion, K. L. 1956 'The Sources of Indian Emigration to Fiji', *Population Studies*, 10, 2, 139–57.

Gilmartin, D. 1995 'Models of Hydraulic Environment: Colonial Irrigation, State Power and Community in the Indus Basin', in D. Arnold and R. Guha (eds.), *Nature, Culture and Imperialism: Essays on the Environmental History of South Asia*, Delhi: Oxford University Press, 210–36.

Ginkel, J. A. van 1991 'Royal Dutch Geographical Society (Koninklijk Nederlands Aardrijkskundig Genootschap)', in G. Dunbar (ed.), *Modern Geography: An Encyclopedic Survey*, London: St James Press, 153–4.

Godlewska, A. 1995 'Map, Text and Image. The Mentality of Enlightened Conquerors: A New Look at the *Description de l'Egypte*', *Transactions, Institute of British Geographers* new series, 20, 1, 5–28.

Godlewska, A. and Smith, N. (eds.), 1994 *Geography and Empire*, Oxford: Blackwell.

Goerg, O. 1998 'From Hill Station (Freetown) to Downtown Conakry (First Ward): Comparing French and British Approaches to Segregation in Colonial Cities at the Beginning of the Twentieth Century', *Canadian Journal of African Studies*, 32, 1, 1–31.

Goring, R. 1992 'Hinduism', in R. Goring (ed.), *Chambers Dictionary of Beliefs and Religions*, Edinburgh: Chambers, 218–19.

Graham, B. and Nash, C. (eds.) 2000 *Modern Historical Geographies*, Harlow: Pearson Education.

Green, A. S. 1901 'Mary Kingsley', *Journal of the African Society*, 1, 1–16.

Gregory, D. 2004 *The Colonial Present*, Oxford: Blackwell.

Griffiths, I. 1996 'Permeable Boundaries in Africa', in P. Nugent and A. I. Asiwaju (eds.), *African Boundaries, Barriers, Conduits and Opportunities*, London: Pinter/Cassell, 68–84.

Griggs, P. D. 1985 *A Dream in Trust. The Centenary History of the Royal Geographical Society of Australasia*, Queensland, Incorporated, special issue of the *Queensland Geographical Journal*, third series, 8, 1–185.

Grimshaw, P. and Sherlock, P. 2005 'Women and Cultural Exchanges', in N. Etherington (ed.), *Missions and Empire*, Oxford: Oxford University Press, 173–93.

Grove, R. 1995 *Green Imperialism. Colonial Expansion, Tropical Island Edens and the Origins of Environmentalism 1600–1860*, Cambridge: Cambridge University Press.

    1996 'Indigenous Knowledge and the Significance of South-West India for Portuguese and Dutch Constructions of Tropical Nature', *Modern Asian Studies*, 1, 121–43.

    1998 'The East India Company, the Raj and the El Niño: The Critical Role played by Colonial Scientists in Establishing the Mechanisms of Global Climate Teleconnections 1770–1930', in R. H. Grove, V. Damodaran and S. Sangwan (eds.), *Nature and the Orient*, Delhi: Oxford University Press, 301–23.

Gründer, H. 1988 'Christian Missionary Activities in Africa in the Age of Imperialism and the Berlin Conference of 1884–1885', in J. Wolfgang,

J. Mommsen and R. Robinson (eds.), *Bismarck, Europe, and Africa. The Berlin Africa Conference 1884–1885 and the Onset of Partition*, Oxford: German Historical Institute/Oxford University Press, 85–103.

Gueye, M. 1990 'African Initiatives and Resistance in West Africa, 1880–1914', in A. Adu Boahen (ed.), *General History of Africa*, vol. VII: *Africa under Colonial Domination 1880–1935*, abridged edn, Paris: UNESCO, 55–71.

Guha, R. and Gadgil, M. 1989 'State Forestry and Social Conflict in British India', *Past and Present*, 123, 141–77.

Guha, S. 2003 'The Politics of Identity and Enumeration of India c. 1600–1990', *Comparative Studies in Society and History*, 45, 1, 148–67.

Hall, C. 2002 *Civilising Subjects. Metropole and Colony in the English Imagination 1830–1867*, Cambridge: Polity Press.

Hardiman, D. 1995 'Small-Dam Systems of the Sahyadris', in D. Arnold and R. Guha (eds.), *Nature, Culture, and Imperialism: Essays on the Environmental History of South Asia*, New Delhi: Oxford University Press, 185–209.

1996 'Usury, Dearth and Famine in Western India', *Past and Present*, 152, 113–56.

Harley, J. B. 1988 'Maps, Knowledge and Power', in D. Cosgrove and S. Daniels (eds.), *The Iconography of Landscape*, Cambridge: Cambridge University Press, 277–312.

2001 *The New Nature of Maps. Essays in the History of Cartography*, ed. P. Laxton, Baltimore, MD: Johns Hopkins University Press.

Harlow, B. and Carter, M. 1999 *Imperialism and Orientalism: A Documentary Sourcebook*, Oxford: Blackwell.

Harper, M. 1999 'British Migration and the Peopling of Empire', in A. Porter (ed.), *The Oxford History of the British Empire*, vol. III: *The Nineteenth Century*. Oxford: Oxford University Press, 74–87.

Harris, R. C. 1977 'The Simplification of Europe Overseas', *Annals of the Association of American Geographers*, 67, 4, 469–83.

2002 *Making Native Space. Colonialism, Resistance and Reserves in British Columbia*, Vancouver: University of British Columbia Press.

2004 'How Did Colonialism Dispossess? Comments from an Edge of Empire', *Annals of the Association of American Geographers*, 94, 1, 165–82.

Harrison, M. 2005 'Science and the British Empire', *Isis*, 96, 56–63.

Hartwig, C. W. 1991a 'Sierra Leone', in J. S. Olsen (ed.), *Historical Dictionary of European Imperialism*, Westport, CT: Greenwood Press, 554–6.

1991b 'French West Africa', in J. S. Olson (ed.), *Historical Dictionary of European Imperialism*, Westport, CT: Greenwood Press, 235–6.

Harvey, D. 2003 *The New Imperialism*, Oxford: Oxford University Press.

Hastings, A. 1994 *The Church in Africa 1450–1950*, Oxford: Oxford University Press.

Haynes, W. T. 1991 'Ferry, Jules François Camille', in J. S. Olsen (ed.), *Historical Dictionary of European Imperialism*, Westport, CT: Greenwood Press, 214–16.

Headrick, D. R. 1988 *The Tentacles of Progress. Technology Transfer in the Age of Imperialism 1850–1940*, Oxford: Oxford University Press.

Heathcote, R. L. 1975 *Australia*, London: Longman.

    1991 'Australia', in G. S. Dunbar, *Modern Geography. An Encyclopedic Survey*, London: St James Press, 6–8.

Hechter, M. 1975 *Internal Colonialism: The Celtic Fringe in British National Development, 1536–1966*, London: Routledge.

Heffernan, M. J. 1989 'The Parisian Poor and the Colonization of Algeria during the Second Republic', *French History*, 3, 4, 377–403.

    1994a 'The Science of Empire: The French Geographical Movement and the Forms of French Imperialism, 1870–1920', in A. Godlewska and N. Smith (eds.), *Geography and Empire*, Oxford: Blackwell, 92–114.

    1994b 'A State Scholarship: The Political Geography of French International Science during the Nineteenth Century', *Transactions, Institute of British Geographers* new series, 19, 21–45.

    1995a 'French Colonial Migration', in R. Cohen (ed.), *The Cambridge Survey of World Migration*, Cambridge: Cambridge University Press, 33–8.

    1995b 'The Spoils of War: The Société de Géographie de Paris and the French Empire', in M. Bell, R. A. Butlin and M. J. Heffernan (eds.), *Geography and Imperialism 1880–1940*, Manchester: Manchester University Press, 221–64.

    1998a 'The Changing Political Map: Geography, Geopolitics, and the Idea of Europe since 1500', in R. A. Butlin and R. A. Dodgshon (eds.), *An Historical Geography of Europe*, Oxford: Clarendon Press, 140–80.

    1998b 'Geographical Societies', in G. Good (ed.), *Sciences of the Earth: An Encyclopedia of Events, People, and Phenomena*, vol. I, New York: Garland, 273–7.

    1998c *The Meaning of Europe: Geography and Geopolitics*, London: Arnold.

    2001 '"A Dream as Frail as those of Ancient Time": The Incredible Geographies of Timbuctoo', *Environment and Planning D: Society and Space*, 19, 2, 203–25.

    2003 'Histories of Geography', in S. L. Holloway, S. P. Rice and G. Valentine (eds.), *Key Concepts in Geography*, London: Sage, 3–22.

    2004 'Commercial Geography and Inter-war French Politics: Louis Marin and the Société de Géographie Commerciale de Paris', in A. R. H. Baker (ed.), *Home and Colonial. Essays on Landscape, Ireland, Environment and Empire in Celebration of Robin Butlin's Contribution to Historical Geography*, London: Royal Geographical Society/Institute of British Geographers, Historical Geography Research Series 39, 180–97.

Henderson, W. O. 1993 *The German Colonial Empire 1884–1919*, London: Frank Cass.

Hepper, F. N. 1986 'Jardin des Plantes', in G. Jellicoe, S. Jellicoe, P. Goode and M. Lancaster (eds.), *The Oxford Companion to Gardens*, Oxford: Oxford University Press, 299–300.

Heuman, G. 1999 'The British West Indies', in A. Porter (ed.), *The Oxford History of the British Empire*, vol. III: *The Nineteenth Century*, Oxford: Oxford University Press, 470–93.

Ho, E. 2004 'Empire through Diasporic Eyes: A View from the Other Boat', *Comparative Studies in Society and History*, 46, 210–46.

Hobson, J. 1902 *Imperialism: A Study*, London: James Nisbet.

Hochschild, A. 1998 *King Leopold's Ghost*, New York: Houghton Mifflin.

Hoffenburg, P. H. 2001 *An Empire on Display: English, Indian, and Australian Exhibitions from the Crystal Palace to the Great War*, Berkeley: University of California Press.

Hoisington, W. A. 1995 *Lyautey and the French Conquest of Morocco*, Basingstoke: Macmillan.

Holdich, T. H. 1901 *The Indian Borderland 1880–1900*, London: Methuen.

Honigsbaum, M. 2001 *The Fever Trail: The Hunt for the Cure for Malaria*, London: Macmillan.

Hopkins, A. G. 2002a 'Introduction: Globalization – an Agenda for Historians', in A. G. Hopkins (ed.), *Globalization in World History*, London: Pimlico, 1–10.

2002b 'The History of Globalization – and the Globalization of History', in A. G. Hopkins (ed.), *Globalization in World History*, London: Pimlico, 11–46.

Houben, V. J. H. 2003 'Southeast Asia and Islam', *Annals of the American Academy of Political and Social Science*, 58, 8, 149–70.

Howe, S. 2000 *Ireland and Empire: Colonial Legacies in Irish History and Culture*, Oxford: Oxford University Press.

2002 *Imperialism. A Very Short Introduction*, Oxford: Oxford University Press.

Howell, P. 2000 'Prostitution and Racialised Sexuality: The Regulation of Prostitution in Britain and the British Empire before the Contagious Diseases Acts', *Environment and Planning D: Society and* Space, 18, 321–39.

2004: 'Sexuality, Sovereignty and Space: Law, Government and the Geography of Prostitution in Colonial Gibraltar', *Social History*, 29, 444–64.

2005 'Prostitution and the Place of Empire: Regulation and Repeal in Hong Kong and the British Imperial Network', in L. J. Proudfoot and M. M. Roche (eds.), *(Dis)Placing Empire. Regulating British Colonial Geographies*, Aldershot: Ashgate, 175–97.

Hudson, B. 1977 'The New Geography and the New Imperialism, 1870–1918', *Antipode*, 9, 12–19.

Hughes, M. J. and Phillips, N. 2001 'Evolution of the Victorian Gold Province: Geological and Historical', *Victorian Historical Journal*, special issue on 'Victoria, 150 Years of Gold', 72, 1–2, 134–58.

Hugill, P. J. 1993 *World Trade since 1431*, Baltimore, MD: Johns Hopkins University Press.

1999 *Global Communications since 1844. Geopolitics and Technology*, Baltimore, MD: Johns Hopkins University Press.

2005 'Trading States, Territorial States, and Technology. Mackinder's Contribution to the Discourse on States and Polities', in B. W. Blouet (ed.), *Global Geostrategy: Mackinder and the Defence of the West*, London: Frank Cass, 107–24.

Hugon, A. 1993 *The Exploration of Africa from Cairo to the Cape*, London: Thames and Hudson.

Hull, I. V. 2005 'The Military Campaign in German Southwest Africa, 1904–1907', *German Historical Institute Bulletin*, 37, 39–44.

Huxley, E. 1941 *East Africa*, London: William Collins.

1998 'Introduction', to Mary Kingsley, *Travels in West Africa*, 3rd edn, London: Dent, Everyman Classic, 1–10.

Hyam, R. 1988 'Empire and Sexual Opportunity', *Journal of Imperial and Commonwealth History*, 17, 83–9.

1990 *Empire and Sexuality: The British Experience*, Manchester: Manchester University Press.

Ilahi, S. 2003 'The Radcliffe Boundary Commission and the Fate of Kashmir', *India Review*, 2, 1, 77–102.

Ileto, R. 1994 'Religion and Anti-Colonial Movements', in N. Tarling (ed.), *The Cambridge History of Southeast Asia*, vol. II, part 1: *From c.1800 to the 1930s*, Cambridge: Cambridge University Press, 193–244.

Iliffe, J. 1995 *Africans: The History of a Continent*, Cambridge: Cambridge University Press.

Imhoff, E. van 2004 'Education at Home: The Age-Specific Pattern of Migration between the Netherlands and the Former Dutch East Indies around 1930', *Demographic Research*, 11, 12, 335–56.

Irwin, I. 2006 *For Lust of Knowing: The Orientalists and their Enemies*, London: Penguin.

Ishemo, S. L. 1995 'Forced Labour and Migration in Portugal's African Colonies', in R. Cohen (ed.), *The Cambridge Survey of World Migration*, Cambridge: Cambridge University Press, 162–5.

Jackson, S. P. 1978 'The South African Geographical Society, 1917–1977', *South African Geographical Journal*, 60, 1, 3–12.

James, D. and Schrauwers, A. 2003 'An Apartheid of Souls: Dutch and Afrikaner Colonialism and its Aftermath in Indonesia and South Africa – an Introduction', *Itinerario*, 47, 3–4, 49–80.

James, L. 1994 *The Rise and Fall of the British Empire*, London: Abacus.

Jeal, T. 1996 'David Livingstone: a Brief Biographical Account', in J. M. MacKenzie (ed.), *David Livingstone and the Victorian Encounter with Africa*, London: National Portrait Gallery, 11–78.

2007 *Stanley: The Impossible Life of Africa's Greatest Explorer*, London: Faber.

Jennings, E. T. 2005 'Visions and Representations of French Empire' [review article], *Journal of Modern History*, 77, 701–21.

Jepson, P. and Whittaker, R.J. 2002 'Histories of Protected Areas: Internationalisation of Conservationist Values and their Adoption in the Netherlands Indies (Indonesia)', *Environment and History*, 8, 129–72.

Johnson, N.C. 2006 'Cultivating Science and Planting Beauty: The Spaces of Display in Cambridge's Botanical Gardens', *Interdisciplinary Science Reviews*, 31, 1, 42–57.

Jones, M. 2002 'Measuring the World: Exploration, Empire and the Reform of the Royal Geographical Society, *c.* 1874–93', in M. Daunton (ed.), *The Organisation of Knowledge in Victorian Britain*, Oxford: Oxford University Press for the British Academy, 313–35.

2003 *The Last Great Quest. Captain Scott's Antarctic Sacrifice*, Oxford: Oxford University Press.

Kain, R.J.P. and Delano-Smith, C. 2003 'Geography Displayed: Maps and Mapping', in R. Johnston and M. Williams (eds.), *A Century of British Geography*, Oxford: Oxford University Press for the British Academy, 371–428.

Kaminsky, A.P. 1991 'India', in J.S. Olsen (ed.), *Historical Dictionary of European Imperialism*, Westport, CT: Greenwood Press, 302.

Katz, R.W. 2001 'Sir Gilbert Walker and a Connection between El Niño and Statistics', *Statistical Science*, 17, 1, 97–112.

Katzenellenbogen, S. 1996 'It Didn't Happen at Berlin: Politics, Economics and Ignorance in the Setting of Africa's Colonial Boundaries', in P. Nugent and A.I. Asiwaju (eds.), *African Boundaries: Barriers, Conduits and Opportunities*, London: Pinter, 21–31.

Kearns, G. 1993 'Fin de Siècle Geopolitics: Mackinder, Hobson and Theories of Global Closure', in P.J. Taylor (ed.), *Political Geography of the Twentieth Century*, London: Bellhaven Press, 9–30.

2003 'Nation, Empire and Cosmopolis: Ireland and the Break with Britain', in D. Gilbert, D. Matless and B. Short (eds.), *Geographies of British Modernity*, Oxford: Blackwell, 204–28.

2008 'Mapping Irish Colonialism: A Round Table', *Journal of Historical Geography*, 1, 138–44.

Kearnshaw, R.N. 1925 revision of J. D. Roger, *Australia*, vol. VI of C. P. Lucas (ed.), *A Historical Geography of the British Dominions*, Oxford: Clarendon Press.

Keay, K.J. 2000a *India: A History*, London: HarperCollins.

2000b *The Great Arc*, London: HarperCollins.

2005a 'The Mekong Exploration Commission, 1886–88: Anglo-French Rivalry in South-East Asia', *Asian Affairs*, 36, 3, 289–312.

2005b *Mad about the Mekong. Exploration and Empire in South-East Asia*, London: HarperCollins.

Kelly, M. 2006 'Introduction' to special issue on 'Writers, Intellectuals and the Colonial Experience', *French Cultural Studies*, 17, 2, 131–5.

Keltie, J. S. 1893 *The Partition of Africa*, London: Edward Stanford.

Kennedy, D. 1996 'Imperial History and Post-Colonial Theory', *Journal of Imperial and Commonwealth History*, 24, 3, 345–63.

2005 *The Highly Civilized Man. Richard Burton and the Victorian World*, Cambridge, MA: Harvard University Press.

2007 'British Exploration in the Nineteenth Century: A Historiographic Survey', *History Compass*, 5, 6, 1879–1900.

Kennedy, P. 1989 *The Rise and Fall of the Great Powers. Economic Change and Military Conflict from 1500 to 2000*, London: Fontana.

Kenny, R. 2007 *The Lamb Enters the Dreaming: Nathanael Pepper and the Ruptured World*, Carlton North, Victoria, Australia: Scribe Publications.

Kern, S. 1983 *The Culture of Time and Space, 1880–1918*, Cambridge, MA: Harvard University Press.

Kerr, I. J. 1997 *Building the Railways of the Raj 1850–1900*, Delhi: Oxford University Press.

2001 'Introduction', in I. J. Kerr (ed.), *Railways in Modern India*, Delhi: Oxford University Press, 1–78.

2003 'Representation and Representations of the Railways of Colonial and Post-Colonial South Asia', *Modern Asian Studies*, 37, 2, 287–326.

Kertzer, D. I. and Arel, D. 2002 'Censuses, Identity Formation, and the Struggle for Political Power', in D. I. Kertzer and D. Arel (eds.), *Census and Identity: The Politics of Race, Ethnicity and Language in National Censuses*, Cambridge: Cambridge University Press.

Killingray, D. 1994 'The Influenza Pandemic of 1918–1919 in the British Caribbean', *Social History of Medicine*, 7, 1, 59–87.

Killingray, D. and Roberts, A. 1989 'An Outline History of Photography in Africa to ca. 1940', *History in Africa*, 16, 197–208.

King, A. D. 1976 *Colonial Urban Development: Culture, Social Power and Environment*, London: Routledge.

1999 '(Post)Colonial Geographies: Material and Symbolic', *Historical Geography*, 27, 99–118.

King, R. 2005 'Orientalism and the Study of Religions', in J. R. Hinnells (ed.), *The Routledge Companion to the Study of Religion*, Abingdon: Routledge, 275–90.

Kingsley, M. 1998 *Travels in West Africa*, 3rd edn, London: Dent, Everyman Classic.

Klotz, M. 2005 'The Weimar Republic. A Postcolonial State in a Still-Colonial World', in E. Ames, M. Klotz and L. Wildenthal (eds.), *Germany's Colonial Pasts*, Lincoln: University of Nebraska Press, 135–47.

Knox, P. and Agnew, J. 1989 *The Geography of the World Economy*, London: Arnold.

Kraly, E. P. and McQuilton, J. 2005 '"The Protection" of Aborigines in Colonial and Early Federation Australia: The Role of Population Data Systems', *Population, Space and Place*, 11, 225–50.

Krüger, G. 2005 'Coming to Terms with the Past', *German Historical Institute Bulletin*, 37, 45–9.

Kuczynski, R. R. 1937 *Colonial Populations*, London: Humphrey Milford.

Kumar, D. 1997 'Colonialism and Science in India', in H. Selin (ed.), *Encyclopaedia of the History of Science, Technology, and Medicine in Non-Western Cultures*, Dordrecht: Kluwer Academic, 223–5.

2006 *Science and the Raj*, 2nd edn, New Delhi: Oxford University Press.

Kumar, M. S. 2005 '"Oriental Sore" or "Public Nuisance": The Regulation of Prostitution in Colonial India', in L. J. Proudfoot and M. M. Roche (eds.), *(Dis)Placing Empire. Regulating British Colonial Geographies*, Aldershot: Ashgate, 155–74.

Laffey, J. F. 1969 'Roots of French Imperialism in the Nineteenth Century', *French Historical Studies*, 6, 78–92.

1974 'Municipal Imperialism in Nineteenth-Century France', *Historical Reflections/Réflexions Historiques*, 1, 81–114.

1975 'The Lyon Chamber of Commerce and Indochina during the Third Republic', *Canadian Journal of History*, 10, 325–48.

Lamb, C. 2000 *The Africa House*, London: Penguin.

Lambert, A. 1995 'The Shield of Empire, 1815–1895', in J. R. Hill and B. Raft (eds.), *The Oxford Illustrated History of the Royal Navy*, Oxford: Oxford University Press, 161–99.

Lambert, D. 2005 *White Creole Culture, Politics and Identity during the Age of Abolition*, Cambridge: Cambridge University Press.

Lambert, D. and Lester, A. 2004 'Geographies of Colonial Philanthropy', *Progress in Human Geography*, 28, 3, 320–41.

2006 'Introduction. Imperial Spaces, Imperial Subjects', in D. Lambert and A. Lester (eds.), *Colonial Lives across the British Empire. Imperial Careering in the Long Nineteenth Century*, Cambridge: Cambridge University Press, 1–31.

Lane, S. 2008 'Editorial: Living with Hazard and Risk', *Geography*, 93, 2, 66–8.

Larkin, J. A. 1982 'Philippine History Reconsidered: A Socioeconomic Perspective', *American Historical Review*, 87, 3, 595–628.

Legg, S. 2003 'Gendered Politics and Nationalised Homes: Women and the Anti-Colonial Struggle in Delhi, 1930–47', *Gender, Place and Culture*, 10, 7–27.

2005 'Foucault's Population Geographies: Classifications, Biopolitics and Government Spaces', *Population, Space and Place*, 11, 3, 137–56.

2007 *Spaces of Colonisation. Delhi's Urban Governmentalities*, Oxford: Blackwell.

Lejeune, D. 1993 *Les sociétés de géographie en France et l'expansion coloniale au XIXe siècle*, Paris: Albin.

Lenin, V. I. 1948 *Imperialism: The Highest Stage of Capitalism*, new edn, London: Lawrence and Wishart.

Lester, A. 1998 *From Colonization to Democracy. A New Historical Geography of South Africa*, London: I. B. Tauris.

2000, 'Historical Geographies of Imperialism', in C. Nash and B. J. Graham (eds.), *Modern Historical Geographies*, London: Prentice Hall, 100–20.

2001 *Imperial Networks. Creating Identities in Nineteenth-Century South Africa and Britain*, London: Routledge.

2004 'Trans-Imperial Networks: Britain, South Africa, Australia and New Zealand during the First Half of the Nineteenth Century', in A. R. H. Baker (ed.), *Home and Colonial. Essays on Landscape, Ireland, Environment and Empire in Celebration of Robin Butlin's Contribution to Historical geography*, London: Royal Geographical Society – Institute of British Geographers, Historical Geography Research Series 39, 125–38.

2005 'Humanitarians and White Settlers in the Nineteenth Century', in N. Etherington (ed.), *Missions and Empire*, Oxford: Oxford University Press, 64–85.

2006 'Colonial Networks, Australian Humanitarianism and the History Wars', *Geographical Research* (formerly *Australian Geographical Studies*), 44, 3, 229–41.

Lever, C. 1992 *They Dined on Eland. The Story of the Acclimatisation Societies*, London: Quiller Press.

Levine, P. 2003 *Prostitution, Race and Politics: Policing Venereal Disease in the British Empire*, London: Routledge.

2007 *The British Empire. Sunrise to Sunset*, Harlow: Pearson Longman.

Limoncelli, S. A. 2006 'International Voluntary Associations, Local Social Movements and State Paths to the Abolition of Regulated Prostitution in Europe, 1875–1950', *International Sociology*, 21, 1, 31–59.

Livingstone, D. 1987 'Human Acclimatization: Perspectives on a Contested Field of Inquiry in Science, Medicine and Geography', *History of Science*, 24, 359–93.

1991 'The Moral Discourse of Climate: Historical Considerations on Race, Place and Virtue', *Journal of Historical Geography*, 17, 413–34.

1992 *The Geographical Tradition*, Oxford: Blackwell.

1994 'Climate's Moral Economy: Science, Race and Place in Post-Darwinian British and American Geography', in A. Godlewska and Neil Smith (eds.), *Geography and Empire*, London: Blackwell, 132–54.

2003 *Putting Science in its Place*, Chicago: University of Chicago Press.

Lloyd, T. O. 1984 *The British Empire 1558–1983*, Oxford: Oxford University Press.

Lonsdale, J. 1999 'East Africa', in J. M. Brown and W. R. Louis (eds.), *The Oxford History of the British Empire*, vol. IV: *The Twentieth Century*, Oxford: Oxford University Press, 530–44.

Lorcin, P. 2004 'Teaching Women and Gender in France d'Outre-Mer: Problems and Strategies', *French Historical Studies*, 27, 2, 293–310.

Louis, W. R. 2006 *Ends of British Imperialism*, London: I. B. Tauris.

Low, E. C. 1991 'Chad', in J. S. Olson (ed.), *Historical Dictionary of European Imperialism*, Westport, CT: Greenwood Press, 123–4.

Low-Beer, D., Smallman-Raynor, M. and Cliff, A. 2004 'Disease and Death in the South African War. Changing Disease Patterns from Soldiers to Refugees', *Social History of Medicine*, 17, 2, 223–45.

Lowenthal, D. 1997 'Empires and Ecologies: Reflections on Environmental History', in T. Griffiths and L. Robin (eds.), *Ecology and Empire: Environmental History of Settler Societies*, Edinburgh: Keele University Press, 229–36.

Lucassen, L. 2007 'Migration and World History: Reaching a New Frontier', *International Review of Social History*, 52, 89–96.

Lutyens, M. 1991 *Edwin Lutyens*, London: Black Swan.

Lynn, M. 1991a 'British Expansion in West Africa: The Gold Coast and Nigeria, 1840–1914', 'British Expansion in East Africa – *c*. 1840–*c*. 1914', both in A.N. Porter (ed.), *Atlas of British Overseas Expansion*, London: Routledge, 105–9.

    1991b 'British Policy, Trade, and Informal Empire in the Mid-Nineteenth Century', in A. Porter (ed.), *The Oxford History of the British Empire,* vol. III: *The Nineteenth Century*, Oxford: Oxford University Press, 101–21.

McAloon, J. 2002 'Gentlemanly Capitalism and Settler Capitalists: Imperialism, Dependent Development and Colonial Wealth in the South Island of New Zealand', *Australian Economic History Review*, 42, 2, 204–23.

McCaskie, T.C. 2004 'Cultural Encounters: Britain and Africa in the Nineteenth Century', in P.D. Morgan and S. Hawkins (eds.), *Black Experience and the Empire*, Oxford: Oxford University Press, 166–93.

McCracken, D.P. 1997 *Gardens of Empire: Botanical Institutions of the Victorian British Empire*, Leicester: Leicester University Press.

McCrone, D. 1997 'Unmasking Britannia: The Rise and Fall of British National Identity', *Nations and Nationalism*, 3, 4, 579–96.

McEwan, C. 1995 ' "The Mother of all the Peoples": Geographical Knowledge and the Empowering of Mary Slessor', in M. Bell, R.A. Butlin and M.J. Heffernan (eds.), *Geography and Imperialism 1820–1940*, Manchester: Manchester University Press, 125–50.

    2000 *Gender, Geography and Empire. Victorian Women Travellers in West Africa*, Aldershot: Ashgate.

McGibbon, I. (ed.) 1997 *New Zealand Historical Atlas*, Auckland: Bateman.

Macinnis, P. 2007: *Australia's Pioneers, Heroes and Fools. The Trials, Tribulations and Tricks of the Trade of Australia's Colonial Explorers*, Sydney: Pier 9.

Mackay, D. 1985 *In the Wake of Cook: Exploration, Science and Empire, 1780–1801*, London: Croom Helm.

    1997 'The Kauri Harvest. Timber and Gum in the North, 1860s to 1920s', in M. McKinnon (ed.), *New Zealand Historical Atlas*, Auckland: Bateman, plate 48.

McKay, J. 2004 *Showing Off. Queensland at World Expositions 1862 to 1988*, Rockhampton: Central Queensland University Press and the Queensland Museum.

MacKenzie, J. M. 1984 'The Imperial Exhibitions', in J. M. MacKenzie, *Propaganda and Empire. The Manipulation of British Public Opinion, 1880–1960*, Manchester: Manchester University Press, 97–119.

1988 *The Empire of Nature. Hunting, Conservation and British Imperialism*, Manchester: Manchester University Press.

1995a *Orientalism. History, Theory and the Arts*, Manchester: Manchester University Press.

1995b 'The Provincial Geographical Societies in Britain, 1884–1894', in M. Bell, R. A. Butlin and M. J. Heffernan (eds.), *Geography and Imperialism 1820–1940*, Manchester: Manchester University Press, 231–43.

1997 'Empire and the Ecological Apocalypse: The Historiography of the Imperial Environment', in T. Griffiths and L. Robbin (eds.), *Ecology and Empire*, Keele: Keele University Press, 215–28.

1999 '"The Second City of the Empire": Glasgow – Imperial Municipality', in F. Driver and D. Gilbert (eds.), *Imperial Cities*, Manchester: Manchester University Press, 215–37.

Mckenzie, C. 2005 '"Sadly neglected" – Hunting and Gendered Identities: A Study in Gender Construction', *International Journal of the History of Sport*, 22, 4, 545–62.

McKeown, A. 2004 'Global Migration, 1846–1940', *Journal of World History*, 15, 2, 155–89.

Mackinnon, R. 2003 'Roads, Cart Tracks and Bridle Paths: Land Transportation and the Domestic Economy of Mid-Nineteenth-Century Eastern British North America', *Canadian Historical Review*, 94, 2, 1–23.

McKinnon, M. 1997 'Gold Rushes and Goldfields', in I. McGibbon (ed.), *New Zealand Historical Atlas*, Auckland: Bateman, 43–4.

MacLeod, R. 1982 'On Visiting the "Moving Metropolis": Reflections on the Architecture of Imperial Science', *Historical Records of Australia*, 5, 1–16.

2000 'Introduction' to special issue on *Nature and Empire: Science and the Colonial Enterprise*, *Osiris* 2nd series, 15, 5, 1–13.

Macmaster, N. 1995, 'Labour Migration in French North Africa', in R. Cohen, (ed.), *The Cambridge Survey of World Migration*, Cambridge: Cambridge University Press, 190–5.

McNeill, J. R. 2003 'Observations on the Nature and Culture of Environmental History', *History and Theory*, 42, 5–43.

Maddrell, A. 1996 'Empire, Emigration and School Geography: Changing Discourses of Imperial Citizenship', *Journal of Historical Geography*, 22, 373–87.

Madeira, A. I. 2005 'Portuguese, French and British Discourses on Colonial Education: Church–State Relations, School Expansion and Missionary Competition in Africa, 1890–1930', *Paedagogica Historica*, 41, 1–2, 31–60.

Marechal, P. 2005 'La controverse sur Léopold II et le Congo dans la littérature et les médias. Réflexions critiques', in J.-L. Velluc (ed.), *La mémoire du Congo. Le temps colonial*, Brussels: Musée Royal de L'Afrique Centrale, Tervuren, 43–50.

Marlay, R. 1991a 'Sumatra', in J.S. Olsen (ed.), *Historical Dictionary of European Imperialism*, Westport, CT: Greenwood Press, 594–6.

    1991b 'Dutch East Indies' in J. S. Olson (ed.), *Historical Dictionary of European Imperialism*, Westport, CT: Greenwood Press, 183–5.

    1991c 'Ceylon', in J.S. Olson (ed.), *Historical Dictionary of European Imperialism*, Westport, CT: Greenwood Press, 588–9.

Marsot, A.G. 1991a 'Egypt', in J.S. Olsen (ed.), *Historical Dictionary of European Imperialism*, Westport, CT: Greenwood Press, 193–5.

    1991b 'Algeria', in J.S. Olsen (ed.), *Historical Dictionary of European Imperialism*, Westport, CT: Greenwood Press, 9–12.

    1991c 'Morocco', in J.S. Olsen (ed.), *Historical Dictionary of European Imperialism*, Westport, CT: Greenwood Press, 411–13.

Martin, D. 2006 'Missions and Empire', *Journal of Religion in Africa*, 36, 2, 224–30.

Martin, G. 1999 'Canada from 1815', in A. Porter (ed.), *The Oxford History of the British Empire*, vol. III: *The Nineteenth Century*, Oxford: Oxford University Press, 522–45.

Martin, P.M. 1995 *Leisure and Society in Colonial Brazzaville*, Cambridge: Cambridge University Press.

Mason, K. (ed.) 1944 *The Belgian Congo*, London: Naval Intelligence Division, Geographical Handbook Series.

Massey, D. 2005 *For Space*, London: Sage.

Meinig, D.W. 1982 'Geographical Analysis of Imperial Expansion', in A.R.H. Baker and M. Billinge (eds.), *Period and Place. Research Methods in Historical Geography*, Cambridge: Cambridge University Press, 71–8.

    1986 *The Shaping of America: A Geographical Perspective on 500 Years of History*, vol. I: *Atlantic America, 1492–1800*, New Haven, CT: Yale University Press.

    1993 *The Shaping of America: A Geographical Perspective on 500 Years of History*, vol. II: *Continental America, 1800–1867*, New Haven, CT: Yale University Press.

    1998 *The Shaping of America: A Geographical Perspective on 500 Years of History*, vol. III: *Transcontinental America, 1850–1915*, New Haven, CT: Yale University Press.

    2004 *The Shaping of America: A Geographical Perspective on 500 Years of History*, vol. IV: *Global America, 1915–2000*, New Haven, CT: Yale University Press.

Michaud, J.L. 1991a 'The Gambia', in J.S. Olsen (ed.), *Historical Dictionary of European Imperialism*, Westport, CT: Greenwood Press, 241–2.

    1991b 'Uganda', in J.S. Olsen (ed.), *Historical Dictionary of European Imperialism*, Westport, CT: Greenwood Press, 642.

Middleton, D. 1991a 'Women in Africa', in J. Keay (ed.), *The Royal Geographical Society History of World Exploration*, London: Paul Hamlyn, 102–3.

1991b 'Africa', in J. Keay (ed.), *History of World Exploration*, New York: Mallard Press, 89–127.

Mill, H. R. 1930 *The Record of the Royal Geographical Society 1830–1930*, London: Royal Geographical Society.

Mitchell, T. 1988 *Colonising Egypt*, Cambridge: Cambridge University Press.

Mohapatra, P. P. 2007 'Eurocentrism, Forced Labour, and Global Migration', *International Review of Social History*, 52, 110–15.

Montefiore, A. 1913 *H. M. Stanley the African Explorer*, 9th edn, London: Partridge.

Moor, J. de 1998 'Annual Review of Dutch Expansion Studies', *Itinerario*, 22, 4, 106–20.

Morgan, P. D. and Hawkins, S. 2004 'Blacks and the British Empire: An Introduction', in P. D. Morgan and S. Hawkins (eds.), *Black Experience and the Empire*, Oxford: Oxford University Press, 1–34.

Mosse, D. 2003 *The Rule of Water. Statecraft, Ecology, and Collective Action in South India*, New Delhi: Oxford University Press.

Muller, J. 1953 'History of the South African Geographical Society', *South African Geographical Journal*, 35, 3–15.

Naranch, B. D. 2005 'Inventing the Auslandsdeutsche. Emigration, Colonial Fantasy, and German National Identity, 1848–71', in E. Ames, M. Klotz and L. Wildenthal (eds.), *Germany's Colonial Pasts*, Lincoln: University of Nebraska Press, 21–40.

Newby, E. (ed.) 1975 *The World Atlas of Exploration*, London: Mitchell Beazley.

Newitt, M. 1995 *A History of Mozambique*, London: C. H. Hurst.

Nicholls, N. 1997 'What are the Potential Contributions of El Niño–Southern Oscillation Research to Early Warning of Potential Acute Food-Deficit Situations?', *Internet Journal of African Studies*, 2, available at: www.bradford.ac.uk/research/ijas/ijasno2/nicholls.html.

Nicolai, H. 1994 'Les géographes belges et le Congo', in M. Bruneau and D. Dory (eds.), *Géographies des colonisations: XVe–XXe siècles*, Paris: L'Harmattan, 51–67.

Nimschowski, H. 1986 'Semi-Colonial Expansion into Morocco 1871–1898', in H. Stoecker (ed.), *German Imperialism in Africa from the Beginnings until the Second World War*, London: C. Hurst, 127–35.

2004 'Geography in Belgium', *Belgeo*, 1, 33–44.

Nobles, M. 2002 'Racial Categorization and Censuses', in D. I. Kirtzer and D. Arel (eds.), *Census and Identity: The Politics of Race, Ethnicity, and Language in National Censuses*, Cambridge: Cambridge University Press, 43–70.

Nogué, J. and Villanova, J. L. 2002 'Spanish Colonialism in Morocco and the Sociedad Geografica in Madrid', *Journal of Historical Geography*, 28, 1, 1–20.

Nordmeyer, W. 1998 *Die Geographische Gesellschaft in Hamburg 1873–1918. Geographie zwischen Politik und Kommerz*, Mitteilungen der geographische Gesellschaft in Hamburg, Band 88, Hamburg: Geographische Gesellschaft.

Northrup, D. 1999 'Migration from Africa, Asia, and the South Pacific', in A. Porter (ed.), *The Oxford History of the British Empire*, vol. III: *The Nineteenth Century*, Oxford: Oxford University Press, 88–100.

Nowell, C. E. 1982 *The Rose-Coloured Map: Portugal's Attempt to Build an African Empire from the Atlantic to the Indian Ocean*, Lisbon: Junta da Investigacões Científicas do Ultramar.

Nugent, P. 1996 'Arbitrary Lines and the People's Minds: A Dissenting View on Colonial Boundaries in West Africa', in P. Nugent and A. I. Asiwaju (eds.), *African Boundaries, Barriers, Conduits and Opportunities*, London: Pinter/ Cassell, 35–67.

O'Brien, P. P. 2001 'The Titan Refreshed: Imperial Overstretch and the British Navy before the First World War', *Past and Present*, 172, 146–69.

Oddie, G. A. 2001 'Indian Christians and National Identity, 1870–1947', *Journal of Religious History*, 25, 3, 346–66.

Office of Population Research, 1945 'French Indo-China: Demographic Imbalance and Colonial Policy', *Population Index*, 11, 2, 68–71.

Ogborn, M. 1998 *Spaces of Modernity. London's Geographies 1680–1780*, New York: Guildford Press.

Ogden, P. E. 1998 'Changes in Population and Society, 1500 to the Present', in R. A. Butlin and R. A. Dodgshon (eds.), *An Historical Geography of Europe*, Oxford: Clarendon Press, 182–8.

O'Hara, S., Heffernan, M. and Endfield, G. 2005 'Halford Mackinder, the "Geographical Pivot", and British Perceptions of Central Asia', in B. W. Blouet (ed.), *Global Geostrategy: Mackinder and the Defence of the West*, London: Cass, 90–106.

Olson, J. S. 1991a 'Réunion', in J. S. Olson (ed.), *Historical Dictionary of European Imperialism*, Westport, CT: Greenwood Press, 521.

1991b 'Mauritius', in J. S. Olson (ed.), *Historical Dictionary of European Imperialism*, Westport, CT: Greenwood Press, 401–2.

1991c 'Portuguese Empire', in J. S. Olson (ed.), *Historical Dictionary of European Imperialism*, Westport, CT: Greenwood Press, 502–4.

1991d 'Spanish Empire', in J. S. Olson (ed.), *Historical Dictionary of European Imperialism*, Westport, CT: Greenwood Press, 580–2.

1991e 'Malaysia', in J. S. Olson (ed.), *Historical Dictionary of European Imperialism*, Westport, CT: Greenwood Press, 384–5.

Omissi, D. E. 1990 *Air Power and Colonial Control: The Royal Air Force, 1919– 1939*, Manchester: Manchester University Press.

Opoku, K. A. 1990a 'Religion in Africa during the Colonial Era', in A. A. Boahen (ed.), *General History of Africa*, abridged edn, vol. VII: *Africa under Colonial Domination 1880–1935*, London: James Currey, 217–28.

1990b 'Colonialism in Africa: Its Impact and Significance', in A. A. Boahen (ed.), *General History of Africa*, abridged edn, vol. VII: *Africa under Colonial Domination 1880–1935*, London: James Currey, 327–39.

Osborne, B.S. 2003 'Constructing the State, Managing the Corporation, Transforming the Individual: Photography, Immigration and the Canadian National Railways', in J.M. Schwartz and J.R. Ryan (eds.), *Picturing Place. Photography and the Geographical Imagination*, London: I. B. Tauris, 162–91.

Osborne, M.A. 2000 'Acclimatizing the World: A History of the Paradigmatic Colonial Science', *Osiris* 2nd series, 15, 135–51.

Österhammel, J. 1997 *Colonization: A Theoretical Overview*, Princeton, NJ: Wiener.

Pakenham, T. 1991 *The Scramble for Africa, 1876–1912*, London: Weidenfeld and Nicolson (Abacus).

1992 *The Boer War*, London: Abacus.

Palmer, A. 2000 *Colonial Genocide*, Adelaide: Crawford House.

Pandey, C. 2003 *Remembering Partition: Violence, Nationalism and History in India*, Cambridge: Cambridge University Press.

Pankhurst, R. 1966a 'The Great Ethiopian Famine of 1888–1892: A New Assessment, Part 1', *Journal of the History of Medicine and Allied Sciences*, 21, 95–124.

1966b 'The Great Ethiopian Famine of 1888–1892: A New Assessment, Part 2', *Journal of the History of Medicine and Allied Sciences*, 21, 271–94.

Park, C. 2005 'Religion and Geography', in J.R. Hinnells (ed.), *The Routledge Companion to the Study of Religion*, Abingdon: Routledge, 439–55.

Parker, M. 2007 *Panama Fever: The Battle to Build the Canal*, London: Hutchinson.

Pater, B. de 2001 'Geography and Geographers in the Netherlands since the 1870s: Serving Colonialism, Education, and the Welfare State', in G.A. Dunbar (ed.), *Geography: Discipline, Profession and Subject since 1870*, Amsterdam: Kluwer, 153–90.

Pawson, E. 1990 'British Expansion Overseas c. 1730–1914', in R.A. Dodgshon and R.A. Butlin (eds.), *An Historical Geography of England and Wales*, 2nd edn, London: Academic Press, 521–4.

Peake-Jones, K. 1985 *The Branch without a Tree. The Centenary History of the Royal Geographical Society of Australasia (South Australian Branch) Incorporated. 1885 to 1985*, Adelaide: Royal Geographical Society of Australasia.

Peluso, N.L. and Vandergeest, P. 2001 'Genealogies of the Political Forest and Customary Rights in Indonesia, Malaysia, and Thailand', *Journal of Asian Studies*, 60, 3, 761–812.

Peper, B, 1970 'Population Growth in Java in the 19th Century: A New Interpretation', *Population Studies*, 24, 1, 71–84.

Phillips, R. 1997 *Mapping Men and Empire. A Geography of Adventure*, London: Routledge.

2002 'Imperialism, Sexuality and Space. Purity Movements in the British Empire', in A. Blunt and C. McEwan (eds.), *Postcolonial Geographies*, London: Continuum, 46–63.

Philo, C. 2005 'Sex, Life, Death, Geography: Fragmentary Remarks Inspired by "Foucault's Population Geographies"', *Population, Space and Place*, 11, 325–33.

Pirie, G. 2004 'Passenger Traffic in the 1930s on British Imperial Air Routes: Refinement and Revision', *Journal of Transport History*, 25, 1, 63–83.

Ploszajska, T. 1999 *Geographical Education, Empire and Citizenship: Geographical Teaching and Learning in English Schools, 1870–1944*, London: Royal Geographical Society – Institute of British Geographers, Historical Geography Research Series.

   2000 'Historiographies of Geography and Empire', in B. Graham and C. Nash (eds.), *Modern Historical Geographies*, Harlow: Pearson Education, 121–45.

Pollock, A. 1991a 'Anglo-Egyptian Sudan', in J. S. Olsen (ed.), *Historical Dictionary of European Imperialism*, Westport, CT: Greenwood Press, 16–19.

   1991b 'Ethiopia', in J. S. Olson (ed.), *Historical Dictionary of European Imperialism*, Westport, CT: Greenwood Press, 203–5.

   1991c 'Mozambique', in J. S. Olson (ed.), *Historical Dictionary of European Imperialism*, Westport, CT: Greenwood Press, 414–16.

Pollock, N. C. and Agnew, S. 1963 *An Historical Geography of South Africa*, London: Longmans.

Porter, A. N. 1991a 'Britain and the Partition of Central Africa', in A. N. Porter (ed.), *Atlas of British Overseas Expansion*, London: Routledge, 114–16.

   1991b 'Communications: Imperial Airways, 1918–1950', in A. N. Porter (ed.), *Atlas of British Overseas Expansion*, London: Routledge, 163–7.

   1994 *European Imperialism 1860–1940*, London: Macmillan.

   1996 'Empires in the Mind', in P. J. Marshall (ed.), *The Cambridge Illustrated History of the British Empire*, Cambridge: Cambridge University Press, 185–22.

   1999 'Trusteeship, Anti-Slavery, and Humanitarianism', in A. Porter (ed.), *The Oxford History of the British Empire*, volume III: *The Nineteenth Century*, 198–221.

   2002 'An Overview, 1700–1914', in N. Etherington (ed.), *Missions and Empire, The Oxford History of the British Empire Companion Series*, Oxford: Oxford University Press, 40–63.

Porter, B. 1996 *The Lion's Share. A Short History of British Imperialism 1850–1995*, 3rd edn, Harlow: Addison Wesley, Longman.

   2004 *The Absent-Minded Imperialists. What the British Really Thought about Empire*, Oxford: Oxford University Press.

   2007 'Did He Puff his Crimes to Please a Bloodthirsty Readership?', Review of T. Jeal, *Stanley: The Impossible Life of Africa's Greatest Explorer*, London: Faber, in *The London Review of Books*, April, 9–10.

Powell, J. M. 1970 *The Public Lands of Australia Felix*, Melbourne: Oxford University Press.

   1976 *Environmental Management in Australia 1788–1914*, Melbourne: Oxford University Press.

1977 *Mirrors of the New World: Images and Image-Makers in the Settlement Process*, Folkestone: Dawson.

1986 'Approaching a Dig Tree: Reflections on our Endangered Expedition', *Australian Geographical Studies*, 23, 3–26.

1988a *An Historical Geography of Modern Australia: The Restive Fringe*, Cambridge: Cambridge University Press.

1988b 'Patrimony of the People: The Role of Government in Land Settlement', in R.L. Heathcote (ed.), *The Australian Experience: Essays in Australian Land Settlement and Resource Management*, Melbourne: Longman Cheshire, 14–24.

1993 'MDB': *The Emergence of Bioregionalism in the Murray-Darling Basin*, Canberra: Murray-Darling Basin Commission.

1995 'The Empire Meets the New Deal: Interwar Encounters in Conservation and Regional Planning', *Geographical Research*, 43, 4, 337–60.

1997 'Enterprise and Dependency: Water Management in Australia', in T. Griffiths and L. Robin (eds.), *Ecology and Empire: Environmental History of Settler Societies*, Edinburgh: Keele University Press, 102–21.

2000 'Historical Geographies of the Environment', in B. Graham and C. Nash (eds.), *Modern Historical Geographies*, London: Longman, 169–92.

2004 'Global, Local and Personal: Recent Transactions in Environmental History', *Australian Geography*, 35, 1, 111–17.

2007 '"Dominion over Palm and Pine": the British Empire Forestry Conferences, 1920–1947', *Journal of Historical Geography*, 33, 4, 852–77.

Prashad, V. 2001 'The Technology of Sanitation in Colonial Delhi', *Modern Asian Studies*, 35, 113–55.

Prendergast, D.K. and Adams, W.M. 2003 'Colonial Wildlife Conservation and the Origins of the Society for the Preservation of the Wild Fauna of the Empire (1903–1914)', *Onyx*, 37, 2, 251–60.

Prest, J. 1981 *The Garden of Eden*, New Haven, CT: Yale University Press.

Price, A. Grenfell 1939 *White Settlers in the Tropics*, New York: American Geographical Society Special Publication 23.

Prickett, N. and Stokes, E. 1997 'The Invasion of Waikato', in M. McKinnon (ed.), *New Zealand Historical Atlas*, Auckland: Bateman, 38.

Prochaska, D. 1990a *Making Algeria French. Colonialism in Bône, 1870–1920*, Cambridge: Cambridge University Press.

1990b 'Approaches to the Economy of Colonial Annaba, 1870–1920', *Africa: Journal of the International African Institute*, 60, 4, 497–523.

Proctor, J.D. 1998 'Geography, Paradox, and Environmental Ethics', *Progress in Human Geography*, 22, 2, 234–55.

Purvis, M. 2004 'Evading the Octopus Clutch of the Monopolists: Co-operative Ventures in West Africa', in A.R.H. Baker (ed.), *Home and Colonial*, London: Historical Geography Research Group of the Royal Geographical Society – Institute of British Geographers, 153–64.

Quanchi, M. 2006 'Photography and History in the Pacific Islands', *Journal of Pacific History*, 41, 2, 165–73.

Rajan, R. 1998 'Imperial Environmentalism or Environmental Imperialism? European Forestry, Colonial Foresters and the Agendas of Forest Management in British India 1800–1900', in R. Grove, V. Damodaran and S. Sangwan (eds.), *Nature and the Orient*, Delhi: Oxford University Press, 324–72.

Rangarajan, M. 1998 'Production, Dessication and Forest Management in the Central Provinces 1850–1930', in V. T. King (ed.), *Environmental Challenges in South-East Asia*, Richmond: Curzon, 575–95.

Ranger, T. 2001 'Colonialism, Consciousness and the Camera', review article in *Past and Present*, 170, 203–15.

    2002 'Christianity and Indigenous Peoples: A Personal Overview', *Journal of Religious History*, 27, 3, 255–71.

Ratliff, W. G. 1991 'Belgian Congo', in J. S. Olson (ed.), *Historical Dictionary of European Imperialism*, Westport, CT: Greenwood Press, 50–1.

Ribeiro, M. C. 2002 'Empire, Colonial Wars and Post-Colonialism in the Portuguese Contemporary Imagination', *Portuguese Studies*, 18, 132–214.

Riffenburgh, B. 1994 *The Myth of the Explorer: The Press, Sensationalism, and Geographical Discovery*, Oxford: Oxford University Press.

Roberts, A. D. 1986 'East Africa', in A. D. Roberts (ed.), *The Cambridge Economic History of Africa*, vol. VII: *From 1905 to 1940*, Cambridge: Cambridge University Press, 649–701.

Robinson, R. 1988 'The Conference in Berlin and the Future in Africa, 1884–1885', in S. Förster, W. J. Mommsen and R. Robinson (eds.), *Bismarck, Europe and Africa: The Berlin Africa Conference 1884–5 and the Onset of Partition*, London: German Historical Institute and Oxford University Press, 1–32.

Robinson, R. and Gallagher, J. with Denny, A. 1961 *Africa and the Victorians: The Official Mind of Imperialism*, London: Macmillan.

Robinson, R. and Gallagher, J. 1962 'The Partition of Africa', in F. H. Hinsley (ed.), *The New Cambridge Modern History*, vol. XI: *Material Progress and World-Wide Problems, 1870–1898*, Cambridge: Cambridge University Press, 593–640.

Roche, M. 1997 'From Forest to Pasture', in M. McKinnon (ed.), *New Zealand Historical Atlas*, Auckland: Bateman, plate 47.

    2002 'The State as Conservationist, 1920–1960. Wise Use of Forests, Land and Water', in E. Pawson and T. Brooking (eds.), *Environmental Histories of New Zealand*, Melbourne: Oxford University Press, 183–99.

Rockel, S. J. 2006 *Carriers of Culture. Labor on the Road in Nineteenth-Century East Africa*, Portsmouth, NH: Heinemann.

Rodger, N. A. M. 1998 'Guns and Sails in the First Phase of English Colonization, 1500–1650', in N. Canny (ed.), *The Oxford History of the British Empire*, vol. I: *The Origins of Empire*, Oxford: Oxford University Press, 79–98.

Rollins, W. H. 1993 'Imperial Shades of Green: Conservation and Environmental Chauvinism in the German Colonial Project', *German Studies Review*, 22, 2, 187–213.

Rotberg, R. I. 1971 *Joseph Thompson and the Exploration of Africa*, London: Chatto and Windus.

Ryan, J. R. 1995 'Imperial Landscapes: Photography, Geography and British Overseas Exploration, 1858–1872', in M. Bell, R. A. Butlin and M. J. Heffernan (eds.), *Geography and Imperialism 1820–1940*, Manchester: Manchester University Press, 53–79.

1997 *Picturing Empire. Photography and the Visualization of the British Empire*, London: Reaktion Books.

2005 'Photography, Visual Revolutions, and Victorian Geography', in D. N. Livingstone and C. W. J. Withers (eds.), *Geography and Revolution*, Chicago: Chicago University Press, 199–238.

Said, E. W. 1978 *Orientalism*, London: Penguin.

1993 *Culture and Imperialism*, London: Chatto and Windus.

Salazar, P.-J. 1991 'Lyautey, Marshall', in J. S. Olson (ed.), *Historical Dictionary of European Imperialism*, Westport, CT: Greenwood Press, 372–3.

Sanderson, J.-P. 2000 'La Congo Belge entre mythe et réalité. Une analyse du discours démographique colonial', *Population*, 55, 2, 331–55.

Sanderson, S. L. 1998 'East and West in the Development of the Modern World System', *Itinerario*, 22, 25–39.

Sandner, S. and Rössler, M. 1994 'Geography and Empire in Germany, 1871–1945', in A. Godlewska and N. Smith (eds.), *Geography and Empire*, Oxford: Blackwell, 115–27.

Schelhaus, B. and Hönsch, I. 2001 'History of German Geography: Worldwide Reputation and Strategies of Nationalisation and Institutionalisation', in G. Dunbar (ed.), *Geography: Discipline, Profession and Subject since 1870: An International Survey*, Dordrecht: Kluwer, 9–43.

Schneider, W. 1990 'Geographical Reform and Municipal Imperialism in France', 1870–80', in J. M. MacKenzie (ed.), *Imperialism and the Natural World*, Manchester: Manchester University Press, 90–117.

Schuylenbergh, P. van 2005 'Les parcs nationaux du Congo Belge', in J.-L. Velluc (ed.), *La mémoire du Congo: le temps colonial*, Brussels: Éditions Snoeck/ Musée Royale de l'Afrique Central, 155–8.

Schwartz, J. M. and Ryan, J. R. (eds.) 2003 *Picturing Place. Photography and the Geographical Imagination*, London: I. B. Tauris.

Schwartzburg, J. E. 1991 'South Asia', in G. Dunbar (ed.), *Modern Geography: An Encyclopedic Survey*, London: St James Press, 166–8.

1992 'South Asian Cartography', in J. B. Harley and D. Woodward (eds.), *Cartography in the Traditional Islamic and South Asian Societies*, Chicago: University of Chicago Press, 295–509.

1997 'Maps and Mapmaking in India', in H. Selin (ed.), *Encyclopaedia of the History of Science, Technology, and Medicine in Non-Western Cultures*, Dordrecht: Kluwer, 571–3.

Scott, H. S. 1938 'Education', in W. M. Hailey (ed.), *An African Survey*, Oxford: Oxford University Press, 1207–1308.

Seeley, J. R. 1883 'Tendency in English History', Lecture 1 of *The Expansion of England. Two Courses of Lectures, First Course*, 2nd edn, London: Macmillan, 1–19.

Seligmann, M. S. 1995 'Maps as the Progenitors of Territorial Disputes: Two Examples from Nineteenth-Century South Africa', *Imago Mundi*, 47, 173–83.

Shaw, G. and Hudson, P. 2002 'Edge of Empire: Transnationalism and Identity in Wellington, New Zealand, ca. 1860–ca. 1920', *Landscape Research*, 27, 1, 51–66.

Sheppard, E. 2005 'Constructing Free Trade: From Manchester Boosterism to Global Management', *Transactions, Institute of British Geographers* new series, 30, 151–72.

Sherrill, P. T. 1991 'Canada', in J. S. Olson (ed.), *Historical Dictionary of European Imperialism*, Westport, CT: Greenwood Press, 109–12.

Shulman, M. R. 1991 'Zanzibar', in J. S. Olsen (ed.), *Historical Dictionary of European Imperialism*, Westport, CT: Greenwood Press, 677.

Sidaway, J. 2002 'Postcolonial Geographies. Survey–Explore–Review', in A. Blunt and C. McEwan (eds.), *Postcolonial Geographies*, London: Continuum, 11–28.

Simmons, I. G. 1993 *Interpreting Nature. Cultural Constructions of the Environment*, London: Routledge.

Simo, D. 2005 'Colonization and Modernization. The Legal Foundation of the Colonial Enterprise; A Case Study of German Colonization in Cameroon', in E. Ames, M. Klotz and L. Wildenthal (eds.), *Germany's Colonial Pasts*, Lincoln: University of Nebraska Press, 97–112.

Simonsen, D. G. 2005 'Accelerating Modernity. Time-Space Compression in the Wake of the Aeroplane', *Journal of Transport History*, 26, 2, 98–117.

Smith, N. 2003 *American Empire: Roosevelt's Geographer and the Prelude to Globalization*, Berkeley: University of California Press.

Smith, T. 1999 '"A Grand Work of Noble Conception": The Victoria Memorial and Imperial London', in F. Driver and D. Gilbert (eds.), *Imperial Cities*, Manchester: Manchester University Press, 21–39.

Smith, V. A. 1914 'Political Geography, Government and Administration', in A. J. Herbertson and O. J. R. Howarth (eds.), *The Oxford Survey of the British Empire*, vol. II: *Asia*, Oxford: Clarendon Press, 242–95.

Smyth, W. J. 2006 *Map-making, Landscapes and Memory: A Geography of Colonial and Early Modern Ireland c. 1530–1750*, Cork: Cork University Press.

2008 'Maps, Modernity, and Memory', *Journal of Historical Geography*, 1, 162–70.

Soubeyron, O. 1994 'Imperialism and Colonialism versus Disciplinarity in French Geography', in A. Godlewska and N. Smith (eds.), *Geography and Empire*, Oxford: Blackwell, 244–67.

Stafford, R. A. 1989 *Scientist of Empire. Sir Roderick Murchison, Scientific Exploration and Victorian Imperialism*, Cambridge: Cambridge University Press.

1999 'Scientific Exploration and Empire', in A. Porter (ed.), *The Oxford History of the British Empire*, vol. III: *The Nineteenth Century*, Oxford: Oxford University Press, 294–319.

Stamp, G. 2004 'Lutyens, Sir Edwin Landseer (1869–1944)', in H. C. Matthews and B. Harrison (eds.), *Oxford Dictionary of National Biography*, Oxford: Oxford University Press.

Stanard, M. G. 2005 'Selling the Empire between the Wars: Colonial Expositions in Belgium, 1920–1940', *French Colonial History*, 6, 159–78.

Steinmetz, G. and Hell, J. 2006 'The Visual Archive of Colonialism: Germany and Namibia', *Public Culture*, 18, 1, 147–83.

Stiebel, L. and Etherington, N. 2007 'Fantasy Maps', in N. Etherington (ed.), *Mapping Colonial Conquest: Australia and South Africa*, Perth: University of Western Australia Press, 41–65.

Stockwell, A. J. 1991a 'Britain in India, to 1939', in A. N. Porter (ed.), *Atlas of British Overseas Expansion*, London: Routledge, 168 70.

1991b 'Britain and the Pacific', in A. N. Porter (ed.), *Atlas of British Overseas Expansion*, London: Routledge, 142 4.

1999 'British Expansion and Rule in South-East Asia', in A. Porter (ed.), *The Oxford History of the British Empire*, vol. III: *The Nineteenth Century*, Oxford: Oxford University Press, 371–94.

Stoecker, H. 1986a 'German East Africa', in H. Stoecker (ed.), *German Imperialism in Africa*, London: C. Hurst, 93–113.

1986b 'The annexations of 1884–1885', in H. Stoecker (ed.), *German Imperialism in Africa*, London: C. Hurst, 21–38.

1986c 'Cameroon 1885–1906', in H. Stoecker (ed.), *German Imperialism in Africa*, London: C. Hurst, 62–82.

1986d 'Cameroon 1906–1914', in H. Stoecker (ed.), *German Imperialism in Africa*, London: C. Hurst, 161–74.

1986e 'The Historical Background', in H. Stoecker (ed.), *German Imperialism in Africa*, London: C. Hurst, 11–20.

1986f 'German East Africa 1906–1914', in H. Stoecker (ed.), *German Imperialism in Africa*, London: C. Hurst, 148–60.

1986g 'The German Empire in Africa before 1914: General Questions', in H. Stoecker (ed.), *German Imperialism in Africa*, London: C. Hurst, 185–216.

Stoecker, H. and Nimchowski, H. 1986 'Pre-1914 Efforts to Secure a Larger Share: 1. Morocco', in H. Stoecker (ed.), *German Imperialism in Africa from the Beginnings until the Second World War*, London: C. Hurst, 230–48.

Stokes, E. 2002 'Contesting Resources. Māori, Pākehā, and a Tenurial Revolution', in E. Pawson and T. Brooking, *Environmental Histories of New Zealand*, Melbourne: Oxford University Press, 35–51.

Stoler, A. L. and Cooper, F. 1997 'Between Metropole and Colony. Rethinking a Research Agenda', in F. Cooper and A. L. Stoler (eds.), *Tensions of Empire. Colonial Cultures in a Bourgeois World*, Berkeley: University of California Press, 1–56.

Studdart, J. (ed.) 1943 *Indo-China*, Naval Intelligence Division, Geographical Handbook Series, BR 510, Cambridge: Cambridge University Press, 211–55.

Sturgis, J. L. 1991a 'The Expansion of Settlement in Eastern Australia to 1835', in A. N. Porter (ed.), *Atlas of British Overseas Expansion*, London: Routledge, 70–2.

1991b 'New Zealand', in A. N. Porter (ed.), *Atlas of British Overseas Expansion*, London: Routledge, 74–6.

Sugirtharajah, R. S. 2001 *The Bible and the Third World*, Cambridge: Cambridge University Press.

Sutton, K. and Lawless, R. I. 1978 'Population Regrouping in Algeria: Traumatic Change and the Rural Settlement Pattern', *Transactions, Institute of British Geographers* new series, 3, 3, 331–50.

Taillemite, É. 1992 *Bougainville à Tahiti*, Paris: Société des Océanistes, Dossier 14.

Tarling, N. 1999 'The Establishment of the Colonial Regimes', in N. Tarling (ed.), *The Cambridge History of Southeast Asia*, vol. II, part 1: *From c. 1800 to the 1930s*, Cambridge: Cambridge University Press, 1–74.

Tayman, J. 2006 *The Colony. The Harrowing True Story of the Exiles of Molokai*, New York: Scribner.

Terry, M. 1988 'Terre Napoléon', in W. Eisler and B. Smith (eds.), *Terra Australis: The Furthest Shore*, Sydney: Museum of Sydney, 153–6.

Thomas, M. 2005 *The French Empire between the Wars: Imperialism, Politics and Society*, Manchester: Manchester University Press.

Thomas, N. 1994 *Colonialism's Culture: Anthropology, Travel and Government*, Cambridge: Polity Press.

Tickell, A. 2004 'Negotiating the Landscape: Travel, Transaction and the Mapping of Colonial India', *Yearbook of English Studies*, 34, 1, 18–34.

Tinker, H. 1995 'The British Colonies of Settlement', in R. Cohen (ed.), *The Cambridge Survey of World Migration*, Cambridge: Cambridge University Press, 16.

Tolen, R. J. 1991, 'Colonizing and Transforming the Criminal Tribesman: The Salvation Army in British India', *American Ethnologist*, 18, 1, 106–25.

Townsend, M.E. 1941 *European Colonial Expansion Since 1871*, Chicago: Lippincott.

1974 *Origins of Modern German Colonisation 1871–1885*, New York: Howard Fertig.

Trocki, C.A. 1994 'Political Structures in the Nineteenth and Early Twentieth Century', in N. Tarling (ed.), *The Cambridge History of Southeast Asia*, vol. III: *From c.1800 to the 1930s*, Cambridge: Cambridge University Press, 75–126.

Turnbull, C.M. 1999 'Formal and Informal Empire in East Asia', in R.W. Winks (ed.), *The Oxford History of the British Empire*, vol. V: *Historiography*, Oxford: Oxford University Press, 379–402.

Vantemsche, G. 2005 'L'empreinte du colonisateur belge sur l'économie congolaise', in J.-L. Vellut (ed.), *La mémoire du Congo: le temps colonial*, Brussels: Éditions Snoek, Musée Royal de l'Afrique Centrale, 83–91.

Vecoli, R.J. 1995 'The Italian Diaspora, 1876–1976', in R. Cohen (ed.), *The Cambridge Survey of World Migration*, Cambridge: Cambridge University Press, 114–22.

Velde, P. van der 1995 'The Royal Dutch Geographical Society and the Dutch East Indies, 1873–1914: From Colonial Lobby to Colonial Hobby', in M. Bell, R.A. Butlin and M.J. Heffernan (eds.), *Geography and Imperialism 1820–1940*, Manchester: Manchester University Press, 80–92.

Vellut, J.-L. (ed.) 2005a *La mémoire du Congo. Le temps colonial*, Brussels: Éditions Snoeck/Musée Royale de l'Afrique Centrale.

2005b 'Regards sur le temps colonial', in J.-L. Vellut (ed.), *La mémoire du Congo. Le temps colonial*, Brussels: Musée Royal de l'Afrique Centrale, 11–22.

Vernon, C. 2007 'Projecting Power on Conquered Landscapes: Canberra and Pretoria', in N. Etherington (ed.), *Mapping Colonial Conquest: Australia and Southern Africa*, Crawley, WA: University of Western Australia Press, 146–77.

Vessuri, H. 1994 'The Institutional Process', in J.-J. Salomon, F.R. Sagasti and C. Sachs-Jeantet (eds.), *The Uncertain Quest. Science, Technology and Development*, Tokyo: United Nations University Press, 168–200.

Veth, P.J. 1879 'The Dutch Expedition to Central Sumatra', *Proceedings of the Royal Geographical Society and Monthly Record of Geography*, new monthly series, 1, 11, 759–77.

Vigilante, T. 2001 'Analysis of Explorers' Records of Aboriginal Landscape Burning in the Kimberley Region of Western Australia', *Australian Geographical Studies*, 39, 2, 135–55.

Wallerstein, I. 1974 *The Modern World-System*, vol. I: *Capitalist Agriculture and the Origins of the European World-Economy in the Sixteenth Century*, London: Academic Press.

1980 *The Modern World-System*, vol. II: *Mercantilism and the Consolidation of the Modern World-Economy, 1600–1750*, London: Academic Press.

1989 *The Modern World-System*, vol. III: *The Second Era of Great Expansion of the Capitalist World-Economy, 1730–1840s*, London: Academic Press.

Walmsley, D. J. 1988 'Space and Government', in R .L. Heathcote (ed.), *The Australian Experience: Essays in Australian Land Settlement and Resource Management*, Melbourne: Longman Cheshire, 57–67.

Walshe, A. P. 1986 'Southern Africa', in A. D. Roberts (ed.), *The Cambridge Economic History of Africa*, vol. VII: *From 1905 to 1940*, Cambridge: Cambridge University Press, 544–601.

Washbrook, D. A. 1999a 'India, 1818–1860: The Two Faces of Colonialism', in A. Porter (ed.), *The Oxford History of the British Empire*, vol. III: *The Nineteenth Century*, Oxford: Oxford University Press, 395–421.

1999b 'Orients and the Occidents: Colonial Discourse Theory and the Historiography of the British Empire', in R. W. Winks (ed.), *The Oxford History of the British Empire*, vol. V: *Historiography*, Oxford: Oxford University Press, 596–611.

Weaver, J. C. 2003 *The Great Land Rush and the Making of the Modern World 1650–1900*, Montreal: McGill-Queen's University Press.

Webster, A. 2006 *The Debate on the Rise of the British Empire*, Manchester: Manchester University Press.

Wesseling, H. L. 1996 *Divide and Rule. The Partition of Africa, 1880–1914*, Westport, CT: Praeger.

2004 *The European Colonial Empires 1815–1919*, London: Pearson Education.

Wesso, H. 1994 'The Colonization of Geographic Thought: The South African Experience', in A. Godlewska and N. Smith (eds.), *Geography and Empire*, Oxford: Blackwell, 316–32.

Wesso, H. and Parnell, S. 1992 'Geographical Education in South Africa: Colonial Roots and Prospects for Change', in C. Rogerson and J. McCarthy (eds.), *Geography in a Changing South Africa. Progress and Prospects*, Cape Town: Oxford University Press, 186–99.

West, R. 1972 *Brazza of the Congo. Exploration and Exploitation in French Equatorial Africa*, London: Jonathan Cape.

Whitcombe, E. 1995 'The Environmental Costs of Irrigation in British India: Waterlogging, Salinity, Malaria', in D. Arnold and R. Guha (eds.), *Nature, Culture, and Imperialism: Essays on the Environmental History of South Asia*, New Delhi: Oxford University Press, 237–59.

Whitehead, C. 2005a 'The Historiography of British Imperial Education Policy, Part I: India', *History of Education*, 34, 3, 315–29.

2005b 'The Historiography of British Imperial Education Policy, Part II: Africa and the Rest of the Colonial Empire', *History of Education*, 34, 4, 441–54.

Williams, D. 1962 'Clements Robert Markham and the Introduction of the Cinchona Tree into British India', *Geographical Journal*, 128, 431–42.

Williams, G. 1985 *When Was Wales?*, Harmondsworth: Penguin.

Williams, G. 1998 'The Pacific: Exploration and Exploitation', in P.J. Marshall (ed.), *The Oxford History of the British Empire*, vol. II: *The Eighteenth Century*, Oxford: Oxford University Press, 552–75.

Williams, M. 1969 'The Spread of Settlement in South Australia', in F. Gale and G.H. Lawton (eds.), *Settlement and Encounter: Geographical Essays Presented to Sir Grenfell Price*, Melbourne: Oxford University Press, 51–64.

1974 *The Making of the South Australia Landscape*, London: Academic Press.

1988 'The Clearing of the Woods', in R.L. Heathcote (ed.), *The Australian Experience*, Melbourne: Longman, 115–26.

1994 'Environmental History and Historical Geography', *Journal of Historical Geography* 20, 1, 3–21.

1997 'Ecology, Imperialism and Deforestation', in T. Griffiths and L. Robin (eds.), *Ecology and Empire. Environmental History of Settler Societies*, Keele: University of Keele Press, 169–84.

1998 'The end of modern history?', *Geographical Review*, 88, 2, 275–300.

2003 *Deforesting the Earth. From Prehistory to Global Crisis*, Chicago: University of Chicago Press.

2004 'William Light (1786–1839)', in *Oxford Dictionary of National Biography*, Oxford: Oxford University Press.

Wilmot, S.E. 1914 'Vegetation', in A.J. Herbertson and O.J.R. Howarth (eds.), *The Oxford Survey of the British Empire*, vol. VII: *Asia*, Oxford: Clarendon Press, 76–112.

Wilson, H.S. 1977 *The Imperial Experience in Sub-Saharan Africa since 1870*, Minneapolis: University of Minnesota Press.

Withers, C.W.J. 1999 'Geography, Enlightenment, and the Paradise Question', in D.N. Livingstone and C.W.J. Withers (eds.), *Geography and Enlightenment*, Chicago: University of Chicago Press, 67–92.

2001 *Geography, Science and National Identity: Scotland since 1520,* Cambridge: Cambridge University Press.

Withers, C.W.J. and Livingstone, D. 1999 'Introduction: On Geography and Enlightenment', in D.N. Livingstone and C.W.J. Withers (eds.), *Geography and Enlightenment*, Chicago: University of Chicago Press, 1–32.

Withers, C.W.J., Finnegan, D. and Higgit, R. 2006 'Geography's other Histories? Geography and Science in the British Association for the Advancement of Science, 1831–*c*.1933', *Transactions, Institute of British Geographers* new series, 31, 433–51.

Wolfe, P. 1997 'History and Imperialism: A Century of Theory, from Marx to Postcolonialism', *American Historical Review*, 102, 2, 416–17.

Wood, D. 1997 'Maps and Mapmaking', in H. Selin (ed.), *Encyclopaedia of the History of Science, Technology, and Medicine in Non-Western Cultures*, Dordrecht: Kluwer, 549–54.

Wood, J. D. 2006 ' "The Last Frontier": Rationalizing the Spread of Farming into the Boreal Woods of Canada, c. 1910–1940', *Canadian Geographer*, 50, 1, 38–55.

Woodham, J. 1989 'Images of Africa and Design at the British Empire Exhibitions between the Wars', *Journal of Design History*, 2, 1, 15–33.

Woollacott, A. 2006 *Gender and Empire*, Basingstoke: Palgrave Macmillan.

Worboys, M. 2000 'The Colonial World as Mission and Mandate: Leprosy and Empire, 1900–1940', *Osiris*, 2nd series, 15, 207–18.

Wright, G. 1987 'Tradition in the Service of Modernity: Architecture and Urbanism in French Colonial Policy, 1900–1930', *Journal of Modern History*, 59, 2, 291–316.

  1997 'Tradition in the Service of Modernity: Architecture and Urbanism in French Colonial Policy', in F. Cooper and L. Stoler (eds.), *Tensions of Empire: Colonial Cultures in a Bourgeois World*, Berkeley: University of California Press, 322–45.

Wright, J. K. 1957 'The Field of the Geographical Society', in Griffith Taylor (ed.), *Geography in the Twentieth Century*, 3rd edn, London: Methuen, 543–65.

Wrigley, C. C. 1986 'Aspects of Economic History', in A. D. Roberts (ed.), *The Cambridge Economic History of Africa*, vol. VII: *From 1905 to 1940*, Cambridge: Cambridge University Press, 77–139.

Wynn, G. 2002 'Destruction under the Guise of Improvement? The Forest, 1840–1920', in E. Pawson and T. Brooking (eds.), *Environmental Histories of New Zealand*, Melbourne: Oxford University Press, 100–16.

  2005 'D.W. Meinig and the Shaping of America', *Journal of Historical Geography* 31, 610–33.

  2006 'Timber Trade History', in *The Canadian Encyclopedia*, Historica Foundation, available at: www.thecanadianencyclopedia.com.

  2007 *Canada and Arctic North America. An Environmental History*, Santa Barbara, CA: ABC-CLIO.

Yeoh, B. S. A. 1992 'Municipal Sanitary Ideology and the Control of the Urban Environment in Colonial Singapore', in A. R. H. Baker and G. Biger (eds.), *Ideology and Landscape in Historical Perspective*, Cambridge: Cambridge University Press, 148–72.

  2000 'Historical Geographies of the Colonised World', in B. Graham and C. Nash (eds.), *Modern Historical Geographies*, London: Prentice Hall, 146–66.

  2003 *Contesting Space in Colonial Singapore. Power Relations and the Urban Built Environment*, 2nd edn, Singapore: Singapore University Press.

Young, R. J. C. 2003 *Postcolonialism. A Very Short Introduction*, Oxford: Oxford University Press.

Zimmerer, J. 2005 'Annihilation in Africa: The "Race War" in German Southwest Africa (1904–1908) and its Significance for a Global History of Genocide', *German Historical Institute Bulletin*, 37, 51–7.

Index

Page numbers in italics refer to illustrations.